Christiane Floyd   Heinz Züllighoven
Reinhard Budde   Reinhard Keil-Slawik
(Editors)

Software Development
and
Reality Construction

With 20 Figures

Springer-Verlag

Berlin Heidelberg New York
London Paris Tokyo
Hong Kong Barcelona
Budapest

Christiane Floyd
Technische Universität Berlin, Institut für Angewandte Informatik, Sekr. 5 – 6,
Franklinstraße 28/29, 1000 Berlin 10, Fed. Rep. of Germany

Heinz Züllighoven
GMD, Institut für Systemtechnik (F2), Postfach 12 40,
W-5205 Sankt Augustin 1, Fed. Rep. of Germany

Reinhard Budde
GMD, Institut für Systemtechnik (F2), Postfach 12 40,
W-5205 Sankt Augustin 1, Fed. Rep. of Germany

Reinhard Keil-Slawik
Technische Universität Berlin, Institut für Angewandte Informatik, Sekr. 5 – 6,
Franklinstraße 28/29, 1000 Berlin 10, Fed. Rep. of Germany

Illustrations by Claudia Weiler-Kühn

CR Classification (1991): D.2, H.1, H.5, K.4, K.6

ISBN 3-540-54349-X Springer-Verlag Berlin Heidelberg New York
ISBN 0-387-54349-X Springer-Verlag New York Berlin Heidelberg

Library of Congress Cataloging-in-Publication Data. Software development and reality construction / Ch. Floyd ... [et al.], eds. p. cm. Includes bibliographical references and index. ISBN 3-540-54349-X (Springer-Verlag Berlin). – ISBN 0-387-54349-X (Springer-Verlag New York) 1. Computer software–Development. 2. Human–computer interaction. I. Floyd, Christiane. QA76.76.D47S633 1992 005.1–dc20 91-43082

The use of general descriptive names, registered names, trademarks, etc. in this publication does not imply, even in the absence of a specific statement, that such names are exempt from the relevant protective laws and regulations and therefore free for general use.

Typesetting: Camera ready by author

45/3140 - 5 4 3 2 1 0 – Printed on acid-free paper

Preface

The present book is based on the conference *Software Development and Reality Construction* held at Schloß Eringerfeld in Germany, September 25 – 30, 1988. This was organized by the Technical University of Berlin (TUB) in cooperation with the German National Research Center for Computer Science (GMD), Sankt Augustin, and sponsored by the Volkswagen Foundation whose financial support we gratefully acknowledge. The conference was an interdisciplinary scientific and cultural event aimed at promoting discussion on the nature of computer science as a scientific discipline and on the theoretical foundations and systemic practice required for human-oriented system design.

In keeping with the conversational style of the conference, the book comprises a series of individual contributions, arranged so as to form a coherent whole. Some authors reflect on their practice in computer science and system design. Others start from approaches developed in the humanities and the social sciences for understanding human learning and creativity, individual and cooperative work, and the interrelation between technology and organizations. Thus, each contribution makes its specific point and can be read on its own merit. But, at the same time, it takes its place as a chapter in the book, along with all the other contributions, to give what seemed to us a meaningful overall line of argumentation. This required careful editorial coordination, and we are grateful to all the authors for bearing with us throughout the slow genesis of the book and for complying with our requests for extensive revision of some of the manuscripts.

The way the book evolved also made great demands on everyone engaged in its production. We are especially indebted to the following persons whose commitment and excellent work enabled the book to be brought to a successful conclusion:

Claudia Weiler-Kühn, our illustrator, who was willing to devote her time and attention to understanding our abstract ways of thinking;

Philip Bacon, who translated or polished up many of the texts written by non-native authors;

Daniela Wegge, who compiled a significant portion of the bibliography;

Doris Fähndrich, who coordinated production of the book. She created the technical environment based on LaTeX and eventually assumed sole responsibility for the layout of the text as a whole. The extraordinary care and patience she showed here have greatly contributed to the overall quality of the book.

Finally, we would like to thank *Hans Wössner* of the Springer Verlag who went to considerable lengths to accommodate our rather unconventional ideas concerning the book's design.

Christiane Floyd, Reinhard Keil-Slawik
Technische Universität Berlin (TUB)

Reinhard Budde, Heinz Züllighoven
Gesellschaft für Mathematik und Datenverarbeitung (GMD)

Berlin and Sankt Augustin, August 1991

Table of Contents

Prologue

Proscenium

A stage. The curtain is down. Christiane emerges from behind the curtain. She is carrying this book in her hand.

Christiane
This is a book about human questions in computer science. Questions such as: What are we actually doing in our work? What assumptions do we rely on? What claims can we really meet? How do we view human beings in relation to computers? What is the impact of the computer in use? How can we promote quality? What kind of social changes do we bring about? To what extent is information technology conducive to human development?

The authors of this book share the conviction that a deeper understanding of these issues is essential for guiding responsible action in science and design. In working on this book, we have proceeded from the assumption that there can be no single theoretical framework providing answers to the set of the questions raised above. All of us approach them from our own perspectives, shaped by our experience in life, by our work and through our interaction with others. We realize that even the way we select and formulate our questions reflects our particular perspective, while you, the reader, proceed from yours. We would like to encourage you to pursue your own questions and to promote discussions in your own personal context.

Heinz *(joins her.)*
This is a book about our parts in a play. A play in which there are many actors. A play about science and software development. Let us take a look behind the scenes to see the way this play is staged and the effects and illusions that are created during its performance.

And you, the reader of our book, shall not only be the spectator – cut off from the action by an imaginary "fourth wall" and embarking on this book as if merely watching our play. Instead, it is our intention to involve you in the development of the book and show you how the play evolved.

It all began with Christiane and me giving a joint seminar.

The Small Bang

The curtain rises. January 1987. A seminar room at the Technical University of Berlin. Students sitting at tables. One of them is standing and appears to be speaking to the rest. Christiane and Heinz sit down at a table in the corner.

Christiane

It was a seminar on Evolutionary Methods of Software Development. But we wanted to go beyond the traditional approaches. Thus it came about that one of the students was giving a paper on constructivist ideas. While listening – not very attentively – we wrote little notes to each other exploring the possibility of organizing a conference on the epistemological foundations of software development.

To be precise, I wrote a note to Heinz asking if he and his colleague Reinhard Budde would organize such a conference.

Heinz

I should never have ventured on a project of this sort without the support of my old friend Reinhard. Luckily, he agreed to join in.

Christiane

As for me, it was clear from the start that I would ask my close colleague Reinhard Keil-Slawik to join us, too.

Heinz

And he also agreed. So we were now a nucleus of four people who wanted to organize this conference. As later became apparent, this configuration was not without its problems. We worked at geographically different locations and our respective degrees of acquaintance varied. This caused tensions which we had to learn to cope with.

They both get up and walk to the edge of the stage. The curtain falls.

Reinhard B. *(enters from the wing.)*

This is a book about the computer. The computer is the main object of our work. But what are we actually doing when we work with a computer? What does it mean to develop programs for other people and use them on a computer? What sort of interplay is there between human existence and computers? These are the questions we wished to raise at the conference and in this book. We realized that here computer science as a discipline was being asked about the way it sees itself. But a project of this sort was not feasible, we felt, without help from representatives of the humanities, who are much more experienced in such questions. After all, had any computer scientist made a coherent attempt to tackle these issues? Who would be prepared to do so in the context of such a conference?

Reinhard K.-S. *(enters from the wing.)*

This is a book about people. Formalisms and programs are meaningless without the people who develop and use them. But how can we arrive at a notion of quality for computer programs that is geared to human values? And to the

meaningful embedding of artifacts in human activity? Are humans merely
the unreliable component in the overall system – a component that needs
to be eliminated? Are not error and repeated attempts to succeed rather an
inexhaustible source of learning and inspiration? It was these learning processes and their relation to human values that we wished to develop at the
conference and in this book. But, in our attempt to do so, we became aware
of a field of tension opening up before us: To what extent should the computer claim our attention here? Or should we confine ourselves to looking at
the people working with it?

Christiane

We each had our own particular background to contribute to the project. I
had always been keenly interested in philosophy and was looking for ways
of integrating my work in computer science with deeper personal concerns
of mine. My attempt to understand software development as a process gave
rise to epistemological questions I felt the need to pursue.

Heinz

Having been a student of the humanities, it was quite natural for me to draw
on these disciplines in my endeavour to establish adequate foundations for
computer science. I had become aware of the importance of experiment and
communication in software development while engaged in work on prototyping with Reinhard.

Reinhard B.

While studying physics, I had learned to be on my guard against a naïve
notion of experiment in which – irrespective of the measuring process – objective data are collected from an objective reality. I now wished to tackle
the questionable view of software design in which – irrespective of the design process – objective data are transformed without this affecting their
meaning.

Reinhard K.-S.

An important aspect of my work has always been the endeavour to establish
foundations for a human-oriented design of information technology. I see this
as both a scientific problem and as the goal of my political work and practical
projects I am engaged in outside the university.

Christiane

To begin with, the only way of circumscribing the theme of the conference
was to draw up a catalogue of questions with which to approach potential
participants.

Heinz

We were faced with the problem of establishing contact with people likely to
be sensitive to these questions of ours. The best way to do this, it seemed,
was through personal connections. First of all, we had to win the support
of other committed participants so as to form an extended nucleus around
which a yet larger group might crystallize.

Christiane

This extended nucleus comprised the coordinators, many of whom also became authors of this book. They helped to illuminate the theme of the con-

ference from different perspectives in computer science and to find other
prospective participants in their own professional environments.

Heinz

It was mainly our friends in Europe whom we approached. They were, after
all, within easy reach, and that meant less organizational problems.

Reinhard K.-S.

Our aim, however, was to organize a truly international conference. It was
to be small, but at the same time to offer a considerable degree of variety.

Reinhard B.

It was important to us to address the questions we had raised by reflecting
on our everyday work.

Christiane

And it was our explicit aim to take account of different schools of thought
and philosophical traditions.

Heinz

A particular problem was finding responsive participants in the United States.
So Christiane's sabbatical, which she was planning to spend over there, came
at a very opportune time.

Christiane

A research scholarship on the "Epistemological Foundations of Software Development" enabled me to go to California and delve once again into a research environment I was already acquainted with.

Heinz

The rest of us agreed to press ahead with the organizational preparations
for the conference.

California Dreaming and German Chaos

*The curtain rises. February 1988. A comfortable room in Palo Alto. In front of the
window a gigantic Californian oak. Christiane lounging on a sofa. Next to her a
telephone. On each side of the stage a telephone booth; one is labelled Berlin, the
other Bonn. In the Berlin booth stands Reinhard K.-S.; in the Bonn booth, Heinz
and Reinhard B.*

Christiane

I had the rare opportunity to shape these six months of basic research in accordance with my evolving needs and interests. While getting re-accustomed
to the golden light of California and the gentle slope of the coastal hills, I
became a visiting scholar at Stanford and Berkeley. I was thus able to take
part in the academic life of both universities.

In the course of discussions with specialists from diverse fields – whose reaction to the conference was very positive – I saw individual topics of interest
gradually fitting together to form a whole, like pieces in a mosaic. I began
to perceive *what* the topics of the conference would be.

Even more important, though, was *how* the conference was to be conducted.
This became clear to me in my encounter with the cyberneticist Heinz von

Foerster, who helped me understand the dialogical, self-organizing nature of the processes involved and encouraged me to find novel ways of facilitating them.

Reinhard K.-S.

Meanwhile, the organization in Germany was making only sluggish progress. From her lofty station of euphoric serenity, Christiane was forever mentioning new names in our weekly telephone calls. And each name brought with it more ideas and suggestions for shaping the conference. But with each new addition, other names disappeared from the list.

Reinhard B.

As this wave of constantly changing names washed over us, we found ourselves beset with difficulties on every side. There was no indication that the conference was settling down on a stable course. The question of its financing was still open. The coordinators were growing uneasy because there was scarcely a single concrete idea in sight about the form the conference was to take.

Reinhard K.-S.

So I tried to mediate between Bonn and Palo Alto without ever really understanding what the problems were all about.

Heinz

We began to seriously question the feasibility of the whole project. Finally, I talked at length to Christiane on the phone. I told her that Reinhard and I were contemplating opting out of the whole thing.

Christiane

This conversation had a shock-effect on me. I realized that the idea I could withdraw from the organizational preparation of the conference for six months just like that had been quite illusory. As if self-organization meant that a project like ours would organize *itself!* No, what we needed was to organize *ourselves!* And each of us was indispensable for establishing and upholding this joint venture of ours.

Heinz

It cost Christiane a great deal of effort to persuade Reinhard and me to hold on until she returned from California.

All walk to the edge of the stage. The curtain falls.

Reinhard K.-S.

Then there began for all of us a period of very intensive work during which we managed to re-establish ourselves as a group and consolidate the conference in terms of its scientific programme, its participants, its financing and organization.

Christiane

We had long since realized that this was to be no ordinary conference. We now began to focus more and more consciously on the concordance between form and content. The key to the whole thing was to see the conference as a network of potential dialogues growing out of the preparatory process, borne by all the participants, and enriching one another on a mutual basis.

Heinz

We wanted to stage a conference at which people with differing interests, views and professional specialties could meet, talk and spend time together. Conversations rather than speakers monologizing up front; changing roles rather than rigid rituals.

Reinhard B.

But how could we encourage scientists to take up issues evidently impinging on their work, yet not belonging to their professional specialties? How were we to promote conversations between such diverse participants?

Heinz

Then it dawned on us that, to communicate, we have more than one means of expression at our disposal.

Once upon a time in Café Einstein

The curtain rises. Summer 1988. Café Einstein – a restaurant with a garden shaded by apple trees. The four protagonists sit down at a table with the members of the organizing committee.

Heinz

To begin with, we talked about music and dance. Art and culture as living forms of expression and as a potential means of communication among the participants.

Christiane

We wanted the participants to feel at ease. The first meal we had together was particularly important for me. I spent hours over the seating order, working out how best to help the participants get to know one another.

Reinhard K.-S.

And then there was the play. To be truthful, I was in doubt about whether this sort of thing would work. To open the conference, we staged a play, together with the coordinators and some of the participants, on the themes of the conference – and that without a fixed script, without much experience, and without the whole troupe having had the opportunity to rehearse together!

Christiane

Right up to the last moment, I was terrified of the risks involved. But I wanted to do away with the traditional conference opening.

Heinz

There we were then, sitting in this café with its curious mixture of Vienna charm and Berlin gruffness – just the right atmosphere for concocting this play of ours. And so we sketched out a sequence of scenes in episodic form, based on a fictitious case study of software development, casting conference participants in the various roles. The different threads of the action were drawn together in a series of intermezzi featuring a narrator Alice who gradually emancipates herself in the course of the play.

Reinhard B.
Sketches, pantomime, speaking choirs and puppet plays were to help make up for the actors' lack of professionality. Furry mice and icons had to be provided for a graphic user interface; props and scenery had to be organized.

Reinhard K.-S.
Once the basic idea of the play was born, other ideas and suggestions kept on rolling in. A conference as a fair of ideas for all those participating.

Heinz
The conference itself as a carefully staged event.

The four protagonists walk to the edge of the stage.

Christiane
And that's how the play, and the play within the play, was organized. The stage was erected, the foundation of what was plannable laid, and now everything was set for variety and creativity to unfold.

Reinhard B.
The framework was built ready for the self-organizing stability to materialize. It provided the form for insights to emerge.

Reinhard K.-S.
We rehearsed the brief episodes that were designed to spin and keep alive the communication web between the conference participants. We set out to transform the ideas into a sequence of events that led from the conference to this book.

Christiane
And these events cannot be separated from the people who initiated and sustained them. These were, first of all, the coordinators who prepared the conference in terms of its scientific programme.

Exeunt. Enter, crossing the stage in single file: Thomas Christaller, Wolfgang Dzida, Heinz K. Klein, Werner Langenheder, Klaus-Peter Löhr, Kalle Lyytinen, Susanne Maaß, Bernd Mahr, Lars Mathiassen, Horst Oberquelle, Arne Raeithel, Dirk Siefkes.

Reinhard B.   *(walks downstage.)*
And then there were our friends who helped us in organizing the conference.

Exit. Enter, crossing the stage in single file: Michael Castner, Guido Gryczan, Christine Harms, Karlheinz Kautz, Karin Kuhlenkamp, Rainer Mantz, Karl-Heinz Sylla.

Heinz   *(walks downstage.)*
We have already pointed out that art, culture and sport were not merely part of a peripheral programme at the conference. But words can scarcely do justice to the variety and impressiveness of the cultural offerings by professional artistes and conference participants.

Exit. Enter, crossing the stage in single file: the Australian didjeridoo-player Mat-
thew McGrath, the dancer Bob Rease & Company, Thomas Christaller and his
Aikido Partner J. Exeler, Dieter Hermes and his bands Blo' Job and Fair Share,
the magician Brunetti, the pantomime artist Geza Melczer-Lukacs & Company,
the pianist Norbert Finke, Don Knuth with his pile of organ music and Markku
Nurminen with his flute, Jan Witt with his Homunculus slides, and Heinz-Otto
Peitgen with a case full of beautiful fractals

Reinhard K.-S. *(walks downstage.)*
And, finally, it was the participants as a whole who made the conference
such a unique event.

Walks to the centre of the stage where the following persons congregate:
Klaus Amann, Brigitte Bartsch-Spörl, Gro Bjerknes, Reinhard Budde, Rodney M.
Burstall, Rafael Capurro, John M. Carroll, Michael Castner, Thomas Christaller,
Wolfgang Coy, Klaus Dässler, Bo Dahlbom, Wolfgang Dzida, Christiane Floyd,
Heinz von Foerster, Klaus Fuchs-Kittowski, Dafydd Gibbon, Joseph A. Goguen,
Thomas F. Gordon, Guido Gryczan, Volker Hammer, Christine Harms, Bernd
Hellingrath, Wolfgang Hesse, Johannes Joemann, Karl Kautz, Pentti Kerola, Heinz
K. Klein, Donald E. Knuth, Wolfgang Küpper, Karin Kuhlenkamp, Kari Kuutti,
Gernot B. Längle, Werner Langenheder, Klaus-Peter Löhr, Alfred Lothar Luft,
Kalle Lyytinen, Susanne Maaß, Bernd Mahr, Rainer Mantz, Lars Mathiassen,
Bengt Nordström, Markku I. Nurminen, Kristen Nygaard, Horst Oberquelle, Er-
hard Oeser, Peter Padawitz, Jürgen Pasch, Gordon Pask, Carl Adam Petri, Arne
Raeithel, Anton J. van Reeken, Fanny-Michaela Reisin, Douglas T. Ross, Dirk
Siefkes, Jan Stage, Risto Suitiala, Edda Sveinsdottir, Karl-Heinz Sylla, Walter
Volpert, Jan Witt, Gerhard Wohland, Heinz Züllighoven.

They wave to the audience. The curtain falls.

Christiane *(enters from the wing.)*
The book cannot be a substitute for the experience of the conference. But it
allows the variety of themes addressed there to be treated in a more mature
form. And the book is intended to carry further the spirit of the conference.

Heinz *(enters from the wing.)*
The management, the people behind the scenes and the actors have now
been introduced and are ready to go. The book can begin.

Exeunt. The curtain rises.

Part 1

Thinking About Computer Science

Christiane

We think about computer science against the background of our scientific tradition. This can be traced back to the Greek philosophers whose ideas have shaped Western thought.

Heinz

Right up to the development of the computer – which is why we have sent it to "The School of Athens". Our illustration is based on the Renaissance painting of the same name by Raphael.

Reinhard B.

During the Renaissance, there was a turning back to Antiquity for inspiration, and of this modern scientific thinking was born. Not long afterwards rationalism and empiricism emerged as schools of thought.

Reinhard K.-S.

The painting is magnificent. But it depicts an idealized world. A world of the élite. Without contradictions. Without needs. Without any relation to life.

Reinhard B.

The Ancient Greeks' view of the world was contemplative. It was not until modern times that technology acquired its fundamental importance. The natural sciences were geared to mastery and control.

Heinz

Science felt that its only commitment was to a dispassionate truth, and technology was associated with the supposedly objective progress of humanity.

Reinhard K.-S.

Dispassionateness, objectivity, belief in progress – these claims still exist today, though only as ideals. They do, admittedly, help us to shake off existing constraints, but science and technology are invariably tied to the prevailing interests.

Christiane

In the illustration, the computer has taken the place of a thinker. Just as computer science takes its place in the rationalist tradition, which originated in the School of Athens with Socrates, Plato and Aristotle.

Heinz

It was there that rules for thinking were first sought and the separation of mind and body postulated. In computer science, the attempt to view thinking as rule-governed and to automate it is evident at every turn.

Reinhard B.

And with it the illusion that human thought can be divorced from bodily experience and social relatedness.

Reinhard K.-S.

But also rooted in Greek philosophy is dialogical thinking. This was characterized by discourse – something which has been widely lost at our universities.

Heinz

These dialogues, though, were little more than monologues held by the teacher, the student being confined to the rather minor role of giving cues.

Christiane

With this book of ours, we wish to promote a different sort of dialogue. And this part with its two widely differing chapters is meant to help to initiate this dialogue.

Heinz

In the first of these chapters, Christiane gives a thematic introduction, which we as co-editors all largely endorse. She raises fundamental questions that are taken up and developed in different ways in subsequent chapters.

Reinhard B.

These questions concern the relationship between humans and computers, the understanding of software development as a human activitiy and the integration of computers in human action. They point to the necessity of questioning the traditional view computer science takes of itself.

Reinhard K.-S.

And Christiane relates basic assumptions, concepts and open questions in computer science to ongoing discussions in the philosophy of science.

Christiane

The second chapter is Don Knuth's account of the errors he made while designing TeX. We have placed it in the introductory part because we consider the willingness to reflect on our own practice to be a magic key to a deeper understanding of the issues underlying our work.

Heinz

Acknowledging our errors means rejecting the myth of rule-governed thought postulated by the rationalist school.

Reinhard K.-S.

The rationalists see errors as deviations from the rule which must be avoided.

Reinhard B.

But what do we mean here by errors? Is it possible to make errors with respect to a system that is still under development? Who decides what is to be considered a correct system, and what an error? Is it an error to have made a non-optimal design decision? Is the traditional category "error" appropriate when considering construction processes?

Reinhard K.-S.

For us, error situations are events we learn from. They help us to identify our limits and deepen our insights. In this sense, errors do not relate to a predefined rule; rather, it is the "error" itself that helps us to realize what we are actually seeking to achieve.

Christiane

The idea, then, that concepts have a fixed meaning proves illusory. We obviously have to reconstruct traditional concepts so as to make them fit our concerns.

1.1 Human Questions in Computer Science

Christiane Floyd

In this introduction to our book, my aim is to provide a common platform for the chapters that follow. I will outline the main issues at stake, as I see them, in order to motivate the variety of themes taken up later on, and to show how they are connected. In contrast to subsequent chapters, I will not give comprehensive references to background literature here, but confine myself to bringing out a few seminal publications, which were inspirational to many authors of this book. I will start by commenting on the motto "Software Development and Reality Construction" which was coined as a suggestive phrase to indicate the range of questions relevant to us.

1.1.1 Software development and reality construction

We focus on *software*, since we consider it to be pivotal in the intertwining of computer technology and the human world. Through software we tailor computers to meet specific purposes, through software we model mental processes to be simulated on the computer, through software we establish the conditions and constraints for people working with computer based systems. Software is a product with unique attributes, and its development calls for new ways of working together that we do not yet fully understand.

Software is tied up with our thinking in a particularly intimate way. We meet fascinating challenges in building formal models and setting up artificial worlds. We struggle to find sophisticated ways for delegating some of our mental faculties to the computer. We come up against our limits in dealing with complexity. We are faced with our own proneness to errors. We see our assumptions, values, and relations to others mirrored in our technical work. We model and make rules for ourselves and for others to follow. Through software we control the computer and, indirectly, strive to control the human context where the computer is used.

Software development is meant here in a very general sense, with no restriction to any particular class of programs or development setting. Some contributions are based on the experiences of researchers working as individuals, others refer to routine production in industry. Most contributions in this book deal with software used by people as part of their work. Such software embodies knowledge from an area of human expertise, and serves to enact information processes on the computer, thereby replacing traditional ways of handling information, and allowing more elaborate processes to be carried out by people with the help of the software.

Thus, even though our focus is on software development, we are also concerned with *software use*, where the computer appears as an artifact in various human contexts. In fact, we consider software development and use to be inherently related, so that one domain cannot be adequately considered without taking the other into account. The term software *development* suggests the *evolutionary* nature of this process, which typically involves cycles of design, implementation, evaluation and revision.

The phrase *reality construction* has been chosen so as to evoke the spirit of recent discussions in the humanities, where it has become a vehicle for focussing attention on *our active role* in constituting what we hold for real. Thus, in applied epistemology, reality construction refers to cognitive processes, in which we bring forth what we perceive and know. In developmental psychology, it relates to the gradual formation of conceptual schemata shaping the cognitive faculties of the growing child. In sociology, this phrase refers to social processes instrumental in establishing and transforming social reality. In the philosophy of science, it concerns processes of intellectual inquiry leading to scientific insight.

The phrase seems provocative to many, as it takes issue with the notion of *reality* dominant in European thinking. The latin root for this term, "res", means "things" or "affairs". It suggests that what is "real" is *given* in terms of things or affairs, which exist "out there" independently from us. This is compatible with the rationalistic tradition in epistemology, which views cognition as *matching* the things or affairs constituting reality as faithfully as possible in the mind. It is also connected to the basic postulate of modern science stating that the properties of the observer should not enter into what is observed.

For example, a software developer analyzing an organization with a view to proposing a software system to support its information processes, is often encouraged to start from the "real world", conceived in terms of the entities and actions constitutive of the information flow in the existing organization. These are supposed to be "given", while the software developer's task is to analyze, to abstract and to elaborate a correct model that can be manipulated by the computer. While this may be difficult to do, the task itself – *discovering* the correct description – is supposed to be clearly defined and independent of the software developer as an individual. Also, his or her responsibility in carrying out this task is restricted to matching the real world in the model with the greatest possible care.

This picture changes drastically, when we acknowledge our active role in bringing about what we hold for real, which is the key to constructivist thinking. The emphasis now is on the *observer* constituting the way he or she sees reality and *inventing* a suitable description. Thus, the software developer is portrayed as making *choices* in an open situation, where there is more than one possibility. When developing the product software, we make choices in selecting the aspects we consider relevant for modelling, in making available modes of interaction with the computer, in determining the software system's architecture, in the way we use the technical resources for implementing the system. Moreover, we make choices in anticipating how the computer will be embedded in its use context and in creating facilities and constraints for users and other concerned parties. And lastly, we make choices in how we conduct the development process itself.

Only a small part of these choices do we make explicitly, more often they are implied by the course of actions we take and, perhaps, even come about by our lack of awareness for potential alternatives or our unwillingness for coping with them and making conscious choices. Also, our choices are constrained by our interaction with others. When seen in these terms, the task of the software developer clearly involves reference to the individual software developer. Through our choices, we constitute the process of development, the product, and the possibilities for its use. In paying attention to our making choices, there is, at the same time, also an emphasis on our responsibility for seeing possibilities and making choices. Thus, the ethical dimension of our activities is always present and included in the discussion.

In constructivist thinking, the ontological question of what *is* is placed in relation to the epistemological question of what *we can know* in a poignant way. Only what we can know is accessible to us, and it is accessible in those terms in which we know it. The seemingly safe ground of the given reality reveals itself as built up in processes of our own making.

Constructivist authors vary in what concretely they mean by reality construction and in the degree to which they regard reality construction as primordial. The use of the term *construction*, though established, is also misleading. It seems to suggest an unwanted arbitrariness for individual experience and action, and to deny our embedding in the world around us. However, our individual reality construction is interacting with that of others, building up on those before us and grounded in the endless recursion of human (co-)evolution.

Cognition, then, may be viewed as bringing forth concepts and insights *fitting* our experience and *viable* for obtaining our aims in open situations where we interpret our needs. It is shaped by our perspective and unfolds against a background or meaning horizon coloured by our tradition, our interests and our life experience. The main points of current controversial discussion concern the relation of my own reality construction to yours and that of others, and the interleavement between our scope for reality construction and the so-called objective world of nature shaped by socio-cultural evolution.

In this book, we do not aim to contribute to the ongoing discussion of constructivist thinking. Neither do we wish to single out a particular constructivist position as the proper one. Individual authors clarify how they relate to constructivist thinking, and which shades of meaning associated with this term they value or reject. In fact, several of them are explicitly rooted in other schools of thought ranging from Hermeneutics to Marxism, and accept constructivist thinking only to the extent that it corroborates or enriches their own world-view.

However, constructivist thinking is applied here in one way or another to several interleaved domains of interest:

- to the process of *software development* which lends itself to being understood as *design* in constructivist terms,
- to the technical result of software development, the *execution of programs* which may be characterized as *constructed reality*,
- to the social outcome of software development, the *human reality of the use situation* resulting from the application of computer programs in a given context,

- to the *emergence of scientific insight* in computer science and other disciplines dealing with questions of design,
- to various *epistemological approaches* providing insights for understanding software development and use,
- to *social reality* in general, shaped and transformed increasingly by the development and use of computer based systems.

Moreover, the way the whole book is made reflects important elements of constructivist thinking, exemplifying, as it does, the use of key notions such as perspectivity, process-/product-complementarity and self-organization.

The remaining sections of this introduction serve to elaborate the set of questions concerning software development and computer science that provided the motivation for working on this book.

1.1.2 Reality and human cognition

Whether or not an "objective reality" exists is unanswerable and, according to some, uninteresting. There is, however, increasing evidence that "objective cognition" of the world is impossible, since human cognition is inherently selective and embedded in the processes of biological and social evolution.

Current arguments in biology, neurophysiology, epistemology and the social sciences suggest a view of human cognition, according to which some of its most important facets are:

- It is profoundly affected by human perception as developed in biological evolution.
- It is geared to human needs arising in situations, and therefore action-oriented and interest-governed.
- It is shaped by the history and experience of the individual, the community and the species.
- It is mediated by the language, methods, procedures and tools we use.
- It leads to deeper insights by merging different perspectives.

Understanding human cognition affects computer science in various ways: it helps us draw the line between aspects of intelligent behaviour that can be modelled in the form of computer programs and the full human cognitive experience; it provides a basis for understanding the cognitive processes arising both in the development and in the use of computer programs; it urges us to think about the potential impact of the computer as a thinking tool in human cognition; and lastly, it leads us to an increasing awareness of what it means to pursue computer science as a scientific endeavour.

1.1.3 Cognitive interest underlying scientific endeavour

In recent years, there has been a growing concern about the assumptions and the world-view underlying, in particular, the natural sciences as we know them, and extending from there to a considerable extent into the humanities, the social sciences and into everyday thinking.

The traditional way of thinking in science rests on dichotomies contrasting, for example, man and nature, mind and matter, facts and values. It assumes the existence of an objective reality, which can be studied by an observer without the observer affecting the result of the observation. Its primary concern is to discover truth, all questions related to values and human needs being regarded as outside the realm of scientific inquiry. It emphasizes analytical thinking, experiments and proofs as basic elements of scientific methodology. Scientific interest serves to further the domination of man over nature and over fellow human beings.

In contrast, a new understanding of science is currently gaining ground, which is sometimes characterized as a new paradigm. Motivated by recent developments both in the physical and biological sciences, it suggests new ways of overcoming the traditional dichotomies, and emphasizes the unity of human beings and nature. It embodies an awareness of how the observer constructs reality by the act of observation, how the questions we ask influence the answers we get and how we interpret them. It transcends the reductionistic view of the established paradigm by offering systemic ways of practice and extends the ethos of establishing truth by that of promoting life. And it replaces the quest for domination and control by that for preservation and nurture.

If this new understanding of science becomes accepted as a basis for technological development in our society, it may contribute bringing about changes which seem urgently needed.

Computer science is firmly rooted in the established scientific paradigm, as is evidenced by its theoretical teachings as well as its professional practice. In view of the shortcomings of this approach, it is faced, like many other sciences, with the demand for richer ways of thinking.

1.1.4 Computer science as a scientific discipline

To date, computer science has failed to make explicit its underlying assumptions. They can, however, to some extent be inferred from the emergence of computer science in its historical context and from the way in which theory formation is interleaved with practical experience in technological development.

Computer science originated, on the one hand, from the need to carry out complex computations during the Second World War; and, on the other hand, from the invention of a machine, the digital computer, capable of carrying out such computations. As a consequence, it has emerged from the beginning as both "computing" science and "computer" science. That means, it views itself as a formal and an engineering science, relying strongly on the traditional scientific paradigm as outlined above.

Moreover, the computer has quickly become a widely used *metaphor for understanding human cognition* both within and outside of computer science. Equating human beings with computers in important ways is explicit in the claims raised to date by researchers in artificial intelligence. It is also implied by traditional approaches in fields like software engineering, requirements engineering or human-computer interaction, where methods tend to assume a machinelike behaviour on the part of both software developers and users. In view of the increasingly subtle interrelation between people and computer programs, these assumptions need to be re-examined.

An important aspect of computer science is that it deals with *creating reality*: the technical reality of the programs executed on the computer, and the conditions for the human reality which unfolds around the computer in use. Therefore, the conceptual categories "true" and "false" it relies on are not sufficient in themselves. We have to go beyond them by finding categories for expressing *the felicity of our choices*, for distinguishing "more or less desirable" as we proceed in making distinctions and decisions in communal design processes. This is essential for dealing with quality in software development and use.

The need to relate the technical reality of computing to the human reality of our own thinking and interacting is also reflected in the basic concepts used in computer science. We find specific patterns of conceptual confusion here, which can be traced to pervasive problems:

- The need to clarify both similarities and differences in phenomena pertaining to human beings and computers, as in "intelligence", "information", "communication", or "dialogue";
- the need to reflect the complementarity of ongoing processes and their outcome or products as in "design", "error" or "quality";
- the need to differentiate between entities emerging in evolutionary processes and formal artifacts created to meet specific purposes as in "language" or "system".

Common usage, however, tends to equate the different shades of meaning contrasted here. Since our choice of basic concepts strongly affects the claims we make about computer science and its possible achievements, our conceptual confusion has already spread far beyond computer science into everyday thinking with unpredictable effects.

Lastly, it must be noted that, to a considerable extent, computer science creates and modifies its own object of investigation. Computer scientists themselves develop formal models and description techniques for technical systems developed by computer scientists; they also develop ways of thinking about and evaluating the systems thus derived, which in turn lead to new developments.

Thus, while the fundamental assumptions underlying scientific work are questioned only to a limited extent by computer scientists, it may be argued that computer science motivates such questions in a particularly challenging manner.

1.1.5 Human beings versus computers

The driving force behind computer science was the rapid advance of information technology, accompanied by a public willingness to attribute far-reaching powers to the computer. From the beginning, this development has given rise to questions about the relationship between human beings and computers in terms of their capabilities and their desirable interaction. These questions remain unsettled to this day and have a strong bearing on our thinking and public decision making. They come up in different ways:

- Intellectually: Are human beings in their cognitive faculties similar to computers?
- Technologically: Can computers, in principle, be likened to human beings?
- Morally: How should computers be allowed to interfere with human affairs?

There is no scope here for treating these questions in depth. Yet, I find it indispensable to bring them in the open, since the stand we take on them profoundly affects the issues raised in this book. Also, we need to see them as intertwined, wherever decisions concerning the development and introduction of information technology are made. Our understanding of the relationship between human beings and computers necessarily influences what we think of as desirable ways for the use of computers. Thus, while these questions may remain the topic of interesting academic speculations for some time to come, they are of basic importance in social reality construction here and now, and have a decisive influence in shaping tomorrow's computerized world.

Equating human beings and computers is in line with recurrent attempts in the history of European thinking to use machine models for *understanding human beings*, and is reflected even in the colloquial use of language today. At the same time, it has emerged in a cultural background, where machine metaphors are applied at different levels to *prescribe the desired behaviour* for individuals, groups, or social bodies such as large organizations, and portray predictable routine performance as a mould for individuals to cast themselves onto. Computability has almost become a modern moral category, a vehicle for discussing the validity of decisions for action in human terms.

Equating human beings and computers rests on singling out the human faculties for *rational thinking* and *functional behaviour*, considering them on their own, and abstracting from their connection with other modes of experience. The fundamental assumption here is that human cognitive faculties can be meaningfully discussed without taking account of our embodied and social nature constituted in the process of co-evolution of all living beings. There are important socio-cultural roots for this idea in the whole of Western civilization, leading up to a historical situation in the past decades, which made the discussion about the relationship between human beings and the newly invented computers, urgent and significant.

The craving for rationality as a basis for conducting human affairs, inherited from Greek philosophy, was formulated into a programme for human progress in the Age of Reason. However, the hope for the fulfilment of this programme was profoundly shaken in the twentieth century. On the personal level, the discoveries of psychoanalysis have confronted us with disturbing limitations in controlling our own rational behaviour. On the political level, the violent social upheavals and the horrors of warfare and totalitarian regimes have infringed upon the lives of vast numbers of people and shaped the thinking of a whole age. Thus, faith in human rationality has declined, and the computer appeared as a desperately-needed rational authority beyond human passion and error.

Moreover, in an age of fear and international confrontation, the computer provided the basis for a key technology enabling the policy of deterrence. It helped accomplish prestigious space missions and promised the illusion of global protection. While the striving for control is intrinsic in modern science and technology, the computer comes in as a quasi-intelligent and quasi-autonomous agent allowing us to exercise control on an unprecedented scale. It can be programmed to handle formerly unimaginable complexity and to function in settings where humans could not survive. Thus, in an age where the possibility for international understanding seemed forever blocked, the computer was taken as a technological guarantee for safety.

The computer has even acquired a mythical significance for many people lost in a disenchanted world. Beliefs in a future governed by machine-implemented rationality, in beings originally created by us but later developing on their own, thrive on myths taken from antique sagas and the ancient religions. They are reflected, in particular, in the roles cast out for mankind in connection with computers. Here, Man no longer sees himself in the image of God, but, on one hand substitutes for God as the creator of intelligent living machines, on the other hand likens himself to Machines taken as models for desirable behaviour. According to some, intelligent machines would even eventually take over, set up constraints for humans and treat them as the inferior beings they supposedly are, forever unable to attain their own perfection.

We might be tempted to relegate such ideas to the realm of science fiction. But we find their trace in scientific papers and official research programmes discussing progress in information technology as desirable in its own right with no reference to human concerns. Thus, while upholding the unshaken belief in scientific and technological progress, the established stand on the relation between people and computers tends to be coloured by a pessimistic view of human affairs, and lends itself to the development of technology in a direction that is potentially destructive to the future of human life on earth.

Unlimited beliefs in the computer have found their critics early on, but it takes time for their voice to gain ground in scientific discussion and in public decision making. Their seminal work has helped many of us shape our thinking and formulate our own positions. The most articulate critics were Hubert Dreyfus who, in his book "What Computers Can't Do"[1], furnished a profound philosophical critique of the claims raised by Artificial Intelligence, and Joseph Weizenbaum who, in "Computer Power and Human Reason"[2], voiced an urgent moral appeal to the scientific community to examine its role in developing a potentially destructive technology.

Dreyfus drew on the whole history of philosophy and on arguments taken from biology, psychology and linguistics for pointing out what he saw as unalterable differences between human thinking and the rule-governed symbol ma-

---

[1] [Dreyfus, 1979]
[2] [Weizenbaum, 1977]

nipulation carried out by computer programs. As a result of his detailed analysis he outlined the limits for the potential capabilities of computer programs based on the symbol-manipulation paradigm of traditional Artificial Intelligence. While his argumentation was extremely rich and subtle, his conclusions were met with a mixture of applause and skepticism. In particular, his statement that fundamental limitations of computer-implemented intelligence could, in principle, not be overcome, was rejected by some as pertaining only to the technology we know at present, and being speculative with respect to future developments. Later on, Dreyfus, in collaboration with his brother elaborated a practice-oriented account of his view of human expertise geared towards supporting public decision-making about the application of current computers in support of human skills in our society[3].

In contrast, Weizenbaum took no issue with the claims purported by leading researchers about what computers could do, but addressed the moral issues inherent in an unlimited development and use of computing technology. Speaking like a prophet, he outlined in no uncertain terms the possibility of technology-induced doom and drew the attention of scientists and programmers to their role in contributing to the dehumanization of our social lives brought about by computer technology. Starting from his own experience with the program Eliza he had developed, he showed how easy it was for claims equating human beings and computers to gain social reality by people being willing to attribute human-like qualities to computers. On a large scale this would enable mechanisms of surveillance and control to be computer-implemented and even induce us to entrust vital decisions such as the use of weapon systems to computers with unprecedented destructive potential for our whole civilization.

I see these two books as sharing a common perspective on the world of computing, focussing on advanced research in Artificial Intelligence, and expressing messages complementary to one another. While they provide important inspirations for the issues at stake in the present book, their focus is far away from the everyday world of developing and using computer programs in ordinary settings.

1.1.6 Programming as a human activity

Our understanding of the activity of programming influences the way in which we carry it out, the priorities we set and the methodological support we seek. Thus, it also shapes the results we obtain. In computer science, however, the nature of programming as a human activity has so far received little attention.

In traditional programming methodology, the activity of programming is portrayed as solving given problems. Programs are studied as mathematical objects with intricate formal properties, divorced from the human context of their development and use. Methods are seen as rule systems for finding a solution, starting from an abstract specification and matching it by a correct program derived in steps of refinement and transformation. Large scale software develop-

---

[3] [Dreyfus and Dreyfus, 1986]

ment is treated as the production of a set of programs designed to meet fixed requirements, proceeding in a sequence of separable stages.

Many software developers, educated in traditional programming methodology, experience a painful clash between trying to adhere to their teachings and what actually seems sensible to do. Even less are they prepared for the social role they find themselves in. Computer programs emerge as the outcome of complex human processes of cognition, communication and negotiation, which serve to establish the problem to be dealt with and to anticipate the meaningful embedding of the computer system in its intended use context.

Programming as a human activity takes place in diverse settings. Distinct professional traditions have evolved around problem classes typical for certain application areas. Skill in programming is defined in terms of mastering specific languages, methods and technical environments. Programming involves dealing with people in a variety of roles giving information, making demands and setting constraints. It rests on the software developers' ability to invent relevant ways of using computer technology in the actual situation. It implies constructing formal artifacts to be embedded in the unique application context at hand.

In discussing programming as a human activity, the starting point for several contributions in this book is Peter Naur's view of programming as *theory building*[4]. Theory building here refers to ongoing human processes of increasing our understanding for an area of concern. Theory is what enables us to cope intelligently with questions and problems as they arise. In software development, theory building pertains to the global task of finding ways in which computer technology can meaningfully be applied to meet the customer's demands. Theory building, in this sense, happens as a continuous process. It is enfolded in the totality of activities involved in communicating with the customer, in establishing the requirements, in selecting the technology to be used, and in designing, implementing, using and evaluating the software. Thus, theory building is inherently tied up with the people carrying out software development, be they individuals or teams. Naur draws some radical conclusions. There can be no right method for theory building, as each process unfolds in a unique way. The "life" and "death" of a program depends on the availability of its developers, who alone possess the theory enabling them to make meaningful modifications and enhancements. The role of a software developer is primarily that of a consultant advising the customer.

While Naur provides a stimulating and provocative view of the conceptual and technical aspects of our work as software developers, he says little about its social quality. He leaves open, how we can build a theory shared by a community, even less does he account for how we become instrumental in bringing about a transformed social reality for all people affected by computer based systems.

Kristen Nygaard, by contrast, has studied *programming as a social activity*[5]. He sees software development as a cognitive activity shaped by *perspectives*. Perspectives provide view-points, from which we structure the cognitive pro-

---

[4] [Naur, 1985b], see also [Naur, 1991].
[5] [Nygaard, 1986]

cesses we are involved in. Perspectives, in Nygaard's sense, make us understand the development situation in social terms (as harmony or conflict between the participants); they stand for conceptual repertoires used as a basis for software development (for example object-oriented programming); and for anticipating the use situation (for example the "systems perspective" versus the "tool perspective"). The concept of perspective, as elaborated concretely by Nygaard, is not easy to work with. On one hand it subsumes many different phenomena under the notion of perspectivity, on the other hand it takes no account of the implicit perspectivity always present in subjective authenticity. However, the idea of perspectivity, illustrated by him in its many forms, is undoubtedly basic for illuminating design with others and for others.

The views of Naur and Nygaard are related to many efforts reported in this book. They imply a shift of emphasis from regarding software development as problem solving and production to viewing it as *design*. Design relates the human reality where the computer is to be embedded to the technical reality of the emerging computer program. It is a constructive process, carried out by the people involved in a unique way. It is constituted by their perspectivity and their interaction, by their understanding of the development situation and their anticipation of the use reality. In design we make choices. We create worlds for ourselves or for others to inhabit.

1.1.7 Computer programs in the human world

Traditional computer science does not concern itself with the application of information technology in the human world. This is revealed both in how it views its own scope, and in the approaches admitted into scientific discussion. In particular, the treatment of software development concentrates on development divorced from use. This provides no scientific platform for considering how programs as artifacts can meaningfully be embedded in human activity – although practising computer professionals act as designers for such artifacts.

Thus, the design of computer artifacts tends to be techno-centred: the computer as an artifact is perceived from the developer's perspective and the users are controlled by computer-implemented rules set up by the developers. Human competence on the part of the users is reduced to their ability for operating programs correctly, everything else being an error, and outside the scope of consideration for designers.

Software developers get little guidance for understanding the *use-situation*, where people are carrying out their work with the help of the computer. Therefore, they have no basis for evaluating whether the results of their design appear felicitous there. An adequate consideration of the embedding of computer programs in the human world does indeed require us to go scientifically beyond the formal and mathematical methods provided for in traditional computer science, and to open ourselves to approaches from the humanities.

The approaches developed there for understanding human learning and communication, individual and cooperative work, and the interrelation between technology and organizations, provide a starting point for dealing with the problems at stake here. However, these approaches mostly have been developed with no specific concern for computing. Therefore, we face the task of selecting suitable approaches and tailoring them to the needs of our discipline. As the intertwinement between computer technology and the human world takes place in a variety of contexts, elaborating an adequate understanding for it becomes an extremely challenging task.

In studying the connection between the development and use of computer artifacts, we need to take the following aspects into account:

- the *social granularity*, i.e., are we interested in individuals working with the computer, in groups communicating or cooperating via the computer, in organizations being transformed by the introduction of computer technoloy or in its effect on even larger social agglomerates?
- the complementarity between *theoretical understanding* and *methodical support* for practice, i.e., are we looking for descriptive or prescriptive approaches, and how can these two be combined to infer a suitable orientation for design from a deeper understanding of the use-situation?
- the *type of human activity to be supported* by computer technology, i.e., how can we understand the interleavement of computerized and other work-steps, what kind of pre-understanding is relevant, what metaphors for the computer can best express human meaning for its use in the context at hand?

These problems can be understood and evaluated quite differently in terms of various philosophical schools. For example, the widely discussed book "Understanding Computers and Cognition" by Terry Winograd and Fernando Flores[6] focusses on the embedding of computers in organizations which are viewed as networks of conversations. Winograd and Flores analyze the assumptions underlying conventional computer science in terms of the rationalistic tradition in philosophy, whose fundamental influence they demonstrate in how we think of language, of decision making, of human learning and cognition. In order to transcend the limitations of the rational tradition, they incorporate elements from three schools of thought:

- Hermeneutics, in a somewhat adapted version of Heidegger's philosophy,
- Constructivism, as expressed specifically in the new biology of Maturana,
- Language Philosophy, as found in the speech act theory of Austin and Searle.

By combining these and tailoring them to the problem of design, they elaborate a platform for understanding conversational processes and the role of the computer artifact in supporting them.

Many authors in the present book take off from Winograd and Flores in one way or another. We share with them the concern for providing an adequate foundation and orientation for design. However, our scope and approach differ from theirs in many ways. The most important difference, in my opinion, is that we do not aim at building up one coherent platform for treating all questions relating to design. Instead, individual contributions deal with different levels of

---

[6] [Winograd and Flores, 1986]

social granularity, focus on certain types of human activity to be supported and bring out the relevance of distinct philosophical schools for illuminating specific aspects. This is a conscious choice on our part, as it serves to show the variety of relevant perspectives, whose elements can be combined in manifold ways for coordinating our understanding of design as needed in different contexts.

1.1.8 Towards a foundation for practice

In closing this introduction, I would like to point out that there is no computer science independent from us. Computer science is *what we make it*. Every professional is instrumental in bringing forth computer science. While we are constrained in whatever situation we work, we also have the scope and the option for making choices. Through our choices we shape our own understanding, we set priorities in our scientific work, we produce the technology that reflects our design, and we create conditions for ourselves and others who inhabit a computerized world.

The computer science we know to a large extent still sees itself as a formal and engineering science *only*, and disregards the fundamental human questions raised here. Though the term "Informatics" is widely used in Europe, it does not yet imply a conscious strive towards a more encompassing approach. While the traditional self-understanding may have been appropriate at the time when computer science originated, it does not provide a sufficient basis for viable decisions on developing and using computer technology today. The authors of this book would like to contribute to providing more adequate foundations for practice in science and design.

One key to such deeper understanding is the willingness to reflect on our own practice. Therefore, some of us open up and show how we see our own work, our professional role and our personal motivation. We acknowledge the full human reality of our lives as the basis for scientific work.

However, understanding does not take place in individuals alone. It is shaped by our involvement with others, by the mutuality of complementary view-points allowed into discussion and by reaching insights through dealing with differences and conflicts. Also, we tailor our insights so as to meet our needs and express our values. For this reason, this book offers a variety of view-points in contributions by different authors, some of whom make their values explicit, and not all of whom agree. Thus, the reader is invited to form his or her own opinion.

We should not expect definitive answers to our questions here, but learn to raise them together in more relevant ways, as they apply to individual situations. We need this conversational foundation for working together towards designing computer technology with a view to promoting human development.

Acknowledgements

This chapter draws to some extent on an earlier version, used as a thematic introduction for the conference at Schloß Eringerfeld. I would like to thank my former co-authors Werner Langenheder and Dirk Siefkes for their contribution and my co-editors Reinhard Budde, Reinhard Keil-Slawik and Heinz Züllighoven for helpful discussions.

1.2 Learning from our Errors
Donald E. Knuth

I've always believed that one of the best ways to learn is by a process of trial and error. Indeed, one of my favorite poems is the following 'grook' by Piet Hein:

> The road to wisdom?
> Well, it's plain
> and simple to express:
> > Err
> > and err
> > and err again
> > but less
> > and less
> > and less.

Furthermore, I've often recommended[1] that people keep records of their mistakes, so that such a learning process will be enhanced.

During the past 12 years I had a golden opportunity to practice what I preached, as I was developing and maintaining the TeX software system. I kept track of all changes made to TeX, including the corrections made when the program was originally being debugged. Afterwards I decided that my error log was so instructive, I should not keep it a secret – although it was, of course, quite embarrassing. It seemed to me that the presentation of a true-to-life list of errors might be the best way to help other people learn the lessons that my experiences with TeX have taught me. So I prepared a long paper[2] containing a complete listing of the errors I had noted down.

Of course no single project can be expected to illuminate all the aspects of software development. But the error log of TeX seems to provide useful data for understanding the problems of crafting a medium-size piece of software. It's hard to teach students the concept of "scale" – the enormous difference between textbook examples and larger systems – but I think that a reasonable appreciation of the complexity of a medium-size project can be acquired by spending about two hours reading through a complete log such as the one in my paper.

My error log begins with all the corrections I made while debugging the first version of TeX, which was a program consisting of approximately 4600 statements in an Algol-like language. The log ends with all the changes I made as TeX was becoming a stable system, as TeX began to have more than a million users on more than a hundred varieties of computers. By studying the log you can see all the stages in the evolution of TeX as new features replaced or extended

---

[1] [Knuth, 1968, p. 189]
[2] [Knuth, 1989]

old ones – except that I did not record the changes I made when I rewrote the original program 'TEX78' and prepared the final one, 'TEX82'.[3]

Altogether the error log contains 867 entries so far. I've tried to analyze this data and to introduce some structure by assigning each of the errors to one of 15 categories:

A   Algorithmic Anomaly
B   Blunder, Botch
C   Cleanup for Consistency
D   Datastructure Debacle
E   Efficiency Enhancement
F   Forgotten Function
G   Generalization, Growth
I   Interactive Improvement
L   Language Liability
M   Mismatch between Modules
P   Promotion of Portability
Q   Quest for Quality
R   Reinforced Robustness
S   Surprising Scenario
T   Trivial Typo

Categories A, B, D, F, L, M, R, S, T are *bugs*, which definitely needed to be removed from the code; categories C, E, G, I, P, Q are *enhancements*, which improved TEX but were not obligatory. I consider both bugs and enhancements to be *errors*, for if I had designed a perfect system in the beginning I would not have made any of these changes and my error log would have been empty.

The most important lessons I learned can be summarized in the following theses, which my paper defends and explains in detail:

(1) TEX would have been a complete failure if I had merely specified it and not participated fully in its initial implementation. The process of implementation constantly led me to unanticipated questions and to new insights about how the original specifications could be improved.

(2) TEX would have been much less successful if I had not used it extensively myself. In fact, when TEX was new I thought of 100 ways to improve it as I was typesetting 700 pages over a period of several months, at a nearly constant rate of one enhancement per 7 pages typed. (On the other hand, the new ideas ceased when I went on to type hundreds of additional pages; 700 was enough! I got most of the later suggestions from other people, and I was able to appreciate them because of my own experiences.)

(3) TEX would have been much less successful if I had not put considerable effort into writing a user manual for it myself. The process of explaining the language gave me views of the system that I never would have perceived if I had merely designed it, implemented it, and used it.

---

[3] Those changes were summarized briefly in another publication for early users [Beeton, 1983].

(4) TEX would have been much less successful if I had not scrapped the first system and written another system from scratch, after having the benefit of several years' hindsight.

(5) TEX would have been much less successful if I had not had the voluntary assistance of dozens of people who regularly gave me feedback on how to improve everything. The network of volunteers eventually became worldwide, perhaps because I decided that TEX should be in the public domain.

(6) I recommend that everybody keep an error log such as the one I kept for TEX. The amount of extra time required is negligible (less than 1%), and the resulting records help us to understand ourselves and our fallible natures.

(7) The methodology of structured programming reduced my debugging time to about 20% of what it was under my habits of the 60s. Furthermore, structured programming gave me enough confidence in my code that I did not feel the need to test anything for six months, until the entire system was in place and ready for testing. Therefore I saved considerable time by not having to do any unnecessary prototyping.

(8) Although certain features of programming languages can justly be considered harmful, we should not expect that eliminating such features will eliminate our tendency to err. For example, 12 of my errors can be ascribed to misuse of **goto** statements[4]; but that accounts for only 1.4% of the total, and I also made mistakes when using **while, case, if-then-else**, etc.

(9) TEX proved to be highly reliable and portable because it was subjected to a "torture test," which is quite different from anything a sane user would write but which really tries hard to make the system fail. We should strive energetically to find faults in our own work, even though it is much easier to find assurances that things are OK.

My experiences agree well with Peter Naur's hypothesis[5] that programming is "theory building," and they strongly support his conclusion that programmers should be accorded high professional status. But I do not share Naur's unproved assertion that "reestablishing the theory of a program merely from the documentation is strictly impossible." On the contrary, I believe that improved methods of documentation[6] are able to communicate everything necessary for the maintenance and modification of programs. I think it's fair to claim that more than 100 people, perhaps more than 1000, now understand the "theory" of the TEX program after merely reading its documentation[7]. For I have seen numerous examples of electronic communications in which many people have demonstrated such knowledge by making excellent special-purpose extensions to the existing code and by giving highly appropriate advice to users.

Therefore I now look forward to making further errors in my next project.

The preparation of this paper was supported in part by National Science Foundation grant CCR-86-10181.

---

[4] [Knuth, 1974]
[5] [Naur, 1985b]
[6] Which I have called "literate programming"[Knuth, 1984, Bentley, 1986].
[7] [Knuth, 1986]

Part 2

Living Computer Science

Christiane

The traditional pursuit of science is such that the scientist, as a human being, remains invisible. The observer stays in the background; the results of his work are to the fore.

Reinhard K.-S.

The only thing that counts is the ostensibly objective result, which is measured in terms of dispassionate truth. We have come to realize that science is also a social process.

Reinhard B.

But the scientific establishment denies this and drives many scientists into seclusion.

Christiane

And, for the computer scientist, this seclusion is frequently reinforced by exclusive concentration on the computer when designing systems.

Heinz

This mastery of the computer is precisely what is marvelled at by the public. A feeling of wonder in the face of technology is nothing new. The illustration portrays a sage of the Athens School inside an ancient Chinese planetarium. Even in Antiquity, astronomers and astrologers were marvelled at.

Christiane

But the very fact of their being marvelled at makes it difficult for scientists to open themselves and point out their limitations and needs ...

Reinhard K.-S.

...and convey to us an idea of the personal strivings and motivations underlying their professional work.

Reinhard B.

We are aware of the gap between living reality and what we are doing in computer science. We are building our own ivory tower, as it were – designed to contain that which is controllable, formal and, at the same time, new and fascinating.

Heinz

But, beyond this technical fascination, it is human beings that are constantly bringing themselves face to face with us. They are looking for ways of making themselves understood.

Reinhard K.-S.

Take, for example, the interplay between teaching and learning. For the student, it is only the lived truthfulness of the teacher that guarantees the veracity of the results obtained.

Christiane

This is exemplified in the contribution of Peter Löhr who writes about his poignant sense of the division between technical and human concerns in computer science; about his enthusiasm as a scientist and his malaise about the way computerization threatens to alienate human life. Some would not hesitate to devise an algorithm for consoling a crying child.

Reinhard B.

By emphasizing the human element he is adressing an issue that is of significance to many computer scientists. But truthfulness is not only essential in our dealings with students, but also in our own professional work.

Christiane

Joseph Goguen introduces himself as a practising Buddhist. He draws parallels between Hermeneutics and ancient Buddhist teachings, showing how the resulting insights can be directly applied to the study of scientific texts. Interpretation is regarded here as a path to be followed by practice.

Heinz

What I find striking is that some of the theoreticians among the scientists are the very people who identify themselves with a spiritual orientation.

Christiane

Rod Burstall, too, writes as a practising Buddhist. He sees the individual's personally emergent view of reality as "reality construction" and shows how working at the computer – with its one-sided emphasis on mastery and control – influences the reality of relations between human beings.

Reinhard K.-S.

These two contributions are of a predominantly introspective nature. But there is a certain tension between spritiual and social concerns that cause us to turn our attention to external matters.

Christiane

In his autobiographical account, Kristen Nygaard highlights the intertwinement of research interests and social concerns in his scientific work. His commitment to workers' interests has led to new technical approaches as well as to trend-setting legislation for computer-supported work.

Heinz

What we see here is one way of integrating scientific concerns into life as a whole. But, depending on the individual personality, this integration may take place in a variety of ways.

Christiane

Douglas Ross sees his life as the gradual emergence of an overall view of nature, to which he gives the name PLEX. And he sees this process of epistemological discovery as incorporating both his scientific work and his private life. PLEX constitutes for him a universal frame of reference, but one which he finds difficult to convey to others.

Reinhard B.

Unfortunately, only male views are represented here. We tried in vain to secure a contribution from a woman other than our co-editor.

Christiane

I think, we should bring in our female experiences of living computer science. We might be able to help give science and technology a new orientation. An orientation not towards mastery and control, but towards common life and survival on this planet.

2.1 The Technical and the Human Side of Computer Science

Klaus-Peter Löhr

A scientific discipline, like any other field of human activity, is shaped by various factors such as individual achievements and discoveries, social context, economic pressure and, last not least, fashion and trends. For most disciplines, it is not too hard to give a comprehensive description of their essence, for instance, "computer science deals with principles and practice of construction, programming and application of digital computers". A deeper understanding, however, has to cover origins, history, folklore and so on, and cannot be gained without taking into account all the aforementioned influential factors.

The complexity of the issue asks for a scientific approach or, at least, scientists would ask for it, and the computing profession has indeed come under the scrutiny of social scientists. While their efforts are certainly necessary and yield valuable insights, we may suspect that, on the one hand, the social scientist lacks technical insight into the subject; on the other hand, there is a bit of a vicious circle in every self-referential activity: can a scientific approach be adequate for understanding a scientific discipline?

I am not able to give final answers to such questions. I contend, however, that we would understand computer science much better if we would just listen to what the scientists say about themselves, their motivations, their ambitions, their perceived constraints and their opinions on the interdependence of the technical and the human side of their profession.

Unfortunately, though, there is not much to listen to. Computer scientists are basically engineers, often with a strong mathematical inclination. Their disposition towards analytical thinking, abstraction, formalisms et cetera is reinforced during their studies. The curricula are devoid of non-technical subjects; the human side of computer science is confined to optimization issues such as programming productivity and human-computer interaction. Students are not trained to meditate on their science from a broader perspective and are not encouraged to take up a stance about social responsibility and professional ethics.

Note that this situation may be regarded as only a symptom of a deeper problem – the often-deplored split between the "two cultures" (sciences and humanities). This is a vast issue which I do not intend to get lost in here.

I do intend, however, to give some personal reflections on the technical versus the human side of our profession. Like most of my fellow scientists, I am no expert on this subject either. I studied mathematics because I enjoyed it at high school. Our curriculum had no connection at all with the humanities. After having finished my university degree I worked with computers and found mathematics more and more boring because I could not accommodate to the wide gap between mathematics and reality. Computers and programming seemed to be "the real stuff". In particular, I considered programming at the hardware/software interface to be the most 'real' programming. So I got attracted to operating systems – only to recognize that I was again far from reality. After having worked as a computer scientist in the operating systems field for several years I realized that systems programming was software development after all, and also became interested in programming languages and software engineering.

This kind of motivation may be typical for quite a few so-called systems people in computer science and computer engineering. They want to build something. Often they are not genuinely interested in applications and run the risk to do "l'art pour l'art". For example, computer engineers have built all kinds of parallel computers over the years, only to find out that they didn't have sound principles for programming them. This sort of confusion is not untypical for computer science (although encountered in other disciplines as well). Its roots lie in the personal motivation of people who simply enjoy solving difficult problems and building interesting artifacts.

Everybody knows that a wide variety of problems can be solved automatically with the aid of computers. The computer scientist also knows that it is of vital importance to apply the automation principle to information technology itself. The evolution of operating systems from heavy reliance on operators towards complete autonomy is a point in case. Programming languages are another example. Early assembly languages or early Fortran were claimed to be "automatic programming systems" (there even was a programming language called "Autocoder"). This may sound silly today, but made some sense when many programmers were using machine code and introducing symbolic locations relieved them of the burden of managing memory addresses.

Today, the shift from imperative to declarative programming represents another important automation step. This has already been noticed by keen vendors who advertise systems that they claim make the dream of automatic programming come true. I saw a system that "automatically generates programs from specifications" – it was just a compiler for a functional programming language. We all know that the notion of automatic programming should be confined to mean generating programs from non-executable specifications; but of course a functional program does many things 'automatically' that the imperative programmer has to do manually.

Now everybody will agree that progressing from assembly languages to declarative languages is indeed 'progress' (whatever connotations any of us may associate with this word). Software engineers are happy with this kind of progress, and we will see more of it in the years to come (for example, automatic support for configuration and version management, or for program transformation). But what about automation outside computer science, that is, the computerization of society?

As an example, would you call the ISDN 'progress'? It is obvious that ISDN unifies and simplifies communication techniques and has substantial economic benefits. But do we really need it? Does it bring progress in the sense of a better quality of life? If not, do the technical and economic benefits outweigh the dangers of an infrastructure that is more prone to abuse than our present non-integrated systems?

An even more thought-provoking example is transmission of moving images. Do we need this for a better quality of life? Or will it just bring about the ultimate TV society?

The computer scientist is not prepared to answer such questions. He (probably 'he' rather than 'she') is not even prepared to ask them. He has a strong bias towards computerized solutions – for all kinds of problems. This is not just because he likes building computerized systems but also because he feels that automation is good for his job – so why not for all jobs?

In conference talks in the seventies, the majority of overhead transparencies were drawn by hand. Only once in a while we were bored by those polished advertising things from industry. In the meantime, we made progress – we got the Mac. Now, where have all these entertaining personal transparencies gone?

People are noticing, though, that perfect slides are boring. Recently, I saw a desktop-published slide with a sort of 'shaky' font which gave the impression of handwriting (at least for a second). Think about it. It reminds me of the robot to help the elderly which will probably be designed to have some 'human touch'.

The enormous versatility of computers can often obscure the fact that a computerized solution is just not adequate, especially if people are involved. It would then be penny-wise but pound-foolish to make the computer system more 'human' or to improve the man-machine interface. Note that the inability to judge adequacy is caused by lack of sensibility and education, not morality. There are well-meaning computer professionals who want to save the world with computers; I feel uneasy about them. My point is that computer scientists should learn, during their studies, the art of self-confinement, a judgement of computer adequacy, a feeling for "convivial tools" (as Ivan Illich has called it) and "small systems" (a term adapted from Eric Schumacher by Dirk Siefkes[1].).

One might argue that this is a rather idealistic view. In reality, information technology means big money and international competition. Research and development are heavily influenced by the huge funding programs we know from Europe, the US and Japan (with the special military twist of the Americans). This funding is geared towards competitiveness in information technology, with the underlying assumption "the more high-tech, the better".

I am not denying that economic and political factors do shape computer science. But I maintain that scientists have a potential to make the human side of computer science much more visible than it is today – and education is the main requirement for this.

Don't think that I am enthusiastic about education. I remember a recent oral examination where the subject of algorithmic problem solving came up. I do treat this subject at length in my introductory courses, emphasizing that many problems are not amenable to algorithmization, and giving examples. In order to provoke a statement about the nature and limitations of algorithms I asked the student: "Do you know an algorithm for consoling a crying child?" To

---

[1] See Chap. 4.2

my dismay, the student began talking about actions like taking a tissue, wiping the child's cheeks and so on; he just had not grasped the essence of the question. The lesson I learned from this was that although we try hard we must try even harder.

For me, amalgamation of technical and human issues in teaching remains a permanent challenge. Often, I am carried away by the attraction of a technical subject, so that not much time is left for reflection about the human side of the subject. Sometimes I feel in danger of only paying lip service to the principles I am advocating. But the effort is worthwhile. Students are generally sympathetic; it is a new learning experience for them – and for me as well.

2.2 Hermeneutics and Path

Joseph A. Goguen

2.2.1 Introduction

Hermeneutics is the study of interpretation, particularly the interpretation of linguistic texts, but also of human experience in general, since this can be seen as both "textual" and "linguistic" in appropriately broad senses of these words.

The works of Heidegger, Gadamer and others[1] say many interesting things about the nature of interpretation and its philosophical implications, but they contain very little for the person who wants to learn how to do interpretation better, or for the person who wants to know how to teach others how to do it; the *practical* dimension is missing from this tradition. There is a striking difference between *philosophy*, which is content to make distinctions and debate issues, and a *path* which provides practices and guidelines for practice, constituting a way forward which is nevertheless based on acknowledging where we are.

Interpretation is a demanding discipline, encompassing essentially everything we are and everything that is. Its practice has the potential to open us up to what we are and what our world is. What is missing is a set of *guidelines* that tell us how to deal with the problems that inevitably arise, and other practices that are less involved with conceptual content and have the possibility of sharpening our general mindfulness and awareness.

This short paper suggests that perhaps Buddhism, and in particular Mahayana Buddhism, can supply this missing practical element. (The word "*mahayana*" means "great path" in Sanskrit, and describes the tradition from which Zen and Tibetan Buddhism have sprung, among others.) The result is that the activity of hermeneutics, that is, of interpreting, can also be a path, by interpreting the term "hermeneutics" sufficiently broadly.

2.2.2 The paramitas

To be a good interpreter, I believe that it helps to be a "good person" in roughly the same sense expressed in Buddhism by the "six paramitas." The word *paramita* means "other shore" in Sanskrit, and refers to action which is not selfish, and which thus transcends this shore of the river of confusion and neurosis. Some hint of this may perhaps be glimpsed in the following brief characterizations, which have been specialized to the interpretation of a text which you should think of as coming from your own time and place:

---

[1] [Heidegger, 1962, Gadamer, 1976] and [Palmer, 1969]; Palmer gives a relatively accessible summary of this tradition.

1. *Dana*, which means generosity in Sanskrit, is the joy of discovering that you don't have to impose your own conceptions on the text, that you can afford to be open to it, that you can give up your conceptual (and preconceptual) territory.

2. *Sila*, which means discipline or morality, is that you don't have to make any special effort, you already have (what is called in ethnomethodology[2]) "member's competence": you are sufficiently grounded in your own tradition and in that of the text to begin work on it, and you are inspired to do so. There is no need for dogma, and you can work with what is actually there.

3. *Ksanti*, or patience, is that you don't have to "succeed," i.e, to satisfy your own, or anybody else's, expectations about the interpretation; you can therefore go at the speed which is proper to the task, and not worry about whether what you discover will be "acceptable".

4. *Virya*, or energy, is to work with what is given, with what you are and what the text is (including the whole context of the text and of yourself); you completely accept the tradition of the text, and then you work from there, without, however, being bound by 'conventional wisdom.' You can actually take delight and inspiration in whatever contradictions and difficulties may arise.

5. *Dhyana*, *chan* [in Chinese], *zen* [in Japanese], or meditative awareness, is to be completely absorbed in the text, without distinguishing between yourself and it, but being fully aware of the environment of the text and of yourself. Your horizon merges with that of the text; or perhaps there is no horizon, that is, no center and no fringe.

6. *Prajna*, or transcendental knowledge, is the precision of discriminating awareness, which is willing and able to recognize and to cut through your preconceptions, as well as those in the text; you can learn from mistakes without worrying about ability or inability, superiority or inferiority. This is "stable awareness" rather than confused awareness.

These characterizations were obtained by combining my interpretation of Trungpa Rinpoche's treatment of the six paramitas[3], with my interpretations of Heidegger, Gadamer and others. These aspects of interpretation (or of meditation) do not necessarily arise in strict sequential order, but there is still a sense in which they build on one another, so that *prajna* is the fruition of the others.

2.2.3 Confusion

The word "confusion" is used here in a somewhat technical sense, referring to mind that is *not* characterized by the paramitas. This is our ordinary confused mind, which sometimes mislays pens and papers, and is often misled by its own hopes and fears.

---

[2] See [Trungpa, 1976].
[3] Cf. [Turner, 1974].

It is important to note that non-confused mind arises by transcending confused mind; clarity does not come to us from some separate pure realm of its own. It arises from accepting what actually happens to us, and working with it as it is, rather than as we wish it were. As Heidegger[4] says,

> when something ready-to-hand is found missing, though its everyday presence has been so obvious that we have never taken any notice of it, this makes a *break* in those referential contexts in which circumscription discovers. Our circumscription comes up against emptiness, and now sees for the first time *what* the missing article was ready-to-hand *with*, and *what* it was ready-to-hand *for*. The environment announces itself afresh ... [and] is thus lit up.

In textual interpretation, this has a very practical meaning: the feelings of confusion, attraction, or aversion which we experience while reading a text, while not necessarily reliable in themselves, are the *energy* that we have for working with the text; they are the breaks in the seemingly seamless seas of meanings that can help us get deeper into the world of the text.

2.2.4 Hermeneutics as path

Without an intimate awareness of how one's own mind works, especially how one's emotional and conceptual baggage get in the way of seeing things as they are, it is difficult to transcend one's confusion and actually use it in textual interpretation. Such an intimate awareness of the confused functioning of mind is difficult to obtain, and according to most Buddhist traditions, the practice of meditation is the most effective way forward.

Indeed, most Buddhist teachers insist that it is necessary to practice meditation in order for paramita practice to be meaningful, because it is necessary to develop the qualities of "mindfulness" and "awareness" first. This kind of meditation practice does not aim to produce either a hypnotic trance state, or to control the restlessness of mind; it is not concentration. Rather, mindfulness-awareness meditation takes as its subject something very simple and natural, such as breath. Mindfulness is attention to what is actually there, "one pointed," direct and precise. Awareness is the context, the space, within which mindfulness happens. This is not at all a matter of calculating or of grasping for meaning. As Trungpa Rinpoche[5] says,

> Mindfulness provides some ground, some room for recognition of aggression, passion and so on. Mindfulness provides the topic or the terms or the words, and awareness is the grammar which goes around and correctly locates the terms. Having experienced the precision of mindfulness, we might ask the question of ourselves, "What should I do with that?

---

[4] See [Heidegger, 1962].
[5] See [Trungpa, 1976].

What can I do next?" And awareness reassures us that we do not really have to do anything with it but can leave it in its own natural place. It is like discovering a beautiful flower in the jungle; shall we pick the flower and bring it home or shall we let the flower stay in the jungle? Awareness says leave the flower in the jungle, since it is the natural place for that plant to grow. So awareness is the willingness not to cling to the discoveries of mindfulness, and mindfulness is just precision; things are what they are.

Or in the words of Heidegger[6], "we should *do* nothing, but rather wait."
In this way, one comes to see the nature of the mind; that is, meditation is the interpretation of mind. Thus, the path of hermeneutics is the path of meditation. Of course, Buddhism is concerned with one's whole life, not just with how one interprets texts; but because one's life can be viewed as a text, these concerns are quite closely related.

2.2.5 Hermeneutics in the practice of science

There are many ways that the paramitas might be relevant to the practice of science. Perhaps the most obvious is also the most personal: the scientist might practice meditation, and hence change the way he relates to everything, including science. But let us consider something simpler and more direct, reading a scientific paper by Dijkstra[7], which is the basis for a course at Oxford which I have been teaching.

As it happens, Dijkstra has not been one of my favorite authors; so the first paramita, *dana* or generosity, has a particularly pointed meaning here: I should drop my prejudices and open up to the text; insofar as I succeed in this, my experience will both be more pleasant and more accurate; just that realization brings a sense of relief. Of course, I must also be aware of what I already know and do not know as I work with the text, and this is *sila* or discipline. *Ksanti* or patience means not only that I should be willing to work through any technical difficulties that may arise as I read, but also that I don't have to compete with the author.

Virya or energy arises as I actually do all this; if I've got the first three paramitas right, there will be no particular pain or frustration to this process, but rather it will be natural and self-energizing. This leads to *dhyana*, awareness, in which I can be authentically engaged with the text and its context, including other related texts and my own being. This does not mean that I must accept everything the author says; on the contrary, I am now in a position to appreciate it properly and fully, both its strengths and weaknesses, as well as my own; this is *prajna* or discriminating awareness.

And what did I learn? The paper is very concise, clearly and compellingly written, has excellent examples, and has stood the test of time (this can be

---

[6] Cf. [Heidegger, 1966].
[7] [Dijkstra, 1975]

seen by comparison with other *CACM* papers from that year, and also from the large literature that it has inspired). However, I was irritated that the author paid no attention to logical foundations or to model theoretic semantics, and gave no indications of the limitations of his methods; also, I kept wondering how to formulate things more algebraically. Eventually, I discovered that the issue of foundations is rather subtle (something like infinitary logic, as explored by Engeler in the 1960s, is needed), that the model theoretic semantics is awkward, that the approach works poorly for large programs (since no account is taken of modules or of data structures), and that category theoretic formulations have already been given[8]. Also, I discovered that worry about all of this got in the way of my appreciating the elegance of the language design, the beauty of the examples, the motivation in terms of programming style, and the richness of the research that this paper opened up. So in the end, I learned something about myself as well.

In discussing interpretation, we are not talking about discovering some objective truth about a text. Rather, there is a very intimate relationship between the interpreter and the interpreted, in which each is uncovered to the extent that the enterprise succeeds. As Heidegger says, "interpretation is never a presuppositionless grasping of something given in advance."[9] Indeed, it is typical that we can learn the most about ourselves from those texts, or parts of texts, where we have the strongest reactions.

2.2.6 Emptiness and beyond

Buddhism might perhaps be described as a participatory phenomenological hermeneutics of mind, leading to the experience (not just the idea) of non-duality between self and other, and between mind and body. In contrast, traditional science is a hermeneutics of other, which already presupposes subject-object duality.

The traditions of meditation and hermeneutics that we have been discussing are not consistent with this classical version of science. In particular, Heidegger presents a stinging critique of the Western metaphysical tradition, including science and technology.[10] Heidegger's hermeneutics opposes the idea that there are *objects* already given in the world, which are *observed* by *subjects*; it opposes the ideas of control and manipulation, whether for material or intellectual gain; and it opposes our usual idea of *idea*, a pre-existing intellectual structure which we see only dimly, as on the walls of Plato's cave. Similar views can be found in Buddhism.

Both Buddhism and science are complex evolving systems, with no ultimate commitment to any particular dogma, belief or theory; instead, each is united by its commitment to particular methods and by immersion in its particular historical tradition. Both are characterized by debate, and by the growth of

---

[8] For example, in [Manes and Arbib, 1986].
[9] See [Heidegger, 1962].
[10] Cf. [Heidegger, 1977c].

insight. And contemporary science may even be developing some appreciation for the inseparability of subject and object.[11]

In Buddhism, "emptiness," or *shunyata* in Sanskrit, refers to this non-duality of self and other, that is, of subject and object. These are our two most basic and generic concepts, and without them, all other concepts are also empty. *Shunyata* is thus an opposite to Plato's doctrine of ideas. But *shunyata* is not a doctrine of nihilism. Indeed, without concepts, the world can shine forth more brightly. For if we ask, "Are self and other the same? Or are they different?" we find that they are neither the same nor different. For in any experience of self and other as being the same or different, self and other necessarily arise together. As Hayward[12] says,

> as the mutual dependence [of objects] with the perceiver is felt, they shine with a spacious but self-luminous quality that is at the same time empty of inherent existence. This luminosity that is beyond concept is the fullness of *shunyata*.

Similarly, Heidegger says in "The Origin of the Work of Art"[13], of a Greek temple set in a valley, that it

> causes [its material] to come forth for the very first time and to come into the Open of the work's world. The stone comes to bear and rest and so first becomes stone; metals come to glitter and shimmer, colors to glow, tones to sing, the word to speak.

Acknowledgements

First of all, I thank Vidyadhara, the Venerable Chögyam Trungpa, Rinpoche for whatever little I know about Buddhism. I also thank Prof. Rod Burstall of the University of Edinburgh, Dr. José Meseguer of SRI International, and my wife Kathleen, for many helpful comments and conversations, and both Naropa Institute and the Center for the Study of Language and Information at Stanford University for partial support and for stimulating environments. Special thanks to Dr. Charlotte Linde, from which I learned much of what I know about discourse analysis and sociolinguistics.

The basic text of this piece was found buried in my computer file system; it was written about 1976 for a course on Discourse Analysis that I taught at Naropa Institute with Dr. Charlotte Linde. It was then lightly edited at SRI in 1988 for distribution at the *Conference on Software Development and Reality Construction*, and was put into its present form at Oxford in early 1990.

---

[11] See [Hayward, 1987] for more discussion along similar lines.
[12] [Hayward, 1987]
[13] [Heidegger, 1971]

2.3 Computing: Yet Another Reality Construction

Rodney M. Burstall

For the past twenty-five years I have been working as a Computer Scientist, for the last fifteen I have put a considerable amount of effort into the study and practice of Buddhism, under the general direction of Trungpa Rinpoche, a Tibetan Buddhist teacher. These two points of view are not easy to reconcile, although both have the same basic attitude of "try it and see if it works". But all of us have a work life and a personal life to live, sometimes separate, but sometimes mingling, with intrusions of kindness into the office or of electronics into the home. The boundary, like all frontiers has its pains, so it seemed worthwhile to try to dissolve it a little and accept an invitation to write something about all this. Perhaps the Buddhist point of view will seem foreign or unacceptable to you, but it may be worthwhile to remember that there is more than one way of looking at our computing world.

2.3.1 Reality: cultural and computational variants

In the Buddhist tradition there are two veils which separate us from enlightened mind

- Conflicting emotions,
- Primitive views of reality.

Working with computers and working with other people who work with computers, we develop our own particular attitude to our emotions and our own particular view of reality, or own particular style as the computing community. This style affects both our working lives and our personal lives. It runs a good deal less deep than our inheritance of Western European (Greek/Jewish/Christian) culture or Japanese culture, or whatever we happen to be landed with; but because the computer metaphor is a powerful one it probably has a significant influence on the way we see our world. I would like to open up here some discussion of our computer-influenced view of reality.

It is hard for us to see that we have a particular reality. We just think it is the reality, perhaps not quite perfectly revealed to us. We can get a glimpse of other people's realities from reading Social Anthropology, or poetry or novels[1],

---

[1] For example "Hanta Yo", by Ruth Beebe Hill, or "The World is not Enough" by Zoe Oldenbourg, or "The Tale of Genji" by Lady Murasaki, or "Njal's Saga" by an unknown Icelandic author.

perhaps from reading Greek Philosophers or Early Christian Fathers. I do not mean their description of their reality, their philosophical dicta. I mean how to feel as they feel, how to see as they see.

Our European reality has moved from the Medieval Christian world, concentric spheres surrounded with celestial realms, a view which we now find puzzling and remote, through a Newtonian world of empty space and point masses inclined to linear motion, to an incipient view of our earth as a rather fragile organism.

In the Buddhist tradition it is very central that our reality is constructed, as opposed to the commonly held opinion that it is given or uncovered. The root cause of our confusion, distress and anxiety is that our view of reality is distorted by our dispositions, based on past anger, desire and stupor. These create our habitual misinterpretation of the world through the bias of our own neurotic emotions, our continual reference point of self.

From the standpoint of Computer Science or Artificial Intelligence the idea that we construct our reality makes a lot of sense. The naïve view that you tell a computer what to do and it does it is far removed from our experience of programming languages and operating systems. Every byte of input is interpreted with respect to many kilobytes or even megabytes of lexical and syntax tables, command interpreters, page tables, indirect addresses and what have you. A robot arm/TV camera set up cannot possibly work without some programmed-in notion of visual and manipulative model, and it is only able to see or act in terms of this model.

Another way in which computing helps to suggest the relativity of our framework of reality is the difference between programming language or operating system paradigms. Imperative languages, functional languages and logic programming languages, each provide a different means of expressions, a different notion of computation.

But what is the style of thinking inculcated by the usual practice of computing? Computing systems seem to be totally understandable; you start with a general notion of what is supposed to happen and work your way down through module documentation to the high level language code and eventually even to the object code produced by the compiler. It is all there; you can spell it out. So the computational viewpoint suggests the possibility of completely grasping and mastering our world in a formal framework of concepts and definitions.

I would like to suggest here some of the ways in which our involvement with computing may bias our overall point of view, leading to additional confusion and pain in our lives, both our working lives and our personal lives. I am not seeking to indict the computing view and replace it with some other doctrine, rather to see that it is just a particular perspective which should not solidify into yet another version of "reality". To quote Hayward[2]

The ... "discovery of insight" is realizing and trusting in the causal efficacy and interrelatedness of the world. It is direct, penetrating insight into causal relationships of the relative world so that one begins to see

---

[2] [Hayward, 1984]

how much is presupposed and taken for granted in our usual experience of the ordinary world. With this discovery the practitioner need not cling either to particular reference points for perception, or to logic in an attempt to sustain only his own viewpoint. He can begin to adopt various viewpoints without partiality.

2.3.2 Computing as power and control

In working with a computer we interact with a small world, partly of our own creation, in which we have a special role. We are the agent who makes things happen. In this world we play the role traditionally assigned to God. We have complete power and our aim is to control everything that happens in this world. The better we are at programming the more nearly we approach total control over what happens. Bugs are an unfortunate accident which further perseverance and skill will eliminate. Everything in this world is open to our inspection, and in principle we can have complete knowledge. We can strip away levels of complexity, expanding macros, looking at object code, at the very bit-patterns. There is some bottom level, the hardware level as a programmer sees it, at which we have complete information about the whole situation.

This is almost a caricature of the basic attitude of Western science which is dedicated to extending our control over the world, placing us as nearly as possible in a position of omnipotence. We might say that we are indulging in Technotheism, technology as a means to achieve god-like control of the universe. The computer enables us to simulate this, precisely by creating a world in which we enjoy complete control. It is all very exciting, and undreamt of power is just around the corner. Byte Magazine, for example, gives the flavour of this. I find it very seductive.

Contrast this with an attitude of respect for other inhabitants of our world, other people, animals or forests, a view of the world in which we do not have some distinguished role. In such an attitude we are open to the richnesss of phenomena over which we have no dominion. Think of sitting on a hillside watching the clouds move through the sky, as opposed to sitting at your terminal.

2.3.3 Living in our heads

Working with computers we have a strong tendency to retreat inside our heads. We live in an abstract symbolic world with little or no connection with our bodies. We certainly have a mental representation of our bodies, mind-body, as it is called in some Buddhist traditions, but we may pay almost no attention to body as a sense of heaviness, of touch, of solidity. This is a reflection of our tendency to ignore the earth and our connection with ground.

One way in which this manifests is the kind of intent absorption which we can experience working at a terminal. Outer stimuli are shut off, as we hunch over the keyboard. Gaps rarely occur and it may be hard for us to find the space to restructure our thinking. Taking a fresh look at what we are doing, even at the level of restructuring part of the program we are developing, can be difficult. We simply do not have the space to do that.

This confined, groundless feeling seems to continue after we stop work. It reinforces our search for entertainment. We shut off our perceptions, and we are unwilling to switch modes to interact with a world of taste, smell or bodily feeling. This can be quite painful and neurotic, a sort of disembodied restlessness, and it is hard to shake off. The groundlessness encourages the speediness, the lack of gap; our world is small and full, like a video game. Compare this with the feeling of contact with body and earth as expressed by Trungpa Rinpoche[3]:

> Imagine that you are sitting naked on the ground, with your bare bottom touching the earth. . . . Earth is always earth. The earth will let anyone sit on it, and earth never gives way. It never lets you go – you don't drop off this earth and go flying through outer space.

We cannot just switch off this state of mind but we can become somewhat aware of it and how it affects the people around us.

2.3.4 Conceptual thought

A striking difference between the computational tradition and the Buddhist tradition is the place assigned to conceptual thought. In the former it is the be-all and end-all, in the latter it has a subordinate role.

Almost everything we work with in computing is at the level of concept, logic or language. We come to think of mind as functioning in slightly sugared Lisp or Prolog, a central process tidily building and moving around data structures. Consider what happens when we give a seminar. From a naïve computer point of view this is transmission of data down a channel. A stream of bytes is to be transmitted from the speaker to the audience; we have to ensure correctness and completeness. So we make some transparencies faithfully transcribing our formulae. We worry whether we will have enough time; should we skip some parts? We use LaTeX and invent major and minor headings. This leaves us little time to think about the audience:

- Who are they?
- What do they know already?
- What problems do they have?
- How would this material be helpful to them?

The main thing is to get the bytes from the disc to the laser printer and then into their heads.

A caricature? But it is the way the task looks from a computing perspective. Of course we have enough natural intelligence and life experience to be not completely limited by this. Nevertheless the caricature has a ring of truth in it, at least from my own experience.

---

[3] [Trungpa, 1984]

If we examine the detailed working of our mind through meditation practice, we first notice a tumultuous sea of internal dialogue, disorganized and uncontrollable. But as we persevere we also note the possibility of non-verbal awareness. The conceptual thread is not the lifeline needed to keep us conscious; we can rest in a state of non-conceptual awareness for some longer or shorter period of time. Staying alive, the maintenance of our being, is no longer identified with conceptual thought.

2.3.5 Awareness

We normally focus on the conceptual content of our mind; working with computers tends to reinforce this tendency. We assume that the way to dispel ignorance is to accumulate more data; this at least seems to be an implicit assumption in much of our education system. Outside areas like sport or surgery, acquiring skills is a less prestigious matter than learning facts. This is noticeable in Computer Science education where knowledge may be rated more highly than programming ability. Indeed we think that we can make people better programmers by describing to them more sophisticated methods of program development.

Coming a long way behind knowledge acquisition, even behind skill acquisition is the cultivation of awareness. In the Buddhist traditions however awareness is regarded as a prime antidote to ignorance. There are some things we have never learnt, but there are many more that we "know" or could perceive but which are outside our awareness. We read the newspaper while our wife/husband quietly sobs across the breakfast table, so to speak. Less dramatically we exclude from consciousness all the nuances of other people's feelings and states of mind, and all the small sights and sounds which convey the brilliance of the phenomenal world.

Even in terms of our trade, if computing teaches us excessive respect for data and conceptual thought at the expense of awareness, we lose the ability to accomplish our computational goals.

Awareness of other people

Worthwhile computing almost always means working with other people, as a member of a team, directing research or obtaining funding for it. What proportion of our PhD study is directed to cultivating our ability to be aware of others, to tune in to their minds and their perception of a situation? Even two people working together on a research problem or on developing a programming system, create all sorts of fixed positions, ownership of ideas and unwillingness to retract. It is very painful to give up our ideas. If we do not have some awareness of this situation and the demands it makes on our generosity, progress is really difficult.

Awareness of atmosphere

More subtle perhaps is awareness of atmosphere, in a meeting or a seminar. What is the temperature, when has the atmosphere become inert, dead, when has it sparked again? We all perceive such things and use them to help us communicate, but they are not thought of as "real", like the agenda or the minutes. Our rationalist and computational bias tends to blind us to such phenomena, even though our everyday experience forces us to be somewhat sensitive to them.

Awareness of energy in a situation

Intuitively we can pick up on the energy in a situation. We know when a group of people are fired by a good research idea. We can feel the change in atmosphere in the work place, the liveliness of the people. Sometimes we can notice how this liveness gets blocked. Our skills in conducting or assessing computing projects depend largely on our sensitivity to such atmosphere, and in our informal chat we often refer to it. But in a "rational", "methodical", "well-structured" world view, there is no reference to it. We deny the very skills which are most important to us.

I really believe that well-meant attempts to assess research more objectively, to set up in advance goals and measures of success, are often flawed because they ignore such considerations. The conceptual structure cannot encompass the fluidity and delicacy of the phenomena.

The space of awareness allows insight to arise. Not deductive reasoning, but the sort of sudden flash with which we are all familiar when we are working on some mathematical or computational problem, or even choosing a birthday present. Methodologies of programming which deny the role of intuitive insight in program development, imposing a process of remorseless top-down handholding, seem stultifying and unproductive. In the same way systems for program development based on partly automating formal reasoning are much more likely to be helpful when they provide a vehicle for us to express our intuitive insights into a problem than when they try to take over the reins; just as a screen editor is useful because it makes it easier for us to say what we want to say, without trying to impose a rationale on our creativeness.

Wilber in his book "A Sociable God"[4], suggests, with justice I believe, that our culture dismisses everything other than rational thought as inferior, magic or myth, based on emotion and primitive logic. Certainly the mythic level of football crowds, patriotic wars or religious struggles is something which should be cooled by the application of reason. But he asserts that there are levels of consciousness transcending rational or conceptual thought. Of these the sort of panoramic awareness which can see a whole situation at once stands as an example; this is not a supernatural power but one which we all have to some degree and which we can cultivate. Another example mentioned above is being in tune with subtle energies in a human situation. These are powers which our culture ignores or devalues. We may be concerned lest computer culture lead us further in this denial.

As to the means of cultivating awareness and insight, many are on offer, including for example the Buddhist practice of Shamatha-Vipashyana (peacefulness-awareness) meditation which I am practising. The main thing is to experiment

---

[4] [Wilber, 1983]

for oneself, with some guidance, and discover what seems to work. But the starting point, motivating any such endeavour, is to take a critical look at out present situation.

2.3.6 Conclusions

I have not tried to suggest that we should regard computing as some kind of evil trap which will warp our minds in a way hitherto unknown to man. Computing carries a great deal of energy in our current culture, and it fuels our curiosity and inventiveness. But in order to fully enjoy its possibilities we need to appreciate the way it can subtly influence our frame of thought. The recognition of this influence does not itself free us; but it may provide a starting point for us to look for ways of working with computers without being entrapped by a limited perspective based on desire for control and exclusive reliance on conceptual thought.

Acknowledgements

It has been difficult for me to write this – my first and very clumsy attempt at anything of this kind. Nevertheless I am grateful for the opportunity to attempt to put into words something of the tension which I feel between my working life and what little I have been able to learn of the Buddhist path. This tension can be creative, inspiring further effort at practice and understanding. It is something of a relief to share it with others who may find it reflected in their own lives.

I would like to acknowledge my debt to my computational colleague and fellow Buddhist student Joseph Goguen for many years of discussions; to Han de Wit of the Free University, Amsterdam, and Sherab Chodzin for trying to sharpen my mind; to my wife Seija and my daughters Kaija and Taru for companionship on this path; to my colleagues at Edinburgh Computer Science Department for their tolerance; to Christiane Floyd for asking me to contribute to this book. Finally I express my profound gratitude to Ven. Chogyam Trungpa Rinpoche for his wisdom and kindness.

2.4 How Many Choices Do We Make? How Many Are Difficult?

Kristen Nygaard

I have been asked to write about some of the choices I have had to make as a scientist – choices relating to social responsibility. This is a very dangerous task, since it may easily become a tale of a battle between evil and good, with oneself as the hero. In fact, I do not know how to avoid that trap: there have been battles with very much to lose, and one had to mobilize a strong belief in the cause one was fighting for.

Some people believe that scientists lead a noble life, aloof and relieved from conflicts, escaping annoying decisions, only guided by the quest for new discoveries and truths, so different from the tumultuous and hazardous existence of a businessman. Other people, like myself, would rather state that being engulfed in the research and development jungle, one is sometimes longing for the peace and safety of the marketplace. This is only a general remark, and my paper will not live up to any expectations raised by it.

Informatics (computer science) and Operational Research (OR) emerged as sciences in the wake of the last world war. I started at the University of Oslo in 1945, with computing in 1948, programming around 1950, and with Operational Research in 1952. I got my cand. real.-degree in Mathematics in 1956, having worked (mostly full time) at the Norwegian Defense Research Establishment (NDRE) since 1948. From 1956 on I had the task of building up the use of OR in the Norwegian Defense. I was active politically from 1945 on in the non-socialist but left-oriented party "Venstre" ("The Left", corresponding to, say, the left wing of the British Liberals).

For me, informatics and OR have always been closely related, and I tend to see many tasks in informatics from the perspective of OR. I left OR in the mid-1960s, however, mainly because the OR community in my opinion became too obsessed with optimization and too little with decision support, and because it failed to realize that a thorough knowledge and mastery of the computer is a necessary part of competence in OR.

A major and, at the time, largely undebated assumption in the development of the post-war culture was that "technological progress happens, it is politically neutral – and *good!*". (The concern about atomic weapons was one of the exceptions.) In Operational Research, however, the situation was somewhat different: The task was to find the best use of men and equipment, *dependent upon a stated set of objectives*. If the objectives were modified, the "best use" changed. Also, the development of new equipment had to be fine tuned to a proper understanding of the objectives of the decision-makers. And those objectives could be highly political, particularly in the military field. The application of OR techniques to conflicts between interest groups *within* organizations was an idea dear to an OR researcher.

Our OR work turned out to be quite successful, and that created an unexpected conflict. I wanted OR to be a science and our work to be research, providing support for decisions made by those having the responsibility for the activities we analyzed. I discovered that many in the military establishment were only too happy to have the researchers point out "the correct solution" to some of the hot issues, and that my Director at the NDRE was only too happy to see a development that gave more power to his institute. I tried to counter this by being very careful in pointing out which conclusions could be validly drawn from our work and also the factors that we had not taken into account. I felt that unless we did, both OR and the decision structures would be undermined.

The military people appreciated this attitude after some clarifying discussions. The conflict with the Director developed further, and as a consequence I left the NDRE in 1960 to build up the Norwegian Computing Center as a research institute in computing and OR.

The conflict also made me aware of corresponding problems in keeping democratic control in the planning processes in Norwegian politics, both at the local and at the national level. As a result, a debate was initiated among planners about our professional role, and I once more went into party politics. (At the time when Simula was finished, I was the chair of my party's Strategy Committee. Soon after I became a member of the 5–person top leader group of the party whose parliamentary group then participated in the Norwegian coalition government.)

When the first version of Simula, Simula I, was made available in the spring of 1965, it was immediately used in a series of jobs in Norway and, even more, in Sweden. It was of course fascinating to see the tool we had developed being put to practical use and influencing the design of organizations and production facilities.

It was evident that the Simula-based analyses were going to have a strong influence on the working conditions of the employees: job content, work intensity and rhythm, social cooperation patterns were typical examples. The impacts clearly tended to be negative. Not surprising, since the analyses were founded upon a Tayloristic view of management.

My own sympathies were with the employees, and the question was unavoidable: Should I continue to support the propagation of a tool that to a large extent was used against those to whom I wanted to show my solidarity?

As I have said, it was not at all a new experience for me that research had implications in politics. But these had mainly been consequences from one world into another, relating to commonly hailed democratic ideals. I was active in the research world and in the political world, but they were separate.

Now matters were different: The demand I had to make was that analyses should be made as in Operational Research. The "best use" of labour and equipment ought to be evaluated both from the objectives of management *and* from the objectives of the employees, taking into account that these objectives normally were at least partially conflicting. The alternative "best" solutions should then, in my opinion, be communicated to *both* management and labour.

I realized of course that this demand would not be accepted by the users controlling the resources for the applications of Simula in business and production planning. When I tried to state my views, I was not taken seriously, as expected. The question then became: May more realistic alternatives be created?

I could not disinvent Simula, and I also believe that computers enrich the set of feasible social structures. I did not believe that I could find "a general solution". In the beginning of 1967 I decided to contact the Trade Unions and propose the building up of competence in information technology within their ranks.

As it happened, the Trade Union School at the same time had decided to ask me to lecture on a course named: "The Trade Unions Facing the Future". The lecture was followed by many more, and it was quickly understood that it was necessary for the unions to develop an information technology policy. A discussion group was formed, and it is interesting to note that a large fraction of the young trade unionists in the group are among the top leaders of the Norwegian Trade Unions today.

Politically, the end of the 1960s were also for me quite eventful. I started doubting my engagement in traditional party politics, and left the Liberal Party when I realized that I had become a socialist. I was the chair of the committee on environment problems within the Norwegian Association for the Protection of Nature for a couple of years, and I worked closely with socially outcast alcoholics in an alternative institution experiment. Both tasks showed me other realities, very different from those I had known before.

You have observed that the main personal pronoun used till now has been "I". This does not mean that I was working alone. On the contrary, nearly all my work has been done in teams. But the decisions discussed above were made by me. From 1967 on I became a member of a group within a broad, democratic movement genuinely representing the interests of the workers. (In Norway unionization is at the 80% level.) It was no longer a question about what I felt was good for other people, but instead participation in a collective effort to shape a strategy for all of us.

The group members came from a wide range of sectors in the society: Job shops, chemical plants, transportation, white collar work, hotels and restaurants, the public sector. I was the only researcher in the group and had for that reason special functions in our work. But the other members had their own areas of competence, equally important for the task.

We first discussed possible consequences of the imminent introduction of information technology in various sectors, then how we should build up our own competence. We never considered building that competence by teaching to union members the curriculum used by programmers, engineers or managers.

Knowledge is organized for a purpose and reflects the world view of the authors in terms of corporate values, power structures, objectives to be achieved and so on. Uncritical acceptance of such material would make us brainwash ourselves. What we needed was a reevaluation of the use of information technology based upon the world view of the union members, emphasizing solidarity, industrial democracy, safe employment, safe working conditions, decent wages and so on.

Since no such exposition of information technology existed, we concluded that it was a research task to produce one. In Norway the Royal Norwegian Council for Scientific and Industrial Research supports a wide range of projects in information technology, and the Norwegian Iron and Metal Workers' Union decided on its convention in 1970 to apply for money to "evaluate planning, control and data processing, based upon the perspective of organized labour" and to ask the Norwegian Computing Center (where I was working) to carry out the project.

This was the first project application of its kind to the Research Council. It was handed over to its Committee for the Mechanical Industry which, no surprise, had its offices in the building of the association of the employers in that industry. Their responses, internal discussions and attempts at getting control of the project have recently been published in a research report. They are interesting, but the end result was that the Iron and Metal Workers' Union got the funding and the Norwegian Computing Center got the contract.

In order to understand what happened behind the scene, one has to be familiar with the Norwegian labour market situation which, at least till recently, has been rather different from, say, the US and the British situation. The Norwegian Unions have been both stronger and also more actively interested in having a responsible influence upon company policies. As a result, the employers accepted that all information about the planning, control and data processing systems in four selected company sites were made available to the Iron and Metal Project team.

This does not at all imply that there was no resistance and conflict surrounding the project or the other projects referred to. Those stories do not, in my opinion, belong in this paper.

The Iron and Metal Project turned out to be very different from other projects. Not only did the shift from a managerial to a labour perspective generate a range of new observations and insights, even the basic criteria for achievement had to be reconsidered.

The project was organized as usual with a steering committee which, as usual, was expected to do next to nothing. In our committee we had key union people. From the very start it became the forum for thorough policy discussions where necessary mutual understanding and consensus about main decisions was established.

Associated with the project were four local unions at four companies, distributed over the country. They were intended to function as reference forums, sources for information and criticism. The group at the Norwegian Computing

Center consisted of two researchers, and we had a very active and helpful contact person in the national union offices acting as our most important advisor.

Our first plan for the project was presented to the steering committee, the local unions and even to the national board of the Iron and Metal Workers' Union in the spring of 1971. It was well received, and well conceived (we believed). We intended to examine the planning systems being used in the four companies, interview the local union members about what they wanted (and did not want) from the systems. Then we would examine the possibilities for modifications of the systems to make them conform better to union objectives. From this we wanted to extract guidelines both for system design and for trade union policies relating to new systems.

During the summer 1971 I felt more and more uneasy about this plan, but I could not spot what was wrong. Gradually it dawned upon me that our strategy would produce some reports about systems, and two researchers who had knowledge *on behalf of* the union members. The reports and the knowledge would not be linked directly to the action possibilities of the local unions, and no action strategy would be developed and tested by the unions themselves. No comprehensive learning process was incorporated, and the interviews would be of limited value when no serious knowledge had been built among the members.

The reorientation was painful, but eventually we chose to tell the steering committee that we had to completely change the project plan. I hope that similar choices will not turn up too often in the future.

The key decision was the acceptance of the following statement:

> *"In most research projects the results of the project may be said to be what is written in the project reports. In this project another definition will be applied: We will regard as results actions carried out by the trade unions, at the local and national levels, as a part of or triggered off by the project."*

The statement was even, at the insistence of the researchers, made subject to vote and passed unanimously.

The immediate consequence was that the local unions got a new and pivotal role. The task was to create knowledge-building processes locally, and to initiate action relating to the local situation, supported by analyses made by the researchers and working groups of local union members and elected shop stewards. The researchers became consultants and participants in a mutual learning process.

Each of the four local unions formed working groups. Approximately 30 members participated at each site, split into groups of 6–8 members. Each local union selected tasks they wanted done, and the results of their work appeared in reports, to a large extent also written by the unionists. The reports were presented at meetings with the rest of the members, and important decisions were subjected to ordinary decision-making procedures.

One of the unions made a "Company Policy Action Program", concentrating upon the planning of work within the union itself. Another made a comprehensive study of a production control information system, and succeeded in modifying the system in a number of important ways. The other two unions also produced interesting results, according to the above definition.

The main result of the project was a self-sustaining process which did not depend upon the presence of external researchers and project money. In 1975 an agreement (the "Data Agreement") was signed between the Trade Union Congress (corresponding to, say, AFL/CIO) and the National Federation of Employers, stating the right for the trade unions to be informed and participate in the development and introduction of computer-based system impacting upon their working conditions. They got the right to elect specialized shop stewards ("data shop stewards") to work with information technology issues. There are about 2000 data shop stewards in Norway today. They also have the right to negotiate privacy issues. We do not have many, if any, information systems spying upon their users.

What we gained in terms of general knowledge was a much better understanding of system development and cooperative knowledge-building processes. Today these insights are more relevant than ever, particularly in the area labelled "Computer Supported Cooperative Work".

A standard question during the numerous confrontations with "mainstream" people in the 1970s was: "Do you agree that your work with the unions is politicized research?"

Our standard reply: " You may get the answer you want – 'yes' or 'no' . If you regard the research along traditional lines going on in research institutions as politicized, reflecting the interests of management – then the answer is 'yes'. Our research is also political. If your regard traditional research as non-political – then the answer is 'no'."

The Iron and Metal Project was followed by other trade union projects carried out along similar lines, in Denmark, Sweden and Norway. A number of gifted young researchers were running these projects together with trade union members. A community sharing a common basic perspective on system development emerged and was joined by other competent scientists doing other kinds of projects.

We felt that the effort we were engaged in was urgently needed, and that it was necessary to avoid that any single person became indispensable. This was easy to state but somewhat less pleasant to experience: When two Danish colleagues told me that we for the first time had been asked to give a one-week course at the Danish Trade Union School, I enthusiastically started to discuss how we should do the course. I got no response, and finally they told me that they had decided that I should not participate, except perhaps during the last day. Cooperation with Danish unions should be handled by Danish researchers. Yes.

I have been criticized for not using more time in the 1970s to promote the Simula language. Many other people have done a much larger job than I. It was a conscious choice. Should a single idea or project use up your whole life as a researcher? Simula (and object oriented programming) is like a child: You have helped create it, you are responsible for its young years, you must see to that it gets a chance to succeed. Then your responsibility ends. You may be proud of it, wish it well, but realize that it will develop on its own and is no longer your property. Your duty is now to care for the new baby and then for any future children.

In addition, the Iron and Metal project demanded attention. My intention was initially to supervise the activities in that project. Then I had to realize, as my boss and a colleague strongly pointed out to me, that a failure for the project would mean that it would be the last of its kind. I had to work full time for nearly three years.

When the project was finished, the results had to be turned into an activity which could survive as an ongoing and integrated part of trade union work. To contribute to the initiation of similar activities in Sweden and Denmark was regarded as having second priority. This implied that the dissemination of information about the project in the scientific community only got third priority, and the researchers in the project never published any comprehensive account about the Iron and Metal Project in English. Much has been said about the projects by others, but I still feel that many of the most important insights have not been recorded properly. The original reports in Norwegian are still being referred to but, I suspect, never read. Reference lists are mostly proofs of awareness of what one ought to have read, and Norwegian is understood by less than 15 million people (and spoken by less than 5 million).

I regret this situation, particularly since I believe that much of our hard-gained practical experience in how to do this kind of research is just as relevant for publication today as then.

After the Iron and Metal Project it became important to make what had been understood about the system development process and the societal implications of information technology a part of academic teaching and research on information systems. As a part of that process I ended up as a university professor (there were additional reasons) working in teams with students – now colleagues – trying to build up an alternative curriculum in system development.

A main problem was to get our field accepted as first-class research. It was at that time frequently referred to as "boxology". Informatics is populated with people like myself, having a background in mathematics, natural sciences or engineering. Most of us share a common arrogance on behalf of our fields and a lack of understanding of social sciences and philosophy, two areas providing essential knowledge for any serious approach to system development. A strategy was definitely called for, even if colleagues at our own institute supported us.

The first part of that strategy was to make our courses very real-life oriented, with theory that was both demanding and useful in practice, and very tough. The second part was to be always active in explaining, arguing, defending, attacking when necessary. The third was to embark upon sufficiently ambitious (and thus risky) research projects.

The fourth was an agenda for myself: I decided that I would have to stay active both in traditional informatics (programming languages) and in system development, and also acquire and keep updated "hands-on" familiarity with important new developments (workstation hardware and software). If I succeeded, everyone would have to admit that we at least had some real qualifications. (In addition all three areas are great fun.) Or, more seriously: My work in languages could be used to legitimize our work on system development. This may sound silly, and perhaps it is. But it has worked.

Reading this paper I start wondering. How many basic choices were really made? The political work combined with the implications of Simula led to the Iron and Metal Project. The Iron and Metal Project led to cooperation with unions in other countries and to the building of our approach to system development. We had to try to introduce those ideas to education and academia.

The basic Simula ideas were generalized in the Delta system description language, providing a first platform for the unifying efforts and further generalization attempted in the BETA programming language and for general concepts in object oriented programming. The integration of information technology in professions created the need for an examination of extensions to the concepts and languages of these professions, the agenda for the SYDPOL project. (The project changed content, but that is another story.)

The movement from traditional party politics to work at grass root level helped in shaping the participation and knowledge-building strategy of the Iron and Metal Project. That strategy combined with BETA and the development of the modern workstations created an important part of the research agenda for a large ESPRIT project proposal: The O-4 Proposal (Object Oriented Office Organization) with cooperating teams from France, Great Britain, Denmark, Greece and Norway. We did not get the project, but the agenda remains and has to be carried out in the years to come.

How many basic choices were really made? How many were difficult? When I try to remember, I feel that most choices were consequences, and that those remaining seldom were difficult. We had burnt so many bridges behind us that few options were open – a good strategy for keeping yourself in shape under pressure.

I have not given the names of all the persons who have been doing the work referred to in this paper. They are too many, and I will only say this: The Iron and Metal Project was carried out by approximately 120 persons. Two were researchers, one was working at the national union level, the rest were local shop stewards and union members. To work in such a project demands a different kind of self-discipline and understanding of your own role than traditional projects. To make this well understood in academia is next to impossible. One has to be exposed to it through own participation. The cooperation in the Iron and Metal Project certainly is one of the most valuable and significant experiences of my work.

2.5 From Scientific Practice to Epistemological Discovery

Douglas T. Ross

2.5.1 On the *being* of reality

Nothing doesn't exist. That is *the* **First Definition** of Plex – a scientific philosophy whose aim is *understanding our understanding of the nature of nature*. Plex does not attempt to understand nature *itself*, but only our *understanding* of it. We are *included* in nature as we do "our understanding", both scientific and informal, so we must understand *ourselves*, as well – not just what we *think* we are, but as we *really* are, as *integral, natural* **beings** *of nature. How* one "understand"s and even who "we" are as we *do* "our understanding" necessarily is left completely open, for all that must arise *naturally* from the very *nature* of nature.

The "we" in question must include *all* "beings", material or immaterial (relationships and states, for example), physical (obeying physical laws) or not – not merely us *sentient* beings (human or otherwise). For Plex I adopt the obsolete reflexive meaning of "to **understand**" *vt : 6: obs :* to know how to conduct (oneself) properly" [Webster's 1961 Unabridged] . Whatever a "being" may **be**, its "understanding" of nature determines its *role* in the scheme of things – that overall *scheme* of things **being** "the nature of nature"which therefore is the *confluence of all* those *"understanding"*s. [For example, a *purely magnetic* "being" would couple with nature *only magnetically*, for that would be the full extent of its understanding. To *it*, something non-magnetic would be Nothing, and it would conduct itself accordingly.]

Plex is a *scientific philosophy*. Instead of claiming that *science* is so powerful that it can *explain* the understanding of understanding in question, we take *understanding* as the *open* question, and set about to determine what *science* results. [It turns out to be precisely the science we use every day, so nothing need be discarded or overturned – but many surprises result. Some very simple explanations for some very important scientific observations arise naturally in the course of Plex development. For example, from the First Definition, there are several Plex proofs that **there was no beginning**, contrary to Stephen Hawking's statement that "this idea that time and space should be finite without boundary is just a *proposal*: it cannot be deduced from some other principle." (*A Brief History of Time*, p. 136.) The very concept of a "big bang" is strictly an inherent *artifact* of our science's *view* of the nature of nature. There *was* no "initial instant" of time.]

Axioms are assumptions. Plex has no axioms – only definitions. (Only) Nothing is assumed to be known without definition, and even *that* is "by definition", for the complete epistemology of Plex is that

Only that which is *known by definition*
is **known** – by definition.

– for *without* a definition for something, we only can know it as Nothing. Without even a *definition* of "definition", the same is true – we know Nothing! So **Nothing is the Ultimate Knowledge** – by the above definition of what is **Known** – without any assumption at all, including this assumption of no assumption – *inherently!* All else is *penultimate* to that knowledge – purely *non-Nothing*.

Definitions *themselves* are non-Nothing, of course – each being *unique* in its non-Nothingness. But that which thereby is defined may be Nothing, in which case the *name* of that which is defined is synonymous with "Nothing", which (with the *naming quotes*) signifies the *name* of Nothing. There may be synonymous expressions for any *specific* definition. The First Definition of Plex is unique, but "Nothing **isn't**" and "Nothing does not-exist" are synonymous with it, for that which Nothing "does" is "not-exist"ing! – where "doing" concerns the *conduct* or *role played* in the scheme of things. Nothing is the role of Nothing, for it can neither *effect* nor *affect* any conduct. That is why the First Definition is *first* – because the entire *scheme* of Plex may be definitively expressed as "Nothing **isn't**; Plex is what Nothing **isn't**". Or, since that First Definition (here expressed synonymously) *itself* is non-Nothing, it *itself* is Plex, at first!

With *every* definition, including the First, the pure non-Nothingness that isn't Nothing (i.e., Plex itself) becomes *cleaved* into that which *satisfies* the definition versus that which does *not*. By definition, that which satisfies the definition is **known** – as what it **is** (by that definition), where:

If a definition, D, *defines* X, then Y **satisfies** D if and only if Y is X.

[Notice that X satisfies D, by definition.] Thus, for any X, the **ultimate definition** of X is its **self-*definition***, which is expressed in natural language as "X is X" – to which any *reference to* X is synonymous. [For any *non-Nothing* X, its ultimate definition (as distinct from the "X is X" universal *expression* of it) is **X** *itself!* For *Nothing* X, since there *is* no "self", this Ultimate Definition definition *is* quite properly *degenerately* satisfied, so it *does* hold "for any X" – even Nothing!] We can *express* the cleavage of "Nothing **isn't**" as:

	Nothing is what **isn't**	
versus	Plex is what Nothing **isn't**	
i.e.,	Nothing is what **isn't**	– a definition
versus	Plex is what **is**	– a *self*-definition

The "**isn't**" of the cleavage is not *itself* Nothing (it *has* a self-definition, for if it did *not*, there would *be* no cleavage) and therefore cannot be the Ultimate Knowledge *itself*. *But it is* **Nothing-by-definition** *within* the Plex cleavage! Thus the self-cleavage provides not only the self-defined Plex that **is**, but *couples* it to *its* very *own* **Nothing boundary** that **isn't**!

The **isn't** *boundary* of Plex is a perfect *model* of the Ultimate Knowledge, where M models A **if M answers questions about A**. To the extent that *any* question about A is (correctly) answered by M, M models A. For the *Nothing boundary*, the answer to *any* question is Nothing – so it *perfectly* models *knowledge* **of** the Ultimate Knowledge , i.e., the knowledge of Nothing. Since *Nothing* is known *without* definition, it is **Plex itself** that is (self-)known by the First Definition. Thus Plex is *complete* as to knowledge-by-definition.

2.5.2 Possibility and meaning

There *is* no one *best* or *fixed* definition sequence for Plex, for *other* definitions may intrude *between* the First Definition (and sometimes even *before* it!) and any other definition. But there is special interest in the *Possibility Definition sequence*, for it ensures that the science that evolves in Plex concerns only that which is *possible*. By definition, any *impossible* imaginary-world's definitions and derivations, however elaborate and intriguing the imaginings they yield may be, are synonymous with "Nothing"! Thus there is only *one* reality – the reality of *possible* realities – which is called **Actual Reality**. It self-defines itself, so there *is* only one – and this is *it!* – with us in and of it, understanding our understanding of it through Plex. So here is the **Possibility Definition**:

A **possibility** is that which *may* (but need not) **be**.

If it **is**, it is non-Nothing; but it *may* be Nothing, while still being (merely) *possible*. We may think of the **may be** and the **may not be** of a possibility as the two *states* of that possibility. The coupling between the Possibility Definition and the First Definition is apparent, for these states match the **is** versus **isn't** (self-)cleavage of Plex. So Plex *itself* is a possibility.

Meaning is the essence of understanding, whether verbalized or not. The **Meaning Definition** couples *directly* to the Possibility Definition and is marvellously subtle:

A *possibility* is **meaningful**, by definition
– its *meaning* **being** its *possibility*.

Thus **Meaning is a possibility**; for even if meaning is Nothing, meaning still is *possible*. (Nothing **cannot** be, so the Nothing/*not*-Nothing dichotomy is the impossibility/possibility dichotomy.)

Meaning is the essence of *understanding*, and **language**, when used for **communication**, is the *conveyor* of meaning. A meaningful thought is *thought*, is **written** down so that it can be mulled and checked, and then is *read* aloud as a **spoken** message – a *signal* which is *received*, is *perceived* as meaningful, is *written* down and mulled and checked, and thereby is **understood** as meaningful *thought*. That is a complete model of how meaning is communicated from *sender* to *receiver*. The model is totally recursive, for in **thinking**, the sender and receiver are *one*, and **memory** is the vehicle for the written-language mulling and checking.

To *apply* this model to the study of Plex requires that the *simplest possible* (and therefore the most *general*) **Language of Thought Itself** be defined so that it couples naturally to *meaning* as already defined by the Possibility Sequence of Plex. It takes both *written* and *spoken* forms. The crucial step is the *(Co-)Definition* of the **Possibility of Inequality**:

> For thoughts that are "equal",
>> their *quality* is their *equality*;
>> Nothing is their *inequality*.
> For thoughts that are "**not equal**",
>> Nothing is their *equality*;
>> they *themselves* are their *inequality*.

The **quality** of a possibility is the **superposition** of its *possibility* with its *meaning*, so the reference to *"themselves"* for *inequality*, above, provides the inherent coupling of these *thought-language* definitions back to the *self-definitions* (of various *"itself's"!*) of the Possibility Sequence of Plex. By careful work, the definitions rigorously prove the following scenario: Because of the *impossibility of impossibility*, only Nothing is *only* Nothing, while *all else* is *not* only Nothing. This is the *possibility of possibility*. It is *because* of the possibility of possibility that the *impossibility of possibility* is not *merely* Nothing but is *the* Nothing *possibility* (which is the possible Nothing) *of possibility*, but this is the only *possibility of impossibility* (which it also is).

Thus the possibility/impossibility *dichotomy* provides

$$
\text{possibility} \left\{ \begin{array}{ll} \text{impossibility of impossibility} & \text{Nothing} \\[4pt] \left. \begin{array}{ll} \text{impossibility of possibility} \\ \text{possibility} \quad \text{of impossibility} \end{array} \right\} & \text{"Nothing", name-only} \\[10pt] \text{possibility} \quad \text{of possibility} & \left\{ \begin{array}{l} \text{non-Nothing \textbf{and}} \\ \text{not-name-only} \end{array} \right. \end{array} \right.
$$

The surprising (perhaps even amazing) *consequence* of all this is that

> Although   *meaning*   may be Nothing
>   and   *meaning of meaning*   may be Nothing
>   the   *meaning of meaning of meaning* **cannot be Nothing!**

This is a direct consequence of the *fact* that, by the definition of *"possibility"* given,

> Although a   *possibility* **may not be**,   by definition,
>   and the   *impossibility of impossibility* **can not be**,
>   the   *possibility of possibility* **can't not be!**
> – leaving *actually* only *the* sole possibility, which is
>   the   **possibility of possibility of possibility !!!**

The **possibility of possibility** does not satisfy the definition of "possibility", and therefore is *not a possibility* (even though the reading of this *expression* for it *sounds* like it is one) – for it has no **may not be** *state*! It is what is called **"verity"**, in Plex – the **ontological** equivalent of the "tautology", which is a *logical* expression which evaluates to *True* regardless of the values of its variables, whereas a *verity* **is** what it **is**, regardless of its constituent quality. (Ontology is "theory of **being**".) Thus the *sole possibility* is the **possibility of verity**, and we can understand that *all* non-Nothingness (which is Plex, with us *in* it) is the *natural elaboration-by-definition* of the **may be** state of that possibility – the *self-knowing of Plex!*

2.5.3 A personal note

Plex is my very *life* – and has been all along, I suspect. From a creative and inquisitive childhood, sampling all the arts, crafts, and sciences, through a strong liberal-arts background, to pure mathematics and electrical engineering – I found myself swept into the very exciting dawn of the *computer age* in my first graduate-student summer job, in 1952. Just as my marriage to Pat in the January break of my senior year at Oberlin had been the perfect choice, my change to part-time Special Student status, while embarking on my full-time professional career at MIT, can be seen as inevitable, when viewed from today's vantage point. There is an exquisite economy in the doings of nature, and for a long time, now, I have been firmly convinced that, whoever I may *really* be, my *role* in the scheme of things has been to initiate the discovery of Plex, not by chance, but as what I *do*, simply because I'm *me*.

I have received great gratification, satisfaction, and some occasional welcome recognition for a reasonably successful career, to date – academic, professional, entrepreneurial, and simply personal. But my *understanding* of all that is that at each stage, what I was *doing* in working so hard with and through others, *fulfilling* each other as we *did* so many exciting and worthwhile things, was merely the then-current *vehicle* for a single, ongoing process of **living through the discovery of Plex** [my survival (living-through), my livelihood (living *through*), and my life itself (*living*, through ...)].

From early childhood, I often have been more aware of and interested in how I went about *solving* a problem than about the problem itself. We all go through that stage – the crude distortion of the crayon drawing is *inconsequential*, except as evidence of the *accomplishment!* In my work, I found that my greatest success came when I could envision a generalization, solve it, and apply that "systematized solution" to the special case at hand. When the generalization applied only as a crude distortion, that was inconsequential, for the elegant *specific solution* was lasting *evidence* of accomplishment. In my early programming work on the MIT Whirlwind Computer, a pattern of solving large and complex problems by an intimate mixture of many small simple solutions, logically controlled by adaptive parameterization emerged. Building languages and tools for an interactive man/machine problem-solving environment and applying them to massive data reduction, to the APT System for programming numerically controlled tools, and then to Computer-Aided Design (CAD) required innovations in every aspect of what now are called Computer Science and Software Engineering. In the white heat of that fecund and stimulating environment, and with my background, being a pioneer came naturally.

By the late 1950s I had coined the name "Plex" for my philosophy of problem-solving, and was actively using it to devise and explain our solutions in these many areas. I stressed that *data + structure + algorithm* could model and solve any problem. Applying Plex principles (molecular structures are built step-by-step from atomic beginnings) to the subject of *language* yielded my Algorithmic Theory of Language (ATL), which soon was followed by methods and tools for generating specialized problem-oriented languages to order. By the late 1960s we had a complete Software Technology, with many active users, and were boot-strapping the AED System (Algol Extended for Design) to a variety of large computers.

In 1969 I and key colleagues left MIT to found SofTech, Inc., now grown to a public company of some 600 people, nationwide. In the early years we continued to extent our tools, methods, and skills into new areas. By delegating to others, I remained very active technically, and my Plex research led to the new field of **Structured Analysis**, as the primary vehicle for a new thrust into Computer-Aided Manufacturing (CAM). The basis for SofTech's SADT^{TM} Structured Analysis and Design Technique (and its government-promoted version, IDEF-0), it was the last widely-accepted offshoot of Plex development, and also the source (since 1974) of my personal focus on the philosophical *fundamentals* of Plex.

I have skimmed through this litany, here, because I think it is important to realize that Plex is not some weird, personal eccentricity of mine, but comes from this long history of practical achievements. No sudden career change turned me toward outlandish obscurity, seeking to explain the universe itself, on a *whim*. It simply is that from all these years of focus on what is going on *behind* the scenes, I have discovered that **nothing can (or need) be left out!** In fact, although I don't know where the actual working papers are in my files, it was precisely that *pun* that thrust me into Plex fundamentals from my early study of Structured Analysis fundamentals!

I was attempting to use SA to model its own semantics and had derived a hexagonal (or cubic) model of the interfaces of its three interface types. ["You can't design an interface from only one side" is an old maxim of mine!] I finally became convinced that *one* of the six *must be Nothing!* I had *both* 1.) Nothing can be left out (yielding the hexagon), and 2.) Nothing *isn't* – i.e., that *one* component *is* left out! (in the *interpretation* of the hexagon) so it must be a *pentagon!* Shades of Bucky Fuller's geodesic dome! – said I, but was unable to complete the connection, then – and thousands of C-pages later [chronological working pages, this one being C8849], my discovery of Plex fundamentals continues to this day!

The early C-pages are a swirl of varieties of word-, picture-, and combined-language models (some in eight colors, and of startling beauty) as I have pursued my quest seven days a week in every available moment snatched from my other activities. Some are pure poetry, when only words are rich enough to carry the ideas – and *every* model is full of *puns* (verbal, visual, and conceptual), for nature *has* no structure, allowing *all possible* structure. Most of these early and hyper-elaborate models I developed purely through the elegance of their structure, simply marveling at what they disclosed, with only the faintest glimmerings of what they might mean. They spewed forth from me, whole, unbidden, and complete – self-stopping – and only years later would I come to understand them or even *believe* the interpretation I then could give. It sounds spooky, I know, and it has taken me a long time to get used to it, but as I said – I *live* Plex, and seem to have done so all along.

So as the 1980s rolled around, with SofTech growing rapidly, going public in 1981, and my extracurricular Plex research becoming increasingly productive, but more esoteric, I became aware of an increasing sense of responsibility to both my local circles and to the world at large to focus on what only *I* could do, while gradually releasing what reins I still held, letting others do things more *their* way, and accepting the results. In 1985 I slashed my SofTech income, so my Plex research would not be a burden on the company and was welcomed back at MIT as a (paid only if I lecture) Lecturer in the Electrical Engineering and Computer Science Department, so I now wear two hats. But it has turned out that even MIT is not yet ready for SA much less Plex, so my main focus continues to be on the research itself, as I generate book after book on Plex in my office at home, in order that Plex will be ready when the world is ready for it!

2.5.4 The rigor of Plex

Although I miss the bustle of actively leading and inspiring others, and it is lonely working entirely alone, I am content. With *no readers* for the last several years, I progress at my own maximum pace. I am my own best critic, and although I seldom make blatant errors, the repair of each weak point invariably leads to still deeper insights and results (sometimes a whole new book further interrupts completion of the others). By now I am very good at what I do, and post-1985, I know *why* things work out so well, which adds to my confidence in Plex.

To my surprise, in 1985 I discovered that the *reason* my methods worked so well was that, although I hadn't *realized* it, I was practicing precisely the *standard, accepted* **rigor of formal systems** – *but* **backwards!** The key concept (going *forward*) is that of providing a *valuation* for linguistic expressions by providing a "Satisfies" predicate, linking them to the structured model. Only by thus *linking* language *and* model, can questions of *completeness* and *consistency* be addressed – and **that is as formal as any formal treatment gets!** I do just the *opposite*. For Plex, the model comes first, and the language is only and precisely the *minimum necessary* to express just what *shows* in the model. A sequence of models, each related to the earlier ones, builds up a rich formal-language capability and a *very* deep understanding – all supported by the models, in which the definitions can be checked and rechecked in every detail.

It is necessary that *only* **Picture Language Models (PLMs)** be formally shown. **No-Rule Seeing** of the *Picture* ensures that every relation that shows is a *Language element*, but **there is no separate translation** into other terms *to obtain the* **meaning**, for *it is* **what shows** – *Modeled* by the picturing itself. Only with *both* seeing *and* saying matched so that **meaning is modeled** (using the definitions given earlier) is a picture a PLM. Multiple modelings (word and picture *puns*) are inherent and intentional, by the **Plex Paradigm** (from the little-known *alternate* meaning of the word: paradigm (n) 1: Example, pattern 2: An example of a conjugation or declension showing a <u>word</u> in <u>all</u> its inflection <u>forms</u>. [Webster's 1961 Unabridged]). Because of No-Rule Seeing, the *scene* presented by any PLM is the **superposition** of all *possible meanings*, any one of which may be selected for study.

The important point is that Plex is *not* merely *just as rigorous* as the accepted level of rigor for formal systems; Plex is *not* **informal** in contrast to these **formal** systems (in spite of the *seeming*-informality of the word-play inherent in Plex). The rigor and formality of Plex **is the accepted formality and rigor** – just viewed and carried out backwards, or in Plex terms – **opposite but the same!**

2.5.5 Scope and relevance of Plex

Pursuit of the deep foundations of Plex leads inexorably to the rigorous PLMing of language, meaning, and thought, itself, at one pole (with which this essay *began*), through counting (which must be defined) and all of mathematics, to the physical spacetime reality of the universe, itself, on the other. Many startling insights result, such as this question and answer regarding the *information* of Information Theory:

> How many *binary digits* are required
> to encode **one bit?**
> Answer : **3/2**
> because the value of the *half-bit* is 3/4 !!!

– which ultimately results from the fact that in *actuality*, when you don't have something, it is *not* the case that you *have* it *but* it is Nothing – it is that you **don't have** it; whereas when you *do* have something, that is because you **don't have** what it *isn't!* In the original Plex cleavage, "Ah got plenty o' Nothin', an' Nothin's plenty fo' me!" – for there, *too*, those are *opposites that are the same!* For *that* stage, the Plex saying is:

> < it > is Nothing but a < nothing > named "it"

where **"it"** is our name for whatever currently is relevant (< all of relevance> is < <u>it</u> >, where <u>word</u> is the Plex quotation notation for the *concept* of the word whose *name* is "word", with the *meaning* < word >). Here is the

> Definition for "not it" :
>   **Given**< <u>it</u> > , < it > , < not it > –
>   **only** < not it > is
>   *every* meaning *other than* its name.

A consequence of *verity* (which can't not **be**) is that, for *any* "it", when $<$ it $>$ is required in order for $< \underline{it} >$ to be what$< \underline{it} >$ **now** is (loosely, when its time has come!) – there $<$ it $>$ **is!** Physical time progressing forward in an expanding universe is a consequence.

The *reason* that the bit has value 3/2, rather than the (perhaps-)expected value, 1, is the same reason that there only is **reference** *sequence*, rather than *reference* alone or *sequence* alone, in Plex. In both cases, **reality** *intrudes!* The "extra 1/2" value quantifies the contextual *coupling* of $<$ it $>$ to $< \underline{it} >$, when we point and declare "That's it!". To be *actual*, such a *reference* must persist in *spacetime* [actually, at the *deepest*, **thought-only** level, in what I call **"thime"** – the foundational level where *place*-like (*there*) and *time*-like (*time*) *coincide*], and a fact of Plex is that **there was no beginning**, as each $<$ now $>$ similarly is coupled to its $<$ before $<$ now $>>$. All follows from that First Definition: Nothing doesn't exist – the ultimate, driving, creative *breaking of symmetry*.

2.5.6 The meaning of any word

I close with the Plex resolution to Plato's *ideals* [*"general objects"*, in modern parlance] – which is the way that (and why) *meaning* **works**:

Let each *use* of the meaning of any chosen word be synonymous with "point", i.e.,

$$\text{Let} < \text{point} > \; = \; < \text{any word} >.$$

Then the following propositions are to be proved:

P1) Let **points** be such that, *except for* identity,
       they *all are* **indistinguishable**.
P2) Let there **be** *only* points.
P3) Let the **world** be the *collection of* **all** points.
P4) Then *the* identity *of a point* is the *collection of* **all other** points.
P5) And *every* point *is the* **whole** *world*.

[P4 can *only* begin with "Then", so all follows from the "Let"s of P1 –P3 !]

2.5.7 Proof that every point is the whole world. (P5)

 I $n = 1$: A world of one point is the whole world.
 II Assume the theorem is true for $(n - 1)$ points. $(n > 1)$,
       i.e., for any collection of $(n - 1)$ points, every point is the whole world.
III To prove the theorem for n points given its truth for $(n - 1)$ points
       $(n > 1)$
       (a) The identity of any one point, p, in the collection is a collection of $(n - 1)$ points, each of which is the whole world, by II.
       (b) The identity of any other point, q, i.e., a point of the identity of p, is a collection of $(n - 1)$ points, each of which is the whole world, by II.

     (c) The identity of p and the identity of q are identical except that where the identity of p has q the identity of q has p. In any case p is the whole world by (b) and q is the whole world by (a).

     (d) Hence both p and q are the whole world, as are all the other points (if any) in their respective identities (and shared between them).

     (e) Hence all n points are the whole world.

IV   For n = 2, I is used (via II) in IIIa and IIIb, q.e.d.

V   Q.E.D. by natural induction.

NOTE: In the Fall of 1984, a Graduate seminar on Plex was offered in the MIT EE/CS Department, but soon ceased for lack of student interest. That was the first public presentation of this 1975 proof . Because counting and the natural numbers do not exist in Plex foundations, but must be derived, the preferred proof for Plex uses the See and Say PLM methodology (– disclosing each point to be a *viewpoint*, in and of the world).

2.5.8 Coda: We must understand our understanding of the nature of nature

This is more than a mere play on words. It would be presumptuous if not preposterous to say "We must understand nature." Even the more reasonable goal to "understand the nature of nature", in which we would settle for studying the properties of reality without, perhaps, having any real understanding of the (theological?) purpose or deep meaning of existence, is too presumptive. In fact, most ontological studies, in whatever field they may be based, seem to suffer from this over-reaching of what seems to be our station in the scheme of things. Only when the goal is made two layers removed and only when it is personified with "we" and "our" do we arrive at a proper stance. We are, to be sure, in and of the world of nature, but quite literally, the world is what we make of it. Not what we make it, but what we make *of* it. We cannot foist our viewpoint on nature, but without a viewpoint, there can be no nature for us.

Nature itself seems hard enough to understand, for it has a habit of overturning each successive and, up to then, successful theory or science. Our understanding is itself a participant in nature, and certainly one of its least-understood aspects. Why, then, set that as the primary goal? It would indeed be presumptuous and foolhardy to approach the matter biologically, attempting to study brain and mind as a scientific exercise. But there is another path open – one that, when it is pursued, shows surprising promise and progress relative to the effort spent thus far.

In this brief essay I sketch the opening steps along this path, in the hope that others will join in the exploration. The primary style of approach is not to make a frontal (prefrontal?) attack on our understanding of understanding, but rather to assume, until forced to think otherwise, that the fundamental nature of nature must be simplicity itself – that the rich complexity that is so apparent is an artifact of sheer magnitudes. The known measurements of physics show that there are roughly the same number of powers of ten above us (to the cosmic reach) as there are below us (to the depth of sub-atomic particles). We (i.e., man and his sensory world) are in the middle of a vast scale of complexity. We will assume that that complexity is merely fantastically profligate simplicity. We will assume, until shown otherwise, that if there be a "law of nature", that there is just one law, and that it operates intact and in toto throughout this vast scale. We seek to understand our understanding of that law, and if the law is to be simplicity itself, then so also must be our understanding.

We must take nothing for granted. And I mean that exactly and literally. We must and do take the non-entity as our starting place. We adopt a posture of aggressive humility, lower our head, and step off along the path starting from nothing at all. In no way intending to play God, and always open to changing our stance and direction when forced to, nonetheless if simplicity it is to be – then there is nothing simpler than nothing. So that is where we start. Then, if we are indeed careful with our reasoning at each step, so that we truly *do* understand our understanding in toto, then whenever we encounter some aspect of the nature of nature that goes counter to that understanding, we can retrace our steps and know exactly what must be altered to proceed.

That was issued April 1976, referencing "some views, tested and still evolving over a twenty-year period", even then. In this current essay, I have done my best to present my most recent view of the opportunity of Plex, in the hope that it can become a proper part of the agenda for the future. It is a completely rigorous *scientfic philosophy*, by now, and I feel an intolerable burden of responsibility to still be the only person in the world (to my knowledge) pursuing it, in spite of my efforts to enlist others *even as responsive readers*. I expect that most readers also will not know what to make of my current effort, and will opt not to invest the time and effort to respond. But I hope that at least *some reader someplace* might accept the challenge to join me in this work which I think is very important.

---

* An annotated bibliography of writings on Plex may be obtained from
Mr. Ross c/o SofTech, Inc., 460 Totten Pund Road, Waltham MA 02154 or
c/o MIT, Cambridge MA 02139.

Part 3

On Reality Construction

Christiane

In this part of the book, we take a look at constructivist thinking. But
without attempting a comprehensive treatment – or even a systematic classification – of different constructivist approaches.

Heinz

What emerges is not a coherent picture with a clear message. Just as in the
illustration, the reader finds here building blocks and facets which he himself
must put together in order to construct his own picture.

Reinhard B.

It also becomes apparent that when using the term "reality construction"
one may have in mind quite different schools of thought whose common
features and whose interaction with other philosophical schools cannot be
fully dealt with here.

Reinhard K.-S.

To my mind, that smacks too much of Dadaism: everything is possible, and
what already exists is negated. What about *Radical Constructivism*, for example, which we originally took as a basis for our work. As far as the different
approaches are concerned, I see a thematic break between the first two chapters of this part – which belong to Radical Constructivism – and the third
chapter dealing with social reality construction and treating the theme on a
much broader basis.

Christiane

I have come to the conclusion that Radical Constructivism does not exist
as a single well-defined platform, but merely as a lively discourse of views
between individual authors differing from one another in a number of important points. This I consider a direct consequence of constructivist thought.
Given the fundamental importance of the observer here, every constructivist
position reveals itself as tied to the individual observer. Moreover, we are
primarily concerned with the emergence of insights, not with ready-made
positions.

Reinhard B.

At all events, Constructivism did play a special role in the preparation of
the conference and this book. To begin with, it was important for addressing
potential participants, but then it became the subject of harsh criticism itself.

Heinz

You are referring specifically to Maturana and to Winograd and Flores'
adoption of his ideas. He is the first to come to mind when talking about
Constructivism. But his approach with its biological basis fails to give adequate consideration to social aspects. This is also pointed out in some of
the other chapters of this book. None of the authors borrows directly from
Maturana.

Reinhard B.

Christiane's dialogue with Heinz von Foerster and her own separate contribution are concerned with cybernetic approaches in applied epistemology tailored here to illuminate the process of design.

Heinz

As one of the key authors of Radical Constructivism, Heinz von Foerster has developed the principle of self-organization and applied it to the social sphere. Unlike Maturana, though, he does not emphasize the closedness of systems in the sense of autopoiesis, but rather their embeddedness in their respective context.

Christiane

For him, the dialogical involvement with others is of crucial importance. This means that interpersonal reality and also the ethical dimension of our actions are always taken into account.

Reinhard K.-S.

Drawing on these ideas, Christiane views software development as design. She describes design as a self-organizing, dialogical process in the course of which a gradually materializing web of design decisions is stabilized.

Heinz

Design is seen here as an insight-building process. Other facets of design are taken up in later chapters of this book.

Christiane

In contrast to this, Bo Dahlbom's contribution looks at reality construction as a comprehensive social process, examining the overall social context in which software development takes place. He shows how the idea that reality is socially constructed finds expression in the two great modern philosophical movements, the Enlightenment and Romanticism. The interplay between these two movements, evolving dynamically up to the present day, constantly creates new conditions under which reality emerges and technology is developed and utilized. To master it, though, political action is required. And here, too, the limits of constructivist ideas become apparent.

3.1 Self-Organization and Software Development

Heinz von Foerster and Christiane Floyd

C. Heinz, since I first sought you out in my quest for epistemological foundations of software development, I have enjoyed finding myself in continuing communication with you. In the course of our conversations off and on, my original topic has gradually evolved and taken shape between us. But we have also touched on more fundamental issues such as the nature of human understanding and our dialogical involvement with others. I have learned with great profit to appreciate your ideas and apply them to my fields of interest.

You have also taken a strong hand in shaping the conference on which this book is based. We opened the scientific programme of this conference with a dialogue, which is the basis of this paper. Later we have decided to arrange the paper in the form of a dialogue.

I think, we need to make explicit that the resulting text is not itself a dialogue. It is an arrangement of sediments from our actual dialogues designed by us so as to please our readers. The actual dialogue processes take place between the lines. Do you agree to that?

H. No, rather *above* the lines. Floating. The spirit of your conference. And whatever lines you include in your final product, the book, you will not be able to hide from readers our affinity, the engine that is driving our dialogue.

C. I am very happy to acknowledge this marvellous affinity between us.

My main concern is to explore with you the relevance of your approach to constructivist thinking for understanding software development. The key notion here is *self-organization*. Heinz, I would like you to say a few things about self-organization.

H. Christiane, you have self-organized me already before the opening of this conference so carefully that I felt I had become your constructed reality. And I can understand you well, for this conference was for you, as I sense it, not only an affair of the mind but also of the heart. When you invited me to participate, I must confess I had no idea what role you thought I might play. But when I saw your programme, the people I would encounter, the place where we would meet, the topics we would discuss, I felt that, for me too, this would become an affair of the mind and of the heart.

Therefore, before I get to the historicals and the scientificals concerning the notion of self-organization, let me take care of my sentimentals.

It is 40 years now since Norbert Wiener's *Cybernetics* was published, and it is only a few months less since I met this extraordinary and modest man

in the flesh, together with John von Neumann, Gregory Bateson, Margaret
Mead, and so many others of the crème de la crème of American science.
It was at the now legendary Macy Conferences on "Circular-Causal and
Feedback Mechanisms in Biological and Social Systems". I had arrived in
New York perhaps two weeks before this conference, and my English vocabulary comprised not more than 25 words. Since I even had difficulties just
to pronounce the title of the conference, I found a moment to suggest to
the group a shorter title, namely to call it "Cybernetics", with the sub-title
"Circular-Causal and Feedback Mechanisms ..." etc. Everybody accepted
with applause this proposal which paid tribute to Norbert Wiener; and he,
deeply moved, left the room to hide his tears.

I am telling this to you as if it were yesterday, but none of these people are
alive today; I am the only one here to tell the tale. When I reflect upon this,
I feel as if I were a living fossil who was there, and who can tell you now
how it was and what we thought would become of it.

C. I would like to take the opportunity to pay tribute to *you* and gratefully
acknowledge your contributions to *our* conference. In fact, the phrase *living fossil*, coined by you to refer to yourself, was later taken up by many
participants with love and admiration. But go on with your story about
self-organization.

H. For me the notion of self-organization is deeply embedded in that of cybernetics and vice versa, but I recognize that many others do not feel that
way.

In my case, I can easily trace my sense of the complementarity between
cybernetics and self-organization to my fascination with the logic of circularity, along the lines of circular causality, recursive functions, closure,
self-reference, paradox or, in its modern cloth, non-linear dynamics, chaos
theory and others. I see these conceptual buds popping out at various times
from the main body of cybernetic thought.

As I said before, my enthusiasm for circularity was not equally shared by
all of my early fellow cyberneticians. When the organizers of the Macy Conferences on Cybernetics asked me to write a preface for the transactions of
these conferences[1], I jumped at the chance to celebrate the peculiarities of
circular causality.

Circular causality – in contrast to orthodox, linear causality – can only be
perceived to operate within a two-dimensional manifold. But, surprisingly,
instead of having gained a degree of freedom from this dimensional expansion, we have lost one, for now the value of the end must be the same as
that of the beginning. This condition has the amazing consequence that,
very much like in Schroedinger's wave equation whose solutions assign to
the electrons in an atom certain discrete orbits around the nucleus, it carves
out from an infinity of potential solutions a finite set of actual solutions. The
convergence towards these dynamically stable solutions reduces the spectrum
of possibilities and uncertainties: order emerges.

---

[1] [v. Foerster et al., 1949]

I remember the unhappiness of my editorial friends who found my flight of fancy too esoteric, and who persuaded me to write with them a more down to earth (I thought, a somewhat pedestrian) piece.

You can now imagine how much I enjoyed meeting Gordon Pask.

Your conference marks, *almost to the day*, the 30th anniversary of my first meeting with Gordon Pask. It was at the Deuxième Congrès International de Cybernétique in Namur. After my presentation, people came up to me raving about an extraordinary leprechaun who opened up new vistas on cybernetics, teaching and learning. Searching through Namur, I finally found him in a coffee house surrounded by a swarm of the curious and inquisitive, listening attentively. I wormed my way through the crowd, and after a few minutes I knew why they were listening; and after a few sentences of our dialogue, I knew I would ask him to join us at the Biological Computer Laboratory at the University in Illinois. Thus began my friendship with Gordon Pask, a friendship that will last to the end of our lives.

The following year Gordon was with us in Illinois, and because of his kaleidoscopic contributions to the concept of self-organization, he was nicknamed "Mr. Self-Organization". This period, and others that followed, were most productive for all of us. Gordon wrote several seminal papers[2] and then, of course, there are his wonderful drawings for my *order from noise* principle[3].

C. This was 30 years ago, you say? What has happened in the meantime?

H. A lot! For instance, the preparation of this conference. You perceived that it was to become a self-organizing system, a process that would establish new links, may they be personal, social or conceptual; that would generate dialogues during the conference, generating in turn meetings, seminars, groups, and I don't know what else, and you don't either! Nobody would have dared to think that way 30 years ago.

C. To me and to my co-organizers it still seemed quite daring to think that way today. And we had little guidance when putting this thinking into practice. As far as I can see, there is a gap between the ideas on self-organization presented by you and others in the literature, and the level of concreteness required for basing our actions on these ideas in complex social endeavours, such as conducting software development projects or organizing this conference. When preparing it, we had to find ways to bridge that gap, relying essentially on our intuitive understanding, on our loyalty to one another and our willingness to take risks.

But then you accused me – or should I say made fun of me – for having "self-organized you" before the opening of the conference.

H. I meant to make fun of you, not to accuse you of having self-organized me. In fact, I wanted to make fun of both of us for self-organizing one another by using the ambiguity of this very notion that sets the notion in motion. It is the act of "priming the pump", of the "initial ignition", of the "initials"

---

[2] [Pask, 1960, Pask, 1962a, Pask, 1962b, Pask and v. Foerster, 1961]
[3] [v. Foerster, 1960]

as Francisco Varela would say[4], the "first distinction" as George Spencer Brown would say [5], or "nucleation" as Gordon would say.

This is one of Gordon's important points: one must have (if one is a constructivist) or there must be (if one is a naïve realist) *nuclei* for self-organization to take place at all. Clouds are self-organizing systems, but for the individual water droplets to form, they need particles, dust, ions, or whatever, as nuclei for condensation: the seeds. All the participants are the seeds for your conference and, as an old self-organizing systems conférencier, I know that they are very fine seeds indeed.

C. Yes, we are quite confident of that, too. However, the way you speak about self-organization just now, illustrates only too well my difficulties in trying to gainfully apply this notion to social processes.

You draw an analogy between a cloud and the interactive processes amongst the collection of people gathered at a conference (it might as well be the collection of people involved in software development) pointing out similarities in terms of the capacity for self-organization.

To me, the dissimilarities between these two assemblies are so profound, that I find it difficult to draw fruitful conclusions from the analogy. Viewed as a system, a cloud – belonging to the non-living world – is quite different from a collection of people interacting in a given context.

Also, my relation to these two systems is radically different: I am a mere *observer* of the cloud, but I am a *participant* in the social processes at this conference. In fact, with my co-organizers, I have created the conditions in which these processes can unfold. While I can make a description of the cloud, I take a share in how the processes at this conference actually come about. Nucleation must mean initiating processes between people here.

And in saying that I have self-organized you, you even go a radical step further: you apply this notion in a dialogical sense between you and me.

H. There were in these 30 years many developments in the way we look at the notion of self-organization and in the way this notion itself acted – and still acts – as a catalyst upon fundamental transformations of our theory of knowledge. You have illustrated some of these developments by drawing your distinctions just now.

In the early days of euphoria, when we thought we had "discovered" this fascinating notion of self-organization, we directed all our attention to the *assessment* of organization, and didn't pay any attention to the *assessor*, or to the semantic booby traps that are wired into the concepts of *self* and of *organization* as well.

For instance, I have become only recently aware of the pun latent in "self-organization". For I may talk about that critter over there who – as it looks to me – is now self-organizing, but it could also mean that it is I who am organizing myself. Let's talk about the critter for a moment, and of his

---

[4] [Varela, 1975]
[5] [Brown, 1969]

magical feat to organize himself, and we shall see that we are, in fact, talking about our own magical powers to organize ourselves.

When we use the verb "to organize" in connection with self or something else, we imply that the organization of that something changes, usually from lower to higher states of organization. We also imply that *organization* is *measurable*.

The two components that come to mind, when one thinks about more or less organization, are *complexity* and *order*. In the Jurassic period of the information age the dinosaurs at that time jumped at the possibility of defining a metric for *order* based on its close conceptual relationship with its measurable cousin *redundancy*.

Since redundancy goes from 0, for perfect chaos, to 1, for perfect order, let redundancy and order stand for one another interchangeably. That is, if by knowing one thing about an organization you still know nothing about the rest of it, there is chaos, redundancy is 0; but if by knowing one thing about an organization you know it all, this is the perfect state of order, it's paradise: redundancy is 1.

C. But Heinz, I find this confusing. You are now using terms from physics and information theory, as you do in your original paper on self-organization[6]. I can follow your argument on its own terms, but it's not obvious to me how it applies to the critter. And, when thinking of the social world, this is a horrific prospect. In your state of perfect order there is no freedom of choice: this is hell! How can you call it paradise?

H. Don't forget that I'm talking about the insights of the dinosaurs of the information age and, please, ignore the labels "chaos" and "paradise" for the time being. Look at the numbers 0 to 1, disorder to order, and allow me to use the language of physics a little longer.

As you know, redundancy goes up when entropy goes down, but the Second Law does not allow this to happen in a thermodynamically closed system. Hence, self-organizing systems must be *open to let the flow of energy activate potential organizational changes*. And what you need to pay attention to is that, when the system's maximum entropy goes up, redundancy, i.e., order, goes up as well. Since maximum entropy is connected through the logarithmic function to the number of distinguishable states of the system, this implies that the *number of distinguishable states of the system increases*.

Going back to the critter, this means: By distinguishing other, additional states, that is, by calling upon my cognitive skills, by drawing more distinctions, I, the inventive observer, am constructing a new reality, now inhabited by a system, or better, by a critter who is more organized, yet even richer in his possibilities than he was before.

This doesn't sound like paradise. But it seems to me to be more interesting.

C. It seems to me, you are saying that *your understanding of the critter is richer*: it allows for a greater richness of the critter's possibilities You don't

---

[6] [v. Foerster, 1960]

appear to be saying anything about the critter himself, independent of your understanding of him.

Meanwhile, I am determined not to lose sight of my concern for understanding and conducting social processes such as software development or the organization of this conference, in terms of self-organization. We need to return to this later.

But first tell me: Why don't you say anything about what the critter *is?*

H. This would be arguing along the lines of *ontology.* I bring up ontology here, because you will get the argument from ontology again and again. It is the argument from "as things are", or "as it is", as if one could ever find out what *is.* The flavour of this argument has not changed since the 17th century, when the primary "it" was, of course, God, and the task of the ontologists was to prove that *He is.* In the past 200 years that task has changed: the "it" is now the world, and ontology tells you how the *world* is.

C. What's wrong with that?

H. That you can't do it.

C. Why not?

H. Because I can only speak about my experiences, they are the primary cause.

C. And the world?

H. And the world is the consequence.

C. How do you see then the connection between what you call the primary cause and its consequences?

H. That is *the* epistemological question.

C. You bring up a new term here, *epistemology.* Can you explain it?

H. It is Greek: *epi* means "up", "above", and *histamein* means "to stand"; hence *epihistamein* means "upper-standing". The English, apparently, prefer to see things from below, so they speak of "under-standing"; thus, epistemology is the science, study, theory of understanding. But since a theory is to provide an understanding of that what it is the theory of, epistemology is *understanding understanding.*

C. I'm not understanding your "understanding understanding"; can you say it differently?

H. When you asked me for the connection between experience and world, I would probably have said that any circular process, any recursive process, when operating on an entity, produces that entity, where these "entities" themselves can be operations, processes, etc.

C. This is very abstract. You now refer to mathematical notions of recursive functions as a general basis for understanding mental processes. In order to concretize your notions, we need to identify the relevant specific processes, and the entities produced by them in any given field of interest, and demonstrate their recursive nature. — Can you help me by giving an example?

H. Language may be a good case. Ask "What is Language?" and the answer must have been contained in the question, for otherwise the question could not have been asked. Moreover, language speaks about itself: there is a word for language, namely, "language", a word for word, namely, "word", etc.

And then there is of course the hermeneutic circle: the meaning of a word is established through its context – *Zusammenhang*, as Frege called it[7]. But context, in turn, is built through words.

C. Don't you get the argument that this never-ending circularity is a *de facto circulus vitiosus*, that it is, in essence, an attention diverter for hiding the flaw in your upside-down epistemology, where experience is the cause and the world the consequence, instead of being the other way around?

H. Of course, I'm getting these arguments all the time, and in all shades. And understandably so. Because it is not more than 20 years ago that the ancient philosophical rejection of the *indefinite regress*, an operation that was believed to lead to nowhere, was replaced by an understanding of recursive functions that lead indeed to somewhere. They lead to those stabilities that evolve, emerge, arise, come to the fore, become manifest, for instance, in the phenomenon language, "as a coordinating agent for actions among conversing human beings" as Terry Winograd and Fernando Flores would say[8] or become even *objects* as I would say[9]. Objects in the sense that they stand as tokens for stable behaviours, "Eigen-behaviours" as these stable dynamic equilibria were then called. Today, however, one speaks of "fixed points", "attractors", even "strange attractors", when referring to these recursively stable states.

C. This implies that when applying your ideas to my fields of interest, I would have to tailor these notions to fit for instance the processes at this conference or the processes of design involved in software development. I need to look for the relevant recursive operations in action here and for the specific stabilities that they give rise to.

The interactions between the participants of this conference may be taken as recursive operations giving rise to stabilities in terms of richer distinctions and common insights leading to further interactions.

In the case of design, I have argued that the making and revising design decisions are recursive operations and the resulting web of design decisions the emerging stabilities[10].

In doing so, I may find a way of *understanding* these processes better as an observer. Even more, I am interested in *facilitating* these processes as a participant.

But, let us first continue to discuss your arguments on epistemology.

---

[7] [Frege, 1950]

[8] [Winograd and Flores, 1986]

[9] [v. Foerster, 1981b]

[10] Floyd, Chap. 3.2

H. You spoke about my upside-down epistemology, where experience is the cause and the world the consequence, implying that there must be a right-side-up epistemology, where the world is the cause and my experiences are the consequences.

You were right: this is, in fact, the popular, or should I say, orthodox position. This is the position of an observer who thinks he is separated from the world, looking as through a peephole at an unfolding universe, and who believes that he reports unequivocally to us all about this unfolding universe. It is the delusion of *objectivity* and *truth*.

C. You are using very strong words.

H. Not strong enough. By separating oneself from the world, one separates oneself from others as well. Hence, one thinks that one can, without consequences for oneself, tell others: "Thou shalt ..." or "Thou shalt not ...". Or take objectivity: "The properties of the observer shall not enter into his descriptions." How can this be? Without his faculties to observe and describe, there would be no descriptions in the first place.

C. And how about truth?

H. Christiane, it's a millipede we are talking about, so brace yourself. Truth? It's impossible! First, because it is impossible to describe anything unambiguously, for it is the listener and not the speaker who determines the meaning of an utterance; and second, because we can never check the truth of a report, for nobody knows what *is*, or *was*, we only know what is experienced.

No, Christiane, we cannot use this epistemology.

C. So you would say that this is the wrong epistemology. But how can we do without the notions of objectivity and truth? Does this not imply that everything is arbitrary? Do you have an alternative to offer? Is your epistemology the right one?

H. Wow! Four questions at once! Let me postpone for the moment my view on right and wrong epistemologies and turn to your question of how we can do without objectivity and truth.

Since objectivity and truth are only recent inventions, we must have done pretty well without them before. *Aletheia* in Greek means "that which is not obscured" (*a* not, *lanthanein* to hide). From the context in which aletheia appears, one thinks it can be translated with "truth", though "evidence" may be semantically closer, for here being true is not the opposite of being false, but of being hidden. There is a fascinating analogy in German where the word for "perceiving" is "wahr-nehmen", that is "taking-a-hold-of".[11]

C. And when I perceive what is not, is that an illusion, a hallucination?

H. By way of an answer, let me refer to our great perceptologists Francisco Varela, Humberto Maturana[12] and others, who insist that there is no distinction between perception and hallucination. When, in delirium tremens,

---

[11] The root for this word in old German is the now obsolete "wahr" as in "Gewahrsam".

[12] [Maturana, 1978]

I see white rats running up and down the walls, white rats *are* running up and down the walls. Too bad for the others who don't see them.

C. Did you say earlier that you would give me your view on my question about right and wrong epistemologies, or did I have a hallucination?

H. I don't know. We have to ask the others.

Be that as it may be, my view on this question is that it belongs to those questions that are in principle undecidable. The fascinating thing is that the question: "Is the world the primary cause and my experiences the consequence, or are my experiences the primary cause and the world the consequence?" is in principle undecidable. It is like asking the question: "How did the universe begin?" Nobody was there, and there is no way to find out. Nevertheless, we have many answers: a creation a few thousand years ago; a big bang a few billion years ago; the wedding of chaos with darkness, whence everything came forth; etc.

C. You said that these are in principle undecidable questions, and yet you give me plenty of answers. What is going on here?

H. What is going on here is that it is precisely *those* questions, that are in principle undecidable, that *we* can decide.

C. Why?

H. Because those that are decidable, for instance, "Is 208796 divisible by 2?" we cannot decide, they have already been decided by the choice of the framework in which they are asked. However, with in principle undecidable questions we have the freedom to decide, and with this freedom we now have the responsibility for our decision.

C. Does that mean, that we have the freedom to decide whether or not we consider the world or our experiences as primary; that we have the responsibility for this decision; and that your stand on epistemology is a result from your choice, which I may or may not follow?

H. Precisely!

C. In our daily lives, questions of the fundamental kind you have just mentioned rarely become explicit as the basis of our actions. Your distinction between decidable and in principle undecidable questions would have to be drawn on a much smaller scale. Are there in principle undecidable questions coming up in ordinary situations?

Looking at software development again, we need to concern ourselves with questions that may crop up in design. While functional software requirements tend to be decided in advance by the choice of the framework in which they are asked, issues of software quality are determined by decisions for which we take the responsibility in design.

Thus, our way of constructing a reality as inventive observers, the metaphors we use, the distinctions we make and the flexibility we allow for, give rise to quite different possibilities for people to interact with software.

Is this a variation of what you once called an ethical imperative: "Act always so as to increase the number of choices"[13]?

H. Of course, very much so. The spirit of this "imperative" is to encourage an "opening", a "seeing", an extension of one's antennas, a refusal to take things for granted, a questioning of "necessity". Ever since Jacques Monod came up with his famous book *Chance and Necessity*[14], it has become popular to think of chance and necessity as the two complementary poles in a conceptual whole. But the complement to necessity is not chance, it is *choice!*

You touched on this point just now, when you talked about creating different possibilities for people to interact with software, about constructing our reality as inventive observers, about the way we use metaphors and so on.

Christiane, all this is so different from the earlier obsession with telling you how it *is*, the ontological thinking. It is quite clear to me that you and the participants of your conference are not so much interested in what *is*, but in what *can be created*. This explains your pre-occupation with self-*organization*, with reality *construction*, with *inventing* and the like, all generative processes, conceptually linked to the notion of choice.

Listen to one of your philosophical brothers, the existentialist José Ortega y Gasset: "Man does not have a nature, but a history.... Man is no thing, but a drama.... His life is something that has to be chosen, made up as he goes along, and a man consists in that choice and invention. Each man is the novelist of himself, and though he may choose between being an original writer and a plagiarist, he cannot escape choosing.... He is condemned to be free...."[15].

Constructivism and related ways of thinking deal with *ontogenetics*, the science of becoming. They touch domains that are untouched, and untouchable by ontology, the science of being.

C. I remember that when I first gave you my paper on paradigm change in software development[16], where I point out the complementarity between processes and products, you immediately brought up ontogenetics, since looking at design as a process emphasizes how software is made up by us as we go along, and how we assume responsibility when providing possibilities for computer-supported action for ourselves and for others. This responsibility is connected to our awareness that there are human choices to be made in design.

On a very deep level, you said you make a choice in considering your experiences as primary cause and the world as consequence. What persuades you to do so?

H. This choice connects me inseparably with my world and with others. Whenever I act, not only *I* change, but the universe as well. Notions of reflexivity,

---

[13] [v. Foerster, 1981a]
[14] [Monod, 1972]
[15] [Ortega y Gasset, 1961]
[16] [Floyd, 1987]

of self-reference that turn on themselves, that preserve the tie between observer and observed, speaker and speech, and partners in dialogue, form the
core of this position, and the only commandments that make sense are: "I
shall" or "I shall not...".

C. How do you then account for dialogue?

H. When I read Martin Buber's *Das Problem des Menschen* I was most moved
by the last paragraph of his book[17]. When I translated it from the German
into English I tried to preserve the force and the spirit of the original. May
I read it to you?

C. Yes, please do.

H. "Contemplate the human with the human, and you will see the dynamic
duality, the human essence, together: here is the giving and the receiving,
here the aggressive and the defensive power, here the quality of searching and
responding, and always both in one, mutually complementing in alternating
action, demonstrating together what is is to be human. Now you can turn to
the single one, and you recognize him as human for his potential of relating;
then you can turn to the whole and recognize it as human for the richness
of relating. We may come closer to answering the question: what is human?,
when we come to understand him as the being in whose dialogic, in whose
mutually present two-getherness, the encounter of the one with the other is
realized at all times."

C. I can now understand what you meant when you said that I "self-organized"
you, and I join you happily in acknowledging the dialogical human reality
you refer to. It seems our task, then, to find ways for making this dialogical
reality come to life in all our endeavours, including professional activities
such as developing software.

Clearly, "self-organizing one-another", to put it in your terms, does not refer to manipulation and control. Rather, it means to create and maintain
conditions allowing the richness of human relations to unfold in dialogical
networks, with a view to increasing the possibilities of choice for all.

But I must confess that your expression "self-organizing someone" sounds
unnatural to me. We seem to leave the conceptual domain of reality construction, unless it be joint reality construction with you, in the sense of
sharing reality in the web of all dialogical relations we find ourselves in.

---

[17] [Buber, 1961]

3.2 Software Development as Reality Construction

Christiane Floyd

Reality = Community
(Heinz von Foerster)

3.2.1 Introduction

I would like to present a view of software development as an insight-building process in terms of multiperspectivity, self-organization and dialogue, drawing on epistemological ideas that have emerged from the discourse in Rational Constructivism.

I have come to this view in the course of my recent research on epistemological foundations of software development[1], which was motivated by many years of preoccupation with software development methods in my research, teaching and project practice. It was during this period, first in industry and since 1978 at the Technical University of Berlin, that I began to question the validity of the established models of thought in software engineering as the sole foundation for our work as computer scientists. I gradually became convinced that we need to arrive at a sufficiently rich understanding of software development if we want to facilitate it with methods in a meaningful way.

My doubts apply, in particular, to the following basic assumptions of the discipline: its view of software development as the *production* of program systems on the basis of fixed requirements; the separation of production from use and maintenance; the division of production into linear phases; the almost exclusive use of intermediate results in the form of documents; the view of methods as rules laying down standardized working procedures to be followed without reference to the situation in hand or the specific groups of people involved; and the one-sided emphasis on formalization at the expense of communication, learning and evolution. The resulting critique of software engineering has been elaborated in a number of papers[2].

I will gladly concede that I know of scarcely any author today who still accepts these assumptions without reservations. They are looked on rather as ideals that can only be approximated in practice. There have, however, as yet, been few efforts to develop conceptual alternatives to the established tradition of thought in software engineering.

---

[1] This research was funded by a grant from the Stiftung Volkswagenwerk enabling me to spend my sabbatical term in Palo Alto from September 1987 to March 1988.
[2] Cf. [Floyd, 1981, Floyd and Keil, 1983, Floyd, 1984, Floyd, 1985a, Floyd, 1987].

One of my reasons for questioning the validity of this tradition were the glaring contradictions between what it postulates and the reality of software projects in both industrial and academic settings, despite the fact that many of these projects were ostensibly conducted along traditional lines. I by no means wish to contend that the production view of software development is irrelevant. But it does seem to me to hold only in part – for specific, well-defined partial goals – failing to do justice to software development as a whole.

Another reason for my doubts about the validity of the established view was its failure to take into account the quest for quality[3] in software development. Ultimately, it neglects to provide any sort of foundation for human-oriented system design.

It seems to me a richer view is needed here. And it was this realization that induced me to seek for suitable epistemological foundations for software development. Such foundations must help us to understand specific, communally sustained, coordinated processes of cognition in which different domains of reality meet. In these processes, abstract – and at the same time highly complex – results are obtained, and the emergent technical reality of the software is interwoven with the social reality of its production and use. These processes take place against a background of social conflicts, changing needs and limited resources and lead to insights regarding the desired software and its use.

The soundest alternative thought model available, to my mind, is Peter Naur's view of programming as "theory building"[4], which has been very influential in shaping my own ideas. However, Naur says little about what theory building consists in. And he does not account for the interpersonal nature of communal theory building.

As I see it, software development is, first and foremost, a specific instance of *design*. By design I understand the creative process in the course of which the problem as a whole is grasped, and an appropriate solution worked out and fitted into human contexts of meaning. To paraphrase Naur: Software development is an activity of overall design with an experimental attitude[5].

To establish foundations for design, I draw here on epistemological insights that have emerged from the constructivist discourse, notably on the work of Heinz von Foerster and Gordon Pask[6]. Their ideas are, I feel, particularly conducive to understanding the process of software development as design.

In the following section, I begin by outlining the postulates of the established software engineering tradition, subsuming them under the general term *production view* of software development. My aim is to show that these postulates are of a perspective nature. They were *invented* from a particular viewpoint to highlight a particular facet, necessarily obscuring others. Which brings us straight to a key insight of constructivism.

---

[3] A phrase coined by Don Knuth in his reflections on the errors he made in the development of the TEX system (Chap. 1.2).

[4] See [Naur, 1985b] and Chap. 1.1.

[5] [Naur, 1974, p. 296]

[6] See Chap. 3.1.

In Section 3.2.3, I introduce some important elements of constructivist thinking and relate them to our present subject. I refer specifically to the school of thought labelled Radical Constructivism. Of interest to us are the insights it provides concerning the emergence of knowledge in different areas. Our task will then be to explain, in the light of these insights, the specific types of cognitive processes that are important for software development.

In Section 3.2.4, I attempt to elaborate a suitable concept of design for software development. Design is not primarily tied to predefined goals, but is governed by the quest for quality.

In Section 3.2.5, I then go on to unfold the design space. It consists of the interlaced domains of reality – application, methods and means of implementation – that are *constructed* during design. Unlike the production view, there is no assumption here of a phase-specific, temporal transition from one domain of reality to another; we are dealing rather with a vibrant structure of ever new and ever finer distinctions, "dancing", as it were, in time.

In Section 3.2.6, the cognitive processes taking place in design are characterized as a web of decisions linking together the domains of reality important for design. The viability of a design decision is determined through its evaluation. Where feedback is permitted from the evaluation to the design process, we have *closure*, the results of design again forming the basis for its further development. Successful design is marked by a stabilization of the web of design decisions through revisions.

What we have said so far also applies to design processes carried out by individuals. In Section 3.2.7, though, we go on to look at communal design implemented in terms of dialogically organized cooperation. This allows for a conscious dialogical orientation of design in which the "I and Thou" of software development is acknowledged in the basic relations "I develop software with you" and "for you" and implemented in terms of dialogically organized cooperation. This orientation directly incorporates the element of responsibility in our technical work.

In the final section, I examine the way this view affects training, project organization as well as the development of methods and tools for software development.

What emerges, in general terms, is a view of design as consisting of interlocking, living processes that are sustained by us, that may atrophy, degenerate or unfold. Their unfolding presupposes both sufficient autonomy of design and the ability and willingness on the part of those involved to engage in multiperspective reflection.

3.2.2 Software Development as production – a view and its limits

In this section, I wish to outline what are to me the essential issues and show how I set about tackling them. A practicable approach to epistemological inquiry in our domain has been shown by Winograd and Flores[7]. The established view, the authors argue, only appears to be self-evident to us as long as we remain within the rationalisitic tradition, which is characterized by them in terms of its postulates and underlying assumptions. (Actually, we are not only concerned here with the rationalistic tradition as a theory about our way of thinking, but also with the realistic tradition as a conception of reality.) This tradition, however, like any other, involves a certain "blindness" by obstructing our view to its underlying assumptions.

Winograd and Flores translate the notion of rationalistic tradition into more concrete terms by deriving from it assumptions relating to different subject domains. Related specifically to the domain of software development, it justifes the following assumptions:

- There is a given reality "out there" which we come across during software development. By analyzing the facts of this reality, we obtain requirements for the software.
- The essential task of the software developer is – starting from the problem defined in that reality – to find a correct solution in the form of a program system.
- It is possible to separate the production of software from its use. Software engineering is concerned with the production of software on the basis of fixed requirements.
- Software production is based on models representing reality. Models should map reality correctly.
- The whole process is largely independent of individuals. For one and the same problem, different developers should arrive at the same results. The developers should be interchangeable.
- Communication should be restricted and regulated via fixed interfaces. The division of labour can be worked out on an ad hoc basis. Subject to technical feasibility, any desired parts of the production process can be automated.
- The developer's responsibility covers – only – proper construction of the product in accordance with the requirements specification. Any ethical considerations that go beyond this are quite separate from the technical aspects of the work.

The view of software development reflected in these assumptions has been instrumental in bringing about impressive advances in programming methodology, in generating controllable models for project execution, and in promoting the development of tools on this basis. It allows us to understand important aspects of software development prior to initiation of the development process, to sub-

---

[7] [Winograd and Flores, 1986]

sequently assess more or less completed projects – or to "fake" a rational design process as suggested by Parnas[8].

It fails, though, to offer any help in understanding the software development processes actually going on in a given situation – processes relating to the emergence of insights into the functionality, implementation and usability of programs. Indeed, the production view is misleading, suggesting as it does that we can (must) proceed from fixed requirements and can derive a program system from these (ideally, in accordance with fixed rules).

The production view highlights one important facet of software development, eclipsing others. In my opinion, it obstructs our view of design. The pervasive nature of design and thus the key role occupied by it is also recognized by other authors. Winograd and Flores, for instance, have given their above-cited book the subtitle "A New Foundation for Design".

Questioning the rationalistic tradition necessarily involves examining other epistemological approaches. I shall confine my attention here to constructivist ideas. They fit in perfectly with the facet I have chosen to focus on: *software development as an insight-building process.*

3.2.3 Entering into the constructivist discourse

Studying constructivist approaches was no easy matter for me. They call for a radical process of rethinking which I can only accomplish step by step. In addition, the available primary literature on the subject is heterogeneous and chiefly concerned with domains outside my own particular sphere of interest. This is due to the fact that the key insights have been derived from a variety of sources, including biology and developmental psychology, and subsequently applied to the social sphere. But retracing this process is not our concern here. Nor are we able, within the present context, to explore just how far these insights can be applied to other spheres.

Radical Constructivism as a school of thought has grown out of Cybernetics and is closely related to chaos theory. What we are dealing with here is the emergence of phenomena, in our case with cognition as the emergence of insights. Since there is no one overall, clearly elaborated constructivist position, but rather a variety of related approaches – differing quite considerably in detail – that blend into a common mind[9], one can justifiably speak of a constructivist "discourse"[10]. The various authors are involved in the ongoing scientific discussion within their own particular disciplines, but they go beyond the "what" of their respective subject to look at the "how" of the emerging insights, discovering as they do related patterns within the different disciplines.

It would be asking far too much to expect me to give a proper introduction to constructivism within the present context. Nevertheless, I shall attempt to

---

[8] [Parnas and Clements, 1985]

[9] [Bateson, 1980]

[10] This is reflected in the German title of an excellent survey on Radical Constructivism, cf. [Schmidt, 1987].

outline at least its essential fundamentals in order to be able to refer back to them later on.

According to constructivist views, our cognitive faculties are ultimately rooted in the biological nature of the human being and his co-evolution with all other living beings. Bateson, an important pioneer of constructivism, postulates the essential unity of mind and evolution[11]. Maturana and Varela consider cognition to be inherently tied up with life[12].

Mind, in this sense, not only characterizes the individual human being, it is also encountered in other living systems. Mind is also invariably related to something. Thus, mind characterizes the way communities interact with respect to common concerns. For example, a group of people interacting in a project when developing software might exhibit mind. Here, deeper insights emerge by careful contrasting and coordination of individual contributions.

In constructivism, a distinction is made between epistemology and ontology in a subtle way. Constructivism teaches us that we construct what we know; it makes no mention here of being. In constructivist thinking, cognition is not concerned with images mapping a given reality; instead, we construct knowledge in such a way as to make it fit our purposes. Von Glasersfeld suggests talking about the *viability* of our knowledge rather than about truth or falsehood.[13] This notion seems quite natural in connection with design.

An essential element here is the introduction of the *observer*. Cognition is invariably tied to an observer[14]. Observers can only perceive what they are in a position to perceive. Communication between observers takes place in consensual domains that are mutually accessible.

Also tied up with this is the concept of perspectives. A *perspective* is the totality of assumptions about relevant aspects of a specific subject domain from a common viewpoint. Perspectives are not necessarily tied to individuals. People adopt different perspectives at different times. Between two or more individuals, common perspectives are formed[15].

Perspectivity necessarily entails *blindness*. I cannot see what I cannot see from my perspective. It is impossible to eliminate this blindness. An important prerequisite for the emergence of deeper insights is self-reference (see below) and the interaction (crossing) of perspectives.

Constitutive elements of cognition are *distinctions* and *indications*[16]. Complex cognitive processes consist of webs of interlocking distinctions, each relating to different perspectives, and their recompositions into a coherent whole[17].

A key concept here is *self-reference*. While in logic it results in paradoxes, it is fundamental to an understanding of living entities. Self-reference requires operational closure. All this means, in basic terms, is that the results of an

---

[11] [Bateson, 1980]
[12] [Maturana and Varela, 1980]
[13] [v. Glasersfeld, 1987]
[14] [v. Foerster, 1984, Maturana and Varela, 1980]
[15] [Pask, 1976], see also [Bråten, 1978].
[16] [Brown, 1969]
[17] [Pask, 1976]

operation are themselves elements of its domain of definition. This supplies the conditions required for the recursive application of operations.

In operationally closed and energetically open systems, the system's behaviour is determined by the recursive coupling of operations, with several levels of consideration interacting. System behaviour is stabilized by reference to eigenvalues that give rise to system-specific eigenbehaviour. This results in self-organization leading to the emergence of higher orders in systems. This is the essence of the "Order from Noise" principle formulated by von Foerster[18].

Living systems are characterized by the fact that, during the course of their existence, they continuously reproduce their own organization[19]. Autopoiesis takes place in a medium. The autopoietic system and the medium condition one another. I avoid giving here an assessment of how this concept can be usefully applied also to social systems, as the current discussion about this point is strongly controversial. For example, rather than regarding software projects as "autopoietic beings" using systemic notions as Joseph Goguen does[20], I will confine myself to considering closure at the level of processes.

Self-reference also plays a major part in the emergence of insights. Perspective blindness can be overcome by self-reference. Once I see that I am blind, I can see again. Self-reference is also amenable to mathematical treatment[21].

An essential and repeatedly emphasized aspect of constructivism is that ethics can never be divorced from the consideration of cognition and action[22]. This is ensured not by explicitly laying down norms about what to do, but rather by viewing cognition and action as being sustained by us as individuals. This leads to von Foerster's ethical imperative: *Act always so as to increase the number of choices.* In my opinion, this can be applied directly as a guideline for designing software development projects as well as computer-supported systems.

According to von Foerster[23], acknowledging others involves making a decision. It causes us to emerge from our monologue and enter into a dialogue. Dialogue means adopting the other's perspective. Closure, then, occurs through the other. I see myself through the eyes of the other.

This step towards living in dialogue[24] is of crucial importance in implementing constructivist ideas in our dealings with others. It leads to the view "Reality = Community"[25] selected as an epigraph for this contribution. According to Bråten[26], our cognitive faculties as a whole are geared to dialogue.

Well, that was, of necessity, a rather rudimentary and fragmentary crash course in constructivism. I have attempted to convey something of the pleasure I experienced as I gradually came to grasp what it is all about in my dialogue

---

[18] [v. Foerster, 1984, p. 17]

[19] "Autopoiesis" is the term coined by Maturana in [Maturana et al., 1974].

[20] See Chap. 5.1.

[21] [Varela, 1975, Varela, 1987]

[22] [v. Foerster, 1984, v. Glasersfeld, 1987, Maturana and Varela, 1980]

[23] [v. Foerster, 1984, p. 307]

[24] The term is used here in the sense of Buber [Buber, 1984].

[25] [v. Foerster, 1984, p. 308]

[26] [Bråten, 1988]

with Heinz von Foerster[27]. I feel at home with these ideas. They tie in with my own everyday experience both privately and professionally, and they seem to me to open up far-reaching prospects for a desirable design of our life in the community.

My subject proper begins with our recognition that the view of software development as production is an invention. Thus, the prevailing view of the subject of the software engineering discipline turns out to be constructed reality. It is useful for understanding certain aspects of software development, but of no use for others. It is therefore important to contrast it with other views.

3.2.4 Software development as design

To begin with, I should clarify what I mean here by design. It will not do to simply adopt an existing definition of design. What I shall endeavour to do instead is to construct a concept of design to fit my fundamental concerns. In other words, I would like you to join me in drawing a number of distinctions in order to arrive at a useful characterization of design in software development.

By design, we mean a specific type of insight-building process that is geared to producing feasible and desirable results within a particular domain[28]. The domains in question may differ widely. We normally only speak of design when there are concerns we wish to fulfil, limited resources at our disposal, and different implementation options open to us.

Design in software development is of a distinct nature and subject to special conditions. Software is characterized by an interplay of several unusual features, relating to both the nature of the product[29] and its embedding in human contexts of meaning[30]. Software exhibits an extreme degree of complexity, thus calling for equally complex construction processes. It consists of a uniform, abstract building material, is therefore plastic and, in principle, of unlimited revisability[31]. It must be machine-processable, i.e., complete down to the last detail, consistent and formally free from error. It is not amenable to sensory perception and can therefore, in the last analysis, only be evaluated once in use. It creates social contexts for human actions, which are shaped by the technical properties of the product.

Design thus links different worlds: the social world of the application in question, the technical world of the means of implementation, and the formal world of methods and concepts.

In order to elucidate the meaning of design as we understand it here in all its essential richness, we have to consider the way this concept is used in different contexts. As a rule, we distinguish between design and implementation.

---

[27] See Chap. 3.1.

[28] In German, the two terms "Entwurf" and "Gestaltung" are used to approximate the meaning.

[29] See [Parnas, 1985] and Keil-Slawik, Chap. 4.4.

[30] See [Ehn, 1988] and Reisin, Chap. 7.3.

[31] See Coy, Chap. 6.3 and Budde/Züllighoven, Chap. 6.2.

We design something. The result is subsequently implemented. Occasionally, we call the result of a design process "the design", focussing here on the external features of an object. That is too narrow a view, though. We also speak of design in a broader context when we have in mind the overall process of organizational and technical system development.

Design should be understood here in a processual sense: the results of design are incorporated into the design processes from which they were obtained. Design relates not only to external features, but also to the functionality of the program system under development and its embedding in human contexts of action. Design also includes the provision of suitable tools and methods for the specific software development situation and for project organization.

I should now like to illuminate design in software development from a number of different angles. I apologize in advance for my rather abstract wording. This is due to the fact that I begin by characterizing design in terms applicable to both individual and communal instances of design. I do not make a distinction between the two until later on, in Section 3.2.7.

3.2.5 The design space as an unfolding of interlaced Domains of Reality

The production view implies looking on software development as a sequence of phases, ideally to be run through linearly. Each phase is concerned with a specific object: first of all, analyzing the requirements of the application; then, on the basis of this, elaborating a specification of the future system, defining what is to be done without prescribing how the system will work; and, finally, deriving the program from this.

It is here that the domains of reality relevant to design implicitly enter into the picture:

- the world of the applications whose concerns are relevant to software development and from which we derive requirements for the software,
- the world of the means of implementation – in our case technical information systems including existing software,
- the world of methods and concepts which we use in the same way as maps to guide us in linking concerns with means of implementation.

The phase model prescribes just one path through these worlds: that starting from fixed requirements and following predefined methods to arrive at the implementation of a given system. Ideally, this path should be followed only once with respect to the overall product software.

The design view involves a process of rethinking here. Temporal progress should be separated from the domains of reality. These are not processed in temporal succession, but are present and linked at every point in time. Moreover, there are no preordained domains of reality; these are constructed in the course of the design process. This means:

- We do not analyze requirements; we construct them from our own perspective[32]. This perspective is affected by our personal priorities and values, by the methods we use as orientation aids, and by our interaction with others constructing requirements from their perspective. Requirements are governed by perspective. In most cases, they reflect differences in perspectives and are subject to temporal change.
- We do not apply predefined methods, but construct them to suit the situation in hand. There are no such things as methods per se – what we are invariably concerned with are processes of situative method development and application. We select methods and adapt them. What we are ultimately doing in the course of design is developing our own methods.
- We do not refer to fixed means of implementation that only take effect later on when working out the details of implementation decisions. Instead, we construct the meaningful use of means of implementation by testing, selecting or complementing what is already available.

To postulate the existence of a predefined path through these worlds is misleading. It would only be possible to follow such a path if all the relevant decisions had already been taken. But then there is no place for design.

3.2.6 Design as a web of decisions

Design is *rooted in concerns*. These concerns induce us to set goals that are to be attained with the help of specific means. By drawing this distinction between concerns and goals, I wish to anticipate any discrepancy between what is ostensibly to be attained and what proves to be desirable[33]. Design is normally initiated with a view to set goals, the point of departure being an already established web of decisions linking the concerns considered relevant for attaining the goals set with provisionally designated means of implementation.

Nevertheless, there is no fixed foundation for design, nor is it determined by predefined goals. The concerns may change during the design process. The means of implementation may prove inadequate. The predefined goals may turn out to be misleading or be considered no longer valid. To this extent, design may be regarded as *goal-free*. Design creates its own foundations and sets its own goals.

Design calls for an interplay of different faculties: besides a command of methods, what is needed is an awareness of the potential of the means of implementation and a sensitivity to the changing concerns of the application.

Design presupposes a range of options and scope for playfully exploring these options. In other words: design can only take place where a sufficient range of op-

---

[32] See Reisin, Chap. 7.3.

[33] According to the constructivist view, the notion of goals should be treated with caution. In [Schmidt, 1987], von Glasersfeld is quoted that what ever can honestly be set as a goal may be derived from the need to sustain autopoietic organization. We mean something similar when we speak here of concerns.

tions is available for making the relevant distinctions. Design requires autonomy
if a genuine choice is to be made.

Design consists of a web of *design decisions* which, taken together, make up
a proposed solution. Not all necessary design decisions are taken consciously.
Frequently, it is not until the proposed solution has been evaluated that it becomes clear which decisions will be needed and which consequences failure to
take them will imply. The importance of explicit design decisions has been emphasized in particular by Parnas[34]. However, he only considers design decisions
as a basis for modular design. Design, of course, involves a wealth of other decisions. They link concerns and means of implementation with a view to attaining
the goals considered valid within a specific context. This results in building up
complex structures of interwoven decisions. These must be intrinsically coherent
and, overall, viable. Their emergence is *specific to the individual design process*;
it is not determined by the given problem. Instead, the problem itself is grasped
in the course of the design process. Design is determined by the perspective of
those sustaining the design process and by the constraints imposed upon them.

The viability of design is determined by a number of different factors, which
are frequently difficult to reconcile: whether the decisions match the concerns;
whether the web of decisions covers all elements of the problem that are considered essential; whether meaningful use can be made of the means available;
whether the goals set are attained. These distinctions are made by an observer.

Design is thus based on a wealth of correlated distinctions concerning what is
"good" (desirable). There emerges here an interplay between proposed solutions
and their evaluation. What is "good" is determined in the course of the process
by what those involved consider to be "good". The criteria for such distinctions
are derived from the concerns relevant to design.

Design can only fully unfold where decisions that have already been taken
can be revised on the basis of their evaluation; in other words, if the results of
design again become themselves the starting-point for design. This is how closure
in design comes about.

Decision-making, evaluation and closure are interleaved and take place on different levels: in individuals, on an informal level; when developing and checking a
proposed solution; during joint critical appraisal; when practically implementing
a decision; during testing; during use.

Closure involves admitting our errors and learning from them[35], offering and
accepting constructive criticism, abandoning erroneous goals and recognizing
changing concerns. Closure means the continuation of design.

Design is successful as a whole if the web of design decisions is stabilized
in the course of revisions; in other words, if it withstands evaluation and is
acknowledged as "good" by those involved despite changing concerns.

Design is, then, always *multiperspective*, even where pursued by individuals.
This is due to the linkage of concerns, means of implementation and methods,
to the different evaluation criteria, and to the interplay between design, imple-

---

[34] [Parnas, 1972]
[35] See Knuth, Chap. 1.2.

mentation and use that is an important prerequisite for closure. Design requires multiperspective reflection.

3.2.7 Dialogical orientation in design

This section focusses on software development with others and for others – the form socially effective software development normally takes. It is to be seen here as *potentially dialogical*. The "I and Thou" of software development is concealed in basic relations such as "I develop software with you" and "I develop software for you". Teamwork in software development can be viewed as a network of this sort of basic relations. The specific network of relations between the people involved, unfolding in time, is constitutive in design.

If we acknowledge this fact and attune ourselves to it, we come to a consciously dialogical orientation. We can decide in favour of accepting the "you" and make provision for it. This means accepting the other, not instrumentalizing him[36]. The essential activity then takes place between me and the other: we develop *jointly*. We look for ways of thinking that will enable us to understand our common reality, and for forms of work that will help us to completely unfold this reality.

In the light of the prevailing practice in software development, this may sound absurd. As we know, software development is widely used as an instrument for exercising power and control. Software projects are managed along bureaucratic lines and controlled by means of tools. Teamwork is characterized by rivalry and lack of coordination. Failure to recognize these facts would indeed be absurd. But we are not obliged to regard this an unalterable state of affairs.

On the contrary, I consider far-reaching changes in the way software development is practised to be imperative if we are to strive for quality and human-oriented system design. I consider such a reorientation to be necessary not only for "humanitarian reasons" – as if the technical work could be performed at least equally well without taking others into account. As I see it, communal design has no chance of unfolding without this reorientation. This also seems to me to be in agreement with Goguen's views on projects as "autopoietic beings"[37].

For this reason, we at the Technical University of Berlin have been working for a number of years now to reorient software development towards a notion of system design that takes account of human needs. These efforts have led to the development of the approach STEPS[38], which has been elaborated in cooperation with other scientists and tried out in academic project situations, in the context of method development, and in practice[39].

I now go on to describe in constructivist terms the ways of thinking and forms of work that have shaped our experience.

---

[36] According to [Buber, 1984].

[37] See Chap. 5.1.

[38] Software Technology for Evolutionary Participative System development, see [Floyd et al., 1990].

[39] PEtS Project, see [Floyd et al., 1989a] and Chap. 7.3.

"Dialogical orientation in design" is one way of characterizing cooperation both among developers and with users. In our experience, there are such common features. But we must also be able to differentiate between the two cases. We distinguish then between

- dialogical design among developers – by which I mean jointly working out a proposed solution together with others[40], and
- jointly creating computer-supported contexts of action with users[41].

Dialogical design involves working out a desirable tentative solution between myself and others, taking design decisions on a joint basis, and bringing about closure with consideration being given to the perspectives of all parties. This means that, instead of developing my model in accordance with my evaluation criteria – objectifying and enforcing these where possible – I should endeavour to be receptive to the perspectives of others. Instead of upholding my own model monopoly[42], to which others must conform, it is up to me to take up all the other perspectives and allow them to interact.

There is little methodological support for this. Most of the methods I am familiar with are of a monological nature (strictly speaking, they postulate a pseudo-objectivity, failing to acknowledge the designer's perspectivity)[43]. In a dialogical design process, we must assume that each contribution is of a provisional nature; that cooperating designers entertain different expectations with regard to the process as a whole, setting different priorities and applying different evaluation criteria. In dialogical design, we must also acknowledge existing conflicts and jointly overcome them.

Dialogical design must succeed in weaving together these perspectives in such a way that the web of decisions emerging during the design process is borne jointly. This involves meaningfully alternating between individual and cooperative work, offering and accepting constructive criticism, exploring the consequences of proposed design decisions, evaluating results multiperspectively and revising them jointly – until gradually a stable solution emerges that is endorsed by all parties.

The basic prerequisite for dialogical design is trust. This can only develop where the interests of those involved are taken into consideration. Moreover, it presupposes a willingness on the part of all parties, especially the project manager, to create and maintain a socially supportive milieu.

Dialogical teamwork cannot proceed from any implicit assumptions; it must lay its own foundations for cooperative work. This involves cooperation in establishing the project, in assigning tasks and responsibilities, in synchronizing and coordinating work, and in laying down conventions and standards for work

---

[40] This is elaborated by Jürgen Pasch in [Pasch, 1989, Pasch, 1991].

[41] This is elaborated by Michaela Reisin in [Reisin, 1990] and in Chap. 7.3. She, however, speaks not of "dialogical" but of "cooperative" design.

[42] [Bråten, 1973]

[43] One exception here is SADT with its concept of viewpoints and the author-critic-cycle (see Ross, Chap. 2.5). However, SADT fails to provide means for bringing the different perspectives into interaction with one another.

within the team. But it also means jointly working out an authoritative project view of the basic documents and of the concerns, priorities and evaluation criteria valid in each case.

Dialogical design calls for the conscious development of a project language, linking the relevant domains of reality in a way that everyone is able to follow.

Joint goals must be set and revised during the ongoing process as the respective situation demands.

Cooperative work calls for commonly accessible and jointly maintained "external memories"[44] such as project files and diaries, recording the currently valid foundations of work and jointly taken decisions, so as to enable the decision process to be reconstructed in the case of revisions.

In contrast to the assumptions underlying the production view, dialogical design calls for rich communication between all the parties involved. Information must be continuously collected and disseminated, new viewpoints must be incorporated, and evaluations must be made from ever new perspectives.

The distribution of work tasks must always take place with reference to a jointly upheld overall view, and results obtained individually must be jointly validated. This process can be given technical support in the form of prototyping, the emphasis here being on mutual learning on the basis of preliminary implemented versions.

The measures outlined here are basically geared to facilitating the unfolding of a "Project Mind" and the emergence of a shared perspective.

3.2.8 Concluding remarks

Although I have only been able to outline software development as design in broad terms, I should like to finish off by showing what the results will be, should we be willing to accept this view and make proper provision for it. It offers us a conscious orientation for our theoretical and practical work.

Applied to training, it will mean equipping students with the knowledge and skills required for design.

As regards the development of methods, it will involve elaborating flexibly adaptable concepts and techniques supporting cooperative work with other developers and users. Also, a cooperative, flexible and incremental work-style will be an important factor in tool development.

Project organization will also promote cooperation in design. This means as much autonomy as possible to enable us to incorporate the element of responsibility; it means the creation of a dialogically oriented working milieu enabling shared perspectives to be formed; a division of labour that allows us to arrive at and evaluate joint design decisions; and finally, the conscious integration of revisions allowing closure in design.

Accepting and implementing this view means designing design. Undoubtedly, we still have a very long way to go before arriving at the sort of societal conditions

---

[44] See Keil-Slawik, Chap. 4.4.

that will allow this to take place on a large scale[45]. That makes it all the more important – by way of a contribution to desirable social changes – to outline practicable approaches to design, using as a guide our common experience of quality and human-oriented design, and to explore these approaches and prove their suitability.

Acknowledgements

This section is of considerable importance because the ideas set out in this chapter were developed in dialogical processes. In other words, they were made possible and given concrete form by cooperation, conversations and intellectual discussions with a number of people, all of whose names I am unable to list here.

The technical experience on which this contribution is based was gained since 1978 at the Technical University of Berlin in a research milieu organized along cooperative lines, and it has been substantially supported by my co-workers. My special thanks are due to Reinhard Keil-Slawik, Jürgen Pasch and Michaela Reisin and all others who have contributed to our methodological approach STEPS.

Important insights were derived from the research work I did during my stay in Palo Alto in 1987/88 and from the work involved in organizing and holding the conference on "Software Development and Reality Construction".

A considerable help to me in writing this contribution were the valuable discussions I had with Michaela Reisin. I learned a great deal from the continual and conscious crossing of our perspectives.

For enabling me to make a tentative entry into the constructivist discourse, I am indebted to three scientists for their intellectual guidance, encouragement and kind support. Stein Bråten showed me the door to this world of thought and was an invaluable help in finding my bearings there. My attempts to understand Gordon Pask's theory, and his personal support in these attempts, have helped me to acquire key insights. And last but not least, Heinz von Foerster has been a great inspiration to me and instrumental in shaping the essence of the ideas presented here.

---

[45] The masters of design are to be found in the Scandinavian countries. Their theoretical and methodological approaches – along with strategies for societal implementation of these approaches – can provide us with important insights for our own work (see [Floyd et al., 1989a].

3.3 The Idea that Reality is Socially Constructed

Bo Dahlbom

"Die Philosophen haben die Welt nur verschieden *interpretiert*; es kömmt darauf an, sie zu *verändern*."

3.3.1 Introduction

Constructivism, the idea that reality is socially constructed, has recently invaded the field of software development. Producing software, designing computer applications, installing systems, reorganizing work patterns, are all constructive activities which, more or less directly, contribute to changing the world we live and work in. A clear understanding of the idea of reality construction is then a way to understand what one is *really* doing as a software developer. Such an understanding should be easy to obtain in view of the current popularity of the idea. It is not. The main reason for this is that most proponents of constructivism today brandish it as a weapon in a humanistic campaign against technology. Doing this they not only fail to see the truly technological nature of the idea of reality construction and the vital roles played by technology in all constructions of reality, but they also manage to alienate many of the practitioners whose practice they want to enlighten.

To claim that reality is socially constructed is to claim not only that reality is constructed, as opposed to "given" or "simply there", but also that this construction is social as opposed to, say, natural, private, or technical. In the recent vogue of social studies of science, constructivism is thus used to combat the hegemony of the natural sciences by showing that a social understanding of concept formation and knowledge acquisition is fundamental to our understanding of reality. Similarly, the current interest in social studies of technology aim at showing that changes of reality initiated by engineering become real only to the extent that they are socially realized.

In a world becoming ever more filled with technical artifacts, the idea that we construct our reality is not that outlandish. But when constructivists argue that reality is socially constructed they are not thinking of the construction of buildings, bridges and highways using concrete and steel. They are thinking of mental rather than material construction, of interpretation rather than material change.

The importance of interpretation, of the meaning we give our world, is underrated in a technological age stressing material goods and values. But acknowledging the importance of mental constructions should not make us forget the reality of material construction. As I try to spell out the complexity of the idea that reality is socially constructed, by sketching its history, by looking closer at some of its major advocates, and by drawing out its implications for software development, my major task will be to warn against such forgetfulness.

I will take you on a tour through the idea of reality construction by travelling back and forth between the two intellectual strands in the process of modernization: the Enlightenment and Romanticism. The major part of our tour will be spent in the land of Romanticism, accepting without argument the kind of irrealism propounded by constructivists like Nelson Goodman, Richard Rorty and Jacques Derrida. But throughout I will try to give the Enlightenment its due by pointing out the important roles of technology in the processes of reality construction: in material constructions, as a basis for thought experiments, as provider of intellectual tools, and as a source for constructivist ideas in general.

In the first two sections the distinction between material and mental construction is introduced and discussed, first, in terms of a distinction between engineering and construction, between industrial production and craft. Secondly, the background of this distinction is traced in the opposition in our culture between the ideas and ideals of the Enlightenment and Romanticism. In the next two sections I then try to show how closely related these two forms of construction really are. Section 3.3.3 tries to show that material construction is always mental by discussing the dependence of facts on theories, of objects on ideas. In Section 3.3.4 the task is the complementary one of showing how thinking relies on material artifacts.

In Section 3.3.5 our understanding of constructivism is deepened by a close reading of some recent philosophical contributions. Section 3.3.6 aims to make clear that a socially constructed reality has all the properties we are accustomed to attribute to reality. In Section 3.3.7 I argue that the constructivist idea really is the idea of technology, and I discuss how science is now changing as it begins to appreciate this idea. Section 3.3.8 finally tries to pull all the threads together in a recommendation for all of us, who would like to see a computerization on human terms, not to be content with trying out different interpretations of computer technology.

Before we begin I would like to stress the importance of processes of construction in nature, of "natural reality construction", to counter the Romantic tendency to make of construction a human privilege. The idea of human world-making makes good sense when it comes to theorizing about society. And everything we care for is (automatically) socialized. But the fact that social reality is constituted by the institutionalized conceptions of its members does not mean that social theorizing can forget about material conditions, be they technological, biological or physical. And when it comes to nature, the idea that it is our conception that counts is, to my mind, an example of ridiculous *hubris*. We are nothing but tiny flecks in the surface of the grand and forbidding construction of nature. Our constructions of nature weigh lightly in comparison with nature's constructions of us.

3.3.2 Industrialization and the social construction of technology

We use technology to change our natural environment and we use it to change our societies. The automation of manual labour has made much more effective our attempts to change nature to our liking. The tremendous social changes brought about by this industrialization are largely side-effects. Information technology plays an important role in industrial production, but its current major role is in changing relations between people: as a technology for expression, communication and social control.

Our conception of how technology brings on changes derives from our experience of industrialized manual labour. We act as if information technology can be used to change social organizations along the very lines of how industrial technology has changed our natural environment. Computerizing an organization, we tacitly assume, is pretty much like fertilizing a field: a matter of introducing the right cause in order to get the desired effect, a matter of good engineering.[1]

This does not mean that in software development people are unaware of complications resulting from dealing with human beings. But many system developers like to think of them as just that – as complications in a process that has a fairly simple causal character of engineering a change. They want to think of those complications as really beyond the business of system development. Just as pollution is a political rather than an industrial problem, software developers should not worry about such complications as long as they produce good systems, they say.

Of course it is true that without such simplifications of complex processes, one can do nothing. A complex process can only be competently handled by divided labour. But not just any simplification will do, and sometimes it becomes necessary to take a hard look at the total process in all its complexity in order to rearrange the division of labour. In the eighties there has been a growing, now rather widespread appreciation that system development (like industrial pollution, medical care, etc.) is in dire need of such a "holistic" going over.[2]

System development projects are relatively small-scale, planned attempts to use computer based information systems to change social organizations. The practice and theory of system development is only beginning to learn the complexities of such tasks. One of the first lessons learned was that using information technology to change an organization should not be viewed as a process of engineering. For reasons of democracy such a perspective would be degrading and for reasons of making profit it would be silly so to underestimate the complexity of social response to technical change.[3]

On a more general level these issues are studied by the growing field studying technology and social change. Traditionally, such studies have often been studies

---

[1] See the discussion of this and similar examples in [Dahlbom, 1987].

[2] See, e.g., [Mathiassen, 1984, Lyytinen, 1986, Winograd and Flores, 1986, Bjerknes et al., 1987, Ehn, 1988, Bjerknes et al., 1990] and, of course, this volume.

[3] An influential version of this argument can be found in [Checkland, 1981].

of how technology has changed society thus inviting technology determinism: a developing technology will have social consequences for us to foresee and then live with. To counter this deterministic view one can try to change the perspective. Rather than looking at society from the viewpoint of technology one can choose to study technology from the viewpoint of society. In system development this means to approach the computer based system from the viewpoint of the receiving organization rather than the other way around.

Such a shift of perspective is currently under way in European technology studies, going by the name of "The social construction of technological systems" or the "SCOT" programme for short.[4] In this programme one sets out to study local environments in which technologies are developed, how general social conditions make a certain technology appreciated and profitable and determine its direction of development, in short, how social conditions, material and ideological, influence the development of technologies.

In all this there is an underlying thesis to the effect that the fate of a technology depends on how people conceive of it, what they know about it, their attitudes to it, their values, etc. Sometimes the phrase "the social construction of technology" is interpreted much more strongly to mean that a technology is what its users conceive it to be. This strong interpretation is attractive (to some) in view of the power over the technology it gives the users. It turns technology into a democratic phenomenon: it is not the experts who design the machines that really make them but we, the users. Rather than being complications in a causal chain of engineering, the users turn out to be the real designers. The strong interpretation is attractive, as well, for its *idealism*: technology can be changed, oh so easily, by rethinking it, by changing our ideas about it, by "positive thinking".

An appreciation of the idea that technology is socially constructed by its users will change one's conception of such a business as software development. The heart of that business can no longer be a *product*, a system, produced by professional software developers, since the properties of that system will be determined in its use. Software development becomes an open-ended *process* in which the software developers play a marginal role.[5] But in all this there is a neglect of the current process of industrializing software production, a process working against user-involvement. Information technology has increased our possibilities for industrializing manual labour, but it is also beginning to make reasonable an industrialization of intellectual labour, including the production of information technology itself.

When the construction of software is a process taking place in projects, in the field, as a craft, using prototyping, resulting in systems tailor-made for a specific customer, the users can play an important role in the design process.

---

[4] This research programme is inspired by the so-called "strong programme", an influential constructivist approach in recent sociology of science. Both programmes are described in [Bijker et al., 1987]. Recent works in this vein are [Latour, 1987] and [Latour and Woolgar, 1986].

[5] Cf. [Floyd, 1987] for a clear formulation of the nature of such a change.

But with a growing software industry producing ready-made system solutions, there will be less and less opportunities for individualized system analysis and design work in the field. Standardized software will replace the works of craft and the users will enter the process of software development consequent to the purchase of an advanced software product package.[6]

That package may of course be tailorable by the users to satisfy their specific needs, but the constraints on that tailorability will be set by software industries competing in a market. As users of computer software we will be in the situation we are now when we move along the aisles of the supermarket trying to pick one out of thirty, virtually identical, laundry detergents all giving our children allergies. Noticing that the distance between the user and the producer will grow as the industrialization of software production proceeds, we must realize that the process of software development is *two* processes rather than one. Stressing the user involvement by worrying about the design of field projects should not make us forget the importance of gaining power over the process of software development in the software industry.

The industrialization of software production means that when we think of software development as "social construction of technology" we must be careful to pay attention both to the social reality of software use *and* the social reality of industrial production of software. If the former is mainly a process of ideology construction, of attitudes, learning, habits, and the like, the latter is primarily a material construction of a product, subject to economical and technical constraints. The idea that technology is socially constructed is valuable in making us see clearly that changing society cannot be conceived as a form of engineering. But if the idea makes us play down the importance of material construction work and underestimate the significance of the ongoing industrialization of intellectual work, then that idea will do the users of computer software more harm than good.

3.3.3 A changing world

The modernization of Europe is a drawn-out process, clearly visible in the 16th century, but not really gaining momentum until the 19th century. It is a complex process of change, transforming a traditional society of peasants, craftsmen, clergy and landlords into the industrialized society we see around us. It has become common to collect the various, often conflicting, ideas involved in this process into two major intellectual strands: the *Enlightenment* and *Romanticism*.

The philosophers of the Enlightenment dreamed of a world ruled by reason, governed by science and technology. They formulated this dream, their "project of modernity", as a programme for democratization, secularization, and industrialization, all three conceived as elements in a rational transformation of society. As the philosophy of a rising bourgeoisie class, this project made its forceful impact on European societies in *La grande revolution*.

---

[6] See my discussion in [Dahlbom, 1990].

Romanticism grew out of that revolution, inspired by it, but giving it a different, emotional interpretation: revolutions were not just means to ends, but ends in themselves. Romanticism turned not only against the authoritarian rule of a feudal society, but also against the rule of the commonplace in an Enlightened society. Its means were the humanities, artistic expressions by individual genius, an inspired anarchy. Its values made Romanticism an easy prey for various elitist movements.

As elements in the modernization process, both the Enlightenment and Romanticism wanted to change the world, society and man.[7] But whereas the Enlightenment had a fairly clear idea of the ends of modernization, Romanticism was programmatically vague and open-ended. This difference can be traced back to fundamentally different conceptions of knowledge. The Enlightenment is a goal-directed, problem-solving, cognitive enterprise in search of the objective truth about the world, society and man, on which to found its projects of change. Romanticism is a process-oriented, inspired, expressive movement inviting us to participate in bold constructions of uninhibited utopias. The Enlightenment has a strong sense of reality. Romanticism pushes further the frontiers of the possible. The Enlightenment, as an epoch in our history, is the era of map-making, Romanticism of world-making. The Enlightenment makes maps to be used in a cumulative rearrangement of the world. Romanticism views these maps as largely counterproductive, providing support for a world well lost, and prefers to debunk that world by demonstrating its ephemeral nature as construction and supplant it wholesale with a brave new world.

In a stable, traditional society, reality is created by God for man to dwell in and worship Him in. What is worth knowing are the principles, the order laid down by the creator, and man himself is subject to that order. He cannot change it. Every real change is authored by some divine, creative power. Nothing *really* happens unless some divine power wills it to happen. All else is mere appearance. The idea of change so fundamental to the process of modernization is not an easy one to accept for a traditional society steeped in the notion of a divine *order*. "Change" smacks of "chaos", and the Enlightenment has to begin its revolution of this society by viewing change as only realizing the true, natural order.

The Enlightenment moves cautiously from the Christian idea of a world recently created to a world with a billion-year-long history of construction, from the Aristotelian idea of an unchanging, ordered and teleological nature to Darwin's conception of fortuitously evolving organisms, from a fixed human nature to a human being almost infinitely malleable by learning. In all these areas the change is a change in the conception of the *nature* of nature, man, and society. It is as a result of scientific research into the nature of phenomena that these are seen to be changing rather than stable. Change is understood as the lawful rearrangement of unchanging elements. Every extension of the idea of change is accompanied by ideas of a more fundamental stability, of conservation.

---

[7] At the same time they correct one another on this score. Romanticism can be used as a basis for a conservative reaction against an uninhibited process of enlightened rationalization. From an enlightened standpoint it is often important to warn against Romantic excesses.

In a lawfully changing world there is a place for *engineering*. Knowing the laws of change in nature, society, man, we can use this knowledge in physical, social, educational and genetic engineering. The Enlightenment idea of a man-made, constructed, *artificial* world is the idea of applying science in designing nature, society and man. From Bacon's *New Atlantis* to Skinner's *Walden Two*, engineering is understood as the competent *control* of a determinate nature.

With Romanticism caution is abandoned. Taking seriously Giambattista Vico's daring conception of society as freely constructed by its members, the Romantic philosophers argued against notions of a fixed nature, be it of nature, society or man. These philosophers were led by their line of reasoning to lose interest in the way the world is in favour of an interest in how we *conceive* the world. Or, better, to identify the way the world is with our conception of it. Making a major point of the observation that our world is shaped by our experience, these philosophers wanted to change our world by changing our experience. New worlds could be constructed, they argued, not by engineering and control, but by new ways of looking and thinking, the construction material being spiritual rather than material.

The decisive move in this argument is what Immanuel Kant called his "Copernican Revolution" – from the Enlightenment theory that our conception of the world is a representation of a ready-made nature "out there" to the transcendental theory that nature is constituted by our conception. By this ingenious move, Kant wanted to avoid the skeptical conclusion that if our access to the world is limited to our representation of it, we have no guarantee that these representations are accurate or, for that matter, that there is a world out there. If nature is our construction, we don't have to worry about our access to it.

By claiming that the fundamental concepts we use in constructing nature are fixed, Kant made sure that natural science had a secure foundation in *one* nature, characterized by the necessary truths of Euclidean geometry and Newtonian mechanics. This idea was soon to be abandoned by the Romantic philosophers taking off from Kant. By making the fundamental concepts relative to culture, the construction of reality came to be seen as a historical process. The necessary truths turned into social conventions, and the interest gradually shifted from the nature of reality to the social process of constructing multiple realities. Kant's transcendental *Kritik*, searching for first foundations for science, changed into *Kulturkritik* and *Ideologiekritik*.[8]

Trying to bring together the two strands of the Enlightenment, rationalism and empiricism, Kant inadvertently managed to prepare for a much deeper split in our culture. His "Copernican Revolution" gave our minds a decisive role in our search for knowledge, replacing Descartes' rather passive mirror of nature with an active world-maker. This "revolution" was to have a tremendous impact on the humanities and the social sciences, but it left members of the natural science community cold. The result was a split between a natural science and

---

[8] In their own different styles, with their own different motives, Marx, Nietzsche and Freud were the major instigators of this change. Heidegger, Lukács, Mannheim and the Frankfurt school are some of the inheritors in our century.

technology guided by Enlightenment ideals *and* an approach to the study of
society and culture based on Romantic ideas.

This split between *Naturwissenschaften* and *Geisteswissenschaften*, between
"positivism" and "hermeneutics", was unfortunate in contributing to a division
into what C. P. Snow called "two cultures". But it was fortunate in the sense
of being a powerful source of discussion. The philosophical tug of war between
an Enlightened interest in *reality* and a Romantic interest in our conceptions of
reality has moved back and forth. In 20th century philosophy the Romantic interest in *Weltanschauungen*, conceptual schemes, has continued to grow. Today,
when we can look back upon two decades of Romantic ("postmodern") attacks
on Enlightenment ideas ("modernism"), it is safe to say that, within philosophy,
Romanticism maintains the strongest position.[9]

When we leave the philosophy seminar behind, however, and enter the business of software development, Enlightenment ideas still dominate. Systems are
judged by their accuracy in mapping their target domain. If we are unhappy with
this situation, if we are oppressed by the conservative elitism of experts designing systems "mapping objective reality", and want to turn software development
into a more democratic, constructive enterprise, we may turn to philosophy and
a Romantic world view for support. But liberating as this move may seem at
first, giving us a view of technology as having the properties we conceive it to
have, there are dangers ahead.

3.3.4 The mental nature of material constructions

When impressed by Enlightenment ideals we speak of constructing the world,
we mean it literally. We want to build cities and highways, schools and sports
arenas, develop technology, give everyone an automobile, a washing machine
and a personal computer, make the country grow. We want to change society by
reforming it, by giving it a new form. Material constructions are the most visible,
and eager to see results we will tend to stress material aspects, building a welfare
state. This does not mean that material values dominate the Enlightenment. On
the contrary, material reforms are only means to more spiritual ends such as
justice, liberty, equality, democracy, education, meaningful employment, love and
self-respect. The problem is only to make sure that changes in these directions
are *real* changes. For the Enlightenment wants real changes – not just talk.

The Romantic idea of reality construction is very different. When the Enlightenment plans its construction projects, Romanticism will speak of the possibilities for a new society based on a new kind of people. Against the Enlightenment idea of a fixed human nature, of the members of society as fairly constant

---

[9] It should be clear by now that the Enlightenment and Romanticism are both systems
of thought and epochs in our history. They continue to fight for domination. They
tend to coincide, roughly, with periods of economic growth and stagnation respectively. The period from the Korean war to the Oil Crisis (the '50s and the '60s) was a
period of Enlightenment. Since then (the '70s and the '80s), Romanticism has ruled,
but times seem to be changing again.

and known resources (and consumers), Romanticism counters with a belief in an unfathomed capacity of human beings to change, develop, grow. Against the Enlightenment project to reap nature of its fruits by developing a material culture, Romanticism counters with a project of human growth, of spiritual culture.

To use the expression "reality construction" to characterize both an Enlightened project of material construction and a Romantic project of spiritual growth is of course confusing. Nothing has come to seem so separate in our culture as engineering and art. Putting together bricks is real construction, the Enlightenment will argue, while putting together ideas is at best metaphorical construction. But even the most down-to-earth engineer has come to feel uncomfortable when making such a statement in view of the current widespread agreement that this item of common sense is false.

In science, to give just an example, it has become commonplace to question the objectivity of scientific facts and appreciate the role of theoretical interpretation. Even such a lowly object as an ordinary brick is always *seen through a theory* and thus we cannot put bricks together without putting ideas together. To say that there is theory involved even in our handling of bricks is to say that there is room for variation in our conception of bricks. Our objective reality is not so objective after all. It only seems objective as long as we stay in the company of people sharing our theory.

This 20th century critique of the idea of an objective, given reality, has spread outside the intellectual debate in philosophy, art and science. The Enlightened engineers have learned their lesson by the very difficult process of losing credibility, of seeing their skills questioned by a moral majority. Their stubborn insistence on real change today seems quite impressive considering the difficulties of success. For what the Enlightenment engineer wants is of course not just any old material change, but one with a certain meaning. Unless the new schools mean a better education, the automobile and nuclear plant a better life, etc., the change is only real in an ironic way. But how do you make sure that the material change you bring about will mean what you want it to mean? How do you know that the ones you do the reforms for will interpret them the way you intend them to? When you begin taking such questions seriously, it is only because you have been forced to appreciate that reality is in the eye of the beholder.

Once we have begun to question our natural attitude of taking our immediately perceived reality for given – be it by way of personal experience, modern physics, philosophical argument or a course in anthropology – we realize that bricks are no more (or less) real than ideas. As long as we all agree on what the world is like we can attend to the bricks and forget about ideas. But when ideas begin to vary we have to worry about them in our reality construction projects. The neat separation into material and mental construction breaks down. What is literal construction and what is only metaphorical is no longer so obvious.

Of course, no one is surprised by hearing that material construction projects involve ideas – in the planning, execution, interpretation and evaluation of processes and products. What we tend to forget is the fact that those ideas may cause disagreement on what we have achieved, to what purpose, with what success, that is unresolvable. And that therefore material construction projects always are mental construction projects as well. But then again, don't we all know that the successful engineer always is a good artist, or has the use of a good designer group and a good advertising agency? Of course we do, but the more Enlightened we are, the more distasteful we find those "artistic" aspects of our work. Mental construction is a way of faking it when one is unable to make something real. That people continue happily to prefer bad technology can only be explained by the negative influence of mental constructions.

The Enlightenment idea of a project, of a goal-directed effort to change the world, involves planning, an ability to think what is not, to imagine situations that are (as yet) unreal. Putting together ideas in order to imagine goals, we mentally construct a reality later to be materially constructed. And when the material construction has done its job we have to mentally interpret the result and relate it to our goals, knowing well that no project will be true to plan. For the Enlightenment it is material construction, what technology can do, that counts. For a Romantic the mental construction phases are the most important: what human beings want to do with the technology.

We don't have to study the introduction of high-tech in pre-industrialized countries, or ponder the conservative nature of the automobile, to see that a Romantic perspective can be illuminating (and lucrative). With such a perspective we will be struck by the futility of technology, of our material constructions, in a number of everyday situations. Children playing with pine cones, sticks and stones will, for example, construct a reality almost by imagination alone, and fancy prefab toys add nothing to the play. Who is to say that the traffic jam constructed on the living room rug becomes more real when the cars are powered by batteries rather than by a child's imagination?

When a child plays with toy cars, those cars are both symbols for real cars and real cars in a constructed reality. Bricks and ideas are certainly very different but the bricks are suffused by our ideas and sometimes act as symbols in our thinking. The processes of material and mental construction are intertwined and impossible to separate. Our material constructions use materials with colours, textures and shapes which are laden with culture and our thinking rely on material support for illustration, inspiration and communication.

But software development is no child's play, the software engineer will reply. And we can see how this debate between material and mental constructivists will go on. But enough is enough. Let us be content here to observe that a software development project is a very complex mixture of material and mental constructions in which it is important to pay heed both to technical constraints and human inventiveness even if it is impossible to obtain a neat separation between what technology does and what human beings want to do with the technology.

3.3.5 The material nature of thinking

To construct is to "put together" and the acts of construction as well as their results differ widely depending on what it is we put together: bricks, ideas, words, notes, etc. That such putting together is "social" can mean that people do it together, orienting their individual contributions to those of other contributors. More interesting is perhaps the idea that constructions of reality are social because what we put together are social objects, cultural artifacts, rather than natural objects. Indeed, it may seem like a good idea to classify constructions in terms of categories such as material, mental, natural, social, artificial, depending on the types of objects used in constructing. Things are more complicated, however, as we shall see when we look more carefully at these categories.

It is easy to see that the material construction projects we undertake are social, both in the sense that they involve several people *and* utilize materials and tools that are the results of previous processes of construction. It is important to realize that mental construction projects, as well, are social in both these respects. When we appreciate the extent to which thinking is a social rather than individual activity and a cultural rather than a natural process, the material nature of our mental constructions become visible.[10]

It is only within the last decades that social scientists have begun to pay serious attention to how organizations think, learn, remember, forget, etc. Our thinking about thinking has been so dominated by the idea that it is an individual, mental process as to block out the obvious fact that most of the thinking going on is more profitably ascribed to organizations than to individuals. But wait a minute! Certainly, thinking is a *mental* process, a *brain* process, and organizations don't have minds, not to say brains. I am not denying that (here). What I am saying is rather that thinking is like traffic: individuals drive the cars, but to understand the traffic in a big city we had better look at what is going on as a system, an organization.

One way of appreciating this point is by seeing that thinking is an activity which, like so many other activities in our modern society, has undergone a process of industrialization. What used to be an individual craft using fairly simple tools has become a complex production process performed by organizations relying on advanced rule systems, planning, division of labour and high technology. Like so many other activities, thinking survives as a craft, but the thinking that really matters in our modern society is almost exclusively organized, institutionalized.

There are several obstacles hiding this fact from our view. One is our tendency to think of thinking as a process in the mind or brain. As a brain process thinking is a *natural* process, and this makes it difficult for us to see that thinking today is about as artificial as anything else – communication, production, consumption – in our modern artificial world. Just as our society will grind to a halt when

---

[10] This lesson has been hard to learn. One exception to the general blindness to the social and cultural nature of thinking is the Russian school in psychology, now generally referred to as "activity theory". See the contribution by Arne Raeithel in Chap. 8.4.

our artifacts break down, so thinking would reduce to next to nothing were we to suffer a breakdown of our *intellectual* artifacts. What could we think, how could we reason, if we did not have words, figures, books, diagrams, concrete examples, slide-rules, algebra, logic, Lisp or legal aid?

Thinking of thinking as a brain process makes us think of human intelligence as natural (in spite of the fact that most so-called intelligence tests measure artificial capacities like vocabulary and numerical ability). This has made the discussion of research on artificial intelligence more confusing than it need be. Once it is seen how artificial human thinking is, to what extent it relies on cultural artifacts, the AI-project is seen as a rather mundane attempt to automatize artifacts, in this case intellectual tools rather than manual ones, but so what? And we realize that calculators are exemplary instances of artificial intelligence.

Another obstacle to seeing the cultural nature of thinking is the dominant role played by visual perception in our attempts to understand thinking. Thinking is conceived as a sort of looking (with the mind's eye), a fairly laid back observing of the thoughts passing by in the stream of consciousness, or at best a more active looking around, doing some sort of inventory or search. The thoughts appear or are found rather than being produced or constructed. This view of thinking has always had its rival in a more active notion of thinking (and consequently perception), but this rival did not become a serious contender until Kant and Romanticism.

The naïve theory of how we get to know the world has not even discovered that perception is a process: just open your eyes and there the world is. The Greek philosophers were not that naïve. They thought of perception as *imitation*: the world somehow impressing its form upon a passive mind. Galileo was moving away from this view of thinking as an imagistic, pictorial imitation, when he argued that "the book of nature is written in a mathematical language," but mathematics to Galileo was Euclidean geometry – still pictorial. It was up to Descartes to take the decisive step to algebra as medium of representation, algebra as our language of thought, which he did by inventing analytic geometry.[11]

When we use mathematics as our language of thought, our thinking about the world can no longer be understood as pictorial imitation. Algebra is a cultural artifact, constructed by the Arabs, and a theory about the world couched in the language of algebra is similarly a constructed artifact, a cultural object. This was by no means clear to Descartes, nor to his followers. The status of mathematics as *Truth* stood in the way of an appreciation of the cultural nature of mathematical thinking. Rationalists from Leibniz to Wittgenstein treat mathematics as a natural rather than a conventional phenomenon, dreaming of *the* ideal mathematical language, with a logical form mirroring the form of the world.

The cognitive science of the last three decades, including artificial intelligence research, lean in this rationalist direction. Major turbulence has been created

---

[11] Thus there is in Descartes a clear formulation of the idea, so important in artificial intelligence research, that thinking is calculation or computation. [Haugeland, 1985] has a nice discussion of this idea.

by such issues as if we think solely in words or also in images – the implicit presupposition being that thinking is a natural phenomenon. In spite of all the work going on in AI on constructing artificial languages, it is most unusual to find someone arguing that human thinking itself is an artifact, done in whatever medium found suitable.

When the Romantic philosophers turned to action rather than perception in search for a model for thinking, they first viewed thinking as an *expression* of our human nature. Our mental processes, including perception, are then taken as starting point in a search for the innate principles of the human mind. Such was the program initiated by Kant and it lives on in much of contemporary cognitive science. Such a program certainly thinks of thinking as a constructive process, but it attends primarily to the predetermined aspects of that process in search of a general theory of the mind.

As we move from viewing thinking and perception as processes of imitation to more complex representational processes to processes of expression, man's contributions to his view of the world increase. But to say that man *constructs* his world becomes a forceful claim only when we take the further step of realizing that this construction is determined by culture. If knowledge is a *natural* phenomenon, if knowledge is obtained by a natural process, it makes little sense to speak of reality construction. But if knowledge is *cultural*, an artifact made by man to his infinitely varying measures, then it begins to make sense to speak of knowledge, truth and reality as constructed. That is why it is so important to stress that reality construction is *social*.

To say that thinking is a process of social construction is then to express a view very different from the standard view of thinking as a natural process in the mind or brain. It is to claim that thinking is regulated by social norms, that much thinking is better understood as a socially organized process involving several individuals (and of course their brains) with an organization as "the thinking thing". It is to claim that the process of thinking relies on intellectual tools and materials supplied by culture, some of which are internalized but a great deal of which are provided by the environment. It is to claim that the symbols, categories, elements we use in our thinking are drawn from our social, natural and artifactual environment, and put together to make worlds, new artifacts made possible by, and making possible, new worlds.

But can reality really be an artifact? Well. . . In sociology there is a growing discipline called "social problems research".[12] Much of the research in that discipline wants to look at social problems as socially constructed. The standard procedure, then, is to "deconstruct" social problems by showing how the one or the other phenomenon of long standing, say the battering of children, in a certain social setting becomes identified or defined as a social problem. Here one obviously operates with a contrast between an objective fact, the battering of children, and a social artifact, child abuse. Distancing oneself from the social problem under study, it can be viewed as socially constructed against the background of more objective phenomena. It is of course possible to carry such

---

[12] [Schneider, 1985] is a short review of this discipline.

a distancing process further, applying it to the phenomenon of child battering itself, then seen perhaps as socially constructed by the science community. But how far can such a process of deconstruction be carried? Will it not have to stop eventually, confronted with a real as opposed to an artifactual reality?

One way of answering this question is to choose a more humble attitude to our tradition of theorizing about thinking. Rather than claiming that the move from imitation to representation to expression to social construction is a move from mistaken ideas about thinking to the true theory, one then takes more seriously all these attempts at understanding thinking. That our view of the world is socially constructed does not mean that it isn't also obtained through processes of imitation, representation and expression.[13]

3.3.6 The philosophy behind

A great deal of the theoretical discussion in the social sciences is today dedicated to analyzing constructivism and its consequences. Influential empirical work in such areas as the sociology of science and social problems are guided by the idea of reality construction. This idea has been a central topic for philosophical debate in the last two decades, approached in different fashions by French, American and German philosophers. It has even entered biology through attempts to base a constructivist approach on biological ideas of self-organization. It has played a major role in the culture debate over "postmodernism" ranging from topics in architecture to politics. Social constructivists are happy to see the current projects of deconstruction and reconstruction going on in Eastern Europe.

Its current popularity notwithstanding, the idea that reality is socially constructed has a long and complex history in our culture. The first proponent of social reality construction we know of was the great sophist Protagoras (500 B. C.) with his "homo mensura" sentence: "Man is the measure of all things, of the things that are that they are, and of the things that are not that they are not." His major opponent was, of course, Plato, who despised the sophists for relativizing truth and made Protagoras a major target of attack. The battle has been raging ever since.

I have no intention of charting this history here. In the previous sections I have tried to indicate some of the complexity of the ideas involved. My purpose was twofold. I wanted to prepare for the main thrust of my argument to the effect that an appreciation of the fact that reality is socially constructed should not blind us to the importance and interdependence of all the various constructivist processes going on, be they material or mental, natural or social. I also wanted to prepare for a presentation of a handful of recent philosophical contributions to constructivism. The following is not intended as an introduction to these

---

[13] Notice that it is a foursome of theories with wide applicability. You can use them to say interesting things about almost any arena of (human) activity. Art is an obvious case, but so is software development.

thinkers. Compressing their complex systems of thought into a few paragraphs I try to give a flavour of what these thinkers say and how they say it.[14]

Peter Berger's and Thomas Luckmann's *The Social Construction of Reality* is probably the most influential recent source for constructivist ideas. This little book is a major effort of synthesizing such ideas within the field of sociology. Berger's and Luckmann's project is an attempt to place the sociology of knowledge, the study of the social conditions of knowledge, at the core of sociological theorizing: "The basic contentions of the argument of this book are ... that reality is socially constructed and that the sociology of knowledge must analyze the process in which this occurs." (p. 13).[15]

The construction of reality is a continuing dialectical process involving three moments: externalization, objectivization and internalization. "Society is a human product. Society is an objective reality. Man is a social product." (p. 79). The objective social reality is constructed through habitualized actions constituting institutions. Language, in the form of everyday conversations, plays a central role both in establishing and legitimizing institutions. The institutions are integrated into a social *system* only through the process of legitimation. This legitimation, involving the use of "symbolic universes" is "faced with the ongoing necessity of keeping chaos at bay... *All* societies are constructions in the face of chaos." (p. 121).

Berger and Luckmann distinguish social reality from nature. Biological facts, characteristics of the human organism and its environment "serve as a necessary presupposition for the production of social order." (p. 70). Such facts impose limitations on man's construction of his social reality and of himself as a social being. Through reification, i.e., "the apprehension of human phenomena as if they were things" (p. 106)... "the world of institutions appears to merge with the world of nature." (p. 108) Reification is not "a perversion of an originally non-reified apprehension of the social world." (p. 107). On the contrary, the realization that the objective social reality is a product of human activity comes rather late in history and in any individual's life. "Roles may be reified in the same manner as institutions." (p. 108). In a modern, industrialized society, however, with social division of labour and social distribution of knowledge, there will be "an increasingly general consciousness of the relativity of *all* worlds, including one's own." (p. 192). In such a society reification is less of a threat, and

---

[14] In order to indicate some of the complexity of the background of the idea that reality is socially constructed, I have chosen Peter Berger and Thomas Luckmann [Berger and Luckmann, 1967] as representatives of the phenomenological movement founded by Edmund Husserl, as interpreted by Alfred Schütz, with firm roots in German idealism; Nelson Goodman as an example of an analytic philosopher building his constructivism on Bertrand Russell's idea of "a logical construction of objects" as developed by the logical positivist Rudolf Carnap; Richard Rorty as an American pragmatist reaching his version of constructivism through John Dewey, the later Wittgenstein and Heidegger; and, finally, Jacques Derrida and a constructivism coming out of the structural approach to language and other social phenomena, originated by Ferdinand de Saussure. Quite a mouthful.

[15] Page references are to the Penguin edition (1967).

individuals not only play at "being what they are *not* supposed to be. They also play at being what they *are* supposed to be – a quite different matter." (p. 192).

Berger and Luckmann brush aside the philosophical problems of the status of "reality" and "knowledge" (p. 13f). Proceeding from a phenomenological, everyday conception of reality, they can treat nature as "really real". A minute's reflection on this issue will, of course, lead one to question such a "reification" of our conceptions of nature. What is it that makes our knowledge of nature less susceptible to sociological analysis than our knowledge of the social world?

"Nothing" would be the answer from the philosopher who more than anyone else has contributed to a deeper understanding of the conditions of reality construction. I am thinking, of course, of the Harvard philosopher Nelson Goodman and the way he comes forth in books like *Ways of Worldmaking*[16] and *Of Mind and Other Matters*[17]. Not that Goodman is particularly interested in discussing the social aspects of reality construction. Being in spite of everything an exemplary representative of modern analytic philosophy, Goodman rarely comments on the fact that man is a *zoon politicon*.

Goodman sometimes characterizes his philosophical position as "irrealism". This position "sees the world melting into versions and versions making worlds, finds ontology evanescent, and inquires into what makes a version right and a world well-built." (p. 29). There is no world out there, independent of us.[18] There are only versions made by symbols of all kinds, and true versions make worlds. "The world of a true version is a construct; the features are not conferred upon something independent of the version but combined with one another to make the world of that version." (p. 34). "The worldmaking mainly in question here is making not with hands but with minds, or rather with languages or other symbol systems. Yet when I say that worlds are made, I mean it literally" (p. 42).

Worldmaking is a matter of categorization: distinguishing elements, categorizing them by function, uniting them into wholes. Categories are symbols, elements of linguistic and other symbol systems, and Goodman has been particularly interested in artistic symbol systems.[19] Worldmaking can be compared to the construction of material artifacts. And just as we cannot make such artifacts any way we like, so our worldmaking is restricted. "Making right world-versions – or making worlds – is harder than making chairs or planes, and failure is common, largely because all we have available is scrap material recycled from old and stubborn worlds. Our having done no better or worse is no evidence that chairs or planes or worlds are found rather than made." (p. 42f).

All this is pretty straightforward, but Goodman goes on to claim that "many world versions – some conflicting with each other, some so disparate that conflict or compatibility among them is indeterminable – are equally right." (p. 39). Ver-

---

[16] [Goodman, 1978]

[17] [Goodman, 1984], quotations below will all be from this latter book in which Goodman comments on critics and expands on his views.

[18] "while the underlying world... need not be denied to those who love it, it is perhaps on the whole a world well lost." (*Ways of Worldmaking*, p. 4)

[19] See his *Languages of Art* [Goodman, 1976].

sions are right or wrong – or, more specifically, when the symbols are linguistic, true or false – not by corresponding or failing to correspond to an independent world "out there". "Nevertheless, right versions are different from wrong versions: relativism is restrained by considerations of rightness. Rightness, however, is neither constituted nor tested by correspondence with a world independent of all versions." (p. 39).

So by what is rightness constituted, by what is it tested? "Rightness of categorization, in my view, derives from rather than underlies entrenchment." (p. 38). This, no doubt, is the weakest point in Goodman's philosophy. He has nothing of substance to say on the matter of entrenchment.[20] Some categories, or systems of categories, survive but why they do so we cannot say, except that they "fit" together. They get entrenched in our culture, and that is it.

It is Goodman's strength that he accepts this consequence of his reasoning without flinching. Having rejected realism in the sense of a categorized world "out there" in favour of a position where all categorization is our doing, correspondence theory is out. "Not all differences between true versions can be thought of as differences in grouping or marking off within something common to all. For there are no absolute elements, no space-time or other stuff common to all, no entity that is under all guises or under none." (p. 36). All the structure there is in the world is man-made, and structure is all there is to the world.[21]

Coherence is no live option, "for a false or otherwise wrong version can hold together as well as a right one" (p. 37), and what remains as a possible candidate for truth is then only functionality. Now this would seem a likely candidate in view of Goodman's comparisons between worldmaking and the making of artifacts. And, indeed, there are hints in that direction in his comments on the notion of entrenchment – entrenchment as adaptation – but there is also explicit rejection of this option, e.g., in *Ways of Worldmaking* (p.122f). Functionality is much too simple-minded as a criterion or definition of rightness in view of the wealth of variety of kinds of versions Goodman is able to keep simultaneously in view.

Constructivism is a powerful idea for fulfilling the philosophical task *par excellence*: that of questioning the obvious. It is a liberating tonic for anyone – like Kierkegaard, Nietzsche or Sartre – feeling oppressed, or nauseated, by a reality too much taken for granted. But driven to its extreme, constructivism sweeps away the very foundations of our existence, resulting in a Kundera-like experience of "the unbearable lightness of being".

If one sometimes gets this experience when reading Goodman, it dominates the reading of Jacques Derrida. According to Goodman, we use scrap material from past worldmakings in making our worlds. We have a tendency to take this material at face value, it's old enough to give us a feeling of acquaintance. We think we know what we mean by what we say, we feel at home in our thinking, in our conceptual worlds. Categories get entrenched by fitting together.

---

[20] What little there is, is in [Goodman, 1979, Chap. IV].

[21] "The many stuffs – matter, energy, waves, phenomena – that worlds are made of are made along with the worlds." (*Ways of Worldmaking*, p. 6).

Derrida is out to shatter that comfortable feeling, by striking at categories, often dichotomies, at the very foundation of our reality construction.

Once reality is seen to be a culture relative construct, the critique of culture turns into a "reconstruction of reality". That is, a current reality is criticized in favour of a more or less utopian alternative. But unlike his predecessors, Nietzsche, Husserl and Heidegger, Derrida is not out to reconstruct reality but to *deconstruct* it. And worse than that he wants to deconstruct the philosophical project of deconstruction itself, thus leaving us no foundation whatsoever. To give only one example, it has become common coin to recognize that our thinking is metaphorical through and through. But sitting there in our smugness, saying fashionable things like "Of course the computer is not *literally* a tool or a telephone or a processor...", Derrida will come around and deconstruct, i.e., pulverize, the very dichotomy literal-metaphorical on which we were basing our insight. No wonder, he has been criticized for advocating a most extreme kind of *nihilism*.

The American pragmatist Richard Rorty , author of *Philosophy and the Mirror of Nature*, is one such critic. Basing his critique of postmodern French nihilism on a very American trust in a liberal, political praxis, Rorty wants to steer clear of constructivist excesses. Chaos, as Berger and Luckmann would say, the lightness of being, is held at bay by the stability of liberal political institutions. This democratic praxis is primary to philosophical theorizing about human nature and the good society. That praxis is the foundation upon which intellectual adventures in science, philosophy and culture at large can be staged, as long as they leave that praxis untouched. It is that praxis that decides what is knowledge, truth, virtue and beauty, not the theories that philosophers so seriously struggle to put together. And the essence of that praxis is "free speech", an ongoing conversation.

The philosophers of the Enlightenment searched for first foundations for science, ethics and politics, for infallible *methods* by which to attain objective *truth* and *justice*. When Romantic ideas dominate philosophy, this quest is abandoned. Methods are scrapped, truth is dissolved. Reality, truth and justice are socially constructed subject to cultural variations. There are no natural rights. Nothing is absolute. This can either result in a nihilistic degrading of science, ethics and politics, as only different arenas for the power struggle of reality construction, or, on the contrary, in an upgrading of the philosophically naïve *practice* of science, ethics and politics. The practice is strong enough to need no foundations, no philosophical support. It needs no codified method, no absolute truth. True to his American heritage, Rorty has an unshaken trust in practice.[22]

---

[22] Habermas, Foucault and Rorty are good examples of these three positions. See [Rorty, 1984] for a discussion of the differences between Habermas' Enlightened search for foundations, the nihilism of modern French postmodernism, and the belief in practice characteristic of American pragmatic philosophy.

3.3.7 Reality is a social artifact

Our world is becoming ever more artificial, our reality more of a human artifice. But that the world we live in is an artificial world, constructed by us, does not make the world any less stable than were it a natural world. Things (Latin "res"), i.e., middle-sized material objects, are our paradigm cases of reality, and artifacts are real to the extent that they resemble things, i.e., are "reified".

Artifacts differ with respect to their "thingishness", their objectivity, independence and stability, of course. *Material* artifacts, such as tools, machines, works of art, roads, buildings, are (at least) as real as rocks and bodies. *Social* artifacts, such as organizations, institutions, roles, persons are less tangible but still reified enough to be treated as objective and independent, often being annoyingly stable. *Ideal* artifacts, finally, such as scientific theories, world-views, programs, ideologies, norm systems are the least concrete of our constructions, getting their stability from their material and social implementations.[23]

The insights that the material world, the social world and the ideal world are all socially constructed grows on European man, in starts and leaps, as major strands in the process of modernization. The expansion of technology, industrialization, moves man's material support from nature towards the artificial. A growing awareness of society as constructed, as in Thomas Hobbes' idea of a social contract, goes hand in hand with democratization. The idea that man makes himself, of a person as a work of art, makes room for ideas of personal liberty. The transition from Plato's world of objective, unchanging ideas to the belief in culture as constructed is long and tortuous, and has still a long way to go in such areas as that of mathematics.

As one of the mainsprings in the modernization process, the idea that reality is socially constructed has formidable power. That reality is *constructed* means that it can be deconstructed and reconstructed. The realization that a phenomenon is an artifact, the result of human construction, may undermine one's trust in its reality. The power of God is undermined when we realize that we have constructed him rather than the other way around. Similarly our belief in the objective truth of science is shaken by seeing how theories are constructed by people using material from their personal history and social setting.

But it is easy to overestimate the power of the idea that reality is constructed. Social practices are inert, difficult to change and difficult to control. That reality is *socially* constructed means that changing it is more easily said than done. To the individual it is generally more correct to say that reality *has been* constructed than to say that it *is* constructed. The practical inertia of social construction gives its products their stability, their *reality*.

---

[23] When we talk of "social reality construction", we might of course mean the construction of *social artifacts* as I use the term here. We might, like Berger and Luckmann, be interested in pointing out that a study of social systems modelled on the natural sciences runs the risk of forgetting the task of analyzing the process of constructing those systems. The way I understand the phrase is, of course, as making the stronger claim that *all* of reality is socially constructed. This is a large claim, amounting to a thorough "social-cognitive" turn, from reality as nature to reality as a social artifact.

Practically speaking, a socially constructed reality is just as real as a reality that just *is*. To interpret the move from an objective, natural reality to one that is socially constructed as a liberation from external control is to misjudge the power of social norms. Social determinism, e.g., is not easier, or more difficult, to escape from than biological determinism, even if you believe that the former is "merely" constructed and the latter "really" real. To show that a phenomenon is conventional rather than natural will liberate you only to the extent that nature is more difficult than conventions to change. But only the most cursory glance at social norms and institutions will reveal their power.

Take the notion of "objectivity", for example. If this concept is understood along the lines of "really there", "representing reality" or suchlike, the realization that knowledge is constructed will make us wary, and we will move towards a use of the term "objective" as meaning "intersubjectively agreed", "conventional" or the like. But this latter type of "objectivity" is not threatened by stories about the construction of knowledge, and will soon be indistinguishable from the former type. Hobbes did not for a minute believe that the social norms were undermined by the observation that they were conventions, part of a contract, rather than natural rights and duties. Constructivism is not an exhortation to deconstruction. Nihilism, anarchy, or revolution are not the consequences of a constructivist revelation. And an appreciation of the fact that reality is socially constructed is not a decision to begin constructing reality, but the appreciation that we have always done so and always will.

The construction of artifacts is subject to norms, guided by values. To think of construction as engineering means stressing the functionality of the artifact. What matters most is that it works. To think of construction as scientific is to subject it to the norm of truth. To think of it as art means to stress its aesthetic, edifying, or communicative aspect. To think of construction as politics means to stress its power to control. Our construction of reality, of conceptual schemes, scientific theories, social institutions, information systems, software, computers, can be subjected to all these values, depending on what aspect we want to stress.

The realization that human activity is fundamentally constructive – in art, science, technology or politics – does not in itself come into conflict with any of these values or norms. That these norms are seen themselves to be socially constructed is no reason to abandon them. It may give us a deeper understanding of the projects of art, science, technology and politics, but with that understanding we can go on as before.

The idea of constructing reality is intertwined with the idea of changing it. The possibility of change is a strong motive for believing in the idea of reality construction. When constructivists argue against a science that sees itself as mapping reality, or more generally against the Cartesian idea of knowledge as representation, the vehemence of their argumentation derives from the fear they feel that such ideas support reification and stand in the way of change. A picture is painted with two opposing camps, one standing for a free and self-organized world, democratically constructed by persons with emotions, the other for a deterministic world, ruled by technology, understood only by experts through objective, cognitive representations.

But if there is some truth to that picture, the diagnosis is certainly mistaken. A representational theory of knowledge does not stand in the way of change, nor is constructivism a short cut to democracy. The Enlightenment philosophers argued quite forcefully for the exact opposite: that only by representing the world did you have a chance to change it deliberately, and that an unbridled constructivism left you in the hands of construction elites. Those arguments can of course be countered. And my point is a different one. The understanding that reality is socially constructed, that the power of science and technology is socially rather than naturally founded, will not in itself threaten that power. Truth may have served an ideologically important role as science was breaking away from the Church, but in our times science is powerful enough to manage without that ideology.

When we realize that the natural, objective world is really a social, intersubjective one, there is no loss in determinism, external control or expert rule. The freedom gained by the possibility of multiple perspectives is lost when perspectives are seen as powerful institutions. Our artificial reality gains its stability, its reality, from the stability of social norms. The practical inertia of social institutions plays the role of the physical inertia of matter, and it plays it well. That the world is socially constructed does not make it any less important to map that world. For what is Berger's and Luckmann's theory, of how we "internalize" the social reality we grow up in, but a theory of representation? The very theory of knowledge as representation lives on as an important element within a general idea of knowledge as reality construction.

Likewise there is no conflict between a theory attributing knowledge to persons and a cognitive theory about how our brains represent the world, as long as we don't believe that a cognitive theory can tell us what is known and what is not. We can construct our brains with innate ideas, categories and perceptual constraints and still hold that what is known is socially settled. As constructivists we may very well claim that worlds are made without restrictions and truths are always relative to a world, but then go on to argue that it is vital to determine the extent of restriction and variation in world-views within the world we've made.

All this seems to come down to the rather boring conclusion that "philosophy leaves everything as it is". But boring or not, I think it is important to realize that reconstructions of reality, in the sense of redescriptions or reinterpretations, mind-blowing as they may seem to those who experience them, achieve nothing by themselves. It is what we *do* that counts and we are all masters at adjusting wildly varying descriptions to the very same actions. Constructivists will argue that when descriptions change the actions will change too. But that is not always true.

There is something frightening in the constructivist belief in the power of descriptions or interpretations. Accustomed to a wealth of conflicting descriptions given of our everyday most mundane actions, most of us go through life skeptically playing with different descriptions, perspectives, frameworks, moving happily within the elbow room thus provided. This is Rorty's point, namely that it is only against this background of habits that the dramas of ideology are staged, that we do our philosophizing about the meaning of the universe and everything. Unless we change those habits nothing is really changed. But those habits can rarely be changed by words alone. Our strength, our autonomy, lies exactly in this our resistance to "propaganda". That a rose is a rose by whatever name is nothing we should grieve for.

3.3.8 Science as construction

That it is *reality* that is socially constructed means that the scientific enterprise to study reality retains its importance. The enterprise to map an objective reality is not superseded but complemented. On the one hand the objective, in the social sciences, is to construct theories, classifications and descriptions, which adequately map the systems of artifacts constituting social reality. On the other hand, the fulfilling of this objective is itself a social process of artifact construction, a contribution to the constitution of that reality. These two objectives are difficult to keep separate. It is impossible to analyze ideologies without contributing to the production of ideology.

In the natural sciences the foundations for research are laid by some sort of general framework, system of categories, conceptual scheme, or paradigm, constituting the general characteristics of reality. Such a framework is generally taken for granted, upheld by the scientific community, transmitted to new members as part of the socialization to a natural scientist. Research is done within such a framework, and consists in filling in the details, chartering the white spaces.

Questioning the framework, asking "external" questions, is a major undertaking of radical nature. Normal science stays comfortably within the socially prescribed framework, tackling "internal" questions only. External questions are open-ended, bewildering, philosophical, since they concern what reality it is we are examining. Internal questions are normal, have definite answers, provided of course that they don't strike at weak points in the general framework. In the latter case it is often wise to back off unless one has the courage to take on a revolution.

As it is in science, so it is in other kinds of human activity, including technology. There is always a choice between acting within the given framework and trying to break out of it. Or, rather, there is always a choice between what framework to act within. A technology designed to fit a certain reality will, when successful, strengthen that reality. It therefore becomes important to determine *whose* reality it is one wants to tailor the technology to. In our kind of society the default choice will almost always help propagate a reality organized by principles leading to injustice and exploitation. Constructivism gets some of its power from its capacity to help you avoid making that default choice blindly. If reality is socially constructed, constructed by "us", it becomes important to be one of "us".

A general appreciation of the constructive nature of science will change your notions of scientific truth and objectivity, but it will not change the practice of doing science. That practice will only change if there is a change of methods and techniques. There is such a change of practice going on right now and it is of a constructive nature. It is spurred by the growth of technology in general and by a rapidly increased use of computer technology in scientific research in particular.

Notice that the similarity between a socially constructed reality and one that just *is* hinges on the fact that the latter too is constructed, only not by us. The material artifact is the bridge between a natural and a social reality. When we stress the materiality of social constructions and the constructed artificiality of everything that is, the difference between nature and culture decreases. Technology as successful producer of material artifacts plays a leading role in this game. I would even go so far as to argue that the idea of reality construction at heart is a technical idea, a generalization of the very idea of technology. Romanticism is a take off on the Enlightenment idea of technology, art is really irresponsible technology.

Technology has given science an interest in how things function, how they are made, constructed, designed. As a result we have changed our conception of nature from that of a stable typology, to be once and for all adequately categorized, to that of a constantly changing, ongoing construction. The realistic enterprise to identify the structure of nature, to "carve nature at its joints", loses some of its force as evolutionary thinking makes us realize that those joints are the result of a constructive process in constant flux. Our interest in what nature is like becomes subordinated to an interest in what is possible. It is all right for a biology with book-keeping as an ideal to catalogue the life forms that have happened to evolve on earth, but modern, Darwinian, biologists ought to be more fascinated by what is biologically possible.[24]

The conception of nature as a constructive process gives to man the opportunity to interfere with, and contribute to, the construction of nature. But such a contribution demands more powerful capacities of imagination than we mortals have. For a while we have satisfied our wish to contribute to the construction of nature by direct interference. Rather than trying to imagine the consequences of certain actions we have made *experiments* and observed the consequences. The use of mathematics to simulate complex processes has certainly aided our imaginary powers, but now, with the use of computer technology we have really obtained a prosthetic imagination.

The telescope and the microscope changed science by magnifying our powers of perception. Computer technology plays a key role in a current development of science by extending our powers of imagination. As the telescope and microscope opened worlds to study that were previously unknown, so the computer will mean a shift in our scientific attention. The new worlds that now will begin to fascinate us are all the possible worlds, all the worlds that could be constructed. And we realize that all those worlds together make up reality, that there is no reason to single out the one world that happened to be constructed, and call *it* reality. Science cannot be content to study that world as it crumbles around us.

---

[24] And they are finally beginning to be so, as witnessed by the contributions to the volume on *Artificial Life*, edited by [Langton, 1989].

Like technology it should instead teach us more about what could be, a type of future studies as it were, in the sense of constructions of possible futures. There is nothing much we can do about the past.

3.3.9 The politics of reality construction

We have already heard Goodman claim that his idea of worldmaking is one of making worlds "not with hands but with minds, or rather with languages or other symbol systems." Goodman is true to the "linguistic turn" taking place in philosophy in the 20th century. If we go back to the Romantic philosophers, their idea of worldmaking was one of consciousness "constituting" worlds. Their means of construction were *concepts* which were thought of as mental entities, somehow deeper than language. As we move into our century, the philosophical notion of a concept changes. The pragmatists want to think of concepts as behavioural dispositions, practices, or rules of action, but most contemporary philosophers agree with Goodman that concepts are fundamentally linguistic in nature.

Thus, the modern contributors to the idea of reality construction we have looked at – Berger and Luckmann, Goodman, Rorty, Derrida – all stress the importance of language as a means for worldmaking. This move from consciousness to language (and action) is a move from private to public, from individual (or transcendental) constitution to social construction. It is a move from "subjective" to "objective" construction in Berger's and Luckmann's sense of externalized objectivization in social institutions.

There is in all this an unfortunate neglect of the more mundane but, to my mind, more important making of worlds "with hands", as Goodman puts it. The Romantic instigators of the idea of reality construction were idealists – they really believed that ideas make the world go round – and the dominating trend in current conceptions of reality construction is likewise idealist in nature. The historical heritage may explain why this is so, but it is still difficult to understand how, having made the move from subjective consciousness to intersubjective action patterns and language, from individual self-expression to institutionally controlled reality maintenance, current exponents of reality construction ideas give to technology such marginal attention. It makes good sense, of course, to stress the importance of mental worldmaking in the face of a widespread and naïve reification of technology. Technological determinism with its boring talk of "consequences of this or that technology" must be countered, but this cannot be done by turning one's back on the objectivization of social reality in technical artifacts.

Rather than trying to fight the reification of technology by pointing to the importance of our conceptions, to the fact that use of technology is socially constructed, one should take a more serious interest in the social processes of technical construction, in the secret ways of high-tech institutions and the game of technology politics. The reason is, of course, that the latter institutions are the most powerful instruments in determining our conceptions of technology and its use.

Technology plays a twofold role in our construction of reality. Only by materially realizing our mental constructions does it make sense to develop them further. We formulate our imagined goals, whether it is a car, a summer house, or a spouse, but as long as they remain unrealized they tend to cramp our thinking. Once realized, however, our mind can soar again, imagining new goals, since all the goals we reach will leave us unsatisfied. Technology, or rather its material artifacts, also plays a more direct role in our thinking as support and medium. Technology supplies our thinking with its tools, such as books, calculators, pen and paper, etc.

What this comes down to is an appreciation of the complex interplay of forms of reality construction, both private and public. And, an appreciation of the importance of worldmaking by hands in the construction of reality. The widespread and deep-rooted reification of technology cannot be neutralized by reference to a general theory of mental reality construction. It has to be taken seriously as a social phenomenon, and used to our advantage as constructivists by active participation in the production of technology.

The objectivization of a socially constructed reality is powerful to the extent that there are intersubjectively shared norms or criteria of rightness. The functionality of technology is such a criterion that is hard to match. Thus our tendency to reify technology. It is real because it works so well at holding chaos at bay. It is all very well to argue that all worldmaking is of the character of *fiction*, a matter of turning ideas into worlds, but the strategic power of this argument stumbles in the face of the *facts* of a powerful technology. The reification of technology is an indication of the power and success of technical reality construction. Freedom from technological determinism is not won with a theory of mental construction, but by a fight for power over the production of technology. The strategy cannot be to see the social construction of reality as a means for taming an existing technology, but rather to see the production of technology as the most powerful method of social reality construction.[25]

Thus, the primary remedy against oppressive computer technology lies not in the strengthening of a multiplicity of different perspectives or organizational structures, unless these are seen as means towards changing the technology. System developers should concentrate on the objective of producing good technology rather than on working with organizations faced with bad technology. Philosophical perspectives and organizational competence is all very well, but these are toothless weapons in the struggle for a computerization on human terms.

The major lesson to be drawn from the idea of social reality construction is not one of increased freedom, but rather a strategy for utilizing the freedom we have. To see that science and technology are socially constructed is to realize the importance and role of social institutions in the production, justification, and legitimation, of science and technology. It is to realize the importance of construction as opposed to interpretation, or the constructive element in all

---

[25] If enough of us decide that there are no bombs, there won't be any. But the most powerful strategy, except for occasional charismatic mass manifestations, to make us so decide, is to stop making bombs.

interpretation. And it is to realize the importance of being one of the ones constructing, of the role of power in the construction of reality.

To stress that reality construction is a *social* process, is to stress the importance of the process of objectivization, of the use of intersubjectively available means of construction. It is to make the individual's ability to rethink his or her situation and his or her world dependent on the social institutions of that world. Reality can be changed by changing our conception of it, but institutionally grounded conceptions are powerful forces in delimiting our individual freedom. Technology constitutes an important element in such institutional grounding, the most important element in our kind of society.

And when technology is being produced by worldwide, multinational companies, the construction of our social reality is largely out of our hands. We can always pretend, of course, by carving out local niches, that there is room for self-organized reality construction. And as a countermeasure to apathetic acceptance of technological determinism such self-organized reality construction is valuable. But there lies great danger in making such happenings, be they under the name of "user-oriented system development" or "local democracy", the major undertaking for a discipline of system development. In the long run that would only result in a disillusioned acceptance of the fact that technology really determines our lives and that we can't do anything about it. Taking Marx seriously we cannot be satisfied with providing local *interpretations* of a given, international technology, but must struggle for real power over the constructive production of that technology, i.e., power to *change* it.

Acknowledgements

I am grateful to, among others, Christiane Floyd, Kristo Ivanov, Lars-Erik Janlert, Ingvar Johansson and Thomas Söderqvist for comments, and to the Swedish Council for Planning and Coordination of Research for economic support.

Part 4

Learning to Know

Reinhard K.-S.

We live in a time when terms such as "information processing", "communication technology" or "knowledge engineering" have become common usage, and yet we know so little about what it really means to know and understand something and to deal with it appropriately.

Christiane

In our everyday practical work, we as computer scientists use, as a matter of course, terms relating to human thought. Words like "information", "communication" and "knowledge" each have a well-defined technical meaning. But its relation to human reality remains unclear.

Reinhard B.

And this is what makes it so surprising that the search for foundations of computer science in the humanities is frequently met with astonished disbelief or dismissed outright.

Christiane

It seems we must first of all demonstrate what might be the good of such foundations.

Reinhard K.-S.

So far, computer science has implicitly relied on the premise that thinking goes on "inside the head", the brain being seen as a processor for rule-based symbol manipulation. Crucial aspects are neglected: the interplay between head and body, the emergence of knowledge as a social process, the role of artifacts in cognition . . .

Reinhard B.

What are required, then, are sufficiently rich perspectives, which the humanities can supply. They need tailoring to the issues concerning computer science so as to be adequate for understanding processes of constructing and dealing with formalisms in our specific domain.

Heinz

There is, however, no established body of knowledge we can fall back on here. Initial findings resemble a jigsaw puzzle more than a finished picture. As in the illustration, we handle pieces without really knowing how they fit together.

Reinhard K.-S.

But unlike the puzzle, although we are already able to construct well-turned parts, we have no idea what the finished picture looks like. This is a general metaphor for creative processes of cognition. The pieces used by us are artifacts incorporating previous findings in the form of "external memories". In the course of construction processes, we fit them together to produce new artifacts.

Christiane

Interlaced learning and communication processes take place on a variety of levels: when pushing forward the boundaries of scientific knowledge; when developing software in the context of projects; when using the computer in work procedures . . .

Reinhard K.-S.

...and this part of the book is intended to help us understand such processes. Klaus Amann examines how knowledge is generated, mediated and established in a social process. For example, we are only able to understand an experiment by following the steps involved, and at the same time constantly explaining the way things are meant and why they take this and not that form.

Heinz

Knowledge, then, neither exists merely in a person's head, nor is it contained – independently of people – in a document. Knowledge is a social entity, manifested in "external memories". But it then depends on human individuals who have their own thoughts about it. Incidentally, this is also in keeping with hermeneutic ideas.

Reinhard K.-S.

We have to create the conditions for the generation and communication of knowledge. Dirk Siefkes shows that, even in the case of a mathematical proof, the essential quality is not to be found in the formal derivation steps, but in the degree of commitment with which people combine the formal How of a derivation with the Why of its purport.

Reinhard B.

Commitment presupposes a desire to think; it calls for motivation and individual free will.

Reinhard K.-S.

But this "being free to see" is at the same time both a chance and a constraint. Jack Carroll emphasizes the fact that we cannot deduce the design of an artifact from psychological invariants we may find when studying human behaviour. Hence, we have to study the ecology of the task-artifact cycle, he argues, if we wish to improve our understanding of design and usability of artifacts.

Christiane

That would seem to tie in closely with your ideas. In the final chapter of this part, you investigate the role of artifacts in software design. By reference to our biological and cultural heritage, you establish an ecological perspective that allows you to derive some principles for the design of artifacts that are meant to support human communication and learning processes.

Reinhard B.

We still have a long way to go as far as implementing these ideas in computer science is concerned. But we already have an inkling of what we have yet to learn. After all, finding out what you don't yet know is what science is all about.

Heinz

The following parts will look at tentative attempts to carry these ideas into the realm of computer science.

4.1 Scientific Expertise as a Social Process
Klaus Amann

4.1.1 The social organization of expertise

In a research project in the sociology of science I study knowledge strategies used by experts in acquiring and changing complex and innovative knowledge.[1] The goal is to analyze problem solving strategies in real-world contexts and to describe the forms of their social organization.

The starting point of such a description of the social organization of problem solving strategies is the assumption that it cannot be appropriately understood as long as one tries to think of the action of experts in terms of the activities of *individual experts*. If we analyze social fields as domains containing knowledge which is at the disposal of experts, we have to make this knowledge more accessible in order to be able to represent it in formal systems or models. In addition, the means of its interactive accessibility in a social context have to be determined. In contrast to the mere possession of knowledge and the competence to use it, accessibility is the result of a social setting, not of "sediments" in individuals. On the one hand, this is recognizable in the socialization of experts, on the other hand, in their socially bound behaviour.

The stages of becoming an expert as described by Dreyfus and Dreyfus[2] presuppose a *social context* in which there *are* experts, who in turn conduct their negotiations with a novice and an advanced beginner in an already existing *setting*. It takes not only *embodied competence* to be a "master" but also a *workshop* which enables him to act competently. So one can say that an expert's means and his ways of conveying his competence are not just linguistic explanations but in a specific way they are meaningful objects and manageable tools. Master and workshop provide by the interaction (the use) of competence and "tool" an outline of competent behaviour, the behaviour of experts.

An advanced beginner will not reach the stage of competent problem solving until he can demonstrate in social encounters that he has mastered the established use of the means at hand – both linguistic means: the ability to talk intelligibly on certain subjects, and instrumental ones: the ability to produce

---

[1] This research has been made possible by a grant from the Deutsche Forschungsgemeinschaft (project: Complex Knowledge Processes). The areas we chose are research groups in molecular biology and high energy physics.

[2] [Dreyfus and Dreyfus, 1986]. The authors' differentiation of these stages of becoming an expert is based on an individualistic concept of knowledge which is isolated from the social contexts in which knowledge exists and takes effect. Presumably this is due to their epistemological, partly speculative approach with its lack of empirical testing of experts' action.

something. However, it is not this knowledge as such that can be demonstrated but only its *use*. The status of an expert is tied to a field of interaction. In such a field it is *conferred* on somebody. There is a connection between the feature of this status as something conferred and the *responsibility* for competent action, which is also acquired in the process of an expert's socialization. "Being responsible" and "being conferred" are not simple property conditions but *social mechanisms* which organize natural knowledge systems. "Being conferred" implies that opportunities to act personally remain connected to their locally based use.

This also applies to the competence embodied in the "master" which is realized in its use in the social context of the "workshop". However, this is not a matter of a mere reification of established action patterns but of dealing with objects whose meanings and methods of handling have to be regarded as non-established. The everyday notion of an expert comprises as an essential element such an ability to deal with something *new*, with open, confusing, unexpected situations.[3]

This involves activities with a 'creative' relationship to the basis of somebody's action and the possibility to modify this basis, i.e., meaning relations, in two directions: First, a given situation is made comparable with earlier, similar cases by identifying "the essence" of this given situation. It is then dealt with accordingly within the limitations of someone's action potential. Second, the given context of action and knowledge is changed as a result of modifications to practices and to the ascription of meanings.

Embodied competence then appears as a necessary but not sufficient condition of such modifications. They require a change of practices and meanings which were established and used interactively, i.e., a change of the actual basis which only made possible the division of concrete and linguistic labour. Consequently, their successful use necessitates prior negotiations on these changes. So the character of embodied competence as something conferred in a social field of action is a bar to any autonomous changes to the collectively established basis of this competence. Before such changes can again become effective as conferred competence, they first have to *gain acceptance* socially. Apart from the convincing demonstration of a modified use, the acceptability both of a corresponding course of action and of the interpretation of its consequences must be negotiated. Thus the modifications established in an expert's activities can only become an effective part of experts' action if there is agreement within a field of experts and if these modifications are generally adopted. Just like the acquisition of established competence, reaching a consensus is accomplished by negotiation.[4]

These considerations lead me to deny the identity of expertise and knowledge of experts, which is assumed by those developing expert systems as well as their

---

[3] In [Dreyfus and Dreyfus, 1986] this ability constitutes the highest stage of an expert.

[4] Is it conceivable that an individual expert develops a practice which is both mastered by nobody else but himself and regarded as expertise in dealing with particular phenomena? Yes, but only as long as he is considered to be the only expert in this practice.

critics, and which is suggested by concepts taken from cognitive psychology. Putnam – until recently one of the main advocates of the "computational view of the mind"[5] – takes the problem of the relationship between reference and mental representations to show that all mentalistic theories ignore the "social dimension of meaning – the division of linguistic labor",(p. 88). He adds the pointed formulation that "Meanings aren't 'in the head'"(p. 73), and finally: "knowing what the words in a language mean (...) is a matter of grasping the way they are used. But use is holistic; for knowing how words are used involves knowing how to fix beliefs containing those words, and belief fixation is holistic."(p. 119) This view that meaning is not in the head points us to the fact that meaning is created and exists only in a *speech situation*.

The production of meaning is not just a matter of linguistic work but also the result of object-oriented action in the world. Competent action of human experts implies non-linguistic handling of meaningful objects. Following Putnam, I would say: *expertise* is nowhere in the body of experts (neither in their bodies nor in their minds). Expertise is an emergent phenomenon of social and local practices in a real world context. To regard experts as "containers" of expertise leads to an objectivistic and mentalistic reduction of natural knowledge processes. This reduction is at the bottom of all problems we know from discussions of artificial expert systems: the acquisition problem, the rule application problem, the meaning problem, the implementation problem, the learning problem and the interaction problem. To provide further arguments for the independence of local expertise as the form in which natural expert systems are socially organized, I shall now use results from my own research.

4.1.2 Expertise as locally and interactively accomplished 'thinking'

What I find in observing scientists at work is not just a link between thinking and language, but a link between thinking and talk, more precisely *shop talk*. What difference does this make? When embedded in talk, thinking is interactively accomplished. It exploits the power of discourse to bring forth features of the phenomena which, once on the table, may be very suggestive, and thus may facilitate or simply imply certain conclusions. Put loosely, the move is from inference to conversational implicature[6]: what we get instead of mentally-induced problem solutions are conversationally induced utterances which, among members of the appropriate science culture, may trigger certain previously non-obvious interpretations or performance recommendations. We have identified several interactionally accomplished inference 'machines' at work in the research groups observed: procedural implicature, optical induction, the oppositive device, and

---

[5] [Putnam, 1988]

[6] This way of putting the matter draws upon a possible but not very clear distinction between "inferences" as logical accomplishments and what Grice calls "conversational implicature" which in our reading rests upon convention and cultural knowledge [Grice, 1975].

thinking aloud patterns.[7] Scientific thinking as it appears in scientific work has a prosthetic structure.[8] It employs devices other than mental activities to elicit and facilitate conclusions. One such device is the interactional inference machinery of shop talk. The pervasiveness and the sheer amount of shop talk is striking in the sciences observed. It is plain that work gets accomplished in shop talk, and that shop talk must be considered a technical instrument of knowledge production just like the more familiar experimental apparatus and machines. We found several recurrent patterns of talk that ostensibly accomplish inference tasks. Most widespread among these appear to be procedural implicatures and the oppositive device. Two of the devices identified are argumentative, the thinking aloud pattern and the oppositive device, with the latter being adversarial while the former is not. To some extent, argumentative patterns 'feed upon' or overlay other conversational patterns; the patterns described are not mutually exclusive. For example, participants may draw visual inferences and make optically-derived claims in the service of their argument. Arguments are often backed by episodic reasoning, as are conclusions in all devices. Episodes are one of several narrative elements in scientists' spoken discourse, other elements being stories and reports. Two shop-talk routines are attached more heavily than others to the objects around which the conversation turns: optical induction and thinking aloud. In thinking aloud, speakers turn away from hearers and face the object while they sketch out arguments, identify issues ("problems") and formulate experiences or conclusions – all apparently in making their clues from the object. In optical induction, the same close connection between object and talk occurs in a more literal sense: by the way it looks, how it is positioned in relation to other observables, etc., the object "suggests" a conclusion. Yet both patterns rely, like the first two mentioned, on the presence of other speakers: They are realized through talk.

In identifying these patterns of talk, we paid attention to the phenomenon that complex problem situations tend to become *interactively dissolved* in shop talk.

In a further study on the fixation of (visual) evidence[9] we address the question of the conversational routines and inference machineries in terms of which *seeing* becomes socially organized in talk. Conversational inference devices are employed as participants run into problems in recognizing visual objects, in determining, say, the identity of 'traces' on data displays. With the help of these devices, participants develop a sense of "what was seen" on these data displays. Through montage, this sense of what was seen is transformed into evidence. Both processes constitute what we have called the fixation of evidence. Evidence is here the aesthetically enhanced, carefully composed rendering of flexible visual

---

[7] In [Amann and Knorr-Cetina, 1989] we regard inference 'machines' as vehicles of thinking. Apart from mental operations there seem to be mechanisms of thinking in scientific inquiry where thinking has less of a cognitive structure (in the sense of mental calculations) but rather a speech act and particularly a dialogue structure.

[8] For an interesting study of "prostethic" forms of thinking in lay persons solving everyday arithmetic problems see [Lave, 1985].

[9] [Amann and Knorr-Cetina, 1988]

objects that, through the meandering interrogatory processes of image analyzing talk, have been embedded and entrenched in procedural reconstructions, local experiences and in the landscape of the data display.

The analyses of the interactively organized fixation of evidence as well as of the organization of thinking through talk make it obvious that experts coping with complex, naturally occurring problems continuously include local features in their collective mechanisms of interpretation and persuasion.

I shall discuss one of the learning phases I studied as an example of how scientific novices acquire competence in dealing with corporeal knowledge through negotiations with the advanced scientists in the lab. The following excer[220zpts from a transcribed dialogue show how novices learn to carry out what is described in so-called lab protocols.

Excerpts from an explanation during radioactive labelling of nucleic acid molecules

A explains what B has to do with the steps listed in the protocol:

... The colour you see/ you see because then that is [...] you see that this here for example/ the blue runs ahm runs with the nucleotides or around...

... I would just spin it down ah, because there are quite a few counts here sticking on the top...

... Well then you have a volume of two/ fifteen or twenty or whatever and here. loading with a pipette isn't it/ take care now I've just done this/ that this one/ begins to run dry you know it from the columns...

... Here take this one for loading and ahm, don't smear it on the wall that the drop is really there/
B: right in the middle okay?/
A: yeah exactly...

... Okay that's what I meant/ now put it there in there above isn't it so and ah so n/ to suck it up take the 200/ it's always annoying when they pull off, fill in very carefully...

... And these are mostly green ones from the dyestuff and that's what I don't take anymore. Green....

In contrast to the protocols, which only sometimes refer to perceptible matters, the accomplishment of the procedures are accompanied by personal demonstrations and comments on visibilities and observabilities. The entire experimental process during this learning phase dissolves into a complex flow of perceptibilities and quite small manipulation details that must be coordinated in order to successfully accomplish any given step.

Everything that happens when objects and their meanings are dealt with in this example – by means of demonstration and imitation – constitutes the basis on which a procedure laid down in documents can succeed in its locally established meaning. Documented knowledge alone offers only an insufficient framework for the development of expertise. Only the successful demonstration of the use learnt in negotiation with other experts allows a competent expert an autonomization of his activities as a part of local expertise.

4.1.3 The possibility of standardized expertise

Ascribing expertise to people is an established form of dealing with knowledge. People (but occasionally also machines or automats) are collectively treated as if their activities as experts were completely determined by their competence as socialized participants. One prerequisite is the responsibility of individuals, which follows from their place in a local context of social relationships. This in turn requires the existence of clearly delimited areas with a standardized, i.e., a collectively accepted repertoire of activities. In natural expert systems such a repertoire is the outcome of a long-term occupation with delimited or delimitable areas of phenomena or problems. These areas become "encapsulated" by a standardization of situation interpretations. As soon as a situation can be interpreted as "similar" with respect to the applicability of a standardized procedure, no more (collective) interpretation and determination of the next steps are needed.

However, such an encapsulation or standardization is preceeded by varied processes to stabilize procedures. It is followed by activities which serve to maintain a once established standard (and to modify it). Standard activities in turn are maintained in local contexts of action. In the empirical sciences this local base is the lab, which comprises objects, people and procedures. Standards are maintained because they are embodied in procedures: partly in instruments, tools and machines, partly in personal competence. These procedures contain fixed interpretation patterns for experimental effects, the "data". The application of such procedures includes checks to make sure deviations from the fixed course of action remain interpretable *within* a procedure. So standardized procedures consist not only of a standardized course of action but also of a standardized repertoire of interpretations of deviations. This facilitates the treatment of something standardized as an entity with a fixed meaning.

Yet this (seemingly static) procedure remains open to constant modification in the case of experimental action in changed contexts. In the course of the research process the range of interpretations of experimental effects is often imperceptibly modified. On the material level, reductions and simplifications are implemented, new case histories extend (or restrict) the meaning of procedures and their effects, which were made visible.

These modifications are processed in the local context of the lab, and this shows that even something standardized is subject to changes in procedures. In the lab, collective activities serve to integrate changes. Communicative relationships and *work at the lab* – at contextual features – lead to a *dynamic* stability of these procedures and their respective expertise. Procedural knowledge of dealing with and interpreting case histories as affiliated patterns of a standardization is continuously circulating in this setting and the procedures are tied to this knowledge. In the course of collective learning processes, which are organized, e.g., through the types of shop talk and fixation of evidence mentioned above, they are incorporated into the standard repertoire. So constant implicit changes, among others of rules for the application of rules and of the knowledge base of scientific expertise, take place in such a research process.

4.1.4 Compulsory standardization in artificial expert systems

Right from the start existing expert systems emphasized the possibility to standardize and to individualize expertise. In this case expertise is exclusively modelled as the interaction of knowledge and the way experts (individuals) deal with it. The expert system itself is presented as an aggregate of several experts' stocks of knowledge and their ways of dealing with them, a "superexpert" who in principle has to know more than the experts who answered questions when the knowledge was gathered. So here the successful modelling of expertise requires the possibility to explicate completely all steps an expert takes while solving a problem. And this requires a model of an expert who has all these steps autonomously at his disposal, independently of any interaction in his field. In a number of domains this seems to be possible and we can identify domains in which expertise seems to be entirely transferred to individuals. If we take for example medical expertise, it is possible to extract rules and knowledge and to model individualized expertise. A precondition of this is that experts themselves must have advanced the standardization of procedures and the stabilization of local contexts of action to such an extent that the interpretation and the ascription of meaning works like a "reading" of unambiguous signs. In previous learning and ascription processes the interpretation was fixed in such a way that the potential range of uses of instruments and objects was eliminated. When an artificial expert system is developed for a field, some areas are created in which only predetermined procedures and uses of knowledge are admitted and unrepresented knowledge becomes meaningless. The stocks of knowledge incorporated in an expert system – propositional knowledge and knowledge of rules – replace after their implementation the kinds of procedures previously needed. Other procedures are applied before or after the introduction of expert systems in these areas. So by applying fixed rules, the artificial expert system is treated like an expert who can and must always read sensory data as unambiguous signs of objective events. The unambiguity of signs is brought about by their earlier assignment to interpretation rules.

To make this work, only certain formats of "input data" are admitted. A user of such a system is called upon to remove ambiguities, whereas the system provides interpretations, so that data can be processed within a scope for interpretations limited by fixed rules. At the other end, the result of this processing is transferred into the "natural" situation. It is thus made accessible and can then be dealt with in the usual processes. The success of such an artificial expert system depends on a trick: It is to put through compulsory standardizations, i.e., to have cleaning-up phases *prior* to the use of such a system. The social field in which the system is going to be used has to standardize the input according to the built-in rule application rules and must keep it constant. So the artificial expert system extends itself to a formalization of its users' activities. This must be achieved before the use of such systems can yield results useful for subsequent activities.

The cleaning process has secondary effects on the use of the respective systems. To what extent can the construction of reality encapsulated in an implemented expert system be kept stable within its field of application? Or to put it differently: to what extent can the data to be processed be kept identical with respect to the ascription of meanings implemented in the system?[10]

The fixation of knowledge calls either for the exclusion of modifications or for mechanisms in the system which can cope with change, i.e., a system capable of learning and of changing meaning patterns.[11]

It then becomes obvious that the social implementation of an artificial expert system is substantially more than merely substituting an artificial expert for a natural one. It changes the character of expertise. A new social reality is produced and natural practices are newly formed and standardized. However, there is not yet a difference in quality to other technical automation processes. A difference does not exist until one tries to individualize and automatize expertise which is based on necessarily local, collective and ambiguous phenomena.

As we have seen above, this kind of expertise requires two types of competence on which natural experts can rely: learning competence and discourse competence. Both types are tied to the social participant role of experts. Learning competence results from the possibility of changing the organization of one's individual knowledge through one's own and the others' experience, i.e., to modify meaning structures in the course of their use. A prerequisite of discourse competence is participation in the collective determination of modified meaning structures. For both types of competence it can be said that they *cannot* be modelled in an artificial expert system but must be incorporated by human experts' intervention from the outside.

4.1.5 Conclusion

Our discussion of results from research on natural expert systems clearly indicates that up to now the social foundation of knowledge systems has hardly touched upon the thinking about conditions of modelling. This also applies to critics of such systems, insofar as they share the individualistic concept of knowledge.

The introduction of the concept of social expertise opens up the systematic possibility of interpreting knowledge and activities of experts as socially and locally bound phenomena. This shows that the real problem in modelling expertise is not the acquisition of knowledge – propositional knowledge and knowledge of rules – but the fact that the status as an expert is socially constructed. Looked at from this point of view, the independent existence of 'objective facts' suggested by the seeming stability of knowledge systems turns out to result from the work of social stabilizing mechanisms. The attempt to represent a knowledge system

---

[10] 'Keeping something identical' or 'stable' does not refer to the technical device but to the (social) context of action into which it is 'fitted'.

[11] A weaker case would be a modification implemented externally and without causing problems, so that it could be carried out during a user's actual work with the system.

in a machine replaces or externalizes these social construction processes by a static disambiguation of locally and socially bound meaning structures. So their usability within natural knowledge systems is restricted to fields of action which are fixed to such an extent that results of such systems can be treated as valid results. In this respect they are tools which replace personal action. Their ability to function properly depends on whether their use of incorporated inference mechanisms can be treated and justified as situationally appropriate. In other words, it depends on whether in social contexts of use their products are still regarded as valid interpretations.

A methodological extension in the analysis of natural expert systems is needed to show where the limits of knowledge systems are. The study of natural expert systems will have to include not only the collection of documented knowledge and the accompanying practices of experts (the latter by interviewing them) but also the systematic observation and analysis of the social use of local expertise.[12] As to the implementation of artificial expert systems as tools, it will have to be studied to what extent the future environment of these systems – the social place of their use – will admit such a formation of expertise and which consequences this will have on its organization.

---

[12] The methods to investigate empirically natural problem solving which are employed in the lab studies mentioned above provide a suitable set of methods for such studies. See [Amann and Knorr-Cetina, 1991].

4.2 How to Communicate Proofs or Programs
Dirk Siefkes

4.2.1 An opening question

Why is formalization so much fun to do or to talk about, and so boring to listen to? How excited most of us get when we prove a new theorem or develop a program, or even more when we explain it to someone else! The "someone" may be a fellow researcher, or a class of students, or the audience at a conference. But do we show the same excitement if we are the someone, but are not ourselves involved in the question, or at least active in the field? Why do students shun mathematical lectures? Why do we fall asleep during a talk? With writing and reading papers it is not so different. Or am I the only one who loves to do mathematics, but tries to avoid reading the papers of others?

Any formalization seems to have this effect: it makes things easier, but less fun. On the freeway we drive smoother than on secondary roads, but have trouble to stay awake. To follow another person's formal built-up is like that: we go straight ahead, fenced in, no decisions are necessary or even wanted. When on the other hand we search for a proof or design a program, we have to be creative. The situation is similar with writing or talking about a result: When we reproduce a proof, we re-live the excitement of finding it – or of understanding it if it is not our own.

So this is an easy answer to the question I started with: Following our own path is fun, being ordered is not. Gregory Bateson[1] describes the dual pair of form and process. Processes happen. They happen in given forms, as cars run on roads; and they produce forms, as traffic results in freeways, which in turn allow increased traffic. We formalize to impose order in the world, and thus to give orders to others. When I present a proof, the others have to believe me; they even have to follow my way towards the theorem. When I write a program, it is first the machine that has to follow me. But soon it is the other guy who has to, especially when I am a theoretician.

There is much effort now in software engineering to replace, or at least to complement, the product-oriented view by the human-centred view[2]. What kind of anti-thesis is this? How is it possible that people concentrate on products instead of humans? My product is my baby, that is, an image of myself. In presenting it, I put myself into the center without having to blush. As Gordon Pask formulated it in a conversation during this conference : "The prevailing view in science is the I-I-I-perspective as opposed to the I-you-perspective. This is what needs to be changed."

---

[1] [Bateson, 1972, Bateson, 1980]
[2] See for example [Nurminen, 1988].

How can we hand over what we have learned if not in the form of a product? Is there a way to induce the processes we have gone through, in the partner? Again, this sounds like a moralistic question. What has formalization got to do with morals? It seems that my rash answer to the opening question – as rash answers tend to do – posed new questions rather than answering the old one.

Let us start afresh from safer ground with a more traditional question.

4.2.2 What is a proof?

Every logician can answer that one: proofs are trees. In a proof we proceed from axioms, assumptions, hypotheses through logical steps to the statement to be proved. Thus the proof tree contains the axioms at the leaves, the logical steps at the branching points, and the theorem at the root. Quod erat demonstrandum.

Such proofs do not occur in praxis, as every logician would admit. In principle, however, any mathematical proof could be broken down into logical steps, and thus changed into a tree. We just have to blow away the accidentals, delete the ephemeral, concentrate on the essentials, work out the underlying structure, and bingo! there is the proof tree – as illustrated in Fig. 4.2–1.

Mathematicians proving theorems proceed on a different level. Not because they are careless or lazy, but because by a formal proof they would not prove anything. We could check its correctness, even by a machine. But we would be unable to understand it, and thus would not understand the theorem.

Traditionally one distinguishes between rational and rhetorical speech. In rational speech we "prove" something; that is, we proceed from evident axioms to derived assertions in self-explanatory steps. Everyone in his right mind has to accept what we say. In rhetorical speech we try to "make clear" our ideas directly, by referring to personal experience, using pictorial language, and drawing analogies, in order to convince the audience. Whether we succeed depends more on how we say it than on what we say. In particular we ourselves do not have to believe in what we say. In the rational tradition rhetoric becomes the art to fool the audience; a "rhetorical question" is a fake question.

Paul Feyerabend[3] mocks the rational tradition when he explains why it has been so successful. "Proofs are stories that tell themselves" is his definition. Story-tellers had better have their stories well told if they want people to believe them. Persons proving a statement on the other hand need not take such pains: The concepts they work with are so general that they already contain the whole argument; thus it develops by itself. In his books[4] Feyerabend demonstrates that the scientist himself does not proceed rationally, but rather like an artist: following the fashion, subject to partialities, looking for advantages. Is the mathematician proving a theorem an artist, too?

Obviously, we are never completely rational when we do a proof. The axioms themselves cannot be proved; we have to "show" them directly, in rhetorical

---

[3] [Feyerabend, 1984]
[4] [Feyerabend, 1975, Feyerabend, 1981, Feyerabend, 1984]

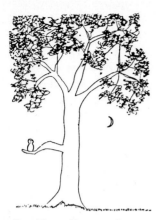

Consider a live proof:

blow away the accidentals,

delete the ephemeral,

concentrate on the essentials,

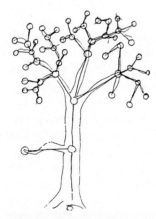

work out the underlying structure,

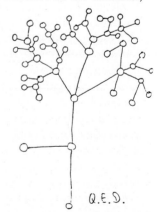

bingo, there is the proof tree!

Fig. 4.2–1. How to turn a live proof into a proof tree

speech. Therefore – Ernesto Grassi[5] concludes – rhetoric is primary; from it we get the framework onto which to pin the rational arguments.

How about the steps in a proof? Are they logical, formal, rule-governed? We saw above that such formal proofs do not occur in praxis, since we would prove nothing that way. Also we could not, even if we wanted, transform a non-trivial mathematical proof into its logical equivalent; it would simply be too complicated. And if we could, the transformation would not be formal. Thus, also within a proof we use informal arguments, that is rhetoric.

Finally we cannot find a proof, formal or informal, through formal arguments. This is the problem with unrestricted automated theorem proving. One tries to program an activity that is not formalized and, in my opinion, not formalizable. Even if one day such a program should produce a non-trivial theorem, few mathematicians would believe it, since they could not follow the proof. To date, many mathematicians do not believe in the proof of the four-colour-conjecture, since a good part of it is carried out by computer. This does not imply, however, that automated theorem provers could not be helpful tools for checking assumptions in restricted applications.

What then are formal proofs good for? A formal proof is a mathematical object, and thus can be investigated mathematically. For example, in order to prove that something is not provable I have to use a formal notion of proof, and thus a logical formalism. To prove that something is provable, however, I just have to set up a proof by which I convince the others. How do I convince another person?

4.2.3 When does a proof make sense?

Before I can convince someone, I have to make her or him understand what I want. "I do not understand what you say. It does not make sense to me." is the worst answer I can get. Only if my proof is understood, my audience can agree. Or disagree, and I can try again, or take back what I said. Understanding comes first, truth or falsity later. When does a statement make sense?

In his logical writings Gottlob Frege distinguished between 'sense' and 'meaning'[6]. 'Meaning' is easy in mathematics: The meaning of a name is the person or thing named; the meaning of a program is the function that we compute by it; the meaning of a statement is its truth value. With 'sense' Frege is less explicit. Two names for the same person have the same meaning, but one of them might be affectionate, the other insulting; thus they differ in sense. Similarly the same proof may make sense or not, depending on the way it is set up or told. But what is this 'same proof'? And why can a proof, really the same one, make sense to someone, and make no sense to someone else? 'Sense' does not seem to reside in the proof, but to flow from its communication.

---

[5] [Grassi, 1980]

[6] See his paper "Sinn und Bedeutung" [Frege, 1892]. 'Bedeutung' is often translated in a more technical sense as 'denotation' or 'reference'. Like Frege, I stick to the term 'meaning' as used in everyday language to catch the informal connotations.

"Sense appears in the form of a surplus of references to further possibilities to experience and to act", defines Niklas Luhmann in "Social Systems"[7]. My partner says something. If it does not make sense to me, I have three standard ways to react: to ask for an explanation, to pretend understanding, or to break off the conversation. If I understand, however, there are numerous possibilities to continue. The situation has become richer. A piece in a conversation makes sense, if it enables the partners not only to follow but to go ahead.

Thus, the elementary actions in a proof are not the logical steps, but information that enables or induces the partner to take a step himself. We could call these pieces the sense-bearing units of a proof. They are not part of the proof, but of our attempt to communicate the proof. They have to be recreated each time I tell a proof, between the audience and myself.

Not enough possibilities to continue a conversation is one extreme. Too many, another: my statement makes no sense, because the audience cannot connect with it. Between these two extremes, the conversation has to flow. In my papers[8] I call such a way to give a proof the 'small systems way'. Not the proof itself is small nor the group I talk to, but the way we communicate. What makes sense depends on what we want and like, what means we use and what rules we obey, as much as on what we know. Excess or defect in any of these bearings makes the system too big or too small, respectively. Which way we go depends on us, whether we are many or just two or one.

A long proof is always hard to understand; or to find, for that matter. I have to break it into pieces which the audience can digest. This way I can induce in my partners the processes I experienced when I first did the proof. Only then can they change the proof. And only what can be changed makes sense. Recall the thesis in the beginning: Nothing is fun if we are just ordered, if we cannot act ourselves. I have to tell the proof in such a way that it opens the view of the listener. Knowledge just thrown on someone can be a burden. Questions are a better present.

Normally we speak locally: about a situation at hand, within a system. Sometimes we speak globally: about the world, in general terms. In particular we speak globally in science, philosophy, religion, art, and when we are drunk; we want to say something that applies everywhere, to everyone. Only global concepts can be formalized. If we forget that, we produce not formalism but confusion.

For example, 'true' is a local concept, 'true in a situation' is global. We cannot determine by a general rule whether what people say is true. If we trust them, we believe. If we do not, we look for a proof. "True is what is the case", says Wittgenstein. We look out of the window to see whether it really rains. But this principle of logic works only for the global concept 'true in a situation'. If we cannot inspect reality directly, we have to ask for a proof, and are back to the local problem. Can we trust what other people say? The less we do, the more we force them to make global – logical – steps. 'True' and 'trust' have the same Indo-European root: 'deru' – 'to last' – 'dauern' in German. 'Tree' has the

---

[7] [Luhmann, 1987, p. 93, translated by the author]
[8] [Siefkes, 1991]

same root. This is different in German, 'wahr' is what lasts in court – "was sich bewährt"; the only tree here is the juridical oak.

When I globalize my statements I end up in a language where I have to follow fixed rules in order to maintain the desired universal meaning. Such languages come clothed quite differently: There are the ritual languages of religion and sports, the esoteric languages of philosophy and science, the "artificial" languages of art, and the formal languages of mathematics. They all fall under the same contradiction: Intended to be global they are restrictive. Using them I have to obey their rules, and can address only the initiated.

What I have learned in a small system on the other hand should be useful everywhere where I manage to build up another small system. How then can we apply global concepts in small systems? We have to learn that 'global' and 'local' like the closely related 'big' and 'small' are not properties of concepts, but ways of usage.

4.2.4 Techniques of proving

In a social system we continuously have to reduce the complexity – of the system and of its environment – to stay alive[9]. Complex is anything that we do not understand. If we make ourselves understood, we reduce the complexity, and increase our ability to communicate. Thereby we create subsystems, and thus a richer structure. For a proof this means: carve out parts that make sense in themselves, then combine them sensibly. Let me make these observations more concrete by collecting a few principles which mostly will be common ground, but are rarely stated explicitly[10].

First, do not do the proof bottom-up. In computer science trees grow upside down: root in heaven, leaves on the ground; a brain-made reality as shown in Fig. 4.2–1. Computer scientists distinguish between bottom-up and top-down programming. When one works top-down, one starts with the meaning (as understood by Frege), with the function to be computed. One breaks this goal into subgoals which are somehow related, works on those in turn, and so on downwards, until on the lowest level one writes the actual programs, which then only have to be connected. Working bottom-up one proceeds just the other way around: one starts by writing pieces of code which one glues together by more code until the program is finished. A bottom-up proof starts with numerous little definitions and lemmata, which are pieced together by propositions and further lemmata, until at the end one states the theorem and proves it by combining lemmata 7, 17, and 27. Quod erat demonstrandum. Of course, nothing is demonstrated that way. When reading such a proof all the way up one is busy with statements one does not understand, since one does not know where they lead to. After one is through, one has to go over the proof a second, and likely

---

[9] This is [Luhmann, 1987] again.

[10] Donald Knuth has lectured extensively on this theme; see his "Mathematical Writing"[Knuth et al., 1989].

a third time. Or one reads the proof backwards, which makes for hard reading. Why not do the proof top-down in the first place?

Second, do not do the proof purely top-down either. Indeed, reading top-down one has to carry along concepts that have no meaning yet; one has to accept statements that are not yet proved; one has to understand techniques with which one has not yet worked.

How then are proofs to be done if neither top-down nor bottom-up? A familiar technique is depth-first top-down: Single out a concept or a substatement of the theorem, explain that, and go down locally with that technique. One cannot go very deep, however, since then one loses the connection, vertically and, what is worse, horizontally to the other mine shafts. In his nice little book "Utopies réalisables"[11] the architect Yona Friedman introduces the idea that communication chains have a maximal length (and branching width), and on this ground calculates the maximal size of communicating groups. Another architect, Christopher Alexander, uses these principles, although in a quite different spirit, when he investigates the problem of designing large projects[12].

Another technique is to proceed from the particular to the general. Do special cases first, not for a superficial motivation, but completely. Then generalize stepwise. The completeness proofs for logic programming in my book[13] are an example of this method. Again, if the special cases are not general enough, they might not be typical, and the chains become too long and will be difficult to deal with.

The best way then is to combine the bottom-up and the top-down approach. In accordance with the remarks at the beginning of this section select units and give them sense: explain the concepts, try the methods on comprehensible cases, work out the details. Combine such units in a similar way. This happens regularly when (and only when!) you try to communicate with others on the proof, since then you have to change your view on the matter. Proceeding in an analogous way in software engineering is called 'prototyping'. In my paper "Prototyping is Theory Building"[14] I investigate prototyping in art and in mathematics, and propose to use it in theory building.

Third, beware of technical lemmata. If you cannot name and formulate what you want to do, you may not have understood it yourself. If you cannot describe the underlying principle so as to make the lemma self-contained, how shall it make sense to anybody else?

Fourth, do not begin with a list of preliminaries and notations. Nobody will read it beforehand anyway. Introduce these things where they are needed, and collect them in an appendix if you feel like it. As somebody (Feyerabend?) once remarked, the sections "What every reader ought to know" often are the dumps for material the author himself does not want to think about.

---

[11] [Friedman, 1976]
[12] See his book [Alexander, 1964].
[13] [Siefkes, 1990]
[14] In [Siefkes, 1991].

Fifth, show courage, be negative! It is customary in science to write "on what there is", and not on what there is not. Every good fiction writer gives his hero some bad properties, and some good streaks to the mean guy. This technique is important to give shading to the persons, and thus depth to the picture. Why should a scientific paper be shallow? In a proof state not only the truth, but also what is false; why you took this turn and not that one; why you define a concept this way and not the other; tell which paths led you astray. Work out the non-theorems as carefully as the theorem. Thereby you save the reader wrong steps, and keep them documented for your own sake as well. Show him the paths you did not take; maybe he is the one to succeed on them. Read what Rudolf Arnheim writes in "Visual Thinking"[15] about figure and ground.

Finally, be careful about how you write. "The proof shows ..." Nonsense! Have you ever seen a proof raise its hand, and point at something. By using the phrase "By the proof I show..." (or "we...", or "she shows...") I leave no doubt who does the job. If "the program computes the function" or "the computer solves the problem", who gets the merits? And who is responsible? Even more nebulous is the passive form: "By the proof it is shown...". Now the subject has vanished altogether, and the action with it. By a verb I describe what happens, by a noun who or what makes it happen. But how can I, if I do not choose the actor as the subject of the sentence, and do not let the verb reveal the action? We scientists are guilty more than anybody else if everyone's sentences stagger from too many too heavy nouns and suffocate from too few verbs. We love to describe states instead of talking about actions, and everyone's reality changes accordingly. To counteract this tendency the physicist David Bohm in his book "Wholeness and the implicate order"[16] proposes to speak in the "rheomode": to turn all words into verbs, to "re-levate" the relevant.

4.2.5 Proofs and programs

Can we apply to programs what we have learned about proofs? Is there an analogy? – By a proof we prove a theorem, by a program we compute a function. Wrong, says the software engineer; a program serves to help to solve a task by computer. But, says the mathematician, the computer is a deterministic machine, and thus produces a unique output to each input; in this sense a computation realizes a function, and the program defines this function. Thus, this first analogy between proofs and programs rests on a mathematical abstraction.

We saw above that a mathematical proof is never formally given, since it purports to convince other people. By contrast, a program has to be executed on a machine, and thus is completely formal. From this contrast springs a deep difference between mathematics and computer science. In mathematics there is "the" mathematical language, which everyone acquires and uses in different styles. And then there are logic formalisms as extreme formalizations of this language. The connection between the two levels is quite unclear, as discussed in the beginning.

---

[15] [Arnheim, 1969]
[16] [Bohm, 1983]

Actually there is no need to clarify it, since logic formalisms are not practically used. In dealing with computers on the other hand one uses many levels of formalization, from the highest-level programs down to the machine code. These computation formalisms correspond directly to the logic formalisms discussed above, where the elementary units now give rise to computational steps instead of logical ones, and the levels are formally related through compilers. They need not concern us here unless we want to design or discuss programming formalisms and compilers. The relation between problem situations and high-level programs is relevant for our discussion. Since these programs are still formal and have to be correct in every detail, computer science abounds in methods, ideas, and theories how to get there from informal description: diagrams, documentations, mathematical formalisms.

In the 1970s the catchword was "structured programming". A well structured program is less likely to contain errors, or to be misinterpreted by the user. This structure, however, is formal, is part of the program. In this approach, therefore, attention is paid mainly to the product – the structured program – and not to the process of programming or communicating about the program. In his paper[17] Donald Knuth claims an era of "Literate Programming" to follow the decade of structured programming. He develops a system, WEB, by which informal writing in programming is as well supported as the development of the formal program.

How to write sensible programs has become a big issue in software engineering. How to write programs sensibly seems to me the actual question. When one really wants to communicate about the program and the programming task, one cannot go top-down from the task to the finished program. Thus this "waterfall model" is replaced by the "cycle model" where one cycles through alternating phases of writing the program and trying it out, to enhance its quality by communicating about it[18]. "Prototyping" is of great help here. This is the technique of singling out a self-contained unit – horizontally or vertically, see above – and doing it first. This way one learns about the project as a whole, in particular through communicating with others, for example with a potential user. As the software engineer said in the beginning of this section: A program is important not in itself, but as a means to solve a problem. The main task is not to write correct programs, but to convince others and oneself that the program works as wanted. Programming is discourse, resulting in texts that we call software, is the view of the linguist Dafydd Gibbon[19]. It is a literary activity then. Programming in this way can only be done in small systems[20]. It will result in smaller programs, too, since nobody understands the large ones.

Some computer scientists say that a program counts for nothing without a correctness proof. Since programs are formal, they use formal methods for programming. Thereby they make programming a mathematical activity. This

---

[17] [Knuth, 1984]

[18] See for example [Floyd, 1987, Keil-Slawik, 1987b, Floyd and Keil, 1983] and Chap. 4.4.

[19] See Chap. 8.3.

[20] See Sect. 4.2.3.

may be helpful for explaining abstract programming languages. But it is a mistake to believe that the communication problem might be alleviated that way. Whether programs are understandable depends less on the characteristics of the programming formalism than on how it is used. "Until we acknowledge the dialectical, creative, and living dimensions in programming, we shall be doomed to participate in software processes that are unwieldy, unpleasant, and ineffective," formulates Joseph Goguen[21]. As early as 1979 Richard DeMillo, Richard Lipton, and Alan Perlis[22] maintained that formal proofs do not help much in convincing others of the correctness of our programs (and theorems); rather we have to argue convincingly, repeat our points, gain credit. Programming is a social activity.

It is an inherently human activity, Peter Naur says in his paper on "Programming as Theory Building"[23]. What programmers know about their work cannot be recovered from the program nor from the documentation. Too much is gone into the programmers' heads and finger tips, into their way of using programs and writing new ones, into the theory that lives and dies with them.

So this is the analogy between proving and programming: both the mathematician and the computer scientist work towards a formal product, and both are in danger of loosing contact with their environment by doing their work in a formal way. In both areas prototyping as described above is helpful: Learning and talking about the formal goal by considering a special case, a representative aspect, or a typical example. Mathematicians have always done this without talking much about it; today they could learn from computer scientists: become conscious about the problem at hand, do something about it.

Whatever part of a proof I really understand, I can wrap up as a unit, and talk about it separately. And conversely: By identifying and naming sensible parts of a proof, I understand better both the parts and the whole proof. This is common mathematical experience: A proof first found is poorly understood, and as a rule contains errors. Only by discussing it with others I comprehend it better; lecturing and writing on the proof provide still higher levels of understanding.

4.2.6 Why formalization anyway?

Now I can try to settle a misconception which may have loomed in the background with many readers: that I disdain formalization, and would rather see it thrown out. I do not. Recall the Bateson pair of form and process. We experience processes, but we cannot communicate them (not even to ourselves). We have to formulate (sic!) them first. This need not happen verbally. We humans have a wide range of ways for communication available, ranging from the secretive whisperings of our bodies, or even thoughts and dreams, through the pronouncements of art and the chatter of everyday conversation to the formal statements of science. Formal mathematics is just on one end of this range. But

---

[21] See Chap. 5.1.
[22] [DeMillo et al., 1979]
[23] [Naur, 1985b]

in every act of communication we wrap up an experience, and by this very act – whether verbal or not, conscious or not – give it a unity, and thus make it an element of our communication system. For this reason, there are always experiences we do not communicate about, since we do not want to endow them with this special status[24].

Formalization thus is a special case of formulation. It provides a sharp tool without which mathematics would not have evolved. Formalization is the vehicle on which science rests, computer science in particular. We divest a word of the meaning it has acquired through our experience, and instead set up rules about how to use it[25]. We separate form from process, by giving a new precise meaning to the word. Thereby we can be sure that other people use it the way we want it, and thus compactify our communication. To use a tool with such skill is much fun. I often tell my students that the only reason not to like mathematics is to be afraid of it. And rightly one should be afraid of a sharp tool if one has to use it without really knowing how.

This is only one side of the coin, however. I may change the meaning of a word, but I have to take care not to throw out the sense along with the meaning. Human communication is sense-bearing and sense-born. Luhmann goes as far as to say that for a sense-carrying system nothing can be without sense. If what I say does not make sense to my audience, they will get bored. Being bored makes sense, too, for a while, but before long they will start to play games, or get afraid. I would spend my time better if I played games, too.

The English language is helpful here: what I say *has*, or has not, meaning; but it *makes*, or does not make, sense. Meaning is a property. I can change it, take it away, assign it to programs(!), hand it over like a coconut. I cannot lay my hands on the sense. Sense happens. In a communication it happens between the partners, and thereby constitutes the communication. Thus, following again Luhmann[26], communication is self-referential: by talking and listening the partners create a sensible conversation, but no talking and listening is possible in a situation that does not make sense already. Therefore an act of communication always refers back to itself as being a communication.

This self-referential balance is especially rickety in a formal environment, say in proving a theorem. When someone tells me a story, I connect what I hear to familiar experiences. Thus, I engage in creating the experiences while listening. When I listen to a proof, I have to connect to an artificial world of man-made meanings. This is hard work, which takes time. A formalism is reality coded through long chains of formal steps. What we gain in space – compactness of speech through precision – we spend in time for coding and decoding.

Again this is common ground: One cannot learn mathematics by listening. While listening one has to follow the steps being told, thus recreating the experiences the teacher went through. Only in this way one can re-live the fun, too.

---

[24] See [Luhmann, 1987].

[25] This is how Ernesto Grassi [Grassi, 1980] formulates it, following the Italian humanist Vico.

[26] [Luhmann, 1987, Chap. 4]

Of course, it is not the same fun. If I induce my partner to work on a problem I solved, he knows that I know the solution. Thus, as in a good story, it is not the solution which matters but the way towards it. First the steps on the way, and then the whole way, have to be comprehensible. Then neither the talker nor the listener have fun on their own; the fun is in the joint going. Never write *'Quod erat demonstrandum'* under a proof! admonishes Imre Lakatos[27]. The proof is first, and you create the theorem through it. By QED you can only signal: This way I convinced myself of the theorem. Now what do you make of it? But always start a proof with DEQ: *Demonstrandum estne?*

A conversation does not follow a planned course, thus it seems to have no structure; it is structured by the themes the participants choose. What themes do we follow when we prove a theorem? In a good conversation people talk and listen in turns. Similarly, when designing a system, the designers have to listen to the users explaining what they want, the users have to listen when the designers explain a prototype, the designers have to listen when the users "play" with it, and so forth. Gordon Pask[28] calls his theory of learning systems a 'conversation theory'. The value of a program is not its low complexity or high elegance, but the understanding we gain of it. The value of a theorem is not its truth, but its proof. And a proof is valuable if it makes us listen.

The aim, then, in telling a proof is not to hand it over to the audience, but to aid in solving a problem. We communicate to reduce the complexity of a situation; only what we do not understand looks complicated. Thus, before you can teach me anything, you have to convince me that I really have a problem there. To listen to your lecture is boring if you try to inflict information on me for which I feel no need. "You are always welcome if you want to talk about the weather", says Annie Dillard[29]. You are welcome to me if you want to talk about trees, or splinters, or small systems, or completeness proofs, or nonambiguous computations, or on formal communication. For other themes knock before you enter!

4.2.7 Change and chance

The best exercise in proving is to find a proof. The second-best exercise is to change one. I can change only what I have understood. You tell me a proof. In order to do so, you have to structure it: you select themes on which we can talk sensibly, and you divide the proof accordingly. Thus, you change the big proof into smaller units which I can comprehend. This helps you to understand the whole proof better. Now I can rework the bits, reshuffle the pieces, and get a new proof. This way we both learn. Sense is a surplus of possibilities. Only what I can change makes sense, makes fun.

Now we are at the very center of the seeming contradiction of formal work. I stated in the beginning that we use formalization to narrow down the freedom

---

[27] [Lakatos, 1976, p. 41]
[28] [Pask, 1980]
[29] [Dillard, 1974]

of other people, explicitly by giving orders, implicitly by introducing order. In replacing sense by meaning, and meaning by rules, we take away possibilities for change. Thus, when we do a proof we fight against change; when we talk about it, we work towards change.

Scientists consume time to carve forms out of processes. Processes go on "all the time", forms stay unchanged. Or rather they change so slowly that we experience them as "things". A thing has observable properties which can be described. This results in the distinction between observable object, which is taken out of time, and observing subject, which depends on time and therefore is not part of the observable world. By algorithms computer scientists do not describe processes, but sequences of states which change in discrete steps. Artists generate time, through repetition. In rhymes and verses, in recurring colours and symbols, in creating similarities through their very style, they make us experience time. They do not describe processes either, but activate processes in us.

Algorithms can be run and copied arbitrarily; the copies and the processes generated are all the same. Each time you consider an art object, your experience is different; and if you copy it, something totally different results. Therefore the scientists' symbol of time is the arrow, which leads from one state to another. Scientists describe what was before and after the change, they cannot describe how it happens. The artists' symbol of time is the hoop[30]. Artists do not describe states, but try to make you experience the movement yourself. They do it by creating patterns.

A pattern is a repeated occurrence. For Gregory Bateson to communicate is to create patterns. I say something, you listen. What I say about my experience creates a similar experience in you. This induced repetition unites us. We call the difference between the two parts of the pattern 'information', the whole act 'communication', the difference between before and after the act again 'information'. In communication we operate with a difference in space and a difference in time. This sounds abstract. For more concrete information read for example the chapter on "Style, Grace, and Information in Primitive Art" in Gregory Bateson's "Steps to an Ecology of Mind"[31].

Thus the seeming contradiction in formal work is easily resolved. We have to do our work communicating, as it were. At least we should imagine a partner, if no real one is available. This way we change from the "I-I-I-perspective" to the "I-you-perspective". We cannot make science more humane by extending our descriptions so as to cover the observer or the designer. We cannot describe the observer or designer or user of a system, because this would mean to take them out of time. Imagine people taken out of time! No wonder we end up formalizing the user into a module among others. We can, however, take the user into consideration, if not into the description. Instead of aiming for a perfect description of a technical system, we should try to make people understand our

---

[30] See the strange book "The Sacred Hoop" by Bill Broder [Broder, 1979], and the tiny chapter "Untying the knot" in Annie Dillard's book "Pilgrim at Tinker Creek" [Dillard, 1974].

[31] [Bateson, 1972]

visions, and to understand theirs. This would be a truly humanistic perspective. Markku Nurminen, who coined this last term, compares in his book "People or Computers"[32] the humanistic perspective with the system-theoretical and the socio-technical perspective: "Instead of incorporating models of human activity in the system, let human beings act themselves.... In other words: use real intelligence instead of artificial!".

Of course this is a risky business. People act and react by chance. For this very reason formalization is used in science: to eliminate chance. Why is this so? Can we admit chance in science? We look back into the past and use our memory to understand what is going on by matching events to previous events. We look ahead into the future and use our knowledge to predict what might happen by analyzing our present surroundings. From predicting events it is only a small step to trying to make them happen by establishing the right circumstances. The hope to become able to predict or even evoke events is the main source in our struggle as scientists to understand the world. In situations that are not fully covered by our theories events will happen without our predictions and against our setups. They happen "by chance". Thus, chance comes in as a negative force, which counteracts our work, and thus has to be fought.

Actually, chance can be eliminated only from the "idealized" non-living systems of natural science. A living system cannot be separated from its environment. It operates constantly referring to itself. Therefore it reacts on information from the outside by autonomous decisions, in contrast to the automatic reactions on the physical level. It not only changes continuously, but it changes "by chance", when viewed from the outside. Humberto Maturana and Francisco Varela[33] call such systems 'autopoietic'.

Man seems to be the only living being who can describe the world to others, so that they can learn from the descriptions rather than from their own experiences. As we saw above this is a misleading statement. One cannot learn from descriptions, only from experiences. Thus, learning persons have to use the descriptions to create events from which they gain new experiences. These events can be imagined, or they can actually happen as in solving exercises. Therefore, the best a teacher can do is to provide circumstances that induce such events. Since students are alive, these events do – or do not – happen by chance. The teacher can only hope for them to happen. Thus, for the teacher chance is positive. People are creative if they open themselves to chance events[34].

Lately I walked our dog. When Bobby crossed the road without watching for traffic, a lady explained: "Dogs do not normally recognize moving cars, at least not by sight. Animals move rhythmically. Therefore, for a dog a car does not move at all; first it is there, and all of a sudden it is here." I leashed Bobby. – We are used for a long time to the way cars move, but we miss the exercise.

In a formalism similarly we move , in an ordered, orderly way. But our mind misses the rhythmical movement of being creative, of going in cycles. Actually,

---

[32] [Nurminen, 1988, p. 116]. See also Chap. 7.2.
[33] [Maturana and Varela, 1980, Maturana and Varela, 1987]
[34] See the contribution by John M. Carroll, Chap. 4.3.

we easily miss the movement completely; we do not realize how fast we advance until we hit somebody, or are being hit.

Rudolf Arnheim in his classic "Visual Thinking"[35] and Oliver Sacks in his impressive case studies "The Man Who Mistook his Wife for a Hat"[36] describe and analyze how thinking rests on body sensations. In a formalized environment we have to reproduce everything every moment from the description. In a living system we move continuously. We understand a movement by moving with it, mentally or factually. We understand an action, since we could do it ourselves, or imagine that we could. Our brain is a powerful instrument, but without support from our body and from the people and nature around us it would be of little help. How then can people think that the brain works like a computer, or hope that a computer could ever work like a brain?

Rational speech is powerful. But if it were not embedded in rhetorical speech it would be poor. Let us strive for a rhetoric of mathematics.

Acknowledgements

In the summer of 1988 my colleague Christiane Floyd intrigued me into giving a joint seminar on the book "Social systems" by Niklas Luhmann. From both her and him and from the participants I learned much about communication, which enabled me to help in preparing the conference on which this book is based. In the cleansing atmosphere of Schloß Eringerfeld the participants grew together investigating and practicing formal and informal communication. From the discussions then and afterwards evolved the present paper.

---

[35] [Arnheim, 1969]
[36] [Sacks, 1986]

4.3 Making Errors, Making Sense, Making Use

John M. Carroll

4.3.1 Introduction

The relationship of science to design work in a technical area, for example the design of software and its documentation, is one of those things that gets murkier as one examines it more closely. What is very clear and simple, however, is *why* we want to describe a close relationship between science and design. Our concrete goal is to design better solutions, better software, better instruction. But we neither wish to nor expect that we can achieve this concrete goal through trial and error, through intuition or through magic: We expect that we will have to *understand* how we do what we do in design, so that we can do it deliberately and repeatedly in diverse and novel situations. Moreover, we want to be able to *externalize* our understanding of design practice to be able to teach it to others and to work with it directly to improve it.

Getting from the *why* to the *how* is the challenge. Traditional basic science seeks to develop and externalize an understanding of the world. But its primary goal is *not* to alter the world as found. On the other hand, the traditional design paradigm of craft evolution seeks to alter the world, but does not even address the problem of externalizing the inherent understanding upon which this design capability rests[1].

4.3.2 Science and design in an ecology of tasks and artifacts

A fundamental and quite classical error in understanding the relation between science and design is to assume and to seek a deductive basis in science for design work. This idea pervades attitudes towards design from within the scientific research community, despite a lack of cases of invention, design and development that were driven by deduction from basic science. Practitioners know that things are not so neat; applied scientists know that invention and design *produce* scientific theory as often as they *apply* theory.

In actual cases in which design "deductions" are offered, they are logically underdetermined. For example, Shneiderman[2] refers to George Miller's paper "The magical number seven plus or minus two"[3] on human information processing limitations to derive the prescription that on-line training options be

---

[1] Cf. [Jones, 1970].

[2] See [Shneiderman, 1980, p. 225].

[3] Cf. [Miller, 1956].

presented one at a time. However, there is no possible way to *deduce* this specific design guideline from the specific research and theory Miller presented on the span of absolute judgement and immediate memory. The connection is far more informal: Miller's work called attention to the (perhaps obvious) fact that humans are limited with respect to the information they can manage, but the theory he discussed was far more limited (and contentful). Shneiderman was inspired by the broader theme of limited processing capacity to suggest severely bounding the number of training options that a user ought to have to consider at a time. But this was no deduction.

The so-called systems approach to instructional design is a more extensive example of the same variety. It is remarkable to contrast the Gagne and Briggs second edition[4] of the classic overview of the systems approach with the Gagne, Briggs and Wagner third edition[5]. The two editions both clearly purport a deductive relationship to the psychology of learning, but they appeal to rather different views of what that psychology is: The second edition rests on Skinnerian behaviourism, while the third edition rests on the more modern information processing psychology. Amazingly, both come to exactly the same instructional prescriptions. The reason this can happen is that little or no real deduction was ever involved. The systems approach to instructional design is pure methodological discipline. It has no substantive theory content and no user domain content at all. This is probably why it performs so poorly in producing instruction.

Similar problems are evident in interface design. Newell and Card[6] outlined a "vision" for psychological science in human-computer interaction that amounts to a systems approach for theory-based design of user interfaces. They place heavy emphasis on systematic hierarchical decomposition of human behaviour and experience, and on the production of simple, quantitative, time-and-error-rate descriptions. They wholly ignore the exigencies of human sense-making on the grounds that such realms of human psychology are not amenable to simple description, and hence not to design by deduction[7]. This is like looking for lost car keys under a streetlight, not because the keys are anywhere nearby, but because the light seems better. Their approach has, perhaps not surprisingly, produced little impact on user interface design practice.

Why doesn't design-by-deduction help us produce usable software and documentation for people? The answer is partly a general fact about the relation of science and design, and partly a particular fact about current psychology: The science base in which design deductions must be anchored is too general and too shallow vis-a-vis specific contexts and situations in the world. In basic science, details are abstracted away; in design, they determine success or failure. Scientists want universal principles; designers need concrete examples. However, in bridging from science to design, the details cannot merely be "added back." To a great extent, the science must be redeveloped for each domain of appli-

---

[4] [Gagné and Briggs, 1979]
[5] [Gagne et al., 1988]
[6] Cf. [Newell and Card, 1985].
[7] Cf. [Carroll and Campbell, 1989].

cation. Miller and Shneiderman were both concerned with processing capacity limitations, but not the *same* processing capacities or limitations. In detail, their proposals had little in common.

In the particular case of applied psychology, this mismatch of basic science and design work is aggravated by the fact that the basic work does not so much focus on abstract domains as on *odd* domains. Traditionally, academic psychology has sought to emulate physics and study abstract domains. However, subtracting the concrete meaning from domains of human experience turns out to be fundamentally unlike subtracting gravity from a physical process (in an experiment carried out in deep space). Extending the results of studies of pigeon pecking, nonsense list learning, tachistoscopic perception, etc. to the design of computer applications is hazardous at best, and often just silly. There are thousands of psychological studies of perceiving and comprehending isolated words, sentences and contrived paragraphs, but they are only of peripheral relevance to understanding real communication or, for that matter, to designing usable computer systems and instruction.

> The fact that we do not, and perhaps *cannot* have a deductive science base for software design, entails that we must develop empirical approaches to design: we must identify ourselves *less* with the roles of abstract analyst and detached observer and *more* with the roles of design participant and user. We must understand the detailed structure of the software domains we seek to impact through design: the real tasks and concerns of users. We must codify this understanding in ways that can realistically find use *in design*.

A starting point is to recognize that human interaction with software is embedded in a *task-artifact cycle*[8]: People want to engage in certain tasks. In doing so, they make discoveries and incur problems; they experience insight and satisfaction, frustration and failure. Analysis of these tasks is the raw material for the invention of new tools, constrained by technological feasibility. New tools, in turn, alter the tasks for which they were designed, indeed alter the situations in which the tasks occur and even the conditions that cause people to want to engage in the tasks. This creates the need for further task analysis, and in time, for the design of further artifacts, and so on. Software design, too, is embedded in this ecology of tasks and artifacts.

An example of a task is sending a form letter to customers in Oregon. This task has an articulated structure. It involves composing, typing and revising a text, duplicating copies, putting copies into envelopes, stamping and mailing them. Analysis of the task suggests classes of artifacts that could simplify it, for example, a word processor can simplify the subtask of composing, typing and revising. However, injecting this artifact into the task situation fundamentally alters the situation itself. For example, there may be a variety of specific usability problems in adjusting to the word processor. Analyzing the task of using the artifact can suggest specific revisions in the artifact itself. And even if the

---

[8] Cf. [Carroll and Campbell, 1989].

artifact is unproblematic, it may restructure the constellation of subtasks: perhaps stuffing, stamping and mailing each separate envelope will now seem more tedious. Analysis of this new task situation could suggest further classes of artifacts, for example, electronic mail and network facilities. Attention can then turn to the problem of selecting only the Oregon mailing labels from a heterogeneous listing of mailing labels. This task problem may suggest yet another artifact: a database retrieval facility, and so on.

The importance of understanding user tasks to the design of software tools and environments is recognized in recent work that represents user requirements in user task descriptions. One approach analyzes the nature of specific subskills users must attain and perform to successfully interact with a system[9]. Such qualitative subskill analysis can be useful in guiding early stages of user interface design. Another approach seeks to anticipate aspects of user performance with new interface technologies by studying simulations, for example, of speech recognition[10] or intelligent help[11], *before* actual applications employing these technologies are developed.

4.3.3 Making errors

Errors are an extremely important element of user tasks, one that we must take very seriously if we wish to understand these tasks well enough to design and redesign them. A point that has become quite salient to me is that we have to try to understand errors as situated in a *multifaceted context of problem-solving, learning and design*, if we are to use them effectively to understand user tasks and to provide guidance to designers. We need to go beyond any particular error and understand the context of activity that made the error meaningful, plausible, intelligent. We cannot design merely to filter errors, there are too many of them: we must design to address the bases of error in intelligence and activity.

A key on-going activity in our group is the empirical analysis of state-of-the-art interfaces ranging from traditional character-box, menu-based styles[12] to raster graphics, direct manipulation styles[13]. Our goal is to inventory and describe the most critical usability problems at an appropriate level of detail to provide guidance for software and documentation designers. To a great extent, the problems people have in learning computing systems depend on idiosyncratic details of the particular system. However, we have found that from a moderate level of abstraction, a class of fairly general problem-types emerges. Some of these are listed below:

[9] Cf. [Carroll and Rosson, 1985]. For example, Furnas, Landauer, Gomez and Dumais [Furnas et al., 1983] characterized the need for rich aliasing in the subskill of referring to things by name.
[10] See [Gould et al., 1983].
[11] See [Carroll and Aaronson, 1988].
[12] Cf. [Mack et al., 1983].
[13] Cf. [Carroll and Mazur, 1986].

1. *People tend to jump the gun.* They tend to learn about a system by plunging in and using it. This can work well, if a person has appropriate background knowledge or access to a more experienced user. But it can also be problematic. In our study of the $Lisa^{TM}$ system, we saw several users switch the system on before inserting the tutorial LisaGuide diskette. Switching the system on seems like a good place to start, but in this case it was jumping the gun: to use the tutorial, the system must be booted from that diskette and not from its hard disk. The user who selects Print before having created any data that could be printed, or who selects Application Customizing before having tried the application at all, is similarly jumping the gun.

2. *People are not always careful planners.* As new users, they often become intrigued by functions irrelevant to their actual concerns or take actions without analyzing even their immediate consequences. For example, in our studies of the IBM Displaywriter, we often noticed people selecting Program Diskette Tasks from the initial menu (instead of the more appropriate Typing Tasks, which is the gateway to editing and printing functions). This selection led them away into system maintenance functions that they did not need to use and could not in general understand. In the Lisa system, we saw people place system applications in the Wastebasket, some of them were motivated to confirm that an application had in fact been deleted by throwing away several more. (We saw one learner repeat a relatively simple error sequence over 40 times.)

3. *People are not good at systematically following instructional steps.* New users often very rapidly skip among several sections of a manual, or among several volumes in a training library, following what in essence is an Ersatz procedure that was never intended or designed. They attempt to execute section previews (jumping the gun) and reviews (just to make sure they really understood the section) even though previews and reviews are meant only to be read. More fundamentally, people have trouble following instructions that are ordered *extrinsically*, that is, sequenced in the sense of labeled and numbered steps, but without clearly motivated prerequisite relationships.

4. *People's reasoning about situations is often subject to interference from what they know about other, superficially similar situations.* Learners may spontaneously refer to prior knowledge about typewriters, and erroneously deduce the operation of keys like Spacebar and Return (which often alter text as well as moving the input pointer). Conversely, prior knowledge can override an interpretation that the designer intends. The Lisa system used a Tear off command to generate new objects from templates. Users were able to apply this with some difficulty to stationery pads; some had trouble stemming from their prior experiences of writing on a pad *before* tearing off the current sheet. However, applying the Tear off command to folder objects caused serious confusion: people had never encountered a folder pad before, nor the idea that one obtains a folder by tearing it off from something. Under such uncertainty, users often reach incorrect conclusions about cause and effect relationships in an interface.

5. *People are often poor at recognizing, diagnosing and recovering from errors they make.* New users may queue multiple print jobs or alter the print queue itself without recognizing the consequence until much later when they try to operate the printer and are surprised by the number, sequence and appearance of their output. In the Displaywriter, mistyping a diskette name in an edit or print command had the consequence that the system would prompt for the erroneously-named diskette to be inserted. It was quite unlikely that the user would have already formatted and named a diskette with that particular typo as its name, hence the whole command had to be cancelled. The problem was that the command to cancel that command was itself quite exotic and new users were never taught it. Hence the only remedy they could avail themselves of was to switch off the system and reboot. This error recovery entailed some side effects of its own (any open file would be saved incompletely and with errors necessitating a subsequent diskette recovery procedure).

These are not the sorts of results that standard systematic instruction advertises! Textbooks on the design of systematic instruction[14] present an overwhelming edifice of common-sense psychology: instructional objectives should be clearly articulated, hierarchically decomposed into successively finer requirements for an instructional curriculum; in designing the curriculum, instructional events (previews, practice exercises, tests, reviews) should be carefully sequenced to build skill and understanding, foundations first and then extensions. The basic problem is that mere hierarchy and logical dependency do not provide appropriate constraint: they more or less guarantee the sorts of problems we found, and other problems as well (they entrain very fat books that are expensive to write and to print).

This understanding of user errors is only the starting point for the kind of understanding we need for use in design. We need to get beyond the "misperformance" aspect of the errors to the "intelligent intention" aspect of the errors. For though some user errors arise out of carelessness, in general users are diligently trying to make sense of the situations they are in, and their errors must be seen as part of this activity. In understanding user tasks, we must be no less diligent. We must try to make sense of what the users are trying to do. Unless we understand error in this context and at this depth, it can be of only limited use in design. To seriously design for error, we cannot merely patch over problems, we must understand and solve problems.

4.3.4 Making sense

We find that users are always fundamentally motivated to get something done. Both the organizational context for learning new software and the internalized standards that adult learners have for determining what is worth spending time on bias users against a "learning for the sake of learning" attitude. New users want to get started fast; they like to jump the gun (executing a procedure when

---

[14] For example [Gagné and Briggs, 1979].

it is merely mentioned in an overview); they like to skip around on their own in a training sequence. People want to learn by doing, to reason things out instead of merely reading about them. They resent rigidly structured exercises that often compel them to copy text character for character and then subject them to insincere praise for these forced accomplishments: "Excellent!" They like to test hypotheses that they generate on the fly and to make use of their prior knowledge and reason by analogy. This "active" orientation to learning often badly misfits training designs which are predicated on instructional models that begin with a logical analysis of what needs to learned and then successively decomposes each learning objective into a step-by-step sequence of preview, practice, test, and review[15].

We have considered five characteristic user errors. But we can turn the tables a bit on these five and see them also as indicators of specific human propensities in learning and reasoning. Viewed in this way, the characteristic problems become evidence of a powerful learning strategy. Instead of merely seeing these problems as reflecting deficiencies in systematic instruction, we can ask what they can tell us about human learners that we might use to develop more effective approaches to the design of instruction. The five characteristic problems correspond to five components of a powerful learning strategy, one that covers most cases of human learning quite well:

1. *People learn by doing; they try to act in order to learn.* Psychologists some-times lean too heavily on the metaphor of writing to a disk when they speak about learning, and quite often this metaphor can be innocuous. Clearly, though, there is far more involved. A person learning to use a complex tool like a computer will not succeed by "writing to disk" myriad previews and exercise steps. The person will learn only if he or she can integrate knowing with doing, and ipso facto this can only occur through meaningful action.

2. *People learn by thinking and reasoning; they generate and test hypotheses in order to learn.* The level and kind of activity required for effective learning necessarily involves self-directed thinking and reasoning. Following a num-bered set of exercise steps is neither active nor challenging enough. Indeed, it places people in a double-bind: try to learn, think about what you are doing and you will get off the track, but try to stay on the track and you will mentally go to sleep and learn nothing. Even when our learners attentively followed their training exercises successfully, they sometimes were uncertain about what they had done or why, as one person put it "What did we do?"

3. *People seek to work in a meaningful context and toward meaningful goals.* A desire to get something done is what makes people want to learn a computer tool in the first place. It orients learning effort to practical progress. Perhaps the worst thing instruction can do is to place an obstacle of numbered steps and well-decomposed learning objectives in the way of practical progress. People learning to use an office application system want to do real work – immediately. One learner, using an on-line tutoring facility, complained: "I want to do something, not learn how to do everything."

---

[15] For example, see [Gagné and Briggs, 1979].

4. *People rely on their prior knowledge when they try to manage and assimilate new experience.* Relating what someone already knows to new things makes it vastly easier for him to remember and be able to use new knowledge in appropriate contexts. This enables the rapid extraction of meaning from new situations that is perhaps the most potent aspect of human learning. However, when situations conflict with prior understanding, when they are difficult to interpret given what is already known, then learning is impaired: this powerful effect may not be significantly mitigated by providing a purely structural organization, like learning hierarchies.

5. *People use error diagnosis and recovery episodes as a means of exploring the boundaries of what they know.* Errors play a far richer role in learning than that of problems. An error can be the touchstone for an intellectual exploration, a vehicle for discovering what is known and what is not currently known. In a serious sense, errors are prerequisite conditions for all learning. For such error-based learning to succeed, however, people need to be able to recognize when they have made an error, they need to be able to reason about what caused the error and how it can be dealt with. Systematic instruction typically assumes that learners will follow instructions errorlessly and thereby deprives itself of even confronting the key situation for real learning.

There is a simple, albeit paradoxical way to summarize these points: *just* the things that make people good learners (for example, a desire to make sense and to accomplish meaningful work) also create the learning problems that ruin systematic instruction. People need to make sense in order to learn, but they need to learn in order to make sense[16]. The challenge of designing usable instructional systems is to allow people to make sense of their own learning activity and thereby to refine what they already know and discover new things as well.

These findings called for a new approach to online training, one that seeks to provide an "exploratory environment" for the new user, an environment that affords active involvement in the learning process, one that encourages initiative and hypothesis testing. A major consideration in this approach is user error. Error is a major consideration for any training model, but the standard rote-practice model typically just ignores the problem, printing steps in bold-face and imploring learners to be careful. From an active learning perspective the problem is completely different: errors are expected; they are unavoidable; they are opportunities to learn. If learners are going to take initiative in directing their own learning, they are going to make errors. The problem for designers of training is to manage the consequences of errors so that the greatest possible learning benefit obtains.

A training model appropriate for active learners simply cannot demand that the learner sit at the interface and read. People don't want to do this, and they in fact don't do it. The Minimalist training model we developed takes this hard reality as a starting point. The sheer volume of training material must be minimal: the ever-present sales pitch should be cut (the user has already bought

---

[16] [Carroll and Rosson, 1987]

the system), section overviews, previews, and reviews should be drastically cut (users often try to execute them), far less how-it-works information should be presented (new users don't have to know details of magnetic recording to use diskettes). Installation should be simple (e.g., loading a single diskette). System and tutorial screens should differ as little as possible (tutorial screens often get confusingly cluttered). The overhead of learning the jargon of the training itself should be minimized (e.g., eliminating fine distinctions between "topics" and "chapters" or between "message lines" and "information lines").

Our five characteristic user problems and five aspects of powerful, general learning strategies can be recast as five design prescriptions for usable instruction:

1. *Allow the user to get started fast.* Cut down overhead and repetition; cut down nonessential verbiage; reject the notion that every function must be covered; people never master every function even when every function is covered. Offer the learner meaningful activities as soon as possible.

2. *Rely on the user to think and to improvise.* Encourage but guide user inference; leave out material that can be inferred. Don't try to give the user an understanding when you can allow the user to create an understanding.

3. *Direct training at real tasks.* Introduce real work immediately. Instruction, no matter how well-organized, will fail if it does not support the goals people bring to the learning situation.

4. *Exploit what people already know.* Even if it is possible to learn without analogy, it is too abstract and cumbersome.

5. *Support error recognition and recovery.* Errors cannot be avoided in learning, but they can confuse and frustrate learners. If they are properly managed they may play useful roles.

These principles follow from our studies of user error. But like most design guidelines they are extremely abstract with respect to the context of design. Much of our work in the past decade has been directed at situating these design principles by embodying them in example designs. Our design work provides an existence proof for the principles: that is, it shows that the principles can support design work. More importantly though, our design work provides a communication medium for more concretely communicating what the abstract design principles are all about. In this way, we try to meet the most difficult requirement on research that seeks to impact design practice: to codify understanding in ways that can realistically find use in design.

One line of this design work has been directed at providing explicit, task-oriented guidance in training and help. It has focussed particularly on supporting error recovery and learner-initiated activities[17]. Another line of work has been

---

[17] We developed a kind of quick-reference card for learning by doing (Guided Exploration cards; [Carroll et al., 1985]), a self-instruction manual that stressed learning via inference (the Minimal Manual; [Carroll et al., 1988]), and a (simulated) intelligent help system that provided advice on error recovery (SmartHelp; [Carroll and Aaronson, 1988]).

directed at providing more suitable software environments for new users[18].

Our studies of learner problems were revelatory for us, but we were not the only investigators to notice these problems and we did not develop the deepest understanding of the problems. Indeed, from the standpoint of *knowledge* what we learned was both more and less than a basic science approach might have produced. We did not describe a detailed learning mechanism, but we learned a lot about word processing tasks, and more perhaps than we ever wished to know about the particular systems and applications we worked with. Our understanding was successfully applied because we drove it to application, because we developed the design implications of the work. Better basic science understandings of learning have in general produced far less application.

Our understanding of user learning tasks, via understanding user errors, and our design principles, embodied in design examples, have allowed us to effectively communicate our design approach to others. The minimalist approach is in wide use today in a variety of companies and in a variety of application areas[19]. We believe that it is *because* our approach is so concretely empirical, *because* our analysis of errors, of learning and of minimalist design is so closely tied to example designs and activity directed to real work tasks, that we have been able to make sense of user tasks for designers.

4.3.5 Making use

The work we are all engaged in as software developers and researchers studying software development is making use: we are designing tools and environments that facilitate tasks, and even create new possibilities for tasks. I have argued that to do this we must understand in detail the user's task in ways that can efficiently find use in design. We must have one foot in abstraction: providing endless detail about particular user errors would yield neither an understanding of the user's task nor any insight into how to design a more appropriate software environment for the user. But we must also have one foot securely in the empirical details of the software domain we seek to impact: general learning mechanisms without domain-specific detail and design guidelines without exemplary applications will not help us.

This tension is to an extent endemic to complex activities like design. Conventional science provides uncertain and indirect support to such practical endeavour[20]. However, without some sense of science and abstraction, we are doomed to become lost in the morass of domain-specific, even case-specific details. What kind of science can we have in software development? What kind of science is

---

[18] We developed an interface overlay that blocks typical and difficult errors (the Training Wheels interface; [Carroll and Carrithers, 1984]), a window-management scheme in which task-related data and applications are displayed adjacently (TaskMapper; [Carroll et al., 1987]) and a programming environment for Smalltalk that coordinates multiple views of the user's task (the View Matcher; [Carroll et al., 1990]).

[19] [Carroll, 1990]

[20] See [Basalla, 1988, Hindle, 1981, Laudan, 1984, Morrison, 1974].

appropriate and useful to the sort of endeavour we have been discussing? In my recent work, I have been exploring the proposal that the important scientific objects in our domain might be the same objects that are of practical importance, namely, software artifacts embedded in their situations of use[21].

Software artifacts necessarily incorporate psychological assumptions about their own usability, about their suitability for the tasks that users want to do. Chalkboard systems, for instance, have been introduced on the assumption that users already understand how to use physical chalkboards, and that the chalkboard metaphor will make such systems easier to learn and easier to use than existing systems. Such artifacts have *falsifiable empirical content*[22]: chalkboard systems could turn out to have specific features that impede rather than facilitate learning and performance. By the same token, artifacts support explanations of the form "This system feature has this consequence for usability." In these respects, *artifacts embody implicit theories of human interaction with software.* Indeed, they embody theory of a sort that melds the need for some abstraction with the need for task details and design examples.

Though this proposal is radical, it is also quite parsimonious. It advises that the scientific ontology of a design domain be no more elaborate than the practical ontology that effectively supports design work. It collapses the socially alienating, and usually pointless, distinctions between "developers" and "researchers." In software development, researchers who do not participate as designers and users are in no position to offer useful results; conversely, developers who do not ceaselessly ask how they can improve design practice should not be designing things for people to use. This view of artifacts and their function in software science also opens up new possibilities for usability research. Conventionally, usability research is seen as providing *evaluations* of usability or *descriptive* theories of the user[23]. Neither of these conceptions, however, acknowledges the central role of software design in software research.

If there is any precedent for this claim about artifacts, it would be the view that computer simulations of task performance are theory-like. Simulations are often held to embody psychological theories[24]. In a number of senses, simulations are the nearest neighbour to human-computer interaction (HCI) artifacts. Both depend on computer technology; both embody psychological theories, but are not themselves theories; both are formal entities requiring conceptual interpretation. There are, however, some deep differences. Simulations are used by psychologists for specific research purposes; artifacts are used by a wide range of people to do real work. Simulations and artifacts are also interpreted in different ways. Simulations are interpreted and evaluated by criteria of *descriptive adequacy*[25]: a simulation of problem-solving behaviour may be judged on the basis of how closely it fits the sequence of moves in a verbal protocol, whether it predicts all

---

[21] See [Carroll and Kellogg, 1989, Carroll and Rosson, 1990].
[22] [Popper, 1965]
[23] [Carroll, 1989]
[24] Cf. [Fodor, 1968, Newell and Simon, 1972].
[25] [Chomsky, 1965]

and only the kinds of errors that are observed, etc. Artifacts are interpreted and evaluated by criteria of *usability*.

If artifacts are appropriate media for the expression and development of psychological theories in HCI, the question can be raised whether making the implicit theory explicit leaves the artifact with any distinctive scientific function. On a weak version of the claim, artifacts are a provisional medium for HCI, to be put aside when HCI theories catch up. On this view, we can imagine, at some point in the future, everything important about the workings and the usability properties of an artifact being extracted as an explicit theory in propositional form. Not, of course, that the theory will capture every detail of the artifact; rather, the workings of the artifact can be understood without serious distortion in terms of a central psychological theory or of theories, plus some auxiliary details of *implementation*.

On a strong version of the claim, artifacts are in principle irreducible to a standard scientific medium such as explicit theories. The strong version would hold, for instance, if artifacts truly cannot be understood apart from the situations in which they are used[26]. Small details of user interfaces often have a major impact on usability. Winograd and Flores[27] and Whiteside and Wixon[28] claim that it is impossible in principle to anticipate the effects of such details; many can only be recognized empirically.

The importance of contextual details for usability suggests that HCI may be dealing with *complex phenomena*, as in Hayek's analysis of economics[29]. Economic phenomena are complex because they have many different kinds of determinants. More tellingly, economic phenomena are embedded in history, which Hayek regards as an unbounded, context-dependent process unfolding in time, consisting of unique events. Historical events, in effect, have an unbounded number of types. Finally, economic phenomena essentially involve human preferences, which are subjective, unpredictable, and constantly changing. Hayek concludes that economic theories must be sharply limited in predictive power. The phenomena of HCI appear to meet Hayek's criteria of complexity.

4.3.6 Invention and interpretation as a paradigm for HCI

Where do we go from here? The lesson that we do not and perhaps cannot have a conventional deductive science for software development is an important one. The consequent refocussing of effort on more directly empirical approaches has already proven productive. Merging the roles of researcher, developer and user makes possible the kind of rich and action-oriented understanding we need to have in what is after all a design domain. I described our work taking errors seriously as specific misperformances, as indicators of powerful human learning strategies and as the starting point for design principles embodied in exemplar

---

[26] Cf. [Winograd and Flores, 1986, Suchman, 1987].

[27] [Winograd and Flores, 1986]

[28] [Whiteside and Wixon, 1987]

[29] [Hayek, 1967]

designs. Much current work has this character. I believe we are serving the user better and that in the future we can do better still.

I am personally excited to see that software researchers are learning how to work with artifacts in situations of use as media for developing theoretical ideas about usability. Invention has become a standard research activity. Thus, investigations of naming and reference tasks have produced specific tools and techniques for keyword information systems[30]. Patterns of spontaneous interaction with an electronic mail application have served as the basis for more usable command languages[31]. Analyses of programming plans[32] have been embodied in intelligent tutoring systems[33]. Stu Card and Tom Moran, the original architects of the rather unsituated GOMS model[34], are now also well-known as inventors[35]!

Each of these inventions has evoked considerable theoretical interpretation, and interpretation has also emerged as a new standard research activity. Norman's interpretation of key aspects of the $Unix^{TM}$ operating system is a particularly influential example[36]. Another example is our interpretation of the Lisa interface and on-line tutorial[37]. This type of work has developed rapidly, as is evidenced by contrasting Shneiderman's interpretation[38] of direct manipulation interfaces with that of Hutchins, Hollan and Norman[39], produced only a few years later. In our research group at the Watson Center, we have found that developing interpretations is becoming increasing central[40].

Our hope is that structured interpretations of HCI artifacts in their situations of use offer a vehicle for capturing the psychology of humanly usable software at the right level of abstraction for this design science. Taking artifacts in situations of use more seriously as embodiments of scientific theories and results brings more of practical activity into the purview of scientific analysis. Conceiving of the task-artifact cycle as a basic structure of research activity in software development entrains a new view of science and design. It fundamentally challenges the conventional division of labour, and directs software research, not toward abstract or merely eccentric domains, but toward the real world.

---

[30] [Furnas et al., 1983]

[31] [Wixon et al., 1983]

[32] For example [Soloway and Ehrlich, 1984].

[33] [Bonar and Cunningham, 1988]

[34] [Card et al., 1983]

[35] See [Card and Henderson, 1987, Halasz et al., 1987].

[36] See [Norman, 1981].

[37] [Carroll and Mazur, 1986]

[38] See [Shneiderman, 1982].

[39] See [Hutchins et al., 1986].

[40] Cf. [Rosson and Alpert, 1990].

4.4 Artifacts in Software Design
Reinhard Keil-Slawik

4.4.1 Introduction

"A scientific discipline emerges with the – usually rather slow! – discovery of which aspects can be meaningfully 'studied in isolation for the sake of their own consistency'."[1] This statement made by E.W. Dijkstra was meant to express a specific desire, namely, to achieve basic improvements in software development by means of mathematical tools and concepts allowing us to express algorithms and data structures in an increasingly precise, unambiguous, consistent and complete manner. The question is, however, whether isolated mathematical properties provide the only – and a sufficient – basis for establishing a scientific discipline.

More than twenty years after the term *software engineering* was coined, the aim of turning the development of software into an engineering discipline based on sound scientific principles has only been partially achieved. Despite some progress in the development of more powerful tools and mathematically based specification techniques, the results have often been less promising than expected. Still, the quality of software is only revealed to its full extent once it is in use. Software projects fail to live up to the expectations of developers and managers or the domain experts who ultimately have to use the product. Frequently, up to three or four versions of a software system have to be delivered before it is considered reliable and sound enough to support performance of the tasks in question.

In order to understand and deal with the problems involved here, we cannot view software and its components merely as isolated mathematical objects. Behind such a strict engineering perspective lies the implicit assumption that thinking is a more or less rule-based process performed by our brain on some internally stored representations that embody our knowledge of the outside world. Once we are able to express this knowledge symbolically in the form of documents or machine-executable programs, these artifacts are said to represent or process (create, delete, modify, etc.) it. Thus, a 'transfer' of knowledge can be accomplished by exchanging artifacts, and, by the same token, human information processing can be replaced by machine operations.

However, this view does not reflect the idiosyncrasies of real software development processes. This, as C. Floyd has already pointed out in her introduction[2], involves going beyond what she has termed the traditional scientific paradigm of computer science. And this I shall attempt to do, by reflecting on the role

---

[1] [Dijkstra, 1982, p. 60]
[2] See Chap. 1.1.

of artifacts in design processes, in particular how they serve to support communication and learning. In order to do so, I shall have to touch on some basic philosophical questions concerning how humans acquire knowledge and how they construct and communicate meaning(s).

I argue that *thinking does not take place inside our heads but is an activity that we perform with our heads*. Most of our mental activities need external resources, and very often thinking is merely a grouping or regrouping of objects in our environment. This perspective emphasizes that humans basically use artifacts to acquire knowledge and create meaning rather than to represent it. Knowledge and meaning are attributes of cooperative social processes; they can neither be located in an artifact, nor are they stored in the brain. A document or piece of software can only be said to represent knowledge to the extent that a common framework for interpretation has been established among the parties involved. I present some guidelines for the design of artifacts that are meant to support the establishment of such a framework rather than to represent knowledge.

4.4.2 Engineering software

The technological achievements of our western civilization are chiefly built on the ability to store, modify and retrieve symbolic representations. Without the invention of mathematical formulas, specification standards or technical drawings, engineering disciplines would be practically non-existent. With the invention of symbolic representations, artifacts can be designed that would be too large to be made by a single craftsperson[3]. An important part of any engineering discipline is the development of tools and techniques and the definition of standards allowing us to create suitable design representations. To distinguish the models or representations produced while employing these means from the artifact being designed, I will call the former *design artifacts* and the latter *products*. With respect to the actual design process, the design artifacts can be said to embody the knowledge about the product being designed.

The material of which the design artifacts consist is usually different from that used for the construction of the product. With the exception of physical models or prototypes, they are symbolic representations serving two purposes: They allow the designers to explore the design space and communicate the knowledge about the product that is acquired in the course of design. Since symbolic representations can normally be created and changed with less effort than is required for the construction of their physical counterparts (i.e., the products or physical models), it is often not recognized that design artifacts can only be understood to the extent that the corresponding physical changes are understood. Essentially, this is also true of software engineering.

There is, however, one essential difference: traditional engineering focusses primarily on material structures and their physical effects, whereas software engineering is mainly concerned with symbolic structures and their cognitive

---

[3] [Jones, 1979, p. 124]

effects. The reason for this is that there is only one sort of material: the design artifacts and the product itself are both symbolic representations. Furthermore, programming languages are flexible and powerful means that provide an infinite variety of ways to embody system functions. Hence, the problem was to develop professional standards governing how certain phenomena should be expressed so as to enable them to be generally understood and communicated. Consequently, one of the main concerns was to get rid of the designers' or programmers' individuality and make programs and documents more accessible to other members of the project team.

Phase models and abstract machines

As a matter of fact, ever since *goto's were considered harmful*, the overriding concern has been to turn the *art of programming* into a manageable activity that uses powerful tools and formal techniques and is performed by increasing the division of labour, achieved by assigning specific functional roles to the members of a project team. This means that the knowledge embodied in a program, a program component or document must be accessible by looking at the design artifact or product in question without having to refer to the programmer who wrote it. Only then can the knowledge embodied in a design artifact or the final product be 'transferred' by handing over the relevant document.

In software engineering, the so-called phase model provides the means for combining this view of 'knowledge transfer' with the scientific ideal put forward by Dijkstra. The aim was to dissect the problem domain into isolated chunks with a view to managing software development projects as well as developing research strategies for this emerging discipline[4].

F. Selig first used a phase model to define the specific problem domains with which software engineering is concerned, namely, analysis, design, implementation, installation and maintenance[5]. B. Boehm subsequently introduced the phase model as a project management tool, later advocating its use as the first of *seven basic principles of software engineering*[6]. Using the phase model as a management principle involves three activities, according to Boehm, namely, devising and maintaining a phase plan for the project; combining this plan with a sequential development approach; and finally, using the plan to control the development. This is basically achieved by associating a document (for instance, a program or a specification) with each phase, its completion serving as a milestone in the development process[7]. To allow systematic treatment and separation of the distinct phases, specific tools and techniques had to be developed. Phases became independent domains of scientific enquiry.

---

[4] Software engineering as a discipline matured roughly along the lines of the phase model. Cf. [Freeman, 1979, p. 44].

[5] Cf. [Naur and Randell, 1969, p. 21].

[6] Cf. [Boehm, 1976, p. 1227] and [Boehm, 1977].

[7] The reader should bear in mind that a variety of different phase models can be found in the literature. Since I am here more concerned with the general idea than a specific instance or refinement, I will continue to use the term *the* phase model.

With respect to the design process, the milestones or documents of the phase model are the design artifacts, the installed software representing the product[8]. Since software can be regarded as a mathematical object, the idea is, then, to develop mathematical tools and techniques that allow the designers to specify the behaviour of software in a precise, complete and unambiguous manner. Once such a specification has been written, it is possible to verify whether the implementation meets the specification. Consequently, a specification of this sort can be regarded as an *abstract machine*, since it already determines the input/output relation of the software under development. This notion was originally introduced by Dijkstra as a way of devising a hierarchical software structure by designing complex general operations which are successively transformed into a combination of simpler and more specific operations[9].

The desire to arrive at a hierarchical structure by designing layers of abstract machines implies developing these abstract machines in a specific sequence of steps, because a more abstract machine defines the constraints for realization of the next-lower (abstract) machine(s). Each such step can be interpreted as a transformation from a behaviour specification (i.e., *what* should be achieved) to an implementation (i.e., *how* it is achieved). This *top-down* approach has been advocated with a view to creating design artifacts or programs (functional decomposition) as well as creating a sequence of design artifacts (phase model). According to the latter, an initial set of requirements that defines the problem space is transformed and refined into successive documents until, finally, a system is implemented, tested and installed.

However, a closer look at the idiosyncrasies of software development[10] reveals that the design artifacts cannot represent the knowledge about the product in the way suggested by the traditional engineering perspective.

Top-down considered impossible

According to our modern scientific ideal, knowledge about natural phenomena and physical structures is largely independent of its creating act, i.e., the creators and the specific setting of its creation. The experimental philosophy is a means of ensuring that the observations made and insights gained are independent of the observer. Thus, as long as the phenomena being studied are stable (repetitive) and all those involved adhere to a common framework of interpretation – such as is established, for instance, by education and training – this ideal can, to a

---

[8] In a strict sense, the program code would be a design artifact, and the indispensable user manual(s) would be neither nor. To avoid confusion, I will in most cases refer to both of them explicitly, using the term *document* to denote any of these artifacts.

[9] See [Dijkstra, 1968] and [Dijkstra, 1969, pp. 181–182]. Note that Dijkstra did not combine this document structure with a temporal development structure, i.e., a sequence of transformational steps. In his example of the T.H.E. Operating System, the hierarchical structure was achieved by restructuring the already finished program code.

[10] See also the detailed account given in [Budde and Züllighoven, 1990] and their summary in Chap. 6.2.

considerable degree, be maintained. The same holds for the use of design artifacts in traditional engineering disciplines. But, as I will go on to show, it does not hold for the development of software.

Traditional engineering focusses primarily on material structures and their physical effects, whereas in software engineering we are mainly concerned with symbolic structures and their cognitive effects. There are two main reasons for this difference, which are closely related to each other:

- the highly dynamic nature of the relationship between the form or artifact and the usage context, and
- the high degree of uniqueness on various levels of development and use.

As D. Parnas has pointed out, software in general lacks the degree of repetitiveness which is so characteristic of materials or artifacts in other engineering disciplines[11]. This is due in part to the complexity and dynamic nature of the context.

Traditionally, engineering problems consist in finding a new technical solution for a given function. The functionality of the automobile, for instance, has remained almost the same for more than a hundred years, but the technical implementation has improved tremendously. In contrast, a critical step in the development of software is defining and agreeing upon the required functionality of the future system. In most cases, there are different parties and user groups involved – with different roles and perspectives, and with conflicting interests[12]. Consequently, the specification of requirements may be the result of a complex process of bargaining, negotiation and evaluation. The requirements emerge as a trade-off between various interests and alternatives rather than as a self-contained specification of a technical solution to a well-known problem.

First, initial proposals are prepared and rejected. Then specifications are written and revised. Finally, programs are implemented, tested, corrected and partly restructured before the first version of the envisioned product is released. By the time the system is installed, people's behaviour and their requirements may have changed or will change once the system is in use and its quality is experienced by its users. In general, experience gained in using the system results in new insights and demands. This, M. M. Lehman argues, gives rise to a constant pressure for correction and improvement, and he concludes, "the need for continuing change is intrinsic to the nature of computer usage"[13].

If we regard software as a mathematical object that is interpreted by a machine, its semantics are a static attribute of the program text. Once the instruction sequence is fixed, the behaviour of a program is determined solely by the input. The crucial point for the developers as well as for the users, however, is determining whether a given instruction sequence is appropriate for supporting execution of the task in hand, i.e., finding out which input sequence will produce the desired output in a suitable and comprehensible manner. In addition

---

[11] [Parnas, 1985]

[12] See the personal account given by K. Nygaard in Chap. 2.4.

[13] [Lehman, 1980, p. 1061]

to understanding what the system should do or actually does, it is indispensable to understand what it should not do or what it does not do. Since software embodies a variety of claims and assumptions about the context and the nature of the problems to be solved by introduction of the system at the workplace[14], these properties describing the relations between software and the usage context cannot be expressed in terms of formalisms. Too many mutually influential factors have to be taken into account. The nature of the problem as it is perceived by the designers changes with every new insight, and very often incompatible requirements lead to *design conflicts* that have to be resolved.

The knowledge required for design, then, has to be built up in the course of a tedious and often painful learning process in which the designers learn which aspects fit into their already developed framework and which ones require redesign, correction or restructuring of already existing design artifacts and programs. The reasons and motivations behind such changes, and the arguments concerning how these changes are achieved while maintaining the overall quality of the design, are not part of a program or its specification, and they cannot be documented in their entirety. Programming, P. Naur argues, should not be regarded basically as an activity concerned with producing program text and its associated documentation, but as a human endeavour in which the programmers build up a theory of how the problems in hand can be solved by program execution. Naur concludes that "...reestablishing the theory of a program merely from the documentation is strictly impossible"[15]. Therefore, he argues, the meaning of a program can only be revived as long as there is at least one member of the original development team available. Merely handing over documents does not transfer the knowledge. However, if a document fails to adequately represent the knowledge required to construct the product, then neither a top-down nor a bottom-up approach will be appropriate for design.

We thus face a dilemma. Design artifacts play an essential role in every engineering discipline and therefore in any design process. In software engineering, though, they cannot play the same role as in traditional engineering disciplines. Hence, besides recognizing the problems on a phenomenological level, we must find a way to resolve this dilemma by going beyond the traditional engineering perspective.

Limits of the traditional research strategy

The idiosyncrasies outlined above reveal that software development must be regarded basically as a cooperative learning process. According to J.C. Jones, cooperative learning should be the primary purpose of any design process[16]. But if learning and communication play an essential role, we must deal with this phenomenon in a more systematic way. Tools, techniques and guidelines which are meant to document the result of a learning process are not necessarily

---

[14] See J. Carroll, Chap. 4.3.

[15] [Naur, 1985b, p. 258]

[16] Cf. [Jones, 1986, pp. 120–122].

equally well-suited for supporting the learning process as such. To provide a general framework for this discussion, C. Floyd has introduced the notion of the complementarity of product- and process-oriented views, arguing that the traditional engineering perspective is basically product-oriented[17]. To illustrate the impact and limitations of an exclusively product-oriented research strategy, I will introduce the notion of *learning cycles* and adapt the waterfall model to depict the ideal of this strategy.

The waterfall or phase model shown in Fig. 4.4–1 suggests that there is a 'flow' or 'transfer' from the most abstract kind of knowledge to the increasingly specific details of everyday affairs. The actual knowledge generated within each domain is embodied in artifacts such as textbooks, tools, models or specific experimental settings. Since we are normally used to talking about knowledge only when it is explicitly given, a learning cycle can be characterized as the updating or revision of the respective artifacts. A learning cycle in software development may thus be identified with the production of a new version; in software engineering it may be the development of a new generation of tools or methods. We may also regard the notion of paradigm as denoting a specific instance or kind of learning cycle within a scientific discipline in general. Roughly speaking, a learning cycle corresponds to the restructuring of knowledge about a certain domain that is embodied in an artifact.

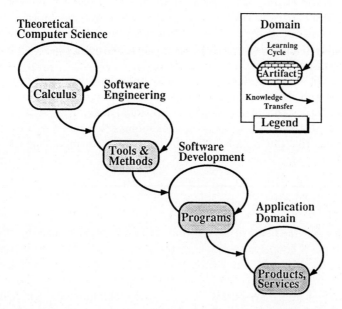

Fig. 4.4–1. The waterfall model of learning cycles and artifacts

---

[17] Cf. [Floyd, 1987].

In order to be able to use methods, tools or a formal specification technique, specific knowledge about the origin and inner structural relations or working principles of the utilities employed should not be required. In other words, the application of a formal specification technique should not require the competence to develop, improve, and maintain the algebraic calculus. Conversely, such competence can only be acquired with sufficient experience in the respective domain. Programmers may be capable of employing a method in which they have been trained, but they may not have the competence to develop methods on their own. And the domain experts may use word-processors to write scientific articles, but they do not have the competence to develop such systems. Hence, the development and maintenance of knowledge within a specific domain is generally associated with a specific role. The general knowledge required for applying this knowledge is acquired through training and education by those professionals who develop and maintain the respective knowledge of that domain.

The waterfall model, as outlined here, highlights the general advantage of any scientific endeavour. In software engineering, however, a crucial problem arises when this model is combined with the notion of abstract machines and a top-down development strategy. If it can be said that a design artifact is indeed a consistent, precise and complete specification of the product to be built, it has to represent all the knowledge required to construct the product. Only *implementation details*, i.e., aspects that do not alter the specification, would have to be added. Consequently, no learning is required for implementing the specification. In this case, it is, in principle, possible to execute the remaining transformational steps mechanically or automatically – i.e, to replace the human implementor by a machine.

In the course of design, where, by definition, these conditions are not given, human operations cannot be prescribed by formal procedures or replaced by machine operations. If, however, the replacement strategy is still in effect, human beings are invariably forced to perform machine-like operations that fit into the overall machine-oriented execution scheme. The typical the-machine-always-performs-better argument actually acquires validity then, because machine-like operations can be better and more reliably executed by a machine. Hence, it should come as no surprise that in software development the above guideline turns out to be counterproductive[18].

We need another perspective; the traditional product-oriented view only allows us to develop replacement strategies. To improve this situation, we have to think about how to support human learning and communication rather than replacing it. Instead of taking it for granted that a design artifact represents the design knowledge, we have to study "how to inform the material with meaning and to extract meaning from the form"[19]. The traditional perspective does not provide an adequate epistemological platform for tackling this problem, because it restricts us to viewing machines and machine-related features as the only frame

---

[18] Various facets of this problem are presented by D. Siefkes in Chap. 4.2 and in [Hoare, 1981, Naur, 1982, Celko et al., 1983, Floyd, 1986, Keil-Slawik, 1989].
[19] [Kay, 1984, p. 41]

of reference. In contrast, I will attempt to outline an ecological perspective by reference to our biological and cultural heritage. In particular, I will examine the role of artifacts as means for acquiring knowledge in an individual and cultural context.

4.4.3 On the evolution of meaningful forms

The notion of meaning is an inherent feature of any life form. The biologist J. von Uexküll was the first to emphasize that the recognition and creation of meaningful forms is of primary importance to every living being. Uexküll invented the concept of the *functional circle*[20] to denote that the meaning of an object is only established through the activities of a living being and has no independent existence of its own. A man, for instance, who is used to climbing up palm trees and has never seen a ladder in his life will not recognize the specific function of this device (its meaning) unless he sees someone using it or tries to use it himself. Uexküll has also pointed out that each living being is adapted with the same degree of perfection to its environment. The simple organism has a simple environment, the complex organism a complex one. Hence, the complexity and richness to which the environment may be differentiated is crucially dependent on the organisms' own inner structures.

These structures originate in an evolutionary process, which means that the more complex structure emerges from the simpler one through an adaptive process with random variations in its reproductive cycles. On the molecular genetic level, Nobel prizewinner M. Eigen and his co-workers have developed an evolution model that describes the origin of biological information as a process of selective self-organization[21]. On a broader level, cyberneticians such as H. von Foerster have developed theoretical models for self-organization and explored their epistemological consequences with respect to a broad range of scientific domains such as biology, psychology, philosophy[22].

In what follows, I will argue that the essence of perception, human learning or design is to create meaningful forms, and that this creation can be characterized as a process of selective self-organization[23].

Creating meaning

On the psychological level, this can be illustrated with reference to the notion of *gestalt*. A gestalt is often treated as a static entity or object. Its theoretical foundation, however, ties in with the notion of *self-organization*. W. Köhler writes: "wherever a process dynamically distributes and regulates itself, determined by the actual situation in a whole field, this process is said to follow principles of *gestalttheorie*."[24]

---

[20] [v. Uexküll, 1957]

[21] Cf. [Eigen and Schuster, 1979, Eigen et al., 1981, Eigen, 1987].

[22] See the selected articles in [v. Foerster, 1985] and Chap. 3.1.

[23] A more detailed account is given in [Keil-Slawik, 1990].

[24] [Köhler, 1935, p. 201]

A gestalt emerges when certain objects or phenomena in the environment are related to each other in a meaningful way. Unrelated physical stimuli are organized to form a coherent whole which can be distinguished from other wholes. The relation or organization as such is not present as a physical stimulus – the perceived gestalt is a construction of the observer. In general, it can be said that we perceive the world by constructing meaningful relations (gestalten). Consequently, we can only perceive what we construct.

However, these constructions are by no means arbitrary, and often not even the individual choice of the observer. The way we relate certain distinct physical stimuli to each other may be part of our subconscious body processes, i.e., fixed action schemes which we cannot influence by our will. The so-called Kanisza triangles[25] for instance, are *virtual* contours, i.e., they have the power to invoke this gestalt, and have been created to serve exactly this purpose. Why this is possible becomes apparent when we acknowledge that as human beings we have a common history and act with the same bodily means in a common environment. Hence, what is a well-adapted perceptual structure for one individual may serve the same need for any other. And what has proved to be useful in an evolutionary process may become some sort of embodied standard repertoire which does not need to be constantly learnt afresh by every individual.

Selection implies that there is a trade-off: we gain effectiveness by being able to react immediately, but pay for this with a loss of flexibility. An optical illusion, for instance, does not disappear when we know that it is one. But we can transcend this limitation. We are able to recognize an illusion through our action, by changing some part of the context and observing how these changes affect our perception of the phenomenon. We provide the required variation through our activities. As J.J. Gibson has pointed out, it is through our action that we can distinguish between what is imagined and what is real, because every close examination of real objects provides new information, reveals new features and details. A mental examination of an imagined object cannot pass this test[26].

Through our activities we are able to create ever new meaningful relations and develop cognitive structures aimed at increasing our ability to relate to the environment such that we can satisfy our needs and pursue our goals in a more flexible manner. A new cognitive structure that is formed neither by imitation nor by trial and error[27] has been called *insight* by the gestalt psychologists, and the process is called *insightful learning* [28].

Insights can be characterized as a restructuring of the perceptual field. For instance, once an ape has come to realize that boxes can be stacked on top of each other or two sticks put together to get a banana which would otherwise be out of reach, it is capable of applying this solution repeatedly, without any hesitation and to any kinds of objects which can be stacked or put together in

---

[25] Cf. [Rock, 1984].

[26] Cf. [Gibson, 1979]. A more elaborate discussion of human action as a validation criterion for reality is given by A. Raeithel in Chap. 8.4.

[27] It should be noted, however, that productive thinking can only take place when all these forms of learning act together.

[28] A brief description can be found in [Hilgard and Bower, 1966, pp. 229–263].

any similar situation. What has been learned by the ape is not how to stack specific boxes, but the general relation that boxes can be arranged on top of each other so as to enable it to climb up and get what it wants.

The same holds for human learning: the meaning of a form – the gestalt – is a construction of the observer. Consequently, it is not the environment that changes, but the way an individual relates the objects and phenomena in its environment to each other to form a meaningful whole – a gestalt, an organization, an architecture, or whatever.

Once an insight has emerged, we have not created yet another cognitive structure, but have revised, modified or enhanced the way we relate the things in our environment to each other. The new cognitive structure supersedes the old one[29]. Hence, gaining experience, learning to better adapt to the environment in order to achieve a goal or to satisfy a need, is not merely a matter of storing more and more cognitive structures in the same way as data is stored in a computer. And problem-solving is not a question of finding an internally stored structure that matches the problem structure. If this were the case, it would take longer and longer to search for the appropriate structure, the more experienced we were. Eventually, we would be unable to react at all; evolution would be a dead end.

Instead, the reverse is the case: the more expert we become in a particular domain, the faster we are able to identify a problem and the closer we come with our first 'guess' to the final solution. This ability is the result of an evolutionary process. Knowledge is historical in the sense that we can only make it explicit and communicate about it properly if we are able to study the learning process which established this knowledge, i.e., the way the individual being related to its environment in its complete course of events[30]. Since we are unable to make such knowledge explicit by expressing it in terms of our actual environment and how we relate the entities (which include, of course, symbolic representations) in this environment to each other, we characterize it as a different kind of knowledge. Basically, it can be characterized as the difference between *knowledge* and *competence* (or *skill*)[31]. In a sense, it can be said that intuition and feeling are our most advanced means of intelligent behaviour[32].

---

[29] This is the same characterization T.S. Kuhn has given (in the addendum of the second edition) to characterize the effect of a paradigm [Kuhn, 1970].

[30] The same holds for biological information. B.-O. Küppers points out that the information embodied in the genes cannot be derived exclusively from the genetic code; it is only given in relation to the environment. In an evolutionary process, it is selectively evaluated against the external information embodied in the environment. Cf. [Küppers, 1983].

[31] Other authors have made this distinction by contrasting different notions, such as *tacit* and *articulate* knowledge [Polanyi, 1967], *knowing that* and *knowing how* [Ryle, 1983], *symbolic reasoning* and *intuition* [Dreyfus, 1979], or by referring to the *paradigmatic* and the *narrative* modes of thought [Bruner, 1984].

[32] On the role of intuition see [Dreyfus and Dreyfus, 1986] and, with respect to software development, [Naur, 1985a].

To sum up: although we characterize an insight in terms of a specific relation of objects or phenomena in the environment, it is always the construction of an individual person. Strictly speaking, knowledge and meaning are neither qualities of the external world, nor are they stored in our brain in the same way as data is stored in a computer. Knowledge and meaning are the ways we relate to our environment. Since they are constituted as self-organizing processes, the creation of knowledge or meaning can neither be controlled nor prescribed. And there is no direct way of transporting meaning or information, giving it to another person as one hands over an artifact, a book or a technical drawing. We can only provide an environment in which the entities that have to be related to each other are present in the perceptual field or within reach.

However, merely relating things in our environment to each other in a specific way does not allow us to transcend the constraints imposed by the given environment and the restrictions of our bodily capabilities.

Artifacts as external memory

To perform so-called mental operations, we are much more dependent on our physical environment, and consequently on our bodily actions, than is generally acknowledged. Our perceptual faculties, for instance, are quite limited. By direct perception, i.e., without starting a counting or calculation process, we can only distinguish up to four items. As G. Ifrah points out, all additive numbering schemes (symbolic representations of the tally system) of different cultures introduce a new symbol by the fifth position at the latest[33]. This allows us to group the symbols on a higher level, thus enabling us to perceive greater numbers more easily under the same perceptual constraints.

Almost every calculation or counting process, however, requires the use of perceivable physical means, be they visible symbols or tangible objects. To begin with, a tally or small calculating stones were used, later on the abacus, the Indian decimal number system (IDNS), and finally algebraic formalisms, Turing machines, formal languages, etc. The word calculus, for instance, stems from the greek calculi which means *chalk pebble*. And the notion of a formal *language* is, according to S. Krämer, already misleading. What mathematicians and computer scientists develop and work with are, strictly speaking, formal *typographies*[34].

The modifications of the physical appearance (states) of artifacts – such as the positions of the pebbles on a calculating board, the marks on a tally or symbols on paper – are an indispensable part of our mental activities. The states of a tool, as well as the calculations performed with a pencil on paper, serve as an external memory which allows us to check the (interim) results, and to reflect on the process as such. Calculating reliably on an abacus, for instance, becomes increasingly cumbersome, the greater the numbers are. Without *storing* intermediate results, i.e., making them perceptible beyond the performing act, checking may become impossible because, with every calculation, the previously

---

[33] [Ifrah, 1987, pp. 169–183]
[34] [Krämer, 1988, pp. 176–183]

achieved result will be destroyed. The only way to check a calculation is to store the result and compare it with another calculation. This problem changes with the introduction of (formal) typographies such as the Indian decimal number system.

When we perform an arithmetic calculation with pencil and paper, we spatially arrange digits on the paper in a systematic fashion to form numbers and columns of numbers representing intermediate results. Where necessary, symbolic operators are inserted. Once we have these physical traces of the process, it is possible to discover structural relations and invariants by relating different calculations to each other. At the end of the 16th century, the invention of algebra and, parallel to this, the construction of the first calculating machines served to represent the then accomplished gestalten and insights by physical means. Both, the replacement of numbers by letters as well as by gears, shafts and cogwheels, are physical embodiments of a relation which formerly had to be established by the human mind for every single calculation.

Now, it is possible to reason on the level of structural relations and make the respective consequences visible. The commutative law, for instance, represents an invariant of the calculation process and can be visualized in the written form:

$$a + b = b + a$$

This expression asserts that the equation holds for all possible instances of a and b within a given mathematical framework. By defining operations that preserve the validity of an equation, this kind of physical representation and its respective operations of generating and arranging symbols in a specific way open up a new realm of thinking. With the invention of boolean algebra, for instance, it became possible to calculate logical deductions.

Finally, a concept such as the Turing machine provides the means to represent the physical operations of transforming and arranging the symbols according to an explicitly given set of rules in the same symbolic medium. Once we are able to describe the symbol manipulation operations as a composition of elementary (atomic) symbol transformation processes, this sequence of transformations can be performed by a machine composed of elementary mechanisms resembling the atomic symbol transformations.

What is replaced by the machine, however, are not the mental activities of forming meaningful relations, i.e., the creation of gestalten, but the physical operations that modify the appearance of the respective artifacts. Once we can describe the invariants of the physical transformation processes that are part of our mental activities, we can try to devise more efficient means to express and technically accomplish the corresponding state transformations.

According to A. Leroi-Gourhan, it can be generally said that the evolution of the human mind is basically the evolution of its expressive means[35]. These expressive means or artifacts embody a new quality. As the result of insightful learning, they are more than the sum of their parts. Neither the invention of zero nor that of the bow and arrow could have been achieved by imitating

---

[35] Cf. [Leroi-Gourhan, 1988].

something which already existed. And there was no sequence of development steps or interim results that enabled the artifact to be deduced systematically.

Again, the notion of external memory is crucial to communication and learning. One essential difference between animals and human beings is not the construction of tools – that animals do as well – but their preservation. This is essential, because only then does it become possible to compare a previously built tool with a new one, to communicate about tools, and to use them as a means for education. All these aspects are essential prerequisites for making progress in the design of new tools. There is no straightforward way to derive a tool which will satisfy a certain need merely by individually performing internal mental activities.

So far, I have emphasized that, owing to their physical nature, artifacts function as external memory, thus facilitating communication and learning. They evolve as part of a functional circle which I have characterized as a process of selective self-organization on various levels, ranging from individual problem-solving through cooperative learning to the evolution of culture. As I have mentioned before, selection implies evaluating a trade-off. I will now discuss this trade-off function in order to identify the features of an artifact that provide the selective advantage.

Flexibility versus iconicity

Two subsections earlier, I have given an example of a trade-off function with respect to embodying human capabilities – for instance, organizing physically unrelated stimuli as action schemes. Such schemes cannot be influenced or controlled intentionally; greater effectiveness is paid for by a loss of flexibility. One could say that, in an evolutionary process, these schemes represent the memory, preserving stereotype behaviour, i.e., fixed action schemes that have proved successful in the sense of leading to a selective advantage in the past.

However, there is only a pay-off as long as the meaning of the scheme is fixed. With respect to the functional circle, this implies that the environment does not provide unanticipated events that would require changing the action sequence embodied in the scheme. If this happens, such an action scheme would lead to erroneous behaviour that might have serious consequences for the individual. But if, as I have pointed out, these schemes are embodied in a more flexible framework of learning, they will enhance the overall flexibility. When they are part of an individual's response to changing environmental conditions, they reduce the amount of cognitive effort required for controlling and performing the overall action, thus freeing the human mind to concentrate on the change pattern. In general, they decrease our dependence on environmental conditions because they give us free time which the human mind can use to develop artifacts. And this – besides offering the already mentioned advantages – may also help us to transcend the limitations and constraints imposed by the inflexibility of these schemes.

If we now view artifacts as the (external) memory of our cultural evolution, we will find that they serve the same purpose. With every new artifact – from the tally to the abacus, the Indian decimal number system, and finally algebra and Turing machines – the sequence of bodily operations required to obtain a result has been reduced. With the tally, every act of making a mark corresponds to the act of counting an object. With the abacus, the spatial arrangement of beads allows us to move one bead into a specific position to replace the respective number of counting acts. The sequentialization of the counting process is reduced by introducing a new spatial structure. With the symbolic representation of numbers, the handling of any number of one to nine beads is reduced to the manipulation of one single symbol (digit). This also allows us to represent the concept of zero as a physical symbol like any other number. Finally, with the invention of algebra it becomes possible to embody the structural properties of an infinite number of calculations in terms of a single symbolic description. By expressing these structural properties through physical forces, it becomes possible to mechanize and later – with the invention of Turing machines and computers – to automate them, i.e., to perform a calculation by pushing a button.

As a result, more powerful operations can be performed in less time, with greater flexibility and reliability. But there is also a new quality: enforced or prescribed sequences of operations that do not allow us to create a gestalt, but which nevertheless have to be performed, are condensed into single objects or operations that can now be flexibly arranged anew and related to each other to form new gestalten or insights. In this sense, the selective advantage in the evolution of artifacts is that prescriptive temporal structures are dissolved by creating physical objects and corresponding spatial structures, or – in more abstract terms – by providing a state space that allows us to find out how we have to relate the states to each other to form new meaningful wholes. With respect to human actions, this cultural achievement can be stated as a general guideline for the design of artifacts:

MINIMIZE THE AMOUNT OF ENFORCED SEQUENTIALITY NEEDED
TO ACCOMPLISH A TASK OR SET OF TASKS.

Enforced sequentiality means either that unnecessary actions have to be performed to form a gestalt or embody it with physical means, or that there is a requirement for certain actions to be performed in a given order. Either one impedes the formation of a gestalt.

Consequently, we can say that artifacts that are meant to support learning must put the user in control, i.e., enable him to plan, control and initiate the sequence of state transformations to be performed. In some cases, however, we may also learn something by following a given sequence such as is imposed by imitation[36]. The individuals still have to create the meaning, but they choose not to control the state transformation of the external memory. This may help stimulate unanticipated insights, but it is too inflexible to provide general support for the learning process.

---

[36] A prescription only works if the individual is willing to follow it, which again is some kind of imitation. We may put pressure on individuals to enforce such a decision, but we cannot enforce insights.

The same holds on the symbolic level: the notion corresponding to imitation is iconicity. We speak of iconicity when the pronunciation of a bird's name closely resembles the sound of its voice, as in the case of the cuckoo. Another more widespread example is the use of icons or pictograms representing an image of the object they denote. Pictograms may promote understanding by referring to an already known visual gestalt, but they do not provide sufficient flexibility for creating new meanings and embodying them in physical means. Thus, part of our cultural development has been the shift from pictorial expressions to languages based on an alphabet consisting of arbitrarily chosen symbols.

This is the price we invariably have to pay for flexibility, namely, that the artifacts we employ become less and less meaningful in the sense that the degree of iconicity is reduced. Each mark on a tally, for instance, represents a counted object. This is no longer the case when arranging beads in a two-dimensional structure by using a calculating board or an abacus. And a digit is of an arbitrary shape that in no way reflects the amount it stands for. Letters in an algebra or cogwheels in a calculating machine dissolve the notion of number and amount even further. And finally, the concept of the Turing machine reduces everything to a sequence of elementary operations by which arbitrarily chosen symbols (the alphabet) are read from and written on to an endless tape.

At every stage in this historical process, the human mind first has to find a way of arranging the visible or tangible objects to form meaningful relations in the specific context of activities. Once we are able to express these relations as perceivable objects by writing down rules and structural expressions, we can perform the physical operations for manipulation in a mechanical way. To obtain the result and to perform the operations, no conscious interpretation is needed, no gestalt has to be established or insight acquired for completion. The operations performed have become meaningless, and they only acquire meaning insofar as they are executed as part of other human activities.

This general view is in accordance with the careful distinction between *data* and *information* as defined by the IFIP[37]. Data can be transmitted and multiplied, but the process which establishes the meaning, i.e., produces the respective information, has to be carried out by every individual anew. Furthermore, data can only be interpreted by establishing conventions and standards. The social processes of defining, revising, applying, reading and teaching such standards and conventions establish a common history among the parties involved; it becomes part of their cultural environment and fosters mutual understanding.

Information, meaning, gestalten or insights are invisible by their very nature and are brought to the surface only through human activity. In order to support this activity, we have to provide artifacts which help us to make the invisible visible[38].

---

[37] A thoughtful account of this definition is given in [Naur, 1974, pp. 18–31]. See also the extensive characterization of information by K. Fuchs-Kittowski in Chap. 8.5.

[38] A. Kay has used the notion of visibility slightly differently, namely, to highlight the difference between the program text (visible) and what will happen during program execution (invisible). Cf. [Kay, 1984].

4.4.4 Designing software

The ecological perspective presented here emphasizes that artifacts are indispensable means for creating meaning and supporting learning and communication. Conversely, the design of a product is basically a process of cooperative learning[39]. To highlight the differences between this and the traditional engineering perspective, I will again use the notion of learning cycles to characterize the research strategy associated with this ecological perspective.

An ecological approach to software development

The basic difference between the ecological and the traditional engineering perspective is that learning cycles *within* software development and use are now acknowledged as primary means for promoting understanding and supporting communication. Its frame of reference is not based on the idea of context-free knowledge that is transferred by the exchange of (design) artifacts, but on the concept of person(s)-acting-in-settings as a specific instance of the functional circle[40]. We can then reconstruct the waterfall model into an ecological model of nested learning cycles as depicted in Fig. 4.4-2.

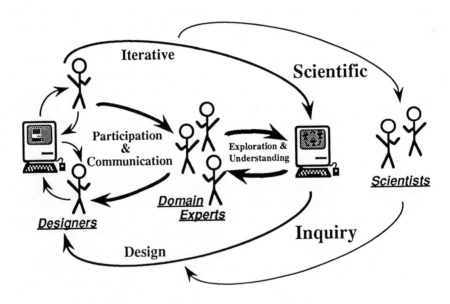

Fig. 4.4-2. The ecological model of nested learning cycles

---

[39] Cf. the definition of design as "the interaction between understanding and creation" in [Winograd and Flores, 1986, p. 4].

[40] This concept has been employed in particular by J. Lave to study and describe *everyday cognition*. See [Lave, 1988] and [Rogoff and Lave, 1984].

In the ecological model, the subjects of study are the processes into which the artifacts are to be embedded, and not the inherent properties of artifacts as isolated entities. To better understand what actually matters in a specific situation and to find better ways and means of supporting the design process, we have to study the human activities of developing and using software.

This is also the basic philosophy underlying the methodological framework STEPS (Software Technology for Evolutionary Participative System development)[41] developed by us at the Technical University of Berlin. In STEPS, it is acknowledged that the quality of software cannot be defined without reference to the development and usage context. This is not only essential for qualitative approaches such as case studies, but for quantitative investigations as well. Software measurements, for instance, can only be understood and interpreted with respect to a specific design setting[42].

The ecological perspective emphasizes that the result of self-organizing processes such as cognition, learning, design, or evolution can only be fully understood by reference to their history. What this means in terms of design is establishing a common history among those who are meant to understand the product. And, since learning and communication are essential for design, a participative development approach is advisable. This requires that the participants are – to a certain extent – able to pursue the matter according to their individual goals, objectives and personal needs. Thus, finding ways of *sharing responsibility*, as explored by G. Bjerknes[43], and developing a *subject-oriented approach*, as does M. Nurminen[44], are not only promising attempts at dealing methodically with the social aspects of design, but also provide ideas on how to improve design of the products.

In his book "Notes on the Synthesis of Form", C. Alexander states: "the ultimate object of design is form". In real-world situations, he points out, the problem with design is that we are trying to invent a form to fit into a context which we do not fully understand. This is especially true of the development of software. Consequently, it is not just a form but a variety of forms which are developed, revised, enhanced, or rejected in the course of software development. Basically, these may comprise the design artifacts which are produced by applying different tools and techniques, prototypes, and eventually the product and its documentation. These forms are related to each other in various ways, and changes in one form have consequences for one or several others. In addition, different people may be responsible for developing and maintaining different forms. Thus, C. Floyd's characterization of design as "a web of design decisions"[45] gives a more appropriate account of the actual process. This web, as it is physically embodied in the design artifacts and products or prototypes, normally changes very dynamically at the beginning, and becomes then more and more stable,

---

[41] An overview is presented in [Floyd et al., 1989b] and [Keil-Slawik, 1987a], see also the contributions of C. Floyd in Chap. 3.2 and M. Reisin in Chap. 7.3.

[42] Cf. [Basili and Perricone, 1984] and, in particular, [Basili and Rombach, 1987].

[43] See Chap. 7.1.

[44] See Chap. 7.2

[45] See Chap. 3.2.

until, at the end of the development process, the final product is released. The general guideline for the development of design artifacts and tools that are meant to support this process is to provide means to embody and maintain the web of design decisions such that the amount of enforced sequentiality is minimized.

On the basis of this view, I will now discuss how this general guideline translates into features and attributes of design artifacts and products.

Improving design

Our task is to devise design artifacts and tools so as to provide sufficient support and sufficient orientation without prescribing the course of actions to be taken. This requires means which allow us to embody gestalten in such a way that they provide a constructive basis for establishing a common understanding of the problems in hand and the desired solution.

Unlike the traditional engineering perspective, where a design artifact is supposed to be unambiguous, consistent, precise, and complete, the general guideline only demands that design artifacts – especially at the beginning of the design process – allow us to embody only those gestalten or items of information which are necessary in the specific situation to continue the (cooperative) learning process – and nothing more. Process-oriented development models[46], prototyping strategies, the development of a project language by establishing a dictionary containing the technical terms of the participants' domain languages – all of these serve this goal, as does the use of *base lines* or *reference lines* instead of phase model milestones[47]. They provide the opportunity to iterate on specifically chosen problem domains or aspects independently and on various levels of detail. In contrast, the phase model approach is transformational: each iterative step comprises the transformation of the whole problem domain.

This difference also applies to the design of products (tools) for the development of design artifacts. A tool may either only accept consistent data records as input, or it may provide a function for checking the consistency or completeness of a specified set of records whenever it seems necessary. The former allows the designer to enter only complete data records that fit into the already developed framework, whereas the latter allows him to store partial results which are not yet consistent, but may nevertheless be useful for exploring the problem.

What all these examples have in common is that they provide means to utilize the external memory to the extent required by the actual needs of the people involved without prescribing the form or structure that should be achieved or the way in which it should be achieved. In the traditional phase model approach, the latter is derived from the structure of the product.

The same idea has been expressed in a slightly different way by D.E. Knuth who has developed a tool called WEB allowing programmers to separate the final structure of the code as required by the programming language from the structure they choose during development to suit their needs and preferences.

---

[46] See [Floyd, 1981, Floyd and Keil, 1983].
[47] See [Andersen et al., 1990, Floyd et al., 1989b].

According to Knuth, the basic idea is to write programs not in order to instruct the machine, but rather to explain to other people what we want the machine to do for us[48]. The point is that now the grouping and sequencing of what forms meaningful wholes in the course of design is left to the designers and their understanding. Thus, the structures as required by the programming language impose less sequencing on their activities.

On a more general level, principles such as *user control*[49] or *minimalist instruction*[50] are design guidelines that serve the same end. And they can be applied to the product as well as to the design of user manuals[51].

As regards development of new products, I wish to point out that the explicit goal of providing support for individual problem-solving and information organization lead to the notion of interactive systems and, eventually, to two basic innovations: hypertext technologies and object-oriented systems. In particular the definition of hypertext as non-sequential text processing explicitly confirms the guideline for reducing enforced sequentiality. Both technologies implement the same basic idea: they allow domain experts to easily embody mentally established relations in physical terms (links, shared code) and build on these embodiments later on. However, besides assessing the essential quality of innovative technologies, the general guideline presented here can also be used to derive more specific design criteria that can be fruitfully applied in the design of use interfaces[52].

4.4.5 Summary

The ecological perspective presented here seeks to provide guidance and orientation in identifying problems and to help direct the search for solutions. It is not meant as a theoretical framework allowing us to deduce or determine the desired properties of either specific design artifacts and products or specific development methods[53]. Nevertheless it does provide some ideas on how to improve the design process.

I have characterized design as a cooperative learning process. The result or outcome of this process cannot be described precisely until the product is finished. The value of any innovation can only be defined once it has been realized and appraised, whether it be a new function or algorithm that is to be implemented, a new method to be used, or a new system to be developed. The same holds for user actions in a learning situation. In a more general sense, it can be said that the meaning of any activity cannot be described precisely until the action has been completed[54].

---

[48] Cf. [Knuth, 1984, Bentley, 1986]; an elaborate example is given in [Knuth, 1986], see also Chap. 1.2.

[49] See W. Dzida, Chap. 7.4.

[50] [Carroll, 1990]

[51] Cf. [Carroll et al., 1987].

[52] A more extensive discussion can be found in [Keil-Slawik, 1990, pp. 47–70].

[53] This substantiates the arguments of J. Carroll in Chapter 4.3.

[54] This is also the central theme in [Weick, 1979].

Since learning is regarded as an evolutionary process of selective self-organization, artifacts that are meant to support this process must provide means to flexibly create and embody gestalten according to the insights acquired by the parties involved. Thus, it is no longer the mathematical attributes of the product that constitute the frame of reference, but the cooperative learning processes that are part of design. Artifacts are viewed as embodying the external memory of human cognitive processes. By studying the evolution of artifacts in a cultural context I was able to derive a general guideline for their design, namely, to minimize enforced sequentiality.

As is the case with all design principles, this guideline can neither be considered in isolation, nor can it simply be optimized along a one-dimensional scale: the more flexible, the better. It is dialectical in its nature because every embodiment of a gestalt – such as the fixation of a problem, the choice of a certain function to be implemented, or a selected module structure – imposes constraints on the subsequent actions and limits the possible choices. On the other hand, without any such fixations no progress could occur. Thus, the crucial question is where and when to draw the line so as to find the right balance between flexibility and stability.

This question can be generally answered by the ethical imperative of H. von Foerster: "Act always so as to increase the number of choices."[55] And this is exactly what should be achieved by minimizing enforced sequentiality. On a practical level, however, it can only be answered with respect to a given context. In the course of developing or employing interactive systems, for instance, this is the analysis of the work environment. However, even then, as I have already pointed out, it is not possible to deduce a solution purely from the needs or requirements. We need the traditional engineering perspective as well. Without the results being produced along these lines, we would not be able to pursue our goals. Every single interactive step, for instance, embraces already a vast amount of formal operations embodying general insights that are invariant with respect to the specific setting or problem – and thus, may not have been derived from the specific context.

Both perspectives – the traditional and the ecological – must be regarded as indispensable for our scientific endeavour. Any practical design activity requires that they be productively combined. Only by their combination can we find appropriate ways of minimizing enforced sequentiality with respect to the development *and* use of software.

Acknowledgements

I would like to thank Christiane Floyd, Rodrigo Botafogo, Kim Halskov Madsen, and Ben Shneiderman for their constructive criticism throughout the various versions of this article. They have been instrumental in shaping my ideas. My thanks also go to Phil Bacon for polishing up the text idiomatically and stylistically.

---

[55] [v. Foerster, 1984, p. 308]

Part 5

Computer Science and Beyond

bintree-base =

     sorts: alphabet
              bintree

     opns: $K1,...,Kn: \rightarrow$ alphabet
              LEAF: alphabet $\rightarrow$ bintree
              LEFT: bintree alphabet $\rightarrow$ bintree
              RIGHT: alphabet bintree $\rightarrow$ bintree
              BOTH: bintree alphabet bintree $\rightarrow$ bintree

Heinz

So this is where we find the thinker supplanted in the first illustration – studying computer science. He is becoming a master of the art of building abstract models.

Reinhard B.

The mathematician sets out to express reality in terms of formal, largely context-free models. The mathematical notion of truth pertains to their internal consistency and correctness.

Christiane

For the engineer, models are related to specific purposes. Accuracy, suitability, testability – these are the criteria that are applied to models.

Reinhard K.-S.

But we also know that such models are set against a human background. On one hand, they embody the interests as well as the insights of the people involved. On the other hand, they are re-interpreted wherever they are used.

Heinz

The models we build for software development have an interesting constructivist aspect as well. By our very analysis of reality we are intervening in this reality.

Christiane

Computer science, traditionally, aims at reflecting reality. But, we must aware that we cannot live up to this claim. Owing to the inherent selectivity of our formalisms, we are only capable of building distorting mirrors, highlighting certain facets of reality and eclipsing others.

Reinhard K.-S.

We are all familiar with the elegance of the upside-down trees used in computer science. We must find ways, though, to properly implant the systems developed by us into their social context.

Christiane

And the cyberneticians' popular adage "data sunt capta" may be of help to us here. It means that we should not view the information we collect during systems analysis as "data" – given to us – but rather as "capta" – seized by us.

Reinhard B.

This leads us on directly to the contributions that go to make up this part of our book. Joseph Goguen, a theoretician in the field of formal specification, demonstrates the limits of formalization and the omnipresence of error. What he has to say sets the scene, as it were, for a critical appraisal and further development of computer science.

Heinz

Heinz Klein and Kalle Lyytinen's contribution translates the "data sunt capta" adage into more concrete terms, illustrating the distorted images of traditional data modelling and proposing ways of minimizing such distortions as are inevitable. The analytical part of their reflections is of particular importance for us as software developers, having to wrestle as we do with the same difficulties in requirements analysis.

Christiane

And, presumably, we should find similar abysses concealed beneath each ostensibly well-defined area of computer science. On closer scrutiny, we find accepted concepts to be hollow; what appear to be established facts turn out to be merely adopted conventions; basic assumptions need questioning. Our work as both scientists and practitioners does not stand on firm ground but on our own constructions. It is a social process borne along by us, like a dance unfolding from nowhere.

Reinhard B.

Pentti Kerola and Jouni Similä discuss the way computer science sees itself as a discipline. They show how discussions about a paradigm change in computer science already have a tradition in the countries of Northern Europe. The different interpretations of the notion of Information Science give a good idea of the variety of approaches being pursued by the different schools of thought in these countries.

Reinhard K.-S.

The chapters included in this part take up many of the ideas – formulated in more theoretical terms in the previous parts – on human learning and communication processes and on the interlacement of practical action with theoretical reflection.

Heinz

One point they fail to address is our call – in line with the holistic principle – for an artistic view of the world to take its place alongside those governed by practical action and theoretical analysis.

There is much talk today about the beauty of fractals and computer graphics. What is lacking, in my eyes, is a look at other aesthetic dimensions of computer science – from the elegance of algorithms to the aesthetics of system interfaces and computer art as an independent field.

Christiane

At all events, this part of the book contains a draft for a self-critique and a process of self-reflection by computer science as a discipline. This must be complemented by an enrichment of computer science's domain of discourse and methodology so as to include consideration of the interactions between humans and artifacts.

5.1 The Denial of Error

Joseph A. Goguen

5.1.1 Introduction

This paper claims that the modern world has developed a kind of arrogance which is damaging the very projects that it seeks to sustain: in proposing methodologies to guarantee the absence of error, we deny the incredible richness of our own experience, in which confusion and error are often the seeds of creation; in this way, we limit our own creativity.

This arrogance is not an isolated phenomenon that is found only in computer science. Indeed, I claim that it arises in a natural way from our preoccupation with and immersion in science and technology, which are strongly oriented toward *control*. The obsession of Western culture with control can be seen in many different areas, including the following:

1. In *myth*; for example, if you know a demon's name, then you can control its behavior (we may relate this to the phrase "knowledge is power").
2. In *science*, which is based upon the idea of the controlled experiment (this is control of the intellectual process, rather than of its result).
3. In our theories of *behavior*; for example, the psychiatrist Ernest Becker has said that "All social life is the obsessive ritualization of control"[1]; see also point 5. below.
4. In *technology*, which seeks to control nature through the application of science, as discussed in more detail later in this paper.
5. In our theories of *information* and *knowledge*; for example, in the "Representational Theory of Meaning", which says that our minds contain representations of external "objects", or in current Cognitive Science theories which posit explicit goals to control behavior, in the same way for both machines and humans[2].

Aspects of the viewpoint common to these items have been called "instrumentality", "teleology", "rationalism", "selfishness", "objectivity", "analysis", "subjectivism", "ego", "positivism" and "conceptualism", depending on the author and the context. The obsession with control is also one aspect of what has come to be called "modernism".

The *denial of error*, that is, the denial of deviation from announced goals, seems to be closely associated with the attempt to maintain control, especially for phenomena that are actually difficult or even impossible, to control. For example, consider the economy of a country, especially one that is highly collectivized.

---

[1] See [Becker, 1973]
[2] See Sect. 5.1.2 below.

The history of science contains many instances of accidental discoveries, for example, that of penicillin. These are often taken as surprising, embarrassing, or amusing, but they actually point to a serious and important facet of scientific knowledge, indeed of all knowledge: its basis is the free play of the mind against the unexpectedly rich worlds revealed within each real situation. The following quotation from Heidegger[3] may be relevant:

> The area, as it were, which opens in the interwovenness of being, un-concealment, and appearance – this area I understand as *error*. Appearance, deception, illusion, error stand in definite essential and dynamic relations which have long been misinterpreted by psychology and epistemology and which consequently, in our daily lives, we have wellneigh ceased to experience and recognize as powers.

Formalism is also a form of control: it attempts to control the use of language, and through that, to control behavior. The tighter and more rigorous the formalism, i.e., the more circumscribed its syntax and semantics, the smaller the domain to which it is applicable. The ultimate in this development may be the attempts of mathematical logic[4] to formally capture the notion of *Truth*; yet the manipulation of uninterpreted tautologies literally tells us nothing, about nothing[5].

Section 5.1.2 below attempts to describe the essence of modern science and technology, loosely based on ideas of late Heidegger, and illustrated with some quotations from Bacon and Newell. Section 5.1.3 discusses the goal of error-free programming, using some work of Dijkstra as an example. Section 5.1.4 considers the goals of software quality, using U.S. Department of Defense procurement procedures as an illustration. Finally, Section 5.1.5 suggests that software development projects could be considered holistically, using some ideas from the so-called New Biology.

5.1.2 Science and technology

At the dawn of modern science, Francis Bacon was obsessed with the concept of what we now call an experiment, using what now seem rather extreme metaphors of torture and the inquisition[6]:

> ... if any expert Minister of Nature shall encounter Matter by mainforce, vexing[7] and urging her with intent and purpose to reduce her to nothing; she contrariwise ... being thus caught in the straits of necessity, doth

---

[3] See [Heidegger, 1959].

[4] For example [Tarski, 1944].

[5] See Chap. 8.1 for some further discussion of meaning, truth and logic along these lines.

[6] [Bacon, 1968]

[7] At the time of this translation, "vex" had much more the connotation of torture, from the Latin *vexare*.

change and turn herself into diverse strange forms of things. ... the reason
of which constraint or binding will be more facile and expedite, if matter
be laid hold on by Manacles, that is by extremities.

Today, this language seems a bit shocking, and of course, no reputable contemporary scientist would want to sound quite so gleefully sadistic about his
work. But perhaps we should give Bacon credit for a degree of honesty that has
been lost to us, as the passage of time has dulled our sense of surprise at the
methods of science and technology. For scientific experiments on animals can be
quite gruesome, and technology has much to answer for in its destruction of the
environment.

The fundamental problem here is not that there are some isolated, unfortunate incidents (e.g., strip mining in the Brazilian rainforest), nor even that there
are potential massive dislocations looming on the horizon, such as the effects of
global warming and deforestation. Rather, the fundamental problem is that man
has come to view nature as a "resource", as something to be used, for his con-
venience and comfort, or against his enemies, or to enhance his prestige through
the acquisition of knowledge. As Heidegger[8] says,

> The hydroelectric plant is not built into the Rhine River as was the
> old wooden bridge that joined bank with bank for hundreds of years.
> Rather, the river is dammed up into the power plant. What the river
> is now, namely, a water-power supplier, derives from the essence of the
> power station. In order that we may even remotely appreciate the mon-
> strousness that reigns here, let us ponder for a moment the contrast that
> is spoken by the two titles: "The Rhine" as dammed up into the *power*
> works, and "The Rhine" as uttered by the *art* work, in Hölderlin's hymn
> by that name. But, it will be replied, the Rhine is still a river in the
> landscape, is it not? Perhaps. But how? In no other way than as an ob-
> ject on call for inspection by a tour group ordered there by the vacation
> industry.

In this way, we lose the capacity to be in the world with a sense of harmony, joy,
or wonder.

The dark edge to science, so clear in the writing of Bacon, has to do with this
fundamental alienation, that is, with man's will to what Bacon called "Dominion
over the Universe", more than it has to do with the subject/object split, or with
any particular difficulties. Bacon was as much the prophet of technology as he
was of science. Let us listen to Heidegger[9] again:

> Today science is admonished to serve the nation, and that is a very nec-
> essary and estimable demand[10], but it is too little and not the essential.
> The hidden will to refashion the essent into the manifestness of its being
> demands more. In order to recapture the pristine knowledge that has

---

[8] See [Heidegger, 1977c].

[9] See [Heidegger, 1959].

[10] Note that in this 1935 passage, "the nation" refers to Nazi Germany!

degenerated into science, our being-there must attain a very different metaphysical depth. It must again achieve an established and truly built relation to the being of the essent as a whole.

Let us now consider an example closer to home, from Artificial Intelligence. Allen Newell[11] proposes a theory of mind based on what he calls a "physical symbol system", which is essentially an automaton, that is, a (mathematical) machine, intended to model the use of symbols. Newell claims that this notion is "the most fundamental contribution so far of Artificial Intelligence and Computer Science to the joint enterprise of Cognitive Science", and that it is "what the theory of evolution is to all biology, the cell doctrine to cellular biology, the notion of germs to the scientific concept of disease, the notion of tectonic plates to structural geology", namely, it is (he hypothesizes) "adequate to all symbolic activity this physical universe of ours can exhibit, and in particular to all symbolic activities of the human mind". The basic definition of "symbolization" is as follows[12]:

An entity X *designates* an entity Y relative to a process P, if, when P takes X as input, its behavior depends on Y.

In this case, X is a *symbol* for Y. I do not wish to dwell on how this definition is too permissive for many applications to science, nor on how it radically excludes most of the symbolism that is important in the arts, humanities and religion, nor on the arrogance of attempting to reduce symbolism in general to causality, but rather, I wish to relate this theory to the themes of control and error which are central to the present paper. Newell says,

A general intelligent system must somehow embody aspects of what is to be attained prior to the attainment of it, i.e., it must have *goals*. ...
A general intelligent system must somehow consider candidate states of affairs (and partial states) for the solutions of these goals (leading to the familiar search trees).

But in order to use the familiar method of search trees, one must not only have a goal that is fixed in advance, but one must also be able to enumerate the possible solutions. Thus, we are dealing here with a form of top-down control that is even less flexible than feedback control, and less able to deal with errors. Thus, despite Newell's desire that his ideal physical symbol system should "behave robustly in the face of error" and "learn from its environment", it is far from clear that it could do so with anything like human intelligence; in particular, it is unclear how it could devise entirely new conceptual organizations in response to its errors, let alone learn such things as compassion.

I do not believe that rigidly mechanistic models, with top-down goal structures, are adequate for explaining human cognition, nor even for explaining how to do science. Although this approach is characteristic of "modern" explanations of science, from the seventeenth century into the twentieth – the so-called

---

[11] In [Newell, 1980].
[12] Ibid.

"Received View" – there is an emerging "post modern" view of science and technology which advocates more flexible organizations, less rigid logics, and more natural control structures. Examples include the so-called New Biology of Bateson, Maturana, Varela and others[13], hermeneutics and other movements in linguistics and philosophy[14], and fuzzy logic and fuzzy control[15]. Within computing, neural nets, highly distributed and open systems, and hypermedia and hyperprogramming may also fit this emerging paradigm.

5.1.3 Error-free programming

What we may call the "Dijkstra School" aims for error-free programming. For example, Djikstra claims that

> we have ... "a calculus" for a formal discipline – a set of rules – such that, if applied successfully: (1) it will have derived a correct program; and (2) it will tell us that we have reached such a goal.[16]

From a narrow point of view, Dijkstra achieves its aim, modulo certain technical difficulties[17]. But its fundamental difficulty is that it attempts to control the programming process by imposing a rigid top-down derivation sequence, working backwards from the initial top-level specification (the "postcondition") to the final code, in which each step is derived by applying a "weakest precondition" (hereafter, "wp") formula.

Perhaps not unexpectedly, this "wp calculus" requires significant human "invention" at exactly the most difficult points, namely the loops. And for most programs that go much beyond the trivial, the insights needed to write the loop invariants are tantamount to already knowing how to write the program; moreover, these insights are more difficult to achieve in the wp context than they would be in a more operational context. Indeed, I have seen good students who had been taught that the wp calculus was the right way to program, become so discouraged over the difficulties that they experienced, that they came to believe that they could never learn how to program and should therefore seek some other profession! In general, such a rigid, top-down ideology inhibits experimentation, the exploration of tradeoffs, accidental discoveries, and so on. Moreover, it can be harmful to students, wasteful of time, reinforcing of an inflexible view of life, and inhibiting to intuition and creativity.

---

[13] See the discussion in Sect. 5.1.5 below.

[14] Again, see Sect. 5.1.5.

[15] For example [Goguen, 1969, Pedrycz, 1989].

[16] [Dijkstra, 1975]

[17] These include the following: (1) there is a gap in the logical foundations, in that the first-order logic used for expressing conditions is not actually sufficiently expressive – something like the infinitary logic proposed by Erwin Engeler in the 1960s is needed; (2) many important programming features are not treated, including procedures, blocks, modules, and objects – in general, all large-grain features are omitted; and (3) data structures, types, variables that range over programs, and variables that range over specifications are all treated in a loose manner.

But we must not get carried away with criticism: It is not that the wp calculus is entirely mistaken or useless, but rather that claims have been made for it that do not take adequate account of its limitations. For example, the wp calculus can be very useful in getting initializations right (many real bugs arise at this point), as well as for simple loops, and I have also found it useful in convincing students that coding can be treated with mathematical precision. Moreover, Dijkstra's *style* is very elegant and careful, his examples are very well chosen, and personally I admire and have learned from these qualities. However, it seems very difficult to scale up Dijkstra's approach beyond programs of more than a few dozen lines.

Let me be clear that I am not criticizing formal methods as such – in fact, I believe that they can be very useful in practice, *especially* for large programs[18], and have myself done research in this area[19] – rather, I am criticizing the tendency to apply formal methods in a rigid, top-down hierarchical manner. In fact, I believe that if appropriate formal methods are used in a flexible, non-ideological way, they can lead to better programs, with greater efficiency and fewer bugs.

But bugs are inevitable. If they don't occur in coding, they will appear in design, specification, requirements, or use; they may arise by misinterpretation of what the customer says, by inadequate modelling of the situation in which the program must run, by inadequate documentation or understanding of the tools being used (such as a compiler for a high-level language), and in many other ways.[20]

Of course, no one wants bugs, or wants to spend any more time than necessary on debugging, because it is difficult and unpleasant. But nevertheless, bugs are interesting and important in themselves: they define the boundary between what is understood and what is not. Hence, they show us where our weaknesses are, and provide opportunities for us to learn and grow.

5.1.4 Software quality

The Brooks Report[21] notes that the procurement process generally used by the U.S. Department of Defense for large software systems is inappropriate for such systems (although they might be reasonable for buying boots, hats, or even rifles): bids are invited on a contract to build a system that meets a given "requirements document", which tends to be excessively elaborate, specific, and

---

[18] This can be achieved by providing formal specification for the *interfaces* between program components, thus greatly enhancing the accuracy of communication between different groups working on different components, and providing a "fire wall" to protect each group from purely internal changes made by other groups. Also, sufficiently powerful mechanisms for parameterization and modularization can greatly improve the reuse of both code and specifications.

[19] [Goguen, 1986, Goguen and Meseguer, 1987]

[20] An overview of some recent debates on the philosophical foundations of formal methods is given in [Barwise, 1989].

[21] [Brooks, 1987b]

optimistic. There is also a tendency for lower bids to win, whether or not they are realistic; and once the contract is let, large cost over-runs are common.

It is important to note that we are *not* talking here just about the processes used internally by a software vendor, but rather about the procurement process *as a whole*, including those processes internal to the *client* as well as those internal to vendor(s), and of course those processes of communication that occur on the interfaces among them. It is convenient to use the terminology of *process models* in this discussion, even though it was originally developed to describe just vendor processes[22]. To be more precise now, it is the government processes of requirements generation and procurement that are rigidly top-down, based on assumptions formalized in the linear structure of a so-called *stagewise model*, which says that a software development project begins with requirements, which then "fall" without essential error into specifications and finally into code. Once the processes internal to a vendor are reached, it is not unusual to see a more sophisticated process models in use, at least a so-called *waterfall model*, which allows feedback between contiguous stages, and perhaps also a single (non-rapid) prototype, or even a *spiral model*[23], which can be sufficiently adaptive to be considered a meta-process model. (Also, note that software procurement is generally less rigid in the commercial sector than in the government sector.) All this suggests that an important topic for further research might be the development of *multi-party* process models, which would allow for different processes within different parties, and for multi-stage interaction between parties.

For large, complex systems, especially if they are unlike anything previously constructed, we can hardly expect to know what is possible or impossible, what is adequate or inadequate, what is expensive or inexpensive, or more generally, what are the design tradeoffs for that class of system. Moreover, it has been found far more expensive to correct errors during the maintenance stage than during earlier stages (by up to a factor of 100)[24].

Thus, it would seem very desirable to debug requirements until they reflect a reasonable compromise between what users want and what is achievable within reasonable cost. The Brooks Report[25] suggests that integrating rapid prototyping with the procurement process might achieve this goal, and thus save vast amounts of time and money. It could also lead to discovering useful capabilities not anticipated in the original requirements document, which are nonetheless relatively easy to provide. It seems very reasonable to suppose that some such more adaptive approach could yield better results than trying to control the entire process of production in advance of exploring the basic pitfalls and tradeoffs that are involved.

The failure of U.S. Government procurement processes to acknowledge the possibility of error in setting requirements is a shocking example of arrogant teleological thinking run wild; even some crude form of feedback control would

---

[22] See [Boehm, 1988] for an overview of this field.

[23] [Boehm, 1988]

[24] Cf. [Boehm, 1981].

[25] [Brooks, 1987b]

be an improvement, and it is amazing that large Department of Defense systems come close to working correctly as often as they seem to.

I think it is fair to say that Software Engineering is presently more like a medieval craft than it is like a modern engineering discipline. This is because modern technology[26] involves the construction of causal calculative theories, and we are only now beginning to develop such theories for Software Engineering. In particular, the relatively neglected, and sometimes maligned, field of formal methods is still at an early stage of development. A promising approach, I believe, is to integrate formal methods with software process models in a way that better supports flexibility and adaptation, rather than mere competition and control.

It may be that such revolutionary techniques as hyperprogramming[27], which involve the multimedia exploration of program structure by visualization and explanation, based on technology developed for formal specification and verification, can be developed to the point where they can be used in a routine way.

What is crucial is to provide environments for software development in which the overall *vision* of the program can be clearly felt at all times, and used flexibly in organizing the programming task. Such a vision is not at all the same thing as a top-down hierarchically structured system of goals, but rather should have an adaptive living quality, in roughly the sense discussed in the next section.

5.1.5 The being of software development projects

Anyone familiar with multi-person software development projects knows that there is a sense in which such projects "have a life of their own": some projects seem healthy and vibrant from the start, and overcome even unexpected obstacles with enthusiasm and intelligence, while others always seem to be disorganized and depressed, suffering, for example, from such symptoms as unrealistic goals, inadequate equipment, poor planning, (seemingly) insufficient funding, faulty communication, indecisive leadership, frequent reorganizations, and/or deep rifts between internal factions.

A software development project is not primarily a formal mathematical entity. Perhaps it is best seen as a *dialogical* or *linguistic* process, an evolving organization of certain informational structures, continually recreating itself by building, modifying, and reusing these structures. In the language of Maturana, this might be described as "development through mutually recursive interactions among structurally plastic systems"[28].

In this view, computers, printouts, compilers, editors, design tools, and even programmers, can be seen as supporting substrates, just as body parts are sup-

---

[26] See [Heidegger, 1977c].
[27] [Goguen, 1990]
[28] See [Maturana, 1978].

porting substrates for a person[29]. Maturana and Varela[30] define an *autopoietic system* to be

> ... a network of processes of production of components that produces the components that: (i) through their interactions and transformations continuously regenerate the network of processes that produced them; and (ii) constitute it as a concrete unity in the space in which they exist by specifying the topological domain of its realization as such a network.

For example, an unhealthy project may struggle for survival by reassigning responsibilities, redefining subprojects, and even trying to reconstrue the conditions that define its success. On the other hand, a healthy project may develop new tools to enhance its own productivity[31].

Autopoietic systems are about as far as we know how to get from rigid top-down hierarchical goal-driven control systems; autopoietic systems thrive on error, and reconstruct themselves on the basis of what they learn from their mistakes. Since organizations naturally strive for their own survival, it would seem natural to study autopoietic software process models.

It is interesting to notice that the discourse which is the life blood of a software project is conducted in a variety of languages, which differ in both their level of abstraction and in their degree of formality. Most discussions are conducted in a kind of pigeon natural language, infused with technical terms and technical ways of thinking. But there are also requirements documents, designs (which may involve graphics), specifications, code, and much more.

I believe that a promising research direction is to apply techniques from hermeneutics to the "softer" areas of the software development process, and particularly to the so-called "requirements acquisition" phase, in which an analyst attempts to determine what the customer really wants. Hermeneutics is concerned with the interpretation of "texts" in a very broad sense which can include programs, dialogues, contracts, live interaction, specifications, history files, proofs, and so on. Another promising application of hermeneutics might be to study the social dynamics of the entire life cycle, or of selected parts of it[32].

5.1.6 Conclusions

Important avenues for further progress in Software Engineering seem to be blocked by our inadequate understanding of the processes involved in developing software systems. It seems that formal methods, despite their power, are

---

[29] Of course, I do not intend these remarks to imply that the group has moral or spiritual priority over the individual, or that people should be viewed as components of systems in anything like the same way that Ada packages can be.

[30] See [Maturana and Varela, 1980].

[31] See [Bateson, 1980, Thompson, 1987, Maturana, 1978, Maturana and Varela, 1987] for more information, and see [Goguen and Varela, 1979, Varela and Goguen, 1978] for some possibly ill-advised attempts at formalization.

[32] See [Palmer, 1969] for an overview of some theoretical aspects of hermeneutics, and Chap. 2.2 for some further discussion along the lines of this paper.

not applicable to some of the most significant aspects of such processes. But it also seems possible that a better understanding may be attained by using some insights from the New Biology of Bateson, Maturana, Varela and others, and from the hermeneutics of Heidegger, Gadamer, and others. A basic step in this direction is to recognize the important role that error plays in any process of construction. The surprisingly widespread belief that it is both desirable and possible to go from requirements to specification, to code, without making any errors, would seem to be a major inhibiting factor to the successful application of formal methods.

Although formal methods can be very powerful when they are properly applied, they also have definite limitations, and formal, rationalistic understanding is only one of many approaches to understanding. Intuition and spiritual understanding are alternatives that seem more important in certain ways. For example, formal methods will never tell us why the U.S. Department of Defense persists in its manifestly wasteful practices. Nor will they explain the success of object oriented programming.

Some specific proposals for further research mentioned earlier in this paper include: the application of hermeneutic techniques to the software development process, both as a method of study, and also as a specific technique for use in the requirements acquisition phase; the development of multi-party process models; the study of autopoietic process models; and the integration of formal methods with such more "organic" process models, through techniques like hyperprogramming.

By some such route, we might go further than merely recognizing the inevitability of error – we might learn to experience our errors as a path that leads to deeper understandings and to better relationships. We must make the programming process not merely tolerant of error, but also able to *take advantage* of the creative possibilities inherent in the interplay between concept and perception. Until we acknowledge the dialectical, creative, and living dimensions in programming, we shall be doomed to participate in software processes that are unwieldy, unpleasant, and ineffective. The denial of error is the denial of life.

Acknowledgements

I wish to thank my wife Kathleen for assistance with preparing this paper, including reading several drafts, undertaking some library research, and providing many helpful comments and conversations. I would also like to thank both the Naropa Institute in Boulder, Colorado, and the Center for the Study of Language and Information at Stanford University for providing stimulating environments in which to think about the kind of issue discussed here.

5.2 Towards a New Understanding of Data Modelling

Heinz K. Klein and Kalle Lyytinen

This paper reviews the fundamental assumptions of current data modelling approaches in the light of the recent debate on conflicting research paradigms. The following four questions are used to identify paradigmatic assumptions about the ontology, language, epistemology and social context of data modelling: (1) What is being modelled? (2) How well is the result represented? (3) Why is it valid? (4) How are data models used in practice? It is concluded that the pursuit of these four questions amounts to a new research programme in data management and that the appropriate metaphors for data modelling are not fact gathering and modelling, but negotiation and law-making.

5.2.1 Introduction

All system developers approach their work with certain assumptions in mind. In data modelling these assumptions concern the nature of the universe of discourse, the nature of the user system, and the role of language and interpretation (sense making) in data modelling. The implications of these assumptions on the outcomes, impact and process of data modelling have not received sufficient attention in research. The goal of the paper is threefold: to raise the awareness of practitioners and researchers about the basic assumptions underlying the practices, tools and methods of their work, to promote reflection on the appropriateness of these assumptions in research on system design methods and tools and to suggest alternative assumptions that can guide research and practice in future with a different set of outcomes[1].

The paper is organized as follows. Section 5.2.2 introduces four basic questions that help to pinpoint fundamental assumptions of different data modelling approaches and explains why these are called "metatheoretical". Section 5.2.3 uses these four questions to analyze the metatheoretical assumptions of current mainstream approaches to data modelling. Section 5.2.4 examines a set of alternative assumptions. It thereby illustrates that the assumptions of data modelling are by no means given and self-evident and therefore they can be subjected to critical re-examination. The conclusions point to the importance of critical reflection on metatheoretical assumptions for further work in data modelling.

---

[1] It has been recognized for some time in the literature that data modelling and knowledge representation are essentially similar. Therefore they share the same fundamental assumptions and the following analysis is of equal importance to both data modellers who build databases and knowledge engineers who build expert systems. But for the sake of simplicity, in the following we speak only of data modelling.

5.2.2 Metatheoretical assumptions defined

The purpose of data modelling is to design a conceptual schema to organize the storage and retrieval of data. The term data model is either a synonym for conceptual schema (as in the phrase "this is our data model for the inventory control system") or it refers to the language in which the conceptual schema is formulated (as in the phrase "we use the relational model"). Typically a data modelling language consists of constructs for expressing data definitions, operations for manipulating data and constraints (such as integrity and privacy constraints). Data modelling is the activity of constructing a data specification by applying the generic abstraction concepts of a data model (language) to a particular application domain. In this paper we are mostly concerned with the assumptions that underlie different conceptual schema (or data modelling) languages and their use in designing a conceptual schema.

In order to identify the assumptions of different approaches to data modelling, we look upon the construction of a data model as building a limited theory of its application domain. This point of view is not new[2] and a number of people have noted that there are important relationships between perception, data, reality and knowledge[3]. Based on this prior work, we can examine the existing approaches of data modelling with regard to four assumptions.

(1) What is being modelled? (ontological question) – This question points to the fundamental assumptions of data modelling approaches about the modelling domain, i.e., about the nature of the universe of discourse. More specifically, by ontology we mean a set of assumptions about the nature of the objects with which software development must deal. There is no accepted terminology for talking about the ontology of software development. Examples of terms used to describe ontologies in software development are entities, relationships, messages, actors, inference rules, facts, speech acts, etc. The ontology of software development also includes some fundamental assumptions about the nature of the application domain, i.e., whether there is a single or several user systems or no "system" at all, whether the primary constituents of each user system are operations, roles, decisions, social action, or speech acts or something else.

(2) How well is the result represented? (linguistic question) – This question points to the assumptions that are made about the nature of the symbolic constructs that are most appropriate and effective to represent the universe of discourse. For example, the relational model recommends normalized tables over record types or sets.

(3) Why is the result valid? (epistemological question) – This question points to the fundamental assumptions that are made on how one can obtain valid interpretations and knowledge about the universe of discourse to be modelled. Experimental modes of schema construction (like prototyping) can be compared with the specification approach as is associated with many versions of the so

---

[2] [Kent, 1978]

[3] [Churchman, 1971, Checkland, 1981, Stamper, 1987, Goldkuhl and Lyytinen, 1984, Lyytinen, 1987]

called waterfall model or systems life-cycle approach[4]. The question of how to cope with uncertain knowledge during system development is, of course, not the only consideration that is important in comparing prototyping and system life-cycle approaches, but it is a good example to demonstrate that different methods sometimes imply different assumptions about knowledge and inquiry in systems design[5].

(4) What is the social context of data modelling? (sociological question) – This question points to assumptions about the relationship between data and action. First, data are related to action because they are used to achieve purposes which in turn are shaped by the context of the social community in which data modelling takes place. Purposes can be latent, which is seen when data are used to supply rationalizations for decision taken with ulterior motives[6]. Second, the relation of data to action is revealed if we interpret the use of data analogous to the use of language.

> "the efficiency of language requires that utterances always be anchored to the unique and particular occasion of their use. In this respect, language is indexical: that is, dependent for its significance on connections to specific occasions, and to the concrete circumstances in which an utterance is spoken." [7]

The same should hold for the efficiency of data. These kinds of socio-linguistic assumptions are not made explicit in the classical approaches to data modelling.

A set of mutually reinforcing answers to these four questions amounts to a metatheoretical position. The term "metatheoretical" is here used to refer to fundamental criteria and standards that support a choice between different methods and tools. This usage follows Oliga[8] who proposes a distinction between methods and methodologies. Methods are concrete procedures for getting things done. A methodology is a higher-level construct which provides the rationale for choosing between different methods. Metatheoretical assumptions are the stipulations and norms built into methodologies[9].

Hence system methodologies are concerned with criteria and principles that help in choosing among different system design methods[10]. The next two sec-

---

[4] Cf. [Davis, 1982, Parnas and Clements, 1985, Agresti, 1986, Boehm, 1988].

[5] Cf. [Churchman, 1971], Gougen, Chap. 5.1.

[6] Cf. [Kling, 1980].

[7] [Suchman, 1987, p. 184]

[8] [Oliga, 1988]

[9] This distinction applies equally to the domain of research as to building systems. A classical example of a metatheoretical debate in research is the conflict between Spinoza (there are four types of knowledge) and Locke (all knowledge comes from experience). This debate continues between the advocates of a realist truth theory and unified ideal of science on the one side and by the proponents of discourse or coherence theory (such as [Habermas, 1973] Truth Theories) on the other.

[10] Examples of system methodologies are [Churchman, 1971] or [Checkland, 1981] and an example of a metatheoretical debate about systems design can be found in [Jackson, 1982b, Jackson, 1982a].

tions articulate the metatheoretical assumptions that support the prevailing approaches to data modelling and the possible alternatives to this as developed in recent research[11].

5.2.3 The mainstream view and the metatheoretical debate

Most current data modelling approaches answer the *ontological* question by presuming that the world is given and made up of concrete objects which have natural properties and are associated with other objects. "Given" means that the world is prior to the existence or appreciation of humans, it is not something which is created through social intercourse. Therefore, this kind of world exists beyond beliefs and social practices of users. The universe of discourse is that part of the real world with which the data model is concerned.

> "A data model is a specification language for representations of the real world." [12]

Similar views have been expressed in the notion of an enterprise model free of bias[13], the van Griethuysen report on "Concepts and Terminology for the Conceptual Schema and the Information Base" [14]. It is also typical of most contributions to the so-called information system proceedings[15]. It should be noted that the above is a specific version of realism, namely one that is based on Tarski's correspondence theory of truth[16]. Whenever the word realism is used without qualification in the following, we mean it in this sense. Otherwise it will be qualified.

The *linguistic* question focuses us on the quality of data models which has been analyzed from two competing angles: linguistic rigor and ease of use. Linguistic rigor emphasizes that data models should be complete, consistent and fully formalized to eliminate ambiguity and allow rigorous inference. From this perspective the ideal data model provides a formal calculus to answer all questions about the universe of discourse. Answers should follow from the axioms and inference rules[17]. To a limited extent this has been achieved for example by the studies on relational completeness[18]. Based on the work of Russell and Whitehead, the *Principia Mathematica* predicate calculus-based formalisms appear very promising to achieve this. It therefore is not surprising that many

---

[11] A similar metatheoretical analysis for the broader area of information systems development is presented in [Hirschheim and Klein, 1989]. [Iivari, 1989] and Kerola/Similä (Chap. 5.3) argue for a reappraisal of the foundations of "information science" as a whole building on related categories.

[12] [Mylopoulos, 1981]

[13] [Chen, 1977]

[14] [v. Griethuysen, 1982]

[15] [Olle et al., 1982, Olle et al., 1983, Olle and Sibley, 1986]

[16] This is explicitly recognized in [v. Griethuysen, 1982, p. 3–7].

[17] [Bubenko, 1983]

[18] [Codd, 1971]

data modelling formalisms were proposed which provided constructs for directly representing the objects, properties and associations of the universe of discourse. One widely used language represents the universe of discourse as entity, attribute and relationship instances[19], but similar ideas exist in the relational model. Data modelling languages also include a simple theory of types in which each instance belongs to exactly one type. The difficulties with this have recently become more widely realized and the type theory has been expanded to include "categories" [20]. However, the semantics of orthodox data modelling approaches are still limited to denotational theory in which the meanings of each term corresponds to the set of objects for which it stands[21]. Consequently, attempts to include more meanings into data models focus on defining constraints that are supposed to reflect real-world structures such as temporal order of events, existence dependencies, object identity and the like[22].

As noted above, the second quality criterion of data models is ease of use. The ease of use characteristic has been applied to explain the popularity of certain types of formalisms such as the E-R model. The ease of use issue has been investigated empirically in a number of studies[23]. However, the criterion has been recognized difficult to apply in that no clear procedure for choosing among different data modelling languages has been proposed[24].

The *epistemology* of current approaches assumes that valid data models can be built by applying proper observation and data collection methods to the application domain (universe of discourse). The data model is like a picture of the universe of discourse. It may have more or less grain to allow for selection, but its accuracy can be determined by checking how well it corresponds to the reality of the universe of discourse. By observing the deficiency of the application, one can infer the likely cause in the specification and correct it. In this way the data model can be tuned over time to improve its correspondence with reality. The same procedure can also be used to adjust it to changing requirements. Whereas data modelling does emphasize user participation in this process of continuing correction and adjustment, the user's role is seen to be limited to two contributions: (i) providing input to the data modellers in form of "raw" data and definitions, (ii) validating the formal specification in the sense of assuring that it corresponds to the true state of affairs. Various devices have been proposed to improve the efficacy of user participation in this sense, for example graphical respresentation aids and walk-throughs. But the application of such tools does not change the fundamental assumption that validation is an accuracy test in line with the correspondence theory of truth.

The *social context* of data modelling is seen as unproblematic. The first assumption is that organizational processes are primarily oriented to maintaining organizational stability and order. The second assumption is that data models

---

[19] [Chen, 1976, Teichroew et al., 1980]

[20] Cf. [ElMasri and Wiederhold, 1985].

[21] [v. Griethuysen, 1982]

[22] For details cf. [Codd, 1979].

[23] See e.g. [Batra and Davis, 1989, Batra et al., 1988].

[24] Cf. [Tsichritzis and Lochovsky, 1982].

are to contribute to given organizational goals through helping with purposeful interventions which serve organizational efficiency and effectiveness. The third assumption is that organizational policy is consistent and well-defined. Policy makers know what they want and how to communicate it well so that policies establish rational preference orderings. Under these assumptions it is reasonable to believe that if data models consistently represent the organization and its environment, this will improve the information that can be used for organizational control. In spite of the emphasis on control, data models are deemed to be politically neutral. If there are conflicts, then it is assumed that they will be resolved by the powers that be. The analyst has no mandate for policy definition.

In summary, the analysis of many current methods and tools of data modelling reveals the influence of "functionalism" [25]. There are two principle sets of assumptions in which this is revealed: a realist ontology coupled with a positivist epistemology and an unproblematic order and regulation view of human organizations. However, from the beginnings of data modelling, these assumptions have not been universally shared[26]. In particular, if we turn to the literature on information systems development in general, we note a lively debate on the dangers of these assumptions[27].

In the research literature on information systems development, it has been recognized for some time that the assumptions made in information systems development are of fundamental practical and theoretical importance, because assumptions affect the way information systems are developed (the process), the design features (the product) or the way they are used (contributing to system success, undesirable consequences or even failure). However, earlier work tended to focus on very specific assumptions[28].

Of special importance for this paper is that the debate has recently also taken a new turn by recognizing the need to explore the most fundamental levels from where assumptions arise. Whereas some fundamental works addressing this points are classics in the field[29], the debate has recently intensified by focusing more clearly on the assumptions that characterize different paradigms or schools of thought in systems development[30].

---

[25] [Hirschheim and Klein, 1989]

[26] [Kent, 1978]

[27] [Capurro, 1986, Winograd and Flores, 1986, Blair, 1990]

[28] For example, [Hedberg and Mumford, 1975] examined the analysts assumptions about users and themselves using the theory x, theory y framework [McGregor, 1960]. [Bostrom and Heinen, 1977] focused on the causes of system failures and identified seven specific assumptions that designers tend to make about users and the scope of analyst's responsibilites and a similar line of thinking was applied in [Lyytinen and Lehtinen, 1987]. Many other thorough analyses of assumptions have been contributed (for a concise review see [Hirschheim and Klein, 1989]).

[29] [Churchman, 1971, Kling, 1980, Checkland, 1981]

[30] [Winograd and Flores, 1986, Hirschheim, 1986, Klein and Hirschheim, 1987, Lyytinen, 1987, Oliga, 1988, Hirschheim and Klein, 1989, Iivari, 1989], and Goguen, Chap. 5.1.

In principle one side in this debate seeks to develop a science of software engineering in the image of the established natural sciences. Their belief is that the success of the natural sciences can be repeated in the area of applied systems development if software engineering emulates the methods of the natural sciences "a more geometrico". To a very large extent, this view is still held by the majority of computer scientists, industrial engineers and academics in the area of information systems. This is reaffirmed by the recent report of the "Task Force on the Core of Computer Science" [31]. It identifies three "major paradigms, or cultural styles, by which we approach our work". The first of this is *theory*, and rooted in mathematics. The second is *abstraction* and rooted in the experimental scientific method, and the third is *design* and rooted in engineering.

> The discipline of computer science is the systematic study of algorithmic processes that describe and transform information: their theory, design, efficiency, implementation, and application. The fundamental question underlying all of computing is "What can be (efficiently) automated?" [32]

This report appears to presume a unified ontology by ignoring that qualitative differences may exist in different application domains; if this were true it would imply that software development can follow the same principles regardless of whether the design requirements arise from physical or human-social application domains. In a unified ontology there is no fundamental difference between operators whether human, machine, or animal, as long as the same function is performed. A prominent supporter of similar views for the areas of AI and knowledge representation, is the Nobel prizewinner Herbert Simon.

However, the view of software development as a branch of applied mathematics that is primarily concerned with the study of algorithms is in conflict with several well established lines of research. For example, a transaction cost analysis of organizational behaviour suggests that data are used opportunistically to influence colleagues and superiors[33]. Hewitt and Gerson and Star[34] show the need to manage ambiguity, inconsistencies and conflict in system specifications. Empirically, the political nature of software development has been demonstrated in Keen[35] through documented cases of counter-implementation strategies. An impressive base of facts and theory gives ample evidence for the social character of software development[36].

Therefore the opponents of the above view[37] argue that the objects of inquiry in information systems development are different from those in the natural sciences, because users, developers and other stake-holders are not natural objects but conscious subjects. Consciousness is a quality which the natural sciences so far have not dealt with. Consciousness is important for data modelling because

---

[31] [Denning et al., 1989]
[32] [Denning et al., 1989, p. 12]
[33] [Ciborra, 1987]
[34] [Hewitt, 1986, Gerson and Star, 1986]
[35] [Keen, 1981]
[36] [Kling, 1980, Hirschheim, 1986]
[37] The view is well expressed in the report [Denning et al., 1989].

information system design is aimed at developing social communication systems and these are always sense-making systems. They are formed around shared meanings. Therefore, the design of information system is like the design of human communities, which requires a different approach than that practiced in mathematics and the natural sciences because they cannot deal with the significance and ethics of differing forms of life. A similar point of view emerges from modern systems theory in that natural systems as studied in physics and chemistry or artificial systems (machines) as studied in traditional engineering or computer science are not "self-referential", that is they do not rely on communication with peers to maintain images of themselves, to maintain their internal structures and to distinguish themselves from the environment. For self-referential[38] systems, either communications or actions are the fundamental building blocks, and this differs from the "elements" and subsystems as typically defined in engineering and the natural sciences. Recent systems theory makes very clear ontological distinctions between machines, organisms, and social and psychic systems[39]. In the following we build on the results that the recent radicalization of this debate has produced.

5.2.4 Four alternative metatheoretical assumptions

The idea that metatheoretical assumptions exist as legitimate objects of scientific investigation is itself controversial and may not meet with universal approval. Metatheoretical statements are only meaningful if one accepts that there is no unified ontology for software development.

(1) The ontological question raises two issues with regard to data modelling. The first is whether the universe of discourse is "given" (is ontologically prior to any human perception or communication) or socially constructed. The second is what sort of "things" one chooses to see in the universe of discourse. Earlier it was noted that the mainstream views tend to view the universe of discourse as given and postulate that the kind of things existing in the universe of discourse are objects with attributes and relationships.

In response to the first question, symbolic interactionism suggests that the universe of discourse is socially constructed through processes of communication in which individuals define their situations. The basic premise is that regardless of whether there are real things out there, they become only accessible through interpretive processes. Often users and analysts may subjectively believe that organizational reality exists, because they have forgotten its human authorship. The process by which this objectivization comes about is called reification[40]. Habituation, language tradition and institutionalization through roles and norms play a key role in this.

Building on these ideas, Boland drew a distinction between the decision model and action-based approach to systems design. The former relies heavily

---

[38] Or autopoietic: cf. Goguen, Chap. 5.1.
[39] Cf. [Luhmann, 1987].
[40] [Berger and Luckmann, 1967, p. 106], see also Dahlbom, Chap. 3.3.

on objective representations and algorithmic manipulations. In the action-based approach,

> "the design of an information system is not a question of fitness for an organizational reality that can be modelled beforehand, but a question of fitness for use in the construction of an organizational reality through the symbolic interaction of its participants. In essence, the information system is an environment of symbols within which a sense making process will be carried out." [41]

Applying this basic idea to data modelling suggests that data models should try to model the language by which users communicate in the application domain. This may be called "the formal language development view" which contrasts with the "reality mapping view" of the mainstream approaches[42]. Language is used for several purposes such as reaching agreement, clarification, concealing or misleading, etc. Much of language use is concerned with interpretation and making sense of one's environment to understand what is happening.

From the formal language development perspective, data models are models of user languages rather than models of reality. User languages are languages,

> "used in a work situation, with the purpose of supporting or changing the working process, the organization of work, the shared knowledge and values, and the social relations constituting the situation." [43]

The notion of a user language coincides neither with a language with special purposes nor with a sociolect (ibid.) but may include elements of both. An example of user language terms are the many acronyms coined by large corporations but also words borrowed from the national language and given a special meaning.

User languages are complex rule systems, many of which are implicit to the speakers. A shift in the modelling focus directs attention to modelling rules that define the syntax, semantics, intentions of messages and, to a certain extent, pragmatics (use situations) rather than given objects and properties. However, it would be unrealistic to expect that complete models of language can be developed, because user languages evolve from the ordinary speaking practices which evade complete specification. The special nature of an information system is that it is built around a language which is more structured and formalized than user languages[44]. Typically, this implies restrictions for the functionality of the information system. Taking this into account, data models partially reconstruct the language by which users understand each other and make sense of their environment.

---

[41] [Boland, 1979, p. 262]
[42] [Lyytinen, 1987]
[43] [Holmquist and Andersen, 1987, p. 348]
[44] [Lyytinen, 1987, p. 15]

A fundamental issue for language modelling is to decide upon the basic building blocks in the universe of discourse (which is the users' language) [45].

Two obvious possibilities are sentences or speech acts. The former is in line with Frege's view of language who proposed that human language can be modelled with predicate logic. If one uses sentences as the basic ontology of language, one could use an entity-attribute notation to model user languages. This would correspond to Frege's sentence view of language, because entities and attributes relate to subjects and predicates in logic. A sentence view of language restricts modelling to individuation, reference and predication.

If language is seen to consist of speech acts rather than sentences, then the focus of data modelling is broadened. A speech act is a basic unit of speech by which a speaker accomplishes some extralinguistic purpose such as obtaining a piece of information (using the speech act of a question) or signalling a commitment (using the speech act of a promise). Searle has hypothesized that there are five basic types of speech acts[46]: questions, promises, assertions (claiming something to be true), declarations (example: giving notice), and expressives (to communicate feelings of the speaker). Basically, modelling a speech act requires respresenting three aspects: what is referred to (predication and reference), intent (illocutionary point) and likely consequences or behavioural outcomes (perlocutionary effects). Entity and relationship models capture at best predication and reference.

From the speech act perspective, data models are models of linguistic discourses that are made up of basic "moves" which correspond to speech acts[47]. Some formalisms for data modelling have been proposed to capture the semantics of simple speech act sequences[48]. An important research issue is how to extend this into more complicated domains, such as policy debates[49].

(2) The linguistic question is concerned with the quality of data models (in the sense of representation languages and conceptual schemata). It interacts with the presumed ontology in the following way. If realism is assumed then data models are means of representing reality. Under this assumption, different data models can be evaluated by applying such criteria as accuracy and completeness. This becomes impossible if the data model co-determines what will count as reality and what is legitimate evidence[50]. This is the case, because from the constructivist perspective data models are one of the means by which a social community makes sense of the environment. It is used to filter the meaningful and important from the unitelligible or insignificant. By helping to maintain a socially constructed reality, a data model guides action through constraining

---

[45] The idea of fundamental linguistic structures has been subject to serious suspicion within the recent post-structuralist criticism: see, e.g., [Hopper, 1987, Tagg, 1989, Macksey and Donato, 1972]. However, this issue is beyond the scope of this paper.

[46] Cf. [Searle, 1979].

[47] [Auramaki et al., 1988]

[48] [Lehtinen and Lyytinen, 1986]

[49] An example of a system designed around the speech act of making commitment is given in the last chapter of [Winograd and Flores, 1986].

[50] [Boland, 1979]

and channelling perceptions, influencing the availability of evidence, suggesting preferred types of evidence, alerting, masking, etc. This would also apply to actions aimed at validation of the data model which thereby becomes circular. Therefore validation can no longer be phrased in terms of finding representations that minimize distortions of true situations or that filter too much or too little of an underlying *given* reality.

The implications of this for data modelling or choosing appropriate data models have not been discussed in the literature. The suggestion that comes to mind is that the role of data models should be seen in a similar light as the role of a theory for a scientific community – a rather controversial topic. Tentatively one might suggest that data models should be formulated in such a way that they help social communication. Ideally, good data models should facilitate communication that is sincere, relevant, clear and well-informed, i.e., it should encourage people to say what they mean, pertinent to the situation at hand, expressed in a way that is congenial to the listeners frame of mind and based on good, defensible reasons. However, such a view is rather idealistic and misses some important points to be discussed next. We will return to it in the concluding part of the paper.

(3) The epistemological question concerns the question in what sense of the word a data model can be more or less accurate or more or less appropriate. We will address this question by way of analyzing data modelling from the perspective of interpretation and sense-making[51].

Hermeneutics is concerned with the problem of interpreting and understanding the meanings of "texts". Anything that potentially has meanings can be considered as a text including "the book of nature". Hence the scientist reading the traces in a cloud chamber is involved as much in a hermeneutic (interpretive) task as the archeologist trying to decipher the famous Rosetta stone. The complex issues raised by the interpretation of natural data are well illustrated by the historical example of Tycho Brahe who was unable to make sense of his own observations on planetary positions. Kepler approached the same data with a different pre-understanding and was able to support his heliocentric theory of the solar system with them[52].

Of particular interest for data modelling are socially created texts. These include "reading" user activities and utterances. Hermeneutics considers the philosophical issues of text interpretation when these are difficult to "read", i.e., opaque or "alien". Organizations and life-forms are such texts (as is well illustrated by the phenomenon of culture shock). Specifically, reading (understanding) an application problem is like reading an alien text, because the analyst has to make sense of things with which he is more or less unfamiliar.

In the following we leave aside further consideration of the implications of hermeneutics for a realist ontology. The reasons for this are practical. While sophisticated versions of realism can be maintained, it is rather difficult to see how

---

[51] Cf. for an earlier treatment [Langefors, 1977, Capurro, 1986]; also related are the references to Heidegger by Goguen in Chap. 5.1 and Chap. 8.1.

[52] Cf. [Kuhn, 1970].

they can be transformed into a practical approach to data modelling. Therefore, we shall not try to defend or refute the viability of more sophisticated positions of realism in data modelling. Rather we will build on the premise that data modelling can fruitfully proceed from a constructivist position. With this in mind, hermeneutic insights suggests that all data models are limited in the following three fundamental ways. The first is that all data models are inescapably biased even though the understanding of bias can be improved through "bracketing". The second is that data modelling involves a meeting of at least two horizons of meanings: it always involves a double hermeneutic. Third, the number of horizons of meanings in complex organizations cannot be predetermined. Hence data modelling has to remain open-ended.

In order to discuss the first limitation, we need to return to the notion of "pre-understanding" which was already used informally in the above example of Tycho Brahe. According to hermeneutics, all interpretation begins with some preliminary ideas or notions (Gadamer likes to call these "prejudices") which amount to a pre-understanding.

From a hermeneutic perspective, there is no difference between pre-understanding, bias or prejudice. Whenever we try to understand something new, like reading the organizational context of system development, we simply start with what we take for granted. Taken-for-granted is what is transmitted to us through culture and its institutions. More specifically, in an organization, the prevailing policies and management ideology will heavily influence the pre-understanding. Further important influences are the professional practices of expert communities which are socially sanctioned through peer norms of different degrees of formality, in the most extreme form through standards. Based on whatever pre-understanding we have, through dialogue, analysis and reflection, we can reach a new understanding. When such a new understanding has been reached, one "hermeneutic cycle" has been completed. In data modelling the pre-understanding is reflected in the fundamental assumptions of the conceptual schema, in particular in the type definitions, integrity constraints and so-called semantic rules (dependency rules).

Interpretation is a continuing process. Each new understanding (not necessarily better) becomes the pre-understanding for the next interpretation and the hermeneutic cycle repeats itself. There is no stopping rule as the meanings of texts constantly changes – as the legal process of law interpretation clearly demonstrates. Furthermore there is no way to assess the quality of pre-understanding, because there is no anchoring point. However, we can try to elicit some of the presuppositions upon which the pre-understanding rests. This is called "bracketing".

An example will help to clarify the idea of bracketing. Assume you are reading a map and have difficulty matching the landmarks that you see to the map. You may say to yourself, well maybe I am not here, but have already overshot my destination. You have now "bracketed" a fundamental assumption. This means, you have identified a fundamental presupposition on which your map reading up to this point rested, put it aside "into brackets" and "pealed it away" so to speak. By attempting to do this systematically, particularly in social communication where different minds look at the same "text" from slightly different viewpoints, several layers of presuppositions may be revealed and bracketed. Again there is no guarantee that this converges or any implication that this leads to an "approximation of reality".

These ideas suggest the following principles that should guide practice, research and methods of data modelling[53]:

a) All data models have a fundamental bias that can be traced to the contingent pre-understandings with which they were built.

b) To some extent, the bias can be made transparent through bracketing, a form of self-critical, reflective dialogue.

c) Bracketing must not be seen as a procedure to decide between fundamentally conflicting preconceptions. Therefore a hermeneutic approach to data modelling is very skeptical of the idea that bias can eventually be substantially reduced or even be eliminated by a process of evaluative error elimination. Gadamer says that complete clarification is an illusion[54].

In applying these principles, the practice of data modelling must take into account the fundamental differences between the separate and unique "horizons of meanings" of such different communities as analysts and users. The "horizon of meanings" is a metaphor that connotes on the one hand openness, as one may gain new horizons by travel, and on the other hand structure, as when we look out towards the horizon things that are close are clearer than things that are further away. Different communities have unique horizons in the sense that when they meet, each faces the problem of interpreting the other in terms of their own horizon and therefore mutual understanding is at risk. However, there exists the possibility of fusing the two horizons and thereby overcoming some of the likely misunderstandings because both horizons are open; i.e., each community, through symbolic interaction, ("being with each other" and "orienting towards their shared problems") can broaden their horizons and "fuse" them to some degree. Applying the notion of *horizon of meanings* to data modelling leads to two further conclusions[55].

a) Each data model merges or "fuses" at least two horizons. Even if users are excluded from the process of analysis, the developers will have to bridge two understanding contexts or "horizons of meanings", i.e., meanings that are shared by two distinct communities, such as users and developers. Both groups have internalized different language games. The situation is symmetrical for the users. If they undertake the development themselves,

---

[53] Cf. [Capurro, 1986] for the area of information retrieval.

[54] Cf. [Gadamer, 1980, pp. 78].

[55] The horizon concept bears some similarity to the term "context of meanings" which is more commonly used, but there are some important differences. Context does not connote the increasing diffuseness of our understanding which becomes vaguer as we move away from the centre of gravity of our life. Neither does context connote so well the openness of the horizon.

they must cope with the fixed horizon of meanings that is embedded in the specification language and modelling tools that they use.

The fusion of horizons in data modelling involves three steps. In step one, the developers must try to capture some of the meanings that are shared by the users and which, initially at least, are "alien" to the developers. In step two, they must translate their understanding into some appropriate formalism. These formalisms carry the implicit claim that, at least in part, they are valid substitutes for the users' existing language games. In step three the formalizations must be retranslated into the users' horizons of meanings and thereby become part of their everyday practices (that is if the fused horizon is accepted as appropriate, otherwise the cycle must repeat itself based on the new pre-understanding). Each step is fraught with many risks that need careful attention and are insufficiently addressed by the usual concepts of walk-throughs, documentation and user "training".

b) The fusion of horizons can be facilitated through systematic "bracketing". The reason for this is that bracketing can be expected to be more effective if it is based on a dialogue between users and developers rather than on internal discussion within each group. This has been realized in particular by Checkland[56] with the concept of constructing alternative "root definitions" that must precede any conceptual modelling. It appears then that the double hermeneutic of users and developers is not only a threat to create rigidities and misunderstanding, but also a chance for improving mutual understanding through dialogue.

There are as many horizons of meanings in an organization as there are distinct user groups. Distinct in this context means that the users have distinct education and professional training and therefore share different kinds of expertise with their own specialized languages and practices. In other words, the centre of gravity of their life interests must be sufficiently different. A good example is that of doctors and nurses in hospitals. Hence the double hermeneutic must be expanded to include multiple hermeneutics. The risk of misunderstandings exists not only between analysts and users, but between different user communities.

This leads to the conclusion that there cannot be overall consistency in an enterprise-wide data model. Of course, there can be a strategic data model of the organization and its horizon can include all of the organization. This simply provides another horizon of meanings, typically that of high-level planning staff. As such, it can provide a basis for a dialogue with other user groups and lead to a fusion of horizons and thereby to organizational learning. In practice, enterprise models may have always been intended to be used in this way. We mention it here only, because some of the data modelling literature suggests otherwise. There have been proposals to construct a consistent enterprise schema whose conventions are to be enforced. In a similar spirit, unambiguous definitions of an enterprise vocabulary and global validity tests of local data bases have been

---

[56] [Checkland, 1981]

proposed. None of this appears as appropriate from a hermeneutic perspective. Similar conclusions follow from the sociology of data use.

(4) Sociological question: In praxis data are not collected to establish truth or do justice to a preferred mode of communication. Data are collected to design action, to give meanings to action and to politically support action taken. Therefore data modelling does not proceed in a social vacuum. In order to structure the discussion we might loosely distinguish between action to design policy (including critique of policy) and action to execute policy, which is often called policy implementation. By policy design we mean the origination of long-term goals, general directives and programs such as are typically on the agendas of boards, legislators and chief executive officers.

It is often assumed that policy-making sets the pre-understanding of policy execution. This is inherent in the models of administrative decision-making of both Simon and Anthony. This, however, overlooks the autonomy of complex bureaucracies, which exists for several reasons[57]. (a) Ambiguous policies facilitate consensus formation to pass policy, allowing different constituencies to support the same policy for different reasons. (b) Organizations often do not have the resources and skills to implement the wishes of policy makers even if they wanted to. (c) Lower-level officials have their own interests and constituents. They view new policies as an opportunity to pursue their own agendas. (d) Policy makers are often unable to specify policies clearly. This overlooks that policy makers do not always know what they want and that conflicting policies are issued. (e) Policy makers often make unrealistic assumptions about the possibility to follow their directives which then leaves organizations to their own devices in implementing them.

In light of this, data modelling, even in support of policy implementation, cannot count on predefined horizons of meanings. It defines and redefines the institutional frame of reference in which policy-making takes place. Therefore data modelling is a political activity which affects the interest of various policy-making groups.

But why is it not possible to separate data collection from policy-making by assigning these tasks to different groups? In fact, this is often attempted. For example the U.S. census bureau has historically been perceived to be non-political. However, its data often turn out to be politically biased[58], because the methods of the bureau lead to a systematic undercount of minorities. This has many political implications and leads to calls to adjust the numbers. But there is no unique method to do so and hence the decision which methods to use and which numbers to get is ultimately intertwined with policy formation.

This point is more generally established by Tenenbaum and Wildavsky with a study on the role of energy data in policy formation.

> As we see it, data, far from preceding policy, are inextricably intertwined with politics; ...it is the policy that one has in mind that determines which data, accurate to what degree, are relevant. ...our conclusions

---

[57] Cf. [Baier et al., 1986].

[58] An example of this is given by [Mitroff et al., 1982].

about the relationship between data and policy may apply to any field of government or company policy[59].

The basic reason for this conclusion is that both data and policies are needed in the hermeneutic (sense making) tasks of policy formation. Data in a very broad sense constrain policy, but only at the extremes. On the other hand, data collected without paying attention to policy are irrelevant, even meaningless. In light of the earlier discussion, it is not surprising that there is an analogy between policies and scientific theories:

> Without considering the political preferences and relationships among people who would make decisions, no intelligent thought, including the selection of data, is possible. Just as philosophers tell us that all facts involved in testing hypotheses are theory laden, so too all data used in analyses are suffused with policy[60].

The theory of data modelling will remain incomplete unless it covers some fundamental principles that govern how data are used in social environments. The development of the ontological, epistomological and linguistic bases of data modelling, no matter how thorough, emphasizes only its rational side. It thereby paints an ideal. In order to complete the picture, the entanglement of data and policy must also be confronted.

5.2.5 Conclusions

We have introduced a number of ideas and stipulations which, if followed up in future research, will not only change many of the current assumptions of data modelling, but also broaden its scope considerably. It was noted that the prevalent metaphor of data modelling is that of a representation that should correspond to reality. In conclusion we propose that a more fruitful metaphor is to view data models as a set of laws and data modelling as the activity by which laws are designed and enacted.

There is a rational side to law making. They should be clear and consistent. They are not necessarily bound by current practices or state of affairs but can be inspired by emancipatory visions. Based on this they can create a new order and establish new domains of jurisdiction. Laws may define what counts as preferred evidence. In practice laws are difficult to interpret, always changing, limited to a certain domain of applications which in turn is never fixed and as a whole certainly not consistent. Hence laws pose serious hermeneutic issues and their validity is difficult to establish. Laws are, of course, one specific type of universe of discourse. It is therefore not surprising that there exist many analogies to our discussion of metatheoretical principles. In fact, the first data modelling project that attempted to formulate a linguistic universe of discourse was concerned with

---

[59] [Tenenbaum and Wildavsky, 1984, pp. 84–84]
[60] [Tenenbaum and Wildavsky, 1984, p. 100]

programming a body of law[61]. If one looks at the rational side of law making, ignoring for a moment its many practical deficiencies, a number of principles suggest themselves that would help to improve the role of data modelling in social communication[62]:

1. Data models should facilitate co-operation for accepted purposes.
2. They should help people to express what they believe to be the case and make them sceptical of beliefs for which they lack evidence.
3. They should provide guidance to formulate reports and arguments which are to the point and available when required[63].
4. They should support a format of communication which is unambiguous, concise and well organized.

Ideally these principles define good laws and good data models. However, in practice, often the opposite can be observed. The reason for this apparent contradiction is that language and epistemology provide little focus on human interest and power. There is much talk of knowledge-based systems and strategic information systems. It must be surprising that there appears to be little inclination to investigate how the design of these systems can be made responsive to the political structures with which they are to interact.

Just as laws lead people to filter information and put their best foot forward, so do the rules of data models. Just as laws are formulated ambiguously to be acceptable to a mixed coalition of supporters, so are data models. Just as laws need to be approved by some sort of due process, so do data models. Just as laws constrain policy making and at the same time are the result of policy, so do data models. Just as laws should be supported by a democratic majority, so should data models, and this may only be possible at the expense of consistency or incompleteness. Just as the interpretation of laws changes with shifting policy orientations, so are data models. As information systems move closer to the centres of gravity of power and political will formation, the entanglement of schema development and interpretation with policy formation and implementation is a subject that can no longer be avoided.

Acknowledgements

An earlier version of this paper benefitted from the sharp eye of Dick Welke for deviations from the topic. The current structure has been influenced by the advice of the editors and a thorough critical reading by Duane P. Truex helped to correct the final wording in many places. All the misconceptions that undoubtedly remain are the sole responsibility of the authors.
The financial support of this work by the Academy of Finland is gratefully acknowledged.

---

[61] British family law, cf. [Stamper, 1983].

[62] They are based on Grice's maxims of conversation, cf. [Levinson, 1983, pp. 101].

[63] This is suggested in the model of argumentation for information systems used by [Nissen, 1988].

5.3 A Reappraisal of Information Science

Pentti Kerola and Jouni Similä

This chapter emphasizes the *informationistic view of science,* and especially of information science. The view accepts the scientifically based cumulative information base as the main goal for science, combining in a natural and balanced manner the theoretical aspiration for truth, the search for applied knowledge and emancipation from old, false conceptualizations. Its philosophical roots are in modified scientific realism and research empiricism (of information science) mainly in the context of a Nordic coeffort.

5.3.1 Introduction – the need for a reappraisal of the foundations of information science[1]

The purpose of this chapter is to summarize one view of the characterizations of information science, and especially human and organization-centred (infological) research into the development and use of information systems[2]. This view was originally based on joint research carried out in the Nordic countries and reported on in the Proceedings of the Scandinavian Systemeering Research Seminars during 1978–89, and more specifically on research at the Institute of Information Processing Science, University of Oulu[3]. Many international connections have been maintained with European IS research groups[4] and with American colleagues[5].

It is evident that the field of information technology and automatic data processing is in a state of mild confusion and uncertainty at present. Competing and conflicting theories and approaches are being put forward[6], most notably as far as terminology is concerned. There is not even any generally accepted

---

[1] Originally we used the longer terms information processing science, information systems science or data processing science. The term information science has been proposed by the editors of this book.

[2] The content is mainly based on the dissertation of Similä [Similä, 1988] which was implemented during the multidisciplinary research project SYKE directed by Kerola [Kerola et al., 1985]. More generally, the term 'infological' has its origins in the research of [Langefors, 1966], who made a fundamental distinction between datalogical (data and technical-oriented) and infological (information, people and organization-oriented) aspects of the development of information systems.

[3] [Kerola et al., 1985, Iivari, 1983, Iivari and Koskela, 1987, Nuutinen et al., 1987]

[4] [Mumford et al., 1985, Buckingham et al., 1987]

[5] [Klein and Hirschheim, 1989, Kerola and Taggart, 1982]

[6] [Mumford et al., 1985]

name for the science itself. For the purposes of this treatise, the term "information science" will be understood as encompassing the whole field of use and development of information systems. The earlier forms and discourses of science seem incapable of analyzing the phenomenon of automatic data processing in its entirety or the knowledge required within it, most pointedly where the computer science paradigm is involved. A new area of knowledge has emerged at the boundary between computer science and the human sciences which requires careful analysis and thought. The science or philosophy of science has rarely been faced with such a hot, dynamic and rich object for analysis.

Information processing research has not delivered the results that have been expected from it in the practical field[7]. According to Lyytinen[8], prevailing research is loaded with the following kinds of "anomalies", i.e., problems which it cannot solve or deal with by following practices consistent with established research standards:

(1) "the delimitation of information systems to comprise technical artifacts and correspondingly the restriction of IS development to engineering aspects";

(2) "the understanding of information as an impersonal, a-historical, a-social formal entity";

(3) "the adherence to bureaucratic rationalism in viewing organizations";

(4) "the neglect of the socio-cultural milieu which has an impact on the development and practical usage of IS";

(5) "the neglect of questions of values in IS development, and associated with this, the neglect of questions of how data serve the purposes of legitimizing social control and power".

It has been necessary to return to the fundamentals, i.e., to the philosophical roots of our research effort in order to express the basic values and foundations of scientific research as explicitly as possible. Different philosophical approaches have been adapted during this evolutionary process, but in this case we utilize the framework of Niiniluoto[9], in which he emphasizes the *informationistic view of science*. This view accepts the scientifically based cumulative information base as the main goal for science, combining in a natural and balanced manner the theoretical aspiration for truth, the search for applied knowledge regarding the various objects of interest and emancipation from old, false cognizances. We introduce in the following the basic features of this philosophical view and its application to information science. Finally we summarize the research effort on a paradigm of infologically-oriented information science and conclude with a discussion of the significance of informationism.

---

[7] [Mumford et al., 1985]

[8] [Lyytinen, 1986]

[9] Professor of Philosophy at the University of Helsinki,
[Niiniluoto, 1980, Niiniluoto, 1983, Niiniluoto, 1987].

5.3.2 The informationistic view of science

Niiniluoto distinguishes three traditional major views of the goals of science. In the *behaviouralistic* view[10], scientific problems are practical decision-making problems and scientific results are prescriptions for action in these situations. The *cognitivistic* view[11] holds that the primary goal of science is knowledge itself, while the *pluralistic* view[12] regards scientific results as a "continually growing ocean of incompatible (and perhaps even incommensurate) alternatives", where "nothing is ever solved, no perspective may ever be eliminated from the total picture".

Behaviouralism in its pure form represents an attempt to analyze the scientific research process without the concept of knowledge. Perhaps, more appropriately, it is characterized as a view according to which scientific knowledge is to be subjected to action. The scientist is understood as a decision-maker or an adviser to a decision-maker. Her/his task is to analyze hypotheses concerning the relevant states of matter with respect to some practical problem, to evaluate the credibility or reliability of these hypotheses and to determine which of the alternatives for action associated with the practical problem are to be recommended in the light of the practical goals. The behaviouralistic model is evidently suitable for the characterization of many activities within the area of goal-oriented applied research or scientific development work. Its suitability as a model for basic research is questionable, however. It maintains that science has no lasting theoretical results – the scientist does not ask what may be known, merely how one should act.

Likewise, it is quite difficult to see how, according to the extreme pluralistic view, scientific results may be utilized as a basis for practical action. While behaviouralism seems to neglect the theoretical side of science, pluralism seems to have forgotten the relation between science and practice – the rationalism of applied science or technology is impossible to understand on the basis of pluralism.

Cognitivism, on the other hand, does not deny that science also functions as a basis for practical action. The modern cognitivist may try instead to show that it is exactly the theoretical pursuit for knowledge, which is apt to lead to knowledge of utmost practical significance. If knowledge is accepted as the only general goal for science, i.e., the cognitivistic view of science is upheld, a classification of science may be performed on the basis of the *interest of knowledge*. In addition to the technical interest, which perhaps would come to mind first when speaking of different interests, there are two other interests[13], namely the *hermeneutical* and the *emancipatory*, which should be considered when characterizing the different fields of science. In addition, according to *verism* (the search for truth), knowledge is in itself a suitable and sufficient interest for sci-

---

[10] [Savage, 1965]
[11] [Levi, 1967]
[12] [Feyerabend, 1975]
[13] [Habermas, 1971]

ence. Niiniluoto provides a table describing the essential features of these four interests of knowledge.

Table 5.3–1. Table, provided by Niiniluoto, slightly modified by us

Interest of Knowledge	Veristic Theoretical	Technical (Theoretical)	Hermeneutic (Theoretical)	Emancipatory (Theoretical)
Function of knowledge	Explanation	Prediction	Understanding	Critique of ideology
Goal	Search for truth	Control of nature and society	Communication and interpretation of tradition	Liberation from false conceptualizations
Typical examples of science	Mathematics, Philosophy	Natural Sciences; Systematic social sciences	Humanistic sciences	Critical social sciences; Psychoanalysis

On the basis of Table 5.3–1 and employing careful reasoning, Niiniluoto proposes an *informationistic* view of science, in which *the information base with its different value, content and argumentation aspects concerning reality* is accepted as the general aim for science. The scientifically based hypothesis or statement has high information content and value if it excludes many potential situations in reality and permits others.

The informationistic view combines in a natural and balanced manner the theoretical aspiration for truth and the search for applied knowledge, both of which Niiniluoto sees as belonging inseparably to the general goals of science. Truth and information are often confused with each other, but they are logically independent, because the information contained in a scientific proposition can be right or wrong in relation to the specified scientific criteria. Informationism maintains that the information content and value of a scientific hypothesis becomes greater, the more daring and improbable it is in its original form. This is quite the opposite of the veristic view, which may be shown to lead to a cautious approach to new theories. The greater the information value of a scientific hypothesis or theory, the more it potentially tells us about reality, and the more information we have concerning reality, the better possibilities we have for explaining phenomena, acting and orienting ourselves in the world, interpreting history, understanding ourselves and liberating ourselves from false conceptualizations.

Likewise the technical, hermeneutic, emancipatory and even theoretical interests of knowledge, when taken separately, are inadequate in themselves for defining science or scientific thinking. Not all "emancipatory" actions are scientific, and the same holds good for hermeneutic interpretations and technical breakthroughs based merely on trial and error or luck without the groundwork of systematic knowledge. But informationism has a more fundamental status in the characterization of scientific thinking. It has a primary role in guiding the search for knowledge and truth concerning reality, and it is only secondarily that the theoretical, technical, hermeneutic and emancipatory interests come into play. Those results of science which have information value usually also have instrumental value in the sense of the technical, hermeneutic and the emancipatory interests of knowledge. *Informationism* becomes thus an 'umbrella concept' covering all four columns in Table 5.3–1.

5.3.3 An informationistic view of information science

The informationistic[14] view of science seems appropriate for information science, not only for the sake of an 'appropriate' terminology, but for the sake of the demands the real world sets for this young field of science at present. What we need especially are daring new theories and concepts and a gradual build-up and accumulation of past scientifically based knowledge into an applicable and comprehensive picture of the field. It is true that in the past the most fundamental interest for information science has been the technical interest of the practical field. The demands placed by post-industrial society on organizations are so startling, however[15], that we need research which will also help us to understand the history of automatic data processing, to adapt ourselves to the new communication society, in which information technology will play a major role in our daily lives, and to liberate ourselves from the false conceptualizations which current and earlier technology has induced us to form. We claim here that the informationistic view of our information science recognizes distinctly different approaches, the hybrid and pluralistic nature of the field and its relation to practice. It provides a suitable starting point for a paradigmatic analysis of the important issues raised above.

The evolution of definitions of information science is instructive. We can distinguish at least three successive phases in these[16]:

(1) Information science studies the analysis, representation and applications of algorithms implementable in a computer.
(2) Information science studies the definition, storage, transmission, processing and use of formal data.
(3) Information science studies the technology, methods, impact and utilization of systematized information processing and its systematization.

---

[14] Please be careful with the different 'variations' on the term 'information'!
[15] [Huber, 1984]
[16] [Iivari, 1983, Nuutinen et al., 1987]

The first definition corresponds to what is generally called computer science[17], but the evolution is not strictly temporal, as some of the first characterizations of computer science in the sense of the second definition originate from the late sixties[18]. The last definition[19] brings the impact of information processing, its management and administration, and the whole process of developing an information and data system into the sphere of information science. There seems to be a clear shift towards research which is more human and organization oriented. Moreover, there seems to be a shift taking place from a strict positivistic interpretation of science towards a radically different "anti-positivistic" perspective, in which the intentionality or purposefulness of human action is understood to distinguish it from the objects of research in the natural sciences in a methodologically significant manner. Causal explanations are not accepted as sufficient or suitable for the inspection of purposeful behaviour, and teleological explanations are needed instead in order to understand human acts and historical events from the viewpoint of their goals.

Comparison of the definitional evolution above with the columns of Table 5.3–1 shows that most emphasis has always been placed on the two leftmost columns, even in the third definition. Today, however, there exists a clear tendency to shift the emphasis more "to the right"[20,21]. The recognition and acceptance of an informationistic view of information science would make this shift explicit and conscious while allowing for a balanced transition phase.

5.3.4 On a paradigm for infological information science

As the title of this subsection suggests, infologically oriented information science has not one, but several competing paradigm candidates. This competition is observed for example in the division of the forums of the science into those dedicated to data base specialists, software specialists, human factors specialists, systemeering[22] specialists, etc.

---

[17] Compare this with the latest definition in ACM [Denning et al., 1989], and compare also Klein and Lyytinen, Chap. 5.2!

[18] [Hamming, 1969, Langefors, 1966]

[19] [Iivari, 1983]

[20] [Mumford et al., 1985, Kerola, 1988a, Kerola, 1988b, Klein and Hirschheim, 1989, Nurminen, 1988]

[21] A National Doctorate Program for Information Science was implemented in Finland in 1985–1990 [Kerola, 1987], financed by the Ministry of Education, comprising three subprograms: Computer Science, Software Engineering Research and Information Systems Science. In the sense of the informationistic view, all of these have skew distributions of emphasis to the left in the columns of Table 5.3–1, but relatively speaking the first two have had very little emphasis on the move to the right. That tendency has been explicit in information systems science, however, but not so strong as it could be from the optimal informationistic viewpoint.

[22] The term 'systemeering' has its origin in Langefors' research, meaning the category of most extensive activities of IS development. The term 'systemeering research' is used in Table 5.3–2 for historical reasons. It could be understood as a synonym for 'infological IS research'.

Iivari[23] has written an up-to-date, thoughtful paradigmatic analysis of the following seven subschools of IS research: software engineering, database management, management information systems, decision support systems, implementation research, the socio-technical approach and the Scandinavian infological[24] approach, based on internationally well-known reference books and papers. The following case of paradigmatic analysis belongs to the last subschool. Its content is of an "ought-to-be" nature and was developed during the early days of the 1980s. It was originally presented in its complete form in the Proceedings of the Fourth Scandinavian Research Seminar on Systemeering[25,26].

5.3.5 Conclusion

In order to summarize the most essential conclusions, we can now pose the question: "What would informationism mean for science in general and for information science in particular?"
According to Niiniluoto the practice of science is to be understood

> *primarily* as a systematic, critical search for information and knowledge
>   concerning reality,
> and in the case of success,
> *secondarily* as serving different interests.

The search for truth alone or scientific information content alone are not sufficient as the main objective of science. The general aim should be the *search for informative truth*. Informationism emphasizes the significance of theoretical basic research. This is important and valuable in itself, but it also forms an indispensable precondition for fruitful, more prescriptive and emancipatory research. Informationism emphasizes 'broad' basic research, which aims at producing well argued knowledge concerning all aspects of reality, and theoretical/philosophical assertions of high information value. The truthfulness of these assertions is then gradually researched and tested. Well-argued, informative hypotheses are not only the most important building blocks of our scientific picture of the world, but also in the long run the most useful scientific knowledge for practical purposes. Theoretical and emancipatory scientific efforts are at the same time both contradictory and complementary in their interrelationships in the context of informationism, the emancipatory results being ultimately rich in their information content, but very 'open' as regards the verification of truth.

---

[23] [Iivari, 1989]
[24] This subschool, in practice, includes many subsubschools, which partially contradict each other.
[25] [Goldkuhl et al., 1981]
[26] The main content is reproduced here in Table 5.3-2 and has been further discussed by [Similä and Nuutinen, 1983].
[27] An information system is characterized here as a professional language.
[28] The informationistic emphasis of the authors!
[29] [Sellars, 1963]
[30] [Sellars, 1963]

Table **5.3–2.** Paradigmatic analysis of systemeering research

---

Ontology:

"Systemeering research (SR) is a subject-object science which studies primary and secondary problems of development, formalization and implementation of language[27] in different contexts including intentional human beings. Therefore SR is subject to historical practice. SR produces methods which are human constructs, represent praxis and are bound to relativism."

Discussion:

"The autonomy of the social dimension must be recognized in the study of the primary and secondary problems of systemeering. The role of the subject-object relations between the researcher and the object of research and between the researcher and the research community must be recognized. The development, formalization and implementation of the languages within systemeering practice and systemeering research must be studied in their social contexts".

Epistemology:

"Due to the ontological assumptions of intentional human beings, genuine teleological explanations are needed with a character of contextuality, partiality and indeterminacy manifested in different modalities. SR includes the *treatment of the relationships between descriptive and prescriptive knowledge as well as between theoretical and practical/operational knowledge within some ethical framework of the researchers.*"[28]

Discussion:

"The role of knowledge in concept and theory formation must be recognized. The Aristotelian notion of the supremacy of the user's knowledge versus the producer's knowledge must be evaluated in the context of systemeering and systemeering research. *Theoretical knowledge (scientific image) must be distinguished conceptually from atheoretical knowledge (manifest image)*[29]. In systemeering practice these two images must be unified into one stereoscopic image. The possibility and role of prescriptive knowledge in systemeering practice must be considered carefully."

Methodology:

"Research methodologies and methods must be adapted to features of empirical reality and research purpose; this implies methodological conditionality and pluralism. Antipositivistic approaches like interpretative methods and action research are required in many situations".

Discussion:

"The applicability of hermeneutic, phenomenological, teleological and positivistic methods must be studied in appropriate contexts. The transcendence of action over collections of rules or methods must be recognized."

Ethics:

"Human beings should be treated as intentional beings and their freedom of choice should be encouraged and supported".

Discussion:

"The fundamental issue of the image of man[30] must be recognized and explicated as far as possible."

As a consequence of the informationistic interpretation of science, the interaction between different categories of science, in the sense of Table 5.3–1, come to resemble a *multiple-level parallel process* rather than the Kuhnian evolution/revolution sequence, and thus a more *balanced* whole. This also has the consequence of *increasing the methodological contextuality and pluralism* in the total process of scientific effort.

What does this mean for the youngest science of our age, information science, and its research trends? The objects of research into information science in reality are in a highly dynamic state and are changing rapidly. The basic, theoretical research in this field should deal with these objects as a whole, interpreted informationistically. Traditional computer science alone is very often interpreted today as theoretical, and the rest as applied research. In this relation, from the informationistic viewpoint, information science is in a state of *imbalance*. In order to improve its direction, the philosophical/theoretical and emancipatory research work implemented in the context of infological information systems research, with its broadest possible selection of objects, would become more important focus area, and one could even claim that it is indispensable for the fruitfulness of other research directions in information science.[31]

---

[31] Conclusions of this type have been reached by other routes by Klein and Hirschheim and Iivari and Lyytinen.

Part 6

Understanding the Computer Through Metaphors

Reinhard B.

We have finally got round, then, to the subject of software development and use – back on home ground, so to speak.

Heinz

And straight to the very crux of software development: reconstructing reality in terms of operative models, while at the same time distilling its conceptual essence.

Christiane

By that, I suppose you mean – to use hermeneutic terms – that we invariably understand the things of reality, in the light of our prior understanding, "as something". That is the germ of the metaphor.

Reinhard K.-S.

We use metaphors to transfer meanings from one object to another. We allow the connotations and implications of metaphorical concepts to act upon us.

Christiane

And this makes us see reality in a different – and frequently clearer – light.

Heinz

The sage in the illustration is contemplating a thing as a tool. And the computer produces an appropriate image taken from the world of the craftsman. The formalism it displays – the program – thus becomes intelligible.

Reinhard K.-S.

But how valid is the metaphor? The screw represented in the computer certainly cannot be turned by any tool the sage might be holding.

Reinhard B.

But the mouse pointer of a graphic editor is a real implement that can be used as a tool in the computer.

Heinz

A good cue for introducing the contributions to this part of the book. The initial ground-probing is done by Susanne Maaß and Horst Oberquelle. They present the metaphors commonly used in interactive systems design and discuss the consequences of using each of these metaphors for the construction and use of such systems.

Christiane

In the chapter you two have co-written, you then take up a specific perspective – the tool and material metaphor – and show its importance for software development in the light of hermeneutic ideas.

Reinhard K.-S.

For me, it is interesting that, even in this relatively technical area of computer science, hermeneutics should be able to play such a significant part.

Reinhard B.

Wolfgang Coy addresses the topic of metaphors from the point of view of the user. From his discussion of the classical machine concept and his analysis of the use situation of application software, he derives his notion of "Soft Engines".

Heinz

He uses this concept to highlight the scope for "plastic" design of software by its users.

Reinhard B.

And then, coming as what might seem a thematic break, we have Thomas Gordon's provocative chapter on Artificial Intelligence.

Heinz

In keeping with the spirit of the book, Thomas avoids getting the reader involved in a fundamental controversy on the feasibility and warrantability of the idea of artificial intelligences, suggesting instead that we look on AI as a metaphor for programming software.

Christiane

I'm very glad to have a contribution here from the AI school, too. Perhaps it can help to give a constructive turn to the often highly emotional controversies waged between the AI and software engineering communities.

Heinz

Which brings us back to discourse as the human and truly scientific form of debate.

Reinhard K.-S.

A positive feature, for me, is the fact that, here, human activity is seen as standing at the beginning and end of software development, enabling us to acquire an understanding of the intervening process of formalization.

6.1 Perspectives and Metaphors for Human-Computer Interaction

Susanne Maaß and Horst Oberquelle

"The underlying premise of modern automation is a profound distrust of thinking human beings. More than any particular technology, this unanalyzed prejudice against people determines the way work is organized.

. . .

We want the computer but not the electronic sweatshop."[1]

6.1.1 Introduction

Computers are becoming omnipresent in the work place. People spend large portions of their time in interaction with computers. Consequently, the design of application systems and in particular of human-computer interaction (HCI) has become a major factor of influence on work contents and working conditions. The design of ergonomic and humane, of adequately demanding and socially acceptable work requires a deep understanding and respect for the properties, capabilities and limitations of the individual. In this context the design of a human-computer interface becomes a late step in a design process that starts with the distribution of tasks among organizational units and among people and the distribution of functions between humans and machines before it arrives at such questions as machine and interaction design[2].

Being part of or even leading such a process of work design is very demanding for computer professionals who most often are educated for its technical aspects only. Preferably the design process should include intense and continuous cooperation with prospective users in order to assess, verify and iterate on their requirements for the new system. Otherwise system designers will act according to their common sense, some prejudice and good will, however with an emphasis on technical considerations. For a long time their products have clearly shown this fact. This has led to all kinds of problems in use. In recent years a research field has formed that focusses on user-oriented design of human-computer interfaces. One of the major insights has been that the user interface has to be conceived and presented in terms the user can understand.

A very common and efficient way of trying to understand and handle new domains is the use of metaphors. Lakoff and Johnson[3] argue that human thinking

---

[1] [Garson, 1988, p. 261–263]

[2] Cf. [Hacker, 1987a].

[3] [Lakoff and Johnson, 1980]

and understanding is fundamentally based on metaphors or metaphorical concepts, respectively. A metaphor most often refers to some well-known domain and allows one to draw parallels between that domain and the current subject of thought or conversation. The better the fit is, i.e. the more details match, the better the new situation or phenomenon can be understood from the outset. However, there will always be a certain degree of mismatch where structures are not comparable, components are missing, or properties do not exist. Metaphorical descriptions can be used to emphasize some chosen aspects of a phenomenon or object while neglecting others, but never to explain the whole. They cannot be considered to be plainly right or wrong, but only so with respect to their context of use. They may also be used in a manipulative manner to blur distinctions or to cause false assumptions.

The use of metaphors can be observed in computer design as well as in use. We speak of *dialog languages, menu-conversation* and *computer intelligence*, we deal with *documents* and *folders, open* and *close windows*; we handle *software tools, store* data, we design *virtual machines* that *process* input and *produce* output. Metaphors may be consciously applied during design to cause a situation of breakdown and detached reflection: design activities are interrupted by the attempt to see the design problem at hand in terms of the concepts the metaphor offers. Imagine, e.g., the difference it makes if you design an interactive system either as a *handy tool* or as a *friendly partner*! Trying to consciously see one thing as another thing opens up a creative potential and different metaphors may lead to completely different solutions[4].

Metaphors, carefully chosen and used to design the interface, can also serve as a learning vehicle in situations of computer use. They make systems self-explanatory or may be used explicitly in user training to explain new systems or additional aspects of systems already in use. The idea is to exploit users' prior knowledge and increase their initial familiarity with the system by presenting its functionality and its handling in familiar terms. Typical examples are the well-known *folders* and *trashcans* in desktop systems or the idea of providing *menus* to choose actions or objects from. Carroll, Mack and Kellogg point out that metaphors help to build useful mental models, even if they are partly incorrect, contradictory or incomplete[5]. If users are not supplied with adequate metaphors they will make them up themselves. It has already been argued that designers should take up the professional languages and metaphors they can observe in the workplace and incorporate them in their designs[6].

Metaphors applied in system design and use stand for certain perspectives. These perspectives, however, may be unconscious to the person who uses a metaphor. A perspective structures the cognitive process, as Nygaard and Sørgaard put it[7]. Looking at things from a certain perspective means highlighting

---

[4] For a detailed discussion of "metaphorical design" see [Madsen, 1988] and [Lanzara, 1983].

[5] [Carroll et al., 1988]

[6] [Madsen and Bøgh-Andersen, 1987]

[7] [Nygaard and Sørgaard, 1987]

certain aspects while hiding others, means seeing certain relations and not others. It provides a frame of reference and consequently influences design and use: To someone who has a hammer everything looks like a nail. So the application of some particular perspective helps one to see more clearly in some respect while blinding to other aspects. To a certain degree this is a desirable effect since it focusses attention. In system design, however, one should deliberately try to take various perspectives in order to get a more thorough understanding of the application and its effects. This is what Nygaard and Sørgaard call multi-perspective reflection. For instance, a decision about the interaction techniques to be provided for users can be taken under the aspect of machine efficiency: short and non-redundant command input helps to save processing time; of learnability and user support: user prompting reminds users of the alternatives they have; of user- and task-adequacy: skilled users need shortcuts for routine tasks. It clearly requires some effort or even training to be able to take different perspectives, since they may be closely coupled with interests alien to the designer or have their origins in disciplines other than engineering. The notion of "perspective" is deliberately set apart from "paradigm" (or "Weltanschauung"), since different paradigms usually exclude each other.

Perspectives set priorities with respect to what is important in human-computer interaction and they take user interests to a larger or smaller degree into consideration; more generally, they imply assumptions about the nature of human beings. These models of humans may be more or less optimistic or pessimistic about people's work motivation and readiness to take responsibilities, their learning abilities and creativity, etc. Taken as a basis for design decisions they will lead to more or less restrictive systems that leave the users with different degrees of transparency and control, of decision latitude and responsibility. In most cases designers are unaware of the rather pessimistic beliefs they hold about users. When explicitly asked about work design in general they tend to offer more liberal views. It is suspected that in the latter case designers mostly think of their own working conditions, while subconsciously assuming different needs and necessities for others[8].

This paper is intended to draw attention to the fact that by designing work situations system designers exercise power. Aware of it or not, they start from certain assumptions about skills and needs of their future users and about the necessities of the tasks those have to accomplish. Focussing on some optimization goals more than on others they will work from a particular perspective – whether they know it or not – and consequently shape working conditions for users. The design process itself will be indicative of their perspective and priorities: the extent to which users are involved, designers' openness for other people's ideas, their willingness to admit crucial gaps in their own knowledge or education. Finally, the metaphors designers use to describe their products to others will be as explicit as they will get about their standpoint and their intentions. We want to shed some light upon the complex interweaving of metaphors used,

---

[8] See the empirical studies of [Hedberg and Mumford, 1975] and [Dagwell and Weber, 1983]

perspectives taken and models of humans held. By pointing out the consequences certain perspectives have for the task- and user-adequacy of the resulting systems we hope to raise consciousness about the designers' power and responsibilities. We propose to designers that they should deliberately take different perspectives themselves or at least to learn to accept and understand the various perspectives of the parties involved in the design process or affected by the design.

In Section 6.1.2 we will present different perspectives from which systems can be designed as well as used. The notion of model of humans will help to characterize these perspectives. We will point out assumptions that underly each perspective and the primary optimization goals that come with it. In Section 6.1.3 we will discuss metaphors that are in use in the field of Human-Computer Interaction and relate them to the perspectives they express. Section 6.1.4 draws consequences for work-oriented and user-adequate design.

6.1.2 Perspectives in system design and use

Many perspectives can be taken in system design as well as during computer use. We are going to present a set of five main perspectives that cover most of the ideas that can be found in practice and in scientific discourse today. Our classification modifies and extends the categories brought forward by Kammersgaard[9].

The traditional machine perspective takes computers as complex devices which can be used by individual users or groups of users similar to mechanical machinery. When applying the system perspective HCI is considered transfer of data between components which have basically the same properties, in particular each component can store and process data according to predefined rules. From the communication perspective you see humans and computers as agents engaged in an interaction similar to a human-to-human dialog. They communicate by means of a more or less shared language. The workshop perspective stresses that a computer can provide a workshop-like work environment that represents tools as well as materials and space. Seeing computer use from the media perspective makes you primarily concentrate on the cooperation process between people that is to be supported by computers, in that the computer serves individuals to communicate or cooperate with each other to accomplish their tasks.

Let us now analyse in more detail what these different perspectives mean for the expectations and the behaviour of users in human-computer interaction, what they mean for the goals designers will follow in order to build a user-adequate system as well as for their main focus of attention and optimization. In addition, it is important to find out what the perspectives reveal about the assumptions designers make concerning future users and their work situations.

---

[9] [Kammersgaard, 1988]

(i) Machine perspective

Seeing the computer as a machine, users will expect to deal with a technical system with given properties and a well-defined input-output behaviour. It may have a rather sophisticated and complex functionality that is non-transparent to its users and may even appear to be acting autonomously. Most users will not try to understand what goes on inside or why input has to be specified in a certain way; neither will they question the output and its format. Like other complex machines, computers get installed by experts and are subsequently used as they are by less (or otherwise) qualified people. Users will not be surprised by difficulties they encounter during system handling. They will call an expert for help.

The idea of building a machine focusses designers' attention on functionality, efficiency, error-free performance, i.e., mainly on the machine as such and less on the situation of machine use by humans. Traditionally there are enough technical problems to worry about and humans are put into the role of a "servant" to the machine (the German expression "Maschinenbediener" is revealing). The ultimate goal is to substitute human labour as far as possible. The extreme idea is that of an "integrated information processing plant" where users will do the remaining bits of work that cannot (yet) be efficiently automated.

(ii) System perspective

Seen from the system perspective the computer is put into the role of an information storage and processing device that is part of the organization's global information and communication structure. The users are seen as having basically the same properties as the automated components of this structure. They can deal with a certain set of data types by means of a set of actions; they can process data according to predefined rules and transfer data to other components of the system. Human-computer interaction becomes data transmission only.

The notion "system" often seems to imply that systems are constructed out of subsystems which consist of subsystems, etc., and thus are hierarchically structured. Organizations need not be hierarchical by necessity; nevertheless, hierarchical structure very often is meant when the system perspective is taken.

Designers who see users as providers and recipients of data will have as a primary goal "to find principles of interaction which speed up the transmission of data ... and reduce the error rate. ... The user interface is seen as just another interface between two components"[10]. Designers will not primarily think about sensible work procedures and working conditions for humans but about optimal information flow, minimal redundancy and the most efficient distribution of data processing tasks between humans and computers. Traditional system analysis methods and description techniques concentrating only on data and control flow support and reinforce this view. Adhering to this perspective means to reduce people's jobs to their algorithmic aspects only and to neglect all other human properties, skills and needs that are important in work situations.

---

[10] [Kammersgaard, 1988, p. 350]

(iii) Communication perspective

From the communication perspective computer use is regarded as a communication process in which the computer shows a communicating behaviour somewhat like humans do. User and computer act as both senders and recipients of messages that are formulated in a language common to both of them. The notions of command language, question and answer, dialog and natural language-like interactions are based on this perspective. Under this perspective it is more the communication process than its contents that is of importance. The primary purpose of messages is to provide information to be stored, to evoke special operations on objects or data, to evaluate stored knowledge, etc. The idea of a general, application-independent form of dialog with general meta-communication facilities (like help functions) to be implemented by application-independent dialog handlers is an expression of the communication perspective.

There are two variants of the communication perspective. The *partner perspective* is mainly found in the Artificial Intelligence community and has as its goal to design systems that act as humanly as possible. It is this variant that Kammersgaard calls "dialogue partner perspective"[11]. The main problem with this perspective is that it obscures the limitations of the computer as a communicating agent and does not make clear who is responsible for its behaviour.

Designers will try to provide natural language interaction and to create the illusion of an autonomous, cooperative, adaptive partner in dialog. So the fact gets hidden that the rules of the dialog are defined beforehand by the designers.

Users will tend to anthropomorphize the computer and overestimate its abilities. They will expect unproblematic natural language interaction and will be surprised by the low degree of flexibility, adaptivity and understanding of their automatic partner. They will especially miss the extremely powerful meta-communication facilities available in human-to-human communication. In case of problems the illusion of a friendly, helpful partner will quickly break down and may even turn into that of an adversary.

The *formal communication perspective* acknowledges crucial differences between interpersonal communication and human-computer communication. Oberquelle, Kupka and Maaß describe the computer as showing a restricted kind of communication behaviour, called "algorithmic communicating behaviour"[12]. This behaviour is preplanned by the designers and then delegated to the machine by means of programming. All factors relevant to interpersonal communication are effective not in the machine but in its designers: they form a mental model of the users as their remote dialog partners, of the language conventions they know and apply, of their intentions in human-computer interaction, etc. In their programs they "freeze" these assumptions and transfer them to the computer. Special problems arise from the fact that users experience systems as a whole. Several parts of an interactive system made by different designers work together to form one virtual communication partner. Inconsistent or contradictory design decisions in different modules will inevitably show at the user interface:

---

[11] [Kammersgaard, 1988]
[12] [Oberquelle et al., 1983]

the virtual communication partner will exhibit an unpredictable and confusing behaviour. The idea that HCI can be considered a special kind of user-designer communication is shared by other authors. Bench-Capon and McEnery stress the fact that the computer acts as a medium[13]. In our view users do not feel as if they communicated with designers; in most cases they will have no chance of ever meeting them in person, but they encounter their product that gives the illusion of a virtual partner.

Taking the formal communication perspective designers will be aware of the limitations of algorithmic communication and of the influence they have on the users' possible actions when they define the interaction modalities beforehand. They will try to make the computer's communicating behaviour as transparent as possible and to avoid unnecessary complexity. In addition, designers have to make sure that their own design of (mostly only) one part of the system will go well with the other parts.

Users who imagine a formally communicating partner will be prepared for unflexible and restricting system behaviour. They will expect meta-communication facilities to a certain degree and will know that the system's apparent intentions, partner model, self-image and interaction conventions are due to its designers who are actually responsible for what is going on at the interface.

Obviously, there are general limitations to what behaviour computers can exhibit and in any case the designers are responsible for what happens. The two communication perspectives admit or stress these facts to different degrees. The partner perspective tries to use the possibilities of algorithmic communication to automate as many aspects of communication as possible – leading to complex and non-transparent systems. The other perspective tries to provide users with comprehensible and controllable support. The ongoing debate about the question whether interactive systems should be adaptive (based on a dynamic internal user model) or only adaptable under user control is mainly a struggle between these two subperspectives.

Both communication perspectives focus the designers' attention on the interaction language. However, designers often tend to expect only very basic communication and language abilities from future users. They forget that people working in some application area develop a very efficient specialized professional language that is in large parts unknown to outsiders. They are experts in their domain. While designing the system, designers should think of themselves as communicating (via computer) with these experts. This would stop them from treating users like children or brain damaged adults.

Successful communication requires mutual understanding of and adaptation to language conventions. When the system is done, users have to cope with the conventions the designers have implemented. This is why already during the design process designers should make sure that they learn and understand well the professional language of their target users so that the system's terminology and conventions do not overly violate users' expectations and do not neglect

---

[13] "People interact through computers not with them."
[Bench-Capon and McEnery, 1989a, Bench-Capon and McEnery, 1989b]

their skills[14]. A communication perspective does not necessarily mean natural language interaction. It focusses attention on the fact that computer and user interact via **some** kind of language.

(iv) Workshop perspective

Looking at a human-computer system from a workshop perspective means viewing an individual as similar to a craftsman who has to make a complete product according to the rules of the craft. To work in a workshop means to handle different kinds of objects:

Materials are transformed from a raw form into a refined product. *Tools* are used in this process, but not used up. They may have *controls* which can be adjusted by the craftsman. *Locations* are objects where other objects can be put. For instance, in the joiner's workshop we may find pieces of wood, nails and a half-finished chair as materials, a hammer and an adjustable plane as tools and the bench, boxes for nails or a tool box as locations.

The work of a craftsman is characterized [15] by:

- deep knowledge of materials and mastery of the tools and procedures developed during intensive apprenticeship and experience;
- permanent control over material and tool with the main attention on the tool's effects on the material, not on the tool itself;
- direct and exclusive control over the space for materials and tools;
- participation in the development of refined tools and the choice of new materials.

The idea of computer systems as workshops has been a basic concept in the pioneering work of Douglas Engelbart already in the sixties, although it was explicitly mentioned as late as 1983[16]. A workshop perspective is also the background of the paper by Budde and Züllighoven[17].

Users working in a computerized workshop will expect to find a situation which is transparent to them, is completely under their control, and extends well-known traditional tools in an obvious way. They will expect that materials, tools, controls and locations are obvious from their appearance, i.e. self-descriptive. They will expect to find tools adjusted to their tasks, but will not assume that a powerful tool can be mastered immediately. They will look for possibilities for adaptation and extension of the tools when their experience is growing or a new situation emerges.

To design a system from the workshop perspective means to start out with a rather respectful view of users: They have to be seen as the application experts from whom designers can (and must) learn about the field of application, its established work procedures, its quality standards and its language. The most

---

[14] For more details see [Maaß, 1984].

[15] [Ehn and Kyng, 1985]

[16] [Engelbart, 1988]

[17] See Chap. 6.2.

appropriate interaction technique for the workshop perspective is direct manipulation, which simulates the manipulation of objects in the real world. Designers will try to make the tools themselves disappear from consciousness during use. They will try to cooperate with users to bring their tacit knowledge into the design process and to use their expertise for evaluation.

The fact that tools can only be developed on the basis of extensive experience with their practical use calls for the use of prototypes. Workshop-like systems are considered open for further modification at any point in time. The real potential of the workshop view is in the development of advanced tools for application experts in cooperation with them. System design for novice users will lead to the provision of only very basic tools.

(v) Media perspective

From a media perspective a computer or computer network is seen as a flexible technical means to support coordination, communication and cooperation among several persons. Cooperation takes place by means of spatial arrangements and connections and by operations and rules for their temporal use.

The computer as a medium combines and extends features of traditional media like mail, telephone, radio or print media. It allows materials to be represented and provides space where materials can be located. It connects persons for the synchronous or asynchronous exchange of materials and messages and allows joint access to shared material. The idea of computers as media for communication has been intensively discussed by Bannon[18]. The view of computers as media providing shared material for cooperation has been stressed by Sørgaard[19]. In addition to the storage, transport and distribution properties of traditional media the computer can be used to flexibly introduce new materials and space, to modify connections and to set up coordination and communication protocols users have agreed upon. In its kernel, it has to behave in a disinterested way[20], i.e., it must not implicitly promote the interests of any individual participant. Since cooperation is a highly dynamic and context-dependent process with frequently changing patterns, the adaptation of the medium must be controlled by the cooperating, responsible persons themselves.

Using the computer as a medium makes users primarily concentrate on the people they work with, on the cooperation processes and on responsibilities. Users will expect the computer to transport their materials and messages without modifying them and to reliably hold material and messages that can be accessed by individuals or groups. They will feel responsible for the parts they control. The programmability of the computer allows users to automate parts of their own work, but they remain responsible for these parts, too. They will try to adapt the medium to the changing needs of their jobs.

When a computer system is being designed from the media perspective, designers will pay special attention to group processes in cooperation of users and

---

[18] [Bannon, 1986]
[19] [Sørgaard, 1987]
[20] [Petri, 1983]

how to support those. The computer as a medium should offer appropriate ways of representing and exchanging various kinds of materials and ideas, e.g., as text, graphics, pictures, sounds. Functions have to be provided to produce new material, to refer to, annotate and build on existing material, zoom in on details, etc. People must be able to contribute easily to conversations, and to send and receive messages. Procedures for turn taking or concurrent work, for discussion moderation and group management have to be thought of. But the system must always be designed as open for adaptation during use. This is a challenge not yet met by existing systems[21]. Nevertheless, designers must be aware that only a small part of human-to-human communication and cooperation can be computerized and that successful computer-supported cooperation is based on good human relations. These can only be established and sustained in direct social contact.

We have presented five major perspectives, mainly in the historical sequence in which they came up. Each perspective is based on a special view of humans, defines a particular human-computer relationship and sets goals for optimization in software design. The perspectives partially reflect those kinds of tasks for which computers have been successfully applied: from strictly formalizable, well-structured tasks to less formal tasks of individual users and further on to group work; from replacement of human work to support of human workers. The question of the adequacy of all these perspectives for certain work situations has not been discussed yet.

We suspect that further perspectives are already in use or will develop as time goes on – our set of perspectives is not in any sense complete. In order to better understand the perspectives presented we will take a closer look at the metaphors that go with them. Unusual new metaphors may be indicators of new perspectives.

6.1.3 Metaphors in design and use

A large variety of metaphors, like *desk-tops, convivial tools, dynamic blackboards* or intelligent *helpful agents*, is used in the context of HCI. Such metaphors make the reader/listener think of concepts, experiences and values that have to do with certain perspectives. So, in studying the metaphors people use, we will get to know more about their underlying views and intentions. In particular, the perspectives introduced in the last section will become clearer.

(i) Machine-oriented metaphors

The basic vocabulary of informatics is full of machine-oriented metaphors, which are part of designers' professional language. Examples are *calculator, data processing, storage, processor, input/output, to run a program*, etc. Programmers

---

[21] For a collection of papers in the quickly developing area of computer-supported cooperative work (CSCW) see [Greif, 1988].

among themselves are used to talking about *virtual machines* they are building and dealing with. By this they abstract from how these software components are internally realized. Also the notion of software engineering expresses the idea of software production as machine construction. Budde and Züllighoven argue that software should be constructed like machines, but appear tool-like in use situations[22].

In public discussions, machine-oriented metaphors are mainly used for two purposes: either to paint a vision of total automation where human beings as potential interference factor have been completely eliminated (as in Computer Integrated Manufacturing), or to point out the inhumane and unforgiving character of computers and of work with computers (e.g., *electronic assembly line, the electronic sweatshop*[23]).

The current discussion on CASE (Computer-Aided Software Engineering) indicates that the idea of an integrated machinery for a complete field of production has reached the designers' workplaces. It will be interesting to see how they are going to react to a machine perspective applied to their own work. The *software factory* seems to be a proper metaphor. But we suspect that successful CASE systems will turn out to be a combination of workshops connected by media.

In user instruction one way the machine metaphor can be of advantage is to explain why users have to strictly follow rules in human-computer interaction: the computer is "just a dumb machine".

(ii) System-oriented metaphors

System-oriented metaphors are rare though the system perspective is the most common perspective for software development. Since the notion of *system* has been developed in close connection with informatics it is often used without metaphorical circumscription. Calling everything a system makes important differences disappear.

Card, Moran and Newell provide an excellent example for system-oriented thinking[24]. In their "Model Human Processor" they describe human cognitive processes by concepts like *storage, processors, capacity, cycle-time*, thus understanding people as information processing systems. Their goal is to optimize the human-computer system with respect to speed, throughput, and error rates.

The equation of people with technical components also becomes obvious in formal languages that are used to describe organizational systems consisting of people and machines. Nets of channels and agencies (or offices)[25] are an example: various active system components, the *agencies*, are connected by passive components, the *channels*. Persons as well as machines may be performing the

---

[22] See Chap. 6.2.
[23] [Garson, 1988]
[24] [Card et al., 1983]
[25] Cf. [Petri, 1980].

actions of an agency. Channels are used to transport or store information. Calling a piece of software an *agency* or *office* makes it appear as a part of a bigger organization. A comparison to a functional unit with a strictly rule-based working clerk or officer as the agent captures the formalized behaviour of the software quite well. On the other hand, comparing humans to strictly rule-based agents means a significant reduction in our view of humans. The development of role/function/action-nets[26] was inspired by the idea that the pragmatic differences between roles (for which always persons are responsible) and associated functions (which can be executed by humans or machines) should be reflected in a new description language in order to overcome some of the deficiencies of traditional system description languages.

(iii) Communication-oriented metaphors

Most communication-oriented metaphors are based on the idea of a *dialog partner*, but stress different aspects and support more or less the aforementioned two variants of the communication perspective.

Describing a computer as an *obedient clerk* characterizes it as inferior to the user. Calling it a *helpful assistant* who "does what I mean"[27] still puts the computer in a subordinate role, but leaves open how far the assistant's knowledge about "what I mean" goes. As long as it only means simple spelling correction that can be switched on and off by the user the metaphor does no harm. However, declaring a computer an *adaptive, intelligent expert* or *tutor* clearly stands for the partner perspective that attempts to make the computer as human-like as possible.

The concept of *help* as such is a metaphor that alludes to a partner relationship. *Passive help* components resemble dictionaries or manuals, they are media-like. They could be more accurately called *descriptions*. *Active help* components realize some kind of adaptive behaviour that makes it difficult for the user to anticipate the system's behaviour and its limitations. *Knowledge-based, intelligent* or *adaptive help* attributes some kind of personality to the computer. In order to inform users about limitations and to leave them in control of the system's behaviour, designers should look for more unpretentious metaphors that stress the differences, not the similarities. For instance, *help* could be replaced by *flexible, extensible descriptions* if implemented accordingly. The system's behaviour in interaction could be called algorithmic or at least formal communication behaviour. The *partner* metaphor should be avoided as far as possible. For example, in the development of the German standard "Principles of Ergonomic Dialogue Design"[28] concepts like *self-explaining* and *error tolerant* were dismissed in favour of *self describing* and *error robust* because it was felt that the former concepts put users in a clearly inferior role with respect to the wise and forgiving computer.

---

[26] RFA-nets [Oberquelle, 1987, Oberquelle, 1988].

[27] See the "programmer's assistant" with DWIM (Do what I mean) principle [Teitelman, 1977].

[28] [DIN66234, 1988]

The recently introduced notion of *user problem-domain communication*[29] differs from the partner metaphor, but still makes the persons responsible for the communication behaviour of the problem-domain (whatever that may be) disappear behind the seemingly objective domain knowledge.

The non-existence of powerful intelligent automatic partners up to now does not seem to influence researchers and funding agencies. The hope for building such systems in a nearby future is still unbroken. From our point of view the question as such, whether almost human-like partners can be built, is the wrong one. The point is not whether we can build such systems, but whether we should do it.

(iv) Workshop-oriented metaphors

The *tool* metaphor is the most prominent metaphor under the workshop perspective. That is why others use it to refer to the whole perspective[30]. But the interpretation of the tool concept has become very broad and general. In informatics people have started to call almost any helpful piece of software a tool. Some call commands a tool, discuss "tools with dialogue capabilities" and see macro facilities as "tool-building tools"[31], thus mixing communication and workshop perspective. Others have called computers as such *convivial tools*, while at the same time promoting the idea of adaptive, knowledge-based human-computer communication[32]. Neither is the tool metaphor appropriate for such systems nor does the attribute convivial taken from Illich seem to be adequate. Convivial tools must be completely transparent to and controlled by their users. Tools able to manipulate their users (as adaptive systems can do) cannot be convivial[33].

The tool metaphor can be useful in that it draws attention to task-oriented system functionality. The study of traditional tools and their characteristics helps to find principles for task- and user-adequate design of interactive systems. It is interesting to see that designers are asking for and are building *flexible power tools* for their own work. Very often, however, the tool metaphor is just used as a catching synonym for simplicity, even for complex integrated systems, in order to play down system aspects that might produce user resistance: Who would be afraid of a tool?

Workshop scenarios integrate and extend the idea of tools, as realized on the Macintosh, for example. *Desktop*, *folders* and *trash-can* provide space and the latter two are movable objects at the same time. *Documents* like *letters, forms, spreadsheets* form the material to be worked on directly by pointing and dragging or by using *tools* like *paint brushes, erasers, rulers*, etc. *Property sheets* represent the many controls which can be manipulated by the users to adjust the system's behaviour to their needs. All objects are graphically represented by icons giving

---

[29] [Fischer and Lemke, 1988]
[30] [Kammersgaard, 1988, Ehn and Kyng, 1985]
[31] [Dzida, 1982]
[32] [Gunzenhäuser, 1982, Fischer, 1983]
[33] Cf. [Illich, 1975, p. 39].

them a visual existence. The illusion of a workshop is supported by the fact that one finds the workplace in exactly the state one has left it in. It is not surprising that help facilities play an inferior role in this environment and that adaptive systems are absent. But even very simple metaphors may be misleading when they are implemented without too much thought. For instance, the *trash-can* icon (and metaphor) of the ATARI suggests that thrown away documents can be retrieved from it, though in fact the trash-can works like a shredder.

Sets of related metaphors supporting a workshop perspective can also be found in other fields of application. Some CAD systems provide drafter's workshops with *paper, grids, templates, pens, palettes*, etc. The UTOPIA project developed a workshop for newspaper layout[34]. Programming of the Macintosh is supported by a *programmer's workshop*[35]. The same metaphor is promoted by Budde and Züllighoven[36]. *Programmer's workbench* and *programming lab* are other metaphors that stand for the workshop perspective.

Simulation systems that are operated by direct manipulation are classical representatives of systems built under the workshop perspective. The Alternative Reality Kit (ARK)[37] drives the illusion of working with real objects to its extreme. Every parameter is represented by tangible objects, e.g., as *knobs, buttons, slider controls* that can be obtained in a *warehouse*. ARK even represents physical laws as objects that can be manipulated. This results in a homogeneous interface, but rather stretches the metaphor of real things.

(v) Media-oriented metaphors

One of the traditional computer applications was to provide central data storage in *data bases*. Another function important under the media perspective, the support of interpersonal communication, was realized in *mail* systems. Only recently have these two functions been integrated in so-called *coordination systems*. Mainly in research settings the idea of supporting human cooperation in groups has been developed. The idea of material sharing is currently being implemented by means of electronic *books, notecards, blackboards* and electronic *bulletin boards*. The goal of communication support is reflected in metaphors like *message*, electronic *mail*, electronic *conferencing*, electronic *meeting*. Recent systems have refined these concepts by structuring the networks of connections (e.g. into *discussions, task forces*, the contents of messages (e.g. *invitations, memos*) and by supporting various patterns of *conversations*.

Calling the coordinated exchange of messages or moderated access to shared material (like a blackboard) a *conference* or *meeting* seems to neglect a factor that is rather important in meetings. Often the explicit exchange of messages is relatively unimportant compared with the development of social relations in the group of participants that happens simply by the fact that they are close to

---

[34] [Bødker et al., 1987]
[35] [Apple, 1987]
[36] See Chap. 6.2.
[37] [Smith, 1987]

each other as humans for a while. Another important feature is confidentiality which is lost as soon as spoken (transitory) communication is made manifest in stored and thus retrievable, modifiable, misusable form.

Metaphors expressing the media perspective and systems that support group work first came up in research settings where the concepts of cooperation and coordination imply a rather balanced distribution of power and responsibilities and shared interests in working groups. The transfer of system solutions from research into commercial settings has been reported as problematic[38]. This has to do with the fact that cooperation and coordination have a different meaning in an environment with hierarchical structure and managerial control. It turned out that systems that were intended to support cooperation among persons with equal rights could be used to make hitherto uncontrollable cooperation processes transparent and more manageable and thus fill one of the last remaining "formalization gaps" in the office. This illustrates the fact that systems that were developed with good intentions and starting from progressive perspectives may have surprising and undesirable effects if the commercial application context has not been correctly anticipated by the designers. It may happen that the original metaphor will stick with the product while in fact raising false expectations with respect to its effects.

(vi) Further metaphors

The workshop perspective is somewhat extended by the *rooms* metaphor[39]: The idea is to provide an individual user with several different work environments that suit his or her various subtasks. Rooms organize collections of windows into related screenfuls of information and functionality. Rooms are connected by *doors* through which they can be entered. A similar idea is promoted by Madsen who suggests using an *office building* approach[40]. A related, but different idea is that of Holt[41]. In his "coordination mechanics" approach he describes organizations as interconnected *work arenas* or *centres* (space) for interacting *bodies* (materials, tools, responsible persons). Coordination is achieved by interactions of responsible persons and other bodies at the common boundaries. In this view computer networks extend the technical basis for coordination by providing space, bodies and means for programmed interactions. The computer provides the "dynamic glue" that binds tasks together into larger, meaningful entities. The organizational structure in space and time can be dynamically developed during use, which gives users more control over their working conditions. In the coordination mechanics approach the idea of "shared material" is rejected since every piece of space belongs to one and only one centre by definition.

Space-oriented metaphors are also used in many hypermedia systems to help users develop a mental model for orientation in complex data spaces that they

---

[38] See, e.g., [Durham, 1988] about the Coordinator system.

[39] [Card and Henderson, 1987]

[40] [Madsen, 1989]

[41] [Holt, 1988]

can *browse* or *walk* or *work* in. *Social browsing* in virtual *corridors* as proposed in the CRUISER project[42] seems to be the most extreme attempt at technically reconstructing social reality.

A rather unconventional way of characterizing the work environment for human-machine interface designers is the *theatre* metaphor presented in "Rehearsal World"[43]. Interface elements are seen as *performers* on *stage* (which is the screen) that can be taught certain parts by the *stage director* (the designer). They can be *rehearsed* individually or in groups to show how they perform together, interacting via *cues*.

Guided tours[44] and *tourist guides*[45] for hyperspaces try to simulate active, helpful agents in the computer.

In both cases the invisible *partners* of the partner perspective are transformed into *visible partners*.

The many space-oriented metaphors as well as the introduction of virtual agents indicate that new *virtual world* perspectives are emerging. They cannot yet be treated in detail.

6.1.4 Consequences for design

The extreme flexibility of the computer allows designers to strive for a variety of goals: maximal automation or control over users, human-like computer behaviour as well as maximal support for highly qualified workers. Accordingly, the resulting systems will constitute very different working conditions for their users; they may turn out to be dequalifying and restrictive, overly supportive and tiresome to work with, or perhaps creativity enhancing, user-adaptable and just right. Obviously, designers are in a powerful position since they are setting the facts the users will have to live with afterwards. Markus and Bjørn-Andersen have pointed out that neither the users nor the designers themselves are necessarily aware of this situation which may range between the two unacceptable extremes of professional manipulation and unintended influence[46]. By our discussion of metaphors and perspectives in design we want to uncover, to question and to influence designers' implicit models of humans and their assumptions about work.

(i) Adequate models of humans and work-oriented design

The view of humans dominating among designers can be characterized as pessimistic: they view them as having little creativity, little interest and motivation for work, and as being afraid of taking responsibility. It seems "natural" to designers to control user behaviour as far as possible, to prescribe work procedures,

---

[42] [Root, 1988]
[43] [Gould and Finzer, 1984]
[44] [Trigg, 1988]
[45] [Fairchild et al., 1989]
[46] [Markus and Bjørn-Andersen, 1987]

to suppress users' own initiatives and to motivate them by economic means only. We believe, on the contrary, that persons who seem to conform to this sad picture should rather be considered a lamentable product of the Tayloristic work organization they have been exposed to, instead of assuming that they are like this by their very nature [47]. The problem is not in the people, but in the inadequate working conditions!

We propose to designers that they deliberately take an optimistic and holistic view of people as a necessary basis for the design of humane working conditions and satisfying work, and choose perspectives and metaphors accordingly. Human beings have to be considered as individuals

- who are bodily present in the world,
- who think and act not only rationally and analytically, but also based on intuitive and fuzzy feelings and social and professional experience, and
- who are social beings who need social contact and cooperation.

Humans live embedded in a biological, historical, cultural and social context. They not only want to earn their living by work, but have a right to self-realization and personal development. People are ready to take responsibility for their work – if they have the chance and get the necessary qualification for it. As skilled workers they also possess a lot of experience and tacit knowledge which should not and cannot be transferred into machines. Such a model of humans is shared by many researchers in Western Europe, especially in Scandinavia, and has been made a starting point for "humanistic", "work-oriented" system design approaches[48]. It is obvious that these design approaches aim for more than what today's good-willing practitioners try to provide: user interfaces that are easy to learn and efficient to use and that have a nice "look and feel".

An optimistic and holistic view of users leads to a new designer-user relationship: designers will act as experts for computers and users will be accepted as experts for work in the field of application.

This view is reflected in work-oriented approaches to system design as they have been similarly characterized by Weltz and Lullies and by Nurminen[49]: Human workers are considered as central agents who have to be supported by a task-oriented job design and by organizational and technical means like computers. The relevant knowledge is bound to the person and the context. Persons are responsible for ordinary as well as for information processing tasks, in which they have to be supported by ("small") computer systems. System development is seen as an evolutionary process focussed on persons and their jobs and user participation is necessary in this process. Hence, the role of designers changes from a "generous god" or "invisible friend" to a real, cooperative partner for users.

In order to transfer these design ideas from research surroundings to commercial applications it will be necessary as a first step to make practitioners aware of

---

[47] Cf. [Weltz and Lullies, 1983].

[48] Cf. [Frese et al., 1987, Volpert, 1987, Nygaard and Håndlykken, 1981, Bjørn-Andersen, 1988, Nurminen, 1987, Nurminen, 1988, Ehn, 1988].

[49] [Weltz and Lullies, 1983, Nurminen, 1987, Nurminen, 1988], and Chap. 7.2.

their models of humans. To convince them that their assumptions might be insufficient or even wrong it may help to confront their models of others with models they hold about themselves. Starting from those metaphors and perspectives they apply for their own working conditions and for desirable computer support may reveal discrepancies and lead to new thinking.

(ii)   User-supportive perspectives and metaphors

Starting from a holistic and optimistic view of humans and keeping humane working conditions in mind, designers should try to choose perspectives and metaphors accordingly. Some perspectives are more suited than others and no single perspective will be sufficient.

The machine and system perspectives neglect or underestimate users' needs and capabilities and should therefore be dismissed. Having the computer appear as a human-like communication partner is problematic as well since corresponding systems tend to become non-transparent and responsibilities seem unclear.

In our view, only those perspectives are acceptable which are based on a view of computers as complementary and supportive to humans. These are at present, as far as we know, the formal communication, workshop and media perspectives. The formal communication perspective is needed to draw attention to language aspects: The language elements that have to be designed for use in human-computer interaction must go well with the professional language of the respective application area. Unlike in human communication, implemented language conventions for HCI cannot easily be modified in dialogue with the system. That is why designers should cooperate with their future users during design in order to learn and negotiate conventions before "freezing" them in their systems. A workshop perspective helps to concentrate on providing appropriate functionality for individual computer use. What is the material the user is going to work with and how could it best be presented? What tools will be necessary and how can they be made adjustable to changing user needs? What can be learnt from the professional experience of people working in the application domain? Since human work always has individual and collective parts, system design for computer-supported work needs the media perspective to complement the other two. From the media perspective the most important questions are, how communication and coordination processes among groups of people can be supported, how to give access to and present shared material and how to send it around.

This kind of multi-perspective reflection about a design problem at hand will give designers a better chance to shape humane working conditions and produce user- and task-adequate systems. Part of this reflection can be done together with users.

When metaphors are used to illustrate system capabilities to users, they at the same time imply something about users and their capabilities. As a consequence of our metaphor discussion we would like to put forth the following rules:

Let us choose metaphors consciously and carefully:

- Metaphors must not prevent system transparency – instead they should help to improve users' understanding and mastery of the system.
- Metaphors should not obscure the dissimilarities between humans and computers by projecting too many human capabilities onto the computer; instead they should serve to create a realistic image of the computer's capabilities and point to its restrictions.
- Metaphors should not transport unacceptably restricted models of humans by comparing humans to machines. They should rather aim at a human-centred understanding of computer-supported work processes.

Acknowledgements

We gratefully acknowledge the constructive comments on earlier versions of this chapter by Susanne Bødker and Liam Bannon, Markku Nurminen, and Reinhard Budde and Heinz Züllighoven.

6.2 Software Tools in a Programming Workshop

Reinhard Budde and Heinz Züllighoven

6.2.1 Recalling our background

When we began, some years ago, building a programming environment for the logical programming language Prolog, the goals we had in mind were predominantly technical ones. Our basic aim was to combine the logical and object-oriented programming styles and to compile a set of tools for constructing Prolog software in a uniform environment. Once we felt we had found satisfactory solutions to the problems involved, we released the programming environment for use by other development groups. We were astounded to find that the external use of our environment led to a number of unexpected problems. We then began not only to eliminate technical errors and inconsistencies, but also to reflect on how it was possible for these problems to arise. The conclusion we reached was that we needed to find answers to a number of questions which went well beyond the original technical problems:

- What are the building blocks of a programming environment and how can they be "invented"?
- What is a good building block and how can it be smoothly integrated into an environment?
- How does an operational building block become an integral part of the developer's daily work?
- What are we doing when we develop a programming environment and what are we doing when we work with it?

Basically, all these questions revolve around an epistemological kernel: How are we as software developers to understand our work and the objects occurring in it? Reflections of the sort expressed in this book by C. Floyd or J. Goguen[1] appear, to us, to rule out any possibility of a formal approach to this particular domain.

The approach we have ultimately chosen to answer this central question consists of identifying different aspects:

- When dealing with programming environments, developers and users adopt different perspectives.
- We view software as consisting of both formal objects and things that we use in our work.

---

[1] Cf. Chaps. 1.1 and 5.1.

- When we formalize, we explain how an object functions; when we work purposively with a thing, we understand what it means.

- To make software executable, we have to make a complete formal description of it. But we can only do this if we have an *initial understanding* of what we are to describe.

Reflecting on these different aspects, it became clear to us that the *starting point* both for designing a programming environment and for understanding this design process had to be an analysis of the *everyday work* of software developers. Nevertheless, formalization is one, though not the only, important task that must form part of the development process. Inspired by the frequently cited book *Understanding Computers and Cognition* by Winograd and Flores, we have looked into Heidegger's notion of "equipment" (*Zeug*) and examined his ideas about everyday ways of dealing with it.

Now, we are told by hermeneutics that, in order to understand our everyday work and in order to be able to express this, we understand things *as something*. We understand a thing explicitly through association with other things that have likewise already been understood. This transference of meanings from one domain to another describes exactly how a *metaphor* works. We thus set out to look for suitable metaphors. This search led us to distinguish between *tools, machines, automata* and *materials* in a *programming workshop*[2]. In what follows, we will explain these terms as metaphors for developing and using a programming environment. It is important for the reader to bear in mind the fact that we are writing about software engineers and their work. That is our point of departure. Meanwhile, our further research work has shown that the chosen metaphors can also be effectively used for developing interactive application systems. W. Coy uses similar arguments when he speaks of soft engines in his contribution to the present book. Coy does not proceed from the professional software developer's viewpoint, but from that of the users, focussing on the use of standard software[3]. Maaß and Oberquelle have shown that there are other metaphors besides this one and have examined the effects this has on questions of usability and quality[4].

Our basic line of reasoning is as follows: We look at our everyday work with the computer and other things of our working environment and find that, in doing so, we adopt different views on different things. And we classify these things as either tools or materials. Then, under the perspective of *construction* and *use*, we establish the connection between software as a machine and software as a tool. We find that software often manifests itself, in use, not as a tool, but as an automaton. Finally, we view the organizational and spatial environment of our work and discuss why we prefer the workshop perspective to the factory perspective to characterize it.

---

[2] The results of this investigation, which go well beyond the scope of this book, can be found in [Budde and Züllighoven, 1990].

[3] Cf. Chap. 6.3.

[4] Cf. Chap. 6.1.

6.2.2 Working with the computer

In our everyday work as software developers, we are used to handling things that are "inside" a computer, such as word processors, editors, interpreters or various types of files. At our workplace, we employ these things in a self-evident way – we frequently talk about them. Generalized statements like "*the* computer is not a tool",[5] which we find in the literature do not tally with our daily experience at work. The things we are familiar with in software development constantly cross the borderline between computer and "non-computer". Take, for instance, a dataset which appears to be lost:

- We look for a specific file on archive tapes which, to be on the safe side, we have stored separately from our workstation computer.
- We look for this dataset on a different computer which we have been using for some time while our workstation was down. Perhaps, we may find an older version "lying around" somewhere.
- We look for the dataset on our desks or in the wastepaper basket, as we have made printouts of various versions.

It is essential in order to understand these various activities, that we regard a dataset as part of our working environment in much the same way as we see the archive tape (which contains it), or the computer (without which it could not exist). In this way, we look both at the computer as a whole ("The dataset has disappeared from the computer") and at its parts ("A moment ago, the file was in the `sdrc` *directory*"). An analysis of the prevailing patterns of dealing with *the* computer shows that we frequently regard its parts and software components (e.g., files, programs, devices) as materials and tools similar to the way we view paper, pencils, file cabinets, and hand tools.

This takes into account the fact that computer use has changed over the last ten years. "Monolithic" mainframe applications are inevitably dying out, and along with them are disappearing working situations in which a user delivers a pack of punched cards to a closed-shop computer department and then has to wait for hours before getting a printed listing. Recently, not only developers but users, too, have adopted a more differentiated view of the computer as consisting of identifiable software components that support daily tasks by means of input routines for order data, billing programs or database services.

6.2.3 Tools and materials

Heidegger characterizes the things that are familiar to us in a working process (das Zeug) in two different ways: They are *in a specific way useful* to us, and, in a given situation, we *take them for what they are*. As we work with equipment, we notice that we use it in different ways – one part of it will, to some extent, *become the object and result of our work*, while another part *serves to produce*

---

[5] Cf. [Wingert and Riehm, 1985].

the result of our work. Let us look at this distinction and what it means in the computer field:

- *The software components that are part of our object of work we will call* programming materials.
  - Materials are characterized by the ways in which we use them as part of the final result of our work. Accordingly, we process, shape, analyze and evaluate materials. When developing software, we come across **programming materials** as components of a software system and its documentation. Examples of programming materials are: an interface specification, comments in a source code file, tuples in a database.
  - Besides this type of programming material, we use additional resources that only contribute indirectly to the final result. Examples of such resources are *tempfiles* with lists of file names and a catalogue of *safe dumps.*
- *The software components that we employ while dealing with programming materials we will call* programming utensils.
  - Utensils are characterized by the way in which they help to produce the result of our work or do so more conveniently. When developing software, we use *programming utensils* like *spelling checkers* and *e-mail systems.*
- *Of the programming utensils,* software tools *are the part of our equipment that we* apply to programming materials *and that are of particular importance for our work and our understanding of it.*
  - Software tools are characterized by the way in which we use them for *processing, shaping and probing* the different types of programming materials. In our view a tool is invariably something *mediating* between us and our materials.
  - In addition, software tools are invariably *signs* of the way we use to do our daily work. They point to our experiences and to familiar working processes and regulations.
  - Another characteristic of tools is their persistency – while we are working on a particular task, we usually perceive them as remaining unchanged, although, we frequently change their settings or "parameters". This persistency is not a predominant aspect of materials or utensils in general.
  - Examples of software tools are: compilers, editors, browsers, and prettyprinters.

It depends on our objects of work and the different settings in which they are used whether we look at software components as materials, utensils, or tools. Thus, we may summarize as follows:

As software developers we process, probe and organize **programming materials** by means of **software tools** and with the support of **programming utensils.**

6.2.4 Working with tools

We have pointed out that tools are crucial to the way in which we work and how we understand our environment. Leaving aside the reduction of the notion of tools to mechanical implements used by the craftsman, we have opened up a variety of different views on the software components of a computer:

> Software as material unfolds when we treat it with software tools. Software is transposed into different sensually perceptible phenomena:

> *Software tools* open up our object of work, the programming materials, as we are dealing with it: thus, software tools are *means for cognition.*

Let us now take a closer look at what it means to work with tools. We frequently find references to the so-called transparency of technical equipment[6]. This aspect is familiar to us when we are handling tools and materials without disturbance. But, at the same time, we realize that these things exhibit distinct characteristics and do not *disappear* transparently. Besides serving a specific purpose, tools and materials appear as things in their own right, useful or harmful to us, but never on their own. Technical equipment requires specific ways of handling which call for practice. Take, for instance, the difficulties a child has to cope with when learning to ride a bicycle, e.g., the problems of balance and coordination; how "natural" this same interplay between the human body and the technical apparatus seems as soon as we have developed the appropriate skills. We have made similar observations with people using a graphical workstation computer and a mouse for the first time: the coordination of arm, hand and fingers obviously had to be subjected to a completely new type of visual control in order to cope with seemingly trivial tasks like selecting an icon or activating a selection menu. Obviously, we learn how to handle tools by working with them – sometimes in experimental or trial situations. And trying to employ tools can result in failure – that is an everyday experience.

Such specific ways of handling tools acquire a kind of autonomy that is evident in the "art" of building and mastering machines and tools[7]. These aspects are of fundamental importance to our work as software developers. We have to look at the different ways and means of *handling* software. And we have to remember that we are frequently confronted with situations in which we have to develop software for other people who are not familiar with software at all.

Thus, we may say that tools, like any other technical equipment, are not confined to opening up the world around us. They are linked to our bodies, extending our senses and giving rise to new forms of movement. In other words:

> Handling *software tools* extends the *sensual perception* of our environment – they help us to *experience* software systems and the world around us.

---

[6] Cf. [Winograd and Flores, 1986, Ehn, 1988].

[7] An impressive elaboration of this aspect is given by R. Pirsig in [Pirsig, 1975].

When we say that the coupling of human beings and technical implements gives rise to new forms of bodily behaviour and new sensual perceptions, we do not mean that these processes strictly follow rational and purposeful dimensions. Let us merely call to mind the sensations and emotions that help us to control and operate a tool or a machine – be it the experience of pain and despair in the case of a car breakdown or accident, or the experience of pleasure and enjoyment we have when playing a pinball machine or riding on a roller coaster.

We may have to get used to the idea that pleasure, pain, emotions and aesthetical feelings in the widest sense are aspects of our ways of dealing with technical equipment, and that these emotions and feelings are neither of secondary importance nor can they be dismissed to the realms of leisure time and amusement parks. Such "ir-rational" emotions and impressions are also familiar to us when dealing with software systems. Anyone, who has ever "got lost" in a graphical computer game will have experienced the fascinating world of "imaginary" appearances with the sometimes far-reaching physical and mental reactions it causes. And they will not be astonished to learn of the similar sensations experienced when constructing and testing "mere" application software.

6.2.5 Tools as artifacts

We have deliberately compared the handling of software tools with that of hand tools. It is customary to oppose the directness and naturalness of our perception to the artificiality of technically mediated signs and models. This position could be characterized by saying: "We perceive the material things around us in a natural way, but we have to be culturally trained to make use of signs and models." We reject this idea by looking at it from a theoretical point of view and contend that we as *human beings* invariably perceive what we call *nature* in a mediated way. Mediation comes in whenever we realize our metabolism with nature by using tools as we shape nature, and whenever we designate and label the things around us.

Adopting this type of theoretical understanding, our bodily motions in a working process may be seen as *artificial* or indirect in varying degrees. What we are likely to overlook is that we are not only confronted with new technical equipment, but also with a new meaning of our own actions. Thus, our motions become *gestures* which are signs denoting a complex technical procedure[8]. This holds, though at the same time we *experience* tools and other technical equipment *directly*.

Consequently, technical equipment does not merely consist of simple objects that we employ and then lay aside again. Technical equipment binds us into a multitude of obvious and hidden links. It transforms our physical and sensual aspects and our body language. The more complex the procedures that are "encapsulated" into technical equipment, the more "abstract" the gestures of our body become. After all, gestures – as the "terms" of our motions – become familiar in our everyday lifes. Like signs, they appear in a double sense: as motor

---

[8] Cf. [Bahr, 1983].

actions of our body, and as symbolic motions, denoting something else. And, as with signs, we both perform and understand them "directly" – if we understand them at all. Who, when switching on the light via a sensor switch, thinks of all the "atomic" actions that have concealed themselves behind this gesture in the course of technological development? There is little or no difference in quality between this aspect of technical equipment and software tools. Software tools merely offer a wider range of gestures via *function keys* and *mouse handling*, but these are by no means more "abstract" or mediated than other gestures. Which experienced user of a graphical workstation computer needs to think about the hardware and software links between moving a mouse and changing the position of the mouse pointer on the screen when clicking an *icon*?

To complete our discourse on the characteristics of work with software tools, we have to look at the tool as a mediator and sign. Technical equipment mediates. This is obvious in the sciences – take, for instance, an experiment with a neutron accelerator – but it is an everyday experience as well. While tools shape , our senses at the same time are informed about the *state of the material* we are working on[9]. While we are concentrating on our task, both our tools and our materials merge into one entity of perception which gives us feedback about state and progress of our work. In this connection, we may justly speak of a *language of tools*.

However, these aspects of information and communication are not only characteristic of the use of hand tools. It is even more obvious that machines shape and organize materials according to their different states; and, at the same time, these states of a machine indicate the states of the processed materials. After all, besides their main functional characteristics, all machines exhibit aspects of signs. The different positions of switches and handles, the pointer deflection of measuring instruments, the changing sounds, these and other signals carry the information guiding operation.

There would appear to be an obvious relation between the signs of a traditional machine and the materials of work, but we still have to be familiar with these signs in order to understand them. Without our ability to operate equipment on a meta-level of signs, we would not be able to work on materials. It is important to note that our everyday ways of employing technical equipment invariably comprise a *level of models*, i.e., of *signs and states*. It is in this sense that we understand the phrase: every tool is a sign for its own use.

Working with a computer, this separation between the thing as such and its meta-level of signs become obvious. "Inside" a computer the materiality of our workpiece loses its dominance and the workpiece becomes a mere focal point of information. Eventually, the level of signs tends to conceal completely the material substratum of information, and thus a software developer usually loses sight of it. The moment of disturbance is when we are reminded of the material level of information, be it a head-crash of a disk, a faulty board or a jam in the local net.

---

[9] Cf. [Bahr, 1983].

Operating a computer and a software system is not substantially different from operating machines or other technical equipment. There is simply a wider gap between the levels of signs of a software system and their material stratum as compared with what we find in a traditional machine. Moreover, we can create new levels of signs based on existing signs within a computer. This would seem to be the main difference. A computer offers not merely a limited set of signs and signals, but a system of signs with the expressive power of a formal language. Further meta-levels come into view, for instance, when tracing a software error within an interactive *debugging tool*. Frequently, this means that we are searching for the reason why, in debugging some application software – which we then take as our material – this debugger shows something that deviates from our expectations. As developers of programming environments, we will eventually find ourselves in a situation where we apply the debugging tool to itself while it is tracing a piece of application software. The number of meta-levels is unlimited. Incidently this example shows that we decide, in a specific working context, what we take as a software tool and what as programming material. Here, we have illustrated that one piece of software can at the same time serve both as a tool (debugger) and as material (debugged debugger).

The most important finding of this last section is:

> *We handle software tools both as material means and on a* meta-level of
> signs.

Summarizing the findings of our reflections on the characteristics of software tools, we may say:

- Software tools *open up* new perspectives of the world around us. They constitute the means for working on programming materials while at the same time indicating the state of the working process and the product by a multitude of signs.
- Software tools *generalize* our ways of handling aspects of the world around us; they organize our actions and condense them into gestures.

6.2.6 The concept of a machine

In this section, we explain the interrelation between using a software component as a tool and constructing it as a machine. In order to understand this distinction, we first have to look at "traditional" apparatus and machines. A prominent characteristic of many technical implements is their *movability*: We have said that tools can only be handled properly in accordance with specific motions of our bodies. Simple mechanical apparatus like the loom or the lathe require this accordance as well. But here it is not movability in the sense of locomotion which is of importance. It is *motion cast into construction*. A movement that is calculable, uniform, repeatable – these are the essential characteristics of motions which are mechanically "fixed" and thus "de-individualized". What is hinted at here becomes predominant in big industrial machinery.

When we speak of technical equipment as machine, we mean for the time being:

> *A machine* is *repeatable motion* which is abstracted from its specific context and cast into construction.

This definition of ours would seem to accord with the essence of the rationalistic image of the machine. The rationality of a machine is shown by its reliability. We can "rely" on a machine, because its motions do not move[10]. But a machine does not incorporate and reify motion as such. Looking at working processes, we realize that machines and *rationalization* cannot be separated. Rationalizing means dissecting human work into purposeful activity and repeated, routinized action. The multitude of possible aims and purposes does not lend itself to generalization or then to rationalization. The objects of rationalization are *routinized actions*, since they can be subjected to standardized process descriptions and mechanization, thereby using the available powers in a more *rational* way. Within this schema, the individual becomes man *power* and is regarded under physiological and quantitative aspects only. Accordingly, individual craftsmanship with its personal skills and human interests no longer counts. What the machine reproduces is the standardized, de-personalized routine aspect of human activities. This process of stripping human activities of all aspects of context, meaning and individuality is called *decontextualization*. Thus, we may say:

> *A machine* incorporates and reproduces the *mechanical reduction* of human activities. It thus *decontextualizes* human activities.

A frequently cited example from industrial production is Ford's assembly line. But we find today's automated factories to be far more revealing. Here, the different positions are occupied either by workers or industrial robots, depending on economical considerations only. The actual interchangeability of human beings and machines illustrates the extent to which decontextualized routines can dominate processes of divided work.

Machine and algorithm

Before entering on further discussion, we wish to underline that we have separated the notion of *machine* from aspects such as power transformation, the mere state-transition of some material, and most of its social context. With this in mind, we now explain our view of *formalization*:

> Formalizing means reducing an activity to its form.

The idea is to make an activity repeatable in order that it may support different aims. Formalizing an activity, then means separating it from its concrete aim and purpose, which leads to a formalism *without any meaning as such*, i.e., the formalism is decontextualized. If we wish to understand an activity as a formal

---

[10] Cf. [Bahr, 1983, Schönpflug, 1989].

process without understanding the *meaning* of this activity, it is crucial that we understand *how* this activity is performed. In order to understand this *how*, we use a language comprising the following parts:

- A finite set of atoms which represent the basic actions of the activity we wish to formalize.
- A finite set of constructors which we use to relate a constructor and a finite set of basic actions to a new action to which we give a name.

We thus *understand* a formalized activity recursively by breaking it down into partial activities and constructors until we arrive at the basic actions. We *formalize* an activity that we have understood intuitively by re-constructing it recursively from basic actions and constructors. We can actually *realize* the result of this process, a formalism, *in a construct* without caring about its meaning: we *build a machine*. The prototype for realizing this notion of a machine and, at the same time, the most general means for denoting its basic actions is a *programming language*.

If, however, we take formalization as a process which reduces meaning, it seems obvious that software, algorithms, and formalisms – like machines – have to be embedded into actual working processes if we wish to restore their meaning. Originally, a formalism comes from the context of purposeful human activities, and in the end goes back into this world, invariably changing it to some degree. Therefore, it is useful to understand formalization as a complementary process of *de-* and *re-contextualization*[11].

We have now outlined the connection extending from familiar activities, via abstractions of an algorithm and its reconstruction in a machine, back to a familiar handling of the machine. To summarize:

> Formalism, formal language, calculus, or algorithm, on the one hand, and *machine*, on the other hand, *essentially mean the same thing.*

When we equate the notions of machine and algorithm, we start from human activities. Leaving aside the purpose of meaningful work, we focus on the routine part of repeated activities. These activities we have decomposed into elementary units and while reconstructing them, we have made them explicit. The formal *decontextualization* and the subsequent explicit *recontextualization* are the essence of our notion of the term *machine*. It is the machine that makes a routine denoted in an algorithm *constructively repeatable*.

When we look at formalization as a *design and construction process*, it is usually complemented by a *process of utilization*:

> Our notion of the term *tool* is aimed at restoring software tools from the formal machines of software construction which can be used in a familiar way in order to arrive at meaningful *results of work*.

---

[11] Cf. [Dreyfus, 1989].

In other words:

> While *using* software, we wish to look on it *as a tool*; and in another
> context, i.e., while constructing it, we wish to look on it *as a machine*.

However, this concept not only describes two different *viewpoints*, but two different *ways of employing* things:

> While using software in our work, we wish to handle it like a tool; but
> while constructing it, we wish to design its parts like a machine.

6.2.7 Machines as tools or automata

Employing software as a tool and a machine – this obviously places demands on software development and use, that are neither evident nor common practice. Thus, we must ask what happens when we use software systems that cannot be handled in an intimate and self-evident way. In order to illustrate this aspect, let us look first of all at the historical predecessors of the computer, the classical automata[12]. The "appeal" of these automata and androids relied on the fact that their internal mechanism was concealed, their gestures and poses astounding onlookers. Their amazement was accompanied by the knowing look of the engineer "behind the scenes". We realize that these automata, which were *constructed as machines*, never worked in the same way as the familiar things they represented; they were intended to *appear as machines* as well.

Let us take a modern automaton, e.g., a vendomat – a machine that reduces operation and control actions to pressing buttons. Once set in action, some "non-transparent" process is executed inside the automaton, presenting us with its output. And we have no further means of influencing this process. We are all familiar with the "comic" situation where the vendomat refuses to dispose the desired item. Confused and at a loss what to do we start banging on the machine and pushing buttoms at random.

If we transfer these reflections to software, we find there are systems which, besides having been *constructed as machines*, also *appear as machines* when employed by their users. Hence:

> Software systems which appear as machines when in use will be called
> automata.

One characteristic of software automata is the fact that our means of control are reduced to presetting parameters. When we push the appropriate button, the automaton sets in motion an internal process which is mostly beyond our understanding and which, hopefully, will terminate in an acceptable result. A profound understanding of software automata is confined mainly to their developers and an in-group of "wizards" and "hackers" who see themselves as adepts. In order to avoid striking a wrong note in this discussion, we wish to make it clear that

---

[12] Cf. [Bahr, 1983, Sutter, 1988].

we frequently choose to operate automata in our everyday work. And for that matter, we do not normally bother to inquire about the process going on inside a vendomat, as long as it spits out the desired packet of peanuts. Similarly, we are not interested in the details of our print server's spooling as long as our graphics and text documents are produced by the laser printer in a reasonable time and are of acceptable quality. This holds for some aspects of our office work. But the situation changes when we are working with a programming environment, because, then, we wish to handle the majority of software components as software tools, and not as automata.

6.2.8 Programming workshop versus software factory

Anyone building a programming environment is faced with the question of the proper kind of overall perspective to choose as a guideline for design. We are aware that it is not enough to provide a variety of unrelated software tools. They have to have their proper location and order, if we wish to make good use of the features and operations they offer. Current discussion on this subject is divided between those favouring a *factory perspective* and those preferring a *workshop perspective*. Today, the dominant perspective is based on keywords such as *software process, software factory* or *CASE* tools[13] evoking the image of an automated, production-line software development process. It is a fair question whether we are not indulging in some kind of nostalgia by using the metaphor of the craftsman.

It is common to take the rather facile view of the historical development of technology as a linear progression of mechanization, from handicraft to manufacture, and finally to the factory. Such a view supposes a "natural" evolution from hand tools (like the hammer) to mechanical machines (like the forge), and eventually to automated production lines (like the rolling mill). In this view, the evolution of technical equipment was complemented by the provision of the proper type of "case" or location (workshop, manufactory, factory).

We believe that the different stages of technological development should be primarily characterized by the means of cooperation and division of labour, and not by the types of technical equipment used. Accordingly, we do not see the crucial difference between a workshop and a factory in the fact that the one contains hand tools and the other machinery, but in the different roles played by the technical equipment within the process of *specialization* and *cooperation*. In the context of a *workshop*, there is emphasis on supporting *individual* activities by employing tools and automata[14]. On this basis, cooperation between workers possessing different skills and qualifications can be optimized. In the context of the *factory*, we find a completely different situation. Here, individual craftsmanship is replaced by appropriate methods, e.g., the division of labour

---

[13] *CASE* = Computer Aided Software Engineering.

[14] We use these terms in line with our definition given in the previous section. An instance of tool, then, might be an electric drill; and of an automaton, say, a photocopying machine.

and specialization in the manufactory, Taylorism and industrial engineering in the factory. In consequence, work becomes routinized and mechanized. In such a setting, human beings increasingly play the role of the unknowing link between a conglomerate of technical implements. To summarize:

- Machinery within a *factory* context objectifies the routinized aspects of human work activities and a specific state of the division of labour.
  By coupling workers and technical implements to form integrated units, industrial machinery reduces individual skills in favour of mechanized routines. The aim is the substitutable worker rather than the specifically qualified expert.
- Tools and automata used within a *workshop* context primarily support *skilled workmanship*.
  Cooperation and the distribution of tasks is maintained by people and not by machinery, although technical equipment may support this process. In this type of working environment, individual skills and abilities can unfold and evolve.

If we look at the work of *software developers*, we find that its characteristics are teamwork, skills and expertise of the individual, and cooperation. Of course, there is a division of labour and specialization, for instance, the attempts to establish *chief programmer teams* and programming pools. Still, there seems to be little chance of arriving at an overall state of routinized tasks which could lead to a sensible "implementation" of this division of labour. There is also little chance of setting up "software production machinery". As evidence of a strong endeavour in that direction, we find there are an overwhelming number of software products available which claim to support individual work and cooperation, and scarcely any products geared to specialization and the division of labour. Thus, we conclude:

> The *tasks of software developers* can be more suitably compared with the *work of a craftsman in a workshop* than with work in a factory.

If we analyze work in a factory we find that, on the one hand, routinized human labour is replaced by mechanical routines and, on the other, that the whole process is aimed at an economical optimization of *re-production*. The things that first come to mind when talking about reproduction are assembly lines turning out huge numbers of items. But even if we look at the small lots within *CIM*, it becomes obvious that the difference lies only in the greater variation of processed materials and in the recombination of the actual working units, there being no departure from the basic principle of repeated mechanical working activities.

The workshop, however, can be characterized by its integration of manual work, coordination, and design. We may well find differing degrees of innovation and creative work within different workshops – depending on the type of products and services offered – but in none of them will we encounter a complete separation of planning, design and construction activities. For our discussion, this means:

- A *factory* is suitable for *reproductive working processes.*
  A factory is geared to economical reproduction of a maximum number of goods which are specified in detail beforehand. Essential planning and design, and even production activities are taken out of the factory.
- A *workshop* brings *planning, design, and construction* activities together under the same roof.
  A workshop is suitable for coping with individual requirements. Its flexible forms of organization promote attunement to individual customer needs and wishes.

In principle, *software development* poses no problems as regards reproduction. Copying programs is a trivial matter, the time factor being negligible. The crucial problems encountered in current software projects centre around planning and development in accordance with user needs and wishes, and coping with complexity, version and variant management. These aspects show a clear orientation of the work of software developers towards handicraft and workshops rather than towards factory operations. We conclude:

> Since *planning, developing and coordination* are the central tasks in software development – and not the mass production of goods – the *programming workshop* may be considered the proper working environment for software developers.

By favouring the programming workshop as opposed to the software factory concept, we are by no means advocating an already obsolete form of social organization of work. It is not our intention to propagate craftsmanship in its historical context, rejecting all types of industrial work. Thus, instead of harking back to the era of craft guilds, we look at aspects of current craftwork involving individual craftsmen produce commodities in cooperation with others. The crucial aspect here is the close relationship between design, production, and evaluation. These activities bear the imprint of both individual and cooperative work. The technical equipment employed in handicraft – be it hand tools, measuring instruments or automata – can be found in various specialized forms that are tailored to the needs of the respective craft. Depending on the requirements of the different tasks and the respective skills of the workers, the utensils and tools used exhibit different degrees of complexity as regards both their purpose and operation. All these facts would seem to justify comparison of the craftsman's use of tools in a workshop with the activities of the software developer. We feel that such a comparison is warranted not only on a metaphorical level. It is the way the tools and other equipment are employed and the similar degree of cooperation and mechanization which suggest the analogy between software development and craftsmanship and which set the context for designing a programming workshop.

If we reduce the factory and workshop perspectives to their technical core, we may characterize their importance for software development as follows:

- A *programming environment viewed as a software factory* is a running program with a pre-defined concept of software development.

This program contains a few *exits*, at which the human resource is supposed to enter data unobtainable from any other (technical) source.

- A *programming environment viewed as a workshop* offers a set of tools, but does not implement an overall strategy of software development. However, it may be used to automate a selected set of familiar and routine activities (such as *change management* or *compilation*).

  Users define working processes by drawing on their knowledge of tasks, materials and tools. The programming workshop "surrounds" the user with sets of tools and automata, each with its own specific application and suitability for a particular type of material.

If we consider the respective long-range aims behind the concepts of factory and workshop, we can see the difference between these two views: The factory stands for replacing human labour by machinery whereas the workshop promotes the enhancement of skills and experience.

6.2.9 The programming workshop as a paradigm

Whether explicitly or implicitly, many software developers are governed in their work by the idea that users must be prevented from making mistakes. They are thus frequently led to the following series of conlusions:

- A major requirement for software is the avoidance of user errors.
- In order to be able to detect such errors, a model for the proper operation of software has to be defined. This model must include the user as a formalized element.
- Once this type of model has been defined, user activities can be checked for conformity to these models.

This is why most software developers think it quite natural to design software with a view to *restricting* the options open to users. For obvious reasons, there is a strong link between this attitude and the industrial notion of machinery, the mechanization of work, Taylorism and the present discussion on *CASE* tools.

Our view of software tools in a programming workshop is based on an emancipatory idea. Tools serve to *extend* the means and skills of users – to enhance what they are able to do, see and understand when employing tools. Users are in full control of their tools, and they are fully conversant with their workshop[15].

The structure of a programming workshop, i.e., its organization, is dependent on the particular working context. Consequently, its structure cannot be predefined in every detail by its developer. Moreover, a programming workshop invariably bears the "imprint" of its users. Names, defaults, configurations, the piles of papers and notes surrounding a terminal and filling the *mailbox* – all of these are concrete indications of the individuality of a programming workshop – which is far more pronounced than one would suspect at first sight.

---

[15] A similar idea of giving skilled users complete command of their work is proposed by Keil-Slawik (Chap. 4.4), by Nurminen (Chap. 7.2) and by Coy (Chap. 6.3).

Work contexts and work styles are rarely adaptable to the formal representations of tool hierarchies and call relations – which, after all, are quite simple interrelations. Take, for instance, the grouping of windows on a screen, their overlapping and the visibility of "relics". They denote interrelations and indicate similarities and characteristic differences in their respective content and manner of operation which can never be captured by a predefined formalism. Therefore, a programming workshop should not fix these arrangements and relations, but should provide mechanisms that help the users to arrange and group the objects and means of work to their liking. These mechanisms should inspire the imagination of users and not be an obstacle to it.

More important still, a programming workshop ought not to force its users into a regulated working procedure which they can only change at a few points and which is scarcely comprehensible anyway. If the programming workshop were an automaton itself, and the user a part of it, then we would no longer be able to speak of the user's responsibility for a meaningful work process, but would have to place *responsibility with the tool developer or the user organization's management that assigned the job.*

Even though users may not be tied to fixed working procedures, this still does not mean that their work is free of restrictions. Programming materials and software tools cannot be employed just as the user desires, nor are the forms of cooperation with others arbitrary.

Our notion of the *workshop* should not be seen as some sort of magic wand that the developer simply has to wave in order to accomplish any desired task. In a programming workshop the work of developers employing different tools is coordinated. Each tool has its place and order in the workshop[16]. Thus, interest must focus on the organization of human work when designing a workshop. This can only succeed, however, if the structure of the workshop is transparent.

Imagine, for instance, a programming workshop where permission to read or write material files can be given by means of an *access tool*. The organization of this workshop does not allow other users to modify reserved materials. Despite this mechanism, tools do not "patronize" users. They do not hide anything, but they are in line with the overall goal of organizing expert work on a team basis. Consequently, the effect of the *access tool* is shown by all tools which can be employed to material files. There may even be other – more "powerful" – tools which can be employed by the experienced user to *consciously* "undo" the effect of the *access tool*. When using the metaphors *tool* and *material*, we emphasize that software tools should never hide or obscure programming materials. By using the workshop metaphor, we indicate that all relevant aspects of a work context should be visible. Hence, the concept of a programming workshop presupposes the *transparent compatibility* of software tools. Generalizing our example, this means that all software tools which can be applied to a par-

---

[16] The aspects of place and order have generally been overlooked in the design of programming environments, but we feel they are of crucial importance. Their close relation to hermeneutic concepts like *nearness, place,* or *orientation* offers developers new and inspiring design criteria.

ticular material invariably show the same effects on that material caused by a specific tool. Familiar tools thus open up an unwonted *perspective* when a new tool is employed. This is why users gain *new potential action* through using new software tools.

Well-designed software tools show their effects but hide details of their construction. *Information hiding* is, in actual fact, a design principle. The "interior" of a tool is hidden, but not the material to which the tool is applied, because effects on materials are not considered irrelevant implementation details. Quite the reverse: many software systems work like *automata* hiding materials once they are set in action by their users. Consequently, the user's scope of activities is narrowed down and the potential risks of an activity cannot be adequately foreseen. We all are familiar with situations in which we try to do a balancing act along the precipice of well-known commands, each unsure step being a nerve-racking experience. Our scope is even further diminished, if new automata are added to the system, bringing with them additional interrelations among system parts – interrelations that we do not understand, but we know, nevertheless, must not be disrupted.

When we speak of the transparency of tools, this does not imply that they will always function without interruptions (or breakdowns) in an imperceptible (transparent) way. More importantly, it means that we are aware of the interrelations between tools and of their specific effects on materials. Transparency of tools is something we will eventually realize in the context of the workshop as a whole. It is, after all, the task of the developers designing the tools within a workshop to arrange equipment, places and environments in a clear and accessible manner and to put up signs indicating where materials and utensils are located. This enables users to work with the software tools of a programming workshop meaningfully and efficiently.

Summary

We have outlined above our concept of tools and materials as metaphors for understanding and designing the software components of a programming environment. Viewing software development from an emancipatory perspective, we feel that the workshop perspective provides a more appropriate basis for design than the factory perspective. The overall idea is to implement new means of work for skilled users, instead of trying to formalize their working processes and thus making skilled workers redundant. We also feel that the validity of idea goes beyond the scope of programming environment design into the field of interactive application systems design and use. A programming workshop along with the tools and materials it provides is not, then, a mere exercise in nostalgia, but a pertinent answer to crucial questions facing software development today.

Acknowledgements
Many thanks to Phil Bacon for translating and polishing up this text.

6.3 Soft Engines – Mass-Produced Software for Working People?

Wolfgang Coy

6.3.1 Engines and machines

We will investigate how the notion 'software engine' may become a useful metaphor for the computer science community, which would reflect the actual status of software practice and which may be understood as a guideline for software development.

The notion of engines and machine systems is closely associated with the industrial revolution after 1750. It is not the analytical disassembly of an engine into machine elements as assumed in the widely used definition of Franz Reuleaux[1] nor the mechanical or logical structure of an engine, but the industrial synthesis of machine systems from engines and machine tools and the associated organization of labour that defines the machine. Industrial production in the factory is intimately connected with this development of machine systems and therefore the organization of labour, engines and machines are closely related notions[2].

6.3.2 Abstract versus real machines

The classical machine of the industrial empires is an artifact, developed as an incarnation of mechanical processes, later enhanced by the power of steam and electricity and other forces. But such a mechanical reduction is an ideological scheme[3], which ignores the fact that machines are not and were never simply material objects. The development of technical artifacts like machines reflect in their material objects the process of human labour under industrial conditions, and technical entities do exist outside human purposes.

Parallel to the mechanical interpretation of the machine there have been continuing efforts in the technical and natural sciences as well in mathematics to define more abstract notions of machines, divorcing this concept from the work process. An important attempt in this direction is the definition of mathematical machines as they were first developed and formalized in the context of the

---

[1] Reuleaux followed Cardano. Many aspects of this development may be found in [Strandh, 1979].

[2] This is developed in some detail in [Coy, 1985].

[3] The philosophers of the Enlightenment, especially Voltaire, but also the encyclopedists, were willingly or unwillingly responsible for this narrow and abstract mechanical interpretation of machines. Cf. [Borzeszkowski and Wahsner, 1980].

'theory of computation' (and formal logic) by Alan Turing. Despite their 'universality' with respect to symbolic computation, Turing machines still reflect a basic work process, namely writing on a paper sheet. But Turing's machines abstract from the writer who is simulated as a mathematical (or more precisely, computable) function. They also abstract from real paper sheets, as the machine tape is immaterial and potentially unbound, and from the contents of work, as they formalize only a general concept of computability. This abstraction is a useful formalization and a precise definition of the rather vague notion of computability; on the other hand it should be obvious that this abstraction is an extremely restricted concept of a machine and that it could be re-introduced to the material world only with this caveat. In fact, it is still an open question what computability means in the physical world, as the role of logic in science is still open to debate.

Following Turing's definition a multitude of mathematical machine notions were defined, especially in theoretical computer science. Abstraction of their basic working mechanism from a material implementation is characteristic for these mathematical machines. They depart from the classical concept of machine, as they no longer rely on a specific hardware implementation. They drop the whole idea of a machine being a piece of mechanics or hardware. From this point of view it appears only consistent to apply these definitions also to software packages. Considering the power of software the name 'engine' was preferred to show that these machines literally move data and software processes. A well known example is the notion of the 'inference engine' that constitutes the prime mover of an expert system. This notion of an engine supports the quite clear separation of the general logical inference process from the application-specific facts and rules (and other entities). Of course the same process seems to occur with translators for programming languages, in word processors or in spreadsheets. They all constitute abstract machines or engines (if the latter notion is preferred).

But the mathematical abstractions including the pure software definition of a machine is as misleading as Rouleux' mechanical definition in terms of machine elements and structure. Both definitions drop the purpose and the use of machines in work environments. Rather in contrast we propose the use of the concept of *soft engines* for programs including their hardware base, *if these artifacts serve people in the work process in such a way that they do not dominate this work by their hardware or software characteristics*. Not every software construct may be seen as a soft engine. Soft engines describe computer programs which become part of the work process and which display the generalized characteristics of tools[4] or media. Both perspectives, tools and media, have been discussed recently[5]. The perspective of a soft engine is not meant to exclude either aspect. Soft engines describe therefore the actual state of professional computing and constitute a guideline for the construction of useful software (and hardware).

---

[4] A transclassical tool in the sense of Frieder Nake [Nake, 1986].

[5] For the tool aspect see [Nake, 1986], for the media perspective see [Winograd and Flores, 1986].
See also Chap. 6.1 where "tool" is presented as a workshop-oriented metaphor.

The engine concept may be seen as directed against the extreme complexity of DP systems, which developed mainly in the directions of universality and abstraction. Universality and abstraction are powerful conceptual guidelines, promising liberation from practical constraints. But they are also misleading if they are over-interpreted. Artifacts of computer science (or informatics as it is called in some parts of the non-English speaking world) are neither universal nor abstract in a strict sense. They are products that were constructed for specific purposes in specific domains, mainly for specific uses in work processes. The universality and abstraction of computer artifacts represent only a failed re-interpretation of the real world of work and labour in the mathematical terms of Turing machines and similar constructs. With the term *soft engine* both aspects should be described more precisely and more modestly as *broad applicability* (versus universality) and as *symbolic transfer* of work situations to computational models (versus abstraction).

If universality is to lead to a tool perspective it must be restricted to broad applicability within a well-defined job context and not permitted a generality in which the applicability of a program is no longer comprehensible to the user. Certainly no one can comprehend the logical consequences of any but the most simple programs, but it is possible to become engaged in a work process, where at least the general purposes of a program within its defined application area may be understood. Word processors are in the class of programs where experienced users develop perspectives of use[6], though there is a broad applicability of word processors. It should be noted that a major goal in the development of so-called *hypertexts*[7] is to prevent the user from being "lost in hyperspace". Other programs with broad applicability are compilers, word processors, spreadsheets or expert system shells[8], but none of these programs may be used *universally* in the work process. The idea of broad applicability is not the result of universal possibilities of Turing machines or their equivalent in programming languages. Broad applicability in the work process is meant to free the user from the necessity to learn to use and interact with many different programs and to unify the use of computers to a reasonable extent. Broad applicability should help to develop a tool perspective – for the developer as well as for the user. It must be noted that a universal Turing machine is applicable to all tasks, but that it will not succeed in the purpose of unifying user interaction reasonably. Understanding user interaction is an art – not a consequence of logic.

While some programs are simply too broad in their perspectives of use, others may be too narrow. A word processor with separate programs for text input, for style definitions, for indexing, for spelling checking and for printing is certainly too narrow in its applicability, but on the other hand it may be observed frequently that useful programs become overloaded with features from version to

---

[6] Though still a word processor may be used for quite unexpected purposes, such as disassembling and reassembling machine code.

[7] Cf. [Coy, 1989].

[8] Cf. [Coy and Bonsiepen, 1989] and [Bonsiepen and Coy, 1990a].

version until they are beyond their appropriate level of use[9]. Broadly applicable programs must be reasonably broad and should be bounded by a social (usually: work) purpose. Broad applicability is never an unrestricted universality, which implements anything that could be easily included. A reasonable balance between the possibilities of a program and its specific purpose must be developed. Programs in work situations are constructed for specific purposes and these purposes should be reflected properly in their design – not more, not less.

Abstraction defines and separates different logical levels. DP systems usually connect a large number of constituents in a wide variety of logical levels to a working structure. Methodological discussions of the correct use of computers focus on the best definition for the level of abstraction. This may be seen in the early development of programming languages (macro-assembler, Fortran, Cobol), operating systems (IOCS, OS/360, THE, Unix), computer architecture (System /360), the GOTO controversy, the discussion of stepwise refinement and other approaches to modular design. Since the complexity of modern computers extends to all steps from digital electronics and switching techniques over logical design, computer architecture, operating systems and programming languages[10] to application-specific programming, the definition of conceptual and logical structure becomes necessary. From the work perspective abstraction demands that the flow of work is transferred to the computer program. A basic step in this direction is the *symbolic transfer of the work environment to the computational model*. In detail this may be a logical structure of the program modules in which the supported work process may be re-identified by the user. It may also be the graphical abstraction of the program's steps with icons, windows and terminal interaction that symbolizes the programmed process. Many control room monitors in complex manufacturing lines are examples of *symbolic transfer*, as control and steering of the manufacturing process is no longer performed directly but at the symbolic model of the machinery. This holds also for the graphical terminals of a CNC lathe. Computer programs are much more suitable for symbolic transfer and many discussions about graphical interfaces, like the desktop metaphor, focus on the idea of symbolic transfer. Spreadsheets are symbolic transfers of cashbooks and this is certainly the main reason for the great acceptance of these programs. Symbolic transfer is the underlying process that leads to the use of metaphors. If soft engines are to support work processes they must show broad applicability as well as symbolic transfer.

6.3.3 Programming a computer or using a computer

Programming in a classical understanding is related to programming languages (or programming notations as Peter Naur prefers to call them), which are to be

---

[9] Anyone who is familiar with the versions I and II of the outline program 'More' will notice such overloading, and the same may be said of Word Perfect 5.1 versus Word Perfect 4.2. Of course, Unix was from the very beginning beyond any appropriate level of understandability – except for some computer science addicts who like it just that way.

[10] Cf. [Coy, 1988].

translated by a compiler or interpreter into executable machine code, which in turn are to be executed on real computers under real operating systems. But command languages have usually nothing in common with the programming languages whose code they are processing. Programmers must therefore learn at least two formalized languages, namely the programming language and the command language of the operating system. And they must understand the underlying application. Using application programs avoids the process of programming but often lacks the flexibility that may result from the proper use of a programming language. There are two obvious ways out of this restriction: to ease the burden of programming or to use more flexible application programs[11].

Among the early attempts to simplify programming were Report Program Generators (e.g., the RPG languages of IBM), i.e., programming languages, which support the programming of subtasks of batch programs by providing fixed formats for data input, data processing and data output. The intention was to simplify the generation of reports based on existing data files; the result can be seen as a reduced version of Cobol, much as early Basic may be understood as a stripped-down version of Fortran. It must be doubted that RPG really eased the programming process by a sequential differentiation of program parts. It seems not to attain a proper level of complexity reduction – something we have learned in the meantime, slowly and painfully. But the adopted strategy of "Keep it simple" is a valuable decision implicit in most successful structural reductions.

Thompson, Kernighan and Ritchie, the main authors of Unix, made "Keep it simple" the guiding principle of their operating system design. Simple procedures like copying, sorting or printing a text file are executed with simple programs, called filters. Filters are (usually parametrized) programs, which transform the standard input file to the standard output file. As Unix command interpreters (shells) may redirect any input or output, including the standard input and standard output and as more complex command structures may be built by forming pipelines of filters, it is easy to program complex work structures without leaving the operating system shell. Programming in a more classical understanding (namely by using programming languages) is reduced and replaced by the function of command structures on the operating system level. This is a real step toward an easier use of computers and also a step closer to highly flexible application programs, though not *every* task may be performed with a command structure as not *every* mechanical task may be done with a Swiss army knife. But the introduction of easily programmable command structures and their extension in the programming language C is the basic contribution of Unix to modern software design, which should not be obscured by long periods of line-oriented (and human memory demanding) interaction, cryptic names[12] and remarkable errors of many Unix filters nor by the misunderstood flexibility of C. Despite its methodological merits, the most influential contribution of Unix to the profes-

---

[11] This is a real dilemma thoroughly discussed in [Brooks, 1987a].

[12] My favourite abbreviation is *dd*, which stands for convert and copy (probably because *cc* abbreviates the C compiler).

sion was probably to offer useful text editing facilities. Together with a relative simple operating system interface UNIX transformed a *general-purpose computer* to a *dedicated word processing machine*. roff, nroff and troff were proud ancestors to many succeeding PC-based word processors like Wordstar and others – though PC-based word processing is now more satisfactory than nroff, troff and TEX. Word processors were the first Soft(ware) engines showing broad applicability within a well-defined job domain and symbolic transfer of the traditional tools of writers to a computer terminal. Together with the hardware, word processors generate a specific, easy-to-use machine for the application-oriented user. Users need not program the computer individually though it can be used for complex and demanding tasks (like desktop publishing).

Although well designed word processing programs are capable of dealing with demanding tasks, many observers found spreadsheets to be the real breakthrough for personal computing – Visicalc being the prototype of this class of application programs[13]. The main characteristic of these programs is the creation of a *user illusion*[14] as a result of successful symbolic transfer, which allows the system's users to relate their paperwork with a dynamic screen image of number and text cells. The several hundred years old Renaissance 'cassa-book' was turned into a dynamic spreadsheet. The prime mover of a spreadsheet is a program generator, which translates the necessary cell computation in a mechanical manner into low-level programs. This process is more or less hidden from the casual or uninterested user. Programming becomes a 'feature' of the application program. Therefore spreadsheets may be viewed as program generators, which allow the user to avoid programming at a low level. Spreadsheets are soft(ware) engines, where the conceptual work at the application level remains the responsibility of the users, though they may not even be aware of the fact that they are programming a computer. Spreadsheets sustain a unique use perspective; the user must learn their use (i.e., programming!) only once and this may be done gradually starting from basic to more advanced features. Since their introduction many more applications, sometimes far removed from bookkeeping, were brought to spreadsheets, e.g., digital circuit simulation or statistical analysis. These applications were almost certainly beyond the imagination of the developers of Visicalc. Modern spreadsheets like Microsoft Excel contain a full programming language with their extensive macro-facilities[15], though casual users will not have the impression that they program in a more classical sense of the word. The basic advantage of such systems is in their broad applicability and their intuitive appeal because of a successful symbolic transfer. Spreadsheets allow the use of software without having to rebuild it from scratch with every new application[16].

---

[13] This was probably because print output did not offer a new perspective to computer users until the advent of cheap daisy wheel and laser printers in the office.

[14] Cf. [Kay, 1984].

[15] Macrolanguages are discussed in [Gates, 1987].

[16] Of course, it is not possible to use any software for all purposes but the construction of reusable software modules seems to be a very promising aspect.

6.3.4 Characteristics of soft engines

Soft(ware) engines, whose first incarnations were discussed above, share several characteristics to be discussed in more detail. This leads to an implicit definition where an explicit definition is still open to coming developments.

(I) *Soft engines are stand-alone application programs and program generators which support interactive work with a broad but specific class of applications.*
The class is *extensive* rather than single purpose (e.g. word processing, spreadsheets, numerical or graphical simulation, symbolic manipulation of mathematical equations or some expert system task). The class is sufficiently specific that a well-understood job can be symbolically modelled by computer means. To use a soft engine is to use a computer, but hardware and software are seen by the user as a unified machine in a tool or media perspective.

Soft engines are interactive *program generators*. They support the user by hiding the actual low-level programming process as far as appropriate and possible. In this sense, they are *very high-level languages* (relative to the present high-level programming languages).

In general, soft engines are *interactive* programs. In some cases a soft engine may be an embedded system as in CNC machines, some CAD workstations or in certain CIM applications, were the interaction is not restricted to terminal interaction. Not every program can be a soft engine; other types of programs are batch jobs or fully automatic systems. The soft engine approach is one design goal among others, though it is considered to be a very important one.

(II) *Soft engines must be usable.*
Usability is not a formal notion, but some negative properties can easily be characterized. Usability demands at least a carefully designed human-computer interface[17], which allows the user to concentrate on the job to be performed instead of focusing the user's attention to the machine (hardware, operating system and program). In this sense the soft engine should help to develop a tool perspective: the user must remain the acting subject of the working situation while the computer remains a technical device, object or medium of the work process.

(III) *There is no need to program a soft engine in order to use it.*
Soft engines are application programs and they may be program generators, generating executable (though in detail hidden) programs for the user, but the user needs not learn a classical programming language with all levels of hardware and operating system.

(IV) *The user may program a soft engine.*
Soft engines are adaptable systems. Adaptability must remain compatible with usability. Programming soft engines is simplified in relation to classical programming languages with macro-structures. The engine may include an interpreter with a simple macro language. Lotus 1-2-3 and Microsoft Excel are examples of

---

[17] Cf. [Nievergelt, 1983].

programs with extensive macro facilities. Apple HyperCard is enhanced by its own programming language HyperTalk (which may be used, though new applications may even be constructed without using it explicitly).

Adaptability does not mean automatically self-adapting systems; these bear the danger that users are irritated and lose their role as the subject of the work process. This would destroy the tool perspective of a soft engine (and therefore destroy the property of being a soft engine).

(V) *Soft engines may be embedded in complex work processes.*
This holds for work processes which use a computer among other tools and resources as well as for work processes where other computer programs in addition to the specific soft engine are used. The necessary interaction between programs is not generally solved today (or solved at all), but the 'desktop' metaphor more and more used with workstations and PCs may be a step in the right direction (despite the fact that most if not all screen desktops are much too small).

(VI) *Not all software products can be soft engines.*
The concept of soft engines seems hardly to be compatible with present mainframe terminals or with process automation. Fully automated systems will not be soft engines as they are not used interactively. Line-oriented CNC terminals may not lead to soft engines as the numeric display of production data will hardly allow the user to concentrate on the work process. Transaction systems with line-oriented terminals can hardly be soft engines as they offer almost no possibility for users to adapt the system to their working conditions and requirements. The notion of a soft engine is therefore a selective one, which describes only one (though one important) aspect of software production – mainly in the mass market of PC and workstation programs.

The (implicit) concept of a soft engine is becoming endemic in more and more working areas, and it seems that the successful application of the stated characteristics of soft engines turns programs into successful programs. Some more recently developed simulation programs like Stella allow the graphical simulation of complex dynamics on the basis of modified state diagrams. This is close to paper and pencil simulation with the enormous advantage of a fully dynamic simulation process. The same holds for some programs for the dynamic manipulation of mathematical equations like Stephen Wolfram's Mathematica. Some expert system shells like KEE and Nexpert Object demonstrate elegantly integrated graphic environments allowing the development and manipulation of stored rules and facts and good visualization of the modelled processes.

6.3.5 Soft engines: A new paradigm for software engineering?

Like all software products, soft engines are very complex entities. Their production should be measured against the known procedures of software engineering – and even more against its deficits. There is a basic distinction in comparison with government or corporate mainframe-based single-purpose solutions still in common use. Soft engines are mass products whose typical hardware is a PC or a workstation. This means that some steps of user-tailored traditional software engineering may not be applied. But the market for standard software is steadily growing. In 1988 nearly two-thirds of the West German software sales were standard software; 18% of the total was for use with PCs[18].

Fully automated versus interactive systems

The basic technical decision for the design of a computer-based system is: Should the system be fully automated or should people use the computer interactively in their work process? Fully automated systems can be applied successfully and there are many industrial systems in which the interaction between humans and computers is reduced to zero. With the growing number of application fields there will be more and more tasks which may not yet nor in any foreseeable future be fully automated, because we do not know how to achieve it or because it is too expensive or sometimes because we do not want it. Among the disagreeable effects of classic DP implementations are systems that try to automate as much as possible and leave the unavoidable 'rest work' to a human operator. This changes the user's role from a working subject to the operator of a machine[19]. Such crippled systems will never achieve the perspective of a tool and therefore they cannot be soft engines. If the encapsulation of the program as a completely automated system is not wanted or not possible or too expensive, the system should be designed explicitly as an interactive program that supports users in their work process. Such systems can and should be constructed with the guideline of a soft engine in mind.

Specific versus unspecific definition of the application

Software engines are, like all software, subject to a software life cycle which extends from the initial specification to product maintenance, though there are some specific constraints. In general the specification of a soft engine is difficult because it is a mass product with a large number of possible applications – some of which may not even be known in advance. Typically there are new applications for spreadsheets from time to time, and fields of application to be explored with simulation engines and expert system shells are hardly foreseeable[20]. The right choice of the initial extent of a soft engine constitutes its main software engineering problem: Which facilities should be included and which should be left out?

---

[18] Cf. [IDC, 1989].

[19] This is not unique to data processing. On the contrary, nearly all factory work may be characterized by the conceptional switch of using a tool to working in a mechanized environment. Marx pointed out that this change of the relation between subject and object defines the industrial factory.

[20] Cf. [Coy and Bonsiepen, 1989].

The absence of faults versus fault-tolerant design

The user interface should offer the skilled as well as the unskilled user a task-oriented engine (as opposed to a computer with an operating system and some application programs). On the other hand this engine should be easily extensible by the use of macro-facilities and it should allow integration in complex work processes.

In the context of the user interface, fault robustness gains major importance. It is obvious that a program must be stable in the presence of faults, recognize the fault and pass an understandable fault message to the user. But the demand for fault tolerant programs is much more. It is an alternative to the implicit technical assumption that programs may be fault-free, an illusion that is contrary to all technical experience. Instead we expect soft engines (like other well-defined software) to be able to work as long as possible even when some elements of the program are out of order. Prerequisite for such *gracefully degrading systems* are complex methods of fault diagnosis like the ones now developed with some rule-based diagnostic systems. This is an active but still largely unexplored area of computer science.

Display of programs versus display of working processes

Another aspect of well-designed user interfaces leads to symbolic transfer as the intuitive visualization of the basic work processes supported by the soft engine. Neither the program structure nor the computer code should be displayed on the screen unless necessary (or wanted). The prominent content of this display should be a symbolic image of the work process. With spreadsheets and word processors this is not too difficult because the image of a paper sheet on the screen is intuitively acceptable. But even this demands a graphic display instead of a line-oriented screen. At Xerox PARC the desktop metaphor was developed that makes the use of computers in an office environment more agreeable. Similar developments may be found in the industrial environment with graphic displays of CNC lathes or with control room monitors of complex production lines. It should be clear that we have taken only the first steps in these directions and that the whole problem of screen-based visualization is by no means solved.

Usability

Fault-tolerant software and an intuitive reflection of the work process are only aspects of the more basic notion of usability. The term usability stands for a design which exhibits a friendly attitude towards the unavoidable faults users make. The computer industry sometimes prefers the term user-friendliness, but the whole issue seems to rest in the PR departments rather than in the engineering departments. Though the terminology is debatable, we cannot take the burden from systems analysts and programmers to develop usable systems. Usability is not simply a technical notion, as an agreeable work situation depends on many technical and social factors. It is not simply the technical design which implies usability of computers in the work environment. But a sloppy design of the user interface almost certainly prevents any satisfying use of the product.

Using a tool versus operating a machine

Introducing soft engines offers users the possibility for task-oriented work and should banish the work resources 'computer' and 'program' into the background of their attention. One approach could be to give the program (implemented as a soft engine) the perspective of a tool[21]. Of course this metaphor, much like the desktop metaphor, is not free of problems – mainly because metaphors should not be stretched beyond their limits. Positive aspects are that they keep the relation of human subjects to the mechanical support of the computer. On the other hand, there are obvious limits. One limit occurs with telecommunication. Even the phone may be handy for many people (much in the sense of Winograd and Flores, who follow Heidegger in his notion of readiness-to-hand), but it may be considered strange to call a phone system a tool. The same holds (even more) for computer networks. Here the idea of a technical medium arises, which allows another description of readiness-to-hand. We should keep in mind that the primary goal of software production is to integrate hardware and software in such a way that it moves to the users' mental background (or vanishes) in the work process. Keeping this in mind permits the design of soft engines.

Soft engines: A new leitmotiv for design

Soft engines may be a new leitmotiv for software design, integrating well proven old as well as some new imperatives. The values of such a redirection of design is not so much in the single characteristics of soft engines but in a wise integration of these characteristics. We have experienced some first and preliminary examples of soft engines. They were constructed without explicitly thinking about a new software design guideline; the next designs may use the framework of soft engines explicitly.

Why is it necessary to change the present direction of software design? Mainly because the 'traditional' methods of software engineering do not cope sufficiently with the social embedding of computers in the work process. The software design process is now in the methodologically unpleasant situation of Feyerabend's "Anything goes" or perhaps even in the worse situation of "Nothing goes (any more)"[22]. The basic issue of the long-lasting software crisis[23] remains open: adapting software production to social reality is still a wide and open field of research. The concept of soft engines is certainly no perfect way out of this situation but it may show a first step in the right direction, at least on the technical side of the problem and restricted to certain kinds of mass product.

---

[21] Winograd and Flores use this analogy, citing Heidegger, stating explicitly that a tool must be present-at-hand. Cf. [Winograd and Flores, 1986] or [Budde and Züllighoven, 1990].

[22] Cf. [Feyerabend, 1975].

[23] Cf. [Bonsiepen and Coy, 1990b].

6.4 Artificial Intelligence: A Hermeneutic Defense

Thomas F. Gordon

6.4.1 Introduction

The field of Artificial Intelligence (AI), from its very beginnings in the 1950s, has been criticized for its name as well as its ambition. Most of the debate concerns the possibility of artificial intelligence and presumes there is indeed some *thing* which *is* intelligence; the only question has been whether or not artificial systems can be built which exhibit, or have, this thing. That is, the debate has remained for the most part within the *rationalistic* tradition. In this section, I would like to explore two alternative approaches to this issue. The first considers the consequences of viewing artificial intelligence as another *metaphor* for computing. That is, perhaps certain kinds of computing systems can be usefully viewed as being *like* intelligent beings in some significant way. An immediate consequence of this view, of course, would be a lowering of the aims and ambitions of the field. The claim that a system displays something like intelligence is surely much weaker than the claim that it *is* intelligent.

However, I will reject viewing AI as a metaphor for another reason. The notion of metaphor presupposes that words do indeed have a core of certain meaning, their literal meaning. The metaphorical meanings deviate from the literal meaning in various ways, by removing some essential element of the definition of the term. By arguing that AI uses the term "intelligence" metaphorically, one would imply there is another, literal meaning.

Instead, I propose taking the lessons of *hermeneutics* seriously by accepting that terms have no static, context-independent, literal meaning. No one use of the word "intelligence" can make an exclusive claim to legitimacy. The focus of the debate about AI should not be its *possibility*, but rather the *suitability* of using the expression "artificial intelligence" in particular social or institutional situations for some particular purpose. Thus, whether or not it is helpful to speak of some computer system as being intelligent, cannot be decided conclusively in the abstract. The risks and opportunities presented by the contingencies of each *case* need to be considered.

This argument turns Winograd and Flores' use of hermeneutics to criticize Artificial Intelligence on its head. Their argument is unpersuasive, as it attempts to restrict and delineate the meaning of intelligence in a rationalistic way, while at the same time denying the validity of this rationalistic tradition. If we accept the lessons of hermeneutics, then we must also drop a naïve correspondence theory of meaning. If intelligence does not denote any particular class of objects, then debates about whether or not certain kinds of machines can be members of such a class become vacuous. However, by abandoning this kind of rationalism, we are left with the task of finding alternative ways to critically examine and evaluate AI systems, while avoiding rationalistic debates about what is or is not intelligence. I discuss three possibilities, based on economics, natural science and law.

Insights from law and jurisprudence will play an important role several times here. For some time now, I have been active in the interdisciplinary field of artificial intelligence and law. In jurisprudence, there is a history of reflection about the nature of reasoning which is comparable in depth and richness to the philosophy of science and mathematics. Within jurisprudence, the limits of a rationalistic perspective have long been appreciated, although the discussion about the consequences of these limits continues. For example, it is recognized that the meaning of concepts is "open-textured" and evolves over time, that normative considerations are of central importance when deciding whether to subsume some event under a general term, and that it is futile to try to construct a "heaven of concepts" for classifying all future events.

Before continuing with a more detailed discussion about these three ways of viewing AI, it may be useful to recall some of the various points of view about the nature of logic. Although the significance of logic for AI is often debated, there does not seem to be much controversy any more about what logic is. This was not always true. I am not well enough acquainted with the history of logic to know why the debate has quieted down; but I doubt it was because the various issues were settled. Has the arena for debating the various issues involved shifted from logic to AI? Stephen Toulmin, in his *The Uses of Argument*[1] listed these positions respecting the subject matter and purpose of logic:

Logic as psychology. Logic is concerned with the "laws of thought", not with pathological, defective thinking processes, but with "proper, rational, normal" thinking, "the working of the intellect of health".

Logic as sociology. Rather than the individual human mind, it is the "habits of inference" which have been "developed in the course of social evolution" that are of interest to logicians.

Logic as technology. Rather than an empirical science about how (healthy) persons actually think, logic is viewed as a craft, a collection of techniques for effective thinking.

Logic as mathematics. Logic is neither science nor art (craft), but a special field of pure mathematics concerned with the properties of an abstract set of objects such as "logical relations".

Logic as "generalized jurisprudence". This is the view developed by Toulmin in *The Uses of Argument*. Logic is concerned with the "soundness of claims", the procedures by which claims are "put forward, disputed and determined". Legal disputes are viewed as just a special case of rational dispute for which the procedures have "hardened into institutions".

---

[1] [Toulmin, 1958]

One could just substitute "AI" for "logic" in the above list to get a list of some arguable positions about the proper subject matter of AI. The formulation of some of the items would have to be modified somewhat. The technology argument, e.g., would have to distinguish between making tools for assisting effective thinking and machines which themselves think. To my knowledge not all of these positions have been taken; the technology and psychology positions have received the greatest amount of support. Of course, as a lawyer, I would be willing to argue that AI, too, can profitably be viewed as "generalized jurisprudence".

6.4.2 The rationalist debate about AI

The usual debate about the possibility of artificial intelligence focuses on three issues: 1) What *is* intelligence; 2) Can, as a matter of principle, intelligent machines be constructed; and 3) If the second question is answered affirmatively, how? Taken for granted in these discussions is the adequacy of the scientific method for addressing these questions. Notice also that here the ambition of AI to construct intelligent systems is understood literally. In the next section we will explore the view that AI is not really about intelligence at all.

With respect to the first question, neither the existence of a thing called "intelligence" nor the possibility of delineating the class of intelligent things in terms of necessary and sufficient properties is called into question. The debate centers around which properties are necessary and which are typically associated with intelligence but not strictly required before one is willing to attribute intelligence to some object. The point of John Searle's "Chinese Room" *Gedankenexperiment*, for example, is that *understanding* is, in his view, an essential part of intelligence[2]. Searle claims he would be unmoved by an AI system which could automatically translate one natural language into another. Even if a computer could be programmed to adequately and convincingly perform this task, he would be unwilling to attribute intelligence to the machine as he is convinced his thought experiment shows that mere performance does not imply understanding.

Also along this line are the arguments claiming an intelligent system must be embedded in the "real world". The claim is that a certain kind of robot might be said to be intelligent, but not for example a chess playing program. Chess programs do not have sensors and manipulators. They transform strings of input symbols into strings of output symbols and the locus of intelligence, according to this line of argument, remains with those persons who interpret these strings in order to make their next move in some game of chess. Intelligence here is viewed as an attribute of autonomous systems struggling to be successful in some environment.

For some, intelligence is a defining characteristic of certain "higher" forms of biological life, humans in particular. From this perspective, no machine can be intelligent simply because a machine is not an animal. That is, the defining characteristics of intelligence are so intimately connected with being an animal that, as a matter of definition, no machine can sensibly be said to be intelligent.

---

[2] [Searle, 1980]

Cognitive science, on the other hand, is based on the premise that it can make sense to talk about intelligence abstracted from biology. (This is what distinguishes cognitive science from cognitive psychology.) Animal and human intelligence are viewed as special cases. This perspective opens the door to defining classes of intelligence where one or more of the defining characteristics of human intelligence are missing. One could postulate a form of intelligence, e.g., where understanding, in Searle's sense, is not required. Perhaps chess machines could be said to display one of these other forms of intelligence. The problem with this strategy is to find a taxonomy of intelligence which is not arbitrary and construed. Why call something "intelligence" if it is not sufficiently related to the common sense meaning of the term?

Whether AI is achievable obviously depends on the particular view of intelligence adopted. In *Understanding Computers and Cognition*, for example, Winograd and Flores deny the possibility of AI by restricting their view of intelligence to human intelligence [3]. The AI projects they criticize do indeed aim to achieve human levels of performance in such domains as natural language understanding.

Following the approach articulated by Rodney Brooks[4], there is a project underway here at the GMD, lead by Christoph Lischka, to construct a small, autonomous, mobile robot displaying the intelligence of a certain kind of lizard. Although the goal is not human levels of intelligence, this project is ambitious enough. Perhaps the robot should be able to catch small insects, for example. Whatever the merits of Winograd and Flores' arguments concerning AI and human intelligence, it remains an open question whether these more modest goals are realizable.

The third issue, how to achieve AI, is too often confused with the second issue, the possibility of AI in principle. Newell and Simon's physical symbol system hypothesis (PSSH) has played an important theoretical role in the history of AI[5]. Its importance is such that the PSSH is often confused with AI itself. Elaine Rich in her textbook on AI, e.g., states that the PSSH lies "at the heart of research in artificial intelligence"[6]. Indeed the central role of the PSSH is so great that those committed to other approaches to constructing intelligent systems, such as some connectionists, claim they are no longer doing AI research![7]

---

[3] [Winograd and Flores, 1986]

[4] [Brooks, 1986]

[5] [Newell and Simon, 1976]

[6] [Rich, 1983, p. 3]

[7] According to Rich, Newell and Simon define a physical symbol system as follows: "A physical symbol system consists of a set of entities, called symbols, which are physical patterns that can occur as components of another type of entity called an expression (or symbol structure). ... At any instant of time the system will contain a collection of these symbol structures. Besides these structures, the system also contains a collection of processes that operate on expressions in order to produce other expressions ... A physical symbol system is a machine that produces through time an evolving collection of symbol structures. Such a system exists in a world wider than these symbolic expressions themselves." The Physical Symbol System

Why should AI be committed to any particular hypothesis concerning the features sufficient or necessary for an intelligent machine? Indeed, why should AI be committed to the digital computer? There should be room within AI for alternative approaches and hypotheses. Physics doesn't stop being physics when a new theory of the universe is proposed. If one views intelligent machines as being the subject matter of AI, then there seems no pressing need to restrict the field to a particular type of machine.

6.4.3 AI as metaphor

It may appear that one way to avoid some of the difficulties of the hard line view that AI is about building intelligent machines is to argue that AI's use of the term "intelligence" is metaphorical: AI systems are not *really* intelligent, they just have some features in common with intelligence. This would allow us to preserve the conventional meaning of intelligence without necessarily limiting AI's ambition regarding the levels of performance to be achieved. The adequacy of the Turing test for testing intelligence would be a non-issue, as real intelligence would not be claimed.

Unfortunately, this argument is not without problems. First, it does not completely avoid the problem of defining intelligence. As AI aspires to be a science, its subject matter needs to be delineated rather more precisely than some unspecified relation to intelligence. The task here is however simpler, as we can be satisfied with a set of features characteristic of intelligence, without being concerned with whether the set is exhaustive or includes all elements necessary for real intelligence. To justify a metaphorical use of intelligence, its literal meaning must be understood to some extent; but it is not necessary to precisely define intelligence in terms of necessary and sufficient conditions. If the claim is made that an AI system *is* intelligent, then the door is open for arguing that some necessary feature of intelligence is missing. The claim that an AI system behaves *as if it were intelligent* is much weaker. The absence of a necessary feature would not rebut the claim.

Secondly, this approach to defining AI is not in the end significantly different from the approach taken in cognitive science. The history of science shows that it is not unusual to apply an everyday word metaphorically to describe a new technical concept. Through use in the scientific discipline the term acquires a new technical meaning. Examples include the terms "field" and "force" in physics.

The use of metaphor has its justification. Languages such as English do not encourage the creation of new terms, and metaphor allows a language to be extended with new senses and shades of meaning for its existing vocabulary. It also allows a new concept to quickly acquire meaning by inheritance from some existing sense of the term. However, the use of metaphor brings with it the risk of misunderstanding. The complete meaning of the prior sense is not carried over

---

Hypothesis (PSSH) is: "A physical symbol system has the necessary and sufficient means for general intelligent action." [Rich, 1983, pp. 3-4]

into the new context, and it may not be apparent just what the metaphorical use of the term is intended to mean.

The main problem with viewing the "I" in AI metaphorically, is that intelligence is an abstract, *open-textured* concept[8]. If intelligence is to be understood metaphorically within AI then arguably the AI community should make an effort to distinguish between the metaphorical, technical use of the term and its everyday, common sense meaning. However, this is easier said than done. Intelligence has no well-understood literal meaning. Our very understanding of intelligence continues to develop along with our research in AI.

William C. Hill has recently argued that, not only is AI a metaphor, it is a poorly chosen metaphor[9]. Hill claims that most AI research has not been about intelligence at all, not even metaphorically, but about constructing new "computation-based representational media", i.e. new forms of communication. He first claims that AI is a phrase such as "horseless carriage, wireless telegraph, iron horse, glass teletype or artificial writing", a phrase which "describes a new technology wrongly in terms of an old familiar one". But unlike these other terms, "artifical intelligence" distracts attention from the new technology's principal use, the computer's potential for improving communication. Actually and "even worse", Hill goes on to say, AI is not like "wireless telegraph" as it describes new technology not in terms of other familiar technology but in terms of mental phenomena, causing irrelevant arguments about the nature of mind and intelligence.

Hill's arguments have a great deal of merit, at least for those of us who, upon reflection, have become involved in AI precisely because they are interested in new forms of effectively representing and distributing knowledge and ideas. However, each of us needs to decide for ourselves where our interests lie, and a great number of AI scientists are indeed principally interested in pursuing the goal of creating intelligent machines.

6.4.4 A hermeneutic interpretation of AI

The arguments outlined above about the nature of AI do not give up what Winograd and Flores call the "rationalistic tradition" of Western science. They view this tradition as being based on mistaken premises regarding the nature of understanding and knowledge, drawing principally for support from Heidegger's hermeneutic theory of understanding, Maturana's theory of perception and cognition and Searle's theory of speech acts. Each of these thinkers arrives at much the same epistemological stance, although they start from very different intellectual traditions. Heidegger is an existentialist philosopher, Maturana a biologist and Searle a linguist.

It would be too much to try to replicate Winograd and Flores' arguments here. It is also unnecessary for our present purposes. I do not intend to challenge or support their position, but to examine some of the consequences for AI

---

[8] [Hart, 1961]
[9] [Hill, 1989]

of accepting their principal conclusions regarding the nature of knowledge and understanding. So, the next few paragraphs will be limited to a summary of this point of view. Although the arguments are difficult and foreign at first, the main insights are not so difficult to grasp when stated informally in everyday terms. Let us start with language.

According to the rationalistic tradition, words have literal meaning. That is, words are thought to correspond to objects in the world. They *denote* things in a context-independent way. Searle's speech act theory challenges this notion by arguing that the meaning of a sentence is always dependent on some particular conversational context or situation. The speakers, their goals and intentions need to be considered when trying to get at the meaning of some "illocutionary act".

I am not sure whether Searle dealt with this aspect of meaning in his work, but the context dependence of meaning implies that words acquire new meaning through use. Words have an "open texture". In the philosophy of law, H.L.A. Hart, especially, stressed this quality of legal terms[10]. His position on this subject is a moderate one in that he asserts that terms do have a core of certain meaning. There are cases where a term is clearly applicable. Open-texture is limited to the boundary.

This brief mention of legal reasoning provides a nice opportunity to shift our attention to Heidegger, who adopted and generalized the term "hermeneutics" from its prior context. Prior to Heidegger, hermeneutics had been the art of interpreting legal and religious texts. It had been an approach to trying to understand the intended meanings of a text long after it has been written, by persons divorced in time, space, language and culture from the text's original context.

Heidegger generalized hermeneutics to the problem of an individual trying to understand his world. Not only is the connection between a term in some language to objects in the world tenuous, so too is the connection between an individual's conceptualization of the world and the world itself. The classification of objects, indeed the identification of objects, does not preexist, but occurs during the process of interaction with the environment. The particular division of the world into objects, properties and classes arrived at depends on a person's unique history, goals and perspective. Contrast this view with the rationalist tradition, where there is thought to be an "objective" view of reality, where the goal of science is viewed as arriving at, by application of the scientific method, the one true theory of the world.

As I understand Winograd and Flores, the relevance of Maturana's work here is that he explains in biological terms the dependence of perception on the structure of the perceiving organism. Compare this with behaviorism, where it is assumed that stimuli can be identified, measured and categorized independently of the structure of the particular organism. Winograd and Flores use Maturana's conclusion that there is no objective perception to support their critique of rationalism.

---

[10] [Hart, 1961]

Let me use the word "hermeneutics" as the general term for this alternative orientation towards understanding and knowledge, without necessarily restricting ourselves to Heidegger's particular interpretation. One difficulty with the hermeneutic viewpoint is that any attempt to convey it must use language, and the conventions of our language are so deeply steeped in the rationalistic tradition that the hermeneutic viewpoint appears mysterious, mystic or even self-contradictory. Any description of the hermeneutic perspective is couched in terms of a theory about perception, knowledge and understanding, which gives the impression that the terms of the theory denote objects in the world and that the theory is subject to verification or, if you prefer, falsification. One plays the game of natural science while refuting the rules of the game. The theory gives rise to the kind of tension experienced with the various instantiations of the Liar's paradox. To understand the hermeneutic perspective, one has to temporarily suspend disbelief as one does when reading a novel or viewing a movie.

In the last section we discussed the possibility of a metaphorical interpretation of AI. The usual interpretation of metaphor does not diverge from the epistemology of the rationalistic tradition. On the contrary, the whole notion of metaphor depends on a distinction between the literal context-free meaning of a term and a novel use which is in conflict in some way with this literal meaning.

Now we are at a point where we can discuss Winograd and Flores' use of the hermeneutic perspective to criticize AI. They argue that AI is deeply embedded in the rationalistic tradition, pointing especially to Newell and Simons' Physical Symbol System Hypothesis. Their interpretation of the PSSH, which I suppose is the usual interpretation, supposes that symbols "can be understood as referring to objects and properties of the world"[11].

There may be a number of ways to rebut Winograd and Flores' treatment of AI. One could argue for another interpretation of the PSSH, for example. Rather than supposing that symbols denote objects in the world, one could hypothesize that symbol processing of a certain kind is a sufficient and necessary condition for higher kinds of intelligent behavior, even though symbols do not denote objects in the world. That is, the PSSH need not imply a naïve correspondence theory of meaning.

Let us focus on another kind of rebuttal here, however. This is my main point: If we accept the hermeneutic viewpoint, then we must also accept that the term intelligence does not denote any particular thing, but may vary in meaning depending on its use within some particular context. One can argue, as lawyers do, that a particular interpretation in some particular context (or case) would lead to certain desirable or undesirable consequences, or create certain risks or opportunities, but not generally, abstracted from some concrete context, that only this or that concept of intelligence is legitimate. That is, if we intend to adopt a hermeneutic perspective, we cannot at the same time use rationalistic arguments to deny the possibility of AI. Hermeneutics requires other criteria for evaluating scientific hypotheses, indeed it presupposes an alternative philosophy of science.

---

[11] [Winograd and Flores, 1986, p. 74]

Of course I cannot pretend to develop an alternative, hermeneutic philosophy of science here. But it may be that such an alternative science would have some characteristics in common with jurisprudence, that the criteria and methods used to evaluate scientific theories would resemble the methods used to decide legal cases. This idea is explored a bit further in the next section.

6.4.5 Evaluating AI systems

Rather than trying to define intelligence in the abstract, and then arguing about whether or not artificial intelligence is possible or desirable, it may be more constructive to focus our attention on the problem of evaluating specific AI systems. An understanding of the limits and potential of AI can evolve through the practice of constructing and using specific systems. Concrete systems, used in specific situations, permit the interests of users and system designers to be taken into consideration.

Again, the legal analogy is useful here. Vague terms are often deliberately used in statutes as a way of deferring decision-making from the abstract setting of a parliament or congress to the courts, where the term can be fleshed out during the process of deciding concrete cases. A constitution may refer to "due process" or a statute to "reasonable cause", without further defining these terms. This is as it should be. Legislatures lack the vision to foresee all the consequences of a law.

Similarly, the field of AI can be characterized very abstractly, as Elaine Rich, for example, does when she writes AI is "the study of how to make computers do things at which, at the moment, people are better". What is or is not an AI system can then be decided, if not definitely, on a case by case basis.

This approach to delineating the field is not merely an attempt to avoid the difficult issue of defining intelligence. Rather, taking the hermeneutic perspective seriously, it is a recognition that concepts like intelligence cannot be defined.

How then can an AI system be evaluated without returning to the futile problem of defining intelligence? Toulmin claims there can be no general domain-independent method for evaluating arguments. The same claim can be made for evaluating AI systems. Which methods are appropriate depends on the interests and goals of the system designers and users. Without striving for completeness, here are three approaches which come to mind:

The marketplace approach. For AI products, an economics perspective may be appropriate. There is no need to decide whether the system really displays intelligence; it is sufficient that some community continues to find the product useful. There is a lot of hype in the AI industry, as in all industries. We in AI should find this no more or less disturbing than in other fields.

The natural science approach. When the purpose of an AI system is to test an hypothesis about some particular cognitive process, then the usual methods of natural science may be appropriate. I hesitate to call this a process of validation. Supporters of Popper's philosophy of science, at least, argue that scientific theories cannot be validated, but at most falsified.

It is not necessary to delve into another discussion about the nature of science here. The only point I would like to make is that the rationalistic tradition has, despite its limits, proven its value. The limits of the rationalistic perspective can be viewed as simplifying assumptions which are appropriate in certain contexts. Apparently, we can ignore the lessons of hermeneutics for certain tasks, just as we can, to use a tired example, get along well with Newtonian physics in our daily lives without resorting to the complexities of the theories of relativity or quantum mechanics.

The legal approach. In the case of knowledge-based or expert systems, especially when such systems are used for making decisions in organizations where the rights and duties of persons in the organization may be affected, it may be appropriate to view the "knowledge base" of the system as a set of laws. The decisions made by such systems must be backed up by cogent argumentation. (This is usually called an "explanation facility".) These decisions should be subject to challenge in some kind of quasi-legal proceeding by the persons affected.

Notice that in such settings, the decisions made by expert systems must be justified by *normative* arguments. Neither logic nor appeals to "cognitive adequacy" are sufficient. Rather, substantial arguments having a legal quality are required. Conflicting interests must be balanced and the appropriateness of subsuming the concrete events of the case under the general terms used in the knowledge base must be addressed.

Formal verification methods can play a role in the above approaches, but cannot themselves offer a complete solution. Formal methods may be used to show, for example, that two forms of representation are equivalent, by constructing a sequence of transformations, known to preserve some relevant property, from one form into the other. Such methods may also be used to derive properties of a knowledge base or program. These formal methods alone are insufficient, as there is no formal way to show that the knowledge structures of an AI system are satisfied by the intended application domain. A stronger statement can be made here. No method, formal or not, can "verify" an AI system generally, abstracted from its application to concrete cases. (Indeed, this is true of all computer systems.) Again, this is an argument from jurisprudence; there is no general method for determining outside the context of particular cases whether the facts of some case are subsumed by the general terms used in the knowledge base. A literal interpretation of a knowledge base will result in unintended or undesirable decisions being made. Knowledge bases, like the law, need to be modified, reinterpreted, and extended as they are applied to particular problems.

The term "verification" is misleading, as its use suggests that there is some way to gain complete confidence in the "correctness" of some AI system. Except perhaps in highly artificial, construed domains, this will never be the case. In practice, there will be arguments for and against the suitability of the system for its intended task, and it will be a matter of judgment requiring the exercise of discretion and interpretation to decide the matter. Thus I have chosen to speak of "evaluating" AI systems. Perhaps "judging" would have been still better.

6.4.6 Conclusion

AI as a field has always had its antagonists. In some countries, notably Great Britain and West Germany, the field was prevented from advancing as rapidly as in the U.S. because of negative assessments of AI's legitimacy or potential, or because of conflict between AI and conventional computer science. After more than 30 years of development, however, I think we can say that AI is here to stay, despite ongoing discussion about the nature of intelligence. I am confident of this for a number of reasons. First of all, there is now a thriving AI industry. These commercial interests will not allow AI to die. Second, this industry is a testament to the fact that AI has indeed created useful technology. It is simply not true that AI has produced no or too few tangible results. (It is true that AI has not fulfilled the promises of some of its promoters, but these individuals should be held accountable for their predictions and claims, not the field as a whole.) Third, our understanding of intelligence is evolving at the same time as AI, indeed because of AI. AI is not bound to any particular hypothesis about the nature of intelligence, despite the historical significance of the physical symbol system hypothesis. Indeed, one could argue that critics of the PSSH are not actually critics of AI, but are themselves doing AI by pointing out the limits of a particular hypothesis, at least if they also go to the trouble of proposing a competing hypothesis. The Dreyfus brothers are a good example here[12]. They may not represent the AI mainstream, but they have played the role of ombudsman within the field. They belong to AI. Finally, one cannot use hermeneutics to attack AI. The hermeneutic view implies that there is no single correct definition of intelligence. The notion of intelligence evolving through the practice of AI is just as legitimate, in its special context, as any other.

Acknowledgements

Many thanks to Joachim Hertzberg, Christoph Lischka, Thomas Christaller and the editors for their helpful comments and suggestions.

---

[12] [Dreyfus and Dreyfus, 1986]

Part 7

Designing for People

Reinhard K.-S.

How can people be the focus of our attention when our real task is to develop formalisms and technical systems? Normally, people are only considered to the extent demanded by the technical development in hand.

Christiane

I'm not sure how widespread this view really is in practice. Of course, there are quite considerable conflicts of interest in system development. I suspect, however, that it's also a matter of ignorance as to the sort of foundations human-oriented system design might be based on. It's not only a question of product design, but also of process design and the design of the use context.

Reinhard B.

We are asking questions such as how the technical design process can be embedded in the social context so as to meet human needs. And yet, today, computer systems are frequently foisted on their users without their having any say in the matter. People's requirements and needs are neither given consideration nor taken seriously.

Heinz

Our approach is perhaps best characterized by comparing the illustration in this part with that in Part II of our book. Here, the people are no longer mere spectators: they themselves become actors in the play. There are, of course, considerable differences in the roles in which the various actors are cast.

Christiane

The sage neither becomes redundant, nor is he recast in a minor role. We continue to need the expertise of software engineers and computer scientists. But we must also acknowledge the fact that we need the know-how of the users and the other groups involved as well. We must develop technology with those affected by it, not against them or on their behalf.

Reinhard K.-S.

But that's where the whole problem starts. For what it means – as Gro Bjerknes points out – is that we have to share responsibility. And that, given the currently prevailing conditions, is not an easy task; it creates problems for all concerned. And yet, it is something that can be learned. Ultimately, she argues, the advantages gained will far outweigh the effort invested.

Heinz

User participation does not, however, mean that there is no longer any call for us as software engineers. We are well aware of the difficulties users experience in suggesting or anticipating technical alternatives. Conversely, we, for our part, must endeavour to acquire a proper understanding of the use situation into which our technical systems are to be integrated.

Reinhard K.-S.

One way of arriving at such an understanding is proposed by Markku Nurminen with his subject-oriented approach. Essentially, his idea is that users must be able to act autonomously and responsibly as the subjects of their work activity. This not only has implications for our approach to design; it also has a direct impact on product structures.

Reinhard B.

And that, surely, means that product structures are not independent of people and the values they hold.

Reinhard K.-S.

It begins with the very way in which a problem is perceived and defined. Michaela Reisin argues that we must view participative system development as a joint theory-building process. She proposes methodological improvements designed to support cooperative theory building.

Christiane

But theory building must go beyond the development process. Not everyone who uses a system can participate in its development. Nor is it possible, before completing a system, to anticipate all the problems that will arise once it is in use.

Reinhard K.-S.

Wolfgang Dzida supports this view, emphasizing that the human being has to be in control of the course of interactions with the system. This is not only important from the point of view of job satisfaction; it is also an essential prerequisite for arriving at an understanding of the system's functionality. Basically, this implies that the designer's job is to provide opportunities rather than to prescribe the course of (inter-)action.

Reinhard B.

As I see it, this question is not confined to software development; it is applicable to any kind of human activity.

Reinhard K.-S.

And that is why we have to know what working and learning conditions are conducive to human development if we wish to design software systems for people. From the industrial psychologist's standpoint, Walter Volpert presents a set of three basic principles which have to be taken into account here. In addition, he proposes a methodical approach to task analysis that places special emphasis on contrasting system operations with human actions.

Christiane

Here, we have a basis for interdisciplinary cooperation. We have to familiarize ourselves with the living and working conditions of the users if we wish to develop useful systems for them. It is not enough simply to know something about system functions and algorithms.

Reinhard K.-S.

Someone who speaks, for instance, only of symbolic representations has already struck the human being from his list of concerns. The language we use sometimes speaks volumes.

7.1 Shared Responsibility: A Field of Tension

Gro Bjerknes

7.1.1 Introduction

Why is it problematic for computer scientists and domain experts to share responsibility for a system development project, even when shared responsibility is a goal for the project?

I will discuss this topic on the basis of experiences from the Florence project[1]. First, I present the Florence project and the organization of the project. Next, I discuss 'shared responsibility'. Thirdly, I tell about three situations in which the dilemma of shared responsibility was visible in some way or another, and finally, I reflect upon our experiences.

My conclusion is that shared responsibility, seen from a computer scientist's point of view, turns out to be a field of tension between control of the project on the one hand, and participation of domain experts on the other hand.

7.1.2 The Florence project

The Florence project was a research project about the development and use of computer systems in nurses' daily work. The original goal of the project was to design programming languages, called profession-oriented languages, based on the professional language of occupational groups. The profession-oriented languages were seen as an offensive strategy for occupational groups to keep control over the use of computers in their work, instead of adjusting the work to computer systems designed from a management point of view. Another hope was to avoid adjusting work to computer systems designed for societies different from the Norwegian one.

The project adheres to a research tradition known as *the collective resource strategy*[2], or alternately as *the critical tradition*[3] of system development in Scandinavia. System development, in short, can be said to be concerned about how to build computer systems that fit the organization in which it will be used.

---

[1] The Florence project was initiated by the system development group, Dept. of Informatics, University of Oslo, and sponsored by The Royal Norwegian Council for Scientific and Industrial Research. The project lasted from 1983 to 1987.

[2] [Ehn and Kyng, 1987]

[3] [Bansler, 1989]

Thus, two important topics are:

1. What does a fit between a use organization and a computer system mean, and
2. How do we carry out system development to ensure that the resulting computer system actually fits the use organization.

The critical tradition in Scandinavia has its its basis in the institutionalized conflict between labour and capital. Hence, these topics have been discussed from a worker's point of view, arguing that capital already had resources to develop computer systems according to their needs. The trade unions were regarded as representatives for the workers' collective, and the first projects within the tradition were carried out in close cooperation with trade unions, aiming at developing strategies for the introduction of computers. However, there are many assumptions built into computer technology, and after a while it was considered necessary to question the technology itself. This led to projects where the goal was to show alternatives to existing technology. The Florence project was one of these projects.

Still, the goal of constructing profession-oriented languages was quite abstract. We also found it difficult to construct a programming language on the basis of natural (professional) languages. Therefore the goal was modified to building a computer system for nurses' daily work. With this goal we could still base our work on a profession, nursing, and we could explore different ways of carrying out system development. In order to build computer systems for nurses' daily work, we had two possibilities. We could do it all on our own, in which case we would have to learn a lot about nursing. Or we could leave it to the nurses to decide what kind of computer applications would suit their work. Then we had to teach the nurses how to evaluate computer systems in relation to their work.

According to the Scandinavian research tradition, we chose the latter and became dependent on the nurses. If we say that the computer scientists represented a technical point of view, and the nurses a work setting point of view, the idea was that the nurses should see the technical solution from a work setting point of view. This view of the computer system should be the basis for design. However, the nurses also became dependent on us, because we were able to evaluate the work setting solutions from a technical point of view by adding our general knowledge of the consequences of computerization.

We wanted to reflect the mutual dependency in the organization of the project, by sharing the responsibility for the project with the nurses. The mutual dependency was reflected in the first period of the project, called 'mutual learning'. This period was inspired by anthropological research methods, introduced by the anthropologist that participated in the project. The goal of these activities was that the computer scientists should learn about nursing, and that the nurses should learn about informatics. The 'mutual learning' period ended with negotiations about the application area of the computer system we intended to build, evaluated on both a nursing and an informatical basis.

7.1.3 The notion of 'shared responsibility'

The notion of 'shared responsibility' was seldomly explicitly stated in the Florence project, it was more like an implicit assumption that guided the planning of the project and the way the project was carried out.

The bases for the concept of shared responsibility are the following statements:

- There are different interests in a project, and the differences are a source of knowledge.
- The different groups are equally necessary.
- The responsibility for the project as a whole should be shared between the participants. To share responsibility means both to give and to take responsibility, according to the situation.

The first two statements can be seen as a political credo. The statements express the importance of the domain experts, in this case nurses. The emphasis on domain experts is closely related to the critical tradition in Scandinavian system development research. The statements also stress the importance of computer scientists. Together the statements express the view that even though domain experts are experts on their own work, computer scientists can contribute to how to build a computer system that fits the work. The third statement seems to be a logical consequence of the first two. However, it proved to be very difficult to share responsibility with the nurses. As the anthropologist in the project put it: "Should the users decide on their own, or should they have democratic system developers who decide for them?"

7.1.4 Three situations

The dilemma of shared responsibility was encountered in three situations:

1. when we decided what computer system to build,
2. when we had serious trouble due to bugs in the computer, and
3. when the computer system was introduced in the work place.

The dilemma appeared foremost in situations where the computer scientists wanted to control the process for one reason or another, e.g. keeping the time schedule, protecting research interests, and at the same time it was imperative that the nurses had control as well, in order to reach the overall goal of the project.

In the first situation, the computer scientists wanted to build a computer system that was interesting from a research point of view. On the other hand, the system should also be a system the nurses wanted to use in their daily work, otherwise there would be no research connected to the study of computer systems in use.

In the second situation, the computer scientists excluded the nurses from the development process by giving priority to programming problems instead of using at least some time to keep the nurses in a kind of busy-wait state.

In the third situation, the computer scientists insisted on leaving the instruction and introduction of the computer system to the nurses. Again, we would have liked to exercise a kind of control to ensure that the system was used. However, we had no means to force the nurses to use the system.

Deciding on what computer system to build

We were determined to let the nurses decide what kind of computer applications they wanted. This was mostly due to earlier experiences: it is hard to motivate a sense of cooperation if the nurses do not judge the proposed computer system to be useful for their daily work. We also would insist on building a computer system for the nurses' daily work. We were not interested in making carbon copies of general administrative or medical systems. And both groups wanted to build a computer system that gave a fair chance to succeed with the available resources.

We decided on the computer system by setting up a negotiating meeting. In the week before the meeting, we were rather nervous. Could we really trust that the nurses had sufficient understanding of informatics to propose a useful computer system? What should we do if there were a total disagreement? Should we try to persuade them in some way or another? Should we set up new negotiations? How should we do this?

Fortunately, we did agree on a computer system. We decided to build a "work sheet system", i.e. the computer system should produce work sheets that were to replace the clipboards that the nurses use during a shift. The clipboards contain all relevant information about the patients in the ward, and they are used as reminders and notepads during a shift. The work sheet system was a small and simple system. At that time, we knew enough about nursing to recognize that even if the computer system was simple, it would interfere with the nurses' daily working routines and the information structures they used in many and complex ways. Seen from a system development point of view, this was a challenge. And, most important, we could rely on the nurses. Our anxiety to leave important decisions to the nurses seemed to be unnecessary.

So, we remained in peace with the nurses. Instead, the decision brought up other conflicts with existing traditions:

- We found ourselves in conflict with the assumptions of what researchers should do. Neither in a research milieu, represented by the financing institutions, nor in the technical milieu, represented by the computer manufacturer, is it acceptable to make simple and useful computer systems. Instead, the systems are supposed to be technically advanced, and result in new and fancy products. This is due to the fact that the (research) goal often is meant to support the development of new Norwegian information technology, which seems to be in opposition to building useful computer systems for particular users.
- The computer system did not correspond to the usual way of using computers in hospitals. The usual way is to make computer systems for the

administration of goods, personnel and patients, to make medical systems for medical doctors or to make statistics for planning. Thus, our computer system represented a new way of looking at the use of information in hospitals. Unfortunately, this is difficult to explain to computer scientists, because they do not know anything about hospitals. And for people in health care, the system corresponded to the way they actually use information, therefore they could not see anything new in it. They could not see that the traditional way of using computers in hospitals often is a mismatch with the way information actually is used.

- Due to the deviation from tradition, another conflict was brought to the surface; namely, two opposing views on how to solve the problems in health care: One side prefers technical solutions, like computer-based medical records, the other side prefers organizational solutions. We were lucky since the larger part of our steering group belonged to the 'organizational' side.

This illustrates that we could rely on the nurses to share responsibility, but that the consequences of shared responsibility are not necessarily accepted outside a project.

Bugs in the computer

The project was behind schedule due to hardware errors, software errors and the fact that we had to explore the limits of the computer tools we were using. During the implementation, we worked at the University most of the time, for several reasons: It was a half hour drive each way to the hospital; at the University we had a workplace, with telephone available all the time, a black-board which we used for planning and writing down design decisions, a proper place for manuals and so forth; in the hospital we had one terminal only, and we always worked in rooms that were designed according to the nurses' needs.

What was the result of this? When we did not have the regular contact with the nurses, they lost the possibility for taking responsibility for the project. We excluded them from the process, even if we did not intend to do so. We just thought that they were not interested in programming and debugging. What happened was that they lost motivation; they could not understand why things took so long. They had seen a prototype made with a text-editor, and they could not understand why it took us such a long time to implement the system; nothing seemed to happen in the project. Thus, it was difficult for them to legitimize the project to the other nurses in the ward. The result was almost a total collapse of the project. We rescued it at the last minute.

This illustrates how easy it is to exclude people from taking responsibility even when the goal is the opposite.

Introduction of the computer system

After teaching the members of the project group how to use the system and making short, written instructions, the responsibility for instruction and introduction of the computer system was completely left to the nurses. Then we left, and we did not show up for half a year.

Since the nurses have been responsible for the suggestion of a useful computer system, it was rather easy for us to let them take the responsibility for introducing and using it. After all, it was not necessary for us to prove to the nurses that the computer system was useful to them.

In the beginning, the nurses were a bit reluctant, and could not believe that we really meant to leave them on their own with the system. But when they got used to the idea, it worked fine. As a matter of fact, their way of organizing instruction was much better than anything we would have proposed. One reason for this was that they exploited the existing organization of work.

The nurses are divided into kernel groups that work the same shift. So the instruction was based on a two-step strategy: One person from every kernel group should learn to use the system, and they should teach the two other nurses in their group when time allowed for it. The nurses were also able to exploit the differences in workload between night and day. So they practised a lot during the night and evening shifts. Where we only saw constraints, they saw possibilities.

This illustrates that the results may be better when we dare to hand over responsibility to others. Still, it was tempting to control the nurses and in this way keep the responsibility for the process, especially when things were going slowly.

7.1.5 An attempt at an explanation

In principle, shared responsibility means both giving and taking responsibility. We found that it was difficult for us to give responsibility. Somehow, we felt that it was easy for us to take responsibility, and that responsibility was easily given to us.

One could ask, why was it important to share responsibility with the nurses if it was so difficult? In belated wisdom, we would say that the notion of 'shared responsibility' was our solution to the field of tension[4] between control and a participative process.

It seems that computer scientists like to have control[5]. However, it is not only computer scientists themselves who expect to control system development; others expect this as well. 'Control' in this setting means that the computer scientists often are in charge of both the computer system and the process of building it. This can prevent user participation in several areas.

- When computer scientists are building a computer system, they want the result to fulfill some quality criteria. To reach the desired level of *use quality*

---

[4] 'Field of tension' is a concept which is inspired by Mao Tsetung's concept of contradictions [Tsetung, 1967]. I have chosen the concept of 'fields of tension' because I like the intuitive meaning of this notion.

[5] Cf. Burstall, Chap. 2.3.

the domain experts[6] must participate in the process[7]. On the other hand, the domain experts' knowledge does not guarantee a computer system with good use quality. This is the reason why both kinds of expertise are necessary in system development[8]. The need for both kinds of expertise creates uncertainty. It seems impossible to determine whether the domain experts have a sufficient background for evaluating a computer system for their own work, and it seems equally impossible for computer scientists to know in advance whether they will have sufficient knowledge about the application area to evaluate the domain experts' suggestions for computer systems. It is quite tempting for computer scientists to reduce this uncertainty by controlling and dominating the system development process. In fact, it is quite hard not to dominate it.

- Even if the computer scientists are responsible for the process, it is possible to *delegate well defined tasks*, like education. Since they are often supposed to be responsible for the overall time schedule, it can be difficult not to intervene if the activity does not proceed as scheduled. In this way, the feeling of control may destroy the involvement of domain experts, because it is somehow contradictory to delegate the responsibility for a task and then control the people who carry it out.

- The computer scientists also have to design and implement the computer system. Of course they have their own time schedules for those tasks. Often they think that the problem to be solved and the specified requirements are well defined, and they do not expect that they will need the domain experts after this point in time. First, it often proves to be wrong that everything was well understood[9]. Second, the computer scientists do not give priority to keeping in touch with the domain experts due to time constraints. If they have to choose between implementing a specification according to time schedule or to contact the domain experts to confirm that the specification is correct from the domain experts' point of view, the computer scientists usually choose to keep the time schedule. In this way, the efforts of the computer scientists to control their own tasks may prevent the domain experts from participation in the process.

In theory, shared responsibility is the field of tension between the computer scientists' and the domain experts' control of the development process. In reality, however, much control is given to or taken by computer scientists. Thus, shared responsibility will be a field of tension for computer scientists between control and participation of domain experts.

Acknowledgements
I would like to thank Reinhard Keil-Slawik for his constructive comments on this chapter.

---

[6] I use the notion 'domain expert' instead of 'user', since the notion of 'user' pinpoints that the most important aspects of people's work is that they use a computer system.

[7] [Rolskov, 1990]

[8] [Bjerknes and Bratteteig, 1988]

[9] [Florence Report, 1985, Sieker and Jensen, 1988]

7.2 A Subject-Oriented Approach to Information Systems

Markku I. Nurminen

The subject-oriented approach is introduced in order to emphasize the role of human subjects in the use of information technology. Subject-orientation brings clarity to the question of control and responsibility. The tasks performed by means of information technology become an inherent part of the user's job. The implications of this ecological principle are explored, in particular with regard to the organization of work.

7.2.1 Introduction

Computers are confusing. We know very well that they are electronic devices which can be programmed to perform predefined tasks. But once the computer is programmed and the execution of the program is started, the computer seems to work by itself. This is confusing because the computer's behaviour is in one aspect similar to human behaviour: it works autonomously without external control.

Sherry Turkle[1] has observed children who use computers. Their confusion was expressed in a debate whether the computers are living or not. The similarity opinion had many good arguments like "People also follow rules, are they not programmed – by their mother and teacher, ultimately by the pope?" Such a confusion makes it justified to bring up the question about the similarity or dissimilarity between computers and human beings. Are these machines really as smart and creative as people? Or are people only well-programmed clones of computers?

In this paper I have chosen as the basis for the discussion the notion of dissimilarity between humans and computers. This seems fruitful because it eliminates many dangers related to the confusion originating in the opposite view based on similarity. If we do not make a sharp distinction between the fundamental nature of computers and people, we are faced with a situation in which the computer appears as a subject. It is typical for a subject that it can act autonomously. But can we also make the computer responsible for the tasks it performs?

In working life we normally assume that the worker has the professional skill needed for doing his or her job and taking the responsibility for the results. It sounds strange if the responsibility suddenly disappears only because there are some computerized tasks included in the job. It is therefore relevant to take as the starting point the entire work situation. Information technology is thus seen

---

[1] [Turkle, 1984]

in its proper context, therefore it does not need any special mysterious status. The worker performs all tasks which belong to the job. Some tasks he or she performs by means of the computer, but he or she is the responsible subject for them as well. For now, we denote this basic as the *subject-oriented approach* in the use of computers. It will be further characterized later in this paper.

I shall first, in Section 7.2.2, describe some factors which have contributed to the appearance of the computer as a subject and point out some problems this has caused. In Section 7.2.3 I shall discuss in more detail what it means to be a subject in general and as the user of information systems in particular. The consequences for job design and design of information systems finally concretize the subject-oriented approach in Section 7.2.4, which is followed by a brief summary.

7.2.2 The birth of the computer subject

No wonder that children were confused since also many adults fail to make the fundamental distinction between people and computers. The Artificial Intelligence community seems often to be confused as well. Inspired by the notion of similarity, Artificial Intelligence researchers are trying to formulate features of human intelligence in a form which can be implemented by means of computer software. In well-defined and restricted areas this approach has the capacity of producing very valuable results, but as soon as the human activity as a whole is taken to be the object of modelling, the dissimilarity comes to the surface: Which is the real subject, the computer or the human?

The problem cannot be defined away by regarding the computer-human-confusion as an animist metaphor which as such is harmless. It does not appear only in the exotic spheres of Artificial Intelligence. It is part and parcel of daily work for numerous users of information systems. If the user of software has no sufficient control over it, the computer and the software grow to be a system subject. Many users are confronted in practice with a situation where the computer really appears as a co-worker. The powerlessness is often expressed in terms like "I ask the system" or "This error was made by the computer".

Another popular area prone to conceptual confusion is object-oriented programming and the corresponding principle of modelling for application software. If we agree that the subject is the person who acts and the object is something which is affected by this, we should be more careful in the vocabulary of object-orientation. It is true that object-oriented programming provides an elegant solution for the problem of integrated representation of data and algorithms by connecting the objects with the methods applicable to them. But the (partly metaphorical) vocabulary also gives the objects some properties which actually belong exclusively to subjects. Objects are capable of sending messages to each other. These messages are not only informative, they are supposed to trigger methods assigned to the receiving object(s). Thus the sending object gets the role of a subject which performs a remote procedure call. Since software designed according to the object-oriented paradigm may perform a large number of such procedure calls without any intervention by the user, the problem of control arises: who is in charge, who is the subject.

As long as objects stand for computer-specific entities in data structures, the operating system or the user interface, the problem is not very serious. But as soon as we describe the entities of the application system (products, customers, budgets, for example), we enter the area which is directly related to the work of the users. There, he or she should have control: the objects should not send messages and trigger actions by themselves. Otherwise we are again faced with the computer-subject.

In the context of (administrative) information systems the autonomous action of the computer is not reflected only in the lack of control of individual users. The information system often also connects different users and thus performs an important part of *organizational coordination*. It is worth noticing that many times there is no human subject doing this coordination, it is left to the system. The subjectivity of the system is further strengthened by the fact that the users are usually not aware of this coordination. They are rather working together with the system instead of the co-workers behind it. This indicates that the system subject has been created as a side-effect of increasing system integration. To illustrate this development, two important changes brought about by integration may be noted.

Initially, computer applications were more or less independent, each having a primary user group. Even if the interface was very primitive, the structure was quite clear: the users delivered their input data to their batch runs on sheets to be punched and fed to the application programs. Afterwards they received the results in the form of printed listings. The coordination between the organizational units took place directly, it was not mediated by the system. The users were "owners" of their systems.

The first step of *integration* implied that a part of the results no longer was returned to the users but stored in the computer centre in order to be used as input to other applications which were owned by other groups of users. As the individual applications grew together, the control – and the responsibility – of the primary users was dissolved. Of course, this step of integration was justified in many rational ways, because it eliminated unnecessary repunching of cards from computer-produced listings. A similar justification may be found also for the other step of integration, the creation of centralized data bases. This eliminated unnecessary sorting and restructuring of data files for the purposes of different applications. As a side-effect, however, it often separated the data base from the users, relying instead on a shared pool of data where nobody actually has the ultimate responsibility. Thus the "ownership" of data disappeared.

Integration does, perhaps, not seem very harmful at the first look. But as soon as something goes wrong, the question of *responsibility* arises. It is not primarily a question of who is guilty. The error must be identified and corrected, and the work must go on. The spaghetti of an integrated system give poor support for straightening out error situations, especially if there are no human subjects having an overview of the whole system.

Similar problems appear in other exceptional situations which are not modelled within the system. It is true that this is not primarily a problem of integrated system structure. It illustrates, however, another feature of the system subject: the computer can perform only predetermined tasks. If the actual task does not fit these, the user is powerless and unable to do anything. The meaningful action of the genuine human subject is prevented. This is likely to have negative effects both in efficiency and effectiveness.

The computer is not a subject in every imaginable use situation. For example, when using an interactive, tool-like application program like word processing or spreadsheet, the user obviously feels like a subject. When inserting a letter in the text, he or she is rewarded with an immediate feedback: the new letter appears on the screen as result of the action taken by the human subject. A similar reward is available when the user adds a formula in a spreadsheet. But when receiving a complex sheet filled with formulas, he or she may be lost. It will take a lot of effort to find out where all the figures come from and how they are calculated. Many administrative systems have similar problems. They are often still more imperceivable, since the spreadsheet and the formulas are not available to be analyzed. In addition, the integration is likely to hide the genuine human subjects behind the system.

The problem is not specific to information technology alone. Automated processes in general are autonomous by definition. The operator has often very restricted control. In this paper, however, we focus on information technology. It seems important that the user of an information should have good control over the system he or she uses. This means several things:

- The user should understand what he or she is doing. This holds for all tasks, both computer-supported and others.
- The user should be able to check the functioning of the system.
- The user should be able to perform exceptional tasks as well. This may imply the possibility to decompose computer functions to smaller primitives, i.e. to shift from automatic to manual control.
- The user should be able to define new procedures from the existing primitives, for example by means of macro generators.

7.2.3 Subject or object?

Our preliminary understanding of subject-orientation was based on the ability of a subject to act autonomously. The discussion above has enriched this view with some aspects, in terms of different forms of control, which support the subjectivity of the worker in the use situation of an information system. Without control we cannot take responsibility for our doings. For example, if the initiative is given the system so that it determines the sequence and contents of the tasks to be performed; and if the user just gives answers when requested by the system, he or she is not very much a subject.

Of course, there are limits to subjectivity. Too much individualism reminds us of sweet handicraft romanticism and is certainly counterproductive in any organization. A nice presentation of these limits is given by Cashmore and Mullan[2].

---

[2] [Cashmore and Mullan, 1983]

They distinguish between two types of factors which restrict the free choice of humans and their capacity to bring about internal and external changes, and relate these factors to different research traditions.

Internal restrictions come from biological and psychological factors. If these are over-emphasized, they lead in the extreme form to a *behaviouristic* research setting, where humans are considered more or less like machines.

External restrictions come from social factors. Social institutions or the logic of historical development determine human behaviour. In the extreme, this approach turns a human being into a cog in the big machine. The rules derived from this view, called *structuralist*, are certainly different from the rules of the behaviourist view, but both of them point to restrictions of the free will.

Surrounded by these two types of restrictions there is the area where voluntarism may survive – to some extent. The name of the research setting studying this area, *interactionism*, describes rather well its character. It reminds us that the freedom of will is never complete, rather it is always shaped by internal and external restrictions. The scope left for the free will may be varying in its size. For subject-orientation this area is very central since there a human being is something more than a machine (as seen by behaviourism) or a cog in a machine (as seen by structuralism). The area is limited already by definition, but it should not be smaller than necessary, says our subject-orientation, not even, when information technology is used.

The subject-orientation has its conceptual origin in the *Humanistic Perspective* presented by Nurminen[3], even if it intends to be more concrete and application-oriented then the abstract frame of reference provided there. The Humanistic Perspective is characterized by its ideal type, an analytical tool called Human-scale Information System (HIS).

The HIS ideal type is completely non-integrated. This implies that there cannot be any centralized data base unless there is a corresponding centralized function with subjects responsible for it. All pieces of data storage belong to a local (ideally personal) system unit. The responsibility for the data has a straightforward solution: the owner of such a system unit is naturally responsible for the maintenance and updating of data as well as for all processing which takes place within his or her HIS unit. The resulting system is built on the basis of subjects rather than objects.

The deintegration implies the possibility for the user to have full control of the storing and processing functions. While these functions earlier used to be external to the work situation, they are now right here: expressions like "this is my data base" and "these calculations are a part of my job" describe how the computerized tasks are an inseparable part of work.

It is true that users still may have computer-supported tasks to perform which are so complex that further de-automation, or decomposition, may be necessary for them to be responsible subjects[4]. Such a de-automation would strengthen the understanding and the control in a situation where the black box danger is

---

[3] [Nurminen, 1988]
[4] See Dzida, Chap. 7.4.

present, i.e. where the user cannot evaluate the outcome of a computer program. In addition, the possibility of decomposition improves flexibility by allowing the user to perform also exceptional tasks. 'Exceptions' belong to normal work situations even if they are regarded as routine. Suchman[5] argues even that "plans are resources for situated action, but do not in any strong sense determine its course".

The decomposition of the information system has other interesting effects as well: it also disintegrates the coordination which was baked within the system. People become visible, they are working together without the disrupting factor of the integrated information system. This means, of course, that the workers with their local system units are not isolated. All channels of communication, even the electronic ones, are exploited, but now they convey human-human communication instead of human-machine communication. The system-subject in the role of the coordinator has disappeared. It is well justified to talk about a social interpretation of the use of information systems.

An example of this kind of a computer-supported work situation may be found in an empirical case analyzed in the research project Knowledge and Work[6]. There was a group of clerks responsible for calculating and paying the salaries for employees of a municipality. Their work was not organized according to a specialization by function. Instead, each clerk performed all tasks in the task lattice. Each clerk had responsibility for a certain group of employees. Each of the groups had different criteria, agreements and rules for the calculation of the salary.

For each employee, the clerk had to maintain a set of permanent data. For each period of payment she collected the salary transactions which determined the payment for this particular period. The calculation, as well as the interpretation of the agreements, was an important part of the job. Even if the clerks worked independently in parallel, they had some similar tasks as well (e.g. advance tax): they were a cooperating team. In terms of system structure, each clerk had a personal subsystem (HIS) of her own, with related functions of storing, processing and communicating.

This case indicates that subject-orientation challenges the very concept of information system. It is not an integrated collection of programs and data bases. It does not make sense to regard the use of information technology separately from the entire work situation. A striking example of this need to redefine the notion of information system is given by Bjerknes[7]. Her research group wanted to design an application system with the starting point in the professional knowledge of the nurses. This implied the selection of a concrete but not very complicated application area. The user interface reflected the daily work of nurses. The specialists in computer science did not, however, consider the selected system

---

[5] [Suchman, 1987, p. 52]

[6] The 'Knowledge and Work' research project worked at the Department of Computer Science, University of Turku, Finland, in 1986–89. It was mainly financed by the Academy of Finland.

[7] Chap. 7.1

interesting or ambitious (for researchers!). This demonstrates how strong the dominant paradigm of information systems often is and how it may prevent us from seeing good and simple alternatives.

The subject-oriented notion of the information system also implies re-thinking many other, underlying assumptions. We are able to formulate new views on knowledge and on human beings, for example. The most concrete part of the reconstructed reality, however, is perhaps the organization of work.

7.2.4 Subject-oriented work with computers

The reinvention of human subjects in the context of information systems not only calls for a new concept of information system. It also gives rise to a revised view of job design. This is a direct implication of the non-integrated system structure which allows for reestablishing the broken connection between the computerized and other tasks of the worker.

In a use situation of an existing information system this means that there no longer is a system external to the work situation. There are individuals and groups doing their work, and they are using information technology to perform some particular tasks. A natural way to design jobs is to connect computer-supported and other tasks by utilizing the symbol function: let the same worker(s) take care of a task and the information related to it. Then, this individual or collective subject has a holistic and unscattered responsibility for a whole.

An example of the subject-oriented organization of work may be given from the inventory[8]. The inventory is run by a group of people with shared responsibility. They receive the products and deliver them (in FIFO order) on request. They also take care of the products while they are in the inventory and of their reasonable physical allocation. They are not allowed to deliver the products before they are released by the quality control in the laboratory. At the same time they also have exclusive responsibility for inventory book-keeping and for local space management in the inventory. These computer-supported tasks are thus an inherent part of the whole job.

Here, the subject-oriented approach combines a set of material tasks together with corresponding information system tasks. The same people are responsible for both of them. This structural solution carries a built-in motivational factor for maintaining high quality of the information system, since the responsible subjects themselves will suffer most from their potential negligence. The same case is analyzed also by Hellman[9]. She points out how important it is to see the context of the information system: its connection to the rest of the work as well as to the organizational coordination between (groups of) people.

This focus on the integral work situation is actually another formulation of the *ecological perspective* advocated by Keil-Slawik[10]. Both formulations express

---

[8] Another case of the Knowledge and Work project.
[9] [Hellman, 1989]
[10] Chap. 4.4

a clear anti-Tayloristic view on organization by trying to reintegrate the tasks of the head and of the hand. From the subject-oriented point of view, however, I am not completely satisfied with the remedy suggested by Keil-Slawik, which relies on a new understanding of system development with user participation as the key feature. It is probably true that traditional methods for information system development are unlikely to produce ecologically sound work situations for the future users. But, on the other hand, participation alone does not guarantee radically new and better use situations, unless the participating people have a clear notion of the basic properties to be demanded from the resulting information system. If the objective of the development group is to design an information system which resembles an assembly line, it probably becomes an assembly line. Thus, the use situation is conceptually more fundamental than the development process[11]. Before specifying the features of the development process we should pay attention to the important properties of the work situation.

If there is no computerized information system separate from the related work, it follows quite naturally that there cannot be a separate information system development either. Rather, there is an organizational change process. The jobs will be changed as a part of this, and one part of their change will be the introduction or modification of information technology. The important distinction is illustrated in Figs. 7.2–1 and 7.2–2.

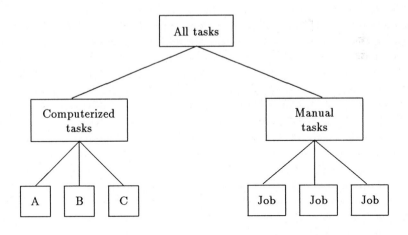

Fig. 7.2–1. The idea of job design in traditional system development

According to traditional, flow-oriented top-down development methods (Fig. 7.2–1), the activities and related information requirements are analyzed until the parts to be computerized can be identified. An analogous situation is created as a result of the design of an organization-wide conceptual schema. In both

---

[11] [Nurminen et al., 1987]

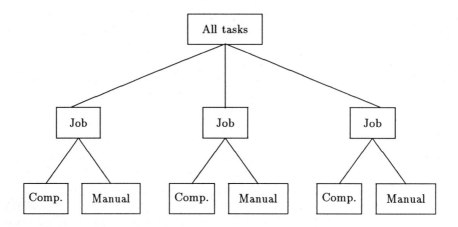

Fig. 7.2–2. The idea of job design in the subject-oriented approach

approaches, it is typical that the question of the remaining manual tasks and job design is raised too late. Then it is normally impossible to make changes in the specifications of the computerized system, which is likely to create problems in the design of meaningful jobs. Another problem which is created by this very procedure is how to re-establish the connections (both logically and physically) between the users and the technical information system.

As presented here, subject-orientation does not give a detailed method-cookbook for the joint design of jobs and information systems. However, the approach gives some good ideas to keep in mind. Its critical power challenges many traditional wisdoms in design traditions, both in job design and in IS design. On the other hand, subject orientation seems to be consistent with many recent suggestions for the design of ideal jobs. In particular the ecological, holistic principle seems to be promising. Let us relate it to Volpert's formulation of good jobs[12].

The holistic principle calls for a mix of computer-supported and other tasks. Jobs consisting only of sitting at the work station will be exceptional. This gives a good ground to variation both in bodily activity and use of sensory capacities. In many contexts it also is likely to provide for and encourage coordination and interpersonal contact. The integrated responsibility for computer-supported and other tasks promotes the broad scope of action.

Even though we have shifted the focus from the computerized parts of work towards the entire work situation, it is not unimportant what the 'computerized' part looks like. A clear subject-oriented system structure alone makes these computer-supported tasks more graspable. But what about the user interface? Does it communicate to the user about the work which he or she is doing?

---

[12] Chap. 7.5

Or does it give details of the system structure – as if the computer work were separate from the rest of the world?

Instead of a review of different types of interfaces I shall comment on the general view of research in this area. Too often, I think, different solutions or suggestions are evaluated in the laboratory. Rather seldom, test persons receive instructions which remind them of a meaningful work task. Yet it is the concrete use situation in which the quality of the user interface ultimately is either confirmed or not. If the connection to this work situation is poor, many solutions, elegant in technical details, will be wasted.

7.2.5 Conclusion

One objective regarding the subject-oriented approach has been to contribute to the demystification of information technology by emphasizing the role of the actor of computer-supported tasks. This social interpretation also led to the ecological program, in which the computer-supported tasks are seen as inherent parts of the subjects' entire jobs.

By improving the controllability and flexibility of the use of information technology, the subject-oriented approach has given a potential promise of improved quality in computer-supported work. For the time being, this promise is not concrete. Future work has to be done at least in following areas.

The properties of subject-oriented information systems must be further specified. On the one hand, the system structure must reflect the organization of work. But on the other hand, it should be flexible in order to allow for reorganizations as desired. The tasks to be performed with the system should be understandable and controllable, and the interface should support the integrated work situation.

The development of subject-oriented systems is explicitly reality construction. It cannot be accomplished separately from the organizational change process. Figures 7.2–1 and 7.2–2 above illustrate the difference between the traditional and subject-oriented approaches. It seems obvious that subject-oriented system development is meaningless without participation of the subjects. Holistic views, conceptual schemas for example, are not useless, but they are not enough. The driving force comes from work and its organization.

Finally, there is an underlying assumption in the subject-oriented approach about the competence of the worker. Computer-supported tasks cannot be under the subject's control unless he or she has sufficient skill for performing them. Such a competence is naturally developed during the participation process. The idea that users may acquire such a competence is perhaps not unrealistic. Today a car driver does not have to be a professional mechanic.

7.3 Anticipating Reality Construction

Fanny-Michaela Reisin

The arguments formulated below are based on the assumption that software development is to be viewed as a work process and can thus be seen as part of the social reproduction process with its historical background. This assumption is useful. It enables us to compare software development with other work processes, and to better understand the characteristics common to all and the ones that are specific to software development.

The most general elements of the work process are the purposive activity or the work activity itself, constituting the subjective side, and its means and products, constituting the objective (gegenständlich) side. My concern here is to pinpoint the subjective and objective elements that distinguish the software development process from other work processes.

My recent research work has led me to the conclusion that software development is characterized by the specific nature of the use objects that are produced and used in the course of this process. The *invariant* means and products, the objective elements of software development, can be identified as software objects and distinctly characterized by their electroenergetic nature and effects. *Software products are typographically symbolized autoprocessual use objects of electroenergetic nature and effect.*

Owing to the purely *electroenergetic nature* of software objects, a fundamental distinction must be drawn between them and all traditional objective means of production and use, which are distinctly characterized by their specific *material nature.*

In view of their *electroenergetic effect*, though, software objects must also be distinguished from all typographic and pictorial objects that, ultimately, are distinctly characterized by their *symbolic effect* only.

Lastly, owing to their *object form*, software products must be distinguished from all *electroenergetic functions and effects* that have previously been produced and used in the course of human activity.

The electroenergetic effect and the object form of software products and their implications for software development have so far been subjected to scarcely any systematic analysis[1].

It is these determinative elements that give rise to a specific instance of the work activities and of the organization of the software development process. And it is on these that we now focus our attention.

If we look specifically at the work activities involved in the development of software objects, we find that any attempt to relate them to conventional mass or series production of new products in accordance with an existing master product will fail. The genuinely human work activity may be defined rather

---

[1] [Reisin, 1990]

as the *creative development* of new (master) objects that have not yet been implemented. Hence, the working process constituted by software development is not well characterized merely as a productive one; it must be viewed quite distinctly as a creative process. The activities consist in creating and implementing genuinely new software objects.

Software development is the creative development of new original objects. In other words it is "original production", which means the work activities are to be characterized as creative and productive as well.

In what follows I focus on the development of software objects whose use purposes are derived from existing work processes of everyday social reality – processes in which they are to be used not only in an indirect manner, but directly as the objects, means or products of work. The development of such objects is necessarily determined as a *cooperative work process involving developers and future users.* This follows from the characterization of software development as a creative work process. As a matter of fact, there is no other way of deriving the use purpose of a new object than by cooperation and communication between the persons who are to use it and the ones who are to produce it. This calls for a specific organization of the development of software objects that are to be embedded in existing working processes, which is generally identified as participative.

These assumptions shape the course of my further argumentation in which I go on to discuss their specific theoretical and methodological implications.

In Section 7.3.1, I give a rough outline of the characteristics of participative software projects.

In Section 7.3.2, I examine the cooperative design process of a new software object. Here, I take up the notion of "theory building" coined by Naur and contrast his view of the theory that must necessarily be built in software development with the concept of *anticipation of purpose* which enables the reflective and creative elements of the work process to be put into a socio-historical context.

In Section 7.3.3, I then go on to outline a methodological approach to cooperative theory building in participative software projects.

I draw throughout on experience gained in the research and development project PETS[2].

---

[2] PETS = Participation, Evolution and Transparency in Software Development for Computer-Supported Work. The project was funded from 1987 to 1990 by the North Rhine-Westphalian Ministry of Labour, Health and Social Affairs under their programme "Mensch und Technik: Sozialverträgliche Technikgestaltung (Man and Technology: Socially-Oriented Technology Design)". It was concerned with the development of a software product to support the staff of the Central Records Office for Collective Wage Agreements at the German Trade Union Federation's (DGB) Institute for Economics and Social Sciences (WSI). The working processes there are to archive and evaluate all wage agreements (6 000 a year, 36 000 altogether) and to publish statistics.

7.3.1 General characteristics of participative software projects

If we agree to characterize software development as 'original development', its work context cannot be compared to either the 'production line' of a manufacturing company or viewed simply as the 'order-processing division' of a software development department. Instead, each software development process involves *the establishment of a project* for this specific purpose for a specified period.

Once it is agreed to establish a project, the project goals are defined, the specific domain of concern demarcated, and the required personnel and material resources determined.

The project goals are generally expressed in normative terms by means of quantitative coefficients. Undetermined factors during initial planning are the structural and qualitative characteristics of the software objects aimed at. Equally unpredictable are the necessary changes in the work processes in which these objects are to be embedded in order to attain the goals. A distinct characteristic of creative and innovative processes is the fact that their result is not determined in advance. A development project's domain of concern is not specified completely at the beginning of the work process, which means that the planned work product, too, can only be determined in outline.

Here, the basic difference becomes apparent between a development project and a skilled craftman's or industrial work context in which a technical product is manufactured. Manufacturing processes – whether they be individual or cooperative – are invariably conducted in accordance with a given master product and production plan. The important thing is to carry out these processes optimally, i.e., by producing the greatest possible quantity in the shortest possible time. The essential requirement here is routine.

Creative work processes cannot be stipulated on a general level. The anticipation of the future domain of reality and the expertise required for designing and implementing it must be established in the course of the project itself. The software objects aimed at and the way in which they are to be used only emerge gradually, and it is only towards the end of the project that their contours become properly visible. Strictly speaking, it is not possible for the means of creative work processes to be determined *completely* in advance, either. Nor is the sequence of work steps to be taken amenable to detailed planning and prescription. Creativity does not evolve continuously, and cannot be expressed in terms of algorithms.

The development of software objects that are used directly in work contexts includes the design of work, and of technology. Evaluation of the specific quality characteristics of work and technology relies not only on general criteria established by industrial scientists, but also on the criteria determined specifically by the existing work processes in a particular area as well as the concrete individual and collective requirements of the future users of the software object. The creative work processes involved in designing a new domain of reality are not primarily of an analytical and constructive nature, but are rather exploratory and experimental. Of significance are not only objective, but in particular subjective factors.

A *participative software project* is a software development project that is organized in such a way as to provide for the participation of users in the development of a new software object. But participative project organization is only a necessary precondition and not a sufficent one. If the software development process involves pursuing goals that are not merely restricted to the product's suitability for a particular purpose, but also include the aim of improving the quality of work and the work products from the point of view of the users directly concerned, then the understanding of the cooperative work processes in software development must go beyond mere user participation in the project.

What participative software projects aim to do is to lay open the subjective and objective elements of the users' work – which have evolved historically in their specific work context – and to construct a new domain of reality on this basis. In particular, they cannot be confined merely to analyzing objective entities, relations, and constraints. It is this fact that gives rise to the need for direct cooperation between developers and users and the tendency to do away with the separation of production and use in software development.

Cooperative work processes are generally characterized by the fact that the persons involved not only react to and correlate objective, concrete factors in the course of their respective work activities, but also necessarily take account of social relations and personal interactions. Focussing attention on the objective project goals, on the concrete means and results of work that are to be changed and used, constitutes only one level of the work context. The other, second level of action is the way the persons involved relate to each other, the way they communicate their respective skills, knowledge, interests and perspectives to each other and coordinate their different work activities. Both of these levels – the object level and the interpersonal level – constitute integral parts of cooperative work processes. They can neither be separated from one another nor reduced one to the other.

The *participative organization* of software development projects aims at the cooperation of the users and developers in the process of determining and designing the use pupose of a new software object.

In the following section, I take a closer look at the developers' and users' cooperative work processes in relation to the anticipative design of a new software object.

7.3.2 Design is theory building

Irrespective of the way in which the performance of software development is described, a common feature of all theoretical and methodological approaches to software engineering is the fact that they attach supreme importance to the work activities involved in the *design* of a new software object.

Recently, emphasis has been given to activities in the course of which the new software object and the domain of reality it circumscribes are anticipated, conceptualized and described. The aim is to make a conceptual distinction between those activities that may be considered to be of a reflective and creative nature, and those that relate to construction and change of 'external reality'. Realization activities are seen as following on logically from anticipative design, and are defined in terms of model construction and implementation. This also implies a changed view of what constitutes *design*[3].

In publications on software development projects in industrial practice[4] and in software development companies[5], there is a call for greater scope to be given in project organization to the informal learning and communication processes, in other words the reflective design processes, than has hitherto been the case.

This differentiation, which has only recently become evident, does, I feel, give due consideration to the specific nature of the work process software development, which I have characterized as an inherently creative process. The crucial element in design is the building of a new theory about a given domain of reality.

The notion of theory building in the context of software engineering

In his paper entitled "Programming as Theory Building", which was published in 1985, Peter Naur presents a perspective which he terms summarily the "Theory Building View". Naur's view has been drawn on by numerous authors in their efforts to emphasize the role of intellectual – and thus subjective – activities in the design process as related to software development. This is my reason for selecting it as a point of departure for my further discussion[6]. Naur's concept of programming embraces "the whole activity of design and implementation of programmed solution"[7] and can therefore also be employed for understanding the corresponding activities in the development of software objects as I see them.

The gist of Naur's approach to programming is: "The proper, primary aim of programming is not to produce programs, but to have the programmers build theories of the manner in which the problems at hand are solved by program execution"[8].

The goals pursued by Naur in adopting this approach are twofold:

(1) He sets out to demonstrate that software development is not confined to programming in terms of production or program formalization in accordance with predefined rules, but must be viewed essentially as an "intellectual" activity. Here, he distinctly highlights the drawbacks of a reductionistic view of programming that focusses exclusively on formalization, using examples to illustrate the implications of such a view also with respect to economic factors such as the costs of program modification and the useful life of programs.

---

[3] [Andersen et al., 1990, Kensing, 1987]
[4] For example ASEA Brown Boveri AG, [Elzer, 1989].
[5] For example Rank Xerox, [Suchman, 1987]; IBM, [Carroll, 1989].
[6] A more detailed analysis of Naur's approach can be found in [Reisin, 1990].
[7] [Naur, 1985b, p. 253]
[8] [Naur, 1985b, p. 253]

(2) He criticizes the traditional view of methods in software engineering. Here, he takes a rather extreme stand "against methods" that, ultimately, neglects the fact that programming is a cooperative activity and, moreover, one that is embedded in a socio-historical process. The consequence is that his reasoning tends to miss its mark: "In the Theory Building View what matters most is the building of the theory ... In building the theory there can be no particular sequence of actions, for the reason that a theory held by a person has no inherent division into parts and no inherent ordering. Rather, the person possessing a theory will be able to produce presentations of various sorts on the basis of it, in response to questions or demands. As to the use of particular kinds of notation or formalization, again this can only be a secondary issue since the primary item, the theory, is not, and cannot be, expressed, and so no question of the form of its expression arises. It follows that on the Theory Building View, for the primary activity of the programming there can be no right method"[9].

In confining himself to the intellectual activities, Naur apparently ignores the external context, the cooperative setting of programming. Although he views programming as a direct cooperative activity, he does not consider possible differences in theory building on an individual level as against a comparable process in a cooperative context. In Naur's reasoning, such a question cannot arise. Programming, in his view, must primarily be "the programmers' building up knowledge of a certain kind, knowledge taken to be basically the programmers' immediate possession, any documentation being an auxiliary, secondary product"[10]. Nevertheless he substantiates his view by referring to discursive processes, which he obviously regards as necessary in the course of programming. The "Theory Building View" is motivated precisely by discursive situations in which the programmers are required to understand, justify or modify a program in virtue of new or changed requirements. He takes it for granted that there is always a shared language and knowledge platform, on the basis of which the persons involved can easily come to an understanding about the meaningful aspects of the world and the program. At this point Naur's approach proves unsatisfactory. After all, the need to build a theory in software projects and to reflect upon it arises not least because of the necessity of reaching a common understanding of the various requirements and different perspectives among the persons involved. Thus the specific implications of cooperation in software development for the process of theory building must be systematically taken into account as well[11].

Naur's approach may justifiably be seen as neglecting the historical process because he divorces the process of software development from the cumulative social "theory building process", and gives it an exclusiveness and uniqueness that is untenable. The understanding of the world that Naur claims is "part of the mental possession of each programmer"[12] and the programmer's ability to

---

9 [Naur, 1985b, p. 260]

10 [Naur, 1985b, p. 253]

11 See also Floyd, Chap. 3.2.

12 [Naur, 1985b, p. 260]

build theories and engage in intellectual and discursive actions are, like it or not, embedded in a socio-historical context. The process of program development and the subjective and objective results obtained by it must be seen in this context and must be able to be reconstructed as constituents of further development if the scientific discourse on it is to remain capable of development and continue to make any sense at all.

The conclusions Naur reaches as a result of his view of theory building, and hence of programming as a whole, take no account of this necessity. I can follow Naur's view that programming and program modifications are not rule-based – which is why they cannot be divorced from the programmer (who is the carrier, so to speak, of the theory), let alone be automated. There is, however, no plausible reason why it should not be considered legitimate to attempt to understand the process of theory building itself, especially if we take it that Naur's aim is to impart a new understanding of programming. In the last analysis, what he proposes is merely another methodological approach.

All the same, I consider Naur's arguments to be highly important. Faced with the fundamental difficulty of grasping what is meant by the term 'creativity', of pinpointing the essence of 'innovation' or identifying a 'theory of innovation and change', the very radicality of his reasoning may prove helpful. Particularly with a view to the creative elements of software development, the aspects of programming that Naur has highlighted – even though he claims them to be intangible – must be systematically reflected upon by software engineering as a discipline. Of course, such guiding insights remain little more than a 'flash in the pan' as long as the conditions for their practical realization are not made explicit.

I continue below to use the term "theory building" borrowed from Naur, but give it a somewhat different connotation. My reason for characterizing certain elements of the software development process as "theory building" follows from the identification of software development as a creative and directly cooperative work process.

Theory building in cooperative work processes

The notion of work embraces "theory building" in terms of both general and specific creative mental activities. Viewed from a historic perspective, 'intellectual' and practical 'activities' make up the notion of work. I therefore view the activity of "theory building" in the frame of a working process in which means of work are newly created for future use.

The concept of *anticipations of purpose* is crucial to my further reasoning because I assume that purposive activities and, hence, anticipated purposes form the basis for the development and implementation of software objects.

Anticipations of purpose can be seen as conceptions, as ideas about essential features of objects for future use and of the activities which they mediate. Hence, in relation to a work activity, anticipations of purpose constitute a conceptual *frame of reference and orientation* to which human beings relate in the course of their activities and through which the *external* activities that are geared to the object acquire their bearings. I view the establishment of a new anticipation of purpose as "theory building" about the use purposes of the future software objects.

The interplay between the conceptual and the productive activities may also be characterized as dynamic feedback between the anticipated purposes and the work object. Perception of the work object during the production process takes place, as it were, *through* the 'idea' of the conceptualized final state aimed at.

This does not necessarily imply that the conceptualized anticipated purpose exists in every case as a fully matured idea – remaining then unaltered throughout the work process – before the production activity even begins.

Klaus Holzkamp assumes that, especially in the early forms of social tool-making, activities based on the anticipation of the use purpose of future work products were mingled in various different ways with trial-and-error activities; findings made by chance were then reutilized. Anticipations of use purpose changed in measure with the resistance offered by the material and the skills of the tool-maker, and only attained a greater degree of clarity in the course of the work process[13].

This assumption can be generalized for genuinely creative work processes right up to the present day. Scientific and technological development projects are characterized by the fact that their underlying idea is undetermined at the beginning of the work process and is evolved in step with the product, so to speak, in the course of the work process itself.

Software development is therefore neither *pure* theory building nor *pure* production; instead, it may be defined as a creative work process in which the anticipation of purpose of a new work object is established in the form of a theory about its use and production and directly implemented in concrete terms.

However, in the context of cooperative work processes, the question is how to establish a new theory that is binding upon all the persons involved, in other words that is shared by them all. The anticipated use purpose cannot merely remain each individual's 'own theory'; it must be adopted by all those involved as a 'shared theory'.

For participative projects, this question must be posed in more extreme terms: How can users and developers, who have no common sphere of experience, build a shared theory about a new domain of reality to which they can refer discursively and from which they can take their bearings in the course of their respective separate or joint activities of constructing, trying out and using a software object ?

In participative software projects, 'theory' means a common and moreover a mutually mediated anticipation of purpose as a frame of reference for the cooperative work processes. This implies that it is possible not only to build a theory on an individual level ("the knowledge a person must have in order not only to do certain things intelligently but also to explain them"[14]), but also on a cooperative level.

---

[13] [Holzkamp, 1978, p. 123]
[14] [Naur, 1985b, p. 255]

Cooperative theory building above all presupposes shared practical experience. This is acquired in cooperative exploration and experimentation and is imparted interpersonally by means of communication and mutual learning processes.

Shared theory is, basically, *communicated individual theory*. The expertise required to determine and evaluate the use purpose of a software object can only be acquired in the course of a communicated, mutual learning process. This applies particularly where not only objective and economic considerations have to be taken into account, but also the individual and collective quality requirements of the users.

The communication and mutual learning processes between developers and users during design constitute the *genuinely creative work processes* from which all other modelling and implementation activities follow and to which they are subordinate. It is in the course of these work activities that, in a sense, a new domain of reality is constructed.

My several years of experience with a continuous and cooperative process of theory building in the course of the PETS project have led me to conclude that new requirements entailing revision of the software version installed at their workplace constantly confront the developers with the problem of understanding exactly what the users want. It occasionally becomes apparent that a jointly established understanding, a shared theory, cannot be simply developed further, but must itself be subjected to revision before the program can be revised.

An important factor here are the differing perspectives of the users and developers with respect to a particular situation, and hence with respect to the aspects of the 'world' they consider of significance – perspectives that remained insignificant earlier on in program development, allowing misconceptions to arise on the part of the developers that bar the way to direct understanding of the new requirements. Here, then, developers and users are again confronted with the tasks of finding a shared theory about the domain of reality in question. The advantage of cooperative theory building, in situations such as this, lies not so much in the theory itself, but is rather derived from a common language platform and skill base for design between the participants that has been established on the basis of joint experience in a practical development situation. One final crucial factor here is the adoption of a proven methodological approach in building a theory about new problems and the implementation of solutions to them in terms of modifications or extensions to the program.

7.3.3 Methodological approach to cooperative theory building

Communication and learning processes are of central importance in design because they go to make up a shared *process of experience* between users and developers.

It is also true, though, that purpose or reality anticipations communicated by exclusively oral means only constitute a transitory mutual basis of agreement. The common knowledge acquired in the course of verbal communication and learning processes is *only sporadically* symbolized. The validity of design goals about which a consensus is established communicatively is limited in space and time. As frames of reference, they remain tied to particular individuals.

Techniques to support cooperative design, such as *Experimental Prototyping*[15], *Mapping*[16], *Simulations, Cooperation Scenarios* and *Future Workshops*[17] promote the evolution of communication and learning processes between the developers and users. They do not, however, support an overall synchronization and coordination of the reflective and creative activities of cooperative theory building in terms of a progressive work process. This calls for means that allow a continuous and stable symbolization of the design knowledge. The process of building a shared theory must be capable of being reconstructed and controlled in its continuity and progress by developers and users alike. Therefore, cooperative processes of theory building must include the production of descriptions symbolizing the current state of the theory in a description language and, thus, indicating its *progress*.

It is precisely the discontinuity of creative work processes that makes it necessary to record the knowledge acquired by the users and developers in communicative feedback and mutual learning activities in terms of a shared theory, such that it assumes, for all parties involved, a degree of permanence above and beyond the immediate communication processes.

Since software development is, in essence, a creative work process, the definitions of purpose, which will only take concrete shape when the software object is being implemented and subsequently used, can be communicated prior to the work processes *only* in the form of a recorded description.

The future domain of reality that is constructed anticipatively in the communication and learning processes must also be symbolized and recorded in order to enable a consensus to be established between those involved about its essential characteristics and the way they are connected. Hence, the notion of 'theory' in participative software projects extends beyond mental processes to embrace a *descriptive product* that the developers and users may agree to adopt as their common frame of reference and as a means of orientation for their respective separate and joint work activities.

The description of this common frame of reference must not necessarily symbolize all aspects of significance of the future domain of reality and software object. If it is to be characterized as a theory, such a description must symbolize the use purposes of the software object anticipated by the users and developers and agreed upon collectively by them.

---

[15] [Floyd, 1984, Reisin and Wegge, 1989]
[16] [Lanzara and Mathiassen, 1984]
[17] [Bødker et al., 1987, Kensing, 1987]

It is therefore crucial that a description resulting from the design process symbolizes the essential characteristics defining the invariant purpose of the cooperative software development process and having a decisive bearing on the implementation and use of the software object. Such a description can be viewed as a shared reference theory and will form the common frame of reference coordinating the cooperative and respective individual work activities.

Only by means of a theory that is *built cooperatively and established on the basis of a consensus* is it possible to ensure that the developers anticipate the purposes pursued by the users as *their own purposes* and embody them in the software object; and, conversely, to ensure that the users recognize in the purposes the developers embody in the software objects their own purposes.

The inner relation between the emergence of a common knowledge and expertise between users and developers during design, and the assessment of the quality of the software object in use is frequently given emphasis in reports on participative software projects[18]. Such a connection has been corroborated by my own practical experience with development projects[19].

I discuss[20] a methodological approach to cooperative theory building that was tested in the context of the research and development project PETS and that essentially comprises the following three stages:

The first stage is to draw up a *Reference Glossary* that can be viewed as a dictionary containing reconstructed and newly constructed terms of the theory language. The Reference Glossary contains the identifier (reference) and the description (referent) of the conceptual terms used while exploring the given and designing the anticipated reality domain. Hence, it constitutes the basic vocabulary of the project's language, which evolves in the course of the process of cooperative theory building.

The second stage is to develop *Reference Schemes* based on the Reference Glossary and other anticipative design, communication and learning processes and symbolizing the essential relations of the software objects' use attributes in the future work processes, the meaning of which is described in the Reference Glossary.

A Reference Scheme is used exclusively to symbolize the anticipated attributes of a software object, the actions that can be performed, the constraints, and if necessary different individual perspectives that have to be taken into account in the context of its use.

In contrast, software objects are viewed in this approach as effective means of work of the future work process and thus of the anticipated domain of reality. A Reference Scheme refers to the use interface of the practically effective software objects and thus to the characteristics and active attributes of their   virtual

---

[18] [Bjerknes and Bratteteig, 1988, Bjerknes et al., 1987, Andersen et al., 1990, Floyd et al., 1989b]

[19] [Floyd et al., 1990, Reisin, 1989, Reisin and Wegge, 1989]

[20] [Reisin, 1990]

use. At the same time, though, it refers to the individual frames of reference of the persons involved in the project and can therefore be viewed as a symbolized *modal* frame of reference on which a general consensus can be reached.

The final stage in theory building is the adoption of a *Reference Theory*. This involves common acceptance by the users and developers of the Reference Glossary and the Reference Schemes previously established as a valid description of the anticipated use purposes of the future software objects. If a description of the anticipated software object is understood by all the persons involved and accepted as a valid representation of the invariant meaning aspects that are anticipated in the course of further cooperative activities, it may be generally accepted as an objectified, modal frame of reference, i.e., as a *shared Reference Theory* and easily justified as such.

Bearing this in mind, I see the building of a shared theory primarily as a *process of abstraction* that takes place on the basis of interpersonal communication in cooperative learning processes. The most important work activities here may be characterized as the reflective and creative exploration of the significant meaning aspects of the existing and future work processes. They are based on the dialogical reconstruction of the respective expert and everyday languages employed by the developers and users, on experimentation and, generally, on common practical experience.

Insofar as they relate to the theory built during design, I emphasize the importance of the reconstruction of everyday language and the construction of the description language by which the newly created meaning aspects of the future software objects are described. The description language called for in each case is brought forth in the course of the theory building process. As they acquire design knowledge, the users and developers establish a sort of common language base.

The essential thing about building a theory in this way is that a common language is established between the developers and users, together with an interpersonally evolved skill and knowledge base, embracing not only the software object, but also the individual perspectives and the different work styles.

The visible result of the cooperative design process is the common frame of reference that is described by a Reference Glossary, symbolized in the Reference Schemes and agreed upon as a valid description that can be viewed as a *shared theory* about the anticipated domain of reality. The orientation function of the theory recorded can only be understood in the context of a common knowledge platform established during design by the developers and users.

The validity of the theory can be verified by all parties involved since it was built, evaluated and jointly accepted by them in the course of a common work process. The language of the theory, the meaning of its terms and rules, can be regarded as having been interpersonally evolved because it was built on the basis of common experience.

The advantage in referring to the everyday and expert language of the users in building a shared theory is that the description of the knowledge base acquired in the design process – though produced by the developers – can be evaluated and revised by the users. The users are able to examine and criticize the description, resulting in feedback that promotes a common understanding of the description and the evaluation of its validity. This helps prevent the developers from 'taking off on their own' at an early stage of the development process.

The description of the theory should not be equated with typographically symbolized software objects. These are, once in use, primarily characterized not by their typographical symbolizations, but by their effects.

However, by typographical symbolization of the effects and, hence, of the effective use meaning of implemented software objects, it is possible to obtain an additional bearing for the description characterized as the theory. For even when implemented in concrete terms, typographically symbolized software objects can be directly related to the theory as its models. This applies throughout the process of software modelling.

After all, the versions of the software objects implementing the common frame of reference may, as models, quite well exhibit characteristics, actions and assurances that go beyond those laid down in the Reference Theory. On the other hand, a software object is determined, ultimately, only in relation to the implicit theory built on the basis of interpersonal communication between the developers and users.

The objects and processes we make use of in reality invariably exists only in relation to a theory. The specification of a 'real thing', its designation and its description are performed in the language underlying the theory.

Objects, relations and situations in everyday reality that are not grasped in real terms and abstracted from, that are not reconstructed and described in terms of language, cannot be communicated on an interpersonal level and cannot therefore be the object of cooperative work processes. Hence, if the means and content of work as well as work activities and products are not subjected to communication and description, they are of no lasting significance in cooperative software development.

7.3.4 Conclusions

If we agree that anticipatory reality construction – and thus theory building in the sense discussed – is always imparted in creative work processes, and if we further acknowledge the fact that software development, as compared with mass production, is a creative and at the same time a productive work process, then we have to draw on the creative elements of the process.

The most important conclusion is, then, the insight that it makes no sense to divide the process of software development into proper work activities, by which traditionally is meant formal construction and correct implementation of the program on one hand, and other necessary – though not proper – working activities comprising communication and learning processes on the other.

In participative projects, cooperative design and thus communication and mutual learning processes, in the course of which individual anticipations are mutually externalized, realized and modified constitute the genuinely creative work elements from which all other modelling and implementation activities follow on. It is in the course of these work acitivtes that the new domain of reality is constructed, not only mentally but also externally. The notion of cooperative theory building for the anticipatory – and thus subjective – side of software development and the concept of a shared theory as its result – though never complete – are of methodological value.

A Reference Theory consisting of a Reference Glossary and a set of Reference Schemes – although it is subject to continual modifications in the course of the project – reflects at all times the state of the theory building process. Together with protocols recording the reasons that led to the various design decisions it is a simple but appropriate concept to support software development as a cooperative working process in the course of the relatively short project-historical and the long socio-historical run. After all, software development projects are part of the societal working process and its evolution.

7.4 On Controllability

Wolfgang Dzida

7.4.1 Introduction

Controllability is regarded as an essential requirement for the design of interactive systems as well as for user-interface design. A system is said to be controllable if the user can influence the selection and sequence of application programs as well as the flow of data and control.

This paper is written from the user's point of view and does not contribute to any technical implementations of controllability. Rather, it is intended to put forward arguments for this requirement, so as to enhance its priority among other requirements, particularly in comparison with the degree of automation a system should achieve. Automation almost always implies that the process to be programmed can be regarded as the "one-best-way" of doing something. In day-to-day work this assumption is sometimes falsified due to exceptional circumstances the user of a program is faced with. But the designer of a program is unable to anticipate all circumstances which determine user activities. When automating parts of those actions the designer should allow for modification of its control flow so as to enable the user to work more flexibly.

Just as the "one-best-way" of accomplishing a task rarely exists, so is there no "one-best-way" of human-computer dialogue. The designer is also overburdened with the decision as to whether "direct manipulation" or other modes of interaction are well suited to individual user needs. Hence, one should leave it up to the user to choose among alternative dialogue styles. Providing multiple ways for users to access application functions increases their understanding and appreciation of control.

Controllability will be examined here with regard to the design of interactive application programs as well as their use by various modes of dialogue. These two domains of controllability correspond to the distinction between "global" control and "local" control[1], with the first being control among dialogue and computational components of the system and the second being control within dialogue.

The first part of this chapter is dedicated to the controllability of modes of interaction, while in the second part an idea is outlined as to how one may improve the potential of a user's intervention into the execution of an application program. Consequences for user interface design are also discussed.

---

[1] [Hartson and Hix, 1989, p. 52]

7.4.2 The user in control of the mode of dialogue

When designing a human-computer interface as part of a computer program, a system developer's effort should not be aimed at an interface providing "the one best way" of interaction. There are some empirical results confirming the assumption that users prefer a dialogue offering individual action strategies. Strongly predetermined dialogue structures were evaluated negatively[2]. In view of this result, let us next investigate the predetermined dialogue caused by an interaction language.

Formal interaction versus "direct manipulation"

The development of software for human-computer dialogues provides a reality which drastically changes the conventional way of handling tools. For a dialogue to be carried out a user is urged to learn and to apply a language which is still quite artificial. Additionally, in contrast to conventional tools the concrete visual conceptualization of what is happening in the machine has been lost. To cope with this intangibility interface designers have invented "direct manipulation"[3] as an interaction concept. The manipulation of a displayed object is "direct" in the sense that the user's action causes an immediate and observable response. Furthermore, the control is achieved by means users have encountered in other contexts; for instance, buttons, scroll bars, or pointing devices. Direct manipulation is not achieved by using an artificial language but by "grabbing" objects. Which mode of interaction is advantageous depends both on the technical sophistication of the user and the complexity of the task.

The user training factor

Whether formal descriptions are useful in human-computer interaction depends on the degree of qualification a user has achieved during user training courses. Of course, untrained users will be unable to manipulate a system by means of a formal language. On the other hand, users who can cope with a formalized level of interaction may work more efficiently. They carry out a mode of operation which is aided by abstract cognitive action schemata. These schemata are more precise and generalizable. Although there is as yet only insufficient empirical evidence available, this mode of operation appears likely to be the most efficient[4]. It can be shown, for instance, that a formal and thereby abstract mode of access to data bases provides more efficient results[5]. Therefore it is at least questionable whether a tangible and convenient mode of use is always the most efficient one. Nevertheless, application programmers tend to design human interfaces under the premise that most people want to interact easily with the system and are

---

[2] [Spinas, 1987]
[3] [Shneiderman, 1987, p. 201]
[4] [Dzida, 1987]
[5] [Katzeff, 1986]

not interested in becoming proficient enough to do their work at a demanding level. However the design of work tasks and the qualification of working persons are aspects which go hand in hand[6]. "Skills are particularly important as prerequisites of control"[7]. Hence, user training is indispensible.

The impact of the training factor on dialogue control can be investigated in the daily work of software engineers, who are undoubtedly the most highly trained group of users. They highly appreciate controllability during their own interaction with the system. For example: provided the task at hand can be represented in terms of a macro (a sequence of commands indicating an action schema), a macro editor is welcome as an interface tool for adapting the control structure of the task steps. Thus, the usual way of user-computer dialogue can be extended. The user is enabled to develop a style of interaction similar to programming. Since the user has access to a programming language, he is in control of the degree of automation of the dialogues. Depending on the user's preference for utilizing action schemas (macros), complex procedures as well as routine tasks can be carried out flexibly.

Sometimes the tendency of work processes to become increasingly formalized, abstract and desensualized is complained about, and it is supposed that abstract and desensualized work activities are less efficient. I do not agree with this assessment, insofar as formalization does not necessarily involve an intangible presentation of an interaction language. In Katzeff's experiment (mentioned above) the formalized data base query language was presented in terms of "Venn diagrams" which are common in mathematical logic and set theory. Provided the user is familiar with the diagrams he or she will be well able to use the formalism as an efficient interaction language. By the way, various engineering disciplines apply graphical though formalized representation languages which can also be used in human-computer dialogue. From this discussion I conclude that it is not always the formal and abstract mode of interaction which causes the user trouble; the lack of adequate training appears to be the real cause.

However, this lack is but one factor affecting the efficiency of an interaction style. The complexity of the task needs also to be considered.

The task complexity factor

As pointed out, abstract action schemata and formal interaction languages enlarge the potential for dialogue control. The advantages of formal interaction languages, however, should not be overgeneralized. Disadvantages may be recognized when taking into account the mental load probably engendered by abstract modes of operation. Therefore, "direct manipulation" has been introduced as an interface conception to visualize those contents of the human-computer dialogue which are tangible and thereby allow more freedom of physical actions on the objects displayed. Thus, a user's cognitive operation needs not stay within the

---

[6] See Volpert, Chap. 7.5
[7] [Frese, 1987]

limits of the abstraction. Operations may be performed with the aid of a concrete and continuous presentation of the objects manipulated. "Direct manipulation" might be favourable when the task at hand is relatively complex. Then the human working memory is active at full capacity and does not welcome the unnecessary mental load caused by a formal interaction language. Visualized objects may play the role of an externalized human information store relieving the internal human working memory from the burden of retaining or remembering[8]. The rationale for this hypothesis points to the distinction between task (work) preparation and task performance. It is the visual feedback provided by "direct manipulation" which reduces mental load during complex work preparations.

On the other hand, a user need not carry on a dialogue in concrete, visualized terms, when dealing with undemanding routine task performance. In this case, it is both the ponderous movement of the manipulation device and the forced stepwise course of action which hampers routinization. Performance in terms of a formal command language appears to be more appropriate then, since the complexity of the underlying task has already been reduced during the preparation phase, and is cognitively available as an abstract action schema. The user can automate this action schema quite easily with the aid of command language facilities, such as command procedures or pipes.

Advice for design

In designing a user interface, both a formalized and the "direct manipulation" mode of operation should be considered. The user should be permitted to decide which mode is purposeful and preferable. It can be shown that the very same human interface feature may affect users differently, depending on the task to be performed[9]. Hence, it is not up to the designer to develop "the one best way" of human-computer dialogue, but to provide for alternative interaction modes. Advantages or disadvantages of modes of interaction cannot be predicted perfectly due to a severe lack of psychological theory on human problem solving in the workplace[10]. Furthermore, it is actually difficult or even impossible to specify *a priori* the category to which to assign a user, since the user is a learning and developing person. A user's preference for any mode of system use may not be regarded as fixed for all time.

7.4.3 The user in control of the application program

At the design level of the traditional system development process, both data flow and control flow must be represented. For control flow, often a graph-structured model is designed, indicating the normal sequence and synchronization of events. At this level, very little may be known about the details of user control needs.

---

[8] [Schönpflug, 1986]
[9] [Hacker, 1987b]
[10] Carroll, Chap. 4.3

Hence, when modelling an application domain there is the danger of over-automating data flow and control flow, with the user's control becoming ancillary to these processes. Controllability, however, is essential in the ergonomic modelling of human-computer interaction[11].

Hartson and Hix distinguish "computation dominant control" and "dialogue dominant control", the first one providing a system "that can be efficient in execution but lacks the flexibility necessary for easy modification of system sequencing"[12]. The second kind of control is dependent on user control inputs. Let us next discuss the design of interactive application systems. I will complain about the preference for designing systems with computation dominant control. This preference is caused at three sources of expertise, producing different kinds of biases.

Biased modelling of reality

At least three sources of knowledge determine the analysis of an application case: 1) the user's expertise in the application field, 2) the formal representation method used in system design to describe the model of the user's application domain, and 3) the engineer's expertise regarding the possibilities of new technology. These three sources of knowledge produce different biases in modelling of reality during systems analysis and design: a) the user bias, b) the methodical bias, and c) the implementation bias.

The user bias is caused by the inability to reproduce knowledge about the application field at all levels of detail and abstraction. Much of this knowledge is private to the user, not because the user is unwilling to describe the tasks and how they are performed, but because of inability. The user knows more than he/she is aware of knowing[13]. With regard to user control of application programs, a block of knowledge needs to be elicited for the design of dialogue functions which indicate such user requirements as how to proceed with a task at hand in readily comprehensible steps, how to receive information for task planning, how to interrupt the dialogue, etc. During system design, however, these nitty-gritty details cannot be anticipated completely. Thus, the model of the reality is biased by incomplete information about user control issues.

Another kind of bias is called methodical bias. In system design, this short-coming becomes evident if one takes into account that most traditional "design" methods are also used as methods for requirements analysis or specification. As a consequence, the outcome of requirements analysis is a representation of the application field mainly from the developer's point of view. Furthermore, methods such as HIPO, SADT or PSL/PSA result in a representation of the application field reflecting the characteristics of the method applied[14]. Thus, the model of reality is biased by leaning the representation towards the methodical

---

[11] See [DIN66234, 1988].

[12] [Hartson and Hix, 1989, p. 53]

[13] Cf. [Feigenbaum, 1977].

[14] [Valder and Weller, 1984]

requirements of system design or system specification. With regard to dialogue dominant control, Hartson and Hix point out that a design representation would result in increased complexity due to the necessity of mixing different levels of abstraction. For the sake of clarity, design representations provide information at an abstract level, thereby hiding details inappropriate to that level. However, when details of local dialogue control are considered, a mixture of abstraction levels takes place, since global control and invocation of functional semantics relates to more abstract levels than local control. "This is especially evident in state transition diagrams where detailed functions such as token level, (syntactic) error processing and help request handling are often found at the same level of abstraction as global transitions among dialogue and computational states"[15].

The third kind of bias in modelling reality is called the implementation bias. On the one hand, systems analysis and design are attempts to elicit and understand the knowledge pertaining to an application domain. On the other hand, specification and implementation deal with the realization of what has been modelled during systems analysis. Understanding an application domain and realizing an application system are activities which should be kept distinct. If this division of developer roles is neglected and the system design is carried out by the implementer, the "system designer" is inclined to understand the application domain from the perspective of his implementation expertise. Swartout and Balzer have pointed out that specification and implementation are inevitably intertwined. Developers who believe in an absolute separation of specification from implementation are overly naïve. Does this also apply to system design? Whereas the implementation bias in system specification seems to be unavoidable because role sharing is impossible[16], the same kind of bias could be avoided in systems design by an organizational separation of roles.

In view of these kinds of design biases, I conclude that in traditional system design "computation dominant control" is given preference over "dialogue dominant control". Thus, controllability has been given little consideration and rarely gets implemented. Less effort has been invested so far in placing global control in the dialogue, because it is assumed that a dialogue-oriented application system "requires increased (possibly substantial) computer systems resources"[17].

A challenge for system design in the future is to go beyond the boundaries of the pure technical system design and consider the user and the computer-system as a whole, thereby enhancing the efficiency of the whole by submitting its technical subsystem to user control. The next paragraph is intended to discuss some ideas about how to improve conventional design techniques with regard to controllability.

Modelling by complementary representations

To address the problems associated with biased modelling of application domains, I propose extending the traditional design approach. Systems analysis

---

[15] [Hartson and Hix, 1989, p. 54]
[16] See [Swartout and Balzer, 1982].
[17] [Mason and Carey, 1983]

can be regarded as knowledge engineering, which is aimed at modelling an application domain in terms of a knowledge domain[18]. Systems analysis thus may bring about a model of the application domain which comprises as usual a representation of data flow and control flow. One part of the model involves instances and conditions of an application domain which can be regarded as normal activity, e.g. the day-to-day data and control flow in an organization. For this purpose traditional diagrams may suffice. Additionally, some "knowledge" about these parts of the domain should be represented, particularly about user control needs and corresponding exception handling.

During the execution of a task, a user is sometimes faced with exceptions and must react to the new situation. The current task may require modification; the means of performance may need to be adapted. Hitherto, little attention has been given to these control needs. But they could be taken as an amendment of conventional design. A complementary part of the model should involve "knowledge" about control needs, particularly about the handling of exceptional cases and heuristic exception handling, which limit or augment the governing of the normal sequence of actions within the user-computer-system. For this purpose, a rule-based representation of the application domain model might be adequate. The rule-based part should comprise "knowledge" about user control issues and automated control flow.

"Most programs are structured so that control is fixed, an entity built into the system, and not readily accessible to the user. But by making control explicit and available for modification, the same program can become more flexible and efficient. In many domains, a production system formalism for representing and using knowledge confers this easy modifiability and understandability"[19].

One might take into account a presentation of data flow by means of conventional diagrams and a complementary representation of control flow in terms of production rules.

Aside from the above points, the knowledge engineering approach does not imply any preferences for rules to be assembled. Even contradictory rules are not prevented from entering the knowledge base. Thus, the systems engineer (knowledge engineer) has the opportunity to gather various facets of an application domain without any prejudice to later design decisions.

One effect of complementary representations may be that the users' domain knowledge will be formulated more precisely, and the impact of a single design or implementation view on the model of the application case can be neutralized. With regard to system design, Winograd and Flores[20] pointed out that we create our world (i.e., our systems) through language. Besides the designer's modelling

---

[18] [Dzida and Valder, 1985]
[19] [Terry and Englemore, 1981]
[20] [Winograd and Flores, 1986]

language, it may have important consequences for design and system use, if the user's language can be considered more seriously in the design of control actions. Rules are close to the language of users.

Objections concerning the use and integration of different languages (representation of data flow differs from that of the control flow) should be taken into account. From the development of knowledge representation systems, however, one can learn that the use of different formalisms no longer causes serious problems. In the case that data flow and control flow are formulated in different formalisms it is possible to integrate them. If this attempt fails, the authors of the Babylon system[21] suggest implementing a meta-interpreter.

Implications for human-computer interaction

The application domain modelling approach suggested may provide significant advantages for the use of a system, and thereby for the "controllability" in human–computer interaction. The user-directed treatment of control issues is aimed at improving interaction during the execution of programs.

As an example, consider the UNIX program "find", which operates on a variety of data. Let us assume that during runtime a user decides to tell the system that certain data need not be considered, in order to avoid unnecessary waiting. To satisfy this user requirement, the user needs to have been informed about which data are under potential operation of the program. Only then would the user be capable of recognizing which kind of data are irrelevant for the operation. Only the user can recognize which data are irrelevant for the operation, and it is most efficient to do this at runtime, because it may be impossible for the user to remember all kinds of irrelevant data in advance (i.e., before executing the command "find"). Unfortunately, the UNIX program "find" does not meet this user requirement; a control facility is missing.

From an ergonomic point of view, a user should at least be able to de-automate an automated process, if it affects an act requiring the freedom to respond to unanticipated circumstances.

Drawing on the idea of rule based control it may be possible to develop a user-interface component allowing the user to govern the system's control flow in terms of rules representing control actions. Unfortunately, however, no such implementation is yet available. Recently, knowledge based system designers have made some progess which could also be applied to design control structures. The key idea of Randall Davis is to separate information about control out of the object-level knowledge and present it explicitly (in meta-rules). "The explicit representation of information about control embodied in meta-rules also makes it possible for a system to reason about that control information".[22] In view of this possibility one may ask whether a user would also be able to reason about that control information.

---

[21] [di Primo and Wittur, 1987]
[22] [Davis, 1980, p. 210]

The prospects for a solution of this problem are not poor, since Kowalski illustrated the separation of logic from control in conventional algorithms. He particularly emphasized that "computer programs will be more often correct, more easily improved, and more readily adapted to new problems when programming languages separate logic and control ..."[23]. Davis came to a similar conclusion: Explicit representation of control information makes a system "more transparent, less prone to what we termed partial order bugs, and easier to modify"[24]. As usual, ergonomic requirements such as "controllability" prove quite well-founded from both technical and economic standpoints.

7.4.4 Perspectives

Designing for controllability appears to be a challenging perspective for computer science and ergonomics. Computer science has been concentrating too much on the automation of offices and industrial environments. Accordingly, modern system development merely follows the old beaten track of industrial changes brought about by conventional mechanical inventions. The operator of this kind of machine was degenerated to an appendage and expected to simply react with relatively passive patterns of behaviour. In the Federal Republic of Germany, a special research programme on the humanization of work was undertaken because of the mental and physical consequences for operators of such machines. There is some hope that we learn from the faults of the past when applying a new technology.

With the advent of "interactive" systems we are now able to utilize the potential of a new technology. Up until now, however, many computer scientists have concerned themselves with adaptive, intelligent programs and planning systems aimed at aiding and controlling the user to perform tasks correctly and consistently, instead of focussing their attention on improving the controllability of machines. Shouldn't the user be allowed to make mistakes and learn from these opportunities? Does Walter Volpert's conclusion in his critique of Tayloristic work design apply that wherever possible, human beings – those rather imperfect and unreliable machines – are to be replaced by real machines?[25] Brown and Newman[26] suggested that system design should focus on the controllability of errors, instead of the minimization of their occurrence – thereby challenging genuine human capabilities, i.e., self-organization of behaviour, flexibility and intelligence.

System designers sometimes argue that people don't want to bother with control issues, since they enjoy the comfort of automation. It should be emphasized that controllability and automation are not necessarily in conflict. The central issue of "controllability" is to what extent a system restricts the control of its

---

[23] [Kowalski, 1979]

[24] [Davis, 1980, p. 219]

[25] See Volpert, Chap. 7.5.

[26] [Brown and Newman, 1985]

user. But it is the user who should decide under which circumstances processes are to be automated, so as to free mental capacity for other tasks.

It also has been objected that controllability exacerbates the complexity of system design as well as system use. Software developers and users, however, seem to be "complexity-reducing beings"[27]. To decrease the complexity of system design the separation of data flow and control flow design issues has proven to be useful. This section has argued that an adequate design language can be applied to help cope with complexity. For system use to become less complex, users almost always prefer applying the concept of "easiness in effort needed for use". This section argues that the complexity of system use can be individually optimized when the user is permitted to decide which mode of interaction or interaction language is appropriate[28]. Frese[29] pointed out a source of confusion in the controllability/complexity controversy. It is not complexity per se but complicatedness which is difficult to control and which leads to degraded performance.

---

[27] [Frese, 1987]
[28] See the paragraph on formal interaction versus direct manipulation.
[29] [Frese, 1987]

7.5 Work Design for Human Development
Walter Volpert

7.5.1 Introduction

In the following sections we present human criteria for the design of working and learning processes to promote human personality development. Taking a global view of this problem means abandoning models which equate human beings with machines or computers. In their place, we propose a perspective on human beings and organizations that is based on the theory of evolution and the psychology of action. From this perspective, we formulate three general principles of evolution, and from them derive nine aspects which are of importance in designing working and learning processes that are conducive to personal development. Finally, we present a guideline designed to enable work tasks to be evaluated in relation to these aspects.

From the psychologist's point of view there is one particular problem requiring special attention in system design: What are the characteristics of a working situation which may be considered conducive to human development, i.e., which promote personality development and allow the worker to satisfy needs and develop skills? And what are the corresponding characteristics of learning situations?

Such questions cannot be answered by empirical means alone. Answering them necessarily requires reflection on different concepts of the human being and undertaking a personal commitment to a particular view of the human condition. Philosophical and anthropological awareness is needed if we are to tackle the concrete, practical issues involved here. But this entails a number of difficulties. Is it possible to develop universally valid criteria for determining what is conducive to human development? Is that not too ambitious an undertaking, and are not the criteria different for each individual?

Even accepting the existence of such difficulties, this should not prevent us from seeking a coherent conception around which a broad consensus might be obtained. We may also aim for some listing of the essential features of working and learning conditions for which a degree of general, supra-individual validity might be claimed. These are the human criteria which practitioners in the field of work design have been calling on psychologists and educationists to provide.

It is obviously still a major problem, even today, to design working and learning processes that are humane and adequate in human terms. One of the main reasons for this is doubtless the prevalent world-view illuminated so critically in the earlier chapters of this book, a view based on the metaphor equating human beings and organizations with machines. If we accept this metaphor, the design of working or learning processes follows well-defined principles. It involves specifying precisely the overall goal; planning in advance the exact procedure to be adopted; specifying it in fixed terms; dividing it up into sequences; and keeping an exact check on the success achieved for each stage. If, at some point, deviant results are obtained, then the program requires branching. This branching must, however, be directed back towards the goal. These are the routines followed in the Tayloristic organization of work and in the behaviourist programming of learning.

There are, of course, alternative lines of research which view human beings and organizations not as externally controlled or cognitive machines, but rather as living beings that have emerged through quite specific processes of evolution and are continuing along their respective paths. One of the research traditions of particular interest in the narrower context of work design is the sociotechnical approach[1].

I shall attempt in the following sections to formulate some basic principles of evolution and derive from them nine aspects or human criteria for the design of working and learning processes. In doing so, I shall refer to more general concepts such as the theories of self-organization[2], activity[3], and action regulation[4]. Here, the following procedure is adopted:

- First of all, I present a very brief (and, necessarily, highly condensed) characterization of human life and action in terms of a 'principle of evolution'.
- I then go on to ask which situational conditions of working and learning correspond to these characteristics. Here, I differentiate a number of aspects in each case and formulate these as arguments addressed to the work designer. The guideline presented in the final section provides procedures for evaluating work tasks in relation to each of these aspects.
- Finally, I try to give some indications of the conclusions which may be drawn or the methodological implications which may be derived from this approach and applied in the design of work-related learning processes, particularly for vocational and on-the-job training.

7.5.2 The principle of personal paths of development

Whatever our exact conception of evolution may be, it invariably presupposes two things: Firstly, that there is a context within which evolution takes place. Basically, this is constituted by the history of the process with its own internal logic, and its surrounding conditions, in a very broad sense. Both give the current process a specific form, and structure its potential for progression – which, in a certain sense, invariably constitutes a restriction, too. And secondly, that there can be no evolution without this progression, i.e., without innovation and self-renewal – factors that are not fully predictable from the context, and for which the terms freedom and autonomy are sometimes used.

---

[1] Cf. [Emery and Thorsrud, 1969].
[2] [Jantsch, 1980]
[3] See Raeithel, Chap. 8.4.
[4] [Volpert, 1989]

Human evolution represents a qualitatively new dimension here. The context is shaped by socio-historical conditions. Self-renewal is translated into potential for autonomous action, into the ability to determine the further course of evolution in accordance with the intentions of the individuals or groups involved. This makes the *personal paths of development* an essential characteristic of human evolution.

So much for the general principle. Let us now turn to the situational conditions which make possible or promote such evolution. There is no escaping from the contextual conditions in which the process of personal development takes place; but there is a significant difference in the degree to which such conditions open up or restrict possibilities for development. Such differences are discussed below in terms of distinct aspects.

The *first aspect* is one to which the work-related social sciences have always paid particular attention when considering the effects of work on learning and development. What is meant here is the *scope of action*. This is the degree to which working people act self-reliantly at the workplace, and to which they are able to make autonomous plans and decisions about goals and the means for attaining them. It is generally recognized that this scope of action is determined primarily by the nature of the work task; its impact on different spheres of human experience and behaviour is well-documented[5]. Using terms from the psychology of action, we speak here of the **regulation requirements** of such work tasks, which are at the same time **regulation opportunities**[6]. The degree of self-reliance provided for in a particular working situation determines (as a rule) the worker's scope for personal development, culminating, in its highest form, in a personal work style, which is what characterizes the especially masterly command over a particular field of work.

This aspect might be paraphrased as follows in terms of an argument: *In order to promote personal development, work tasks must allow for a broad scope of action, i.e., have high regulation requirements.*

If we consider analogous principles for the design of learning processes, we note that such principles are by no means unknown in this sphere. Thus, a brief, fairly general reference to these learning processes will suffice to begin with. It will be a different matter, though, when we turn to look at concrete work-related learning processes, especially in the field of on-the-job training. Here, the design of learning processes would, in most cases, still appear to bear the mark of the very same machine models which determine the way work tasks are shaped. It might, therefore, be useful to reflect on some specific learning methods in this connection.

We turn our attention accordingly to the first aspect, the scope of action. The overall concern here is to ensure that opportunities for self-reliant action in complex situations are considered as both the general goal and, at the same time, a design criterion for learning processes. All learning and educating should promote the emergence of self-reliant action regulation. This self-reliant action

---

[5] Cf. for example [Kohn and Schooler, 1983].
[6] Cf. [Oesterreich and Volpert, 1986].

regulation should be considered the subjective counterpart to the criterion of high regulation requirements and opportunities applied to work tasks. Training methods based on the action regulation theory set out, in this respect, primarily to improve the cognitive regulation basis, in other words the appropriation of techniques for the self-reliant definition of goals and means for attaining them with respect to complex work tasks[7]. Instances of such methods are:

- special training with regard to particularly important theoretical foundations and planning procedures,
- learning aids to be studied and applied on a self-reliant basis,
- directions for coming to terms with the demands of a specific task by making notes, watching experienced colleagues, etc.

The *second aspect*, which is quite obviously connected with the first, is the temporal scope for accomplishing a specific task or 'autonomy in time'. I treat it separately because in practice it plays an important role. It is often found that too tight a schedule for performing a particular task nullifies an otherwise quite generous scope of action.

Every form of social organization of working processes requires an element of timing. However, the temporal disposition margins enjoyed by individuals or groups vary considerably. They are narrowest where work is subject to the tight schedule of a rigid organization run along serial production lines. The temporal scope increases as the time schedules or relevant agreements acquire an increasingly global applicability, and as the periods of time to which they relate are extended (without this necessarily making them any less binding).

Cast in the form of an argument, the second aspect might read: *In order to promote personal development, work tasks require the provision of wide temporal scope.*

Applied to learning processes, this second aspect means the possibility of individualizing learning speeds, such as is the goal of didactic models of external and internal differentiation. It is this principle, though, that is so frequently violated in connection with training in industrial practice, for instance, by behaviouristic learn-step sequences, or by a precisely graded system of training measures which put unreasonable pressures on workers and make it practically impossible for them to catch up once they fall behind.

A *third aspect* of situations that is crucial to the principle of personal paths of development may be termed *structurability*. This refers to conditions which challenge workers:

- to gain insight into, and a mental grasp of, the overall situation, i.e., of the social and technical aspects of the production process;
- to try and develop, on the basis of this knowledge, their own practical experience and personal dispositions, own ways of viewing and interpreting their respective work tasks as well as the difficulties and potential solutions connected with them; and

---

[7] See [Volpert, 1989].

- to develop subsequently their own personal working style, which assumes the character of an intuitive, matter-of-fact confidence which is both effective and non-stressful.

Structurability as a situational feature allows behaviour of this sort, by not only permitting different forms of task interpretation and mastery (already enhanced by the scope of action), but by actually calling for and encouraging in various ways this type of personal structuring.

Worded as an argument, it might run: *Work tasks must provide facilities for developing a personal approach to grasping and mastering demands in terms of structurability.*

This also involves what Ulich[8] calls differential and flexible work design, i.e., responding to individual idiosyncrasies in task interpretation and offering scope for workers to influence the nature of tasks. Individual structurability is closely interwoven with the social organization and technical design of the production process. A machine ideology with its 'one-best-way' dogma rules out any alternative or personal approaches[9]. But the interpretation of the nature of tasks prevalent within a particular organization can encourage such alternative approaches. For example, in the case of computer-related work, the design of the program system may help make the technical process more transparent, thus opening up possibilities for adopting an individual approach in handling it[10].

A similar picture emerges if we turn to look at learning processes. Individual structurability, in the sense of autonomy in interpreting and assessing events as well as in decision-making and action, is one of the basic tenets of the reform movement in education. In contrast, those approaches to work design which follow the machine model adhere to a firmly preordained learning goal and the optimized 'one-best-way' of reaching this goal.

If we go on to consider the learning methods proposed by industrial psychology, mention should be given first of all to the forms of exploratory learning which have recently been shown to be especially relevant to work involving data processing devices[11]. Another aspect of crucial importance here is the use of heuristics or general rules of procedure[12]. These methods are designed to promote the self-reliant and task-optimized mastering of complex situations, and also to indicate how these rules may be abridged and internalized.

The *fourth aspect* is the notion of freedom from regulation hindrances. In practical task performance in organizations, it can be frequently observed that, despite a broad scope of action, performance can be impeded by specific circumstances not inherent to the nature of the task itself. These could, in principle, be eliminated, but it is precisely the scope of action granted the worker which prevents this. The worker is compelled to live with hindrances to task mastery which are rooted in organizational or technical deficiencies and faults, in other

---

[8] For example[Ulich, 1987].
[9] Cf. [Greif and Gediga, 1987].
[10] Cf. Dzida, Chap. 7.4; [Ackermann and Ulich, 1987].
[11] Cf. Carroll, Chap. 4.3; [Greif, 1989].
[12] Cf. [Höpfner and Skell, 1983].

words which 'need not exist'. This results in various forms of additional work effort, including increased action-related risks, which constitute the negative factor mental load. (In contrast, regulation requirements may be seen as the positive, demanding aspect of conditions affecting task performance.) Such hindrances can be further refined into impediments, interruptions and hindrances of various other kinds[13].

The following argument applies to all of these forms: *In order to promote personal development, work tasks must avoid objective hindrances to the work activity.*

In the case of learning processes there are a wide variety of hindrances which may be similarly categorized. Examples of these are inadequate learning aids or unfavourable learning conditions, as well as the difficulties frequently encountered by instructors in industrial practice in clearly specifying and structuring the essential elements of the learning tasks and translating these into guides for action.

7.5.3 The principle of embodied being-in-the-world

We have so far looked at four aspects which are derived from the general principle of 'personal paths of development'. The second general principle of evolution is one which follows from the perspective of the theory of evolution. It needs emphasizing because it is often overlooked in approaches based on the machine metaphor. Take, for instance, the fundamental notion of cognitivism, which is based essentially on equating human thought and action with the processes of a serial digital computer. Here, the perceptive and active human being is viewed as a cognitive decision-making machine, the outputs of which are viewed as changes in the internal model of the machine. By the same token, in mechanistic concepts of organization, the human being is seen as an abstract node in a network of procedures whose functioning is dependent on his fitting in as smoothly as possible into a formalized, abstract and quasi-automatic process.

Embodied being-in-the-world, then, requires particular emphasis as a general principle of human development. Physical existence, real movement and action in terms of intervention and change are the starting-point and objective of all thought and perception. We exist only through our physical embodiment, and we experience the world only through this body of ours and by handling the objects in this world.

But is it not an illusory and anachronistic undertaking to present the work designer with a principle of this sort, faced as we are with the tendency for work processes to become increasingly formalized, abstract and dehumanized – take, for instance, the control consoles in power stations or refineries. To suggest the existence of a quasi-natural force behind such a tendency is merely to fall once again for the machine metaphor. Precisely the work performed by the console operator – together with other jobs like programming CNC machines – may be considered demonstrative of the fact that such abstraction of working activities

---

[13] Cf. [Greiner and Leitner, 1989].

is inefficient and detrimental to the personality of the worker. And, what is more, it may be seen as indicative of the fact that meaningful working activities can only be secured by enriching a task with elements which re-establish in some way a basis for direct practical experience as well as active sensory contact with the production process.

These examples may also serve to demonstrate that enriching work requirements with theoretical, or even scientific, elements does not necessarily involve the loss of the concrete, sensory relation to production. On the contrary: industrial psychologists and sociologists have repeatedly found, particularly with respect to demanding technical work activities (such as those performed by the skilled worker), that integrated and holistic sensory experience, with all its emotional components, constitutes an essential prerequisite for true mastery of a particular activity. Let us consider, for example, the operation of a numerically-controlled machine tool. Here, work quality is highly dependent on the possibilities afforded the operator of experiencing the ongoing process via different senses, and especially through the physically felt feedback from his own intervention. The notion of quality is, in this connection, to be understood both in relation to workmanship and to subjectively experienced work load[14].

Three aspects may now be derived directly from the evolution principle outlined above. These are listed below, consecutively, in the form of arguments addressed to the work designer.

Fifth aspect: In order to promote personal development, work tasks require provision for sufficient and varied bodily activity.

Sixth aspect: In order to promote personal development, work tasks must call for the use of a wide variety of sensory capacities.

Seventh aspect: In order to promote personal development, work tasks must provide for the concrete handling of real objects and ensure a direct relation to social conditions.

If we now relate these aspects to the area of education in general, we address some quite fundamental principles behind the efforts of the reform movement. Of relevance here, too, is the old established principle of learning by doing. It should be stressed that this principle has nothing to do with blind, unreasoning action or tedious drill (with which it is today sometimes – erroneously – associated). Instead, it is concerned with uniting goal-reflection, path-planning and active mastery.

This consideration may also serve to establish a link with learning methods which are designed to promote speech, cognition and imagination processes in the acquisition of skills and the more complex forms of know-how. First of all, though, we have to work these methods 'against the grain', for it is precisely the cognitive element that they emphasize, whereas we are concerned here with physical embodiedness, concreteness and the sensory element. The action regulation theory has, however, always emphasized a close correlation here with concrete, executive action – in contrast, say, to the pure acquisition of knowl-

---

[14] Cf. [Böhle and Milkau, 1988].

edge or the presentation of abstract guides for action. This applies particularly, in the sphere of sensorimotor learning, to the assortment of methods which may be subsumed under the heading **training through internal realization** (training by mental rehearsal, by observation or by verbalization[15]). Generally speaking, we as scientists still know far too little about what goes to make up the specifically human quality of mastery or expertise – characterized as it is by swift, intuitive grasping of situations and a 'feeling' for people and materials – and how it is acquired.

This leads us on to our *eighth aspect*. Cognitive approaches are mostly atomistic, emphasizing the function of rules. They combine individual stimuli to form objects, and individual objects to form situations. And, in the same rule-governed manner, they derive actions from these with the help of a decision-making machine. In contrast, the approach based on the evolution theory highlights the fact that perception, in its original sense, means the holistic grasping of situations, and that action is the direct expression of this process of grasping. In the course of evolution, this has become differentiated in various ways. Especially significant – often particularly difficult or dangerous – elements of a situation are pinpointed and viewed as objects. Intermediate links are inserted into the situation-action interlacement. Instances of these are: the global 'emotional' assessment of the situation as a whole; the cognitive analysis of its component parts and the consequences of potential actions; and the 'deliberate' decision in favour of one of several possible actions. It is important here, though, that the original embedment in a holistic grasping of the situation and the close connection with actions are not (or at least, ideally, should not be) lost in individual human development and in the learning process.

It is, again, precisely this swift and sure assessment of the situation as a whole and the close connection between perception and action on which expertise, the knowledge gained over many years of experience, is based. And it is evidently on this basis alone that intuitive solutions and creative innovations are possible. This is true at least of those areas where, in view of the complexity of the problems involved and the wealth of available knowledge, many years of practical experience are required to come to a proper understanding of the essential issues.

Sufficiently elaborate process models are already available for the basic assumptions relating to a differentiated development based on holistic situation-perception and situation-action interlacement, e.g., the associative or holographic memory. They rest, basically, on the assumption of a resonance process between a current stimulation constellation – corresponding to the situation perceived – and a flexible pattern, 'transported through time' by the individual, (comprising the results of individual experience and appropriation). This pattern includes emotional judgments and programmes of action, and possesses the characteristics of a **schema**, a concept which has long been well-known in psychology. There is a pure or kernel form of the pattern (which can usually be illustrated by a 'prototype') and a range of permitted variation, the limits of which are, in turn, changeable depending on experience.

---

[15] See [Volpert, 1989].

But how can our deliberations help us to derive from this a new argument relating to situations that promote personality development? Forming flexible patterns in a complex domain requires the ability to tackle the same basic issue, problem or task in a number of different guises, in a variety of real-life situations. Reducing this contextual variability – through the standardization of situations – evidently hinders the learning process and the mastery of situations which transcend this standardized range. But the same goes, presumably, for a contextual variability that is, so to speak, vagabond, i.e., not centred on specific requirements and task kernels[16].

Our *eighth argument* might, then, run as follows: *In order to promote personal development, work tasks must be characterized by centred variability, i.e., while the basic structure of the tasks remains the same, they must provide for a variety of different implementation conditions.*

Numerous training methods used in the spheres of work and sport emphasize the need to vary training conditions in order to ensure that patterns of action are flexible enough to meet differing requirements. There is also another type of centred variability in learning tasks which extends and complements their 'horizontal' dispersion about a task kernel. Particularly for the attainment of complex learning goals, a 'vertical' arrangement of learning tasks, reflecting a gradual conditioning to the complexity of the overall action aimed at, may also be considered useful. This conditioning serves to prevent both an overtaxing of capacity and a fragmentation of the learning process. It might be characterized as adapting the task to the development needs of the learner. This procedure is also a familiar one in educational theory and practice. In action regulation theory, it appears in the guise of the **antecedent genetic form** concept. Here, emphasis is given to the holistic and action-related nature of the learning tasks in a graded learning procedure.

Recent successful applications of this principle have been reported by Krogoll et al.[17] for basic training on CNC machine tools, and by Greif[18] for learning a word-processing program. It is apparent that the principle of the antecedent genetic form is of particular importance where new tasks are to be learned in a complex technical context.

7.5.4 The principle of social and societal embeddedness

The definition of humans as a social being is an ancient one, and, if it is to be correct, invariably refers to both their association with others, i.e., direct communication, as well as the determination of individual thought and action by the socio-historical situation.

In the course of historical development and in the process of individual evolution, *social determination* is always essentially mediated by *direct interaction*. Our relations with the world are conditioned by our association with others.

---

[16] For the domain of sensorimotor regulation here [Munzert, 1989].

[17] [Krogoll et al., 1988]

[18] [Greif, 1989]

In this association, our existence acquires its systems of meaning and its developmental impulses. To fulfil the principle of embodied being-in-the-world, it is essential that the social contact is immediate (i.e., non-mediated). In other words, it must primarily take the form of oral dialogue and accompanying body language. Written, and even technically mediated, communication is sometimes unavoidable or even actually useful. It does, however, invariably reduce social relations, making association with others both more abstract and more difficult. For this reason it should not be allowed to gain predominance over other forms of communication.

Our *ninth aspect*, then, might be worded as follows: *In order to promote personal development, working conditions must both provide for and encourage cooperation and direct interpersonal contact.*

This demand is not new to work designers either, at least in terms of acquaintance with the particular wishes of working people. It is, however, difficult to fit such forms of direct contact into organizational forms based on the machine model. And this is why the attempt is generally made – on the grounds of certain unspecified constraints or in order to ensure clarity of organizational structure – to hinder and restrict such contacts. Let us recall here F.W.Taylor's recommendation to suppress any sort of workers' groupings on the grounds that they are not expedient and merely lead to unrest[19].

These considerations can also be applied without any great difficulty to the design of learning processes. The essential features of this aspect are to be found above all in the various forms of group instruction with their different social learning goals. Regarding the structuring of work-related learning on the basis of the action regulation theory, the reader is referred, first of all, to the method of task-oriented information exchange[20]. In this method, workers are encouraged to form groups responsible for producing specific material, mainly manuals explaining how to achieve a proper mastery of their work tasks. This is shown to have a number of effects: not only is there an improvement in task mastery (with respect to both performance and stress reduction), but workers also develop suggestions for improving work design. In addition, the material compiled provides a good basis for on-the-job training of other workers.

A slightly different, complementary approach has been presented by Kötter and Gohde[21]. They are concerned with the question of how working groups can be prepared for production along the lines of the 'group technology model' (so-called 'production islands'). They recommend defining a central task for each group, and requiring them to learn their task in a stage-by-stage process. Here, the connection with the notion of the antecedent genetic form – introduced in conjunction with the previous aspect – becomes apparent.

In discussing this ninth aspect, we have come up against a boundary. This is the transition from system design to organization development. In the sphere of learning, one could, by analogy, speak of the boundary between individual

---

[19] Cf. [Taylor, 1911].
[20] Cf. [Neubert and Tomczyk, 1986].
[21] [Kötter and Gohde, 1989]

appropriation processes with isolatable goals and collective open systems. For our research group, this boundary is an essentially pragmatic one – the guideline presented below is concerned with task analysis only. Confinement to this aspect should not, however, be taken to mean that there are not, beyond this boundary, important aspects relating to working and learning conditions that promote personality development. Nevertheless, the nine aspects outlined above do provide a basis for crossing this boundary with a view to developing common design processes for working and learning conditions. The latter are actually inherent in them.

Detailed consideration of the ninth aspect we have just discussed also implies arriving at *higher-level task-independent communication* and, with that, reflection on the common goals of action above and beyond immediate task performance, thereby addressing more directly the social determination of action. If we avoid restricting the requirements relating to scope of action and structurability, and above all avoid confining these to individuals, scope is enhanced for *participative design of working and learning conditions.* In the same way, groups which accordingly assume responsibility for the individual development of their members are likely, in the long run, to change their work tasks so as to bring them into line with this development. Moreover, they will relate their action to societal (development) processes and, by so doing, pose the question of the 'meaning' of this action.

This idea must be seen from two different perspectives. On the one hand, it refers to *the relation of working and learning activities to other spheres of life,* i.e., to the life-worlds, of individuals and groups. On the other hand, it indicates that working and learning conditions can only be seen as conducive to personality development if they *enable individuals or groups to reflect on the social utility of their action, and hold out the prospect of such reflection yielding positive results.*

7.5.5 The guideline for contrastive task analysis

In our research group we have developed a guideline[22] enabling the system developer to evaluate work tasks on the basis of whether they take into account the aspects or human criteria considered above, and thus whether they are conducive to personality development. The procedures provided by this guideline also make it possible to evaluate future work tasks, i.e., those still at the planning stage. Particular attention is paid here to the question of which subtasks might be transferred to automated procedures, and in which cases this might be considered unreasonable or even detrimental, since it would impair rather than promote specifically human strengths. This is why we speak of contrastive task analysis.

The method used for investigation is the observation interview, which involves asking the user of the guideline (the industrial and administrative practitioner) questions about the work task. The information required for answering these

---

[22] Cf. [Dunckel et al., 1991].

questions can then be acquired by the user in an open dialogue with the working person while observing the work activity.

The guideline comprises two main parts: the general procedure, and the special procedures relating to the above-mentioned human criteria. Each of these parts contains a detailed manual and questionnaire. The manual provides information on the aims and functions of the respective parts or sections, on the procedure to be adopted in the investigation, and on how to deal with the questionnaire.

The *general procedure* is subdivided into four parts. *Part A*, when processed, provides a general picture of the department or *organizational unit* under investigation. The aim of *Part B* is to supply general information about the individual *workplace* and to give a clear definition of the work tasks to be performed at this workplace. *Part C* is designed to provide an initial picture and a more detailed characterization of the individual *work task*. It contains, in particular, the question whether information and communication technologies are of importance for performing the work task, and if so, which ones. *Part D* enables a *rough analysis* of the work task to be made with reference to the *human criteria* formulated above. Particular attention is already paid here to whether any impairment of the human criteria by the information and communication technologies is observable. Part D must be processed separately for each different work task in a particular department or organizational unit. By way of a result, Part D indicates those human criteria which may have to be dealt with in more detail by the special procedures.

The other main part of the guideline comprises *special procedures* which briefly cover the various human criteria outlined above (*Parts E to M*), and another part (*Part N*) summarizing the results of the analysis. Here, too, the essential question is to what extent the human criteria are either impaired by information and communication technologies or supported by them. This second part of the guideline is constructed according to the 'modular design principle', i.e., it also allows for consideration of each human criterion in isolation.

So far, our experience in using the guideline has been promising. It has proved easy to handle and suitable for use in a wide variety of different fields and for work tasks of varying complexity. Depending on this complexity, the analysis of a workplace normally takes between 4 and 6 hours. Moreover, it has been found that the results of the analyses are also seen by industrial and administrative practitioners as being important for system design.

7.5.6 Concluding remarks

Calls for the design of working and learning conditions conducive to personality development take their place today alongside a number of other similar ideas. These point out that people must adopt a different attitude towards conditions of life and identity from the one prevalent so far – based as it is on the dogma of the mechanistic world-view and the inordinate desire for command over behaviour and the world. Such ideas also include questions concerning our relationship to nature and the way we deal with natural resources and energy supplies.

Basically, what we are concerned with is a new view of human beings and the world in which they live, taking account of the whole biological and socio-cultural process of evolution and the shared responsibility of humanity for the quality of their existence. But more so than in the fields of, say, environmental protection or energy management, there exist clear and distinct alternatives to mechanistic ideologies for the design of working and learning processes conducive to personal development. These alternatives cannot simply be disposed of by offering the global excuse that none of them constitutes a 'viable economic proposition'. The design of working and learning processes that promote personality development may be considered an initial test of whether we have a serious concern for a responsible and life-oriented design of technology and the environment.

Acknowledgements

Translated from the German by Philip Bacon. My thanks go to Nigel Nicholson for his helpful comments. The text draws on work carried out in conjunction with the research project *Contrastive Task Analysis*. Other members of the project team are: H. Dunckel, K. Hennes, U. Kreutner, R. Oesterreich, C. Pleiss and M. Zölch. The project is funded by the German Federal Ministry for Research and Technology as part of the research programme on the Humanization of Working Life.

Part 8

Epistemological Approaches to Informatics

Christiane

> We cannot hope to establish adequate foundations for computer science without probing into philosophical traditions concerned with human thought.

Heinz

> As implied by the illustration, a closer look at the computer gives rise to profound philosophical questions. The computer has emerged from human reality and carries this reality within itself. If we wish to understand computer science, we must see it in the context of the history of thought and, at the same time, show how the history of thought is reflected in it.

Reinhard B.

> In the heading to this part of the book, we have chosen to use the term "informatics" to suggest a conception of our science that goes beyond a mere "computer science". For, traditionally, the computer is the focus of attention, human reality being reduced to an abstract image on the computer screen. It dwindles to mere form, vanishing, as it were, in the computer.

Reinhard K.-S.

> In our view, though, informatics should concern itself with the interactions between the formalized technical world of the computer and the living world of the human being, throwing light on ways in which formalisms can be integrated into human action. This would also enable it to adopt an explicit orientation to human values.

Christiane

> Traditional computer science is based essentially on logic. And it fits perfectly into the philosophical school of Logical Positivism. It has developed for itself sophisticated logical calculi to model increasingly complex facts and ideas. And many computer scientists continue to believe that logic is sufficient as a foundation for our work.
>
> But if informatics is to concern itself with interactions between human contexts of action and technically implemented formal artifacts, it must rest on richer foundations.
>
> In his introductory chapter to this part, Joseph Goguen goes into the reasons why computer scientists should address philosophical ideas that transcend the domain of logic – such as hermeneutics, for example – with a view to arriving at a deeper understanding of "truth" and "meaning".

Reinhard B.

> We also need a more comprehensive understanding of language. For language serves not only as a basis for formal calculi, it is also a vehicle for communication among all the parties involved in the meaningful development and use of computer technology.

Christiane

> In the next chapter, Dafydd Gibbon highlights the connections between informatics and the philosophy of language. There is a wealth of correlations

here. Programs are texts; they are written in special languages; all modelling is carried out in terms of language; our understanding of language shapes our understanding of informatics ...

Heinz

... and language also constitutes the means for critical reflection on our work. Thought, language and action are interlocking and inextricably linked to one another by our bodily experience. And our experience is mediated by technology.

Christiane

These interrelations are viewed quite differently by the different schools of thought in philosophy.

Rafael Capurro establishes relations between informatics and hermeneutics, which sees human existence as "Being-in-the-World". He also refers to the ideas of Winograd and Flores, giving a critical appraisal of them from his own standpoint. For him, the key issue is not merely the designability of technology, but our way of dealing with it, which shapes our thinking and our whole lives.

Arne Raeithel looks at the design of computer-supported systems in terms of activity theory. This Marxist school of thought has developed and elaborated a notion of activity geared to social action – computer-supported action representing a special instance of such activity.

Reinhard K.-S.

The activity-theoretical approach is historical. Beyond that, our concern must be to integrate all of these connections into the biological and socio-cultural evolution process.

Christiane

By way of a conclusion, Klaus Fuchs-Kittowski gives a comprehensive treatment of the information concept in biological, social and technical systems. For him, an adequate understanding of the nature of information is the key to a richer notion of informatics and to responsible handling of information technology.

Heinz

This part of the book is pretty hard going. Each chapter needs to be read and appraised on its own merits.

Reinhard K.-S.

Personally, I'm not particularly fond of these elaborate abstract edifices of thought. The book should not end there, but turn back to daily practice.

Reinhard B.

I agree. But that's not something that can be done by adding even more chapters to the book. This book and what it offers in the way of ideas must be absorbed and integrated into our work in science and design.

Christiane

And it is up to each individual reader to constantly rebuild this bridge in terms of his or her own particular context.

8.1 Truth and Meaning Beyond Formalism

Joseph A. Goguen

8.1.1 Introduction

Logic and formal semantics have been enormously helpful in understanding programs and programming languages, and in automating some aspects of the programming process. Therefore computer scientists have good professional reasons to be interested in truth and meaning construed in a narrow technical sense, through symbolic logic and formal semantics.

But computer scientists also need to better understand the processes that create and sustain software, and in particular, the complex relationships between computer systems, individuals, and societies. Moreover, we also need to develop more humility about our own role in the scheme of things. Unfortunately, these problems raise deep questions about truth and meaning which cannot be addressed by formal semantics.

This short paper is intended to suggest why computer scientists might be interested in the work of Heidegger, Wittgenstein and others[1], and to stimulate some further thought about some of the questions that they address. Although Heidegger did not write very much that is explicitly about formal logic, what he did write is quite pertinent, and much of his other work is relevant to questions of meaning in the larger sense. Wittgenstein was concerned with the limits of language, that is, with "what cannot be said". We will see that their views are fundamentally opposed to those of logical positivists such as Carnap, as well as to the whole Anglo-American tradition of analytic philosophy, and in particular, to Russell and Moore. We will also see some interesting parallels to Buddhist philosophy.

At the end of the paper we return to consider what all this has to do with computing.

8.1.2 Heidegger, Carnap and Wittgenstein on "the Nothing" and Dread

This section tells the story of an encounter (in print) between three of the most influential philosophers of the early twentieth century. In 1931, the log-

---

[1] Among the attempts to summarize Heidegger's philosophy that I have found the most useful is [Palmer, 1969]; see also [Winograd and Flores, 1986] for other indications of its relevance to computer science. [Janik and Toulmin, 1973] is an excellent source of background information on Wittgenstein.

ical positivist Carnap[2] took Heidegger's 1929 essay "What is Metaphysics?"[3] as a paradigmatic example of what he called "metaphysical pseudostatements". Carnap's program was to develop an ideal language based on logic, in which all words would refer to observable sense data, experiences or things, and in which a "logical syntax" would guarantee that all sentences are meaningful by eliminating all "nonsensical" combinations of words that are still permitted by grammatical syntax. Such a language would eliminate metaphysics (and much of the rest of philosophy) as well as all literature and poetry, in much the same way that Orwell's "Newspeak" in *Nineteen Eighty-Four* would eliminate all language that is inconsistent with the ideology of Big Brother. As Orwell[4] says,

> Newspeak was designed not to extend but to *diminish* the range of thought, and this purpose was indirectly assisted by cutting the choice of words down to a minimum.

According to Carnap[5],

> The meaning of a statement lies in the method of its verification. A statement asserts only so much as is verifiable with respect to it. Therefore a sentence can be used only to assert an empirical proposition, if indeed it is used to assert anything at all. ... Logical analysis, then, pronounces the verdict of meaninglessness on any alleged knowledge that pretends to reach above or behind experience. ... The (pseudo)statements of metaphysics do not serve for the *description of states of affairs*, either existing ones (in that case they would be true statements) or nonexisting ones (in that case they would be at least false statements).

Specifically, Carnap criticizes Heidegger's use of the word "nothing" in the following assemblage[6], by showing that it violates his "logical syntax":

> What is to be investigated is being only and — *nothing* else; being alone and further — *nothing*; solely being, and beyond being — *nothing. What about this Nothing? ... Does the Nothing exist only because the Not, i.e., the Negation, exists? Or is it the other way around? Do Negation and the Not exist only because the Nothing exists? ...* We assert: *the Nothing is prior to the Not and the Negation. ...* Where do we seek the Nothing? How do we find the Nothing? ... We know the Nothing. ... *Anxiety reveals the Nothing. ...* That for which and because of which we were anxious, was 'really' — nothing. Indeed: the Nothing itself — as such — was present. ... *What about this Nothing? — The Nothing itself nothings.*

---

[2] Cf. [Carnap, 1978].

[3] [Heidegger, 1977d]

[4] See [Orwell, 1989].

[5] See [Carnap, 1978].

[6] The italics and deletions are Carnap's, and it is worth noting that by taking these widely scattered sentences out of their contexts, and by his selected italicization and capitalization, Carnap creates a very distorted view of Heidegger's text [Heidegger, 1977d].

As an example of Carnap's analysis, Heidegger's sentence "We know the nothing" is represented as "$K(no)$" and then claimed meaningless because "nothing" (denoted "no") is used as a noun. But Heidegger says "The nothing is neither an object nor any being at all."[7] Hence, Carnap is accusing Heidegger of something which Heidegger clearly says cannot be done, namely taking "the nothing" as "a something".

Indeed, Heidegger anticipates precisely the sort of attack which Carnap mounts when he says[8]:

> But perhaps our confused talk already degenerates into an empty squabble over words. Against it science must now reassert its seriousness and soberness of mind, insisting that it is concerned solely with beings. The nothing — what else can it be for science but an outrage and a phantasm? If science is right, then only one thing is sure: science wishes to know nothing of the nothing.

This quotation indicates that Heidegger knows he is playing with words. But in order to explore the foundations of something, it is necessary to step outside its bounds. As Wittgenstein says[9], in direct contradiction to Carnap,

> I can readily understand what Heidegger means by Being and Dread. Man has the impulse to run up against the limits of language[10]. Think, for example, of the astonishment that anything exists[11]. This astonishment cannot be expressed in the form of a question, and there is also no answer to it[12]. Everything which we feel like saying can, a priori, only be nonsense ... Yet the tendency represented by the running-up against *points to something*. St. Augustine already knew this when he said: What, you wretch, so you want to avoid talking nonsense? Talk some nonsense; it makes no difference!

(The history of this little passage is interesting. A "sanitized" version appeared in the *Philosophical Review* in 1965 without the first sentence and without the original title, which was *On Heidegger*.)

Unfortunately, Wittgenstein himself did not take St. Augustine's advice to "talk nonsense," and as a result, the *Tractatus* is in some ways very obscure.

---

[7] See [Heidegger, 1977d].

[8] See [Heidegger, 1977d].

[9] See [Wittgenstein, 1978].

[10] Murray explains in [Murray, 1978] that this is a reference to Kierkegaard, who was the first philosopher to give a serious treatment of anxiety ("*Angst*" in German, translated "dread" in the previous sentence) before Heidegger.

[11] This is a reference to the last sentence of [Heidegger, 1977d] which is "Why are there beings at all, and why not rather nothing?" This fundamental theme of Heidegger is, for example, the central question of [Heidegger, 1959].

[12] Although this is a criticism of Heidegger's formulation, the last sentence of this quotation from Wittgenstein suggests that they may not differ so much after all.

In fact, Wittgenstein was rather systematically misunderstood, and hence distorted, by the logically oriented philosophers of the Vienna Circle and the Anglo-American tradition[13]. Russell's preface to the *Tractatus*[14] is a good example, since it criticizes Wittgenstein on precisely those points where his contribution was perhaps most original and significant, namely the pages from Proposition 6.4 onward, which discuss such topics as ethics and the "problem of life".

It is notable that Carnap and Wittgenstein share not only a common interest in logic, science and language, but also in what cannot be said. However, their attitudes towards this area were entirely different: Carnap considered that everything outside his ideal logical language was nonsense without meaning, whereas Wittgenstein considered that everything of the greatest value and interest was contained in this realm. In contrast, Heidegger was not only willing to talk "nonsense", he was willing to break the bonds of language by making up new words, and by using old words in new, often ungrammatical or "illogical" ways to indicate deeper meanings which strictly speaking cannot be said at all, but only pointed at.

Carnap[15] recognized that art operates outside of the strictly verifiable, but he still considered that the metaphysician

> confuses [science and art] and produces a structure which achieves nothing for knowledge and something inadequate for the expression of an attitude. ... The metaphysician believes that he travels in territory in which truth and falsehood are at stake. In reality, however, he has not asserted anything, but only expressed something, like an artist. ... [The statements of metaphysicians] serve for the *expression of the general attitude of a person toward life.* ... Metaphysicians are musicians without musical ability.

Thus, Carnap does not intend to ban everything that falls outside his language, but only to label it meaningless. However, both his view of meaning, and his view of art as expressing a general attitude toward life, are very limited. In contrast, Heidegger says "Art lets truth originate. Art ... is the spring that leaps to the truth of beings ..."[16].

8.1.3 What is "the Nothing"?

It is no coincidence that Heidegger, Carnap and Wittgenstein collide on the issues of "the nothing" and anxiety. All three philosophers can be seen as advancing Kant's program to stem the turgid tide of traditional metaphysics that still today flows on at us from out of the Middle Ages. One major goal of Kant's "critical philosophy" was to show the limits of reason *from within*, that is, using the tools of reason, in order to prevent its misuse. In particular, Kant wished

---

[13] This is clearly explained in [Janik and Toulmin, 1973].
[14] [Wittgenstein, 1922]
[15] Cf. [Carnap, 1978].
[16] See [Heidegger, 1977b].

to separate the realm of reason from that of value. For example, Kant wrote a treatise which denied that there could be any justification for blaming the great Lisbon earthquake of 1775 either on the presence of a few Protestants there (as did many Catholics in Lisbon) or on the adherence of the majority to Catholicism (as did some English clerics).

Kant took subject-centered rationalism to its limit, declaring that we construct objects according to *a priori* given faculties of mind, which include space, time, causality, objecthood, number, affirmation, negation and possibility. This analysis assumes a world of "things in themselves" and an idealized human subject, both of which are unknowable. Thus, Kant's so-called "second Copernican revolution" actually went in the *opposite* direction from that of Copernicus, since it placed man in the *center* again, as the constructor of perceived objects (the phenomena). Since the time of Descartes, this kind of move has been seen as necessary to secure a firm grounding for the objectivity of science.

Wittgenstein's *Tractatus* can be seen as a Kantian critical (i.e., from within) deconstruction of logical positivism, despite its significant contributions to the technique of logic (e.g., truth tables). In particular, Wittgenstein argues that it is impossible to express the meaning of a formal language within the language itself, and instead uses a "picture" theory of meaning in which interpretations can be shown but cannot be said. Russell and Carnap tried to counter this by proposing a "meta"-language in which the meaning of an "object" language can be expressed, and even an infinite tower of meta-, meta-meta-, meta-meta-meta-, ... languages. But as Russell admits in his preface to the *Tractatus*, Wittgenstein's argument seems to apply just as well to such a tower of languages as it does to a single language.

If it is impossible to express the meaning of a sentence *within* its language, then it is necessary to move *outside* the language. This led the later Wittgenstein to investigate the conventions which determine when and how sentences can be used. He called these flexible rule-governed symbol using activities "language games"[17]. They, in turn, get their meanings from the even more flexible and larger-grained patterns of symbol using activities of which they are parts, which he called "forms of life". This point of view is quite different from that in the *Tractatus*, which had simply assumed that the relation between language and reality is one of "picturing" (i.e., representation). But in late Wittgenstein, it is the rules of language games which determine the limits of what can be said.

This whole development, starting from Kant's clarification of the subject-centered approach of traditional metaphysics and science, and proceeding to the work of Heidegger, Derrida, Barthes and other modern French thinkers, can be seen as an ongoing *deconstruction of the self*, which is nothing other than the exploration of "the nothing" as it applies to the knowing subject of Descartes and Kant. The inevitable conclusion is that there is no rational basis for assuming such a subject. Instead, subject and object continually emerge and dissolve together.

---

[17] See [Wittgenstein, 1968].

Many books have been written in the Buddhist tradition about "the nothing," called *shunyata* in Sanskrit[18]. Buddhism says that the experience of *shunyata* is egolessness, the lack of any subject, and says that egolessness is a fundamental fact of human existence. One way that this experience can manifest is described by the Tibetan meditation master Trungpa Rinpoche[19] as follows:

> It is a very desolate situation. It is like living among snow-capped peaks with clouds wrapped around them and the sun and the moon starkly shining over them. Below, tall alpine trees are swayed by strong, howling winds and beneath them is a thundering waterfall. From our point of view, we may appreciate this desolation if we are an occasional tourist who photographs it or a mountain climber trying to climb to the mountain top. But we do not really want to live in those desolate places. It's no fun. It is terrifying, terrible.

No wonder, as Heidegger says, "science wishes to know nothing of the nothing." For science wishes to banish dread and proceed with its objectivity firmly established in the subjectivity of its scientists, reducing "the nothing" to mere negation, which is a rational operation on beings, as opposed to the terrifying emptiness from which beings emerge into authenticity.

However, if Heidegger and the Buddhists are right, it is the possibility of non-being which gives beings their character of luminosity[20], and hence the nothing, i.e., *shunyata*, is not only prior to negation, but also to beings.

The effect of this, as Heidegger says, is to rob logic of its claim to supremacy, and in particular, to rob it of its claim to provide foundations for science and even for mathematics. Indeed, we must conclude that foundations in the sense sought by logicians are simply not possible. The judgements that we make, and in particular negative judgements, are necessarily grounded in our being-in-the-world, and not in any pre-existing unshakable truths, or eternal world of ideal things.

More significantly, we may conclude that it is the finitude, limitation, or mortality of beings which makes them luminous. The fundamental importance of finitude for Being is expressed in the thundering series of questions which close Heidegger's major work, *Being and Time*[21]. The finitude and luminosity of beings are two of the many suggestive points of contact between Heidegger and Buddhism. For "impermanence" (i.e., finitude) is one of the Three Marks of Existence (the other two are egolessness and suffering).

---

[18] One of the most famous is the *Mulamadhyamakakarikas* of Nagarjuna, from around the second century A.D.; a more recent one is *Religion and Nothingness* [Nishitani, 1982] by Nishitani, considered the dean of the Kyoto School of philosophy.

[19] Cf. [Trungpa, 1976].

[20] It is impossible to "define" the experience of luminosity. But perhaps it might be some help to say that it refers to the flickering of beings between presence and non-presence. On the other hand, this may be an example of something which really cannot be said.

[21] [Heidegger, 1962]

8.1.4 What are truth and meaning?

The intimate relationship between truth, meaning and being in the Western philosophical tradition goes back to the ancient Greeks, and is extensively discussed, for example, by Aristotle; these three correspond (roughly) to the Greek words *aletheia, logos* and *on*.

Most attempts to explicate these notions and their relationship have taken as paradigmatic the "eternal" sentences of mathematics (such as "$2 + 2 = 4$"), whose "meaning" is a truth value that is independent of any context in which the sentence might be uttered. But such sentences are exceedingly rare in "earthly" discourse, where meanings can be far more complex than just "true" or "false," and where context has a profound effect upon meaning.

In his essay "On the Essence of Truth"[22], Heidegger criticizes semantic theories that are based on the so-called "Correspondence Theory of Truth":

> "Truth" is not a feature of correct propositions which are asserted of an "object" by a human "subject" and then "are valid" somewhere, in what sphere we know not; rather, truth is disclosure of beings through which an openness essentially unfolds.

That is, according to the Correspondence Theory, a statement is "true" just in case what it asserts is a fact about the world. Although the assertion is made by a (human) subject about some object, the true statements themselves are ideal forms in a Platonic realm that is only dimly perceived by humans. Instead of this, Heidegger says that truth is a process of unfolding, of disclosure. That is,[23]

> The essence of being is *physis* [i.e., appearing]. ... Appearing makes manifest. Already we know then that being, appearing, causes to emerge from concealment. Since the essent[24] as such *is*, it places itself in and stands in *unconcealment, aletheia.* ... The Greek essence of truth is possible only in one with the Greek essence of being as *physis*. On the strength of the unique and essential relationship between *physis* and *aletheia*, the Greeks would have said: The essent is true insofar as it is. The true as such is essent. This means: The power that manifests itself stands in unconcealment. In showing itself, the unconcealed as such comes to stand. Truth as un-concealment is not an appendage to being.

This is a radically different notion of truth from that which we find in logic or empirical science. It has nothing to do with operations of measurement or of verification, carried out by some human subject. Rather, it has to do with authentic presence, with the power of beings to emerge from the nothing. This

---

[22] [Heidegger, 1977a]

[23] See [Heidegger, 1959].

[24] The word "essent" was made up by the translator Ralph Manheim to translate Heidegger's made-up word "Seiende," which (roughly speaking) means "something that exists," an "existent." In this chapter, I have mostly used the word "being" for this.

approach to truth and being does not presuppose a knowing subject, and does not reduce beings to objects of knowledge; for Heidegger and the ancient Greeks, being and truth are pre-conceptual.

It seems clear that from this perspective, "meaning" is not an "object," whether as part of some formal causal theory, as an abstract logical intention, or as some set-theoretic entity. The following may provide some reference points in a search to understand our alternative sense of "meaning":

1. *Meaning is ontological.* All experience is inextricably bound up with Being and with beings, i.e., with luminous appearance. In particular, meaning arises through openness to being, or as Heidegger says, "The essence of truth is freedom"[25].

2. *Meaning is dialectical.* Meaning is only disclosed through engagement with beings, through uncertainty and questioning, through making mistakes, exploring oppositions, and seeking roots[26].

3. *Meaning is historical.* Because meaning is dialectical, it only emerges through time, through the accumulation of questionings, encounters and revealings, in the context of a tradition or lineage[27].

Interestingly enough, recent efforts to extend formal semantics beyond mathematics and science, for example to natural languages, can be seen as embodying (diluted versions of) similar principles. In particular, recent work in philosophy and linguistics has proposed new formalisms for complex meanings that can vary with context, and can model discourse and other interactions. Examples include the work of Montague, using intensional logic[28], the work of Barwise, Perry and others on "situation semantics"[29], of Strachey and Scott[30] on "denotational" semantics, and many other formalisms developed for the semantics of programming languages. But all these theories posit abstract entities, such as "intentions," "situations" or "denotations" that are quite remote from the human experience of meaningfulness, and it is not clear that they can tell us anything important about what it means to be human. In particular, they do not deal with truth as the unconcealment of beings.

On the other hand, it seems clear that these advances are technically useful. For example, they may help us to write programs that are more accurate, more general, more efficient, and more reusable; they may also help us to write programs that can help us in programming. They may even some day lead to machines that can understand and speak the sort of utilitarian languages of which Carnap would approve.

---

[25] See [Heidegger, 1977a].

[26] For some further discussion of the development of meaning, see Chap. 2.2; for more on error, see Chap. 5.1.

[27] See Chap. 2.2 for some related discussion.

[28] Cf. [Montague, 1974].

[29] Cf. [Barwise and Perry, 1983].

[30] Cf. [Scott and Strachey, 1971, Stoy, 1977].

8.1.5 Where are we?

The *Tractatus*[31] concludes with the following mysterious proposition,

> What we cannot speak about we must pass over in silence.

which is perhaps intended as a summary of Wittgenstein's arguments that the meaning of a language cannot be expressed in the language itself.

In a sense, this whole paper has been about that which cannot be said. We first presented arguments against Carnap's narrowly dogmatic "logical syntax" and his rejection of Heidegger as nonsense. While accepting that a line of the kind that Carnap wants to draw can in fact be drawn, we agreed with Wittgenstein that all the most important things lie on what Carnap would regard as the wrong side of it. On the other hand, I cannot agree with Wittgenstein that we must remain silent about these things. Even though they may not make strict logical sense, they are too important not to bring into the open through dialogue.

As an illustration, we tried to explore Heidegger's "nothing" and why it might be prior to negation, with some help from the later Wittgenstein and Buddhist philosophy. This also perhaps gave some insight into the foundations of logic. We next tried to follow Heidegger's approach to truth, beginning with his rejection of the Correspondence Principle, and then moving on to *physis* and *aletheia*, which reveal a completely different perspective from that of formal semantics. We concluded with some pointers toward the meaning of meaning, followed by a short summary of some recent work in formal semantics.

But how does all this relate to computing?

I think we must conclude that the techniques of computer science, such as formal semantics, logic, and even simulation, cannot tell us the *meanings* of computer systems, in the broad human sense of "meaning". This becomes an issue especially for so-called "embedded computer systems". For example, consider the question of what the Star Wars weapons system really means: is it a defense system, as its proponents tend to claim, or is it really an offensive system, intended to provide some protection after a first strike has been launched? Such a question cannot be answered without a careful consideration of social and political factors, as well as a careful assessment of technical capabilities. To remain silent on such issues is to invite manipulation, or even tyranny.

To address such questions, it is not necessary to be "an expert," that is, to have everything already worked out. Indeed, it is not even desirable, because genuine meaning only arises through uncertainty and questioning, even through confusion and error. It is necessary to enter into a dialogue in order for truth to emerge from concealment.

Similar considerations hold for many less dramatic and more ordinary situations. For example, suppose that we are part of a team that is producing a large business system, and one day the customer tells us of an unexpected change in the tax laws, which it turns out will require keeping much more data than had previously been anticipated; unfortunately, this means that the system will

---

[31] [Wittgenstein, 1922]

have to run on different hardware, because the old requirements led to choosing hardware that cannot handle so much data. The customer has trouble understanding why his system will now cost more, and threatens to sue. The head of the company threatens to counter-sue. Some team members panic and consider quitting.

Is there any way that formal semantics can save the day? No, there is not. We will have to negotiate. Of course, formal semantics might play some role, for example, in revising the specifications, but the real meaning of this situation is a human one, involving a conflict of interests between the company and its customer.

Numerous other examples could be given. There are many aesthetic decisions to be made in programming. These are not without meaning. If a program is elegantly designed and coded, then it may be easier to debug, maintain, and reuse.

Also, the members of a programming team have to work together, and the project will only prosper if there is a spirit of friendly cooperation, rather than, say, envy, bitterness, or competition. Formal semantics might be used to specify a component, but anger could cause someone to write it in a particularly obscure way.

In all such situations, it is vital to understand the difference between issues that can be resolved by appeal to formal semantics (e.g., "is this code right?") and issues which cannot (e.g., "is this code elegant?"), and it is vital to approach each kind of meaning in an appropriate way. I would like to think that the philosophy of Wittgenstein, Heidegger, and the Buddhists might be some help in this regard, and I have tried to explain how this might be so. But really, common sense is likely to be more valuable than philosophy here, unless perhaps some antidote is needed against previous large doses of positivistic or analytic philosophy. Moreover, even this would require thinking about things that are difficult or even impossible to say clearly. So I do not imagine that I have done more than provide a few pointers for those who may want to pursue such issues further, and I hope that the reader will take this chapter in that light, and will enjoy looking into some of the original source material, and thinking things through on his/her own.

Acknowledgements
I would like to thank my wife Kathleen and my son Healfdene for reading through several drafts of this paper and providing many helpful comments and conversations. I would also like to thank both the Naropa Institute in Boulder, Colorado, and the Center for the Study of Language and Information at Stanford University for providing stimulating environments in which to think about the kind of issue discussed here.

8.2 Informatics and Hermeneutics

Rafael Capurro

8.2.1 Introduction

The short cut and the long path

Not only the historical development of informatics as a scientific and technical discipline but also its core problems are, *prima facie*, far removed from philosophical developments arising from soft sciences such as hermeneutics, and closer to logic or the philosophy of science. Is the relationship between informatics and hermeneutics of any mutual relevance? What happens when we reflect hermeneutically on the foundations of informatics? Winograd and Flores have made the attempt, and one result was their insight into "the non-obviousness of the rationalistic orientation" of informatics. Consequently, they found themselves "deeply concerned with the question of language"[1].

My purpose is to show why Winograd and Flores have grasped, on the one hand, some key issues of Heidegger's hermeneutics, while at the same time distorting some of his insights, particularly with regard to science and information technology.

Their critique of what they call the rationalistic tradition is based on the following premises:

1. The process of understanding is a never-ending one; it always implies unspoken conditions; it is limited.
2. Language does not represent objective meanings, but is a social process through which commitments are generated.
3. Computer technology is a tool belonging to our being-in-the-world (In-der-Welt-sein): "in designing tools we are designing ways of being" (p. xi).

In opposition to these premises, the rationalistic tradition's view of human understanding is characterized by the idea of representing a so-called objective world through mental processes. Language is considered to be the result of such mental data processing, which is basically autonomous and independent of the social context. Consequently, computers which manipulate language are said to be intelligent, to understand, to think, to be able to replace experts, and so on.

---

[1] [Winograd and Flores, 1986, p. 17].
See the reviews by [Vellino, 1987, Stefik and Bobrow, 1987, Suchman, 1987] and [Clancey, 1987]; also the "Response to the reviews" [Winograd and Flores, 1987] and my review [Capurro, 1987].
On hermeneutics, see [Shapiro and Sica, 1984].

Winograd and Flores criticize this conception. They view computers essentially as tools for conversation, to be implemented as aids where the user's background expectations are confronted with non-obvious situations.

In such situations of what they call **breakdown**, tools are normally no longer of any use. Instead of their **readiness-to-hand** – a Heideggerian concept which I shall explain in detail below – we are confronted with their **presence-at-hand** as objects. By a hermeneutical design of computer programs, some possible breakdown situations can be implemented in order to help the user when something goes wrong with the normal functioning of the system. In other words, the flexibility of the system depends on its capacity for anticipating such situations, i.e., on its capability to remain a tool.

These as well as other insights are important not only for informatics, but also for hermeneutics. But some of them are one-sided. I shall comment below on this one-sidedness. My critique concerns the following points:

a) Winograd and Flores' opposition between hermeneutics and the rationalistic tradition, taking as a basis some key concepts from Heidegger's "Being and Time" and leaving aside their connection to Heidegger's overall project of a philosophical foundation of the natural and socio-historical sciences.

b) Their interpretation of computer-based information systems as tools, taking Heidegger's tool analysis as a foundational paradigm for modern information technology and leaving aside Heidegger's explicit characterization of modern science and technology in his later works.

Is there an opposition between hermeneutics and the rationalistic tradition?

Since the authors devote the first part of their study to discussing specifically some basic concepts of Heidegger's hermeneutics, and since they do so by explicitly avoiding "the twists and turns of academic debate" (p. xiii), i.e., by taking the short cut of popularized accounts, it is useful at least to indicate where the long path might lead to, in order to see to what extent the views arrived at via the short cut are distorted ones. This is particularly the case with regard to Heidegger's tool analysis in "Being and Time" taken as a philosophical basis for understanding computer technology. Moreover, Winograd and Flores' interpretation gives the general impression that Heidegger's hermeneutics is anti-rationalistic. Neither in "Being and Time" nor in his later writings was Heidegger *merely* criticizing modern science and technology; he was looking for a point of view which would allow us to see their specific demarcations. If we take the long path – and I can only point to it here! – then we may learn that there is no such opposition or definite point of view; in other words, that taking the long path means abandoning the illusion of definite borderlines and foundational oversimplifications based on paradigm changes.

Can a tool-oriented view of computer-based information systems cope with the radical ambiguity of modern technology?

Taking Heidegger's tool analysis as a key for the interpretation of modern information technology means distorting both phenomena. What is left aside in this instrumental interpretation is – according to Heidegger's explicit analyses of modern technology – its radical *ambiguity*. Recognizing this ambiguity means seeing the impossibility of surmounting it by trying to master it, because such a project – for instance, by trying to replace an old paradigm by a new one – is based on the premises of what it tries to replace: it is a *petitio principii*. This ambiguity is, as I shall point out in the final section, a key issue with regard to software development, since software is not just a tool, but a specific form of reality disclosure and transformation. The question is, then: what kind of reality are we constructing when we develop software, and what are the limits and chances of such a form of reality construction? In order to perceive such limits, we have to take the long path. This is merely an invitation to take such a walk, not the walk itself.

In the final section, I shall plead for what I call an open constructivism, i.e., for a confrontation of software development with metaphorical forms of reality construction.

8.2.2 Heidegger's tool analysis in "Being and Time"

The task of philosophical destruction

Since Heidegger's phenomenological interpretation of our being as There-Being or Dasein on the basis of a pre-conceptual comprehension of Being (Seinsverständnis) as a condition of possibility for the interpretation of beings, hermeneutics has left the domain of text interpretation to become a philosophical research programme[2].

In "Being and Time" (§6) Heidegger calls the task of questioning the obviousness of a dominant tradition destruction (Destruktion). This term does not have the negative meaning of eliminating the past, but rather suggests the task of criticizing a *present* theory or world view by an analysis of its presuppositions. Since this analysis, being itself historical, cannot be regarded as definitive, we are left with the figure of a circle – a hermeneutical not a vicious one. From a hermeneutical perspective, then, it makes no sense to replace old paradigms by new ones; the question of their destruction concerns the critical appraisal of their forgotten historical roots in order to perceive their limitations. In other words,

---

[2] I am referring to [Heidegger, 1987]: "Sein und Zeit" (1927) (engl. transl. 1987). The best introduction to Heidegger in English is still [Richardson, 1967]. See also [Steiner, 1978] and [Capurro, 1991]). For a brief exposition of some of Heidegger's major works, see [Capurro, 1988]. On Heidegger's interpretation of modern science and technology, see [Kockelmans, 1984] and [Kockelmans, 1985]; [Loscerbo, 1981, Schirmacher, 1983] and [Seubold, 1986].

with the help of hermeneutics we learn to see theoretical and practical traditions and their terminologies as answers to forgotten questions, and we learn how to question the questions themselves, too.

Being-in-the-world and the outside world

Winograd and Flores oppose the dualistic view of the rationalistic tradition, with its conception of a subjective mental world and an outside world of physical reality, to the phenomenological insight into the "more fundamental unity of being-in-the-world (Dasein)." (p. 31). This approach is, in my opinion, diametrically opposed to Maturana and Varelas' radical constructivism, to which Winograd and Flores refer directly, leaving aside the dimension of openness (Offensein) or being-outside (Draussensein) as the way human beings are (which is also the reason why Heidegger chooses the term Da-sein), retaining only the hermeneutical process of understanding, reinterpreted now as an *auto*poietical one. Heidegger also calls our way of being existence (Existenz, Ek-sistenz). This term means being open to a field of possibilities, and it expresses the contrary of what we usually mean when we point to the existence of things, grasping their being as actual being. Thus, we can paradoxically say that human beings are not, but that they exist[3].

In their somewhat eclectic approach, Winograd and Flores fail to see the contradiction between Heidegger's hermeneutics and what I call strong or radical constructivism[4]. The dimension of openness, not that of a so-called external reality, lies at the very heart of Heidegger's "Being and Time". He writes: "When Dasein directs itself towards something and grasps it, it does not somehow get out of an inner sphere in which it has been proximally encapsulated, but its primary kind of Being is such that it is always 'outside' alongside entities which it encounters and which belong to a world already discovered. (...) And furthermore, the perceiving of what is known is not a process of returning with one's booty to the 'cabinet' of consciousness after one has gone out and grasped it; even in perceiving, retaining, the Dasein which knows *remains outside*, and it does so *as Dasein*."[5] This is the exact opposite of an autopoietic system, which "holds constant its organization and defines its boundaries through the continuous production of its components."[6]

---

[3] The term Dasein does not denote an asexual human being. It means the primordial structure of being-with-others as the condition for different concrete possibilities of living sexuality. Human sexuality and the human body are not conceived merely as biological phenomena, but as being within the field of openness, which is basically related to our affections or moods (Stimmungen). See [Heidegger, 1978, Boss, 1975] and [Derrida, 1988].

[4] See [Schmidt, 1987].

[5] [Heidegger, 1987, p. 89]

[6] [Winograd and Flores, 1986, p. 44]

Tools and breakdowns

The way in which we exist in the world is intrinsically a social and a practical one. Through our **being-together-with-others (Mitsein)**, we are immersed in the world, but not just in the common spatial sense we think about when we say a chair is in the room. **World (Welt)** does not mean the totality of beings out there, but the complex and open web of meanings *in* which we live. How do we become aware of the world in terms of the open dimension of our existence in which we are normally immersed? In order to answer this question – and not in order to describe the phenomenon of modern technology – Heidegger shows how, through the negative experience of using tools, the **worldhood (Weltlichkeit)** of the world, i.e., our specific way of being in it, becomes manifest[7]. The phenomenological analysis of our everyday immersion in the world shows human beings as concerned with things in terms of using them as tools. This means that things are inserted into a project, building a structure of references for practical purposes. This implicit purposefulness remains tacit unless a disturbance occurs. Winograd and Flores call such a disturbance **breakdown**, thus simplifying the Heideggerian terminology and missing the point. What happens in these cases is not simply that tools become **present-at-hand (Vorhandenes)** instead of their former practical way of being as **ready-to-hand (Zuhandenes)**, but that the world itself, i.e., the possibility of discovering beings within a structure of references, becomes manifest.

At this point, I would like to draw attention to one oversimplification of Winograd and Flores' short cut. They write: "Another aspect of Heidegger's thought that is difficult for many people to assimilate to their previous understanding is his insistence that objects and properties are not inherent in the world, but arise only in an event of **breaking down** in which they become **present-at-hand**." (p. 36). If we read Heidegger's analysis (§16), we find a very detailed description of different modes of concern in our everyday encounter with entities we use for doing something, through which the phenomenon of world becomes manifest, namely:

---

[7] Heidegger's examples of tools are: "ink-stand, pen, ink, paper, blotting pad, table, lamp, furniture, windows, doors, room" ("Being and Time", p. 97). With regard to the hammer – the example to which Winograd and Flores explicitly refer – Heidegger remarks that there is no real opposition between looking at things merely theoretically or practically, insofar as practical behaviour is not atheoretical in the sense of sightlessness, and, correspondingly, theoretical behaviour is looking without practical circumspection, but not without rules: "it constructs a canon for itself in the form of *method*." (ibid. p. 99). Other examples of tools in this context are shoe and clock. Nature itself is discovered (as environment) in its **ready-to-hand** kind of being from the point of view of toolmaking. Finally, not only the "domestic world of the workshop" but also the "public world" with its "roads, streets, bridges, buildings" is **ready-to-hand**. At the end of his analysis (p. 102), Heidegger remarks explicitly that its aim is not to discover that **presence-at-hand** is founded on **readiness-to-hand**, but to exhibit the phenomenon of the world, which is not just the sum of both characteristics.

a) **Conspicuousness (Auffälligkeit):** when we meet tools as something *unusable*, i.e., "not properly adapted for the use we have decided upon. The tool turns out to be damaged, or the material unsuitable." (p. 102). In this case, we do not merely have an event of breaking down from readiness-to-hand to presence-at-hand, but a case where tools, in their readiness-at-hand, cannot be used. Heidegger writes: "Equipment which is present-at-hand *in this way* is still not just a Thing which occurs somewhere. The damage to the equipment is still not a mere alteration of a Thing – not a change of properties which just occurs in something present-at-hand." (p. 103).

b) **Obtrusiveness (Aufdringlichkeit):** whereas, in the case of conspicuousness, we come up against unusable things *within* what is *already* ready-to-hand, there are also cases in which things are not to hand at all, namely when we *miss* something. In such cases, we look at what is missing in such a way that the more urgently we need it, the more obtrusively it reveals itself. Things *seem* to lose their character of readiness-to-hand *completely.*

c) **Obstinacy (Aufsässigkeit):** finally, we have the case where we encounter things which are neither unusable nor missing, but merely standing in the way. Tools reveal their unreadiness-to-hand, although they are not damaged and although we do not miss them; we just do not need them here and now. They disturb us in such a way that they obstinately call our attention. We must deal with them before we do anything else. The *un*readiness-to-hand means, in this case, that *we* have to do something before we can go on with our concerns.

In all three cases, as Heidegger remarks, tools do not become mere things, i.e., tools show themselves to be *still* ready-to-hand in their presence-at-hand. Readiness-to-hand does not simply vanish. What we experience through these three modes of concern is, therefore, not just the *readiness-to-hand* of tools, but *the phenomenon of the world itself.* Why? Simply because we go thematically *beyond* things, i.e., we discover ourselves as the ones whose nature it is to go beyond things, or whose essence is existence or openness. The experience of the unfamiliarity of tools reveals that we do not just operate *within* a system of thematic and non-thematic references, but are radically (or, as Heidegger says, ontologically) open to Being itself as the horizon of significance, allowing us to discover beings in the modes of concern of readiness-to-hand and presence-at-hand. As one can clearly see, Heidegger's tool analysis does not set out to describe the phenomenon of modern technology – this is precisely what it does not do – and it is not intended to be in pragmatistic opposition to the theoretical view of the sciences.

8.2.3 The existential conception of science

It is important to remember that, when Heidegger reinterprets the whole analysis of our being-in-the-world under the explicit notion of temporality, he gives as an example of authentic existence not only the temporal structure of world discovery under the horizon of purposeful instrumentality, but also the process of scientific discovery (§69). Why? Because science is a kind of disclosure, where man must make *explicit* the preconditions for the discovery of beings, no longer as tools, but as objects. In other words, the scientific disclosure shows the *unity* of man and world. The process of knowing is neither a projection of a worldless subjectivity on an outside reality, nor is there an objective world influencing a subject. It is an encounter, where the project of Dasein is not an arbitrary construction of reality, but always relies on a pre-understanding as the horizon for a specific non-thematic-practical *and* thematic-theoretical approach, enabling human beings, during the encounter, to disclose *their* own structures.

Heidegger insists that the emergence of the theoretical scientific attitude does not simply lie in the disappearance of **praxis** (p. 409). To no longer regard a hammer as a tool, but "as a corporeal Thing subject to the law of gravity" (p. 412), is not the result of a breakdown but of a **change-over (umschlagen)** of our understanding of Being. There is no opposition or even contradiction between taking something as present-at-hand and the scientific attitude, merely because that which is ready-to-hand can also be made the subject of scientific investigation, for instance, economics. The main point is not the modification of the kind of *being of things*, but the modification of *our* understanding of *Being*, i.e., of the way we *project* a priori the horizon that is to serve us as a guide for the disclosure. Heidegger concludes: "When the basic concepts of that understanding of Being by which we are guided have been worked out, the clues of its methods, the structure of its way of conceiving things, the possibility of truth and certainty which belongs to it, the ways in which things get grounded or proved, the mode in which it is binding for us, and the way it is communicated – all these will be determined. The totality of these items constitutes the full existential conception of science." (p. 414) The primordial difference between this type of constructivism and a subjectivist one is that, for Heidegger, Dasein's projects are based on the facticity or **thrownness-character (Geworfenheit)** of Dasein itself. Its being as Being-possible is not a free-floating potentiality but a **thrown possibility (geworfene Möglichkeit)**, already got into *definite* possibilities, being free *for* (not *of*) them (p. 183). As Being-possible, we are a pro-jection, a temporal transcendence, always outside with others within a process of *practical and theoretical* disclosure of beings.

Since Dasein is neither the creator of itself nor of beings, this process of *un*-concealment is, given our finitude (natality and mortality), groundless. To be concerned with *concealment* means ultimately to face death as the horizon that makes all other possibilities of existence come forth as *finite* possibilities. Because of the limited nature of its possibilities, Dasein is not able to comprehend Being under conditions other than finite ones. This way of encountering beings presupposes a being whose mode of being is *to be this encounter itself*, a *temporal being*. We interpret the world as the web of relations in which we are embedded on the basis of a finite or temporal pre-understanding of Being. This is not a solipsistic process. It takes place as listening to others in the way we are originally open to each other, capable of dialogue and communication. Dasein articulates its being-in-the-world, anticipating the structure of beings and letting them appear during the encounter through mood and speech.

8.2.4 Some comments on Heidegger's analysis of modern science and technology

In his later works, Heidegger poses the question of the specific nature of modern science and technology. This is another part of the long path that remains untrodden in Winograd and Flores' short cut and that should be taken into account when reading their critique of the rationalistic tradition using as a basis Heidegger's "Being and Time".

Heidegger on modern science

Heidegger's starting point in his phenomenological analysis of our being-in-the-world is actually a pre-scientific view of our everyday comprehension of beings within a practical perspective or project. This primacy of the practical does not mean, as I have already shown, a devaluation of the scientific or rational view of the world. Science is, in actual fact, a *genuine* possibility of our being-in-the-world. What Heidegger is questioning throughout "Being and Time" is not rationality (or even science) *as such*, but the critical problem as posed by Neo-Kantians: how does a knowing subject emerge from its subjectivity in order to establish contact with an external object in the real world. This Cartesian dichotomy and the corresponding realistic and idealistic positions disappear as soon as our way of being is grasped as being always outside, as There-being. This is the reason why Heidegger does not simply use the word consciousness or subject. We are not, as Medard Boss puts it[8], a capsule-like psyche re-presenting things from an outside world and communicating these representations to other psyches.

The concept of science in "Being and Time" aims at giving sciences an ontological foundation in man's being-in-the-world, instead of their modern transcendental constitution in subjectivity. One should remember that "Being and Time" begins with a reference to the crisis of scientific research (§3) and to the logical precedence of the question of Being in order to be able to distinguish between the different areas in their ontological specificity.

Heidegger's later analyses of *modern* science[9] make explicit the differences between science in Antiquity and in the Middle Ages, showing modern science to be a particular project or dis-closure of Being on the basis of subjectivity. Some of the characteristics of this project are: materialism (= everything becomes raw material), uniformity, functionality, objectivity, calculability, domination, productivity, exploitation[10]. Modern (natural) science reveals nature in its objectivity, but this is not the only possibility for dis-covering it. Heidegger contrasts the conception of subjective re-presentation of beings with his view of human existence as primarily open or receptive to Being. While, according to

---

[8] See [Boss, 1975]. See also [Capurro, 1986] as well as [Capurro, 1985].

[9] See for instance [Heidegger, 1975] and [Heidegger, 1972].

[10] For a more detailed elucidation of these characteristics, see [Seubold, 1986, pp. 218–227].

Heidegger, in Antiquity the projective and the receptive paradigms coexisted, modern science superimposes only the projective standards, now founded not in Being, but in subjectivity and, ultimately, in its "will to power" (Nietzsche). But it is the openness to Being that enables us to inquire into the foundations of beings, as we do in science. We experience this basic dimension in our relation to beings when we regard them and ourselves with the eyes of the artist, i.e., when we open ourselves to the aesthetic dimension of existence. This is, in fact, not just another possibility, but the implicit condition of modern science, and its future, too.

Recapitulating, we could say that,while in "Being and Time" Heidegger was looking for an existential foundation of science, in his later works he became aware of the peculiarity of *modern* science. Whether we agree with this analysis or not, one thing is clear: questioning the rationalistic tradition is not just a matter of changing paradigms. *The pragmatistic will to surmount paradigms belongs closely to the tradition it sets out to criticize.* The change from one paradigm to another is not just like changing clothes. ... This is the reason why Heidegger also prefers the term overcoming (Verwindung) to surmounting (Überwindung) when talking about our relation to Western metaphysics, of which science and technology are the outstanding results. The term Verwindung is related to the way in which we overcome a disease or a pain or the loss of a loved one. It means letting our possibilities come over us, individually and socially, and becoming acquainted with them as something we cannot simply throw away or surmount, according to the different modern idealistic or materialistic theories of progress.

Heidegger's analysis of modern science is closely related to his views on modern technology.

Heidegger on technology

Winograd and Flores refer to the possibility of designing computer technology as a tool, and they do so by reference to the analysis in "Being and Time". Heidegger's analysis of the question of modern technology can be found in his later writings, particularly in "The Question Concerning Technology"[11]. The connection between modern science and modern technology is usually seen in terms of the one – technology – emerging, as applied science, out of the other. Heidegger sees modern science as being already technological. Technology is not a collection of tools to be designed according to a pragmatical idea, but a specific form of un-concealing or disclosure of beings. Where does the specificity of this kind of disclosure lie? Heidegger considers this question with regard to technological disclosure in Ancient Greece and in the Middle Ages, as well as to other forms of non-technological disclosure, particularly art. The first approach leads to the conception of *modern* technology as challenging disclosure (herausforderndes Entbergen). Both art and technology are similar insofar as they bring forth beings which cannot, as in the case of nature, disclose themselves. But, in that case, technology does not exactly mean using tools for manipulating things.

---

[11] [Heidegger, 1977c]

This characteristic – already implicit in the Greek conception of causes or 'aitiai' – becomes predominant in the case of modern technology. Ancient technology was less challenging and therefore nearer to art. The univocity of modern technology accentuates such characteristics as control, by considering things to be in supply (Bestand). Even nature is now being conceived from this one-sided anthropocentric and subjectivistic view, i.e., *everything* is viewed as supply or as 'ob-ject', lying before man's challenging disclosure. Modern technology is a generalized attitude towards the world, whose characteristics are summarized by Heidegger in the single concept: Ge-Stell. This is a word that normally means 'frame', 'stand', 'rack'. An English translation might perhaps be 'framework', as suggested by Mitcham and Mackey[12]. This generalized attitude is not something we can simply change *ad libitum*. It belongs to our Western tradition, and it is particularly interrelated with the non-challenging disclosure of Being we call art. Technology belongs to our destiny, but not in the sense of a tragical necessity or Nemesis. Pessimism and voluntaristic optimism are re-actions which presuppose either the idea of a hidden power behind history, or of man as having such power over reality. Being is not God or its substitute, but merely *the very fact of finite givenness of man and the world in a changing, non-perennial tradition*. For Heidegger, entering into a free relation with technology means being able to see and let coexist *different* attitudes to the world. Instead of surmounting technology or indulging in back-to-nature dreams, he looks for possible forms of its overcoming or Verwindung. According to Heidegger, we have understood what modern technology is when we do not see it *merely* as a tool or as man's activity, but as a kind of world disclosure. At the origin of technology – in Greek 'poiesis' and 'techné' – the character of challenging does not entail the primacy of the non-dominant attitude of bringing forth things. This gives us a clue in our search for a definition of modern technology or, in other words, when looking for a free relation to it. This is, I feel, neither a naïve nor a romantic view of modern technology. And it is not, of course, an anti-rationalistic one!

Heidegger's reflections on information technology may serve as an illustration here[13]. What are the characteristics revealed by information technology as it appears in modernity? Analogously to the view of modern technology as a whole, information technology is not *just* a tool for manipulating language. Nor does it suffice to look on it, as Winograd and Flores do, as a tool for designing human conversations. In actual fact it is what I suggest calling the *information Ge-Stell*. This term is meant to recall the Heideggerian characteristics of technology – and particularly that of challenging disclosure – in their relation to language. This characteristic becomes manifest when we consider language from a non-dominating attitude, as in the case of poetry. The crucial point about modern information technology, as well as modern technology as a whole, is not how to design computer-based systems from the hermeneutical premise that they should be regarded *merely* as tools. According to Heidegger, we can only overcome (verwinden) technology, if we are able to see its *ambiguity*: it looks like a tool, but

---

[12] [Mitcham and Mackey, 1983, p. 26]
[13] For original quotations see [Capurro, 1981].

it is a challenging disclosure of the totality of beings. This is not something we are simply able to change, in the case of information technology for instance through a different kind of software design. We must first learn to see its ambiguity, just as we learn to see our image and the image of things in modern art – say in a cubist picture by Picasso – not as the deformation of an ideal, but as an original perspective of what things are. By the same token, we must learn how to see information technology as the modern challenging perspective of our being-with-others in the world. In other words, we must learn to see it as the perspective it is. Consequently, we must consider this perspective as a genuine possibility to be inserted into the plurality of other possibilities of social interaction. By assuming a certain distance to it, we learn to view it *ironically*, by abandoning the illusion that we could cope *better* with human conversations *merely* by readiness-to-hand design and breakdown programming. We do, of course, need user-friendly systems. But their friendliness does not lie in their *strong* capability to assimilate conversations, but in their *weakness* to do so. By making them suitable for conversations, we may be distorting both.

8.2.5 A plea for an open and weak constructivism: The power of software and the weakness of imagination

Sense and meaning or living metaphors and software development

Information technology, as well as technology in general, can be seen as a threat. And we have good reasons for seeing it in this way, particularly where we use it for transforming all other possible forms of human interaction under the premises of this perspective. Within this approach, we see the originality of the perspective as the only possible one. This is merely the other side of the coin, as we might try to replace or surmount a so-called wrong or deformed cubist picture by a so-called right one. Instead of that, we must educate our eyes to see the information Ge-stell in its own original perspective. Discovering its originality by assuming a certain distance from it, also enables us to see it not as a threat but as a chance.

To show what I mean, I would like to use Paul Ricoeur's concept of living metaphors to illustrate the difference between *world disclosure or reality construction through software technology* on the one side, and *poetical world disclosure* on the other[14]. Ricoeur's ideas are basically related to the distinction made by G. Frege between sense (Sinn) and meaning (Bedeutung)[15]. In the field of poetry, the creation of metaphors can be seen as:

(a) a production of sense, i.e., of expanding language *within* language, or
(b) a heuristic function, discovering new *possible* aspects of reality[16].

This last function is not only one of disclosure (revelation), but also of transformation.

---

[14] See [Ricoeur, 1986].
[15] [Frege, 1892]
[16] [Ricoeur, 1986, p. ii]

Both aspects also appear in a perspectivist manner if we look at the information Ge-Stell, and particularly at the field of software development. In this field, we also have, on the one side, a production of sense, i.e., of expansion of language, but it is mainly an expansion of *formalisms* and it is governed by mainly univocal rules. Unlike literature, for instance, software is primarily limited in its potentiality of sense production. Otherwise, it could not be applied to the referent for which it was conceived. On the other side, software is developed not merely to describe, but to *actually* dominate, i.e., to transform or control specific dimensions of reality. In other words, the relation between the creation of living metaphors – a poem, for instance – and software development can be seen as a *reverse* one: a poem opens up a field of possible sense interpretations and can be used heuristically for the disclosure and transformation of reality[17]. Software development aims at a mainly univocal reduction of the metaphorical sense of language, i.e., it looks primarily for meaning in order to transform or control reality. The will and/or power to dominate reality that is at the basis of a meaning-relation constitutes, in my opinion, the difference between software technology and, say, pure mathematics or logic.

Strong constructivism versus weak constructivism

We need, of course, *both* kinds of creative or constructivist relation to the world, i.e., to the field of open possibilities within given traditions, in order to continue being the finite project we are. If, as a result of a one-sided view of the information Ge-Stell, we see in it the only possible perspective, then it presents to us the illusion of an ideal language, of pure intelligence, of objective information, and so on. But if we have learned to see it as a possible perspective among others, then its claims become weaker, and we learn not to believe that our demands are fulfilled just because we adopt an anthropomorphic terminology. Analogously to the idea of conjectural knowledge in the field of science, we might also begin to see *weak technology as good technology*. We could then consider it *for what it is*, i.e., not primarily as a method for the production of an artificial mind, for instance, nor merely as a tool for conversations. It allows both views because it is an ambiguous project of world disclosure. It adopts the perspective of modern subjectivity and can therefore even try to substitute it. But, at the same time,it does not enable this subjectivity to look behind itself in order to become aware of the thrownness character of its world projects.

My final plea is, therefore, not for modern subjectivity in the form of radical constructivism to be given the tools it needs for the construction of reality as a whole, including human conversations, but rather for this global claim to be questioned – a claim common to the rationalistic as well as to the instrumentalistic tradition. In other words, my plea is for *a weak or open constructivism* through stressing the potentialities of human imagination in a dialogical process of sense creation. Such an open constructivism is the opposite of Maturana and Varela's *auto*poietical systems, which reduce the openness of our being-in-the-world to

---

[17] See [Eco, 1977].

the idea of *ego*centric or closed systems. On the ethical basis of the dialogical experience of openness to each other and to our common world, we can learn how to see computer-based information systems in all their social, historical and cultural ambiguity, reducing in this way their, as well as our own, hermeneutical ambitions. To this extent, I see computer-based systems not as a threat, but as a *chance*: as a chance to insert the originality of the challenging perspective of human interactions into the plurality of other kinds of non-challenging ways of reality disclosure and construction. How can this be done? Well, our Conference on Software Development and Reality Construction was a start.

8.3 Language and Software, or: Fritzl's Quest
Dafydd Gibbon

8.3.1 Fritzl and the problem-solving problem

A linguist surveying the challenging peaks and valleys of the computational cognitive science landscape was awed by the forceful arguments and brilliant solutions offered by various teams of guides to the problem of traversing this impressive terrain. The AI team turned up with its helicopters, the software engineers offered their snowcats, the philosophers brought along a variety of skis designed for a dizzy slalom 'alpine' or a circuitous debate 'de fond'. And the local travel agent (Frame Problems, Inc.) had a special offer of three styles of planning: the checklist plus rules of thumb (risking accidents), the exhaustive step-by-step chart (with the risk of never finishing) and the list of things that don't have to be taken along (with the risk of never starting).

However, being a sociable sort of person and accustomed to linguistic study in the field, the linguist sought out Fritzl, a speaker of an unintelligible local dialect but reputed in the village to be a real expert on the area, and patiently learned enough of the lingo to persuade Fritzl to communicate his enthusiasm for life in this area, explain the interesting features of the terrain, and finally to cross the area together, ending up at Fritzl's favourite hostelry on the other side.

Why is it, the linguist wondered on his return, that so many people ignore the advantages of looking at language closely? Reminiscing, he picks up one of the travel brochures he had perused before the trip[1] and recalls the comments of many of his friends and colleagues about *Zuhandensein* and *Vorhandensein*, which he had not found in the local dialect, and *autopoiesis*, which seemed a big word for explaining how Fritzl and the villagers had survived through the centuries. And he noticed that indeed the language dimension was emphasized in the brochure, but had somehow tended to be overlooked: there were sections on language, truth and the world, on language, listening and commitment, even on listening in a background, on meaning, commitment and speech acts, on formalization as special language use, on breakdown, language and existence, on levels of representation, on understanding language, on artificial intelligence and language understanding, on understanding as pattern recognition, on what it means to understand, and indeed on management and conversation and on tools for conversation!

Surely this would have been enough to allow the specialists to get on with Fritzl? Particularly since one of the authors came to fame with a simulated

---

[1] [Winograd and Flores, 1986]

natural language understanding robot (called Shrewd Lou) and both, as well as others they criticize, are in the business of designing and selling helpful tools for the purpose.

Obviously Fritzl has special knowledge, indeed down-to-earth, flesh and blood skills, which are of great interest, and if we can find special technical languages in which to represent them, and strategies for simulating them, for instance in a silicon environment, then we are in the same business[2]. The linguist, too, will need to exercise his own knowledge in order to describe such a special language, since some of Fritzl's skills are verbal: insofar as he can transmit his own skills to the next generation, he has such a technical language already, and the linguist will need to describe it and translate dialogues in this language into a more comprehensible dialect.

Now, who is Fritzl? Although he may be a court of last appeal, he is no abstract 'homunculus', and certainly not a 'deus ex machina'. Nor is he a personification of the trip designer's 'alter ego' when he sits at his desk and works out examples to illustrate his theoretical predictions.

Fritzl is the fellow who can actually perform the tasks required on an intuitively intentional basis, who can talk about them in a rational, analytic, functional manner to those who listen carefully, and who could, if motivated, be trained to design devices which satisfy or extend part of his own bodily requirements or skills, such as energy storage (his rucksack), protection (his woollen underwear), aids to perception (his hand raised against the glare) and locomotion (his skis and ropes), and high-level symbolic representation systems (his charts and maps). He could, if given the chance, tell experts how to make even better tools for him. However, he would get extremely insulting if anyone suggested that such a device could replace him, or the linguist, for that matter, as a guide to the physical and linguistic intricacies of village life in that area.

This assumes, of course, that Fritzl's consultants had learned his dialect, or taught him theirs. Usually, however, an interpreter is required. So it falls to the linguist to outline strategies for understanding Fritzl and either do the interpreting himself or train others to do so. Naturally, there are other experts with somewhat different specializations who could also do the job: the logician, who would instantly translate Fritzl's words into an unambiguous, completely explicit set of axioms, or the ordinary language philosopher, who would discover the conditions under which Fritzl's statements were at least felicitous, if not actually true, or the sociologist, who would observe Fritzl's everyday verbal and nonverbal activities at his work in detail, uncovering pairwise patterns, or the psychologist, who would either offer Fritzl higher and higher rewards for ever more complicated patterns of behaviour, or make him press buttons on seeing pictures of the mountains, thus revealing his internalized mental map.

But what would the linguist actually do? He would try to account for similarities and differences in the languages used by the participants in the above scenario, explain why Fritzl or the linguist himself and his Consultants have difficulty in understanding each other at different levels of comprehension, and

---

[2] Cf. [Fluck, 1976, Weingarten and Fiehler, 1986].

try to provide a link between the methods of the linguist's colleagues in other disciplines and the details of the forms, meanings and functions of language. And the linguist would not succeed, for the same reason that others would not succeed: his own technical language would be different again, and of course everyone *knows* his language anyway, so who needs a linguist? However, Fritzl had not yet reached this level of self-questioning.

8.3.2 Cognition and computation: the linguistic stance

Regardless of these minor hurdles, the following report on the principles underlying Fritzl's verbal expertise is intended to be generalizable to anyone speaking in any dialect on any topic under the sun. It represents a *linguistic stance* on questions of cognition and the representation and construction of reality; the *intentional, functional,* and *physical stances*[3] appropriate to functional models of computational modelling and, in particular, artificial intelligence, are seen in terms of a *pragmatic* stance, the *semantic and syntactic* stances, and a physical stance towards our models and constructs. The basic ideas underlying this approach may be outlined in terms of the following points.

Cognition and causality: Fritzl's cognitive processes are causally explainable by his biological makeup, and are specific to it[4]. Abstract and concrete computational models of Fritzl are selective, with a shifting selection line, and never fully simulate human intentional properties such as intelligence, but are, rather, conjectural tool-like extensions of his own bodily requirements and skills.

Cognition and representation: Fritzl's cognitive processes, and hence his techniques for constructing realities, including the new one with the linguist in it, are knowable only via their representations in his external symbol systems, which are causally linked to his cognitive processes, i.e., his dialect.

Underlying representations: Fritzl's most fundamental external representation system is his everyday verbalization in speech. Fritzl can write a quite acceptable variety of German, as the linguist soon discovered, but systems such as standard languages or writing are more like highly specialized and context-specific technical languages. To suggest the existence of mental representations inside Fritzl seems somewhat superfluous, though external representations of his hypothetical mental states are a scientific necessity for the self-respecting modern linguist.

Reality and representation: Fritzl's representations of the world and of himself appear to be located (in terms of their main vocabulary fields) on a scale of intention, meaning, form, and physical substance. This closes into a cycle when the linguist observes Fritzl talking. Introspection seems to lead him make utterances which we give representations in terms of the vocabulary field of intentions (we know these, because we have them too). These can be structured in terms

---

[3] [Dennett, 1987]
[4] Cf. [Searle, 1980].

of vocabulary fields covering the meanings and the forms of utterances, and in terms of expressions describing their physical form. An observer could alternatively traverse the cycle in the other direction: she may analyse Fritzl's organs and behaviours, say, in terms of a physicalistic language, extract from this the formal patterns discovered thereby, interpret these in terms of perceived reality in general, and put these into the context of intentions which we attribute to Fritzl. For Fritzl, the frame problem turned out to be a problem of linguistic focussing – foregrounding and backgrounding information – and of stereotypic versus experienced views, of the explication of information so far left implicit, and of coping with vagueness.

Representation and explication: Fritzl's initially indistinct utterances, while perfectly adequate in context, may be replaced in the course of time (under the pressure of the linguist's incomprehension) by more explicit formulations which, while not being exact paraphrases, are intended to say much the same thing but more clearly. And Fritzl's own understanding of the subject matter itself is thereby enhanced. This process may continue cyclically, as in scientific endeavour, becoming eventually so complicated that additional storage media (writing, computers) and access techniques (page numbering, computer programs) may be needed for representing things, and the re-translation into Fritzl's village dialect will have become all but impossible. But external representations are no more than external representations, whether as evanescent movements of the lips, the fingers, or the air, as traces on stone or paper, or as lithographic or electrical patterns on silicon chips. This is not to say that the intellectual equivalent of an optical illusion – the lithoid homunculus – may not be engendered by the qualitative leap in brain support achieved with the aid of the magnification effects of the computer in space and in time.

Language, cognition and commitment: Fritzl's dialectal representations permit not only the reconstruction of the notion of his individual mind and its external symbolic representations, but also a reconstruction of Fritzl as part of a larger conventionally organized, aggregate society which is larger than and differently structured from the individual, though not in any sense an organism in the sense that Fritzl is an organism. Innate tropisms (like the ant building its anthill, Fritzl's balancing movements), learned stereotypic skills (like Fritzl's mountaineering in general, or his friendly greetings, or his pronunciation), creative action (like Fritzl's recognizing an unexpected trap and avoiding it, or explaining how to do so to the linguist) define the mutual strategies of the village society for survival or self-destruction. Some are verbal, some are directly physical strategies.

Language and variety: Fritzl adapts his language to different social contexts as a skill, holistically and without necessarily consciously knowing he does, in a fashion which the linguist can describe parametrically. He mumbles indistinct curses when trying to repair his rucksack, raises his voice when exchanging stories with the other village folk, speaks slowly and with a different vocabulary when explaining things to his visitor.

The important point for this report is, essentially, the last: the parametrization of the variety in Fritzl's speech. His teacher at school apparently tried to convince him, fortunately without success, that his pronunciation was awful, his syntax wrong, his vocabulary miserable and his expression crude. His own common sense told him that he was entirely right to speak as he did in the village, that his pronunciation was perfect, his syntax fine, his vocabulary relevant and his expression appropriate – in short, that he was accepted by the community – and that the teacher's pronunciation was awful, his syntax wrong, his vocabulary ridiculous and his expression quite screwed up. Not only that, Fritzl realized that if he wanted to be a teacher he would have to make some compromises. Moreover, he also realized that if he wanted to play any number of other roles in the community he would have to adapt his language in the same number of ways, without any prescriptive moralizing about whether his language was thereby "better" or "worse"[5].

Actually, some time later, Fritzl wrote to the linguist in puzzlement about all the changes due to the tourists in the village, and that he had somehow come to the conclusion that it was all due to the fact that nobody could understand his dialect. Not only that. He confided that since the specialists had all but succeeded in duplicating him, he had decided to become a software engineer and perhaps construct a new reality for himself in so doing. Moreover, he had already found in the process that whatever language he learned, the same applied: Fortran, Lisp, C, even Prolog. And, though he was hesitant to admit this, he had finally decided to become a linguist. A computational linguist, naturally.

8.3.3 Software as language

The term 'programming language', Fritzl decided, is not a misnomer; a programming language shares most common features with more familiar written colloquial idioms except ambiguity on the semantic side and pronounceability on the physical side. This is sometimes doubted, but the similarities and differences are not fortuitous, as Fritzl discovered.

The forms of a programming language are quite similar to those of other versions of written language. Its smallest units resemble orthographic words, and have their internal spelling which often overlaps strongly that of some natural language. It has a syntax, determining the combinatoric properties and ordering of words. It has a morphology (prefixes and suffixes, etc.), for instance in the form of type indices on variables, or in variable names, which express a kind of co-reference much in the same way that pronouns agreeing in person, number and gender do. It has a textual syntax, stating how to combine sentences into coherent texts.

Not only that, a programming language has a semantics, not just in the formal logical sense of a set-theoretically defined virtual ontology, or in the usual programmer's sense of the runtime values of identifiers, but in a common or garden linguistic sense of having meaning in the contexts in which it is used.

---

[5] Cf. [Gumperz, 1982].

The expression "FRITZL" really means Fritzl, and "SALARY FRITZL" really means Fritzl's salary, unless the programmer is playing with the language, testing, or otherwise combining signs in a syntactically correct but meaningless fashion (as we can in other forms of written language, too).

But what Fritzl found when he turned to linguistics was that the distinctions do not stop at syntax and semantics as in computer science. They continue to pragmatics, as in general semiotics. *If syntax expresses relations between signs in a language, and semantics relations between signs and the world, pragmatics expresses relations between signs and their users,* in traditional semiotics[6]. For Fritzl, with his interest in software engineering, this apparently taboo area came to exercise a considerable fascination, and thus it constitutes the main thrust of the rest of this report.

8.3.4 Systems as texts

Looking back on his third-year software development project, Fritzl recalled what an immense amount of paper he and his team had generated, most of it remaining unread in detail, and was thankful for the sophisticated interactive system he was using to generate his memoirs. More intensely than screens and blinking cursors, he found, the idea of paper still conjured up the notion of pen, writing, and all their associations. And he recalled the different sorts of text (at that time called "hard copy") which they had produced. There were descriptions of various tasks, some informal and some as reports, program listings, test runs, program specifications, inventories, technical documents, and a user manual. And of course there had been all that endless discussion about the right design philosophy, the right implementation strategies, the tiresome bugs, and what the user needed to know. And how Mariandl, a translator he was friendly with at the time, had been appalled by the bad grammar and punctuation of the prompts! Some of these texts Fritzl had kept.

Was there a principle behind all this variation? What was the unifying force behind all these written traces of communicative processes? If there was system behind it all, perhaps one could conceive of the system as a theory – but surely not as the private and ultimately incommunicable theory of an individual programmer or team, as suggested by Naur[7]. Isn't it the conventional property of a serious theory to be explicit, shared by a scientific community and, with a certain finite amount of effort, to be comprehensible? In fact, there appeared to be no theory, but a roughly coherent set of texts around a major theme: perhaps this is closer to Naur's idea.

The core was the program itself, which had a precise syntactic specification. Beyond the local line-by-line details, which made some kind of easily recognizable formal sense, the program as a whole made not the slightest sense, of course. It might just as well have been an ancient and sacred, as yet undeciphered scroll. But given the handbooks, things started to fall into place: whole chunks of the

---

[6] For example [Morris, 1946].
[7] See [Naur, 1985b].

program text were given informal but highly intelligible rules of interpretation, relating them to the world outside. And these interpretations could often be followed, with a little more effort, down to the more local details of the code. So Fritzl found syntactically correct sentences in the program, and remembered that they had actually meant something to somebody a long time ago.

So the different sorts of text varied quite systematically in terms of several parameters: by *form* or syntax (small technical vocabulary and grammar against larger, more picturesque informal descriptive vocabulary), by *meaning* or semantics (more precise, specific, highly delimited, specialized versus more vague, general, informally characterized, widely applicable), and by *function* or pragmatics (instructions to the programmer, the program as a 'template' for the computer to traverse mechanically again and again without variation, the handbook as a set of explanations and instructions for the user). And also by *medium* (written, not spoken, confidential versus published), by *genesis* (explicitly designed versus gradually acquired) and along other dimensions.

What a pity, thought Fritzl, that they had not recorded the oral discussion at that time, as Goguen would have recommended; the special features of spoken language had a particularly intensive effect on finding solutions: how often had he simply described a problem to someone else, hearing only "Really?!" or "Sounds okay to me", for the answer to occur to him just like that. The different kinds of dialogue had been subject to quite different conventions[8].

8.3.5 The pragmatics of utterances

So, Fritzl reasoned further, if software development is largely text production, what roles do these texts and their parts play in the individual acts of text or utterance creation, speech acts, and in the constitution of discourses with whole sequences of such acts? What kinds of speech acts are performed

...by the developer, in producing the software,

...by the user, in using the software,

and who takes the responsibility for these texts or speech acts – promises, threats, explanations, summaries, predictions – in the contexts in which they are used?

To gain an idea of what is involved, Fritzl reviewed some approaches to describing the functions of language. The central approach was speech act theory, with some historical background in other theories, and with some contextualization in terms of higher-level speech activity such as dialogue.

The traditional parametrization of speech acts (acts of writing being more restricted) was based on constitutive factors of communication, such as speech producer and receiver, channel or contact, message, context, and the code used. The "functional" approach started with three functions defined on a quadruple of constitutive factors <Sign, Speaker, Addressee, Context>[9], explicating the

---

[8] Cf. [Coulthard, 1987].

[9] See [Bühler, 1934].

old notion that language is a tool, organon. The three main kinds of function are:

EXPRESSION (speaker, utterance), with values such as emotion, conviction, opinion, belief;

APPEAL (addressee, utterance), with values such as persuasion, insult, fright, impressiveness, rejection;

REPRESENTATION (context, utterance), essentially with referential values: object reference and truth values.

Jakobson[10] extended the factors with somewhat different terminology to include <Speaker, Hearer, Contact, Context, Code, Message>, and defined three more functions (using the term "message" rather than "utterance"):

METALINGUAL (code, message), with values involving marking, commenting on and evaluation of the code itself;

PHATIC (code, contact), with the function of creating, sustaining, closing channels of communication, securing uptake, marking and correcting errors, with both physical and social dimensions[11];

POETIC (message, message), with the idea that some functions of language are aesthetic in a formal sense, with intrinsic and conventional patterning – perhaps "art for art's sake".

These views of the functions of language beyond the individual were greatly refined by contributions from the philosophy and the sociology of language. And it is interesting to see how the contributions of speech act theory within the philosophy of language[12] look somewhat different from the perspectives of different disciplines such as linguistics or philosophy.

From the philosophical perspective, speech act theory may be seen as an attempt to generalize over the semantics of speech acts (as the statement of *truth conditions*) and the pragmatics of speech acts, in particular those which do not, strictly speaking, have truth values (such as baptisms, commands and promises), but have other ethical values in terms of commitment and responsibility. However, their *felicity conditions* are quite similar to truth conditions when looked at in all relevant details.

From the linguistic perspective, speech act theory links up with other levels of representation of language: with the choice of words, details of the choice of sentence structure, the use of speech melody and typography to give contour to the utterance, and with the use of language of different styles, sociolects and dialects under the conditions of different relations of social cooperation, competition, and domination.

A classical, rather detailed exposition of the nature of speech acts is given by Searle. Searle starts from the basic premise of a *Principle of Expressibility*[13],

---

[10] See [Jakobson, 1962].

[11] [Malinowski, 1924]

[12] Cf. [Austin, 1962, Searle, 1969] and many other studies.

[13] [Searle, 1969, p. 20]

which includes what speakers mean, but excludes "certain kinds of effects" on hearers – poetic, emotional, inducing beliefs, etc., contrary to Naur's view:

> "A main claim of the Theory Building View of programming is that an essential part of any program, the theory of it, is something that could not conceivably be expressed, but is inextricably bound to human beings."[14]

The Principle of Expressibility claims:

> ...for any meaning X and any speaker S, whenever S means (intends to convey, wishes to communicate in an utterance, etc.) X then it is possible that there is some expression E such that E is an exact expression of or formulation of X...

This connects to the notion of speech act, i.e., the utterance as having a role in a speech situation, by virtue of what may be termed the "Literal Utterance Principle" (not Searle's term), the point being that some speech acts (e.g., "Yes, of course") are quite inexplicit, and rightly so, in everyday speech:

> ...for every possible speech act there is a possible sentence or set of sentences the literal utterance of which in a particular context would consitute a performance of that speech act.

The importance of the Principle of Expressibility cannot be overemphasized: it underlies the whole of the work of the linguist, but it also underlies the basic strategy of scientific explication in every scientific discipline. Starting from a less well-understood notion, clearer delimitations from other notions and sharper characterizations of the notion itself are developed in terms of technical languages, and ultimately formal languages, including computer programs.

For Searle, the general form of a speech act is $F(p)$, where p ranges over propositions and F ranges over "illocutionary force indicating devices" such as word order, stress, intonation contour, punctuation, the mood of the verb (imperative, indicative, interrogative, subjunctive, etc.), and explicit "performative verbs" such as **apologize, warn, claim, request**.

Speech acts are defined in terms of *constitutive rules* (as opposed to regulatory rules, which channel pre-defined action), which are based on necessary and sufficient *conditions* for the successful and non-defective performance of a speech act. These, in turn, build on **institutional** (conventional, social) as opposed to brute (or physical) facts. Typical institutional facts include observations about speakers and hearers in their discourse roles, rather than in their identities as biological persons. The performance conditions are illustrated by the speech act of **promising** (think of booking an airline ticket as a computational promise by someone – by whom?):

---

[14] [Naur, 1985b, p. 258]

"Given that a speaker S utters a sentence T in the presence of a hearer H, then, in the literal utterance of T, S sincerely and non-defectively promises that p to H if and only if the following conditions 1-9 obtain."[15]

Normal context condition (not Searle's term)

1. Normal input and output conditions obtain (such as knowledge of the language, health, non-play-acting, ...).

Propositional content conditions

2. S expresses the proposition that p in the utterance of T.
3. In expressing that p, S predicates a future act A of S.

Preparatory conditions

4. H would prefer S's doing A to his not doing A, and S believes H would prefer his doing A to his not doing A.
5. It is not obvious to both S and H that S will do A in the normal course of events.

Sincerity condition

6. S intends to do A.

Essential condition

7. S intends that the utterance of T will place him under an obligation to do A.

Uptake condition (not Searle's term)

8. S intends (i-1) to produce in H the knowledge (K) that the utterance of T is to count as placing S under an obligation to do A. S intends to produce K by means of the recognition of i-1, and he intends i-1 to be recognized in virtue of (by means of) H's knowledge of the meaning of T.

Utterance condition (not Searle's term)

9. Semantical rules of the dialect spoken by S and H are such that T is correctly and sincerely uttered if and only if conditions 1-8 obtain.

If discussion of the *commitment* dimension of communication (which Fritzl intuitively understood when he agreed to act as companion through mountainous terrain) is to be concrete, coherent, and convincing, then it requires a detailed explication in terms such as those provided by speech act theory.

---

[15] [Searle, 1969, p. 57]

8.3.6 The pragmatics of dialogue

But the individual utterance is not the be-all and end-all: there are more general *discourse conditions* such as *conventions for cooperation*[16], different discourse roles, different *turn-taking* conventions for conducting meetings, for discussion at the desk, for phone calls, for informal chats in the cafeteria with other colleagues[17].

While Searle concentrated on constitutive rules for speech acts, the *maxims* of Grice might be conceived as *regulatory* rules for the relevance of utterances in the whole discourse context[18], together constituting the *Cooperative Principle* of conversation which is intended to enable the hearer to recognize the intention of the speaker[19]:

Maxims of quantity

1. Make your contribution as informative as is required.
2. Do not make your contribution more informative than is required.

Maxims of quality

1. Do not say what you believe to be false.
2. Do not say that for which you lack adequate evidence.

Maxim of relation

1. Be relevant.

Maxims of manner

1. Avoid obscurity of expression.
2. Avoid ambiguity.
3. Be brief.
4. Be orderly.

The maxims may be related indirectly to Searle's conditions of performance; the sincerity condition is clearly reflected in the first maxim of quality, for example. Informally expressed as these maxims are, their appropriateness should not be underestimated. Each represents an important question in the philosophy of language; for instance, the maxims of manner can be taken to refer mainly to classical problems in semantics: to vagueness or fuzziness, ambiguity, redundancy or tautology, and to the compositionality of meaning. Intelligent application of these maxims enables Fritzl to draw interesting conclusions such as the following:

---

[16] See [Grice, 1975].
[17] Cf. [Sacks et al., 1974, Gibbon, 1985].
[18] See [Sperber and Wilson, 1986].
[19] See [Grice, 1975].

Vagueness is not just "noise" but an essential property of non-technical use of language. Why? Imagine a language game with two people who disagree on some topic, say, on whether Fritzl really knew what he was talking about. Even their definitions of terms are different. Also imagine that they are rather excited, and don't feel like getting on to some higher level of universal "meaning atoms" to which they can reduce their disparate definitions (as true empiricists, they might even refuse to do this on principle). How could they conceivably communicate anything without vagueness? But, through the explication process, they can approximate more and more closely to precision.

Cooperation – like commitment, or responsibility – is not a property of an individual speech actor: "cooperation with", "commitment to", "responsibility for" imply roles in a social aggregate. Just to give an example: imagine Fritzl in his role as chairman of a project negotiation meeting. Simultaneously he may at any given moment participate in the following communicative role structure[20]:

CONTROL: chairman (versus working party member, etc.),
STRATEGY: floorholder (versus audience versus eavesdropper),
TACTICS: addressor (versus addressee versus listener),
PRIORITY: initiator (versus responder, e.g., questioner versus answerer),
CHANNEL: sender (versus receiver),
PROCESS: producer (versus perceiver).

Any of these roles can help to determine when Fritzl gets to speak or relinquishes his turn to someone else, and Fritzl may indeed choose to project structures of this kind on to his software communication strategies as constraints to guide or frustrate the user.

Interaction in communication is governed by a number of dynamic factors, apart from the underlying role structures. One such factor pertains to situation-specific turn-taking principles[21]. How does one know that someone has finished speaking, or wants to speak? The cues (such as tone of voice, ends of sentences, lowering of eyes and hands) and role conditions, differ from situation to situation: meetings, interviews, informal conversations and other kinds of interaction differ in these respects. How does this apply to the interactive principles involved in human-computer-interaction? Fritzl found no easy answer to this question.

Another factor is the typical sequencing of speech acts which is characteristic of specific language varieties. A common case is the speech act *adjacency pair*, such as <Question, Answer>, <Claim, Refutation>, <Request, Response>, which may be generalized to a pair <Initiation, Reaction>. But this is not the whole story. What happens when the language tool slips, as it were, and Fritzl doesn't succeed in making the point he wanted to make? This *breakdown* situation, where the tool becomes simply an oddly shaped object, forces the routine, stereotypic running of dialogue into the consciousness of the participants.

---

[20] See [Gibbon, 1985, p. 407].
[21] Cf. [Sacks et al., 1974].

But there are higher level discourse strategies for coping with this kind of problem, too. These may often be explicated by analysing an existing stage in a dialogue structure in terms of a further pair, involving transitions of various kinds, either to the reaction, or to the next structure, confirming the successful execution of part of the dialogue or its unsuccessful execution, plus a corrective suggestion. A simple case:

A: Where's the mouse?
B: In the corner.
A: Thanks.

The third item is often used to initiate an "uptake loop" of arbitrary length (i.e., until patience runs out), designed to clarify the response:

A: Where's the mouse?
B: In the corner.
A: Which corner?
B: That one.
A: Thanks.

Reactions, too, may be analysed as being prefixed by a transition element:

A: Where's the mouse?
B: Sorry?
A: Where's the mouse?
B: Oh, in the corner.
A: Which corner?
B: Pardon me?
A: ??*!@!!

The so-called "empty words" used in such structures are actually far from empty[22]: they bear a high burden of information about the state of the conversation in terms of the fulfilment of speech act conditions. Moreover, it can be quite dangerous, literally, to assume from one's own conventions that all languages, indeed all varieties of one's own language, share them. The conventions for marking these initiations, reactions, transitions, terminations vary from language to language, and group to group, and indeed situation to situation, though the basic uptake loop structure is constant. And uptake-oriented forms – realizations of Jakobson's *phatic* function of language – figure in effect, though at a crude level, in interaction with software systems, too.

Applications of principles related to those discussed here have been made by Goguen, Linde and others[23]: much communicative interaction is stereotyped, and can be easily modelled. The difficulties arise when in real-time office situations, in industrial plants, in aeroplanes and elsewhere the stereotypes based on role and convention are interrupted by noise or unusual events, and real creative

---

[22] Cf. [Schriffrin, 1987].
[23] Cf. [Goguen et al., 1983].

communication based on partial or background information plus immediately perceived changes of situation is called for. The intricacies of language which allow language users, both speakers and writers, to signal this kind of prioritizing of information – the light and shade of the verbal landscape – are varied and complex and somehow, presumably, require to be taken into account in reconstructions of such realities in the form of computational tools.

8.3.7 Fritzl and commitment

Why is language so often overlooked as a source not only of problems but of stimuli for solutions to problems? The main reason is, perhaps, that we are so practised in its use that its "readiness-to-hand" as a fluently used tool makes it all but unnoticeable. And when it breaks down, thereby laying bare the necessity for following repair strategies, these too, as a rule, are present as higher-level, fluently used tools. Further, when the breakdown is so thorough that the necessity for conscious reflection on the conditions of language use is laid bare, these conditions turn out to be so complex, and the cues for indicating them so varied, that we immediately shy away from them and create our own abstract, simplified pictures of language, preferentially the kind of language that we think (that we think...) that we use ourselves.

It should now come as no surprise to learn that linguists have found out that the way we *actually* use language when it is "ready to hand" as a fluently used tool differs from the way in which we *think* we use it, i.e., a mode in which language is contemplated as an object. We tend to think we speak (and act) according to well-defined norms which we have been trained to think are "good". And in a homogeneous society there may well be no such discrepancy. But society even in Fritzl's village is inhomogeneous in terms of the roles of its members, and at a moment's notice it may become more so, owing to an influx of inquisitive linguists and other tourists. And our prescriptive ideas about how we speak are not descriptions of the reality of skilful, fluent language use.

Writing, too, only makes sense when interpreted in a given context, like Fritzl's software project, where the program only made sense when interpreted with the aid of the handbooks or its developers, and otherwise was simply a pattern imposed on silicon or on the magnetic coating of a disk, a template to be traversed with the aid of minimal amounts of electrical energy, again and again, ever in the same way ('modulo' breakdowns), in response to switches in keyboards, in mouse keys, or in other sensors, and producing light patterns to be interpreted much as other writing is interpreted. Where is the commitment, the responsibility, in such traces? No more in the computer than in the pen Fritzl used to sign his first cheque, but either in the designer of the pen, or Fritzl himself, who both share the responsibility, often in legally defined ways. Breakdown for technical reasons? Never. Though our less privileged successors in the next millenium will no doubt have archaeologists who will be puzzled by millions of tiny silicon replicas of Mosaic tablets, each with hundreds of thousands of simple commandments linked with hundreds of thousands of ANDs and ORs and NOTs.

So, having gone through all of this in order to understand what had suddenly descended on his village, way back then, Fritzl realized that he was right after all: his dialect was just fine. And his command of other languages, and of styles of speech and writing also became, in due course, finely attuned to the contexts in which they were used. The specialists had simply been writing, writing, writing in order to use the advantages of a special kind of storage medium with suitable access techniques in order to support selected aspects of their bodily requirements and functions, including those of their brains.

Thus, Fritzl concluded his report, in the beginning was the word. And, not unexpectedly, in the end, too.

8.4 Activity Theory as a Foundation for Design
Arne Raeithel

In this chapter, epistemological questions will be analyzed as everyday problems that present themselves to people doing any kind of work, including household and other unpaid forms of work. The constant change in the organization and content of such work processes during several identifiable historical stages is acknowledged and taken into account by providing a series of genetic concepts for the construction of an idealized picture of human societal and personal development. This originally Marxist philosophy must be, and is, complemented by recognizing that the cultural dimensions of humanity cannot be found in work processes only. Therefore, in a genetic unfolding of concepts, the more basic category of human activity has to be explicated first. A most important insight along this way is understanding language and other sign systems as *instruments for social and personal self-regulation* that are socially constructed, again in several historical stages.

Thus, the Kantian and timeless framing of epistemological enquiry in philosophy – What are the preconditions for the possibility of gaining knowledge about the world? – is transformed by an activity-theoretical approach into several anthropological, sociological, psychological and biological research tasks: How to model and describe empirically the *development* of the respective types of self-regulation (also called cognitive processes) that enable animals and humans to regulate their activities according to their vital aims and necessities.

Computer science or informatics appears in this perspective as one of the sciences of human self-regulation, mainly concerned with electronic and virtual machines used in this process. Software objects may consequently be seen as predefined constraining contexts ('forms') for sign processes (semioses) mediating between human actors, while at the same time presenting virtual objects and instruments ('means') for self-determined use by the cooperating persons.

8.4.1 Different ways of thinking about computer-supported work

In their book on understanding computers and cognition, Terry Winograd and Fernando Flores[1] used the conceptual tools of three very different schools of thought to construct their new foundation for design: the theory of speech acts proposed by John Searle, the philosophy of Martin Heidegger, and the constructivist theory of natural cognition developed by Humberto Maturana and Francisco Varela. From the choice of these theories, it is already clear that W&F wanted to think about humans and computers in a radically new way.

---

[1] [Winograd and Flores, 1986]: I refer to the authors as W&F.

Using speech act theory, they argued convincingly that the paradigm of producing results by automatic machinery – taken for granted in the usual way of
looking at computers as information processors – must be complemented by the
paradigm of people undertaking and fulfilling commitments through computerized media of symbolic communication. Another possible option would have
been to analyze the paradigm of productive work in industrial or service settings
– used in industrial sociology or industrial psychology – for possible bearings on
computerized work.

Instead, W&F adopted a much less complicated way of looking at work processes: the phenomenology of craftsmen. On the basis of Heidegger's distinction
between ready-to-hand tools and present-at-hand objects, they formulated an
important rule for the design of software: *always prepare for 'breakdowns'*, i.e.,
disruptions in the smooth flow of work with a software object, because these
will happen regularly *even with optimal design*. Computer users expect some
means of re-orientation in cases of breakdown, and designers must supply these
in addition to the target functionality of the system.

Finally, W&F challenged the model of human actors that still seems dominant among software designers: the Cartesian ideal of a rational mind using inner
representations of an 'objective reality' to plan and steer a course of action, applying rational methods and following explicitly given rules. Interestingly, the
option they propagated instead was not taken from the various recent developments in philosophy or psychology of action[2], but was imported to informatics
from biology. Building on the theory of autopoiesis[3], W&F presented a picture
of human agents as self-organized organisms that make sense of their surroundings and are connected to other individuals through 'consensual domains' like
language in a specifically human way.

Put succinctly and with some grains of irony: in W&F's book, man appears as
a speaking animal that loves to bargain. Jürgen Habermas' more comprehensive
theory of communicative action was also mentioned by W&F, but only with
respect to those parts of his work that touch hermeneutics or transcendental
pragmatics. Critical social theory beyond communication research is non-existent
in W&F's book. Furthermore, communication is reduced to verbal or written
language; we find practically no mention of body language, nor of the semiotics
of symbolic representations, and consequently no distinctive concept of models
– instead of using the term 'model', W&F speak (strictly) only of 'systematic
domains'.

But there are important fields of design that are in urgent need of a philosophical clarification of the concept of symbolic representations or models: information systems for planning and decision-making, modelling facilities for natural
scientists including shared data bases, knowledge-based systems for the support
(not replacement!) of experts, media support software for conferences, and so
on. Thus, while W&F's book constituted a significant enlargement of the field of
vision, it should be clear that we have to dig still deeper than W&F were able to

---

[2] See e.g. [Harré et al., 1985, Frese and Sabini, 1985].
[3] [Maturana and Varela, 1987]

in their quest for a new foundation for design. Winograd[4] has explained why the above-mentioned and other possible problem areas were consciously disregarded in their book, admitting this as a 'blindness' of their own approach. To keep the philosophical focus steady on the concepts necessary for founding their important perspective was no doubt a wise decision for writing their immensely readable and visionary book. But, to tackle the broader problems sketched above, a still more general theoretical framework will be helpful, providing a language in which the necessary dialogue can take place between all the disciplines mentioned. The system of concepts inherent in this language must also be applicable to the problem of coordinating the various different perspectives of software designers and users.

And finally: by way of a self-application of this general theory to the important, but much more specialized task of organizing interdisciplinary research work, it should even be possible to formulate a strategy for developing software design itself. After all, the activity of software designers also falls under the same heading of computer-supported work.

My favourite candidate for such a general language and strategy is 'activity theory', a multidisciplinary endeavour in the social sciences and humanities[5]. In what follows, I shall not attempt to give a comprehensive overview of this tradition, but will rather present my own example of a *historical systems approach* to activity theory[6] that was heavily influenced by one other candidate for such a general language and strategy for science, namely, general systems theory – as seen from a Marxist perspective[7].

A diagram of historical connections between philosophical authors

A look back into the history of ideas (Fig. 8.4–1) reveals the intricate connections between the philosophical schools that W&F have tried to integrate. Although many professional philosophers have judged the result of their theoretical effort as a kind of patchwork, my own impression is that these authors have demonstrated that some such integration is important, and that it can be done if we do not keep too closely to our 'home bases' in philosophy.

What the diagram also shows is that my favourite, activity theory, has many common ancestors with W&F's post-modern philosophical orientation in informatics, while the ancestry of mainstream computer scientists (whom I have labelled 'Logicians') is relatively narrow and isolated from both other final nodes. This diagram is a biased representation, to be sure, but I think it mirrors quite well the general mood of the group of authors who produced the present book.

The diagram may also be consulted by the reader whenever historical references are given. And finally, it may be looked on as a backdrop for future discussions in which a more lasting foundation for design might be produced.

---

[4] [Winograd, 1988]
[5] Cf. [Hildebrand-Nilshon and Rückriem, 1988, Engeström, 1990].
[6] [Raeithel, 1983]
[7] Cf. [Blauberg et al., 1977].

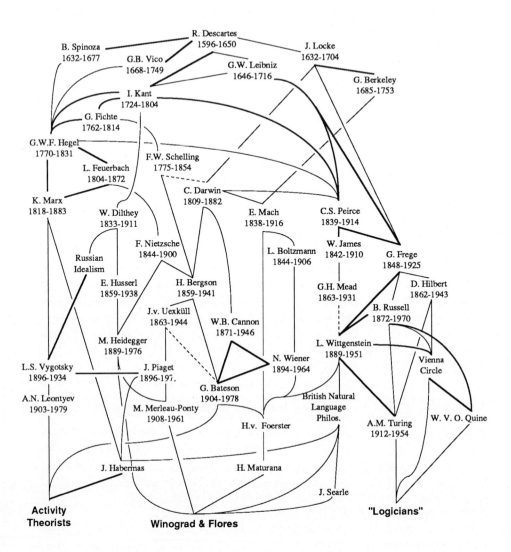

Fig. 8.4–1. Historical connections among philosophical authors

Bolder lines mark discussions, controversies or critique by later workers.
Thin lines show paths of continuing influence.
Dashed lines mark similar orientations, influences are uncertain.

To be really sound, it would have to include also what the 'Logicians' (e.g., the logical positivists) saw more clearly than the rest.

8.4.2 The Marxist conception of human activity

Before going into details about the activity theory, I feel I should give some initial conceptual clarifications of the intended use of the terms 'activity', 'work' and 'praxis' in the following text.

Human Activity: Pursuing subjective ends while producing objective results. – In a Marxist, genetic development of concepts, the notion of activity (*Tätigkeit*) comes first, meaning the living action of humans who try to reach their subjective ends. In this category, all forms of human action can be included, even child's play and school learning. The scientific goal of using this category is to analyze why, how and with what persons do the things they do, and what objective results (*gegenständliche Resultate*) they produce through doing it. These results are at the same time less and more than was anticipated in the intentions – the conscious aims – of the active persons.

In view of this, A.N. Leontyev[8] has proposed distinguishing the contextual process level of *concrete activities* – oriented towards results (objectives) which do not need to be conscious – from *consciously regulated actions*, and these again from the process level of *embodied operations* by which persons realize their aims – again without necessarily being aware of all the details. 'Object-oriented activity' is thus a category that is designed for *subject-centered* study of human actions, their context, and ways of realization.

Societal Work: Activity in societal forms and with a constrained pool of means. – To analyze what Marxists call 'labour' (*Arbeit*), it is not enough to understand human activity from the inside. It is also necessary to reflect upon the objective (i.e., encountered and counter-acting) reality in which persons must currently earn their living. In doing so, we may build the category of societal 'labour' or work – put simply: the daily, recurrent duties of men and women. Now, the activities of persons may be seen as unfolding in definite social forms, which can be essentially characterized by constraints on the available means for action and living.

These constraints are brought about by what Marx has called the societal *distribution* of those means. Here, all the numerous problems of property rights and legislation concerning (not only economic) relations among humans arise. Social forms are, to be sure, present everywhere – not only in wage labour. This means that every activity, when analyzed as to the forms in which it unfolds, is looked at *as if it were societal work* in the sense used here.

Communal Praxis: Cooperative reproduction of means by social re-creation of common forms. – Although many people believe that Marxist thinking ends with the question of who owns the means of production, this is not true. There is another, still more comprehensive category besides activity and work that is

---

[8] [Leontyev, 1978]

designed to include the possibility that *social subjects* (families, groups, institutions, organizations, even whole societies) might try and decide upon the forms in which they will live. But, of course, the really important question here is not how we could build this category of communal praxis theoretically, but how we could invent really new social implements.

This elusive goal of self-determination of human history constitutes the most basic Marxist motive for building an evolutionary theory. The ongoing worldwide movement of inventing and using more human, i.e., smaller and more regionally rooted, forms of immediate or mediated democracy is my own most important reason for optimism in theory building, especially in this historical moment where all totalitarian forms of socialism are in the process of being abandoned for a very long period, preferably forever.

8.4.3 Five essential attributes of human activity

As is evident from the diagram in Fig. 8.4–1, activity theory has a predominantly Marxist heritage that was transformed by applying it to psychological problems, which is, in itself, very important, because the role of persons and their actions was thus much better understood than in other versions of Marxism. The psychological school from which the activity theory arose was founded in the Soviet Union in the 1920s by the Russian linguist and psychologist Lev S. Vygotsky, and was further developed by the psychologists Alexei N. Leontyev and Alexander Luria[9]. The basic category in this theory is 'object-oriented activity' (*gegenständliche Tätigkeit*), a concept that was developed by German Idealism (Kant, Fichte, Schelling, Hegel) and its critics Ludwig Feuerbach and Karl Marx.

In what follows, five attributes of activity are explained in order to convey an initial impression of the content and scope of this complex concept. I keep roughly to the chronological sequence in which the respective attributes were worked out in philosophy and psychology, each time adding a paragraph with illustrations from informatics. Finally, some implications for epistemology are presented.

(1) Activity of a living body – use of 'natural' bodily means

Contrary to Hegel, for whom the most important human activity was thinking, Feuerbach maintained that we humans are living, sensuous beings who live in a natural world that we can apprehend with our senses. Although Feuerbach also stressed praxis, his philosophy was more contemplative than revolutionary. This changed when Marx (who was a Hegelian) read Feuerbach in 1843, and saw this philosophy in his context of political action (he had to emigrate to Paris). In his critique of Hegel and Feuerbach, he formulated the basic tenet that human praxis must be understood as living, sensual activity that produces and changes the physical and social world.

---

[9] See [Wertsch, 1981].

A salient attribute of computerized work is the 'de-sensualization' of human activity[10], i.e., the reduction of the objects and instruments of work to graphical displays of texts or diagrams on computer screens that respond to keyboard and mouse operations. Even in these activities the natural abilities of humans are indispensable, but, of course, they have to manifest themselves as historically evolved skills ('embodied means') – hence the scare quotes around 'natural'.

(2) Activity of an extended body – use of technical, semiotic and social implements

In his political and economic studies, Marx realized that the societally produced implements change the course of history, often against the will of the acting individuals. Accordingly, he understood human activity not only as motion of living bodies, but as activity of *functionally extended bodies* that transforms nature in a qualitatively new order of magnitude (as Vico and Hegel had already seen). Taken together, these extended activities comprise the *mode of production* of a society and are realized in *forms of social intercourse* in which new implements are also used, besides the natural means of communication and cooperation.

'Bodily labour' is therefore always more than mere organismic activity of a living body, and, furthermore, it should not be pitted against 'mental labour', because the latter activity is, of course, also realized by motions of the human body, functionally extended by societally produced means. Only in very rare cases (e.g., Stephen Hawking's) are theorists able to work without external signs and operations, and even then their bodily thought processes are guided by the objective (encountered) characteristics of the 'systematic domains' of thought[11] that have been constructed by generations of other theorists.

As to work with electronic computing devices, this perspective reveals that parts of the virtual machines must be regarded as extensions of the 'dynamic body' of workers. Just as typewriters are handled by secretaries as part of their own extended body, the virtual design tools of a CAD system should be suitable for 'natural' incorporation into the activity of the designers, who are then able to reach and handle the virtual objects "through the interface"[12].

(3) Activity transforms objects, and is transformed by them

Thus the most important insight is that we humans literally *produce a new reality:* Object-oriented activity creates a world full of new objects that physically exist as the material heritage that the next generation has to cope with, and by which the activities of elders and children alike are transformed (contextually co-determined, not predetermined) in turn.

The appearance of the objects and instruments of computer-supported work is produced by the interface that presents virtual objects, and possibilities of

---

[10] [Volpert, 1987]
[11] [Winograd and Flores, 1986]
[12] [Bødker, 1987]

action. The underlying data structures and algorithms are not normally known to the working persons. Therefore, in software design, the correspondence between appearance and effective implementation must be guaranteed as far as possible[13]. Regardless of the quality of software in this respect, we may expect that all new computerized workplaces will produce noticeable effects on the activity structure, and that means the personality, of workers[14].

(4) Activity is itself an object for other activities – therefore social coordination is possible

The self-transformation of human activity is not only brought about indirectly through confrontation with the products of earlier generations, but can also be accomplished by communication and reflection: In this case, the activity of Generalized Others (George Herbert Mead) and its regularity and patterns become the objects of an anticipatory form of activity. In language (oral or written, natural or formal), we can operate with the forms of activity, and thus construe new possibilities of action. Marx has not expanded much upon this *symbolic construction of possibilities*.

The Marxist view that language and other sign systems function like other human implements was mostly developed by Vygotsky. His analysis gives much the same results as the semiotic philosophy of Charles Sanders Peirce. Vygotsky's cultural psychology is also very much like George Herbert Mead's symbolic interactionism (indirectly influenced by Peirce), and it shares the central conviction that meaning is produced and reproduced in social intercourse with the philosophy of the (later) Wittgenstein. Vygotsky has found a very simple formula to express the difference between productive and semiotic means, or put simply, between 'tools' and 'signs'[15]: *Tools and machines have 'external effects' while language and other sign systems are directed 'internally', and thus realize self-regulation.*

Figure 8.4–2 illustrates this methodological rule in three diagrams. Together, they make up Vygotsky's "initial abstraction", i.e., the most simple symbolic form from which the full meaning of *mediated human activity* may be generated by successively more concrete substantiations of the initial elementary relations. Both the structural similarity and the essential difference between productive and semiotic mediation are already visible in this series of diagrams.

To make optimal use of the simple, but essential formula stating the difference between 'tools' and 'signs', we have to distinguish two shades of the meaning of 'internal' with respect to human subjects: Semiotic action has effects 'inside the head'; accordingly it changes thinking, perception and regulation of action – a trivial fact for most modern philosophers. But semiotic action also has effects 'inside social groups', thus changing shared ways of thinking, shared world views, and finally the culturally patterned actions themselves. This profound insight is

---

[13] For example, by the strategy of object-oriented programming: [Bødker, 1987].
[14] [Raeithel and Volpert, 1985], Volpert, Chap. 7.5.
[15] See [Vygotsky, 1978, p. 55]

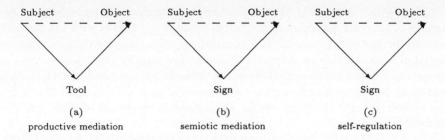

Fig. 8.4–2. Vygotsky's initial abstraction

Diagram (a): A subject wants to produce a mediated effect (dashed arrow) on an object, and uses some 'tool' (bodily means included), on which the subject may exert direct effects (plain arrow), and which, in turn, has direct effects on the object. The other diagrams show that subjects may have mediated effects on other subjects (b) or on themselves (c) by using some 'sign'.

also expressed in Gregory Bateson's magnificent vision of 'mind as a between', as "the pattern that connects" all individual living beings with one another and within themselves through time[16]. Any such social between is internal to the community of actors and constitutes the cultural order[17], i.e., the system of meanings of this community.

While Bateson's wording sounds very strange to many of his readers, Vygotsky's formula might appear much too simple. Indeed, his initial abstraction has to be enriched considerably, as will be shown in Section 8.4.7. But even this initial version will suffice to present a considerable challenge for informatics: If we believe that informatics is essentially the science of mechanization of semiotic processes, then we, as informaticians, have to ask ourselves in the light of Vygotsky's formula: Are we sufficiently aware of our function and effect in social self-regulation? Are we able to correctly perceive the societal changes produced by our own work with our very own ways of evaluation and present methods of assessment?

(5) Activity is essentially social, existing only as cooperation

Of course, informaticians are not the only group of people whose work may have profound effects on the future patterns of cooperation. On the contrary, from attributes (3) and (4) it follows that every individual actor participates in the process of reproduction of the cultural order of some community. Communities, as a rule, are not isolated social systems, but 'interpenetrate' each other in various ways, the more so, the more functionally differentiated the respective society is[18].

---

[16] [Bateson, 1980]
[17] [Sahlins, 1983]
[18] [Luhmann, 1987]

This means, ultimately, that any attempt to analyze the structure and dynamics of concrete activities of individual persons must start with the recognition of the historical, societal and cultural contexts (the 'forms' in a Marxist sense) of human activities. Forms in this sense are socially stabilized patterns of cooperation[19] and provide, as it were, the 'moulds' or 'river beds' in which each and every person unfolds his or her own version of each activity, thus developing the necessary cognitive structures for the conscious regulation of these activites as well[20].

From this, activity theorists have drawn the conclusion that *forms of thinking – of grasping one's own reality and possibilities – develop as internalized forms of actual human cooperation.* If, for the time being, we take this *thesis of internalization* as given, another immediate implication for informatics follows: If computer systems are designed to have an effect on the structure and content of the cooperation of working groups, then they will necessarily also have a constraining effect on what the members of this group will normally think about their world, inside or outside work. This being so, there is some cause for concern about such – as yet quite unforeseeable – future effects of computerized and distributed workplaces.

From the existential position of "Promethean shame"[21], feeling helpless and tiny in the face of the self-produced "Mega-Machine", a person may easily lose his or her usual hold on scientific detachment[22] and drop into the emotional whirlpool of some 'culture-pessimistic' nightmare like George Orwell's "Nineteen-eighty-four", where state-enforced patterns of cooperation predetermine all conceivable actions, if not all thoughts, of individuals. But we may also free our gaze from looking at this fetish – as soon as we realize that it is mainly the emotional commitment and unquestioning anticipatory obedience of a majority of actors that produces the appearance of power and might of totalitarian state authorities. What becomes visible from a more detached position is a variety of interlocking communities and organizations, and a contradictory pattern of conservative and revolutionary forces that cannot be controlled globally at all for more than a few decades.

This realistic view of societies by no means rules out the possibility that forms of human cooperation may be designed locally, in each case for a few concrete working groups only. But these will develop in ways co-determined by all participating persons, and as soon as a new form is successfully stabilized, it may then also be socially generalized either by unsupervised 'imitative' multiplication, or by using the theory produced by the original groups as an internalization of their own praxis.

---

[19] See Sect. 8.4.5.
[20] [Vygotsky, 1978, Ilyenkov, 1977]
[21] Günther Anders
[22] [Elias, 1956]

8.4.4 Epistemological implications of the five attributes of human activity

It follows from these considerations that there is *one most important decision* in each strategy for epistemological enquiry: the primary role conceded or denied to individual human actors in producing human knowledge and effectiveness. My position here is that any post-modern philosophy must be 'threaded' through cultural psychology in order to be able to present a truly encompassing world-view, in which the unity of nature and culture is revealed as a recurrent historical reality, brought about by the social and productive activity of each and every human being.

A psychological phase of enquiry is indispensable because the object domain of psychology coincides with the core of the problem of understanding the relation between nature and culture: Societies consist of human beings, and every one of them starts life as a 'mere' unicellular life-form, developing in the profoundly human environment of the mother's womb. Ontogenesis of humans – the domain of developmental psychology – is a process where the 'natural abilities' or 'gifts' of the child unfold within cultural forms, and all of this must be understood, at least in outline, if the epistemic faculties of humankind are ever to be explained, as Jean Piaget and other evolutionary epistemologists have stressed many times[23].

Thus, the Kantian and timeless framing of epistemological enquiry in philosophy – What *are* the preconditions for the possibility of gaining knowledge about the world? – is transformed by the activity theoretical approach into several psychological, anthropological, sociological and biological research tasks: How to model and describe empirically the *development* of the respective types of self-regulation that enable animals and humans to steer their activities according to their vital aims and necessities.

In Alexei N. Leontyev's early work[24], we find the foundation for a theory of natural cognition and its evolution into human ways of grasping reality. In his later works, he extended this theory by a conception of personality development that builds on the very well known but also quite opaque "sixth thesis on Feuerbach": "... the essence of man is no abstraction inherent in each separate individual. In its reality it is the ensemble (aggregate) of social relations."[25]

I have tried to give an inkling of what this may mean in explaining attribute (4) and the internalization thesis. Leontyev goes one step further and models a personality as a concrete *system* of activities and meanings that is reproduced through the continuous realization of these activities in social cooperation as a contradictory or harmonious whole[26]. It is this holistic process that, in Leontyev's view, produces what the individual experiences as his or her "personal

---

[23] See [Kesselring, 1988].
[24] [Leontyev, 1981]
[25] Marx, cited from [Kamenka, 1983, 157].
[26] [Leontyev, 1978]

sense" of life, or as the lack of a clear feeling of meaning, or as the existentially disturbing revelation that *there is no* one and only predetermined meaning of life on earth.

While Leontyev has concentrated his efforts on the explanation of personal development in cooperative contexts, others have more recently expanded the scope of the activity theory to the whole field of communication[27], to educational processes in or outside school[28], to cross-cultural psychology[29]; in short, a renaissance of the Vygotskian approach to the social formation of mind[30] is well on its way. The development of an interdisciplinary and scientific theory of the formation and development of social, collective knowledge seems now possible, if the many valuable contributions to such an end that have been produced by scholars of other backgrounds[31] are taken into account. In my view, the Marxist approach to societal and cultural development will be able to fulfil this task – precisely because it is going through *a healthy crisis* presently.

New possibilities for political action, for various other fields of praxis, among them the design of computerized work, are being constructed everywhere. To understand all this and to accommodate the activity theory to new societal developments, I have found it necessary to go back to the roots of Marxist thinking in order to reconstruct the basic concepts of this theory. The following section presents what has become of this endeavour.

8.4.5 'Means and Forms': How to understand natural evolution and cultural history

From Hegel's grand vision of the development of objective (i.e., social) Mind or Spirit (*objektiver Geist*) Marxist philosophy has inherited its essential historical orientation. Karl Marx and Friedrich Engels discovered what they took to be the one most important driving force of human history: the dialectics of means and forms (i.e., relations) of production. When Charles Darwin published his theory of natural evolution, Marx greeted it most enthusiastically as a kind of biological backing of his own thinking. And, indeed, the polar opposites of natural variation in bodily means of animals, and natural selection by the conditions of the ecological niche can be seen today as very much akin to the historical dialectics of means and forms. To see this kinship clearly, the co-evolution theories of the New Biology[32] are very helpful, because through them we are able to see that the ecological niches are co-produced by the animal species, in contrast to the received opinion that animals have to 'adapt' to external conditions that exist independently of their activities.

---

[27] [Leontyev, 1981]
[28] [Davydov, 1982]
[29] [Scribner, 1985, Cole, 1988]
[30] [Wertsch, 1985]
[31] For example, [Mead, 1934, Elias, 1987, Bourdieu, 1977].
[32] See [Bateson, 1980, Thompson, 1987].

Operative means: subjective control structures, encountered object processes, and mediated, flexible realization according to perceived conditions

Of course, after acknowledging the basic similarity between evolution and history, the very different time scales of natural evolution and cultural history must be recognized, and also the fact that the necessary structures for cultural reproduction are 'stored' in the world of human artifacts with its most important kernel, the societally produced systems of signs[33]. From this 'storage' humans may take the instruments needed to do their work. It is helpful to distinguish two broad classes here[34]: *means of orientation* and *means of production*. Both classes have precursors in every living species: the perceptual, cognitive and explorative abilities needed in the *orientation phase* of animal activity, and the various skills employed by the animals to reach their species-specific goals in the *realization phase* of activity[35].

In his latest work, A.N. Leontyev has explained at length why it is necessary to conceive of the instruments of work as integral parts of the activity of the human individuals that set them in motion[36]. This amounts to a rule that both orientational and productive instruments should always be analyzed in the context of their use[37], especially if we want to understand innovations that usually start with new ways of using old instruments. In the parallel case of natural capabilities of animals, this rule seems self-evident, since most of their means, disregarding several exceptions like the branches and twigs that beavers use, cannot be 'divorced' from their bodies at all.

In order to understand the use of artifacts in human activity, the general concept of 'operative means' (comprising both orientational and productive means) may be defined as an *operational, functional, and developing system* encompassing the following "three simple moments of labour" (Marx in "Capital"):

(1) The subjective moment, being the regulative, controlling structures that the individual worker has at his or her disposal as cognitive knowledge, and/or as 'mere knowing-how' (implicit but effective knowledge). It is helpful to distinguish "epistemological knowledge" that is ascribed to a person by an observer, from "cognitive knowledge", that the same person may easily communicate to the observer[38]. Implicit knowledge is thus part of epistemological, but not of cognitive knowledge.

(2) The objective moment, being the encountered material (physical or semiotic) process that is transformed into a product, but also has its *Eigensinn* (its proper natural or social dynamics) that is never fully known by the subject of work. Because of this dynamical autonomy from the subject, I propose

---

[33] See [Cole, 1990, Norman, 1991] and Keil-Slwaik, Chap. 4.4.

[34] See [Elias, 1987].

[35] [Holzkamp, 1983]

[36] [Leontyev, 1978]

[37] See [Bannon and Bødker, 1991].

[38] [Bromme, 1988]

to call it 'counterprocess'. In German the word is *Gegenprozeß*, a new term that I have suggested as an abbreviation for *gegenständlicher Prozeß* and as a replacement for *Gegenstand* (object), because the latter term has too many connotations of static physical structures like chairs and hammers. This replacement is especially helpful when reproductive or communicative activities are to be analyzed[39].

(3) The mediating moment, being (recursively) the operative means through which the action of the subject on the object (and vice versa) is realized. This recursive organization ends with the physical contact of subject and object at the most elementary interface. At some quite early level of recursion, the subjects of work lose the possibility of conscious control of all the details, delegating these, as it were, to their 'natural', embodied, self-organizing faculties for orientation or realization[40].

This conceptualization of operative means entails their *relative autonomy* with regard to the subjects that employ them. In the case of animal activity, this again seems self-evident, because we do not usually think of animals as working subjects that regulate their activity with more than simple awareness of their immediate needs and of the ecological conditions pertaining to these. But in our own case, there is still much overestimation of the possibilities of rational control of actions, especially in the design 'philosophies' of mainstream computer science. Activity theory warns against this modern hubris, stressing that all our means for orientation and production must still be controllable by human actors who are, first and foremost, living beings that cannot but rely upon their 'natural gifts'.

What distinguishes human work (and consequently historical development) from animal activities (and natural evolution) are essentially the very different operative means that humans can set in motion. They comprise everything from the most simply produced tools up to today's automated production plants, from verbally transmitted rules for action to computer-based simulation devices. Of course, these means also demand more complicated and flexible control structures, for the implementation of which the human brain has a vastly greater capacity than nearly all other species, and they permit the transformation (but not the ultimate mastery!) of a truly universal realm of counterprocesses, much more than any single animal species can control.

Societal forms: Operational closure and reproductive cooperation patterns

The category of operative means is incomplete without its polar opposite: the societal (international, state-governed, organizational, institutional, cultural, microsocial) *forms of the use* of these means. If we employ the conceptual accomplishments of Second Order Cybernetics[41], we can define societal forms as opera-

---

[39] [Raeithel, 1989]

[40] See [Haken and Stadler, 1990]

[41] von Foerster, Pask, Maturana, Varela, von Glasersfeld; see also Chaps. 3.1 and 3.2.

tionally closed, self-referential systems in the following sense: They consist in a definite selection from all operative means, together with a constraining cooperation pattern among these selected means that may or may not leave open a considerable flexibility and scope for using them. The closure is brought about by including the reproduction of the selected means via other means into this form[42].

It is important to see that the delimitation and selection of means is usually maintained by societal power relations among the cooperating subjects. Consequently, societal forms cannot easily be equated with "autopoietic systems"[43] that are defined as being essentially autonomous. On the other hand, one of the profoundest results of Marxist thinking is the insight that societal forms have a definite autonomy in relation to the humans that produce or try to dominate them without full awareness of what they are doing. Here, then, is food for further thought: How can we discriminate the various grades and shades of autonomy? How can we describe the relations between individual human actors and social systems, both considered as *relatively* autonomous, more precisely and concretely than Luhmann[44] has been able to?

A very important point in the dialectic of means and forms is clear enough, though: Societal forms can be, and usually are, transformed into operative means. As an example, compare the machining shops of the late 19th century, where the cooperative pattern was very much stabilized by social coercion and concomitant self-restraints of the actors, with the newest automatic machining cells, where this pattern has been programmed into the process control computer and the system has thus become a single operative means, supervised by one worker. Another example from the domain of orientational means would be to compare the research activity of a mathematician in the 19th century, who had to follow a quite rigid discipline in his symbolic computations, with today's use of a computer-based "system for doing mathematics": The previous self-constraints of the mathematical actors have been transformed into the programmed rules of the virtual machine[45].

8.4.6 Figurations, actors, and means: Three process levels of collective activity and historical development

What is not so clear is how the *societal production of new forms*, for instance in the wake of technological innovations, is brought about. There are diffusion models of innovation-spreading (analogous to the diffusion of diseases), that allow fairly good predictions of spreading times, but they do not explain why some forms of use of new artifacts spread widely, while others remain a regional speciality. Looked at from an activity-theoretical perspective, models like these do not pay enough attention to the part played by the individuals in these processes.

---

[42] Reproductive closure: [Raeithel, 1983, Chap. 2].

[43] Maturana/Varela

[44] [Luhmann, 1987]

[45] [Wolfram, 1988].

Instead, they concentrate on the relative autonomy of operative means, invoking principles of physical self-organization to explain the emerging new forms.

On the other hand, the definition of societal forms given above is subject to the same critique, and there are comparable deficits in most post-modern epistemologies that picture the development of social patterns of grasping reality as a self-organizing process of autonomous "discourse processes" – i.e., in the terminology used here: of relatively autonomous means of orientation – without explicating the essential role of human actors in 'mediating' (a second shade of meaning of this very general and abstract verb) between means and forms. The remedy for all these deficits is, in my opinion, to be found in the "figurational sociology" of Norbert Elias.

The most revolutionary concept of Elias's theory is called "figuration" and "points to the changing patterns of interdependencies which weave people (both allies and opponents) together, [it] is to be understood as 'a fluctuating, tensile equilibrium, a balance of power moving to and fro, inclining first to one side and then to the other'[46]. At the hub of figurational processes, then, are shifting balances of power"[47]. Using the concepts developed above, we can now state that *the process of societal formation is driven by figurations of human actors*, keeping in mind this observation of Elias, implicitly addressed to orthodox Marxists: "With regard to the distribution of power in a society one can say that monopolization of the means of violence or of the means of orientation, that is of knowledge and particularly of magical-mythical knowledge, plays no less a part as a source of power than the monopolization of the means of production"[48].

Just as we distinguished above an essentially subject-related class of instruments, the orientational means, from a dominantly object-related class (means of production), we should now differentiate between *objectified aspects of societal forms* – the 'uneven' (to put it mildly) distribution of means for living that is constantly reproduced by the balance of powers in international, nation-state or organizational *institutions of violence control* – on the one hand, and the much more *subjectified aspects* that constrain the balance of power 'from within the actors', on the other hand: embodied social rules, habitual inter-individual orientations and so on, whose workings Elias has called *"self-restraint of the actors"*.

Putting everything together, we get the three-level diagram in Fig. 8.4–3, which is – just like the Leontyevian scheme of three process levels of human activity[49] – centered on the consciously acting persons. It has the joint activity of a concrete community, i.e., its figuration, as its *synchronic* context level – in contrast to the biographical and *diachronic* context that is meant by Leontyev's top-level construct, the personal system of concrete activities[50].

---

[46] Elias
[47] [Featherstone, 1987, p. 203]
[48] [Elias, 1987, p. 230]
[49] Sect. 8.4.2
[50] Sect. 8.4.4

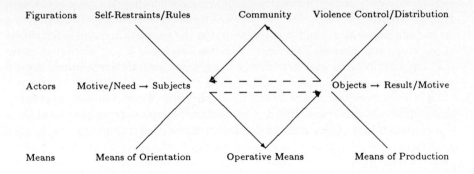

Fig. 8.4–3. Three process levels of collective activity

The actors are motivated by a dual system of 'powers': by their personal needs, developed in the course of their biography, and by the societally defined 'results' or products of the working community. The products are distributed within and between working communities, and this process of fulfilling needs by the consumption of products constitutes a third kind of mediation (upper triangle in the diagram): *contextual mediation* between objects and subjects of work – the dialectical converse of the first kind: operative mediation between subjects and objects (lower triangle).

In the corners of the diagram, we find Elias's four distinct *process universals* "which are common to all societies and with which testable theoretical models of the structure and direction of long-term processes can be constructed. To survive, people who belong to groups have to fulfill a set of elementary functions for each other and the group: the economic function, the control of violence, the development of knowledge, and the development of self-restraints"[51]. In this conception, the highest process level – traditionally called 'superstructure' (*Überbau*) – is not ideational and ideological anymore, like in those orthodox versions of Marxism designed for philosophical warfare. Scientific Marxist enquiry may thus be redirected from a strictly engaged activity, bound to an allegedly clear and self-evident 'class interest', to a much more detached observation of the changing, fluid patterns in which social figurations develop. The results of this enquiry should be understood not as objective facts, but as new means that can be appropriated for the sake of orientation by any of the subjects in need of explanation.

We might add one interesting and straightforward implication: Science appears now as just one special kind of figuration among many others[52], thus the concept of 'scientific communities'[53] can be made much more precise. Furthermore, for the main goal of this chapter, namely the explication of a useful and

---

[51] [Featherstone, 1987, p. 202]
[52] [Elias and Martins, 1982], cf. Amann, Chap. 4.1.
[53] [Kuhn, 1970]

epistemologically sound methodology of design, this diagram may serve as a general orienting scheme, since it contains some essential distinctions enabling us to describe, analyze, and eventually design the organization and instruments of working communities. Yrjö Engeström has developed a very similar diagram that has already been used extensively to organize several "developmental work research" projects[54].

If it were merely concerned with the explication of societal work in general, this section could end here. But it is computerized work that we have to analyze – a commonplace of the present discussion being that computers are symbol processors. Accordingly, we finally have to turn to the question of what symbols and symbolic processes are, and how they could ever have been invented by humans.

8.4.7 Evolution of semiotic self-regulation – From natural signals to symbolic models

It is time to go back to Vygotsky's initial abstraction (Fig. 8.4–2) in which semiotic mediation is eliminated by combining the previously disconnected diagrams into one, and adding retroactive effects. It is easy to name what mediates the effect of the second subject on the first: it is simply another sign. However, it is highly problematic for epistemology to find a good name for the mediational entity that realizes the retroactive effect of the object on the subject. As may be inferred from my using the label 'sign' at this point, too, I am following Peirce in maintaining the *semiotic character of perception and verification of results*.

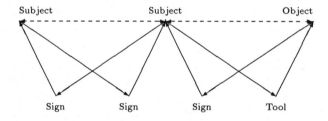

Fig. 8.4–4. Semiotic self-regulation of human activity

This decision entails *stretching* the usual concept of signs and semiotic mediation to also include natural and organismic signals. Objects appear as complex signs that are partially anticipated as an effect of the organism's action, and also contain some parts hinting more or less clearly at the hidden proper dynamics of the object[55]. The difference between anticipated and perceived effects may be easily noticed by all living beings. In the case of humans, most of their effects are realized by using some tool that has been designed beforehand, and therefore usually

---

[54] [Engeström, 1987]
[55] Cf. [Turvey et al., 1990].

leaves very well-known markings on the object of work. In short, the appearances of objects are specified *pragmatically* – a straightforward generalization of the justly famous Pragmatic Maxim of C. S. Peirce[56] to our case.

Up to this point, we have recognized just one undifferentiated class of objects in the eco-world[57] of animals. From a psychological perspective, the most important sub-class of objects consists of the co-specific animals of the same community, because the signals connecting co-specifics constitute a *semiotic sphere of social coordination* completely internal to, i.e., completely self-determined by, the concrete species, and this system of social signs is absolutely necessary for social self-regulation and reproduction, especially for protecting the young ones until they are able to care for themselves[58].

In the present epistemological context, however, another implication of the existence of this semiotic sphere internal to every animal community is still more important: An animal may take the stance of an observer, using the signals specific to its own species to pick up[59] the needs, intentions, and activity patterns of the other members of its community. This possibility rests on the imitative, mimetic abilities of all 'higher' animals (e.g., most mammals) to perceive and re-create in their own activity the bodily postures and gestures inherent in the stream of signals that present a living, familiar, or even intimate subject-object – a partner in social interaction – to the observing animal. Using this ability, the higher mammals, especially the primates, are able to individually learn patterns of coping with natural or social problems from their elder partners, and thus animal traditions, i.e., genuinely social forms of semiotic self-regulation, may evolve in those communities that reproduce for long enough periods without severe disruptions.

It is decisive for understanding communication to recognize that the observed animal need not be aware that his visible motions are being picked up as signs by the observer. This is to say that *mimesis, i.e., being able to observe and recreate activities of others, is the very basis of communication*, not as the dominant but simplified view of information theory would like to have it: being able to 'receive' and 'decode' prepackaged meanings produced by some 'sender'. That the latter model is completely inadequate to understand animal or human communication has been said many times, especially in original work on information theory[60]. It is interesting that this conceptual fact is now more generally accepted as a consequence of the widespread critique of early attempts to understand the use of computers as 'man-machine-communication'.

We now have to take a quick look back into the immediate prehistory of human beings in order to understand the invention of human symbolic communication. The three historical stages of the evolution of human communication described hereafter should be understood as steps in a logical reconstruction,

---

[56] [Peirce, 1968, p. 62]
[57] *Umwelt*, [v. Uexküll, 1957].
[58] See [Bischof, 1990].
[59] [Gibson, 1979]
[60] [MacKay, 1969]

not as events in a 'true story' about the past of humankind[61]. It follows from this logical strategy that the two 'lower' types of modelling must be described in a state of development where the 'higher' types are not yet available. There is not enough space to also present the more complex forms that these basic types of models may take after development and incorporation of later types.

Dramatic modelling: Iconic performance of an activity for the benefit of a community of observers

The ability to mimetically perceive intentions and activity patterns of others may be turned into an *intentional staging of a certain activity* by an actor in order to communicate a complex sign by way of 'body language', including vocal signals and static iconic signs (e.g., line drawings scratched on some surface). Such a *dramatic sign* constitutes a general semiotic type, designating a variety of concrete activities with the same meaning as its tokens. All 'higher' meanings of the following stages thus depend on the "primary language games"[62] of physiognomic communication made possible by the highly developed mimetic abilities of primates and our prehuman ancestors. Recent ethological studies[63] have substantiated the popular belief that monkeys and apes are able to deceive their partners by staging 'dramatic lies'. We may now safely assume that other forms of splitting immediate practical intentions and apparent content of communications were already available to prehumans before development of full syntactic speech.

Discursive modelling: Indexical voicing of stories and the breaking of the time barrier

As Martin Hildebrand-Nilshon[64] has made plausible, the emergence of full syntactic speech is a consequence of the objective demands for complex cooperation strategies arising for a social, food-sharing species like ours that builds and uses permanent home bases for the protection of the very young and the very old. Compared with dramatic modelling, the presentation of a discursive, language-bound model does not allow the immediate pick-up of meaning possible with an iconic sign. Instead the indirect, indexical reference to what is re-presented in signification is constitutive for this stage of communication. But in return for the greater cognitive effort necessary for the interpreters, this mode of modelling affords much greater flexibility in expressing and understanding self-referential messages. For instance, negation of a previous or following utterance is suddenly very easy by using an intra-linguistic index like 'not' or 'taboo'. Furthermore, the multiple and rapid shifts of reference to specific actors of some moving story ('me', 'you', 'the aliens') possible in speech are not feasible in dramatic modelling, except for the most gifted masters of pantomime.

---

[61] See [Latour and Strum, 1986].
[62] [Hintikka and Hintikka, 1986]
[63] [Byrne and Whiten, 1988]
[64] [Hildebrand-Nilshon, 1989]

The possibility of reference to something or somebody outside the actual situation of the communication breaks this temporal boundary and opens up the typically human reaches of time: the duration[65] of memory that reaches back to the times of the elders, the present re-enactment of actual problem situations, and the effective presence of several possible futures – as far as they are expressible in words. The drawback, of course, is that meanings may now no longer be simply picked up from the analogic similarity of signs and objects. Instead, they depend on the continuous social reproduction of the respective language games[66].

Symbolic models as objects for theoretical work

While the gradual emergence of syntactical speech may only be logically reconstructed, being hidden behind the mist of myths and sagas, the last stage in the development of human communication can be pinned down quite precisely by historical-empirical facts. The availability of physical, objectified symbols like the famous clay tokens of Mesopotamia[67] affords to the humans that use them the possibility of pure theoretical and organizational work. While looking for order in the array of tokens, it is not necessary to think about the referenced object domain at all. After having found some interesting or sought-for symbolic result, this alone may be 'de-referenced' to yield a practical bearing. It is clear that human social self-regulation may now develop as rapidly as new 'systematic domains' of symbols can be invented, provided that the operational structure of these domains can be mapped to the operational structure of one or several work tasks.

This general affordance of symbolic models may, of course, be grasped and used only by actors that have enough spare time to become masters in these pure and formal language games. Accordingly, it comes as no surprise to find that symbol systems like mathematics, astronomy and writing were invented mainly by members of the ruling class of archaic state societies, and that this invention was soon accompanied by the first kind of schools known in history. All of this happened well after the invention of agriculture and cattle-breeding, and we might suppose a pressing societal demand for symbolic models some ten thousand years ago, when the growing agglomerations of rural villages in several different regions on earth needed better means to organize, plan and supervise the exchange of goods, the erection of major buildings, the control of waterways, and so on[68]. Space limitations prevent us from looking in detail at the subsequent development of symbolic modelling[69] that finally led to today's electronic symbol processors. We still call these 'computers' because the paradigm of a rule-governed symbol system has always been the computable number.

---

[65] Henri Bergson
[66] Wittgenstein, see [Hintikka and Hintikka, 1986].
[67] [Schmandt-Besserat, 1978]
[68] [Damerow, 1988]
[69] See e.g. [Goody, 1977].

Symbolic computation by virtual machines: a new surface layer of semiotic self-regulation

The developmental path of computational devices appears, in the light of the previous analysis, to wind backwards in history, and may eventually reach the historical roots of semiosis with some as yet utopian technical re-creation of organic self-regulation. At present, however, all we have are virtual machines for working with symbolic models and media that merely *assist in distributing* the more basic kinds of models – predominantly textual representations of discursive models. Today's artificially intelligent software objects emulate just one strictly circumscribed sphere of human activity: rule-governed symbolic computation. There is not one convincing simulation of the next underlying semiotic faculty of humans: the construction, understanding and critical evaluation of arguments in social discourse.

Some bits and pieces necessary for scientific modelling of human discourse in virtual machines might be hidden in the present arsenal of cognitive science. My hunch is that the current wave of connectionist modelling will produce some more impressive advances, because the problem of coping with vagueness and similarity[70] now seems to be solvable by these first specimens of self-organizing virtual machines. All of this is merely of interest for basic research, however, because the excessive claims of applicability, sadly still typical for cognitive science, are simply moves in the language game of bargaining for research grants.

For the design of real-world software objects, it is much more important to know how working communities presently regulate their joint activity[71], in order to eventually come up with support systems that enhance human abilities of semiotic self-regulation. To conclude, a philosophical and psychological sketch of three genetic stages of using symbolic models will be presented that might be helpful for both designers and researchers. There will be no further mention of computers, because they are too recent an invention to have had any discernible impact on these very general and ancient ways of grasping symbolized reality.

8.4.8 Three modes of reflection: primary centering, de-centering, re-centering

Any strategy for human semiotic self-regulation requires for its applicability the basic ability to work with symbolic models, these being again divisible into dramatic, discursive or diagrammatic variants, depending on which of the pure types of modelling is the dominant one. In the following sketch of three stages of using symbolic models, these finer points will not be given consideration.

---

[70] [Rorty, 1961]
[71] See e.g. [Lave, 1988, Suchman, 1987].

The naïve problem-solver: Primary centering, or sorting out symbolized possibilities

As has been stated already, we humans are the only species known to us that may consciously reflect upon their praxis using the contents of a 'second world' of symbolic means and forms. These are, of course, dependent on this very same praxis, because outside society there are no symbols. But, as objects, they are at the same time independent of any single observer, as he or she may use them or overlook them in the course of his or her reflection.

The first mode of such a reflection is entered when the flow of action is broken by events that were not anticipated and the subject must turn into an observer. The surrounding world will be perceived in this mode as a separate, distant array of meaningful things that can be ordered with a view to finding some new direction of action that will realize the original aim in spite of the hindrance that has broken the smooth flow of unimpeded action. All the while the subject remains naïvely centered in him- or herself[72], and is not aware that the appearance of the objects he or she is perceiving is fundamentally brought about by his or her activity. Therefore, the meaning of objects is still inherent to them, i.e., the symbolic structure is inseparable from the perceived reality. The life-world appears as its own symbolic model.

Our normal way of problem-solving thus consists in halting the ongoing realization of our aims, and trying to re-orient ourselves in the space of symbolized possibilities. The things around us have their names on their faces, as it were, and in the middle ages people generally believed in the possibility of simply looking out and 'reading the book of nature'. Since then we have painfully learned to distinguish between this second, exclusively human, world of symbolized meanings, and the first world of sensual and effectual 'things' that appear stable, but are processes with complex dynamics of their own. However, this distinction could never have been reached in naïvely centered reflection, as will be explained next.

The detached observer: De-centered analysis of the functionality of means

A second, de-centered mode of reflection is entered when the subject observes another subject's activity. Taken as the Generalized Other[73], this other subject shows the *relation* of activity and counterprocess, and thus the possibility of functional analysis opens up. In informatics, we learnt some years ago to use the conceptual distinction between algorithms and data structures. In the light of our discussion, this reflects the fundamental distinction of activity and counterprocess in a way that facilitates functional analysis and control.

The subject can even try to see him- or herself from a distance (constructing the Generalized Me), and this shows that the full power of de-centered reflection may only be reached with highly developed symbolic means, because, in the case of a really tough and urgent problem, the flow of activity is so complex

---

[72] Piaget has called this mode 'egocentric'.
[73] G.H. Mead

that it has to be re-presented in a *model* of the process. Such a model shows the relation between activity, counterprocess and the feasible means in a way that frees the reflecting subject from time pressure and allows full exploration of the space of possibilities. When models exist, it becomes possible to understand and productively employ the difference between real, i.e., sensual and effectual, object domains and their analogous symbolic domains.

There is another very important aspect: In this mode of reflection, not only can other persons, their activities and means used be examined – but the natural world may also be represented and analyzed as an ordered and 'lawful' process. It appears that the ability of humans to invent natural science might be a generalization of our ability to observe and understand other humans, a very important point when we try to establish a new, more ecological orientation to our natural surroundings. In a fundamental sense, all pure and much of applied science is dependent upon the de-centered mode of reflection, even though scientific activity cannot be reduced to this, since it is also a personal and interactive praxis and, furthermore, demands choosing among possibilities (see next subsection), not being reducible to the impartial, 'value-free' study of models.

The participant observer: Re-centering, or producing the voice of a community

There is a danger in radical de-centered reflection: The world is 'revealed' as a big network of functional relations that determine the subjects 'from outside' by 'functional laws'. To counter this picture, it is helpful to remember that the symbolic models merely present possibilities and not 'the' reality to us. Therefore, another, still higher mode of reflection is necessary to re-establish the freedom and power of human reality production: We may *choose* (in the fullest sense of the word) from the possibilities to find the ones that *should* be turned into reality, if feasible. In this process of internal argumentation, real and symbolic worlds will be coupled again – after the dissociation brought about by de-centering. A *perspective*, a domain of anticipated reality, may now be constituted that, for its orienting power, is wholly dependent upon the reflecting subject. Of course, the operative means to turn it into an effectual reality have to be available or must be constructed, and it is in them that the proper dynamics of the objects will have to be recognized.

This mode of reflection is once again centered, in its highest form not – like the strategic action of a single economic actor – in an individual subject, but in the community of which the subject is a member. This also means that the split between observing and observed subject that formed the starting-point of the de-centered mode will now be developed into a dialogical relation. In order to enable the collective subject to choose among possibilities, the participants must take turns in *producing its communal voice* that makes the evaluations of possibilities and the options for choice *public between the participants*. The concept of a voice is to be understood in the sense of Mikhail M. Bakhtin[74]. He

---

[74] [Bakhtin, 1981]

was a Russian linguist and literary scholar, most famous for his theory of the modern novel which he analyzed with respect to the multitude of voices that the author brought into a dramatic dialogue.

Eventually, this emergent voice will pronounce the final decision of the community – usually it is not correctly remembered which person produced the decisive utterance; most often it is ascribed to some acknowledged leader. It is only in such a *multi-voiced dialogue* that human subjects may reach the 'highest' level of conscious self-regulation; shared awareness cannot be produced otherwise. Although the paradigm of re-centering is an actual dialogue among people gathering in the same space with the goal of mutual understanding[75], it is important not to restrict the scope of this mode of reflection to *immediate* encounters: Re-centering is, of course, also possible through semiotic means other than speech – as evidence, we might consider the book open before us – although it seems to me that, for *consensual decisions*, the shared presence of participants and the concomitant emotional quality of experience that ensures lasting commitment is necessary.

8.4.9 Conclusion

"Everything that is being said is said by an observer"[76]. The present observer has done his best to participate constructively in the multi-voiced dialogue about epistemological foundations of design between philosophers, social and natural scientists and informaticians. Of course, others will be able to spot some 'blindnesses' inherent in activity theory as in any other perspective. I hope to have shown, though, that we have at our disposal some very general strategies for the progressive elimination of any one blind spot in epistemological vision, as soon as we become sufficiently aware of the blindness itself, of its potentially harmful consequences, and of the resulting need for public re-centered reflection.

Acknowledgements
I wish to thank Michael Cole, Charles Tolman, Liam Bannon, Donald Norman, Jonathan Grudin, Christiane Floyd, Barbara Grüter, Susanne Bødker, and Glen Pate for their very helpful comments in developing the final form of this chapter from the intricate reasoning of earlier versions.

---

[75] [Habermas, 1984]
[76] Maturana

8.5 Reflections on the Essence of Information
Klaus Fuchs-Kittowski

8.5.1 Point of departure

I wish to proceed from the thesis that automation and life, as well as automation and social organization, have to be recognized as a genuine unity of common features and differences.

Information and communication technologies, especially in the area of artificial intelligence still pose deep unsolved problems. Many AI researchers think of expert knowledge as consisting of static structures that can be divided into rules and facts and captured by a representation formalism. They assume that knowledge acquisition is a process translating mental content into symbols, which can be formally operated upon in order to produce specific forms of intelligent behaviour. This paradigm was successful in reproducing some forms of intelligent human behaviour and has therefore been very influential. Today, there is a growing insight that the classical paradigm is too narrow. There is little reason to believe that it will prove possible to build such expert systems in fields where real experts are at work, such as medical staff in critical situations, managers in economic planning, and so on.

All the philosophical and social problems associated with the new information and communication technologies can be directly or indirectly related to one central scientific category. This category is *information*.

It has emerged in biology as hereditary information and behavioural control; in psychology, it is associated with the phenomena of cognition, thinking and memory, as well as with the question of communication and sense in human behaviour; in economics, it gives rise to a key technology; and in informatics it serves as a basis for modelling mental processes.

In philosophy, information has succeeded to the throne of the mind. To some artificial intelligence researchers, philosophy as a whole appears to be "mysticism", and "consciousness" is held to be "largely a nineteenth-century European invention"[1]. The difference between natural and artificial intelligence is allegedly no longer scientifically definable. Hence, what is needed is a deeper understanding of the common features and differences between automata and human beings. Taking account of the richness of human information generation and use can help to widen the classical AI information-processing paradigm.

Reflections on the essence of information are also necessary in order to understand the basic structure and the theoretical and methodological assumptions

---

[1] Cf. [Feigenbaum and McCorduck, 1984, p. 33].

of informatics in general, and of software development and information systems design in particular.

A complex user-oriented information systems design requires practical concepts of information and systems, which must be supplied by the theoretical foundations of informatics. Systems design and software development serve to formalize information and organization in order to replace human action by computer functions. Formalizing information means discarding the contents and the effects of information in human terms, and reducing it to syntactic patterns. Formalizing an organization means replacing the creative nature of a social (actional) system by a signal-controlled system that can be compared with the computer. A human-centred, actional design strategy implies that the application of the computer metaphor to humans and social organizations is inadequate. Thus, a new perspective is called for, transcending the scope of mechanistic expectations about the behaviour of systems and their environment[2].

Up to now, the guiding principle of informatics, and often of cognitive science, has been a concept of human beings, in which the wide diversity of human experience and activity is reduced to information processing and symbol manipulation. This approach assumes that human problem-solving behaviour is based entirely on rigid or heuristic rules and can therefore be classified and predicted. However, it only considers syntactic aspects, ignoring the other aspects and process stages of information inherent in human communication.

The present chapter rests on a view of information derived from an investigation, which was aimed primarily at understanding biological systems[3]. This conceptual work was carried out by myself together with my former colleague Bodo Wenzlaff[4]. We have come to distinguish five qualitatively different levels of organization which support one another. Each level is connected with three aspects – *form*, *content* and *effect* – pertaining to three qualitatively different process stages – *mapping*, *interpreting* and *evaluating* – in the generation and use of information. A synopsis of our view is given in Table 8.5–1, which is used as a basis for our further discussion.

The levels distinguished here become intelligible only if we take into account the relation between information and image. In most cases, information is identified with an image of something, as is illustrated in the common phrase "reception of information" from the environment. We are convinced that patterns of stimuli indeed constitute the basis for the generation and use of information, but that they control the response behaviour of a system only in principle, because in practice the selection of response reactions is much smaller than the set of possible stimulus patterns. We wish to show that on no level of organization does the living organism merely receive information as it exists in the outside world. There is, in this sense, no immediate instructive interaction between the living organism and its environment.

---

[2] Cf. [Fuchs-Kittowski, 1991].
[3] Cf. [Fuchs-Kittowski and Wenzlaff, 1976].
[4] See also [Wenzlaff, 1983].

Table 8.5–1. Generation, use and preservation of information in human communication

		Aspect	Form	Process/Content	Effect
Characterization of information		process stage	mapping	interpreting	evaluating
		resulting in	structure	meaning	behaviour
		linguistic concept	syntax	sematics	pragmatics
		mode of existance	spatial	temporal	spatial and temporal
Levels of organization		Consciousness of Self and of Values	Spatial arrangement of signs in meta-forms (Personal form of language)	Totality of personally selected forms of language	Communication of meaning in personal interaction, creation of values
		Consciousness of society	Spatial arrangement of signs in language (Social form of language)	Totality of socially established forms of of language	Communication of meaning in social interaction
		Consciousness of Environment	Spatial arrangement of objects in the environment	Totality of objects in situations as indivisible qualities	Meaningful reaction to impulse patterns and their cause in the environment
		Nervous System	Spatial arrangement of nerve cells and impulse patterns in the brain	Totality of impulse patterns as an indivisible quality	Interaction of the neurons based on impulse patterns controlling behaviour
		Macro-molecules	Spatial arrangements of molecules and their parts (e.g. DNA)	Totality of molecules, their parts and their connections	Interaction of molecules and their parts on the basis of signals

The principles we wish to argue for are:

- The principle of *irreducibility of information.*
  On none of the levels of organization of living systems can the phenomenon of information be reduced solely to the aspect of form.
- The principle of *no-substance-understanding.*
  Information is not a non-physical substance, a 'thing' whose identity is independent of any physical body to which it may be temporarily 'attached'. Information must be understood as a specific effect and as a relationship.

- The principle of *no immediate instructive interaction.*
  It is insufficient to view the generation and use of information only in terms of a reception of available information from the outside world in order to obtain a direct representation.
- The principle of *information generation and use.*
  Information is generated and used in a process that involves stages of mapping, forming, selecting and interpreting the abstract structure, and evaluating the explicit and implicit semantic content by functionalization (building and maintaining the organismic reactions).
- The principle of *universal interconnection.*
  The aspects form, content and effect of information correspond to qualitatively different interrelated stages in a process of information generation and use, thus constituting a specific form of universal, holistic interconnection.

In our view, informatics has to investigate and to classify informational relationships in their specific quality in an endeavour to achieve a scientific foundation for the function and structure of information as a basic relationship between physical reality and organization. Deeper reflections on the essence of information will lead to a way of thinking that rejects the Cartesian mind-body dualism as well as a mechanistic mapping theory of naïve realism.

8.5.2 Bridging the gap between the formal model and informal reality

Like physics at the beginning, and molecular biology in the middle of this century, informatics is revolutionizing science in the last third of the twentieth century. This revolution is characterized by the fact that it has become possible to analyze highly complex social information processes and systems in terms of their underlying elementary informational processes and structures (formal operations and data structures), to subsequently re-synthesize these elements step by step, and to master them by the rapid development and comprehensive utilization of modern information and communication technologies.

Since the computer can only store and transform formalized images of reduced complexity (or models[5]), and since computer programs are formal or syntactic, humans can only be replaced in such mental activities as can be formalized. But what are the limits of formalization? Human minds form mental content – semantics. Thus, the computer does not replace human information-forming processes, but challenges them and accelerates their social reality and effectiveness by providing reduced models as their basis.

In this context there is a danger of technological reductionism. A formalized surrogate for reality, presented in terms of data, is taken for reality itself and considered as the entire progress possible in obtaining views of the world. Informatics as a science, however, must also develop a synthetic view, because it

---

[5] See [Steinmüller, 1979].

is faced with the necessity of bridging the gap, the field of tension, existing between the formal model and informal reality, between information technologies
as functional systems and the social organizations (actional systems) in which
they are used. Using information technologies in social organizations means operating formal structures in an informal world[6]. Thus, the main theoretical,
methodological and technological problem of this new science is the design of
the relationships between automata as information-transforming systems and
creative human beings in their developing social environment.

Proceeding from the various aspects of information, informatics – by means
of abstraction and modelling – is concerned with different levels of information
generation in social organizations, with basic methods for producing, processing, storing and retrieving formalized social information items, and with general
methods for using them in social organizations in order to master the informational processes and systems of society more effectively. There is invariably a
human process of generating and using information with the stages: mapping,
interpreting and evaluating formal models, corresponding to the aspects syntax,
semantics and pragmatics of information. As J. Searle has stated: "Syntax by itself is neither constitutive of nor sufficient for semantics. Conclusion 1. Programs
are neither constitutive of nor sufficient for minds."[7]

8.5.3 Information as a specific effect

Phenomena like order, information, organization and communicative interaction
have not been studied by the classical natural sciences. Information as a problem
in its relation to physics and organization was first posed by Norbert Wiener in
his famous book "Cybernetics", where he wrote: "Information is information,
neither matter nor energy. No materialism which does not take this into account
can survive the present day."[8] Here, the idea becomes apparent that information
is an effect transcending what had previously been known in physics.

From Wiener's words, some authors inferred that information is a magnitude
independent of substance and energy. On the other hand, we know information to
be a measurable magnitude whose transformation can be described by a physical
formula. This gave rise to a probabilistic concept of information, establishing a
connection between information and physical entropy[9].

The similarity expressed in this formula is, however, insufficient for clarifying
the relationship between information and the natural forces studied by physics.

Furthermore, viewing information as related to physics in no way replaces an
investigation into the connection between information and organization, which is
closely linked with the frequently discussed problem of the relationship between
physics and biology[10].

---

[6] Cf. [Zemanek, 1989].
[7] See [Searle, 1990].
[8] See [Wiener, 1963, p. 192].
[9] This is discussed above all by [Shannon and Weaver, 1949], see also [Szilard, 1929],
[Brillouin, 1962] and [Wiener, 1963].
[10] Cf. [v. Weizsäcker and v. Weizsäcker, 1972, Peil, 1977, Fuchs-Kittowski, 1976].

It is generally recognized today that, despite the success of classical information theory, its application in biology is facing certain limits because it is only concerned with sources and channels of information. Not even technical-logical networks can be given adequate consideration with this concept of information, much less so neural networks. The classical information theory of Shannon can be fruitfully applied to account for some aspects of molecular structures[11], but as it is insufficient for treating the dynamic interactions of complex systems, attempts are being repeatedly made to develop further-going measures of information[12].

The relationship of cybernetics to physics, as well as to biology, is currently a much discussed topic. The extreme positions taken are either that cybernetics can be reduced to physics, or that cybernetics and physics have hardly any point of contact.

Information is embedded in the interaction of the natural physical forces, and it allows a new dimension for determining the way they act. In examining how information is physically possible, the discussion of the essence of information is closely related to physics. In looking at what information brings about, it is related to biology and to all branches of science concerned with the investigation of organization. According to our view, the essence of information can only be grasped if we regard the structure and function of information as a basic relationship between the physical effect of natural forces and organization. We need to recognize that information is itself a physical structure and, at the same time, a force dominating physical structure[13].

Taking such a view, we can avoid one-sided positions that reduce information as an effect to the realm of physics or that hypostatize information as a completely independent magnitude. Thus, we consider information to be a specific effect, which we can describe as follows: On the basis of recognition, reception and processing of environmental states as signals, it is not the physical structures in themselves that cause a direct or indirect response, but rather their meanings which become immediately effective. Hence, we shall only speak of information where it is possible to attribute meaning to a structure, so as to bring about the teleonomical behaviour of a system.

8.5.4 Information as a relation rather than a substance

In studying the essence of information in living systems it became apparent that here information is not simply transmitted in one-sided, directed processes. Instead, the exchange takes place in a meaningful context allowing an evaluation and a creation anew. This evaluation as the central process stage of information has an effect. "The semantic of the semantic is the pragmatic", as E. von Weizsäcker has shown[14].

---

[11] Cf. [Koref, 1987].
[12] Cf. [Völz, 1982, Völz, 1983].
[13] Cf. [Fuchs-Kittowski and Wenzlaff, 1976].
[14] See [v. Weizsäcker, 1972].

In order to understand information, cybernetics has produced models such as the computer metaphor, by which it is possible to grasp some characteristics of information in a first step. In biology, however, we need to pay attention to a basic difference between technical-cybernetic systems and living organisms. The technical self-organizing systems (or machines) as originally considered[15] cannot become self-organizing by themselves. Their self-organization is not caused by a qualitative change of internal states, but solely by the environment, by the inputs actuating the system. Thus, such a machine is not self-organizing on the basis of its inherent contradictions, but must be connected to another machine[16].

Development, on the other hand, is based on the inherent contradictions in matter, which give it the capability of self-motion and self-organization. Hence the models, the metaphors, the concepts tailored to technical-cybernetic systems must be extended and deepened in order to take account of the natural progressive differentiation and development and the generation of information. Thus, when Manfred Eigen discussed the general question of self-organization of matter, he proceeded beyond the limits of the original concept of self-organization for technical systems[17].

The decisive fact here is that information develops by a process of self-selection. Self-organization is not, or not merely, the result of receiving already existing information from the environment, but the result of the emergence and reproduction of biological and pre-biotic macromolecular systems, in the course of which information is increased by the optimization of the selection value in mutual competition.

In accordance with the view predominant today, the nervous system is held to be an instrument used by the living organism to receive information from the environment as a basis for building up a representation of the outside world, allowing the organism to optimize its behaviour. H. R. Maturana and F. J. Varela[18] have shown, however, that it is the nervous system that uses the pattern of stimuli, the incoming signals, to generate behaviour. This means that the structure of the environment only stimulates changes in the structure of the nervous system but does not determine them. In the interaction between a living organism and its environment, the 'perturbations' of the environment do not determine what happens to the living organism; it is the structure of the living organism which determines the changes provoked by the perturbation.

At the one extreme, we have a mechanistic view: the nervous system works with representations of the outside world; information is a substance, and the mind like a vessel receiving and storing information. If we adopt this view, we forfeit the possibility of understanding the nervous system as an operationally closed system with ever new possible structures emerging from one moment to the next.

---

[15] For example in [Ashby, 1960, v. Foerster and Zopf, 1962]. Von Foerster later enriched his concept of self-organization substantially ([v. Foerster, 1985, pp. 4–5]; see also Chap. 3.1).

[16] Cf. [Fuchs-Kittowski and Rosenthal, 1972].

[17] Cf. [Eigen, 1971].

[18] Cf. [Maturana and Varela, 1987].

Maturana and Varela show that it would be a great mistake to understand the nervous system as an input-output system because of its operational closedness. Their view, on the other hand, implies the danger of solipsism. We might be led to the other extreme, eliminating the existence of an environment and holding that the nervous system functions in a vacuum. Maturana tries to solve this dilemma by introducing an observer with a different perspective. He argues that the nervous system should not be seen from either of these two extreme positions, since it works neither in a representationistic nor in a solipsistic manner. One important conclusion is that the computer metaphor for the brain is not only misleading, it is simply wrong[19].

8.5.5 Information and the human mind

Philosophy has long been concerned with the question: What is mind? Ever since Plato declared that mind and body differ fundamentally, philosophers have discussed the nature of mind and the mind-body problem.

It has become fashionable to relate the intellectual and cultural problems of the present day with Cartesian thinking, which relies on a separation of mind and matter, of *res cogitans* and *res extensa*. There is hope now that this gap can finally be bridged. According to Descartes' dualistic theory, mind is a substance, not of a physical nature, but something of which thoughts are made. In the history of philosophy, great efforts have been made to overcome this substance view of mind.

Various monist alternatives to the dualistic concept were developed. An extreme contrary position is adopted by mechanistic materialism, which ultimately denies the existence of mind, regarding mental processes as nothing other than physical processes. Another extreme is postulated by subjective idealism, according to which the physical world does not exist at all, everything being held to be perception.

More recently, philosophy has been joined by psychology, neurobiology, evolution theory and artificial intelligence – to name some of the branches of science striving towards an understanding of the nature of the human mind.

Also, the system of scientific categories developed for describing computers, such as the distinction between hardware and software, has given rise to new views of thought and consciousness, and has compelled various scientific disciplines to think about the human mind more poignantly than before.

Modern research focusses on elucidating the mechanisms of thought and the connection between the mind and the brain. As the brain, in the course of its evolution, became more and more complex, composed of an intricately interlinked network of large numbers of nerve cells, it acquired the capacity to perform increasingly sophisticated functions, culminating ultimately in human intelligence and in mental states such as feelings and beliefs.

The dualistic view suggests that mind is a distinct "non-physical substance" forever beyond the scope of sciences like physics, neurobiology and computer

---

[19] See [Maturana and Varela, 1987, p. 185].

science. This idea underlies the separation of hardware and software in functionalism, the basic paradigm in traditional AI research, but is opposed by cognitive
neurobiology as a basis for understanding the cognitive activities specifically
displayed by living organisms[20].

By contrast, the mechanistic-materialist view holds that mind 'is' the brain.
But even if we were able to give a scientific explanation of the evolutionary and
embryonic origins of the brain in general terms, we would still face the problem
of how to refer to mental states in terms of brain states – electrical activity
patterns in the networks of cerebral nerve cells.

The possibility of such a reductionist explanation of the human mind is rejected by many philosophers, psychologists and neurobiologists because of the
intentional character of mental phenomena and the introspective nature of their
perception. Nevertheless, it gains new momentum in connection with the changing AI paradigm – from functionalism to connectivism. We hold that reduction
as a method is necessary, but that it is too narrow to capture the whole. Mental
phenomena arise in the brain and must therefore, in principle, be explicable in
terms of neurobiological theories. But our view implies that a total reduction –
reductionism as a philosophical position – is not possible in practice.

The reason for this is the extreme complexity of the specific organization
of mental phenomena. This limits the extent to which theories developed to
explain them can be successfully reduced by theories developed to explain less
complex phenomena. This applies, in particular, to the process of generating,
using and preserving information. Higher complexity allows for interactions in a
greater variety of ways, so that new qualities arise as compared with less complex
phenomena.

There are now several competing theories for describing the connection between
the mind and the brain:

- Mind and matter are two (or several) levels of description of a single whole,
  like the levels of hardware and software (Functionalism[21]).
- Learning is a process of behaviour transformation through continuous change
  in the capacity of the nervous system for synthesizing it, rather than a process
  of accumulating representations of the environment (Autopoiesis[22]).
- Mind is not separate from matter, but is a self-organizing quality of matter,
  co- ordinating its spatial-temporal structure (Theory of Self-Organization[23]).
- Mind is not a part of the human being, but the human being as a whole
  embodies mind (Principle of Complementarity[24]). It implies, in our view,
  the consequence that abstract descriptions of mental processes, as obtained
  by applying computer-oriented categories, must be enhanced as soon as they
  are inserted into the general context of studying the human mind.

---

[20] See [Churchland, 1986].
[21] See [Fodor, 1981].
[22] See [Maturana, 1980].
[23] See [Jantsch, 1980].
[24] See [Delbrück, 1986].

In the remainder of this section, we will look at some of these theories in more detail and relate them to our concept of information with its different levels and process stages and to our understanding of the complementarity of part and whole.

From the point of view of functionalism, the essential constituent of mind is not the 'hardware' of which the brain is composed, but the 'software' consisting of the mental processes. As in studying computer applications, we need to distinguish these two different levels of causal description, without being obliged to consider the manner in which the one affects the other. The old philosophical question as to how the mind influences the body simply amounts to an interpenetration of two levels of terms in which the brain level can normally be disregarded, just as we do not usually care how a program brings about the changes required in the circuits of a computer for solving an equation.

It is clear, then, for functionalism that machines can also think and feel, at least in principle. But we need to be very cautious in dealing with the computer metaphor. For one thing, as we see in Table 8.5–1, the levels taken from computer science do not appropriately define the levels of organization in the brain. It is evident here that there are many levels of organization between the uppermost and the intercellular level of molecular dynamics, each level being associated with syntactic, semantic and pragmatic aspects of information.

By contrast, a computer only manipulates the symbols of some formal system according to rules which must be explicit, at least in the program of the virtual machine. Efforts in artificial intelligence research are directed towards finding better heuristics and better algorithms for implementing them on the machine. Since computer programs are formal, they can only take into account the syntactic aspects of information.

The symbols manipulated by the computer may, however, have interpretations that relate them to the outside world. This is the domain of semantics and pragmatics. In general, semantic properties are not formal. The idea that an automatic, formal system with an interpretation such that the semantic aspect will take care of itself – a semantic engine – is possible, that, given the right kind of formal interpretation, a machine could handle meanings, is the driving force behind AI research and cognitive science[25]. But compared to natural language and natural intelligence, mathematics and logic, the basis for formalizable semantics, constitute only a limited and special area.

Thus, cybernetics and computer science introduce new aspects into the mind-body problem, which has been the subject of heated argument over the centuries, and provide new suggestions for addressing it. But they do not really overcome either mechanistic or dualistic positions because of the substance view of information[26] and the separation of psychology from neurobiology[27] implied by the two levels of description.

---

[25] Cf. [Haugeland, 1981].
[26] Cf. [Fuchs-Kittowski, 1983].
[27] Cf. [Churchland, 1986].

A recent development in cognitive science is the emphasis on mental states and their relations with psychology and neurobiology[28]. But we feel that this is not sufficient. The 'vessel theory' of mind itself, based as it is on the substance concept of information underlying the information-processing paradigm, needs to be overcome. This would require a change in the research paradigm of artificial intelligence, probably going well beyond connectivism[29].

We now turn to alternatives to dualism, of which mechanistic materialism – that views everything, including mind, merely as matter in one form or another – is not the main or only possible one. For example, it is well known that semiotics has long called for the semantic or pragmatic aspects of information to be taken into account as well[30]. But since these aspects cannot be represented in terms of bits – and the computer is merely a bit-processing machine – they are often simply disregarded.

The theory of self-organization, on the other hand, views mind not as something separate from matter, but as a self-organizing quality of the dynamic processes which take place in a system and its relationships with the environment. Whereas functionalism essentially identifies mind with information and reduces the discussion of both to syntactic aspects and storable form, the theory of self-organization or self-structuring, as advocated by E. Jantsch[31] among others, understands mind as a dynamic principle organizing information in living systems. Information should neither be identified nor separated from mind.

Returning to our view of information as shown in Table 8.5-1, we need to consider in particular the relationship between information and mind, storage and memory[32], program and thinking, taking into account the specific features of living and social organization, of the processes generating information and creating values in contrast with technical, purely physical systems.

Let us therefore take another look at the aspects of information and their related process stages: the structure or syntax connected with mapping, the meaning or semantics associated with interpretation, and the effect or pragmatics resulting from evaluation. These aspects in their interrelation on different levels of organization of living systems describe the spatial and temporal mode of existence of information as specific stages in a process of generating and using information.

Philosophy has argued a great deal about whether mind should be explained in terms of matter, or matter in terms of mind; but, regrettably, there have been few ideas developed about the mode of existence of mind. The mode of existence of matter, as already recognized by Descartes, is space. The term *res extensa* (the extended thing) is a pointed expression of it. Everything existing in space is matter. But are there any phenomena at all which do not exist in space?

---

[28] See [Berleur and Brunnstein, 1990].

[29] See [Lischka and Diederich, 1987, pp. 21–31] and [Dreyfus, 1979].

[30] See [Morris, 1938, Klaus, 1973].

[31] Cf. [Jantsch, 1980].

[32] Cf. [Elsasser, 1982].

When endeavours were made to define information as necessarily existing in space, astounding successes were initially achieved (as previously with the consistent mechanistic-materialist explanation of the world). Yet every explanation of this kind is inadequate if it tries to dispense with the subjective, the mind, the consciousness.

Instead, we need concrete ways for understanding the mode of existence and performance of mental phenomena or – to put it more modestly – of information in all its aspects and process stages. But not only are we reluctant to ascribe thought and feelings to 'mere' matter, we also find it very hard to ascribe shape and location to minds or ideas. This is because mind does not possess any spatial existence. Only the syntax of an information item can be stored, which again is worthless without its semantics. Therefore, time has to be considered the mode of existence of mind.

According to Hegel[33], "mind appears" necessarily in time, not in the elapse of time as a succession of time points, but in the duration of time, the period available for comparing things with one another. This requires a memory[34]. The main consequence of this approach is that meaning does not exist in space: meaning is not storable, not reducible to its form; it needs a dynamic memory. On the other hand, the meaning of information cannot exist independently of its form[35].

It is fairly clear that today a computer is an automatic, formal system, a physical device capable of communicating and transforming signals and manipulating symbols. The distinction of levels and process stages shown in Table 8.5–1 clearly indicates that the areas in which the computer excels today, or can in future be expected to excel, are all of a special kind. They comprise those fields in which all aspects of information can be fixed, and thus reduced content and effects of information can be formalized. These fields include formal games and routine technical or microworld tasks.

Such a formal system, however, has no consciousness of the environment, of society, or of values. Considering the consciousness of values leads us on to the personal content of language, the communication of meaning as a main means of personal interaction and the creation of new values.

We can also infer that the intelligence manifested in everyday life, especially in art, invention, discovery and creative social interaction, is not merely of the same formal kind, only of greater complexity. Here, we need to take into account all three aspects of information – generating new content and pragmatic purposes for information items, and new values for using information in a human context.

---

[33] See [Hegel, 1964, p. 558, p. 38, p. 560].

[34] Cf. [Bateson, 1980].

[35] Postulating the free existence of meaning would be like postulating the free existence of consciousness, the *Weltgeist* of Hegel.

8.5.6 The interrelation between form, content and effect of information

As we have seen, the phenomenon of information is not reducible to its spatial mode of existence. On all levels of organization of living systems, information is not merely imported from the outside world, nor is learning a process of accumulation of representations; there are distinct stages in the process of generation and use of information. In this section, we look at the interrelation between these stages as it applies to the different levels.

Level 1:

At the beginning of evolution, there was only uninformed interaction. Macromolecules can already do more: they can recognize one another and thus select and be selected. All present-day forms of life have a unified chemical organization, which is manifest in the albumin-nucleic acid interaction as the structure of hereditary information and in the capability of proteins to interpret this structure and to receive and respond to external signals.

Thus, even on this basic level of organization, living organisms receive signals from the environment and form rudimentary meanings in the sense that they have a structure allowing them to respond in a suitable manner. Through the interpretation of the DNA structure by the proteins and their interaction with other structures in the course of ontogenetic development, there arises an explicit and an implicit semantic content of the genetic information which is only produced in the context of the structures realized already.

Hence, even on the molecular organizational level of living organisms, it is necessary to take into account the interrelation between mapping, interpreting and evaluating information in the process of generating, using and preserving information.

Level 2:

It is the task of programs laid down in the nervous system to process signals arriving from the environment. They are attributed a meaning and evaluated so as to produce meaningful behaviour patterns. Here, information is not simply received from the outside world, but an enormous condensation of signals takes place, which amounts to an abstraction bringing out the qualities of things, their meaning.

Connected with this formation of meaning for states of excitement is the emergence of the human mind on the basis of the nervous system. The investigation of the human cortex and of vision shows that the signals are transformed into meanings in a process of selection of specific impulse patterns. Hence, what we see are not primary signals or crude data, but qualities of an object that are abstracted from sensory stimuli and that mean something to us. On this level of living organization, signals are processed in a pre-conscious manner, which is inaccessible to introspection, on the basis of the programs acquired in the course of evolution.

Level 3:

The way the brain works has to become relatively independent of the genome because the relationships between an organism and the environment are only formed in the course of individual life. The nervous system attains such a complexity that, on the organismic behaviour level, the corresponding external stimulus – the perceived sensation – constitutes only a minor part of the entire functional organization. The important thing is that we can attribute meanings to the source of stimulation.

What this essentially implies is that, on this level of organization, we register not only a stimulation on the retina or in the brain, but the actual object of the outside world, e.g., a tree. This is not the result of an accumulation of representations of the environment in the brain; humans can use the objects of the environment to store representations in a continuous process[36]. To the extent that we use the invariant properties of the environment for mapping (encoding) the meanings of information items, the objects of the environment also supply meaningful signals, and it is only in this sense that the human brain 'receives information' from the environment. As a result of a long ongoing process in which objects of the outside world become meaningful, they are able to provoke a cognition.

Level 4:

In the further course of development, a more and more powerful, complex central organ emerged, capable of forming intricate and increasingly free connections, leading to networks of connected internal relationships based on already available information items. To do this, a special mechanism was needed, language emerged, allowing us to represent and freely manipulate concrete facts with the help of a spatial arrangement of signs relying on abstract symbols.

If we accept the principle that information is not simply received from the outside world, we also have to break with the widely-accepted view that language is a vehicle for carrying information. Instead, language stimulates understanding arising in dialogues between people. Information is generated in mutual processes of mapping, abstracting the quality of things, giving rise to their meaning and the possibility of their evaluation.

The brain that has emerged during biological evolution (by pressure of selection) does more than merely adapt the organism to the immediately perceived environment. It enables us to obtain deep insights into the world of mathematics, into the microcosm and macrocosm of matter, as well as into the organization of life and the mind. Building on the results of biological evolution, there began social evolution relying on social experience, making it no longer necessary for individuals to experience everything themselves in order to obtain insights. "Intelligence has to be motivated by purposes in the organism and other goals picked up by the organism from an on-going culture."[37]

---

[36] See also Keil-Slawik, Chap. 4.4
[37] See [Dreyfus, 1979].

Human beings must lay down identifiable and mutually shared meanings in order to transmit informational structures. On the level of social consciousness, insights are needed into the intrinsic laws of natural and social development.

Level 5:

If we are concerned with the self-development of the human personality, then we proceed from the assumption that human beings live in society and follow the social values which have been formed in the process of social development. Values serve to reduce the complexity of human behaviour, of human actions and interests. At the same time, the development of society is also the development of its system of values. Values belong to the pragmatic aspect, the process stage of evaluation of information. They serve to select the meanings of the informational structures in order to produce certain effects in terms of actions.

By means of language and the values created and accepted (not merely transmitted) in social communication, it is possible to say "No" in answer to a request, to say "I don't want to", or to ask "What for?". Reflection on the purpose of individual life and on the goals for self-development of personality determines behaviour in society and the efforts aimed at successful political action.

8.5.7 Information in the relation of mapping, interpretation, and evolution

Mental content is communicated mainly by means of language. Today, we are able to build machines endowed to some extent with this ability. For example,Terry Winograd developed a program capable of decoding the syntax and semantics of sentences pertaining to a narrowly circumscribed world with a limited history[38]. Since then, machine language-processing has made progress and is likely to make further advances in the years to come[39]. However, it has become repeatedly apparent that in natural language the relevant semantic context has no limitations whatsoever, because human meaning is based on the entire conscious and subconscious content of human memory.

Here, we come across a qualitatively new form of universal interconnection. Just as quantum physics had to learn that the motion of an electron is only one aspect of the whole, and just as biology had to learn that living organization does not simply consist of parts which can be analyzed and subsequently recomposed, we need to take into account the interconnection of mapping, interpretation and evaluation as specific and interrelated process stages in the generation, use and preservation of information.

In keeping with the ideas of Max Delbrück[40] – the founder of molecular biology – about the emergence of the human mind, as summarized by G. Stent[41], this means: Mind is not part of a human machine, but rather a quality of the

---

[38] [Winograd, 1972]

[39] See, for example, [v. Hahn, 1986].

[40] [Delbrück, 1986]

[41] [Stent, 1986]

entire human being. It draws on the whole of natural and social evolution and is brought forth by the body as a whole.

Thus, a computer endowed with artificial intelligence and the human mind may be seen as in a dialectical relationship of common ground and differences. Since the mind is enshrined in matter, certain forms of mental processes can be generated by machines, insofar as mental operations are mapped in symbolic form and symbol manipulations can be presented in a formal manner. However, computers are not participants in a social process; they are not personalities whose development is shaped by living a life that involves an interleavement of biological, psychological and social processes.

In studying language, which is open to all experiences of humankind and is shaped by human history, it becomes apparent that in order to understand meanings or metameanings arising in the context of human communication, and in order to form relevant social values, the computer would have to lead a practical life, interacting with the world in concrete sensory terms and having access to the whole realm of the conscious and the unconscious.

Furthermore, concepts such as consciousness and emotion do not only belong to a popular or everyday psychology. The laws governing living matter and the human mind are deeper, wider and at the same time more concrete than the laws and principles of automation. However, by reducing the differentiated features and their interrelations, and by limiting ourselves to a sufficiently crude structure, it is possible to describe specific biological behaviour patterns, as well as selected intelligent human activities, in terms of the behaviour features of technical cybernetic systems and to rely on automata as formal symbol manipulators.

The investigation of biological and human behaviour should, then, be conducted in close interaction with the study of the structure and function of such systems. We should, however, bear in mind that the computer metaphor relies on concepts which abstract from the universal interconnection and that all theories derived from the computer metaphor must be enhanced as soon as they are inserted into the general human context.

If we accept that information items are more complex than their storable material form, then it becomes evident that systems capable of creating and evaluating information cannot be identified with machines.

8.5.8 Conclusion

Elucidating cognitive processes in learning and problem-solving and transforming them into machine-executable functions is an important contribution to the rapid development of modern information and communication technologies. Embedding these technologies in all spheres of our social and even individual life challenges us to focus on sufficiently rich concepts of information.

The phenomenon of information is not reducible to any of its process stages, especially not to its spatial mode of existence as form, structure or syntax. On all the different levels of organization of living systems, information is not merely imported from the outside world, and learning is not merely a process of accumulation of representations. Instead, we can distinguish interrelated stages in a continuous process of generation and use of information.

The interrelation between these stages – mapping, interpreting and evaluating information – constitutes a new form of universal interconnection that requires us to enhance abstract descriptions of mental processes derived from the computational approach of AI as soon as they are inserted into the general holistic context of studying the human mind.

Deeper reflections on the essence of information are required in order to embed the computer with its limited performance into individual human work processes and the overall process of social development in an effective and responsible manner[42]. Since we must formalize information and organization in order to replace human actions by computer functions, informatics and system design must be complemented by theoretical and practical methods allowing us to take account of the creative nature of organization. Informatics must be enriched by consideration of the non-formalizable content of information and human actions which are related not only to realizing functions but also to developing personality and to realizing interests. Thus, understanding information is essential if we are to meaningfully integrate information and communication technologies into society as a whole.

Acknowledgements

This work is only thinkable in the context of my close cooperation with Bodo Wenzlaff. We were united in both scientific and human terms through our discussions on philosophical and methodological problems in quantum physics, cybernetics, biology and computer science. The theoretical focus of our work was the concept of information, the practical concern a humanistic orientation of system design.

The fact that this chapter could appear here is owed to my friendship with Christiane Floyd, built up and maintained for many years across the Berlin Wall. I would like to thank her for many helpful discussions, and Phil Bacon for his substantial contribution to the formulation in English.

---

[42] [Weizenbaum, 1977, Floyd, 1985b, Winograd and Flores, 1986]

Epilogue

Back in the wheels of daily practice

Christiane

During the conference at Schloß Eringerfeld, there evolved a sense of community between people presenting their respective approaches and attempting to arrive at a common understanding of them. We experienced what Gordon Pask calls "the discrete embrace of conversation". But we must try to carry this spirit over into our everyday working life.

Reinhard K.-S.

Computer scientists, though, do not go about their everyday work in castles like Eringerfeld. It remains to be seen whether the ideas and views presented here will find acceptance within the scientific community.

Heinz

Back at work, we were faced again with incongruities, deficiencies and – as the illustration suggests – even with deadlocks. A substantial part of our energy was absorbed by coping with our daily tasks . . .

Christiane

. . . and by meeting our responsibilities in our respective communities. It was most demanding to keep up the spirit of the conference in our situation, and to embark on work on this book.

Reinhard B.

We also encountered unforeseen difficulties while compiling material for the book. Not everything that was said at the conference could be put into writing. Some of the participants preferred not to write anything at all rather than be misunderstood. Others focussed more strongly on their own particular specialty when writing their contribution.

Reinhard K.-S.

Even so, what the conference and the work on this book meant for us was a chance to learn and understand. We set out to address a variety of themes and had to come to grips with our differing ideas on these.

Christiane

The book's taking shape was a slow process. We had to wrestle with our material. And repeated discussions were necessary before a stable structure began to emerge.

Reinhard B.

Most of the contributions were considerably enhanced by their treatment at the conference and intensive subsequent discussions.

Heinz

An aspect of particular significance was the design of the illustrations for the book. Our illustrator Claudia felt the endeavour to arrive at a common understanding to be an essential feature of our collaboration.

Reinhard K.-S.

In some ways, it was like the preparations for the conference. From differing, sometimes conflicting, views, there gradually emerged – through argument and efforts to arrive at a mutual understanding – joint insights into the questions raised.

Christiane

Eventually, we managed to collect a whole range of different approaches illuminating the questions we have raised from various angles.

Reinhard B.

We hope, too, that the intertwinement of these approaches with each other and with related ideas not touched on in this book has become evident.

Reinhard K.-S.

Behind these approaches are numerous different world-views. What emerges is a network of interrelated, complementary ideas that can be coordinated in order to promote human-oriented system design.

Heinz

But, though important, the book is only one result of the conference, which has also inspired further conferences promoting discussion of these themes in a similar spirit.

Christiane

I find myself meeting more and more people who share my conviction that for us as computer scientists there is, in the long run, no getting around the issues raised here.

Heinz

Conversation is of major importance in the process of understanding and design – an insight that is winning increasing recognition in software engineering circles and in other fields concerned with modelling.

Christiane

But we should also give more attention, in our scientific work and in software development, to the ways in which we pursued these issues and arrived at insights into them.

Reinhard B.

We have learned to look not only at the "foreground" of an event – to view a conference not simply as a series of papers given, of working groups and panel discussions.

Heinz

At Schloß Eringerfeld, it was just as much the conversations in the "background" – for example, during meals, around the numerous artistic performances or at the conference bar – that made the conference what it was.

Reinhard B.

And this "background" is essential for a conference to succeed. But we must go a step further: we need to question our view of science in which this distinction is rooted.

Reinhard K.-S.

Work on the book is now completed, but the approaches presented here are meant to open further discussions rather than to provide final answers. We must continue along these lines in our practice of science and design ...

Heinz

... and endeavour to incorporate our ideas in convincing technology development.

Christiane

But to evolve a human-oriented computer science cannot be our concern alone. We would like to invite our readers to help in implementing the ideas put forward here.

We are living in the *age of design*. We should learn to see design as concerned with our dwelling together on earth and oriented towards maintaining and increasing the choices open to us. Therein lies our chance. If we join in common action in the spirit of relatedness, we may hope.

Alice in Cyberland

An evocation of the play staged at the conference "Software Development and Reality Construction". (Inspired by the immortal characters of Lewis Carroll.)

by **Heinz Züllighoven**

Cyberland. The gallery of ancestors and descendents of a hunting seat. On the walls antlers with pointers of stacks. In a remote corner some PCs. On a book-shelf several bulky unwritten manuals and an empty jar labelled "HOMUNCULUS". Alice, pushed into a Rocking Chair, is popped by two Daemons, Peter Pun and Linus Tron, on to the stage. They stop in front of a display case on tiny wheels. On the display a lot of bottles, all labelled "DRINK ME".

Alice

This is a story of computer science, which builds its own reality. Cyberworlds full of strange events and loops.

Linus

Top. *(Alice stands up)* My buffers are empty. I need some clean source.

Peter

You have said that before, but look, there is a rolling bar.

Linus

I was afraid you would say this. Anyhow, let's give it a try.

Each takes a bottle and drinks. The Daemons suddenly shrink like shutting up telescopes and turn into icons on the wall. Then a White Rabbit with 40 dots per inch on its waistcoat comes running in.

White Rabbit

Oh dear! Oh dear! I'm lost! I'll never find my milestones.

The Rabbit takes a PERT chart out of its waistcoat-pocket, looks at it and then hurries on.

Alice

This seems to be the very place where I can learn everything about software development and reality construction. Once I know this, I'll know which direction to take in computer science.

Enter Humpty Dumpty, dragging a huge mouse that is dragging a drawer.

Alice

(Aside). It's him – the great master of systems. He is very clever at explaining everything present-at-hand and using everything ready-to-hand. *(Turns to him).* Sir, would you kindly tell me the meaning of software development and reality construction?

Humpty Dumpty double-clicking the mouse on its nose. The mouse takes out of the
drawer a large index-card with circles, boxes and arcs on it.

Humpty Dumpty

First, you have to understand the world as such. The world is an instance
of an abstract data type. There is one sort "world", one function "change"
and one equation "world = change(world)". Become what you are.

Alice

I don't know what you mean by that.

Humpty Dumpty

When I use a formalism, it means just what I choose it to mean – neither
more nor less.

Alice

The question is, what purpose does a formalism serve.

Humpty Dumpty

The question is, which is to be the master – that's all. *(Exit).*

Enter the White Knight wearing health-sandals and coarse hand-woven clothes.

Alice

(Aside). I guess the problem is very complex. I'll decompose it into subprob-
lems. Here comes a friendly-looking man. He has such a nice smile . Maybe
he can solve the first part of my problem. *(Turns to him).* Sir, would you
kindly explain to me the essence of software development?

White Knight

The great art of software development is to see it as a cooperative human
activity. The technical aspects of reality construction are only marginal tri-
fles.

Alice

Indeed?

White Knight

Let me show you. I have invented a plan for developing ecological software.

He walks over to a PC and hacks in a sequence of keystrokes. The PC beeps and
dissolves.

Alice

I'm afraid you've not had much practice in programming.

White Knight

What makes you say that? I've had plenty of practice. The great art of
software development, as I was saying, is – to be first of all friendly and
well-disposed towards each other. Reality construction is a trifle like this,
you know –

He walks over to another PC and hacks in a new sequence of keystrokes. The PC
beeps twice and dissolves.

Alice

It's too ridiculous! You ought to start practising with computer games, that you ought!

White Knight

Does that kind operate smoothly? *(Aside)*. I'll get one. One or two – several. *(Exit)*.

Enter Tweedledee and Tweedledum each with an arm round the other's neck in a strange loop.

Alice

(Aside). Perhaps it was not such a good idea to start with Software Development before understanding Reality Construction. *(Aloud)*. Sirs, I'm so confused about the things I've heard. Would you kindly tell me if software development is reality construction?

Tweedledee

Nohow, if it was so, it might be; and if it were so, it would be; but as it isn't, it ain't. That's logic.

Tweedledum

Contrariwise, you are confused, because you've begun wrong! The first thing to ask is, 'Is reality constructed?'

Alice

Nobody can guess that.

Tweedledee

Do you know what you are?

Alice

I'm real.

Tweedledum

Nohow. You are only a perturbation of our structurally coupled autopoietic system. If we uncoupled you, where do you suppose you'd be?

Alice

Where I am now, of course.

Tweedledee

Not you! You'd be nowhere. Why, you're only a sort of construction in our reality.

Alice

I'm not. Besides, if I'm only a construct in your reality, what are you in my reality, I should like to know?

Tweedledum

(Laughing). Ditto.

Tweedledee

(Laughing). Ditto, ditto. *(Exeunt)*.

Alice

I know, they are talking nonsense. At any rate, I'd better find someone who can at least tell me what direction to take in computer science.

*A curious appearance in the air. First the notorious grin, then the whole head of
the Cheshire-Cat appears.*

Alice

(Aside). It's the Cheshire-Cat: Now I have somebody really sensible to talk
to. *(Aloud).* Cheshire-Cat, would you tell me, please, which way I ought to
take from here in computer science?

Cheshire-Cat

That depends a good deal on what you want to achieve.

Alice

I don't much care what –

Cheshire-Cat

Then it doesn't matter which way you go.

Alice

– as long as I arrive at a computer science for human beings.

Cheshire-Cat

Oh, you're sure to do that, if you only run long enough. *(Vanishes).*

*Alice begins to run. As she runs, the scene does not change. Alice, quite breathless,
stops exhausted. Then she notices the Wizard of OS who has been sitting quietly in
front of a big terminal all the time.*

Alice

Why, I do believe I have been at this very spot the whole time. Everything's
just as it was.

Wizard of OS

Of course it is. What would you have it?

Alice

Well, in my understanding of computer science, you'd generally get to somewhere else – if you ran very fast for a long time as I've been doing.

Wizard of OS

What a strange notion of computer science. Now, here, you see, it takes all
the running you can do, to keep in touch with the leading edge and stay
where you are. If you want to get beyond, you must run at least twice as
fast!

Alice

I will never succeed. So I'm doomed to stay in this place forever. *(She starts
to cry).*

Wizard of OS

I know what your problem is. I'll give you my memorandum book which will
be a good help.

*He takes an enormous book out of his pocket, hands it to Alice and, with a benign
smile, turns back to his keyboard. Alices starts to turn over the leaves.*

Alice

What a strange book this is. It's all written in a language I hardly understand. Ah, this seems to be a poem. *(She reads it aloud)*

> The road to wisdom?
> Well, it's plain
> and simple to express:
> > Err
> > and err
> > and err again
> > but less
> > and less
> > and less.

It is very pretty. Somehow it seems to fill my head with ideas — only I don't
exactly know what they are.

*Alices puzzles over the poem for some time. Suddenly, the two Daemons deiconify.
When they clap their hands, the floor changes into a matrix of black and white
fields like a chess-board. And again the White Rabbit comes skipping in. Whenever
it hops from one field to another, the dots on its waistcoat invert.*

Alice

Now I understand – I'm in a cyberspace world, of course. Maybe, if I change
my perspective and hop to another field, the words in this book will all go a
different way as well. Let's try it. The list on this page reads:

Turbo	*She hops to*	Hyper
Overhead Projectors	*a white field*	Video Projectors
Operating Manuals		Philosophical Encyclopaedias
AI		Ai-Ki-Do

There is another one on the next page:

Abstract Data Types	*She hops to*	Present-at-hand
Program Verification	*a black field*	Commitments
Software Life Cycle		Self-Organisation
Nassi-Shneiderman		Winograd-Flores

This seems to be the way to do it. I'll try the pretty poem again. *(She hops)*.
It has changed as well:

The road to wisdom?
Well, it's plain
and simple to explore:
  Love
  and love
  and love again
  but more
  and more
  and more.

At this, all sorts of things happen. The two Daemons appear again leading all the rest of the characters in two lines. The two lines advance, set to partners and begin solemnly dancing round and round Alice. A living cybernetic fossil waves its hands like dangling pointers to mark the time.

Alice

Oh, what fun it is. It's a huge game that's being played – all over this cyberworld – if this is a world at all. How I wish I was one of them! I wouldn't mind being a Hacker, if only I might join – though of course I should like to be a Cyber Queen, best.

At this, the whole castle and all the characters except Alice rise up into the air, are transformed into fractals and disappear in a whirl. The memorandum book changes into the manuscript of this book. Alices sits down on the empty stage.

Alice

Oh, I've had such a curious dream! Or was it real? I don't know. And what is this? *(Looks at the manuscript).* It's nothing but a pack of punched cards!

The curtain falls.

Bibliography

Ackermann, D. and Ulich, E. (1987). The chances of individualization in human–computer interaction and its consequences. In [Frese at al., 1987], pages 131–145.

Agresti, W. W., editor (1986). *New paradigms for software development*. IEEE Computer Society Press, Washington, DC.

Alexander, C. (1964). *Notes on the Synthesis of Form*. Harvard University Press, Cambridge, MA.

Amann, K. and Knorr-Cetina, K. (1988). The fixation of (visual) evidence. *Human Studies*, 11:133–169.

Amann, K. and Knorr-Cetina, K. (1989). Thinking through talk: An ethnographic study of a molecular biology laboratory. *Knowledge and Society: Studies in the Sociology of Past and Present*, 8:3–26.

Amann, K. and Knorr-Cetina, K. (1991). Qualitative Wissenschaftssoziologie. In Flick, U., v. Kardorff, E., Keupp, H., v. Rosenstiel, L., and Wolff, S., editors, *Handbuch Qualitativer Sozialforschung*. Psychologie Verlags Union, München.

Andersen, N. E., Kensing, F., Lundin, J., Mathiassen, L., Munk-Madsen, A., Rasbech, M., and Sørgaard, P. (1990). *Professional Systems Development*. Prentice Hall, Englewood Cliffs, NJ.

Apple (1987). *Macintosh Programmers Workshop Reference*. Apple Computer Inc., Cupertino, CA.

Arnheim, R. (1969). *Visual Thinking*. University of California Press, Berkeley, CA.

Ashby, W. R. (1960). *Design for a Brain. The Origin of Adaptive Behaviour*. Chapman and Hall, London. (2nd edition).

Auramaki, E., Lehtinen, E., and Lyytinen, K. (1988). A speech–act–based modeling approach. *ACM Transactions on Office Information Systems*, 6(2):126–152.

Austin, J. L. (1962). *How to Do Things with Words*. Clarendon Press, Oxford, UK.

Bacon, F. (1968). *The Wisdom of the Ancients*. Da Capo Press, Amsterdam. (Facsimile of 1619 translation by Arthur George, printed by John Bill, London.)

Bahr, H.-D. (1983). *Über den Umgang mit Maschinen*. Konkursbuchverlag, Tübingen.

Baier, V. E., March, J. G., and Saetren, H. (1986). Implementation and ambiguity. *Scandinavian Journal of Management Studies*, pages 197–212.

Bakhtin, M. M. (1981). The dialogical imagination. In Holquist, M., editor, *Four Essays*. University of Texas Press, Austin, TX.

Bannon, L. J. (1986). Computer–mediated communication. In [Norman and Draper, 1986], pages 433–452.

Bannon, L. J. and Bødker, S. (1991). Beyond the interface. Encountering artifacts in use. In [Carroll, 1991].

Bansler, J. (1989). System development research in Scandinavia: Three theoretical schools. *Scandinavian Journal of Information Systems*, 1:3–20.

Barwise, J. (1989). Mathematical proofs of computer system correctness. Technical Report CSLI-89-136, Center for the Study of Language and Information, Stanford University, Palo Alto, CA.

Barwise, J. and Perry, J. (1983). *Situations and Attitudes*. MIT Press, Cambridge, MA.

Basalla, G. (1988). *The Evolution of Technology*. Cambridge University Press, Cambridge, UK.

Basili, V. R. and Perricone, B. T. (1984). Software errors and complexity: An empirical investigation. *Communications of the ACM*, 27(1):42–52.

Basili, V. R. and Rombach, H. D. (1987). Tailoring the software process to project goals and environments. In *Proc. 9th International Conference on Software Engineering*. Monterey, CA, pages 345–357.

Bateson, G. (1972). *Steps to an Ecology of Mind*. Ballantine Books, New York.

Bateson, G. (1980). *Mind and Nature. A Necessary Unity*. Bantam Books, New York.

Batra, D. and Davis, J. (1989). A study of conceptual data modeling in data base design: Similarities and differences between expert and novice designers. In DeGross, J., Henderson, J. C., and Konsynski, B., editors, *Proc. 10th ICIS*, number 7 in ACM Transactions on Office Information Systems. Baltimore, MA.

Batra, D., Hoffer, J., and Bostrom, R. (1988). A comparison of user performance between the relational and the extended entity relationship model in the discovery phase of database design. In *Proc. 9th ICIS*. Minneapolis, MN.

Becker, E. (1973). *The Denial of Death*. Free Press, New York.

Beeton, B. (1983). TEX and METAFONT: Errata and changes. Distributed with *TUGboat* 4.

Bench-Capon, T. J. M. and McEnery, A. M. (1989a). Modelling devices and modelling speakers. *Interacting with Computers*, 1(2):220–224.

Bench-Capon, T. J. M. and McEnery, A. M. (1989b). People interact through computers not with them. *Interacting with Computers*, 1(1):31–38.

Bentley, J. (1986). Programming pearls. *Communications of the ACM*, 29(5,6):364–369,471–483.

Berger, P. and Luckmann, T. (1967). *The Social Construction of Reality*. Penguin Books, Harmondsworth.

Berleur, J. and Brunnstein, K. (1990). Recent technical developments: Attitudes and paradigms. In Berleur, J., Clement, A., Sizer, R., and Whitehouse, D., editors, *The Information Society: Evolving Landscapes*. IFIP, New York, pages 384–423. (Distributed by Springer, Berlin).

Bice, K. and Lewis, C. H., editors (1989). *Proc. CHI'89: Conference on Human Factors in Computing Systems*. ACM, New York.

Bijker, W. et al., editors (1987). *The Social Construction of Technological Systems*. MIT Press, Cambridge, MA.

Bischof, N. (1990). Phase transitions in psychoemotional development. In [Haken and Stadler, 1990], pages 361–378.

Bjerknes, G. and Bratteteig, T. (1988). Computers – utensils or epaulets? The application perspective revisited. *AI and Society*, 2(3):258–266.

Bjerknes, G., Ehn, P., and Kyng, M., editors (1987). *Computers and Democracy. A Scandinavian Challenge*. Avebury, Aldershot, UK.

Bjerknes, G. et al., editors (1990). *Organizational Competence in System Development. A Scandinavian Contribution*. Studentlitteratur, Lund.

Bjørn-Andersen, N. (1988). Are 'human factors' human? *The Computer Journal*, 31(5): 386–390.

Blair, D. C. (1990). *Language and Representation in Information Retrieval*. North-Holland, Amsterdam.

Blauberg, I. V., Sadowski, V. N., and Judin, E. G. (1977). *Systems Theory. Philosophical and Methodological Problems*. Progress, Moscow.

Bødker, S. (1987). *Through the Interface. A Human Activity Approach to User Interface Design*. Aarhus University, Aarhus.

Bødker, S., Ehn, P., Kammersgaard, J., Kyng, M., and Sundblad, Y. (1987). A UTO-PIAN experience: On design of powerful computer–based tools for skilled graphic workers. In [Bjerknes et al., 1987], pages 251–278.

Boehm, B. W. (1976). Software engineering. *IEEE Transactions on Computers*, 25(12): 1226–1241.

Boehm, B. W. (1977). Seven basic principles of software engineering. In Infotech, editor, *Software Engineering Techniques*, Infotech State of the Art Report, volume 2: Invited papers. Infotech, Maidenhead, UK, pages 77–113.

Boehm, B. W. (1981). *Software Engineering Economics*. Prentice Hall, Englewood Cliffs, NJ.

Boehm, B. W. (1988). A spiral model for software development and enhancement. *IEEE Computer*, 21(5):61–72.

Böhle, F. and Milkau, B. (1988). *Vom Handrad zum Bildschirm. Eine Untersuchung zur sinnlichen Erfahrung im Arbeitsprozeß*. Campus, Frankfurt a.M.

Bohm, D. (1983). *Wholeness and the Implicate Order*. ARK Paperbacks, London.

Boland, R. (1979). Control, causality, and information system requirements. *Accounting, Organizations and Society*, 4(4):259–272.

Boland, R. R. and Hirschheim, R. A., editors (1987). *Critical Issues in Information Systems Research*. Wiley, Chichester, UK.

Bonar, J. and Cunningham, R. (1988). Bridge: Tutoring the programming process. In Massey, D. and Mutter, S., editors, *Intelligent Tutoring Systems: Lessons Learned*. Lawrence Erlbaum, Hillsdale, NJ.

Bonsiepen, L. and Coy, W. (1990a). Is there really a challenge of expert systems to industrial labour? In [v.d.Besselaar et al., 1991], pages 53–62.

Bonsiepen, L. and Coy, W. (1990b). Szenen einer Krise – Ist Knowledge Engineering eine Antwort auf die Dauerkrise des Software Engineering? *KI*, 90(2):5–11.

Borzeszkowski, H. H. and Wahsner, R. (1980). *Newton and Voltaire*. Akademie-Verlag, Berlin, GDR.

Boss, M. (1975). *Grundriß der Medizin und der Psychologie*. Huber, Bern.

Bostrom, R. and Heinen, S. (1977). Management information system problems and failures: A socio–technical perspective – Part I: the causes. *Management Information System Quarterly*, 1(3):17–32.

Bourdieu, P. (1977). *Outline of a Theory of Practice*. Cambridge University Press, Cambridge, UK.

Bråten, S. (1973). Model monopoly and communication: Systems theoretical notes on democratization. *Acta Sociologica*, 16(2):98–107.

Bråten, S. (1978). System research and social science. In Klir, G., editor, *Applied General Systems Research: Recent Developments and Trends*. Plenum Press, New York, pages 655–685.

Bråten, S. (1988). Between dialogical mind and monological reason: Postulating the virtual other. In Campanella, M., editor, *Between Rationality and Cognition – Policy-Making under Conditions of Uncertainty, Complexity and Turbulence*. Turin.

Briefs, U., Ciborra, C., and Schneider, L., editors (1983). *Systems Design For, With, and By the User*. North-Holland, Amsterdam.

Brillouin, L. (1962). *Science and Information Theory*. Academic Press, San Diego, CA.

Broder, B. (1979). *The Sacred Hoop*. Sierra Club Books, San Francisco, CA.

Bromme, R. (1988). *Der Lehrer als Experte. Möglichkeiten und Grenzen des Expertenansatzes in der Lehrerkognitionsforschung*. Institut für Didaktik der Mathematik, Bielefeld.

Brooks, F. P. (1987). No silver bullet: Essence and accidents of software engineering. *IEEE Computer*, 20(4):10–19.

Brooks, F. P. (1987). Report of the defense science board task force on military software. Technical Report AD-A188 561, Office of the Under Secretary of Defense for Acquisition, Department of Defense, Washington DC 10301.

Brooks, R. A. (1986). Achieving artificial intelligence through building robots. A.I. Memo 899, MIT, Cambridge, MA.

Brown, G. S. (1969). *Laws of Form*. George Allen and Unwin, London.

Brown, J. S. and Newman, S. E. (1985). Issues in cognitive and social ergonomics: From our house to Bauhaus. *Human–Computer Interaction*, 1:359–391.

Bruner, J. S. (1984). Narrative and paradigmatic modes of thought. In *Learning and Teaching: The Ways of Knowing*. 1985 Yearbook of the National Society for the Study of Education, pages 95–115. (Invited Address for the Annual Meeting of the American Psychological Association, Toronto, August 1984).

Bubenko, J. J. (1983). Information and data modeling: State of the art and research directions. In Kangassalo, H., editor, *Second Scandinavian Research Seminar*, Acta Universitatis Tamperensis, Ser. B 19. Tampere, SF, pages 9–28.

Buber, M. (1961). *Das Problem des Menschen*. Lambert Schneider, Heidelberg.

Buber, M. (1984). *Das Dialogische Prinzip*. Lambert Schneider, Heidelberg.

Buckingham, R. A., Hirschheim, R. A., Land, E. F., and Tully, C. J., editors (1987). *Information Systems Education – Recommendations and Implementations*. Cambridge University Press, Cambridge, UK.

Budde, R. and Züllighoven, H. (1990). *Software–Werkzeuge in einer Programmierwerkstatt*. Berichte der Gesellschaft für Mathematik und Datenverarbeitung, Nr. 182. Oldenbourg, München.

Bühler, K. (1934). *Sprachtheorie. Die Darstellungsfunktion der Sprache*. Fischer, Stuttgart.

Byrne, R. and Whiten, A., editors (1988). *Machiavellian Intelligence*. Clarendon Press, Oxford, UK.

Capurro, R. (1981). Heidegger über Sprache und Information. *Philosophisches Jahrbuch*, 2:333–343.

Capurro, R. (1985). Epistemology and information science. Report TRITA-LIB-6023, Royal Institute of Technology Library, Stockholm.

Capurro, R. (1986). *Hermeneutik der Fachinformation*. Alber, Freiburg.

Capurro, R. (1987). Die Informatik und das hermeneutische Forschungsprogramm. *Informatik Spektrum*, 10(6):329–333.

Capurro, R. (1988). M. Heidegger (Works). In Volpi, F. and Nida-Rümelin, J., editors, *Lexikon der philosophischen Werke*. Kröner, Stuttgart.

Capurro, R. (1991). M. Heidegger. In Nida-Rümelin, J., editor, *Philosophie der Gegenwart in Einzeldarstellungen*. Kröner, Stuttgart.

Card, S. K. and Henderson, A. J. (1987). A multiple, virtual–workspace interface to support user task switching. In [Carroll and Tanner, 1987], pages 53–59.

Card, S. K., Moran, T. P., and Newell, A. (1983). *The psychology of Human–Computer Interaction*. Lawrence Erlbaum, Hillsdale, NJ.

Carnap, R. (1978). The overcoming of metaphysics through logical analysis of language. In [Murray, 1978]. (Translated by A. Pap, original in *Erkenntnis 2*, 1931.)

Carroll, J. M., editor (1987). *Interfacing Thought: Cognitive Aspects of the Human–Computer Interaction*. Bradford Books/MIT Press, Cambridge, MA.

Carroll, J. M. (1989). Evaluation, description and invention: Paradigms for human–computer interaction. In Yovits, M. C., editor, *Advances in Computers*, volume 29. Academic Press, San Diego, CA, pages 47–77.

Carroll, J. M. (1990). *The Nurnberg Funnel: Designing Minimalist Instruction for Practical Computer Skill*. MIT Press, Cambridge, MA.

Carroll, J. M., editor (1991). *Designing Interaction. Psychology at the Human–Computer Interface*. Cambridge University Press, Cambridge, UK.

Carroll, J. M. and Aaronson, A. P. (1988). Learning by doing with simulated intelligent help. *Communications of the ACM*, 31(9):1064–1079.

Carroll, J. M. and Campbell, R. L. (1989). Artifacts as psychological theories: The case of human–computer interaction. *Behaviour and Information Technology*, 8:247–256.

Carroll, J. M. and Carrithers, C. (1984). Blocking learner errors in a training wheels system. *Human Factors*, 26(4):377–389.

Carroll, J. M., Herder, R. E., and Sawtelle, D. S. (1987). Task mapper. In Bullinger, H. J. and Shackel, B., editors, *Human–Computer Interaction – Interact '87*. North-Holland, Amsterdam, pages 973–978.

Carroll, J. M. and Kellogg, W. A. (1989). Artifact as theory-nexus: Hermeneutics meets theory–based design. In [Bice and Lewis, 1989], pages 7–14.

Carroll, J. M., Mack, R. L., and Kellogg, W. A. (1988). Interface metaphors and user interface design. In Helander, M., editor, *Handbook of Human–Computer Interaction*. North-Holland, Amsterdam, pages 67–85.

Carroll, J. M., Mack, R. L., Lewis, C. H., Grischkowsky, N. L., and Robertson, S. R. (1985). Exploring a word processor. *Human–Computer Interaction*, 1:283–307.

Carroll, J. M. and Mazur, S. A. (1986). Lisa learning. *IEEE Computer*, 91(11):35–49.

Carroll, J. M. and Rosson, M. B. (1985). Usability specification as a tool in iterative development. In Hartson, H. R., editor, *Advances in Human–Computer Interaction*, volume 1. Ablex, Norwood, NJ, pages 1–28.

Carroll, J. M. and Rosson, M. B. (1987). The paradox of the active user. In [Carroll, 1987], pages 80–111.

Carroll, J. M. and Rosson, M. B. (1990). Human computer interaction scenarios as design representation. In *Proc. HICSS-23: Hawaii International Conference on System Sciences*. IEEE Computer Society Press, Los Alamitos, CA, pages 555–561.

Carroll, J. M., Singer, J. A., Bellamy, R. K. E., and Alpert, S. R. (1990). A view matcher for learning smalltalk. In Chew, J. C. and Whiteside, J., editors, *Proc. CHI'90: Conference on Human Factors in Computing Systems*. ACM, New York, pages 431–437.

Carroll, J. M. and Tanner, P. P., editors (1987). *Proc. CHI + GI '87: Human Factors in Computing Systems and Graphics Interface*. ACM, New York.

Cashmore, E. E. and Mullan, B. (1983). *Approaching Social Theory*. Heinemann Educational Books, London.

Celko, J., Davis, J. S., and Mitchell, J. (1983). A demonstration of three requirements language systems. *SIGPLAN Notices*, 18(1):9–14.

Checkland, P. (1981). *Systems Thinking, Systems Practice*. Wiley, Chichester, UK.

Chen, P. P. S. (1976). The entity–relationship model – Towards a unified view of data. *ACM Transactions on Database Systems*, 1(1):9–36.

Chen, P. P. S. (1977). The entity–relationship model: A basis for the enterprise view of data. In *Proc. National Computer Conference, volume 46, Dallas, TX*. pages 77–84.

Chomsky, N. (1965). *Aspects of the Theory of Syntax*. MIT Press, Cambridge, MA.

Churchland, P. S. (1986). *Neurophilosophy. Towards a Unified Science of the Mind-Brain*. MIT Press, Cambridge, MA.

Churchman, W. (1971). *The Design of Inquiring Systems*. Basic Books, New York.

Ciborra, C. U. (1987). Research agenda for a transaction cost approach to information systems. In [Boland and Hirschheim, 1987], pages 253–274.

Clancey, W. J. (1987). Review of Winograd, Flores (1986). *Artificial Intelligence*, 31:232–250.

Codd, E. F. (1971). Normalized data base structure: A brief tutorial. In Codd, E. F. and Dean, A. L., editors, *ACM SIG-FIDET Workshop on Data Description, Access, and Control*. San Diego, CA.

Codd, E. F. (1979). Extending the data base relational model to capture more meaning. *ACM Transactions on Database Systems*, 4(4):379–434.

Cole, M. (1988). Cross–cultural research in the socio–historical tradition. In [Hildebrand-Nilshon and Rückriem, 1988].

Cole, M. (1990). Cultural psychology. A once and future discipline? In Berman, J., editor, *Nebraska Symposium on Motivation: Cross–Cultural Perspectives*. University of Nebraska Press, Lincoln, NE.

Coulthard, M. (1987). *An Introduction to Discourse Analysis*. Longman, London.

Coy, W. (1985). *Industrieroboter*. Rotbuch, Berlin.

Coy, W. (1988). *Aufbau und Arbeitsweise von Rechenanlagen*. Vieweg, Wiesbaden.

Coy, W. (1989). Après Gutenberg – über Texte und Hypertexte. In Rammert, W. and Bechman, G., editors, *Jahrbuch Technik & Gesellschaft*, volume 5. Campus, Frankfurt a.M., pages 53–65.

Coy, W. and Bonsiepen, L. (1989). Expert systems: Before the flood? In [Ritter, 1989].

CSCW'88 (1988). *Proc. CSCW'88: 2nd Conference on Computer–Supported Cooperative Work*. ACM, New York.

Dagwell, R. and Weber, R. (1983). System designers' user models: A comparative study and methodological critique. *Communications of the ACM*, 26(11):987–995.

Dahlbom, B. (1987). Artificial intelligence and systems development. From design to cultivation. In [Järvinen, 1987].

Dahlbom, B. (1990). Using technology to understand organizations. In [Bjerknes et al., 1990], pages 127–147.

Damerow, P. (1988). Individual development and cultural evolution of arithmetical thinking. In Strauss, S., editor, *Ontogeny, Phylogeny, and Historical Development*. Ablex, Norwood, NJ, pages 125–152.

Davis, G. (1982).] Strategies for information requirements determination. *IBM Systems Journal*, 21(1):4–30.

Davis, R. (1980). Meta–rules: Reasoning about control. *Artificial Intelligence*, 15:179–222.

Davydov, V. V. (1982). The psychological structure and content of the learning activity in school children. In Glaser, R. and Lopscher, J., editors, *Cognitive and Motivational Aspects of Instruction*. Deutscher Verlag der Wissenschaften, Berlin, GDR, pages 37–44.

Delbrück, M. (1986). *Wahrheit und Wirklichkeit. Über die Evolution des Erkennens*. Rasch and Röhring, Hamburg.

DeMillo, R. A., Lipton, R. J., and Perlis, A. J. (1979). Social processes and proofs of theorems and programs. *Communications of the ACM*, 22(5):271–280.

Dennett, D. C. (1987). *The Intentional Stance*. MIT Press, Cambridge, MA.

Denning, P. et al. (1989). Computing as a discipline. *Communications of the ACM*, 32(1):9–23.

Derrida, J. (1988). Geschlecht. Différence sexuelle, différence ontologique. In *Cahiers de l'Herne IX*. L'Herne, Paris, pages 571–595.

di Primo, F. and Wittur, K. H. (1987). BABYLON: A meta interpretation model for handling mixed knowledge representations. In *Proc. 7ᵗʰ Int. Workshop on Expert Systems and their Applications*. pages 821–833.

Dijkstra, E. W. (1968). The structure of the "THE"–multiprogramming system. *Communications of the ACM*, 11(5):341–346.

Dijkstra, E. W. (1969). Complexity controlled by hierarchical ordering of function and variability. In [Naur and Randell, 1969], pages 181–185.

Dijkstra, E. W. (1975). Guarded commands, nondeterminacy and formal derivation of programs. *Communications of the ACM*, 18(8):453–457.

Dijkstra, E. W. (1982). *Selected Writings on Computing. A Personal Perspective.* Springer, Berlin.

Dillard, A. (1974). *Pilgrim at Tinker Creek.* Harper and Row, New York.

DIN66234 (1988). DIN 66 234, Part 8: VDU work stations. Principles of ergonomic dialogue design. German Industrial Norm, Beuth, Berlin.

Docherty, P., Fuchs-Kittowski, K., Kolm, P., and Mathiassen, L., editors (1987). *System Design for Human Development and Productivity: Participation and Beyond.* North-Holland, Amsterdam.

Dreyfus, H. L. (1979). *What Computers Can't Do. The Limits of Artificial Reason.* Harper and Row, New York. (Revised edition).

Dreyfus, H. L. (1989). *Being–in–the–World: A Commentary on Heidegger's Being and Time, Division I.* Manuscript. To be published by MIT Press, Cambridge, MA.

Dreyfus, H. L. and Dreyfus, S. E. (1986). *Mind over Machine: The Power of Human Intuition and Expertise in the Era of the Computer.* Free Press, New York.

Dunckel, H., Volpert, W., Kreutner, U., Pleiss, C., and Zölch, M. (1991). *Leitfaden zur kontrastiven Aufgabenanalyse und –gestaltung bei Büro- und Verwaltungstätigkeiten. Das KABA–Verfahren.* (In preparation).

Durham, T. (1988). Organisational dinosaurs take on a human face. *Computing*, (Nov. 3):40–41.

Dzida, W. (1982). Dialogfähige Werkzeuge und arbeitsgerechte Dialogformen. In Schauer, H. and Tauber, M. J., editors, *Informatik und Psychologie.* Oldenbourg, München, pages 54–86.

Dzida, W. (1987). On tools and interfaces. In [Frese and Sabini, 1985], pages 339–355.

Dzida, W. and Valder, W. (1985). Application domain modelling by knowledge engineering techniques. In Shackel, B., editor, *Human-Computer Interaction – INTERACT '84.* Elsevier, Amsterdam, pages 481–488.

Eco, U. (1977). *Das offene Kunstwerk.* Suhrkamp, Frankfurt a.M.

Ehn, P. (1988). *Work–oriented Design of Computer Artifacts.* Almquist and Wiksell International, Stockholm.

Ehn, P. and Kyng, M. (1985). A tool perspective on design of interactive computer support for skilled workers. DAIMI PB-190, Computer Science Department, Aarhus University, DK.

Ehn, P. and Kyng, M. (1987). The collective resource approach to systems design. In [Bjerknes et al., 1987], pages 17–56.

Ehrig, H., Floyd, C., Nivat, M., and Thatcher, J., editors (1985). *Formal Methods and Software Development, volume 2 of TAPSOFT Proceedings: Colloquium on Software Engineering (CSE).* Lecture Notes in Computer Science, volume 186. Springer, Berlin.

Eigen, M. (1971). Selforganization of matter and evolution of biological macromolecules. *Naturwissenschaften*, 58(10):465–522.

Eigen, M. (1987). *Stufen zum Leben. Die frühe Evolution im Visier der Molekularbiologie.* Piper, München.

Eigen, M., Gardiner, W., Schuster, P., and Winkler-Oswatitsch, R. (1981). The origin of genetic information. *Scientific American,* 248(4):37–56.

Eigen, M. and Schuster, P. (1979). *The Hypercycle – A Principle of Natural Selforganization.* Springer, Berlin.

Elias, N. (1956). Problems of involvement and detachement. *British Journal of Sociology,* 7(3).

Elias, N. (1987). The retreat of sociologists into the present. *Theory, Culture and Society,* 4:223–247.

Elias, N. and Martins, H., editors (1982). *Scientific Establishments and Hierarchies.* Reidel, Dordrecht, NL.

ElMasri, R. and Wiederhold, G. (1985). The entity category relationship model. *Data and Knowledge Engineering,* 1(1).

Elsasser, W. M. (1982). *Biological Theory on a Holistic Basis.* Baltimore.

Elzer, P. (1989). Management von Softwareprojekten. *Informatik Spektrum,* 12(4):181–197.

Emery, F. E. and Thorsrud, E. (1969). *Form and Content in Industrial Democracy.* Tavistock, London.

Engelbart, D. C. (1988). Toward high–performance knowledge workers. In [Greif, 1988], pages 67–78. (Reprint).

Engeström, Y. (1987). *Learning by Expanding.* Orienta-Konsultit, Helsinki.

Engeström, Y. (1990). Activity theory and individual and social transformation. In 2nd *International Congress for Research on Activity Theory.* Lahti, SF. (Opening address).

Fairchild, K., Meredith, G., and Wexelblat, A. (1989).] The tourist artificial reality. In [Bice and Lewis, 1989], pages 299–304.

Featherstone, M. (1987). Norbert Elias and figurational sociology. Some prefatory remarks. *Theory, Culture and Society,* 4:197–211.

Feigenbaum, E. A. (1977). The art of artificial intelligence: I. Themas and case studies of knowledge engineering. In *IJCAI-77: 5th International Joint Conference on Artificial Intelligence.* Carnegie-Mellon University, Pittsburgh, PA, pages 1024–1029.

Feigenbaum, E. A. and McCorduck, P. (1984). *The Fifth Generation. Artificial Intelligence and Japan's Computer Challenge to the World.* New American Library, New York.

Feyerabend, P. (1975). *Against Method: Outline of an Anarchistic Theory of Knowledge.* New Left Books, London.

Feyerabend, P. (1981). *Erkenntnis für freie Menschen.* Suhrkamp, Frankfurt a.M.

Feyerabend, P. (1984). *Wissenschaft als Kunst.* Suhrkamp, Frankfurt a.M.

Fischer, G. (1983). Entwurfsrichtlinien für die Software–Ergonomie aus der Sicht der Mensch–Maschine Kommunikation (MMK). In Balzert, H., editor, *Software–Ergonomie.* Teubner, Stuttgart, pages 30–48.

Fischer, G. and Lemke, A. C. (1988). Construction kits and design environments: Steps toward human problem–domain communication. *Human–Computer Interaction,* 3(3):179–222.

Florence Report (1985). *Gjensiding laering.* Department of Informatics, University of Oslo, Report No. 1 from the Florence Project edition. (Mutual Learning, in Norwegian).

Floyd, C. (1981). A process–oriented approach to software development. In *Systems Architecture. Proc. 6th European ACM Regional Conference, London*. Westbury House, Guildford, UK, pages 285–294.

Floyd, C. (1984). A systematic look at prototyping. In Budde, R., Kuhlenkamp, K., Mathiassen, L., and Züllighoven, H., editors, *Approaches to Prototyping*. Springer, Berlin, pages 1–18.

Floyd, C. (1985). On the relevance of formal methods to software developent. In [Ehrig et al., 1985], pages 1–11.

Floyd, C. (1985). The responsible use of computers: Where do we draw the line? Working paper for the tapsoft conference, Technical University of Berlin. (Also published in *CPSR Newsletter*, Spring 1986 and as CPSR Working Paper, Computer Professionals for Social Responsibility (CPSR), Palo Alto, CA).

Floyd, C. (1986). A comparative evaluation of system development. In Olle, T. W., Sol, H. G., and Verrijn-Stuart, A. A., editors, *Information Systems Design Methodologies: Improving the Practice*. North-Holland, Amsterdam, pages 19–54.

Floyd, C. (1987). Outline of a paradigm change in software engineering. In [Bjerknes et al., 1987], pages 191–210.

Floyd, C. and Keil, R. (1983). Adapting software development for systems design with the user. In [Briefs et al., 1983], pages 163–172.

Floyd, C., Mehl, W.-M., Reisin, F.-M., Schmidt, G., and Wolf, G. (1989a). Out of Scandinavia: Alternative approaches to software design and system development. *Human–Computer Interaction*, 4(4):253–349.

Floyd, C., Mehl, W.-M., Reisin, F.-M., and Wolf, G. (1990). PEtS: Partizipative Entwicklung transparenzschaffender Systeme für EDV–gestützte Arbeitsplätze. Final Project Report, Technical University of Berlin.

Floyd, C., Reisin, F.-M., and Schmidt, G. (1989b). STEPS to software development with users. In Ghezzi, C. and McDermid, J. A., editors, *ESEC '89: 2nd European Software Engineering Conference*, Lecture Notes in Computer Science, volume 387. Springer, Berlin, pages 48–64.

Fluck, H.-R. (1976). *Fachsprachen*. Francke, München.

Fodor, J. A. (1968). *Psychological Explanation*. Random House, New York.

Fodor, J. A. (1981). *Representations: Philosophical Essays on the Foundations of Cognitive Science*. MIT Press, Cambridge, MA.

Freeman, P. (1979). A perspective on requirements analysis and specification. In [Infotech, 1979], pages 41–55.

Frege, G. (1892). Sinn und Bedeutung. *Zeitschrift für Philosophie und philosophische Kritik, Neue Folge*, 100:25–50.

Frege, G. (1950). *The Foundation of Arithmetic*. Philosophical Library, New York. (Translated by J. L. Austin).

Frese, M. (1987). A theory of control and complexity: Implications for software design and integration of computer systems into the work place. In [Frese et al., 1987], pages 313–337.

Frese, M. and Sabini, J., editors (1985). *Goal Directed Behavior. The Concept of Action in Psychology*. Lawrence Erlbaum, Hillsdale, NJ.

Frese, M., Ulich, E., and Dzida, W., editors (1987). *Psychological Issues of Human–Computer Interaction in the Work Place*. North-Holland, Amsterdam.

Friedman, Y. (1976). *Utopies Réalisables*. Union General d'Editions, Paris.

Fuchs-Kittowski, K. (1976). *Probleme des Determinismus und der Kybernetik in der molekularen Biologie. Tatsachen und Hypothesen über das Verhältnis des technischen Automaten zum lebenden Organismus*. Gustav Fischer, Jena, GDR.

Fuchs-Kittowski, K. (1983). Information Organisation und Evolution. In *Proc. IV. Wissenschaftliches Kolloquium zur Organisation der Informationsverarbeitung*. Berlin, GDR, pages 67–127.

Fuchs-Kittowski, K. (1991). System design, design of work and of organization. the paradox of safety orgware concepts, the necessity of a new culture in information systems and software development. In [v.d. Besselaar et al., 1991], pages 83–98.

Fuchs-Kittowski, K. and Rosenthal, H. A. (1972). Selbstorganisation und Evolution. *Wissenschaft und Fortschritt*, 22(7):308–313.

Fuchs-Kittowski, K. and Wenzlaff, B. (1976). Zur Differenzierung der Information auf verschiedenen Ebenen der Organisation lebender Systeme. In Geissler, E. and Scheler, W., editors, *Information, philosophische und ethische Probleme der Bio-Wissenschaften*. Akademie Verlag, Berlin, GDR, pages 317–361.

Furnas, G. W., Landauer, T. K., Gomez, L. M., and Dumais, S. T. (1983). Statistical semantics: Analysis of the potential performance of key-word information systems. *The Bell Systems Technical Journal*, 62(6):1753–1806.

Gadamer, H.-G. (1976). *Philosophical Hermeneutics*. University of California Press, Berkeley, CA. (Translated and edited by D. Linge).

Gadamer, H.-G. (1980). *Vernunft im Zeitalter der Wissenschaft*. Suhrkamp, Frankfurt a.M.

Gagné, R. M. and Briggs, L. J. (1979). *Principles of Instructional Design*. Holt, Rinehart and Winston, New York. (2nd edition).

Gagne, R. M., Briggs, L. J., and Wagner, W. (1988). *Principles of Instructional Design*. Holt, Rinehart and Winston, New York. (3rd edition).

Garson, B. (1988). *The Electronic Sweatshop. How Computers Are Transforming the Office of the Future Into the Factory of the Past*. Simon and Schuster, New York.

Gates, B. (1987). Beyond macro processing. *Byte*, 7(12):11–18.

Gerson, E. M. and Star, L. S. (1986). Analyzing due process in organizations. *ACM Transactions on Office Information Systems*, 4(3):257–270.

Gibbon, D. (1985). Context and variation in two–way radio discourse. *Discourse Processes Special Issue: Special Language Registers*, 8(4):395–420.

Gibson, J. J. (1979). *The Ecological Approach to Visual Perception*. Houghton-Mifflin, Boston.

Goguen, J. A. (1968–1969). The logic of inexact concepts. *Synthese*, 19:325–373.

Goguen, J. A. (1986). Reusing and interconnecting software components. *Computer*, 19(2):16–28. (Reprinted in P. Freeman, editor (1982) *Tutorial: Software Reusability*, IEEE Computer Society Press, pages 251–263).

Goguen, J. A. (1990). Hyperprogramming: A formal approach to software environments. In *Proc. Symposium on Formal Approaches to Software Environment Technology*. Joint System Development Corporation, Tokyo.

Goguen, J. A. and Meseguer, J. (1987). Unifying functional, object–oriented and relational programming, with logical semantics. In Shriver, B. and Wegner, P., editors, *Research Directions in Object–Oriented Programming*. MIT Press, Cambridge, MA, pages 417–477. (Preliminary version in *SIGPLAN Notices*, 21(10):153–162, October 1986).

Goguen, J. A. and Varela, F. (1979). Systems and distinctions; duality and complementarity. *International Journal of General Systems*, 5:31–43.

Goguen, J. A., Weiner, J. L., and Linde, C. (1983). Reasoning and natural explanation. *International Journal of Man-Machine Studies*, 19:521–559.

Goldkuhl, G., Iivari, J., Kall, C.-O., Koskela, E., and Tyllilä, P. (1981). Paradigm factors of systemeering research. In Kerola, P. and Koskela, E., editors, *Report 4th Scandinavian Research Seminar on Systemeering*. Institute of Information Processing Science, University of Oulu, pages 244–246.

Goldkuhl, G. and Lyytinen, K. (1984). Information system specification as rule reconstruction. In Bemelmans, T. M., editor, *Beyond Productivity: Information systems Development for Organizational Effectiveness*. North-Holland, Amsterdam, pages 30–55.

Goodman, N. (1976). *Languages of Art*. Hacket, Indianapolis, IN.

Goodman, N. (1978). *Ways of Worldmaking*. Hacket, Indianapolis, IN.

Goodman, N. (1979). *Fact, Fiction, and Forecast*. Hacket, Indianapolis, IN.

Goodman, N. (1984). *Of Mind and Other Matters*. Harvard University Press, Cambridge, MA.

Goody, J. (1977). *The Domestication of the Savage Mind*. Cambridge University Press, Cambridge, UK.

Gould, J. D., Conti, J., and Hovanyecz, T. (1983). Composing letters with a simulated listening typewriter. *Communications of the ACM*, 26(4):295–308.

Gould, L. and Finzer, W. (1984). Programming by rehearsal. Report SCL 84-1, Xerox PARC, Palo Alto, CA.

Grassi, E. (1980). *Rhetoric as Philosophy*. Pennsylvania State University Press, PA.

Greif, I., editor (1988). *Computer–Supported Cooperative Work CSCW. A Book of Readings*. Morgan Kaufman, San Mateo, CA.

Greif, S. (1989). Exploratorisches Lernen durch Fehler und qualifikationsorientiertes Software–Design. In [Maaß and Oberquelle, 1989], pages 204–212.

Greif, S. and Gediga, G. (1987). A critique and empirical investigation of the 'one–best–way–models' in human–computer interaction. In [Frese et al., 1987], pages 357–377.

Greiner, B. and Leitner, K. (1989). Assessment of job stress: The rhia instrument. In Landau, K. and Rohmert, W., editors, *Recent Developments in Job Analysis*. Taylor and Francis, London, pages 53–66.

Grice, P. (1975). Logic and conversation. In Cole, P. and Morgan, J., editors, *Speech Acts*, volume 3 of *Syntax and Semantics*. Academic Press, San Diego, pages 41–58.

Gumperz, J. J. (1982). *Discourse Strategies*. Cambridge University Press, Cambridge, UK.

Gunzenhäuser, R. (1982). Mensch–Maschine–Kommunikation als Zielsetzung der Informatik. In Endres, A. and Reetz, J., editors, *Textverarbeitung und Bürosysteme*. Oldenbourg, München, pages 75–91.

Habermas, J. (1971). *Knowledge and Human Interests*. Beacon Press, Boston, MA.

Habermas, J. (1973). Truth theories. In Fahrenbach, H. and Rock, W., editors, *Wirklichkeit und Reflexion*. Weinsberg, pages 211–265.

Habermas, J. (1984). *The Theory of Communicative Action*, volume 1. Heinemann, London.

Hacker, W. (1987a). Computerization versus computer–aided mental work. In [Frese et al., 1987], pages 115–130.

Hacker, W. (1987b). Software–Ergonomie: Gestalten geistiger Arbeit?! In Schönpflug, W. and Wittstock, M., editors, *Software–Ergonomie '87*. Teubner, Stuttgart, pages 31–54.

Haken, H. and Stadler, M., editors (1990). *Synergetics of Cognition*. Springer, Berlin.

Halasz, F. G., Moran, T. P., and Trigg, R. H. (1987). Notecards in a nutshell. In [Carroll and Tanner, 1987], pages 45–52.

Hamming, R. W. (1969). On man's view on computer science. *Journal of the ACM*, 16(1).

Harré, R., Clarke, D., and DeCarlo, N. (1985). *Motives and Mechanism. An Introduction to the Psychology of Action*. Methuen, London.

Hart, H. L. A. (1961). *The Concept of Law*. Oxford University Press, Oxford, UK.

Hartson, H. R. and Hix, D. (1989). Human–computer interface development: Concepts and systems for its management. *ACM Computing Surveys*, 21(1):5–92.

Haugeland, J. (1981). *Mind Design, Philosophy, Artificial Intelligence*. MIT Press, Cambridge, MA.

Haugeland, J. (1985). *Artificial Intelligence: The Very Idea*. Bradford Books/MIT Press, Cambridge, MA.

Hayek, F. A. (1967). The theory of complex phenomena. In Hayek, F. A., editor, *Studies in Philosophy, Politics, and Economics*. University of Chicago Press, Chicago, pages 22–42.

Hayward, J. (1984). Perceiving ordinary magic. In *New Science Library*. Shambhala, Boulder, page 268.

Hayward, J. (1987). *Shifting Worlds, Changing Minds*. Shambhala, Boulder.

Hedberg, B. and Mumford, E. (1975). The design of computer systems: Man's vision of man as an integral part of the system design process. In Mumford, E. and Sackman, H., editors, *Human Choice and Computers*. North-Holland, Amsterdam, pages 31–59.

Hegel, G. W. F. (1964). Phänomenologie des Geistes. Leipzig, GDR. (Edited by J. Hoffmeister, original from 1807).

Heidegger, M. (1959). *An Introduction to Metaphysics*. Yale University Press. (Translated by R. Manheim, original *Einführung in die Metaphysik* from 1935).

Heidegger, M. (1962). *Being and Time*. Blackwell, Oxford. (Translated by J. Macquarrie and E. Robinson, original from 1927, German: *Sein und Zeit*. Niemeyer, Tübingen 1976).

Heidegger, M. (1966). *Discourse on Thinking*. Harper and Row, New York. (Translated by J. Anderson and H. Freud, German: *Gelassenheit*, Neske, Pfullingen 1959).

Heidegger, M. (1971). *Poetry, Language, Thought*. Harper and Row, New York. (Translated by A. Hofstadter).

Heidegger, M. (1972). Die Zeit des Weltbildes. In *Holzwege*. Klostermann, Frankfurt a.M.

Heidegger, M. (1975). *Die Frage nach dem Ding*. Niemeyer, Tübingen.

Heidegger, M. (1977a). On the essence of truth. In *Basic Writings*. Harper and Row, New York, pages 119–141. (Translated by D. Krell, original from 1929).

Heidegger, M. (1977b). The origin of the work of art. In *Basic Writings*. Harper and Row, New York, pages 149–187. (Translated by D. Krell, original from 1929).

Heidegger, M. (1977c). *The Question Concerning Technology and other Essays*. Harper and Row, New York. (Original from 1953, German: *Die Frage nach der Technik*. In: Vorträge und Aufsätze. Neske, Pfullingen 1967).

Heidegger, M. (1977d). What is metaphysics? In *Basic Writings*. Harper and Row, New York, pages 91–116. (Translated by D. Krell, original from 1929).

Heidegger, M. (1978). *Metaphysische Anfangsgründe der Logik*. Klostermann, Frankfurt a.M. (Gesamtausgabe, Band 26).

Heidegger, M. (1987). *Being and Time*. Blackwell, Oxford. (Translated by J. Macquarrie and E. Robinson, original from 1927, German: *Sein und Zeit*. Niemeyer, Tübingen 1976).

Hellman, R. (1989). Emancipation of and by computer–supported cooperative work. *Scandinavian Journal of Information Systems*, 1:143–161.

Hewitt, C. (1986). Offices are open systems. *ACM Transactions on Office Information Systems*, 4(3):271–287.

Hildebrand-Nilshon, M. (1989). Intersubjektivität und die Semantisierung des Motivsystems. Psychologische Überlegungen zur Sprachevolution. In Gessinger, J. and v. Rahden, W., editors, *Theorien vom Ursprung der Sprache*, volume 2. De Gruyter, Berlin, pages 249–319.

Hildebrand-Nilshon, M. and Rückriem, G., editors (1988). *Activity Theory. A Look into a Multidisciplinary Research Area*, volume 1 of *Proc. 1ˢᵗ International Congress of Activity Theory*. Hochschule der Künste, Berlin.

Hilgard, E. R. and Bower, G. H. (1966). *Theories of Learning*. Meredith, New York.

Hill, W. C. (1989). The mind at AI: Horseless carriage to clock. *AI Magazine*, 10(2):28–41.

Hindle, B. (1981). *Emulation and Invention*. New York University Press, New York.

Hintikka, M. B. and Hintikka, J. (1986). *Investigating Wittgenstein*. Blackwell, Oxford.

Hirschheim, R. A. (1986). The effect of a priori views on the social implications of computing: the case of office automation. *Computing Surveys*, 18(2):165–195.

Hirschheim, R. A. and Klein, H. K. (1989). Four paradigms of information systems development. *Communications of the ACM*, 32(10):1199–1216.

Hoare, C. A. R. (1981). The emperor's old clothes. *Communications of the ACM*, 24(2):75–83. (1980 Turing Award Lecture).

Holmquist, B. and Andersen, P. B. (1987). Work language and information technology. *Journal of Pragmatics*, 11:327–357.

Holt, A. W. (1988). Diplans: A new language for the study and implementation of coordination. *ACM Transactions on Office Information Systems*, 6(2):109–125.

Holzkamp, K. (1978). *Sinnliche Erkenntnis. Historischer Ursprung und gesellschaftliche Funktion der Wahrnehmung*. Athenäum, Königstein/Ts.

Holzkamp, K. (1983). *Grundlegung der Psychologie*. Campus, Frankfurt a.M.

Höpfner, H.-D. and Skell, W. (1983). Zur Systematisierung von Formen der Übung kognitiver Prozesse – Klassifikationsgesichtspunkte und Darstellung entscheidender Variablen. *Forschung der sozialistischen Berufsbildung*, 17:161–166.

Hopper, P. (1987). Emergent grammar. In Aske, J., Beery, N., Michaelis, L., and Filip, H., editors, *Proc. 13ᵗʰ Annual Meeting of the Berkeley Linguistics Society*. Berkeley Linguistics Society, Berkeley, CA.

Huber, G. P. (1984). The nature and design of post–industrial organizations. *Management Science*, 30(8):928–951.

Hutchins, E. L., Hollan, J. D., and Norman, D. A. (1986). Direct manipulation interfaces. In [Norman and Draper, 1986], pages 87–124.

IDC (1989). Standard–Software gewinnt immer mehr an Bedeutung. *Computerwoche*, 16(52):12. (IDC study is cited in this article.)

Ifrah, G. (1987). *From One to Zero: A Universal History of Numbers*. Penguin Books, Harmondsworth, UK.

Iivari, J. (1983). Contributions to the theoretical foundations of systemeering research and the pioco model. Technical report, University of Oulu, SF.

Iivari, J. (1989). Contemporary schools of information systems development: A paradigmatic analysis. Working Paper, University of Oulu, SF.

Iivari, J. and Koskela, E. (1987). The PIOCO model for information systems design. *Management Information System Quarterly*, 11(9):401–419.

Illich, I. (1975). *Selbstbegrenzung. Eine politische Kritik der Technik*. Rowohlt, Reinbek.

Ilyenkov, E. V. (1977). *Dialectical Logic. Essays on its History and Theory*. Progress, Moscow.

Infotech, editor (1979). *Structured Software Development*. Infotech State of the Art Report, volume 2: Invited papers. Infotech, Maidenhead, UK.

Jackson, M. C. (1982a). The nature of soft systems thinking: Comments on the three replies. *Journal of Applied Systems Analysis*, 10:109–113.

Jackson, M. C. (1982b). The nature of soft systems thinking: The work of Churchman, Ackoff and Checkland. *Journal of Applied Systems Analysis*, 9:17–28.

Jakobson, R. (1962). Linguistics and poetics. In Sebeok, T. A., editor, *Style and Language*. MIT Press, Cambridge, MA.

Janik, A. and Toulmin, S. (1973). *Wittgenstein's Vienna*. Simon and Schuster, New York.

Jantsch, E. (1980). *The Self–Organizing Universe*. Pergamon, New York.

Järvinen, P., editor (1987). *Report 10th IRIS: Information systems Research seminar In Scandinavia*. University of Tampere, SF.

Jones, J. C. (1970). *Design Methods: Seeds of Human Futures*. Wiley, Chichester, UK.

Jones, J. C. (1979). Designing as a creative activity. In [Infotech, 1979], pages 117–133.

Jones, J. C. (1986). *Design Methods*. Wiley, Chichester, UK.

Kamenka, E., editor (1983). *The Portable Karl Marx*. Penguin Books, Harmondsworth, UK.

Kammersgaard, J. (1988). Four different perspectives on human–computer interaction. *International Journal on Man–Machine Studies*, 28:343–362.

Katzeff, C. (1986). Logical reasoning, models and database query writing. The effect of different conceptual models upon reasoning in a database query writing task. Hufacit Paper No. 10, Dept. of Psychology, University of Stockholm.

Kay, A. (1984). Software. *Scientific American*, 251(3):41–47.

Keen, P. G. (1981). Information systems and organizational change. *Communications of the ACM*, 24(1):24–33.

Keil-Slawik, R. (1987a). An ecological approach to responsible systems development. In Jacky, J. P. and Schuler, D., editors, *Directions and Implications of Advanced Computing (DIAC–87)*, volume 1. Ablex, Norwood, NJ, pages 82–96.

Keil-Slawik, R. (1987b). Supporting participative systems development by task–oriented requirements analysis. In Fuchs-Kittowski, K. and Gertenbach, D., editors, *System Design for Human Development and Productivity: Participation and Beyond*. Akademie der Wissenschaften, Berlin, GDR, pages 113–124. (Supplement volume to [Docherty et al., 1987]).

Keil-Slawik, R. (1989). Systemgestaltung mit Aufgabennetzen. In [Maaß and Oberquelle, 1989], pages 123–133.

Keil-Slawik, R. (1990). Konstruktives Design. Ein ökologischer Ansatz zur Gestaltung interaktiver Systeme. Habilitation, Forschungsberichte des Fachbereichs Informatik, Nr. 90-14, Technical University of Berlin.

Kensing, F. (1987). Generation of visions in system development: A supplement to the toolbox. In [Docherty et al., 1987], pages 285–301.

Kent, W. (1978). *Data and Reality*. North-Holland, Amsterdam.

Kerola, P. (1987). Search for national synergy in doctoral education programs of information technology. In Nissen, H. E. and Sandström, G., editors, *Report 9th Scandinavian Research Seminar on Systemeering*. Department of Information and Computer Sciences, University of Lund, SE. (In Finnish, abstract in English).

Kerola, P. (1988a). Integration of perspectives and views in the conception of office and its systems development. In *Proc. IFIP TC8 Open Conference*. University of Singapore.

Kerola, P. (1988b). Reflections of a human cognition and learning theory in information systems use and development. In *Proc. IFAC/IFIP Conference on Man–Machine Systems – Analysis, Design and Evaluation*. Oulu, SF, volume 2, pages 463–466.

Kerola, P. and Taggart, W. (1982). Human information processing styles in the information systems development process. In Hawgood, J., editor, *Evolutionary Information Systems*. North-Holland, Amsterdam, pages 63–86.

Kerola, P., Weckroth, J., Keinänen, J., Komulainen, S., Nuutinen, R., Pankkonen, K., Similä, J., and Tahvanainen, A. (1985). Research on the human–centred methodology of IS development – Summary Report. Technical report, Institute of Information Processing Science, University of Oulu. (In Finnish, abstract in English).

Kesselring, T. (1988). *Jean Piaget*. C. H. Beck, München.

Klaus, G. (1973). Semiotik und Erkenntnistheorie. Berlin, GDR.

Klein, H. K. and Hirschheim, R. A. (1987). A comparative framework of data modelling paradigms and approaches. *The Computer Journal*, 30(1):8–73.

Klein, H. K. and Hirschheim, R. A. (1989). Rationality concepts in information system development methodologies. In Coltersman, W. and Senn, J., editors, *Proc. Symposium on System Analysis and Design: A Research Strategy*. Atlanta.

Klein, H. K. and Kumar, K., editors (1988). *Information Systems Development for Human Progress in Organizations*. North-Holland, Amsterdam.

Kling, R. (1980). Social analysis of computing. *ACM Computing Surveys*, 12(1):61–110.

Knuth, D. E. (1968). *Fundamental Algorithms*. Addison-Wesley, Reading, MA.

Knuth, D. E. (1974). Structured programming with go to statements. *Computing Surveys*, 6(4):261–301. (Reprinted with revisions in *Current Trends in Programming Methodology*, Raymond T. Yeh, ed., 1 Prentice Hall, Englewood Cliffs, NJ, 1977, pages 140–194; also in *Classics in Software Engineering*, Edward Nash Yourdon, ed. Yourdon Press, New York, 1979, pages 259–321).

Knuth, D. E. (1984). Literate programming. *The Computer Journal*, 27(2):97–111.

Knuth, D. E. (1986). *TEX: The Program*. Addison-Wesley, Reading, MA.

Knuth, D. E. (1989). The Errors of TEX. *Software Practice and Experience*, 19(7):607–685.

Knuth, D. E., Larabee, T., and Roberts, P. M. (1989). Mathematical writing. *Mathematical Association of America Notes*, 14.

Kockelmans, J. (1984). *On the Truth of Being*. Indiana University, Bloomington, IN.

Kockelmans, J. (1985). *Heidegger and Science*. Washington University Press, Washington.

Köhler, W. (1935). *Gestalt Psychology*. Liveright, New York.

Kohn, T. and Schooler, C. (1983). *Work and Personality. An Inquiry into the Impact of Social Stratification*. Ablex, Norwood, NJ.

Koref, M. S. (1987). *Statistische Untersuchungen an DNS-Sequenzen – ein Verfahren zum mehrfachen Sequenzvergleich*. Dissertation, Humboldt-Universität, Berlin, GDR.

Kötter, W. and Gohde, H.-E. (1989). Ermittlung von Qualifizierungsvoraussetzungen, –zielen und –konzepten auf der Grundlage der Verfahren VERA und RHIA. In Dybowski, H., Herzer, H., and Sonntag, K., editors, *Strategien qualitativer Personal- und Bildungsplanung bei technisch–organisatorischen Innovationen*. Kommentator, Neuwied.

Kowalski, R. (1979). Algorithm = Logic + Control. *Communications of the ACM*, 22(7):424–436.

Krämer, S. (1988). *Symbolische Maschinen. Die Idee der Formalisierung in geschicht-lichem Abriß.* Wissenschaftliche Buchgesellschaft, Darmstadt.

Krogoll, T., Pohl, W., and Wanner, C. (1988). *CNC–Grundlagenausbildung mit dem Konzept CLAUS. Didaktik und Methoden.* Campus, Frankfurt a.M.

Kuhn, T. S. (1970). *The Structure of Scientific Revolutions.* University of Chicago Press, Chicago. (2nd edition).

Küppers, B.-O. (1983). *Molecular Theory of Evolution: Outline of a Physico–Chemical Theory of the Origin of Life.* Springer, Berlin.

Lakatos, I. (1976). *Proofs and Refutations – The Logic of Mathematical Discovery.* Cambridge University Press, Cambridge, UK.

Lakoff, G. and Johnson, M. (1980). *Metaphors We Live By.* University of Chicago Press, Chicago.

Langefors, B. (1966). *Theoretical Analysis of Information Systems.* Studentlitteratur, Lund.

Langefors, B. (1977). Hermeneutics, infology, and information systems. Technical Report TRITA-IBADB No. 1052, University of Stockholm.

Langton, C. G., editor (1989). *Artificial Life.* Addison-Wesley, Reading, MA.

Lanzara, G. (1983). The design process: Frames, metaphors and games. In [Briefs et al., 1983], pages 29–40.

Lanzara, G.-F. and Mathiassen, L. (1984). Mapping situations within a system development project. An intervention perspective on organizational change. Technical Report, Computer Science Department, Aarhus University.

Latour, B. (1987). *Science in Action.* Harvard University Press, Cambridge, MA.

Latour, B. and Strum, S. (1986). Human social origins. Oh please, tell us another story. *Journal of Social and Biological Structures,* (9):169–187.

Latour, B. and Woolgar, S. (1986). *Laboratory Life. The Construction of Scientific Facts.* Princeton University Press, Princeton, NJ.

Laudan, R., editor (1984). *The Nature of Technological Knowledge: Are Models of Scientific Change Relevant?* Reidel, Dordrecht, NL.

Lave, J. (1985). *Arithmetic Practice and Cognitive Theory: An Ethnographic Inquiry.* University of California Press, Berkeley, CA.

Lave, J. (1988). *Cognition in Practice. Mind, Mathematics and Culture in Everyday Life.* Cambridge University Press, Cambridge, UK.

Lehman, M. (1980). Programs, life cycles, and laws of software evolution. *Proceedings of the IEEE,* 86(9):1060–1076.

Lehtinen, E. and Lyytinen, K. (1986). The action based model of information system. *Information Systems,* 11(4):299–317.

Leontyev, A. (1978). *Activity, Consciousness, and Personality.* Prentice-Hall, Englewood Cliffs, NJ.

Leontyev, A. (1981). *Problems of the Development of Mind.* Progress, Moscow.

Leroi-Gourhan, A. (1988). *Hand und Wort. Die Evolution von Technik, Sprache und Kunst.* Suhrkamp, Frankfurt a.M.

Levi, I. (1967). *Gambling With Truth: An Essay on Induction and the Aims of Science.* A.A. Knopf and Routledge and Kegan Paul, New York.

Levinson, S. (1983). *Pragmatics.* Cambridge University Press, Cambridge, UK.

Lischka, C. and Diederich, J. (1987). Gegenstand und Methode der Kognitionswissenschaft. Symbol oder Neuron – Die künstliche Intelligenz an der Schwelle eines Paradigmenwechsels. *Der GMD-Spiegel,* 17(2/3):21–32.

Loscerbo, J. (1981). *Being and Technology. A Study in the Philosophy of Martin Heidegger.* Nijhoff, The Hague.

Luhmann, N. (1987). *Soziale Systeme. Grundriß einer allgemeinen Theorie.* Suhrkamp, Frankfurt a.M.

Lyytinen, K. (1986). Information systems development as social action: Framework and critical implications. Studies in Computer Science, Economics and Statistics 8, University of Jyväskylä, SF.

Lyytinen, K. (1987). Two views of information modeling. *Information and Management*, 12(1):9–19.

Lyytinen, K. and Lehtinen, E. (1987). Seven sins of systems work. In [Docherty et al., 1987], pages 63–79.

Maaß, S. (1984). Mensch–Rechner–Kommunikation. Herkunft und Chancen eines neuen Paradigmas. Bericht Nr. 104, Fachbereich Informatik, Universität Hamburg.

Maaß, S. and Oberquelle, H., editors (1989). *Software–Ergonomie '89.* Teubner, Stuttgart.

Mack, R. L., Lewis, C. H., and Carroll, J. M. (1983). Learning to use office systems: Problems and prospects. *ACM Transactions on Office Information Systems*, 22(1): 254–271.

MacKay, D. (1969). *Information, Mechanism and Meaning.* MIT Press, Cambridge, MA.

Macksey, R. and Donato, E., editors (1972). *The Structuralist Controversy: The Language of Criticism and the Sciences of Man.* Johns Hopkins Press, Baltimore, MD.

Madsen, C. M. (1989). Approaching group communication by means of an office building metaphor. In Bowers, J. and Wilson, P., editors, *Proc. EC-CSCW'89: 1st European Conference on Computer-Supported Cooperative Work.* London, pages 449–460.

Madsen, K. H. (1988). Breakthrough by breakdown: Metaphors and structured domains. In [Klein and Kumar, 1988].

Madsen, K. H. and Bøgh-Andersen, P. (1987). Design and Professional Languages. Technical report, Information Science Department, Aarhus University, DK,.

Malinowski, B. (1924). Meaning in primitive languages. In Odgen, C. and Richards, I., editors, *The Meaning of Meaning.* Routledge and Kegan Paul, London.

Manes, E. and Arbib, M. (1986). *Algebraic Approaches to Program Semantics.* Springer, Berlin.

Markus, M. L. and Bjørn-Andersen, N. (1987). Power over users: Its exercise by system professionals. *Communications of the ACM*, 30(6):498–504.

Mason, R. E. A. and Carey, T. T. (1983). Prototyping interactive information systems. *Communications of the ACM*, 26:347–354.

Mathiassen, L. (1984). Systemudvikling og Systemudviklingsmetode. DAIMI-PB-136, Department of Computer Science, Aarhus University, DK.

Maturana, H. (1978). Biology of language: The epistemology of reality. In *Psychology and Biology of Thought and Language: Essays in Honor of Eric Lenneberg.* Academic Press, San Diego, CA, pages 27–64.

Maturana, H. (1980). Biology of cognition. In [Maturana and Varela, 1980], pages 5–58.

Maturana, H. and Varela, F. (1980). *Autopoiesis and Cognition: The Realization of the Living.* Reidel, Dordrecht, NL.

Maturana, H. and Varela, F. (1987). *The Tree of Knowledge.* Shambhala, Boulder, CO.

Maturana, H., Varela, F., and Uribe, R. (1974). Autopoiesis, the organization of living systems: Its characterization and a model. *Biosystems*, 187(5).

McGregor (1960). *The Human Side of Enterprise.* McGraw-Hill, New York.

Mead, G. (1934). *Mind, Self, and Society.* University of Chicago Press, Chicago.

Miller, G. A. (1956). The magical number seven plus minus two: Some limits on our capacity for processing information. *Psychological Review*, 63:81–97.

Mitcham, C. and Mackey, R. (1983). Technology as a philosophical problem. In Mitcham, C. and Mackey, R., editors, *Philosophy and Technology. Readings in the Philosophical Problems of Technology*. Free Press, New York, pages 1–30.

Mitroff, I. I., Mason, R. O., and Barabba, V. P. (1982). Policy as argument – a logic for ill-structured decision problems. *Management Science*, (12):1391.

Monod, J. (1972). *Chance and Necessity*. Random House, New York.

Montague, R. (1974). *Formal Philosophy: Selected Papers of Richard Montague*. Yale University Press, New Haven, CT. (Edited and with an introduction by R. Thomason).

Morris, C. W. (1938). Foundations of a theory of signs. *International Encyclopedia of Unified Science*, 1(2).

Morris, C. W. (1946). *Signs, Language and Behaviour*. Braziller, New York.

Morrison, E. (1974). *From Know–How to Nowhere*. Blackwell, Oxford.

Mumford, E., Hirschheim, R., Fitzgerald, G., and Wood-Harper, A. T., editors (1985). *Methods in Information Systems*. North-Holland, Amsterdam.

Munzert, J. (1989). *Flexibilität des Handelns. Theoretische Überlegungen und experimentelle Untersuchungen zum Konzept des Motorikschemas*. bps, Köln.

Murray, M., editor (1978). *Heidegger and Modern Philosophy*. Yale University Press, New Haven, CT.

Mylopoulos, J. (1981). A perspective on conceptual modeling. In Brodie, M. L. and Zilles, S., editors, *Proc. Workshop on data Abstraction, Databases and Conceptual Modelling*. Published in *SIGPLAN Notices*, 16(1), pages 5–12.

Nake, F. (1986). Die Verdoppelung des Werkzeugs. In Rolf, A., editor, *Neue Techniken alternativ*. VSA, Hamburg, pages 43–52.

Naur, P. (1974). *Concise Survey of Computer Methods*. Studentlitteratur, Lund.

Naur, P. (1982). Formalization in program development. *BIT*, 22:437–453.

Naur, P. (1985a). Intuition in software development. In [Ehrig et al., 1985], pages 60–79.

Naur, P. (1985b). Programming as theory building. *Microprocessing and Microprogramming*, 15:253–261. EUROMICRO 84.

Naur, P. (1991). *Computing: A Human Activity*. ACM Press. Addison-Wesley, Reading, MA. (In press).

Naur, P. and Randell, B., editors (1969). *Software Engineering*. Scientific Affairs Division NATO, Brussels.

Neubert, J. and Tomczyk, R. (1986). *Gruppenverfahren der Arbeitsanlayse und Arbeitsgestaltung*. Springer, Berlin.

Newell, A. (1980). Physical symbol systems. *Cognitive Science*, 4:135–183.

Newell, A. and Card, S. K. (1985). The prospects for psychological science in human-computer interaction. *Human–Computer Interaction*, 1:209–242.

Newell, A. and Simon, H. A. (1972). *Human Problem Solving*. Prentice-Hall, Englewood Cliffs, NJ.

Newell, A. and Simon, H. A. (1976). Computer science as empirical inquiry: Symbols and search. *Communications of the ACM*, 19(3):113–126.

Nievergelt, J. (1983). Die Gestaltung der Mensch–Maschine–Schnittstelle. In Kupka, I., editor, *GI – 13. Jahrestagung*, Informatik–Fachberichte, Band 73. Springer, Berlin, pages 41–50.

Niiniluoto, I. (1980). *Introduction to the Philosophy of Science*. Otava, Helsinki. (In Finnish).

Niiniluoto, I. (1983). *Scientific Reasoning and Explanation*. Otava, Helsinki. (In Finnish).

Niiniluoto, I. (1987). *Truthlikeness*. Reidel, Dordrecht, NL.

Nishitani, K. (1982). *Religion and Nothingness*. University of California Press, Berkeley, CA.

Nissen, H.-E. (1988). Information systems development for responsible human action. In [Klein and Kumar, 1988], pages 99–113.

Norman, D. A. (1981). The trouble with Unix. *Datamation*, 27:556–563.

Norman, D. A. (1991). Cognitive artifacts. In [Carroll, 1991], pages 17–38.

Norman, D. A. and Draper, S. W., editors (1986). *User Centered Systems Design. New Perspectives on Human–Computer Interaction*. Lawrence Erlbaum, Hillsdale, NJ.

Nurminen, M. I. (1987). Different Perspectives: What are they and how can they be used? In [Docherty et al., 1987], pages 163–175.

Nurminen, M. I. (1988). *People or Computers: Three Ways of Looking at Information Systems*. Studentlitteratur, Lund.

Nurminen, M. I., Kalmi, R., Karhu, P., and Niemelä, J. (1987). Use or development of information systems: Which is more fundamental? In [Docherty et al., 1987], pages 187–196.

Nuutinen, R., Koskela, E., Iivari, J., and Kerola, P. (1987). Design and implementation experiences of a curriculum for the information systems architect reflected on the IFIP/BCS curriculum. In [Buckingham et al., 1987].

Nygaard, K. (1986). Program development as social activity. In Kugler, H. G., editor, *Information Processing 86 – Proceedings of the IFIP 10th World Computer Congress*. North-Holland, Amsterdam, pages 189–198.

Nygaard, K. and Håndlykken, P. (1981). The system development process – Its setting, some problems and needs for methods. In Hünke, H., editor, *Software Engineering Environments*. North-Holland, Amsterdam, pages 157–174.

Nygaard, K. and Sørgaard, P. (1987). The perspective concept in informatics. In [Bjerknes et al., 1987], pages 371–394.

Oberquelle, H. (1987). *Sprachkonzepte für benutzergerechte Systeme*. Informatik–Fachberichte, Band 144. Springer, Berlin.

Oberquelle, H. (1988). Role/function/action–nets as a visual language for cooperative modelling. In Finkelstein, A., editor, *Proc. IFIP International Workshop on Human Factors of Information System Analysis and Design (WHISAD 88)*. London.

Oberquelle, H., Kupka, I., and Maaß, S. (1983). A view of human–machine communication and co-operation. *International Journal on Man–Machine Studies*, 19(4):309–333.

Oesterreich, R. and Volpert, W. (1986). Task analysis for work design on the basis of action regulation theory. *Economic and Industrial Democracy*, 7:503–527.

Oliga, J. C. (1988). Methodological foundations of systems methodologies. *Systems Practice*, (3):87–112.

Olle, T. W. and Sibley, E., editors (1986). *Information Systems Design Methodologies – Improving the Practice*. North-Holland, Amsterdam.

Olle, T. W., Sol, H. G., and Tully, C., editors (1983). *Information Systems Design Methodologies – A Feature Analysis*. North-Holland, Amsterdam.

Olle, T. W., Sol, H. G., and Verrijn-Stuart, A. A., editors (1982). *Information Systems Design Methodologies – A Comparative Review*. North-Holland, Amsterdam.

Ortega y Gasset, J. (1961). *History as a System*. New York. (Translated by Weyl, Clark and Atkinson).

Orwell, G. (1989). *Nineteen Eighty-Four*. Penguin Books, Harmondsworth, UK. (First edition published by M. Secker and Warbug, 1949).

Palmer, R. (1969). *Hermeneutics*. Northwestern University Press, Evanston, IL.

Parnas, D. L. (1972). On the criteria to be used in decomposing systems into modules. *Communications of the ACM*, 15(12):1053–1058.

Parnas, D. L. (1985).] Software aspects of strategic defense systems. *American Scientist*, (September–October):432–440.

Parnas, D. L. and Clements, P. C. (1985). A rational design process: How and why to fake it. In [Ehrig et al., 1985], pages 80–100.

Pasch, J. (1989). Mehr Selbstorganisation in Softwareentwicklungsprojekten. *Softwaretechnik–Trends*, 9(2):42–55.

Pasch, J. (1991). Dialogical software design. In Bullinger, H. J., editor, *Human–Computer Interaction – Interact '91*. Elsevier, Amsterdam.

Pask, G. (1960). The natural history of networks. In [Yovits and Cameron, 1960], pages 232–261.

Pask, G. (1962a). Interaction between a group of subjects and an adaptive automaton to produce a self–organizing system for decision making. In Yovits, M. C., Jacoby, G. T., and Goldstein, G. D., editors, *Self–Organizing Systems*. Spartan Books, Washington, DC, pages 283–312.

Pask, G. (1962b). A proposed evolutionary model. In v. Foerster, H. and Zopf, G. W., editors, *Principles of Self–Organization*. Pergamon, New York, pages 229–254.

Pask, G. (1976). *Conversation Theory – Applications in Education and Epistemology*. Elsevier, Amsterdam.

Pask, G. (1980). The limits of togetherness. In Lavington, S. H., editor, *Information Processing 80 – Proceedings of the IFIP 8th World Computer Congress*. North-Holland, Amsterdam, pages 999–1012.

Pask, G. and v. Foerster, H. (1961). A predictive model for self–organizing systems. *Cybernetica*. Part I in No.3 , 258–300; Part II in No.4, 20–55.

Pedrycz, W. (1989). *Fuzzy Control and Fuzzy Systems*. Wiley, Chichester, UK.

Peil, J. (1977). Eine Diskussion des begrifflichen Inhalts von "Information" in Kybernetik, Physik und Biologie. In Geissler, E., Scharf, J. H., and Scheler, W., editors, *Diskretität und Stetigkeit von Lebensprozessen*. Akademie Verlag, Berlin, GDR, pages 76–105.

Peirce, C. S. (1968). *Über die Klarheit unserer Gedanken. How to make our ideas clear*. Klostermann, Frankfurt a.M. (Bilingual edition).

Petri, C. A. (1980). Introduction to general net theory. In Brauer, W., editor, *Net Theory and Applications*. LNCS volume 84. Springer, Berlin, pages 1–19.

Petri, C. A. (1983). Zur "Vermenschlichung" des Computers. *Der GMD–Spiegel*, 13(4): 42–44.

Pirsig, R. (1975). *Zen and the Art of Motorcycle Maintenance*. Bantam Books, New York.

Polanyi, M. (1967). *The Tacit Dimension*. Doubleday, Garden City, NY.

Popper, K. R. (1965). *Conjectures and Refutations*. Harper and Row, New York.

Putnam, H. (1988). *Representation and Reality*. MIT Press, Cambridge, MA.

Raeithel, A. (1983). *Tätigkeit, Arbeit und Praxis. Grundbegriffe für eine praktische Psycholgie*. Campus, Frankfurt a.M.

Raeithel, A. (1989). Kommunikation als gegenständliche Tätigkeit. Zu einigen philosophischen Problemen der kulturhistorischen Psychologie. In Knobloch, C., editor, *Kommunikation und Kognition*, Studien zur Psychologie der Zeichenverwendung. Nodus Publikationen, Münster, pages 29–70.

Raeithel, A. and Volpert, W. (1985). Aneignung der Computer oder Telematik–Monokultur? *Zeitschrift für Sozialisationsforschung und Erziehungssoziologie*, (5):7–26.

Reisin, F.-M. (1989). Gestaltbarkeit und Gestaltung von Methoden – Zwei notwendige Bedingungen kooperativer Softwareentwicklung. *Softwaretechnik–Trends*, 9(2):14–26.

Reisin, F.-M. (1990). *Kooperative Gestaltung in partizipativen Software–Projekten*. Dissertation, Technical University of Berlin.

Reisin, F.-M. and Wegge, D. (1989). On experimental prototyping in user–oriented system development. In Bødker, S., editor, *Proc. 12th IRIS: Information systems Research seminar In Scandinavia*. Aarhus University, pages 517–532.

Rich, E. (1983). *Artificial Intelligence*. McGraw-Hill, New York.

Richardson, W. J. (1967). *Heidegger. Through Phenomenology to Thought*. Nijhoff, The Hague.

Ricoeur, P. (1986). *Die lebendige Metapher*. Fink, München. (Original *La métaphore vive*, Paris 1975).

Ritter, G. X., editor (1989). *Information Processing 89 – Proceedings of the IFIP* 11th *World Computer Congress*. North-Holland, Amsterdam.

Rock, I. (1984). *Perception*. Scientific American Books, New York.

Rogoff, B. and Lave, J., editors (1984). *Everyday Cognition: Its Development in Social Context*. Harvard University Press, Cambridge, MA.

Rolskov, B. (1990). Organizational Competence in System Development. A Scandinavian Contribution. In [Bjerknes et al., 1990].

Root, R. W. (1988). Design of a multi–media vehicle for social browsing. In [CSCW'88, 1988], pages 25–38.

Rorty, R. (1961). Pragmatism, categories, and language. *Philosophical Review*, 70:197–223.

Rorty, R. (1984). Habermas and Lyotard on post–modernity. *Praxis International*, 4(1).

Rosson, M. B. and Alpert, S. (1990). The cognitive consequences of object–oriented design. *Human–Computer Interaction*, 5(4):345–379.

Ryle, G. (1983). *The Concept of Mind*. Penguin Books, Harmondsworth, UK.

Sacks, O. (1986). *The Man Who Mistook his Wife for a Hat*. Pan Books, London.

Sacks, H., Schlegloff, E. A., and Jefferson, G. (1974). A simplest systematics for organisation of turn–taking for conversation. *Language*, 50:696–735.

Sahlins, M. (1983). *Culture and Practical Reason*. University of Chicago Press, Chicago.

Savage, L. J. (1965). *The Foundations of Statistics*. Wiley, Chichester, UK.

Schirmacher, W. (1983). *Technik und Gelassenheit. Zeitkritik nach Heidegger*. Alber, Freiburg.

Schmandt-Besserat, D. (1978). The earliest precursors of writing. *Scientific American*, 238(6):38–47.

Schmidt, S. J., editor (1987). *Der Diskurs des radikalen Konstruktivismus*. Suhrkamp, Frankfurt a.M.

Schneider, J. W. (1985). Social problems theory: The constructionist view. *Annual Review of Sociology*, 11:209–229.

Schönpflug, W. (1986). The trade-off between internal and external information storage. *Journal of Memory and Language*, 25:657–675.

Schönpflug, W. (1989). Neue Technik und alter Mensch – Kulturhistorische Wurzeln einiger Schwierigkeiten mit dem Computer. In [Maaß and Oberquelle, 1989], pages 17–35.

Schriffrin, D. (1987). *Discourse Markers*. Cambridge University Press, Cambridge, UK.

Scott, D. and Strachey, C. (1971). Towards a mathematical semantics for computer languages. In *Proc. 21st Symposium on Computers and Automata*. (Also Technical Monograph PRG 6, Oxford University, Programming Research Group).

Scribner, S. (1985). Vygotski's uses of history. In Wertsch, J. V., editor, *Culture, Communication and Cognition. Vygotskian Perspectives.* Cambridge University Press, Cambridge, UK, pages 119–145.

Searle, J. R. (1969). *Speech Acts.* Cambridge University Press, Cambridge, UK.

Searle, J. R. (1979). *Expression and Meaning.* Cambridge University Press, Cambridge, UK.

Searle, J. R. (1980). Minds, brains, and programs. *The Behavioral and Brain Sciences,* 3:417–457.

Searle, J. R. (1990). Is the brain's mind a computer program? *Scientific American,* 262(1):20–25.

Sellars, W. (1963). *Science, Perception and Reality.* Routledge and Kegan Paul, London.

Seubold, G. (1986). *Heideggers Analyse der neuzeitlichen Technik.* Alber, Freiburg.

Shannon, C. E. and Weaver, W. (1949). *A Mathematical Theory of Communication.* University of Illinois Press, Urbana, IL.

Shapiro, G. and Sica, A. (1984). *Hermeneutics. Questions and Prospects.* University of Massachusetts Press, Amherst, MA.

Shneiderman, B. (1980). *Software Psychology: Human Factors in Computer and Information Systems.* Winthrop, Cambridge, MA.

Shneiderman, B. (1982). The future of interactive systems and the emergence of direct manipulation. *Behaviour and Information Technology,* 1:237–256.

Shneiderman, B. (1987). *Designing the User Interface – Strategies for Effective Human–Computer Interaction.* Addison-Wesley, Reading, MA.

Siefkes, D. (1990). *Formalisieren und Beweisen – Logik für Informatiker.* Vieweg, Wiesbaden.

Siefkes, D. (1991). *Kleine Systeme – Lernen und Arbeiten in formalen Umgebungen.* Vieweg, Wiesbaden. (In preparation).

Sieker, J. and Jensen, C. S. (1988). Modsigelser i Designprocesser. Master Thesis, Institute of Electronic Systems, Aalborg University. (Contradictions in Design Processes, in Danish).

Similä, J. (1988). Modelling and analyzing empirically the success of ADP systems use. Dissertation, Acta Universitatis Ouluensis, Series A, No. 196, Institute of Information Processing Science, University of Oulu, SF.

Similä, J. and Nuutinen, R. (1983). On the image of man and its implications for systemeering research. In Nurminen, M. I. and Gaupholm, H. T., editors, *Report 6th Scandinavian Research Seminar on Systemeering.* University of Bergen.

Smith, R. B. (1987). Experience with the alternate reality kit. An example of the tension between literalism and magic. In [Carroll and Tanner, 1987], pages 61–67.

Soloway, E. and Ehrlich, K. (1984). Empirical studies of programming knowledge. *IEEE Transactions on Software Engineering,* SE-10(5):595–609.

Sørgaard, P. (1987). A cooperative work perspective on the use and development of computer artifacts. In [Järvinen, 1987], pages 719–734.

Sperber, D. and Wilson, D. (1986). *Relevance: Communication and Cognition.* Blackwell, Oxford.

Spinas, P. (1987). VDU–work and user–friendly human–computer interaction: Analysis of dialogue structures. In [Frese et al., 1987], pages 147–162.

Stamper, R. (1983). Information analysis in LEGOL. In Bubenko, J., editor, *Information Modeling.* Studentlitteratur, Lund, pages 565–596.

Stamper, R. (1987). Semantics. In [Boland and Hirschheim, 1987], pages 43–78.

Stefik, M. J. and Bobrow, D. G. (1987). Review of Winograd, Flores (1986). *Artificial Intelligence*, 31:220–226.

Steiner, G. (1978). *Heidegger.* Collins, Glasgow, UK.

Steinmüller, W. (1979). Juristische Informationswissenschaft. *Rechtstheorie*, pages 327–345. (Supplement to volume 1979).

Stent, G. S. (1986). Einleitung und Übersicht. In [Delbrück, 1986], pages 11–34.

Stoy, J. (1977). *Denotational Semantics of Programming Languages: The Scott-Strachey Approach to Programming Language Theory.* MIT Press, Cambridge, MA.

Strandh, S. (1979). A history of the machine. New York.

Suchman, L. A. (1987). *Plans and Situated Actions – The Problem of Human–Machine Communication.* Cambridge University Press, Cambridge, UK.

Sutter, A. (1988). *Göttliche Maschinen.* Athenäum, Frankfurt a.M.

Swartout, W. and Balzer, R. (1982). On the inevitable intertwining of specification and implementation. *Communications of the ACM*, 25(7):438–440.

Szilard, L. (1929). Über Entropieverminderung in einem thermodynamischen System bei Eingriffen intelligenter Wesen. *Zeitschrift für Physik*, 53:840–852.

Tagg, J. (1989). Postmodernism and the born–again avant–garde. In Tagg, J., editor, *The Cultural Politics of Post–Modernism.* SUNY Binghamton MRTS, Binghamton, NY.

Tarski, A. (1944). The semantic conception of truth. *Philosophy and Phenomenological Research*, 4:13–47.

Taylor, F. W. (1911). *The Principles of Scientific Management.* Harper and Row, New York.

Teichroew, D., Macasovic, P., Hershey, E., and Yamamoto, Y. (1980). Application of the entity–relationship approach to information processing systems modeling. In Chen, P. P., editor, *Entity–Relationship Approach to Systems Analysis and Design.* North-Holland, Amsterdam, pages 15–38.

Teitelman, W. (1977). A display oriented programmer's assistant. Technical Report 3, Xerox, Palo Alto, CA.

Tenenbaum, E. and Wildavsky, A. (1984). Why policies control data and data cannot determine policies. *Scandinavian Journal of Management Studies*, pages 83–100.

Terry, A. J. and Englemore, R. S. (1981). A knowledge–based approach to the interpretation of protein electron density maps. In Bond, A., editor, *Machine Intelligence*, number 3 in Infotech State of the Art Report, series 9. Infotech, Maidenhead, UK, pages 307–321.

Thompson, W. I., editor (1987). *Gaia – A Way of Knowing. Political Implications of the New Biology.* Lindisfarne Press, Great Barrington, MA.

Toulmin, S. (1958). *The Uses of Argument.* Cambridge University Press, Cambridge, UK.

Trigg, R. H. (1988). Guided tours and tabletops: Tools for communicating in a hypertext environment. In [CSCW'88, 1988], pages 216–226.

Trungpa, C. (1976). *The Myth of Freedom.* Shambhala, Boulder, CO.

Trungpa, C. (1984). *Shambhala: The Sacred Path of the Warrior.* Shambhala, Boulder, CO.

Tsetung, M. (1967). *On Contradiction*, volume 1 of *Selected Works.* Foreign Language Press, Peking.

Tsichritzis, D. and Lochovsky, F. (1982). *Data Models.* Prentice-Hall, Englewood Cliffs, NJ.

Turner, R., editor (1974). *Ethnomethodology.* Penguin Books, Harmondsworth, UK.

Turkle, S. (1984). *The Second Self – Computers and the Human Spirit*. Granada, London.

Turvey, M. T., Carello, C., and Kim, N. G. (1990). Links between active perception and the control of action. In [Haken and Stadler, 1990], pages 269–295.

Ulich, E. (1987). Individual differences in human–computer interaction: Concepts and research findings. In Salvendy, G., editor, *Cognitive Engineering in the Design of Human-Computer Interaction and Expert Systems*. Elsevier, Amsterdam.

v. Foerster, H. (1960). On self–organizing systems and their environments. In [Yovits and Cameron, 1960], pages 31–50.

v. Foerster, H. (1981a). Das Konstruieren einer Wirklichkeit. In Watzlawick, P., editor, *Die erfundene Wirklichkeit. Wie wissen wir, was wir zu wissen glauben?* Piper, München, pages 39–60.

v. Foerster, H. (1981b). Objects: Tokens for (eigen–)behaviors. In [v. Foerster, 1981a].

v. Foerster, H. (1984). *Observing Systems*. Intersystems Publications, Seaside, CA.

v. Foerster, H. (1985). *Sicht und Einsicht. Versuche zu einer operativen Erkenntnistheorie*. Vieweg, Wiesbaden.

v. Foerster, H., Mead, M., and Teuber, H. L., editors (1949). *Cybernetics: Transactions of the Sixth, Seventh, Eighth, Ninth, and Tenth Josiah Macy Jr. Conferences*. The Josiah Macy Jr. Foundation, New York. (Further editions: 1950, 1951, 1953, 1955).

v. Foerster, H. and Zopf, G. W., editors (1962). *Principles of Self–Organization*. Pergamon, New York.

v. Glasersfeld, E. (1987). *The Construction of Knowledge – Contributions to Conceptual Semantics*. Intersystems Publications, Seaside, CA.

v. Griethuysen, J. J., editor (1982). *Concepts and Terminology for the Conceptual Schema and Information Base*. Information System, New York.

v. Hahn, W. (1986). Pragmatic considerations in man–machine discourse. In *Coling 86: Proc. 11th International Conference on Computational Linguistics*. University of Bonn.

v. Uexküll, J. (1957). A stroll through the worlds of animals and men. In Schiller, C. H., editor, *Instinctive Behavior*. International University Press, New York, pages 5–80.

v. Weizsäcker, C. F. and v. Weizsäcker, E. U. (1972). Wiederaufnahme der begrifflichen Frage: Was ist Information. In Scharf, J. H., editor, *Informatik*. Johann Ambrosius Barth, Leipzig, GDR, pages 535–555.

v. Weizsäcker, E. U. (1972). Unterschied zwischen genetischer und Shannon'scher Information. In Geissler, E. and Ley, H., editors, *Philosophische und Ethische Probleme der modernen Genetik*. Akademie Verlag, Berlin, GDR, pages 160–172.

v.d. Besselaar, P., Clement, A., and Järvinen, P., editors (1991). *Information System Work and Organization Design*. North-Holland, Amsterdam.

Valder, W. and Weller, U. (1984). Schwierigkeiten mit der klassischen Systemanalyse. *Angewandte Informatik*, 26(8):323–328.

Varela, F. J. (1975).] A calculus for self–reference. *International Journal of General Systems*, 2:5–24.

Varela, F. J. (1987). Autonomie und Autopoiese. In [Schmidt, 1987], pages 119–132.

Varela, F. J. and Goguen, J. A. (1978). The arithmetics of closure. *Journal of Cybernetics*, 8:125. (Also in Trappl, R., Klir, G., and Ricciardi, L., editors (1978), *Progress in Cybernetics and Systems Research*, Volume 3, Hemisphere Publishing).

Vellino, A. (1987). Review of Winograd, Flores (1986). *Artificial Intelligence*, 31:213–220.

Volpert, W. (1987). Contrastive analysis of the relationship of man and computer as a basis of system design. In [Docherty et al., 1987], pages 119–127.

Volpert, W. (1989). Work and personality development from the viewpoint of the action regulation theory. In Leymann, H. and Kornbluh, H., editors, *Socialization and Learning at Work*. Avebury, Aldershot, UK.

Völz, H. (1982). *Information I. Studien zur Vielfalt und Einheit der Informationstheorie und Anwendung vor allem in der Technik*. Akademie-Verlag, Berlin, GDR.

Völz, H. (1983). *Information II. Theorie und Anwendung vor allem in der Biologie, Medizin und Semiotik*. Akademie-Verlag, Berlin, GDR.

Vygotsky, L. S. (1978). *Mind in Society*. Harvard University Press, Cambridge, MA.

Weick, K. E. (1979). *The Social Psychology of Organizing*. Addison-Wesley, Reading, MA.

Weingarten, R. and Fiehler, R. (1986). *Technisierte Kommunikation*. Westdeutscher Verlag, Opladen.

Weizenbaum, J. (1977). *Computer Power and Human Reason: From Judgement to Calculation*. Freeman, San Francisco.

Weltz, F. and Lullies, V. (1983). Menschenbilder der Betriebsorganisatoren. In Rammert, W., Bechmann, G., Nowotny, H., and Vahrenkamp, R., editors, *Jahrbuch Technik & Gesellschaft*. Campus, Frankfurt a.M., pages 109–128.

Wenzlaff, B. (1983). Information und Gedächtnis – Ein Modell zur Veranschaulichung der Niveaustufen der Information. In *Proc. IV. Wissenschaftliches Kolloquium zur Organisation der Informationsverarbeitung*. Berlin, GDR, pages 3–66.

Wertsch, J. V., editor (1981). *The Concept of Activity in Soviet Psychology*. Sharpe, Armonk, NY.

Wertsch, J. V. (1985). *Vygotski and the Social Formation of Mind*. Harvard University Press, Cambridge, MA.

Whiteside, J. and Wixon, D. (1987). Improving human–computer interaction – A quest for cognitive science. In [Carroll, 1987], pages 337–352.

Wiener, N. (1963). *Kybernetik, Regelung und Nachrichtenübertragung im Lebewesen und in der Maschine*. Econ, Düsseldorf.

Wilber, K. (1983). *A Sociable God: Toward a New Understanding of Religion*. Shambhala, Boulder, CO.

Wingert, B. and Riehm, U. (1985). Computer als Werkzeug. In Rammert, W., Bechmann, G., and Nowotny, H., editors, *Jahrbuch Technik & Gesellschaft*, volume 3. Campus, Frankfurt a.M., pages 107–131.

Winograd, T. (1972). Understanding natural language. *Cognitive Psychology*, 1972(3):1–191.

Winograd, T. (1988). A language/action perspective on the design of cooperative work. In [Greif, 1988], pages 623–653. Reprint.

Winograd, T. and Flores, F. (1986). *Understanding Computers and Cognition – A New Foundation for Design*. Ablex, Norwood, NJ.

Winograd, T. and Flores, F. (1987). A response to the reviews. *Artificial Intelligence*, 31:250–261.

Wittgenstein, L. (1922). *Tractatus Logico–Philosophicus*. Routledge and Kegan Paul, London. (Translated by D. F. Pears and B. F. Mc Guiness, with an introduction by Bertrand Russell, original from 1921).

Wittgenstein, L. (1968). *Philosophical Investigations*. Blackwell, Oxford. (English translation of the 3rd edition by G. E. M. Anscombe).

Wittgenstein, L. (1978). On Heidegger on being and dread. In Murray, M., editor, *Heidegger and Modern Philosophy*. Yale University Press, New Haven, CT. (Translation and commentary by M. Murray. The complete German text first appeared as "Zu

Heidegger" in *Ludwig Wittgenstein und der Wiener Kreis: Gespräche, aufgezeichnet von Friedrich Waismann*, 1967.)

Wixon, D., Whiteside, J., Good, M., and Jones, S. (1983). Building a user–defined interface. In Janda, A., editor, *Proc. CHI'83: Human Factors in Computing Systems*. ACM, New York, pages 24–27.

Wolfram, S. (1988). *Mathematica. A System for Doing Mathematics by Computer*. Addison-Wesley, Reading, MA.

Yovits, M. C. and Cameron, S., editors (1960). *Self–Organizing Systems*. Pergamon, New York.

Zemanek, H. (1989). Formal structures in an informal world. In [Ritter, 1989], pages 1101–1105.

List of Authors

Klaus Amann
(Born 1958 in Germany)
Dr. soc. from the University of Bielefeld. Research and Teaching Assistant in the Faculty of Sociology at the University of Bielefeld.
Research interests: Sociology of knowledge, theory of science, sociology of culture

Gro Bjerkness
(Born 1956 in Norway)
Dr. scient. in Informatics from the University of Oslo. Associate Professor in the Department of Informatics at the University of Oslo.
Research interests: System development

Reinhard Budde
(Born 1951 in Germany)
Dr.-Ing. in Informatics from the Technical University of Berlin. Senior Scientist at the German National Research Center for Computer Science (GMD), Sankt Augustin.
Research interests: Software engineering, object-oriented design and programming methods, programming environments

Rodney M. Burstall
(Born 1934 in Britain)
PhD in Computing and Operational Research from the University of Birmingham. Professor of Computer Science at the University of Edinburgh.
Research interests: Programming languages, logic and category theory

Rafael Capurro
(Born 1945 in Uruguay)
Dr.phil.habil. in Practical Philosophy from the University of
Stuttgart. Professor of Information Science at the College for
Librarianship in Stuttgart. Associate of the Philosophical and
Technical Studies Center, Polytechnic University, N.Y.C.
Research interests: Information science, philosophy of technol-
ogy, hermeneutics, ethics

John M. Carroll
(Born 1950 in U.S.A.)
PhD in Experimental Psychology from Columbia University.
Manager of User Interface Theory and Design at the IBM Wat-
son Research Center Yorktown Heights.
Research interests: Analysis of learning, problem-solving, lan-
guage capacities, human-computer interaction

Wolfgang Coy
(Born 1947 in Germany)
Dr.rer.nat. in Informatics from the Technical University Darm-
stadt. Professor of Informatics in the Department of Computer
Science at the University of Bremen.
Research interests: Computers and society, theoretical founda-
tions of informatics, image processing, computers as technical
media

Bo Dahlbom
(Born 1949 in Sweden)
PhD (Docent) in Theoretical Philosophy from the University of
Göteborg. Associate Professor in the Department of Technology
and Social Change at the University of Linköping.
Research interests: Artifical intelligence and the philosophy of
mind, computer technology and social change, conditions for
benign computerization of society

Wolfgang Dzida
(Born 1941 in Germany)
Dr. phil. in Social Psychology from the Technical University of
Berlin. Senior scientist at the German National Research Center
for Computer Science (GMD), Sankt Augustin.
Research interests: User interface design and evaluation, er-
gonomic office system conception, system developers' workplaces

Christiane Floyd
(Born 1943 in Austria)
Dr.phil. in Mathematics from the University of Vienna. Professor of Software Engineering at the Technical University of Berlin. Research interests: Software development methods, human-centred system design, epistemological foundations of informatics

Heinz von Foerster
(Born 1911 in Austria)
Dr.phil. in Physics from the University of Vienna. Professor Emeritus in the Departments of Biophysics and Physiology, and of Electrical and Computer Engineering at the University of Illinois, Urbana.
Research interests: The study of physiology, theory, technology and epistemology of cognitive processes.

Klaus Fuchs-Kittowski
(Born 1934 in Germany)
Dr.phil.habil. in Philosophy from the Humboldt University at Berlin. Professor in the Department of Theory and Organization of Science at the Humboldt University, Berlin.
Research interests: User-oriented analysis and design of information systems, human-computer interaction, epistomological and methodological problems of information processing

Dafydd Gibbon
(Born 1944 in England)
Dr.phil. in English and Linguistics from the University of Göttingen. Professor for English and Linguistics at the University of Bielefeld.
Research interests: Computational modelling of speech, theoretical lexicology, epistomological foundations of linguistics

Joseph A. Goguen
(Born 1941 in U.S.A.)
PhD in Mathematics from the University of California of Berkeley. Professor of Computing Science at Oxford University, Student of Tibetan Buddhism.
Research interests: Requirements, software engineering, theorem proving, philosophy of computation, massively parallel computer architectures, discourse analysis, the semantics of natural and artificial languages, and computer security

Thomas F. Gordon

(Born 1955 in U.S.A.)

J.D. from the University of California at Davis. Senior scientist at the National Research Center for Computer Science (GMD), Sankt Augustin.

Research interests: Artificial intelligence, legal reasoning, argumentation, abduction, planning

Reinhard Keil-Slawik

(Born 1953 in Germany)

Dr.-Ing.habil. in Informatics from the Technical University of Berlin. Assistant Professor in the Computer Science Department at the Technical University of Berlin.

Research interests: Software engineering, software ergonomics, computer and society, history of computing

Pentti Kerola

(Born 1935 in Finland)

Dr. of Economics and Business Administration h.c. Phil.Lic.. Professor of Information Processing Science at the University of Oulu.

Research interests: Philosophical aspects of information processing, macromodelling of information system development, human-computer interaction

Heinz K. Klein

(Born 1939 in Germany)

Dr.oec.publ.. Associate Professor of Information Systems at the School of Managment of the State University of New York at Binghampton.

Research interests: Socio-theoretic foundations of information systems, application of social action and systems theory, information engineering

Donald E. Knuth

(Born 1938 in U.S.A.)

PhD in Mathematics from the California Institute of Technology. Professor of The Art of Computer Programming at Stanford University.

Research interests: Analysis of algorithms, combinatorial mathematics, programming languages, digital typography, history of computer science

Klaus-Peter Löhr
(Born 1941 in Germany)
Dr.-Ing.habil. in Informatics from the Technical University of
Berlin. Professor of Computer Science at the Free University of
Berlin.
Research interests: Operating systems, distributed systems, soft-
ware development

Kalle Lyytinen
(Born 1953 in Finland)
PhD in Computer Science from the University of Jyväskylä. Pro-
fessor for Information Systems at the University of Jyväskylä.
Research interests: Data modelling, requirements specification,
information system failures, speech-act based models and tools

Susanne Maaß
(Born 1952 in Germany)
Dr.rer.nat. in Informatics from the University of Hamburg. As-
sistant Professor in the Research group on Applied and Socially
Oriented Informatics at the University of Hamburg.
Research interests: Software ergonomics, computer support for
group work, social impact of computing, women and computers

Markku I. Nurminen
(Born 1943 in Finland)
PhD in Computer Science at the University of Turku. Professor
of Computer Science at the University of Turku.
Research interests: Use of information systems as an inherent
part of work situation of its users, system architecture, user
learning, user interface

Kristen Nygaard
(Born 1926 in Norway)
Cand. real. in Mathematics. Dr.h.c. in Informatics from the Universities of Lund and Aalborg. Professor of Computer Science
at the University of Oslo.
Research interests: User-tailorable software that is modifiable
and extendable by the users

Horst Oberquelle

(Born 1947 in Germany)

Dr.rer.nat.habil. in Informatics from the University of Hamburg. Professor for Informatics in the Research group on Applied and Socially Oriented Informatics at the University of Hamburg.

Research interests: Human-machine interaction, user-oriented description languages, tools and methods for interface design and development

Arne Raeithel

(Born 1943 in Germany)

Dr.phil.habil. in Psychology from the University of Hamburg . Assistant Professor in the Department of Psychology at the University of Hamburg.

Research interests: Assessment methods for cognitive psychology, design of computer-aided collaborative workplaces for scientific data analysis

Fanny-Michaela Reisin

(Born 1946 in Israel)

Dr.-Ing. in Informatics from the Technical University of Berlin. Assistant Professor in the Computer Science Department at the Technical University of Berlin.

Research interests: Methods and management concepts for participative software projects, empirical study on software projects, theory of of software and software development

Douglas T. Ross

(Born 1929 in China)

Master's in Pure Mathematics and Electrical Engineering from MIT. Chairman Emeritus, SofTech, Inc., Waltham, Mass., Lecturer in the Department of EE and Computer Science, MIT

Research interests: Rigorous foundations for PLEX, and its application, as in SADT (Structured Analysis and Design Technique)

Dirk Siefkes

(Born 1938 in Germany)

Dr.rer.nat. in Mathematical Logic from the University of Heidelberg. Professor for Theoretical Computer Science at the Technical University of Berlin.

Research interests: Logic, term rewriting systems, complexity theory, philosophical, historical and pedagogical problems of informatics, "small systems"

Jouni Similä
(Born 1951 in Finland)
PhD in Information Processing Science from the University of Oulu. Technical Director at CCC Software Professionals, Oulunsalo, Finland; Area Manager of CCC Greece Ltd.
Research interests: Information systems implementation and use, methods and tools for risk-oriented software project management

Walter Volpert
(Born 1942 in Germany)
Dr.phil. in Psychology from the Technical University of Berlin. Professor for Industrial Psychology and Pedagogics at the Technical University of Berlin. Head of the Institute for Human Science in Work and Education.
Research interests: Psychology of work and action, work design, social impact of information technology

Heinz Züllighoven
(Born 1949 in Germany)
Dr.-Ing. in Informatics from the Technical University of Berlin. Senior Scientist at the German National Research Center for Computer Science (GMD), Sankt Augustin.
Research interests: Software development, object-oriented design, programming environments, prototyping

Printing: Druckerei Zechner, Speyer
Binding: Buchbinderei Schäffer, Grünstadt